THE BEST PLAYS OF 1974–1975

THE
BURNS MANTLE
YEARBOOK

THE
BEST PLAYS
OF 1974-1975

EDITED BY OTIS L. GUERNSEY JR.

*Illustrated with photographs and
with drawings by* HIRSCHFELD

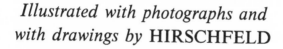

DODD, MEAD & COMPANY
NEW YORK • TORONTO

EDITOR'S NOTE

THE American Theater of the 1970s is an expanding universe; and it's our goal in the 56-year progression of *Best Plays* volumes to keep expanding our grasp to take in every important act and development. New York is still the center of gravity, shooting out its novas and comets to light the outer edges, as well as imploding into itself any worthwhile material developed out on the ever-busier perimeter. But New York too is changing and growing. The off-Broadway movement of the 1960s is becoming in the mid-1970s a mini-Broadway, acquiring some of the commercial theater's problems and limitations along with its advantages. Consequently, the indefinable but very turbulent new galaxy known as "off off Broadway" is mushrooming to take its place and fill the theater's mushrooming need for experimentation and tryout facilities. To document this immense new vitality, we've collected more information on off off Broadway in *The Best Plays of 1974–75* than in any previous volume—or, for that matter, than in any other single compilation we've ever seen. In our OOB section prepared by Camille Croce, we list 85 leading OOB producing groups (as compared to 70 in last year's volume) together with more than 575 of their programs of new or reconstituted plays and musicals, plus the names of their artistic directors and one-line descriptions of their artistic policies. In addition, an article by Marion Fredi Towbin in this volume's "The Season in New York" section sorts out and describes the highlights of the OOB year.

Equally comprehensive coverage on a national scale is provided in Ella A. Malin's listing of regional theater programs in "The Season Around the United States" section, with its complete cast-and-credits entries on new scripts produced in professional theaters in the whole English-speaking area of North America. This listing is embellished with an introduction by the distinguished New England theater critic Elliot Norton and by special closeup coverage by distinguished critics in two American cities which have broad, creative theater movements of their own: Rick Talcove in Los Angeles and David Richards in Washington, D.C.

In other sections of this volume the coverage is of the same order. Broadway and off-Broadway 1974–75 programs are listed as always in magnifying-glass detail and with a high degree of accuracy, thanks in large measure to the invaluable assistance and persistent effort of the editor's wife and the helpful surveillance of Jonathan Dodd of Dodd, Mead & Company, publishers of the *Best Plays* series. Our European Editor, Ossia Trilling, keeps track of Western world theater, listing London programs compiled with the assistance of Barbara Pearce Johnson (with detailed cast-and-credit information on the best of the London season, "Trilling's Top Twenty") and adding his comments on the European theater year in reviews of the British and Continental scenes.

The long list of knowledgeable and dedicated people who have earned the thanks and admiration of the reader as well as the editor for their contributions to this volume includes Rue Canvin, compiler of the necrology, the books and records listings and other coverage, and Stanley Green who has provided a record of cast replacements during the year in long-run and touring Broadway and off-Broadway shows. Others who have helped materially include Jeffrey Sweet, Henry Hewes of *Saturday Review*, Bernard Simon of *Simon's Directory*, Mimi Horowitz of *Playbill*, Hobe Morrison of *Variety*, Clara Rotter of the New York *Times*, Ralph Newman of The Drama Book Shop, the Theater Development Fund, the Off-Off-Broadway Alliance and the many, many patient and forbearing staff members of theater production offices who supply so many of the facts so exactly.

We're also fortunate in having the finishing graphic touches of Al Hirschfeld's drawings of people and plays; of outstanding theater designs by Geoffrey Holder, Rouben Ter-Arutunian, Pearl Somner and Fred Voelpel; and of the photographs of theater in New York and across the country by Bert Andrews, Rhoda Baer, William Baker, Xenophon A. Beake, Michael Eastman, Friedman-Abeles, Robert Alan Gold, Martha Holmes, Ken Howard, Alton Miller, William L. Smith, Ric Sorgel, Martha Swope, David S. Talbott, Thomas Victor and Van Williams.

And finally, it's a very great pleasure to express our gratitude and enthusiasm to the dramatists themselves: the playwrights, composers and lyricists of the best, almost-best and nowhere-near-best new scripts and scores of Broadway, off Broadway, off off Broadway, British, regional and other theater constellations north, east, south and west. Thanks to their talent and determination there was good theater just about everywhere in the season of 1974–75, which the record in this volume goes to prove.

OTIS L. GUERNSEY Jr.

June 1, 1975

CONTENTS

Drawings by HIRSCHFELD

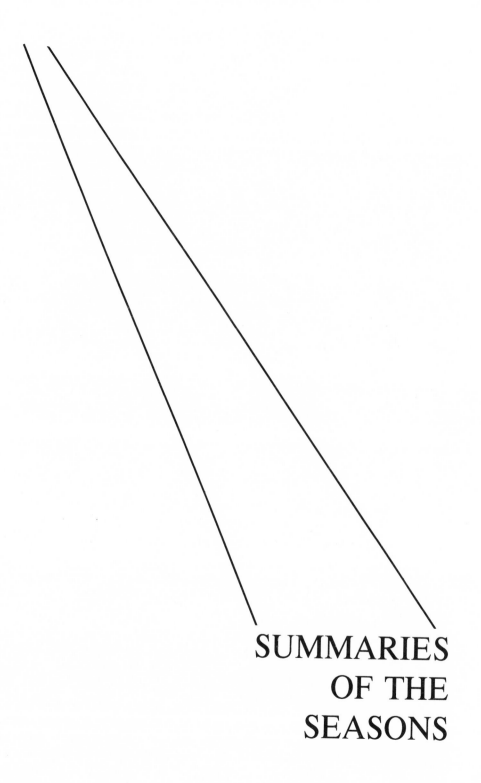

SUMMARIES
OF THE
SEASONS

THE SEASON IN NEW YORK

By Otis L. Guernsey Jr.

THE fabulous invalid sat up and roared this season. The mood on Broadway changed 180 degrees from apathy to excitement. Perhaps there were a few too many more shows than hits, and perhaps audiences turned out in greater abundance than shows good enough to satisfy them. But when all was said and done and the 1974–75 New York theater season an accomplished fact, there was a consensus—more of a *feeling*, really—that a current of energy had suddenly been turned on.

Only a year ago, the show business newspaper *Variety* was dismissing the 1973–74 theater year with words like "dismaying," "a national invalid," "slump" (off 9.15 per cent), "discouraging" and "grim." By mid-season of 1974–75, *Variety's* tune had changed right around from dirge to triumphal march, now resorting to such phrases as "prairie fire," "the box office went wild" (up 25 per cent) and finally just plain "wow!" to sum up Broadway activity.

Asked to comment on the season's quality for better or for worse, leading New York theater spokesmen repeatedly cited the brightening mood ("The sense of excitement"—Anna E. Crouse, president of the Theater Development Fund; "The resurgence of interest on the part of the audience; the general awareness that the theater is still an active and powerful force"—Dore Schary, former New York City cultural commissioner). Their only reservations were the same old headaches that have plagued the so-called invalid for years: the scarcity of new works by American dramatists ("While we all appreciate the high-subsidized imports from England, many of them superb, I would prefer that kind of subsidized effort to come from the various theaters and organizations around our own country"— Richard Barr, president of the League of New York Theaters) and the commercial theater's special, insidious economic strictures ("Some of the most worthy shows don't do business"—Stephen Sondheim, president of the Dramatists Guild; "We still seem to be in a hit-or-flop economy"—Richard Lewine, vice president of the Dramatists Guild).

When the dust cleared we looked back on a Broadway year dominated by British scripts at the box office but not in numbers on the Best Plays list; on an off-Broadway year that staggered toward a dismal foregone conclusion like the dinosaurs in *Fantasia* and then came suddenly to life and began doing hand-springs in the final couple of months. The New York theater's best 1974–75 work was distributed in the ten Best Plays as follows: seven Broadway and three off-Broadway productions; nine plays and one musical; nine repeating authors and one new playwright; three foreign and seven American scripts; of these, two

3

The 1974-75 Season on Broadway

PLAYS (18)

Medea and Jason
Dreyfus in Rehearsal
Vivian Beaumont:
  Mert & Phil
  Black Picture Show
  Little Black Sheep
Tubstrip
Mourning Pictures
Fame
Who's Who in Hell
God's Favorite
ALL OVER TOWN
The Hashish Club
THE RITZ
SEASCAPE
SAME TIME, NEXT YEAR
Don't Call Back
We Interrupt This
  Program . . .
P.S. Your Cat Is Dead

MUSICALS (9)

Mack & Mabel
Sgt. Pepper's Lonely
  Hearts Club Band on
  the Road
The Wiz
Shenandoah
Man on the Moon
Goodtime Charley
The Lieutenant
The Rocky Horror Show
Doctor Jazz

REVUES (3)

The Night That Made
  America Famous
*Clams on the Half
  Shell*
Rodgers & Hart

FOREIGN PLAYS
IN ENGLISH (8)

Absurd Person Singular
THE NATIONAL HEALTH
Hosanna
EQUUS
Royal Court:
  Sizwe Banzi Is Dead
  THE ISLAND
Saturday Sunday Monday
In Praise of Love

SPECIALTIES (3)

Flowers
A Letter for Queen
  Victoria
Marcel Marceau

REVIVALS (18)

Gypsy
Cat on a Hot Tin Roof
Circle in the Square:
  Where's Charley?
  All God's Chillun Got
    Wings
New Phoenix:
  Love for Love
  The Rules of the Game
  The Member of the
    Wedding
Sherlock Holmes
As You Like It
London Assurance
Of Mice and Men
Good News
Dance With Me
Private Lives
Hughie & Duet
A Doll's House
The Misanthrope
The Constant Wife

RETURN
ENGAGEMENTS (3)

Scapino
Brief Lives
Clarence Darrow

HOLDOVER SHOWS
WHICH BECAME HITS
DURING 1974-75

The Magic Show

Categorized above are all the plays listed in the "Plays Produced on Broadway" section of this volume.
Plays listed in CAPITAL LETTERS have been designated Best plays of 1974-75.
Plays listed in *italics* were still running June 2, 1975.
Plays listed in **bold face type** were classified as hits in *Variety's* annual list of hits and flops published
  June 4, 1975.

had their American premiere productions off off Broadway, two in regional theater (the Long Wharf in New Haven) and one in university theater before coming to New York.

The foreign works ran one-two-three in the New York Drama Critics Circle voting for best of bests: *Equus* by Peter Shaffer the winner, *The Island* by Athol Fugard, John Kani and Winston Ntshona the runner-up, with the other of the year's foreign Best Plays, Peter Nichols's *The National Health,* coming in third. The four American Broadway plays on our Best list were Edward Albee's *Seascape* (the 1975 Pulitzer Prize winner), the American playwriting debut of Canadian-born Bernard Slade with the smash hit comedy *Same Time, Next Year,* plus new works by a pair of the American theater's leading authors: Murray Schisgal with *All Over Town* and Terrence McNally with *The Ritz.*

Most of Broadway's 1974–75 musicals were a bit overripe, and off Broadway stole the musical show in the last two weeks of the season with *A Chorus Line* by Michael Bennett, James Kirkwood, Nicholas Dante, Marvin Hamlisch and Edward Kleban down at Joseph Papp's Public Theater (it moved to Broadway as soon as it could run out its subscriptions and get its bags packed). The other two off-Broadway productions on the Best Plays list were Mark Medoff's *The Wager* and Ed Bullins's *The Taking of Miss Janie,* both graduates of off-off-Broadway tryouts. The Bullins play was one of four excellent late arrivals off Broadway, the other three being Leslie Lee's *The First Breeze of Summer* at The Negro Ensemble Company (later moved to Broadway), Jonathan Reynolds's program of one-acters, *Rubbers* and *Yanks 3 Tigers 0 Top of the Seventh* and Gene Feist's *James Joyce's Dubliners.* Other close contenders for Best Plays selection this year were *Naomi Court* by Michael Sawyer, *Philemon* by Tom Jones and Harvey Schmidt and *Diamond Studs* by Jim Wann and Bland Simpson off Broadway; and the British plays *Absurd Person Singular* by Alan Ayckbourn and *In Praise of Love* by Terence Rattigan, Anne Burr's *Mert & Phil* and the musicals *The Wiz* by William F. Brown and Charlie Smalls and *Shenandoah* by James Lee Barrett, Peter Udell, Philip Rose and Gary Geld on Broadway.

Broadway's production decline seemed to have bottomed out. The long dropoff from 84 shows in 1967–68 down to 56 in 1970–71 and 1971–72 and 54 in 1972–73 and 1973–74 was reversed with a total of 62 productions in 1974–75. Of course, it took 18 revivals to reach that figure (and there were 19 last year), but new American play production jumped from ten last year to 18 this, with musicals holding steady with a total of nine.

In the all-important matter of playing weeks (if ten shows play ten weeks, that's 100 playing weeks) Broadway jumped back to a total of 1,101 this year from its historical low of 852 last, perhaps a first step upward toward the 1,200 playing-week plateau of the 1960s. Broadway's total gross from the 52 weeks by *Variety* estimate was $57,423,297, the third-highest in its history, about $1.5 million under the record of 1967–68. Tickets were priced somewhat lower in those days, of course, but the 1974–75 increase of more than $11 million over last year and $13 million over the year before took place without any appreciable rise in ticket prices, which have held the line at the $15 top in recent years, until the musical *Chicago* broke through that ceiling in June, 1975 with a $17.50 top.

The road-show activity of Broadway productions also steadied and started to climb back from its sharp 18 per cent dropoff last season. Broadway shows grossed $50,924,844 on the road in 1974–75 as compared to $45.3 million last year, and this season's combined New York-plus-road gross of Broadway shows of $108.4 million was an all-time high, according to *Variety*. This very large whole contained some extraordinary parts. In September, at Chicago's 4,319-seat Arie Crown Auditorium, a Broadway road show—the musical revival *Irene* starring Debbie Reynolds—totaled up what *Variety* estimates to be the all-time high week's gross: $242,867 for 8 performances at a $12.50 top (and $479,553 for two weeks, also believed to be a record). The previous week's-gross record had been set in 1966 by Carol Channing in *Hello, Dolly* in Oklahoma City. Closer to home

MEMBERS OF "A CHORUS LINE": THOMAS J. WALSH, PRISCILLA LOPEZ, PATRI
WAYNE CILENTO, SAMMY WILLIAMS, RON KUHLMAN, CAROLE BISHOP, CAMERON MAS

—in fact, at the Broadway theater's absolute center—the revival of *The Constant Wife* starring Ingrid Bergman broke the house record of the Shubert Theater for a week's gross of a straight play by taking in $86,100.

Whatever story the numbers may tell, in the theater there's no such thing as a satisfactory season; who'd be satisfied with only 27 new American shows on Broadway—or 37 or 47 or 57? Something more and/or better is always just out of reach, but at least the reach lengthened considerably this season, statistically if not esthetically. Satisfactory? No, but at least encouraging, with the upturn in production and audience response, and with the excitement that arose on both sides of the New York footlights in 1974–75.

RLAND, MICHEL STUART, RONALD DENNIS, ROBERT LU PONE, DONNA MC KECHNIE, MELA BLAIR, NANCY LANE, DON PERCASSI, RENEE BAUGHMAN, BAAYORK LEE

Ups and Downs

In this year of progress for the theater as a whole, individual achievements were sometimes spectacular. After winning the movie Oscar as the year's best actress, Ellen Burstyn went on to win the Tony for her performance in *Same Time, Next Year*. This remarkable, probably unprecedented double accolade raises the possibility that some day there may be a show-biz hat trick, or triple crown winner, or whatever it may be called, for someone who duplicates Miss Burstyn's feat and wins the TV Emmy too. Her stage vehicle was a hard-ticket hit, one of only three shows—the other two being *Equus* and *The Wiz*—which managed to generate that old-time box-office magnetism in a year of many survivors (accounting for those high overall gross figures) but strangely few solid individual successes.

Admiration for the precise timing and characterization of John Kani and Winston Ntshona in the two South African plays they devised with Athol Fugard expressed itself in the Tony Award for best leading male actor, bestowed jointly. Some of the brightest stars of all media chose to appear in New York this season, often in distinguished revivals: Liv Ullmann, Diana Rigg, Angela Lansbury, Maggie Smith, Ingrid Bergman (and with less happy results, Alice Faye) and on the male side John Wood, Henry Fonda, Raul Julia, James Earl Jones and Michael Moriarty. Our scrap book of memorable performances in 1974–75's new shows would also have to include, at a minimum, Robert Preston and Bernadette Peters as Mack Sennett and Mabel Normand in *Mack & Mabel* . . . Anthony Hopkins as the doctor in *Equus* . . . Lindsay Kemp as a mute transvestite in *Flowers* and Richard Monette as a logorrheic one in Hosanna . . . *Absurd Person Singular's* entire sextet of performers . . . Rex Harrison and Julie Harris, stylishly matched in *In Praise of Love* . . . Ann Reinking's Joan of Arc to Joel Grey's *Goodtime Charley* . . . Estelle Parsons as a woman in despair in *Mert & Phil* . . . Charles Nelson Reilly as a celestial errand boy in *God's Favorite* . . . Frances Foster playing yet another stalwart grandma in *The First Breeze of Summer* . . . . . . Rita Moreno and ensemble in *The Ritz* . . . Ted Ross as the Cowardly Lion of *The Wiz* and Frank Langella as the adventurous lizard of *Seascape* . . . John Cullum as the indomitable individualist of *Shenandoah* . . . Barnard Hughes and Cleavon Little at odds in *All Over Town* . . . Kristoffer Tabori as the prime mover of *The Wager* . . . Laura Esterman as a legislative irritant in *Rubbers* and Tony Lo Bianco as the embattled pitcher in *Yanks 3 Detroit 0 Top of the Seventh* (and not overlooking Lou Criscuolo as his catcher, Lawrence "Beanie" Maligma, and the extraordinary ensemble which performed both these plays) . . . the ensembles in the ever-widening circles of *A Chorus Line* and *Philemon* . . . and more, many more, including some like Sam Levene, Ruth Gordon, Dick A. Williams, Boni Enten, Graham Brown, Walter Abel, Eli Wallach, Arlene Francis and Sada Thompson who bore up staunchly in less than favorable circumstances.

Claims that we're drifting toward a directors' theater are supported somewhat by the unusually large number of directors who placed their personal stamp on New York productions this season, many of them accomplished actors and dramatists as well. As in playwriting, the best of directorial bests was British: John Dexter's staging of *Equus*, which won him the Tony (and Dexter also put on a notable *Misanthrope*). Other distinguished visiting directors were Athol Fugard (his South African plays), Frank Dunlop *(Sherlock Holmes)*, Euan Smith *(London Assurance)* and John Gielgud *(Private Lives* and *The Constant Wife)*. The many standouts among our own directors included, for musicals, Geoffrey Holder *(The Wiz)*, Philip Rose *(Shenandoah)*, Gower Champion *(Mack & Mabel,* choreographer as well as director), Arthur Laurents *(Gypsy)*, Theodore Mann *(Where's Charley?)* and Michael Bennett *(A Chorus Line,* choreographer as well as director); and for plays, Arvin Brown *(The National Health)*, Fred Coe *(In Praise of Love)*, Edwin Sherin *(Of Mice and Men)*, Douglas Turner Ward *(The First Breeze of Summer)*, Anthony Perkins *(The Wager)*, Edward Albee (his own *Seascape)*, Robert Drivas *(The Ritz)*, Gene Saks *(Same Time, Next Year)*, Dustin Hoffman *(All Over Town)* and Gilbert Moses *(The Taking of Miss Janie)*. Another choreographer, George Faison, was a Tony-winning standout for his work in *The Wiz*. On the darker side, three of the stage's most accomplished artists succumbed to overreach: Tom O'Horgan *(Sgt. Pepper's Lonely Hearts Club Band on the Road)*, Franco Zeffirelli *(Saturday Sunday Monday)* and Abe Burrows *(Good News)*.

For once or maybe twice, the Broadway producer of the year wasn't David Merrick. It was Adela Holzer, who presented two new comedies *All Over Town* and *The Ritz* and co-sponsored *Sherlock Holmes*. Merrick's season was a distinguished one, with three respectable, if not wholly successful, Broadway productions: *Mack & Mabel, Dreyfus in Rehearsal* and (with Kennedy Center) *The Misanthrope*. Kennedy Center and Roger L. Stevens also helped bring in *Absurd Person Singular* and *London Assurance;* but the year's extraterritorial producing honors went to Arvin Brown's Long Wharf Theater which pioneered *The National Health, The Island* and *Sizwe Banzi Is Dead* before their transfer to New York. Joseph Papp opened his customarily busy season with Anne Burr's *Mert & Phil,* which turned out to be his best work until the last-minute blaze of glory of his two Best Plays and Critics Award winners *(A Chorus Line* and *The Taking of Miss Janie)*. Arthur Cantor brought in three major star vehicles: *Private Lives, The Constant Wife* and *In Praise of Love*. Off Broadway, he continued to hover protectively over Bil Baird's marionette troupe, as its executive producer. Other producers-of-the-year included Kermit Bloomgarden *(Equus)*, Hillard Elkins and Lester Osterman *et al* (the South African plays), Ken Harper *(The Wiz)* and Richard Barr *et al (Seascape)*. All the institutional producers had at least one standout: Circle in the Square *(The National Health)*, The Negro Ensemble Company *(The First Breeze of Summer)*, Chelsea Theater Center *(Yentl the Yeshiva Boy)*, American Place (the Jonathan Reynolds one-acters) and the Roundabout *(James Joyce's Dubliners)*. The producer with the worst luck was Harry Rigby, whose *Good News* revival recorded a $1,500,000 loss, according to *Variety* estimate, the same week the show biz newspaper used the words "prairie fire" to characterize business on Broadway. Alexander H. Cohen also fell short of success with his productions of Peter Ustinov's *Who's Who in Hell* and Norman Krasna's *We Interrupt This Program . . .*, but he distinguished himself with yet another gala TV presentation of the Tony Award ceremonies.

Among designers, Geoffrey Holder clearly earned his best-costumes Tony for *The Wiz* and Carl Toms his for the *Sherlock Holmes* scenery (and his un-nominated costumes for the same show were also noteworthy). John Napier's horses in *Equus* and Fred Voelpel's lizards in *Seascape* ranked high among the year's triumphs. Among costume designs, so did Patricia Zipprodt's *Mack & Mabel*, Pearl Somner's and Winn Morton's *Shenandoah*, Willa Kim's *Goodtime Charley*, Carrie F. Robbins's *Polly*, Theoni V. Aldredge's *A Chorus Line* and Tanya Moiseiwitsch's designs (both costumes and scenery) for *The Misanthrope*. Rouben Ter-Arutunian's *Goodtime Charley* scenery design was a standout, along with Tom H. John's *The Wiz*, Robin Wagner's *Mack & Mabel*, James Tilton's *Seascape*, Boris Aronson's *Dreyfus in Rehearsal*, William Ritman's *God's Favorite* and Lawrence King and Michael H. Yeargan's *The Ritz*.

Impressive as the total 1974–75 box office activity may have been, in the list of individual shows the losses seemed more impressive than the gains. In the present economics of the theater, the bad news happens fast and good news is a long time coming after a production is far enough into its run to have paid off its cost. In these circumstances, according to *Variety* estimate. the long-run *Pippin* was the star performer with a $2,500,000 net profit on its $500,000 investment and still counting. A handful of other holdovers were reported in the black including *A Little Night Music* ($100,000 profit on $650,000), *A Moon for the Misbegotten* ($300,000 on $150,000), *Good Evening* ($100,000 on $120,000), *Scapino* ($15,000 on $50,000) and *The Magic Show*, with the off-Broadway revue *Let My People Come* reported having grossed over $1,500,000 and returned $350,000 on its $10,000 investment. Of this season's new shows, *Same Time, Next Year* (banking a steady $22,500 each sellout week) and *The Wiz* were estimated to be running in the black by season's end, with *Gypsy*, *Absurd Person Singular*, *In Praise of Love*, *Sherlock Holmes*, *Private Lives* and *The Constant Wife* also thought to be over on the profit side.

On the reverse side of this coin, *Goodtime Charley*, like *Good News*, was a debacle on a scale of an estimated $1 million plus (on an $800,000 investment). Other losses reported by *Variety* this season included *Mack & Mabel* ($750,000), *Dreyfus in Rehearsal* (another Merrick show, another $200,000), *Flowers* ($150,000), *Mourning Pictures* ($150,000), *Saturday Sunday Monday* ($275,000), *Fame* ($170,000 of $185,000), *Don't Call Back* ($160,000 of $165,000), *The Night That Made America Famous* ($400,000). *We Interrupt This Program . . .* ($285,000 on $300,000), *P.S. Your Cat Is Dead* ($132,500) and *The Misanthrope* ($70,000 on $175,000).

Even more discouraging was the fact that several of last year's most effective shows ended their runs in the red, as follows: *Noel Coward in Two Keys* (the 1973–74 season's best play, $100,000 loss on its $175,000 investment), *Bad Habits* (a Best Play, $150,000), *Lorelei* ($250,000 on $500,000), *My Fat Friend* ($100,000 on $175,000), the Andrews Sisters' *Over Here!* ($500,000 on $750,000, expected to recoup on the road but cancelled after contractual differences between stars and producers) and *Thieves* ($250,000 on $300,000). And on the roster of 1974–75 dismay, four Broadway and two off-Broadway productions opened and closed at the same performance: the abovemention *Don't Call Back* and *Fame* plus *Medea and Jason* and *Mourning Pictures* on Broadway and *Four Friends* and *A Matter of Time* off. The perversity of famine amid this season's plenty was even more clearly illustrated in the irony of *Dr. Jazz* and *The Lieutenant* receiving multiple Tony nominations in the musical categories while their Broadway runs lasted only 5 performances for the former and 9 for the latter, with losses estimated at $900,000 and $250,000 respectively.

Standing off from the individual achievements of 1974–75 and taking a long look at the loops and whorls of the season as a whole, we conclude that the new sense of excitement isn't merely another show-biz illusion. There's a clearly perceptible resolve, a re-commitment if you will, on both sides of the proscenium. The theater's audience has been rather neglectful in this decade, but now, it seems, they've decided to take another, closer look. The New York theater in its turn —like an old trouper who unexpectedly finds himself with an eager crowd on his hands—has risen to the occasion, throwing together a revival here, pulling in a ready-made show from abroad there, rummaging everywhere for inspiration. The old pro lit the lights, pulled the curtains and somehow created a season that transcended the reality of its statistics. If you look too closely you can see that the props are a bit tacky: too small a number of new plays, too few American authors, a trace of mold here and there around the edges of some of the most popular musicals. If you look behind the scenes you'll find the same problems becoming more rather than less acute in these difficult times: a hit-or-flop economy, discouraged backers, attenuating foundation support, a sleazy theater district, high costs of production, etc. (one problem alleviated in the present circumstances is the high cost of theater tickets; they haven't come down, but inflation has made them seem less costly in comparison to everything else).

Tacky, moldy, problematical or whatever, the good old New York theater came on in 1974–75, put on a show for all those folks out front and left them wanting more. And more is what the theater will certainly strive for next season, when those crowds are certain to come back: more new plays, more inventive musicals, more hits.

And speaking of hits, as we've noted in past *Best Plays* volumes, a "hit" in the true Broadway meaning of the word isn't merely a show that's hard to get into on a Friday night, but a show which pays off its production cost (it may be easy to get into but become a hit by virtue of a movie sale or a profitable road tour). In recent seasons, however, the word "hit" has been losing a lot of its magic. With higher costs hopefully compensated by longer runs, few productions, however popular, reach the break-even point in the season in which they opened. And very often New York doesn't have either the first or the last word on a playscript, as it once did. A good script ignored on Broadway for some strange or special reason may take on brilliantly illustrious life elsewhere on world stages or in other media (a recent example is Ron Clark's and Sam Bobrick's *Norman, Is That You?*, a 12-performance Broadway flop in 1970 but a long-run smash hit on world stages almost everywhere, under various titles). So we make no special point in this resume about which 1974–75 offerings were "hits" and which were "flops" except that this information is recorded in the one-page summary of the Broadway season accompanying this report.

The ultimate insignia of New York professional theater achievement (we insist) is not instant popularity at the box office, but selection as a Best Play in these volumes (a designation which is 16 years older than the Critics awards and only three years younger than the Pulitzer, which began its drama prize selection in 1916–17 with a negatively pretentious "no award"). Our Best Play selection is made with the script itself as the primary consideration, for the reason (as we've stated in previous volumes) that the script is the very spirit of the theater, the soul in its physical body. The script is not only the quintessence of the present, it is most of what endures into the future. So the Best Plays are the best scripts. As little weight as humanly possible is given to comparative production values. The choice is made without any regard whatever as to a play's type—musical, comedy or drama—or origin on or off Broadway, or popularity at the box office or lack of same.

If a script of above-average quality influences the very character of a season by its extreme popularity, or if by some means of consensus it wins the Critics, Pulitzer or major Tony awards, we give consideration to its future historical as well as present esthetic importance to the season as a whole. This is the only special consideration we give, and we don't always tilt in its direction, as the record shows.

On the other hand, we don't take the scripts of other eras into consideration for a Best Play citation in this one, however good they may be or whatever their technical qualifications. As far as *Best Plays* classification and selection is concerned, a script like Maxim Gorky's 1904 *Summerfolk* is a revival and not a new play eligible for a Best Play citation, even though it may never have been produced in New York before and technically had its local "premiere" in the Royal Shakespeare Company production this season.

The Best Plays of 1974–75 were the following, as named previously in this report but listed here for visual convenience in the order in which they opened in New York (a plus sign + with the performance number signifies that the play was still running on June 1, 1975):

The National Health
  (Broadway; 56 perfs.)

Equus
  (Broadway; 253+ perfs.)

The Island
  (Broadway; 52 perfs.)

All Over Town
  (Broadway; 176+ perfs.)

The Wager
  (Off Broadway; 104 perfs.)

The Ritz
  (Broadway; 150+ perfs.)

Seascape
  (Broadway; 65 perfs.)

Same Time, Next Year
  (Broadway; 92+ perfs.)

The Taking of Miss Janie
  (Off Broadway; 32+ perfs.)

A Chorus Line
  (Off Broadway; 54+ perfs.)

Broadway

The conspicuous presence of British plays on Broadway this season was topped by the towering *Equus,* the fifth British script in a row to capture our admiration as the season's best-of-bests (the others being *Sleuth, Old Times, The Changing Room* and *Noel Coward in Two Keys*). *Equus* is a drama of almost classic power, and yet its design is simple and functional as small-town gossip. A psychiatrist (played by Anthony Hopkins), hearing that a stable boy (Peter Firth) has gone berserk and blinded his beloved animals with a steel spike, asks himself how and why such a thing could happen, much as we all do on reading in the newspaper about some seemingly senseless act of brutality. The psychiatrist's calling is not just to shake his head in dismay, but to try to find the answers—and this seeking and at last finding is Peter Shaffer's play, which goes deeper and deeper into the boy's psyche, past ordinary quirks of family strain and religious conviction, until it uncovers dark mysteries of love and worship that have the power to taint other characters.

The physical production was an arena of wooden benches occupied both by the actors (who stepped back and forth into the arena, in and out of their roles) and by a segment of the audience, in order to place no barrier of fourth-wall convention between active and passive witnesses to this ritual. The horses were graceful, bestial and uncannily real as symbolized by actors wearing cage-like suggestions of horses' heads and hooves and moving across the stage in the slow, jointed rhythms of the large animals. John Dexter's direction and John Napier's design (with the mime credited to Claude Chagrin) created a compelling stage illusion of horses and man-horse relationships that was much larger than life, much more illustrative than the presence of a real horse onstage ever could have been, reminding us once again of the great power of the theater at its best. In contrast, the "real" nude love scene seemed to pull *Equus* down to earth. It was just a blurred copy of reality, unworthy of the transcendent images in the rest of this fine play, whose worth was admirably realized by everyone who touched it.

No other drama achieved much stature on the 1974–75 Broadway scene; all other outstanding scripts from home or abroad were more or less streaked with comedy. Even the Athol Fugard-John Kani-Winston Ntshona South African plays—solemn as their overtones certainly were—were devised in the context of the human comedy, not as direct confrontations of drama. *Sizwe Banzi Is Dead* and *The Island* were coupled as a best-play "entry" in the Tony nominations, but we don't do so here because we view them as two full evenings, distinctly separate works. In a sense, they are a canon of work on a single theme—South African racism—developed over a period of time but presented in a single season, under special circumstances. They both ranked high among the year's best, but we don't think it would be appropriate to put them both on the Best Plays list. We've named *The Island* a Best Play rather than *Sizwe Banzi* because it is the stronger literary entity, the other being more mimetic.

A collaborative effort of Fugard, the author-director, and Kani and Ntshona, the performers, the plays were precise in their linkage of word and action and finely tuned in every detail, perfected in the long practise of performance in South Africa, in England, and finally here at the Long Wharf Theater in New Haven and then New York. In *The Island,* Kani and Ntshona impersonated cellmates in a political prison whose last resort of protest lies in the allegory of a two-character version of *Antigone* they're preparing for the annual prison show. Their partnership is placed under great stress when one of them learns he is soon to be set free, while the other will probably rot in confinement. *The Island* was a triple *entendre* of protest against the South African state's racist policies: first in the Creon-vs.-Antigone dialogue about the individual's duty to the state; second in the convicts' selection, planning and presentation of this material in their prison context; and thirdly, in the modern actuality of devising and presenting *The Island* in its authors' native land, where the rules of *apartheid* are so restrictive that Kani and Ntshona must be registered as Fugard's house servants in order to work with his theater group, because "artist" or "actor" isn't accepted as an employment category for South African blacks.

The comedic twists of *The Island*—the curious relations between the two men as they endure their hard time, and their rehearsing and dressing up for the play —put a curve on the script that probably helped get it past official objections. The same was true of *Sizwe Banzi* which begins with a Kani monologue describing the preparations for an inspection of an American-owned factory in South Africa, with the blacks' oppressive working conditions temporarily disguised for the benefit of the American visitors. The heart of the *Sizwe Banzi* matter, though, was the second part: a tipsy laborer considers changing identity papers with a man he finds lying dead in the street, in order to better his condition—but hesitates to do so because this would a sort of suicide, forever destroying the real identity in which he takes pride and comfort. The hard emotional and psychological consequences of tyranny were eloquently expressed in these fine South African stage works which dared to confront problems which wouldn't vanish when the curtain came down.

Another foreign Best Play processed in an American premiere at the Long Wharf before coming to Broadway was Peter Nichols's *The National Health,* which found the means to satirize the assembly-line impersonality of socialized medicine as it becomes ever more mechanized, institutionalized, in order to broaden its democratic base. *The National Health* spread itself across its hospital-ward setting in episodes of fear, hope, cynicism, racism and death, in a sprawling script which sprayed little pellets of satire in all directions instead of seeking to drill a single hole like *Equus.* It cried out for an ensemble performance and received it from Leonard Frey (a sardonically efficient orderly), Richard Venture (a trembling ulcer patient), Rita Moreno (a West Indian nurse) and a large cast portraying all kinds of doctors, nurses and patients caught together on many levels between life and death; all presented under the inspired and inspiring direction of Arvin Brown, artistic director of the Long Wharf.

If this seemed a foreign-play-dominated season, it was because of the high quality of the imports, not their quantity. They numbered eight, the same as last year, all but one of them standout attractions. Terence Rattigan's newest script, *In Praise of Love,* was a bright, mannered comedy (though not billed as one) of deception and counter-deception with very dark shadows of mortality in the background. The husband and wife played by Rex Harrison and Julie Harris have come to terms with each other's eccentricities—his intellectual, hers emotional. There are many layers to be peeled off, however, and the truth was slowly revealed under Fred Coe's meticulous direction as something quite different and quite touching: she has a terminal illness; he knows it and is redoubling his selfish importunities, lest he betray the truth with a hint of sympathy; but she also knows he knows it and goes along with his game so that he won't be troubled. A friend (played by Martin Gabel) was a mirror in which the audience could see reflected its own reaction to the various discoveries in this very smoothly-crafted play.

There were a protracted suicide attempt and other sinister implications including a vicious dog in Alan Ayckbourn's *Absurd Person Singular,* but it was the only one of the foreign entries which forthrightly billed itself as a "comedy" and set its sights firmly upon humor. The play showed three British couples with vastly different backgrounds meeting at each other's houses for Christmas Eve parties over a period of years. The working-class couple (the late Larry Blyden and Carole Shelley) is on the rise, the aristocrats (Richard Kiley and Geraldine Page) are on the descendent, and the other two (Sandy Dennis and Tony Roberts) are muddling through the middle, in these times which are homogenizing mankind along with the milk. All these American actors played their roles with convincing British accents (and ideal ensemble proportion) under Eric Thompson's direction. Blyden in particular achieved a perfect caricature of the not-so-meek who are now inheriting the earth, or at least a few of its luxuries and ostentations.

Another foreign play, *Hosanna,* was an English translation of a French Canadian script by Michel Tremblay about a transvestite and his seedy, leather-jacketed friend. The play is said to be a parable of Canadian politics, but it was theatrically effective on its own, without the political key, in a second-act monologue by the transvestite, powerfully acted by Richard Monette. The eighth imported new script, an Italian family play by Eduardo de Filippo directed and designed by Franco Zeffirelli in an English production by the National Theater, proved somewhat topheavy and lasted only 12 performances.

American authors made a creditable showing side-by-side with their transatlantic competitors. They provided Broadway with 18 new plays this season, four of which were Best Plays, one by a new author. No American work had the shattering impact of *Equus* or the resounding social echoes of the South African plays. Their approach was almost uniformly comedic or melodramatic, and their attitude one of helpless laughter in unfathomable circumstances—certainly a valid concept for the mid-1970s.

Edward Albee's Pulitzer Prize-winning *Seascape* was his best work since *A Delicate Balance,* the lightest in his canon and his first full-scale Broadway directorial credit. His play seemed filled with light and air, as he studied a middle-aged couple trying to work off their post-picnic depression in a lonely oceanside sand dune by trying to figure out what if anything to do with the rest of their lives. They're mismatched in their desires for the future, and the playwright further mismatches them with a pair of humanoid sea-lizards trying to find out whether it would be worth the effort to evolve into land creatures. Each "couple" hopes for more than their past, ordinary lives have afforded. They're willing to try for the brass ring—if it exists. Their confrontation is brittle rather than harsh, with Deborah Kerr as the spokesman for the land and Frank Langella for the sea, and their discourse is prevented from taking on too much weight by Albee's direction. The seascape by James Tilton and the lizard costume designs by Fred Voelpel were as helpful to the play as its staging—even the large, saurian tails seemed to be easily-manageable parts of a living body.

These couples conclude, not unpredictably, that evolution is a game probably worth the candle, even in middle age and considering the loss of peace of mind which is the cost of knowledge. *Seascape* was a pleasant conceit expertly contrived, easily the best American play of the Broadway season and a notch above its nearest off-Broadway rival.

The vein of absurdist comedy yielded riches in two other American Best Plays: Murray Schisgal's *All Over Town* and Terrence McNally's *The Ritz*. They were both comedies of tenacity, with individuals holding to their own concerns in the face of profound disorder, like an earthquake victim saving an ash tray from a falling house. In *All Over Town* an eminent psychiatrist (Barnard Hughes) is sure that California will fall into the Pacific Ocean any day now, but what he's immediately concerned about is the strange case of a young man who has nine children by five different women, all on welfare. There's also a matter of mistaken identity when the eminent doctor assumes that the good breeder is a black man (Cleavon Little) who happens by, when in reality he is a shy young white man (Zane Lasky) who seems harmless and is by some happy magic irresistable to women. Schisgal's play finds fun in everything it can lay its hands on, which under Dustin Hoffman's direction (his professional debut) is plenty and includes sex, sociology, success and everything else brought within range of this energetic and perceptive farce.

McNally's *The Ritz* was a script very similar to Schisgal's in genre, though it was billed as a "comedy" while Schisgal's was billed as a "play"; in tone, not surprisingly, because the producer of both plays was Adela Holzer; and in directorial energy and skill—for Dustin Hoffman read Robert Drivas, though *The Ritz* was certainly not his debut. In it, a helpless fugitive from a gangster family quarrel (Jack Weston) finds himself hiding out, or rather in, at a Turkish bath during a sort of homosexual Homecoming Weekend. It's not long before he finds the kinks of some of his fellow guests more troublesome than his enemy's threats. His guides in this jungle of fetishists include Tony Award-winning Rita Moreno as a Latin Bette Midler trying to get a foot on the first rung of the ladder by performing in this most unpromising place, and F. Murray Abraham as a seasoned veteran of these purple occasions. The point of this as of other McNally plays was that anyone who can keep his sanity in the circumstances we all find ourselves in today ought to have his head examined. As in the three past McNally Best Plays, *The Ritz* made it both absurdly and delightfully.

Another comedy and the biggest straight-play hit of the season was the Broadway stage debut of its Canadian-born author, Bernard Slade: *Same Time, Next Year,* a heterosexual response to the strictures of our times in the assignations of a couple, more or less happily married (to other people), who take an intense pleasure in meeting secretly for a fling once a year in a convenient motel cottage. The audience is privileged to look in on a half dozen such trysts over a 25-year span, each making a comment on its unique time frame of hippies, hipsters, affluence, even of war. As the world knows, Ellen Burstyn played the warm, generous, sometimes affected woman, while Charles Grodin was overlooked by most award givers and nominaters in his equally sure portrayal of a middle-class husband and father torn between his desire to be with it and his deepest instinct against it, whatever "it" happened to be at the time. Gene Saks's direction insured renewed life and a fresh style in each repeat of the situation and made the most of the many verbal and visual jokes—short-range assets which did more for this play than any long-range overview.

This comic spirit dominated American playwriting this season and carried through from the best to the near-best, though sometimes showing its darker side. One of the half dozen new 1974–75 scripts which billed themselves as "comedy" rather than "play" was Neil Simon's God's Favorite, a telling of the Biblical Job tale as though it had taken place in a modern, affluent Long Island suburb. In the first part, Vincent Gardenia as Job is harried by a divine messenger in the fussily, elaborately eccentric person of Charles Nelson Reilly, a wingless but persistent angel who mined the same vein of dark humor that sometimes gives the stripping of King Lear by his daughters a comedic streak. The second part, with Job clinging to his love of the God who pulls his house and his life down around his ears, didn't work comedically and, unlike King Lear, couldn't go forward and make it as drama. The brighter moments of God's Favorite rank with Simon's best work; and if the play as a whole doesn't, it's because it was too adventurous in trying to find a new way of telling the old tale. The playwright's search for a new way of expressing himself was a fault of commission, at least, not of omission.

Another of the season's comedies, Peter Ustinov's Who's Who in Hell, seemed a thoroughly American play regardless of the author's nationality. It had its premiere in New York and pursued a satire of American attitudes in situation-comedy style, with George S. Irving (who has played Richard M. Nixon on Broadway and resembles him in this role) as an American President assassinated together with the U.S.S.R. Chairman (played by Ustinov in portly Slavic grandeur) by a young hothead (Beau Bridges) who in his turn is killed by police and thus joins his victims in an anteroom of eternity. It was a quick-witted script, but it settled too comfortably into its premise and went nowhere. This time the anteroom was an empty office entered through a one-way door (as in No Exit) and left by means of elevators. The last anteroom of eternity of any consequence onstage was a steambath in the play of the same name. This year there were steambaths all over the place, but they had no supernatural significance; they were earthbound in their function, as in The Ritz and the far less successful Tubstrip, which wandered nakedly onto Broadway for a few performances following a national tour.

Across the line and into the realm of drama, Garson Kanin stressed the irony and pathos of believing, in the times just before Hitler, that anti-Semitism was finally dead and buried in civilized Europe, in an adaptation of a French play-within-a-play, *Dreyfus in Rehearsal,* about a Polish troupe rehearsing a drama of the Dreyfus case. The scripts which Joseph Papp's New York Shakespeare Festival brought into the big theater at Lincoln Center were shaded for drama even more than comedy, the first and best being Anne Burr's *Mert & Phil* dramatizing the emotional impact of a mastectomy on a 20-year marriage, constructed in widening concentric circles. Then there was Bill Gunn's *Black Picture Show* depicting the intellectual decay and death of a black poet seduced by ambition and movie money; a shambles of innuendo and grief which wasn't helped by the author's direction of his own play. Finally, in Anthony Scully's *Little Black Sheep,* powerful neuroses worked on the priests in the Jesuit House of Study in New Haven, but none emerged to make a play of it—not even with the added fillip of a visiting nun with a compulsion to take all her clothes off. It was a script with a good deal of muscle but little coordination.

Conventional crime and violence occupied some of theater's attention inside the auditorium as well as outside in the streets this season. *P.S. Your Cat Is Dead* offered up Keir Dullea as a victim first of a burglary and then as the target of an attempted burglary of his emotions, as the thief, having failed to rob him, tries to seduce him. Norman Krasna's *We Interrupt This Program. . .* reached for total audience participation, as a gang of criminals takes over the theater soon after the "play" begins and holds the audience hostage for the freedom of a gang member who is in prison. The action had to be continuous. The sound, by Jack Shearing created the illusion that the mayor, the police commissioner and a whole street full of police cars were milling around, jabbering on walkie-talkies just outside the theater. Broadway proved inhospitable to this pleasantly prickly conceit, but it might do well in production elsewhere. Lance Larsen's *The Hashish Club,* about a bad drug trip, arrived from Los Angeles and departed shortly. *Don't Call Back,* with Arlene Francis as a star who comes home to her New York apartment to find it taken over by a gang of criminal youths including her own son, gave up after only one performance.

In the domain of Broadway musical production, *The Wiz* stood head and shoulders above all its contemporaries, but it didn't have to stand very tall to do so. A hip version of L. Frank Baum's Wizard of Oz story, with a soft-rock score by Charlie Smalls and marvellously inventive design and staging by Geoffrey Holder and Tom H. John, this was distinctly a 1970s show, albeit with a 1930s book which had to be picked up and dusted off from time to time. *The Wiz* began by representing a tornado as a dancer whirling and twirling across a huge empty stage with a strip of black gauze attached to her head, revolving up into the flies —one of the best of its trip-like design fantasies. The season's other rock efforts on Broadway were *Sgt. Pepper's Lonely Hearts Club Band on the Road,* a Tom O'Horgan fancy taking off from the famous Beatles album but never becoming really airborne; and *The Rocky Horror Show,* a lampoon of the movies presented cabaret-style at the Belasco, which was remodeled for that purpose. Andy Warhol ventured into musical production this year with a fantasy of the space age entitled *Man on the Moon,* lasting a little longer than your average moonwalk, but not much; and Harry Chapin also ventured onto Broadway with a revue *The Night That Made America Famous,* a loud, multimedia compendium of those depressing country rock "somebody done somebody wrong songs" about how everything without exception is going to hell in a haycart.

Another standout of the Broadway musical year was another oldie: *Shenandoah*, based on the 1965 James Stewart movie by James Lee Barrett, also the co-author of this Broadway book with Peter Udell (its lyricist) and Philip Rose (its director). This one tells a tale of the Civil War about a widowed farmer, a rugged individualist who refuses to take sides and is determined to keep on raising his large family and let the war go by. It doesn't, of course—it reaches out to take him and his family by the throat. If emotions were always showing on the surface of this show, at least they were *there,* with an attractive score by Gary Geld to give them emphasis.

The historical past supplied all the other Broadway musicals with their fitful inspiration. *Mack & Mabel* looked back at the movies' silent era in a big, impressive show by the *Hello, Dolly!* authors—Jerry Herman and Michael Stewart—with Robert Preston and Bernadette Peters striving mightily in the leading roles of Mack Sennett, the comedy director, and his star Mabel Normand. *Goodtime Charley* took a leaf out of *Pippin's* book and went Gothic with a musical version of Joan of Arc's travails, with Ann Reinking as Joan and Joel Grey as the Dauphin Charles (the Charley of the title), and with a most effective design by Rouben Ter-Arutunian. *The Lieutenant* made a bold attempt to express itself in musical theater terms on the subject of the agonies of My Lai. Finally, *Dr. Jazz* turned inward for a cavalcade of music, tracing the development of jazz in a score mixing old and new numbers, with a slight show-business story for a book. None of these shows was without some spark, but none lit a fire anywhere big enough to warm Broadway.

A much warmer musical pleasure was *Rodgers & Hart,* which also looked backward in a collection of 98 songs by the great composer-lyricist team of the 1920s and 1930s. Subtitled "A Musical Celebration," it was based on a concept of Richard Lewine and John Fearnley which for purposes of statistical classification we can call a revue. The songs poured out—love songs in Part I, satirical numbers in Part II—with Donald Saddler dances but without any inconvenience of a book, performed by an enthusiastic young group under the enthusiastic and canny direction of Burt Shevelove. It was in every way a happy event whose only shortcoming was the lateness of its arrival in a season which could have used its brightly entertaining presence all winter long.

In addition on the 1974–75 musical scene, there were concert appearances by singing stars (among them Frank Sinatra) and rock groups not only in the sports arenas and concert halls but also in some of the larger Broadway theaters, whose owners discovered a season or two ago that a Sammy Davis Jr. or a Liza Minnelli in what amounted to a concert could attract audiences as well or better than such Broadway fare as was available to them. These are "fan" audiences, and one of their objects of adoration this year was Bette Midler, whose appearance at the Minskoff, entitled *Clams on the Half Shell,* was offered as a revue of sight gags, inside jokes and Midler vocals, backed by Tony Walton designs; a little more elaborate than others of its concert-like ilk, enough so, perhaps, to earn the name of "show." Others making concert

FRANK SINATRA AT THE URIS THEATER

appearances on New York stages this season included Charles Aznavour, Tony Bennett and Lena Horne at the Minskoff and Henry Mancini, Anthony Newley, Johnny Mathis and the Fifth Dimension at the Uris, a pair of new skyscraper "theaters" which have proved more useful for making noise than for uttering words.

This season's specialty shows were impressive. Lindsay Kemp's *Flowers,* a tragi-comic program of pantomime imported from London, was a sensitive exploration of transvestism in several phases, said to have been suggested by Genet's *Notre Dame des Fleurs.* Kemp devised, designed, directed and played the leading role in *Flowers.* Another arresting specialty production was Robert Wilson's *A Letter for Queen Victoria,* a mood-establishing but otherwise mysteriously jumbled collection of theater effects of monologue, music, mime, etc., in Wilson's unique style. The list of specialties was further distinguished by the presence of Marcel Marceau for a limited engagement of his Bip sketches and other pantomimes. Return engagements of Henry Fonda in *Clarence Darrow,* Roy Dotrice in *Brief Lives* and Jim Dale in his hit Young Vic production of *Scapino* also added to the season's store of theatergoing riches.

The important part played by revivals in the success of this banner theater year will be the subject of the next section of this report. Meanwhile, here's where we list the *Best Plays* choices for the top individual achievements of 1974–75. In the acting categories, clear distinctions among "starring," "featured" or "supporting" players can't be made on the basis of official billing, in which an actor may appear as a "star" following the title (not true star billing), or as an "also starring" star, or any of the other typographical ego gimmicks. Here in these volumes we divide acting into "primary" and "secondary" roles, a primary role being one which carries a major responsibility for the play; a role which might some day cause a star to inspire a revival in order to appear in that character. All others, be they vivid as Mercutio, are classed as secondary. Our problem isn't definition but an embarrassment of riches as we proceed to choose the single best in each category.

Here, then, are the *Best Plays* bests of 1974–75:

PLAYS

BEST PLAY: *Equus* by Peter Shaffer
BEST AMERICAN PLAY: *Seascape* by Edward Albee
ACTORS IN PRIMARY ROLES: John Kani and Winston Ntshona as John and Winston in *The Island* and as Styles/Buntu and Sizwe Banzi in *Sizwe Banzi Is Dead*
ACTRESS IN A PRIMARY ROLE: Ellen Burstyn as Doris in *Same Time, Next Year*
ACTOR IN A SECONDARY ROLE: Larry Blyden as Sidney in *Absurd Person Singular*
ACTRESS IN A SECONDARY ROLE: Rita Moreno as Googie Gomez in *The Ritz*
DIRECTOR: John Dexter for *Equus* and *The Misanthrope*
SCENERY: Carl Toms for *Sherlock Holmes*
COSTUMES: John Napier for *Equus*

MUSICALS

BEST MUSICAL: *A Chorus Line*
BOOK: James Kirkwood and Nicholas Dante for *A Chorus Line*
MUSIC: Charlie Smalls for *The Wiz*
LYRICS: Edward Kleban for *A Chorus Line*
ACTOR IN A PRIMARY ROLE: John Cullum as Charlie Anderson in *Shenandoah*
ACTRESS IN A PRIMARY ROLE: Ann Reinking as Joan of Arc in *Goodtime Charley*
ACTOR IN A SECONDARY ROLE: Ted Ross as Lion in *The Wiz*
ACTRESS IN A SECONDARY ROLE: Donna McKechnie as Cassie in *A Chorus Line*
DIRECTOR: Michael Bennett for *A Chorus Line*
CHOREOGRAPHER: Michael Bennett for *A Chorus Line*
SCENERY: Rouben Ter-Arutunian for *Goodtime Charley*
COSTUMES: Geoffrey Holder for *The Wiz*

Revivals on and off Broadway

This season as last, New York was a repertory extravaganza, with 37 professional revivals (18 on Broadway, 17 off Broadway and two return engagements of revivals), and who knows how many off off Broadway—perhaps more than 100.

Revivals serve five obvious purposes in the entertainment/esthetic context of the modern New York stage: 1) They provide a known quantity for star performers who might not dare risk failure in a personal appearance in new, untried work; 2) They provide entertainment for audiences as well as occupation for artists during periods when good new scripts are relatively scarce; 3) They test the imagination and muscle of all the theater's interpretive talent; 4) They give audiences an historical perspective on living theater the way a library does on the theater as literature; and 5) They sometimes discover, or uncover, dormant vitality in a vintage comedy or drama to the extent that it outgrows the original concept of the work revived.

The first four purposes were admirably served by the 1974–75 revival activity, the fifth less so than last year, when new productions of *Candide* and *A Moon for the Misbegotten* redefined these works for our theater. The popular success of this season's Royal Shakespeare production of William Gillette's antique *Sherlock Holmes* came nearest to serving such a purpose. It was a redefinition with elaborate scenic, melodramatic, costuming and performing devices adding a new dimension of sentiment, or perhaps camp, to the good old detective play, like the fifth or sixth re-reading of a horror cartoon. The elegantly tilted nostrils of John Wood as the great detective, the fuzzy hair of wild-eyed Professor Moriarty (Philip Locke), the lighted cigar in the gas-filled boiler room were all intended to invoke chuckles of recognition, not gasps of astonishment.

John Steinbeck's *Of Mice and Men* was also reprocessed by casting a black actor (James Earl Jones) in the part of simple-minded, hulking Lennie, with Kevin Conway as his mentor George. The acting, direction (by Edwin Sherin) and design (by William and Jean Eckart) were top-notch, but the added interracial tensions gave little to the drama and actually blurred it in some scenes. Eugene O'Neill's drama of a mixed marriage, *All God's Chillun Got Wings,* was staged by George C. Scott at Circle in the Square with his wife, Trish Van Devere, as the white city girl who marries her devoted black childhood sweetheart and then disintegrates under the pressures of their relationship. It was a sound production, but its most conspicuous revelation was that the playwright didn't have a very strong grip on this weighty subject, by modern standards. The massive musical effort to put *Good News* on a modern pedestal was the conspicuous demise of the year, even with memorable tunes added to the score, the Abe Burrows touch in adaptation and staging, and Alice Faye leading the cast. S.J. Perelman's comedy *The Beauty Part,* long supposed to have been an innocent victim of a newspaper strike in its initial Broadway production, proved to be less than durable in an American Place production off Broadway. Lindsay Kemp's effort to re-examine Oscar Wilde's *Salome* with the addition of mime and other innovative concepts proved not very productive.

The 1974–75 revival season served purpose number 1 by making an international firmament of the New York theater scene, attracting star performers from all over the world to shine with their special colors in specially chosen circumstances: the high-tensile strength and sensuality of Elizabeth Ashley in Tennessee Williams's *Cat on a Hot Tin Roof*... a replay of Jim Dale's *Scapino*... Maggie Smith, embodying frivolity as Noel Coward's Amanda in *Private Lives*... Ben Gazzara throwing verbal punches as Erie Smith in O'Neill's monologue *Hughie* ... the outward style and inward vibrations of Liv Ullmann in *A Doll's House* ... charm and abrasion perfectly paired and contrasted in Diana Rigg and Alec McCowen in *The Misanthrope*... the glow of Ingrid Bergman in *The Constant Wife*... the subtleties of character brought by Michael Moriarty to the title role of *Richard III*.

Revivals also fulfilled the second-named purpose in providing live entertainment where there might otherwise have been a shortage. The great Broadway musical *Gypsy* was given a new look in the successful revival directed by its multi-gifted author, Arthur Laurents, and starring Angela Lansbury, who won a Tony Award for her reinterpretation of the Ethel Merman role. An excellent cast headed by Raul Julia disported itself under Theodore Mann's direction in the Circle in the Square revival of *Where's Charley?* The La Mama Plexus Company settled in for a Broadway run with *Dance With Me,* a comedy with music expanded as well as revived from its earlier 1971 productions at La Mama and the Public Theater.

The Public Theater played its part by inviting other companies to use such of its stages as happened to be empty. The visitors who helped expand Joseph Papp's 1974–75 schedule included the Shaliko Company in distinguished presentations of Bertolt Brecht's *The Measures Taken* (its first professional New York revival) and Ibsen's *Ghosts.* Also visiting downtown was The Manhattan Project in a return engagement of its revival of Samuel Beckett's *Endgame* and a new interpretation of *The Seagull* in the Andre Gregory's troupe's imaginative style. Brooklyn too was the scene of notable revival activity with its Academy of Music hosting the Royal Shakespeare Company, whose Ian Richardson headed a travelling troupe presenting Gorky's *Summerfolk* (its first professional New York production), *Love's Labour's Lost* and an abbreviated *King Lear.* This company also put on a new selection of Shakespearean excerpts on the subject of royalty and monarchy, entitled *He That Plays the King,* in its U.S. premiere. Finally in Brooklyn there was Chelsea Theater Center's amusing *Polly.* a handsome and lively refurbishing of John Gay's musical sequel to *The Beggar's Opera.*

The third major purpose of exercising and stretching artistic muscles was amply served all over town. The visiting Royal Shakespeare production of Dion Boucicault's 19th-century comedy *London Assurance* (about a lordly widower competing with his son for the attentions of a young heiress) was a gem of ensemble stylization, directed by Euan Smith and with Donald Sinden giving one of the season's outstanding performances as the aging suitor. Another British visitor to Broadway, the National Theater's *As You Like It,* stretched its muscles in the concept of this Shakespearean comedy performed by an all-male cast, little more than a stunt in the context of the modern theater. This season's New Phoenix repertory was a triptych of sharp-edged comedies of similar mood but widely differing eras: Congreve's *Love for Love* (directed by Harold Prince in a season which he spent between musicals), Pirandello's *The Rules of the Game* and Carson McCullers's *The Member of the Wedding.*

Off Broadway, Gene Feist's steadily active Roundabout Theater Company expanded into a second theater in its midtown neighborhood by acquiring and remodeling the RKO 23d Street movie house and renaming it Stage Two, the Roundabout's Stage One being its former and retained headquarters at 307 West 26th Street. This organization's busy season of high-quality offerings included four revivals on its busy schedule: Arthur Miller's *All My Sons,* Ibsen's *Rosmersholm,* Sheridan's *The Rivals* and Barrie's *What Every Woman Knows.* Only Joseph Papp's Shakespeare operation comes anywhere near the Roundabout in establishing a New York repertory *presence.* This year in the Delacorte, Papp essayed the seldom-seen *Pericles, Prince of Tyre* with Randall Duk Kim in the title role and *The Merry Wives of Windsor* with Barnard Hughes as Falstaff. In the Newhouse Theater at Lincoln Center Papp followed the distinguished Moriarty *Richard III* with a production of *A Midsummer Night's Dream,* then turned the smaller theater over to the presentation of a new script, thus falling short of his announced ambition to have Shakespeare revivals continuously available to New York audiences in that modest facility.

Finally, purpose number 4—historical perspective on the living theater—is perhaps the most precious byproduct of all this revival activity in New York. No single repertory company could possibly serve so grand a purpose; it is possible only in the large context of a great world theater capital and only in a time when the audience appetite for live entertainment exceeds the supply of satisfying new work. New York City is such a place, and recent seasons have provided such a time. This one was no exception. Here's a list of New York's 37 Broadway and off-Broadway revivals, in the alphabetical order of their authors:

George Abbott (with Frank Loesser)
Where's Charley?

Greg Antonacci
Dance With Me

James M. Barrie
What Every Woman Knows

Samuel Beckett
Endgame

Dion Boucicault
London Assurance

Bertolt Brecht
The Measures Taken

Anton Chekhov
The Seagull

William Congreve
Love for Love

Noel Coward
Private Lives

John Gay
Polly

William Gillette
Sherlock Holmes

Maxim Gorky
Summerfolk

Henrik Ibsen
A Doll's House
Ghosts
Rosmersholm

Arthur Laurents (with Jule Styne and Stephen Sondheim)
  Gypsy
W. Somerset Maugham
  The Constant Wife
Carson McCullers
  The Member of the Wedding
Arthur Miller
  All My Sons
Molière
  The Misanthrope
  Scapino
Eugene O'Neill
  All God's Chillun Got Wings
  Hughie (with David Scott Milton's *Duet*)
S.J. Perelman
  The Beauty Part
Luigi Pirandello
  The Rules of the Game

Laurence Schwab, B.G. DeSylva and Frank Mandel
  Good News
William Shakespeare
  As You Like It
  King Lear
  Love's Labour's Lost
  The Merry Wives of Windsor
  A Midsummer Night's Dream
  Pericles, Prince of Tyre
  Richard III
Richard Brinsley Sheridan
  The Rivals
John Steinbeck
  Of Mice and Men
Oscar Wilde
  Salome
Tennessee Williams
  Cat on a Hot Tin Roof

Off Broadway

Nobody told the off-Broadway theater that 1974-75 was going to be a great year—not until April, that is. Off Broadway just dawdled along until the last three months of the season, when all at once it seemed to get the word and caught up fast.

Once so vital to the experimental side of the New York theater, off Broadway is now priced so high in both production costs and tickets that experiment has become too expensive for both producer and show-shopper. In independent production, this tends to create a mini-Broadway with a repressive hit psychology. And the alternative, the semi-sheltered (by subsidy) institutional production with its semi built-in (by subscription) audiences, was also facing up to hard times of reduced funding from both government and private sources. It was still dominant in 1974-75, however, with 22 of the 30 new American playscripts produced in organizational schedules. On the independent side, there was one Best Play *(The Wager)* and one that came close *(Naomi Court)*—and of course the off-Broadway flagship continued to sail on proudly in the longest run of record in the American theater, as *The Fantasticks* gave its 6,281st performance on May 31 and still counting. There have been 3,788 productions of this extraordinary Tom Jones-Harvey Schmidt musical in all the 50 states and 248 productions in 54 foreign countries.

The 1974–75 Season off Broadway

PLAYS (30)

Negro Ensemble 1974:
In the Deepest Part
  of Sleep
Why Hanna's Skirt Won't
  Stay Down
Naomi Court
Public Theater:
Where Do We Go From
  Here?
The Last Days of
  British Honduras
In the Boom Boom Room
  (revised)
Our Late Night
Kid Champion
Fishing
Chelsea Theater Center:
Hothouse
Yentl the Yeshiva Boy
Santa Anita 42
THE WAGER
Ridiculous Company:
Stage Blood
Bluebeard
Hotel for Criminals
Four Friends
James Joyce's Dubliners
Negro Ensemble 1975:
The First Breeze of
  Summer
Liberty Call
Sugar Mouth Sam Don't
Dance No More & Orrin
The Moonlight Arms &
  The Dark Tower
Welcome to Black River
Waiting for Mongo

American Place:
Killer's Head & Action
Rubbers & Yanks 3
*Detroit O Top of the
  Seventh*
Augusta
Parto
Women Behind Bars
THE TAKING OF MISS
  JANIE

FOREIGN PLAYS
IN ENGLISH (3)

The Burnt Flowerbed
The Advertisement
Bullshot Crummond

MUSICALS (12)

I'll Die if I Can't Live
  Forever
How to Get Rid of It
The Prodigal Sister
Diamond Studs
Lovers
Wings
Be Kind to People Week
Philemon
A Matter of Time
The $ Value of Man
The Glorious Age
A CHORUS LINE

REVUES (5)

Some People, Some Other
  People and What They
  Finally Do
Pretzels
Broadway Dandies
The National Lampoon Show
In Gay Company

REVIVALS (17)

Delacorte:
Pericles, Prince of
  Tyre
The Merry Wives of
  Windsor
Roundabout Company:
All My Sons
The Rivals
Rosmersholm
*What Every Woman
  Knows*
Public Theater:
The Measures Taken
The Seagull
Ghosts
Newhouse Theater:
Richard III
A Midsummer Night's
  Dream
The Beauty Part
Salome
Royal Shakespeare:
Summerfolk
Love's Labour's Lost
King Lear
Polly

RETURN
ENGAGEMENTS (3)

Public Theater:
Alice in Wonderland
Endgame
The Wild Stunt Show

SPECIALTIES (11)

The World of Lenny Bruce
Chelsea Westside:
La Carpa de los
  Rasquachis
The Mother
The Great Air Robbery
Baird Marionettes:
Peter and the Wolf
Alice in Wonderland
Blasts and Bravos
He That Plays the King
The Ramayana
The Dybbuk & Priscilla,
  Princess of Power
The Magic of Jolson

Categorized above are all the plays listed in the "Plays Produced off Broadway" section of this volume.
Plays listed in CAPITAL LETTERS have been designated Best Plays of 1974–75.
Plays listed in *italics* were still running June 1, 1975.

Another independent off-Broadway production, *Godspell,* was was also exhibiting unusual stamina, passing its 1,684th performance, while *The Hot l Baltimore,* not far behind *Godspell* at 943 performances, carried the off-Broadway banner into network television with a half-hour comedy series based on the Lanford Wilson characters and situation.

When the final numbers were in for 1974–75, off-Broadway production volume was up from last year, including a small rise in new American plays (from 27 to 30) and a doubling of new musicals (from 6 to 12), plus a spate of specialties and revues and the previously-reported high level of revival activity. The total off-Broadway programming has been recorded in recent *Best Plays* volumes as follows: 119 in 1969–70, 95 in 1970–71, 87 in 1971–72, 87 in 1972–73, 76 in 1973–74 and finally 81 in 1974–75. As for quality, off Broadway held its own with the abovementioned *The Wager* plus two institutionally-produced Best Plays— *The Taking of Miss Janie* and *A Chorus Line*—plus the close contenders like *The First Breeze of Summer, Yanks 3 Detroit 0 Top of the Seventh, James Joyce's Dubliners, Philemon, Diamond Studs* and *Naomi Court.*

One of the reasons why the off-Broadway season at times seemed less successful than it later turned out to be was that it went somewhat sour for Joseph Papp in 1974–75. Papp's New York Shakespeare Festival is the leading producer off Broadway (and by volume in all New York as well) with five auditoria in the Public Theater downtown, his open-air season in Central Park and his small "off-Broadway" Newhouse Theater in Lincoln Center. At season's end, Papp threw the towel in and his hands up with the announcement that he would abandon off-Broadway production and take over the Booth Theater on Broadway for the production of new scripts. The Public Theater is to be given over to off-off-Broadway-level, work-in-progress, limited-engagement-type productions and the Newhouse to children's theater. Also, in disgust at the lame audience response to his Broadway-scale new-play schedule at the Beaumont, Papp declared further that he plans to turn the big Lincoln Center theater over to revivals.

The heart of this matter seems to be that the off-Broadway production environment has now failed to support even so entrenched and subsidized a group as Papp's, so that he must move up the scale to Broadway or perish. But it's hard to draw any such definite or sweeping conclusion from Papp's 1974–75 season, in which the quality of the plays gave little reason for audience enthusiasm in any corner of the Papp empire for 11 of the 12 months. And Papp has never sustained himself by keeping his hits going off Broadway, he has always moved his successes into the bigger theaters, beginning with *Hair* in his first season at the Public. If he no longer considers himself an off-Broadway impresario, perhaps he is merely one of the last to discover that he never was.

In any case, Papp managed to end his season with a bang as well as a whimper. At almost the year's last second he brought one of the year's best plays into the limelight. Like last season's *Short Eyes,* Ed Bullins's *The Taking of Miss Janie* was developed off off Broadway and later acquired by Papp for commercial showing. *Miss Janie,* like some other Bullins plays, was first produced by Woodie King Jr.'s New Federal Theater at the Henry Street Playhouse. As a result of an agreement announced in April, Papp will now provide input into the New Federal schedule of productions and, in the case of the more successful ones, bring them before a larger public in his uptown or downtown facilities.

The New Federal Theater production of *Miss Janie* was brought to the Newhouse Theater under this agreement. It proved to be Bullins's best programlength script to date (it is a long one-acter, playing without intermission), a parable of race relations in the 1960s in the encounter between a black would-be poet (Adeyemi Lythcott) and his blonde classmate and devoted friend (Hilary Jean Beane) whom he suddenly rapes after years of friendship. Bullins has often used the party as a microcosm of life, a means of mixing attitudes to produce reactions of social conflict and comment. He does so again here, in a play dominated by characters symbolic of both black and white stupidities and by the bad vibes of outside 1960s events such as the shocking assassinations. *The Taking of Miss Janie* has a sharper focus under Gilbert Moses's direction than similar Bullins works—*The Pig Pen* (to which this play is a kind of sequel) and *The Duplex*, to name two; its dialogue has the incisiveness of Bullins's best one-acters. *Miss Janie* won the New York Drama Critics Circle award as the best American play of the year in a close contest with *Seascape*, and it now brings Bullins his first Best Play citation.

Miss Janie was merely a guest in Papp's house, but *A Chorus Line*, also a Critics Award winner and by far the best musical of the season, was a member of the New York Shakespeare production family from its outset. It was a beautifully simple show: on a bare stage sometimes backed with mirrors in which audience and dancers can see themselves doubled (as in last season's *Jumpers*), a Broadway musical director lines up 17 chorus aspirants from which he is going to pick eight for the chorus of his show. Because some of them may have a side or two of dialogue, and to get some insight into their skills and personalities, he asks each of the dancers to tell him something about themselves. The "director" is more often than not a disembodied voice on the public address system, like a god or at least a Delphic sibyl to whom these young people open themselves in awe. They speak in the various idioms of the musical stage, sometimes singing, sometimes joking, sometimes drawing out painfully their secret sexual and other hangups, but more often dancing, for this is a dancers' show as conceived, directed and choreographed by Michael Bennett. It is about dancers, by dancers; incredibly lithe and disciplined bodies driven, it seems, by damaged and overcompensating psyches. They long and strive mightily for the safe and yet exciting, fulfilling anonymity of the chorus line. This theme is expressed in Edward Kleban's sensitive lyrics for a song called "At the Ballet" in which one of these insecure young people notes that in the ballet when you reach out your arms there's always someone there.

Marvin Hamlisch's *A Chorus Line* music is sophisticated, singable, danceable, never missing the mood any more than it would miss the beat. A great charm of this show was its seamlessness, nothing bulging out of proportion, a true ensemble of authorship, staging and performance, running without intermission. Donna McKechnie as a onetime leading dancer now trying to start all over again in the chorus and Robert LuPone as the poker-faced "director" of the show come on a shade stronger than the others, in a production that is as much a blend of performers as of colors in Theoni V. Aldredge's rehearsal costumes or the blend of score and emotion, as near perfect as the unison of a Rockettes finale.

One distinguished guest production and one late-blooming, smash-hit musical —and two Critics awards—not Papp's finest New York season, perhaps, but certainly not his worst. What then of the long list of 1974–75 New York Shakespeare Festival productions that caused him to abandon off Broadway as a concept at the Public and new-play production at Lincoln Center? On the Public's schedule, Michael Weller's *Fishing* and Thomas Babe's *Kid Champion* showed some signs of theatrical vigor. The former, by the author of *Moonchildren*, looked in on a group of now-grown-up moonchildren, functionless and apparently aimless, groping for a meaningful existence and meanwhile taking drugs to pass the time. It at least established an atmosphere, a presence, onstage, as did the Babe play in a series of highly-flavored episodes in the life and times of a popular rock star (and Lindsay Crouse in the former play and Christopher Walken in the title role of the latter gave Public Theater audiences a little more than they found in their vehicles). Also at the Public Theater there was John Ford Noonan's portrait of a transvestite and his friends in *Where Do We Go From Here?*, one of many scripts on this subject this season, and not the best—the best was *Hosanna* on Broadway. There was Ronald Tavel's *The Last Days of British Honduras,* a science-fiction-mystery treatment of the disappearance of Mayan civilization in the 12th century.

Last year, Papp introduced his new-play policy at the Beaumont with David Rabe's *Boom Boom Room,* a blurred, black character sketch of a go-go dancer. It didn't do well uptown, and it didn't do any better downtown this season in a revised version called *In the Boom Boom Room.* Such was Papp's off-Broadway new-play season in 1974–75 (the remainder of the Public's schedule consisted of guest productions, including revivals, by The Manhattan Project and Shaliko). No firm diagnosis of off-Broadway's condition can be made from shows like these —and the same is true of the those uptown at the Beaumont, described earlier in this report. If Joseph Papp meant what he said and has really drawn irrevocable conclusions about the future of off-Broadway and new-play production at the Beaumont from the fate of the shows he presented this season, he is wearing dark glasses to judge a thunderstorm.

The vital signs of independent off-Broadway production are a more reliable indication of its general health than any institutional play schedule—and unfortunately these continued to decline in 1974–75. The truth is as simple as a thermometer reading: production costs have risen in multiples, so exprimentation is ruled out at the source; and ticket prices have risen so high ($8.50 for *The Hot l Baltimore,* $8.95 for *Diamond Studs,* for example, and not extraordinary ones) that audiences can't afford adventure, either, and support only the smash hits. This might be called the Broadway syndrome, and there's no doubt it is far advanced off Broadway too, where in 1974–75 there was only one Best Play in independent production as compared with three last season. This was *The Wager* by Mark Medoff, a script as sophisticated as Medoff's 1974 Best Play *When You Comin' Back, Red Ryder?* was elemental. *The Wager's* leading character is a graduate student (most forcefully realized in Kristoffer Tabori's performance), an intellectual gymnast who has deliberately dominated and suppressed every emotion within himself and is now capable of total dispassion—almost. He treats his fellow-students like flies placed there expressly for him to pull their wings off. He bets that his athlete-roommate can't seduce the married student next door without inciting her husband to murder and then does his best to induce both actions, the seduction being a kind of flagellation because he's rather drawn to the woman himself. She is openly and confessedly interested him him, but of course he won't respond to either her hints or, finally, her open pleas. *The Wager* was tried out off off Broadway last year and directed off Broadway this year by Anthony Perkins in a production which was only one interpretation—albeit a good one— of a subtle script that will have a different color in each production in theaters around the world. The fact that it couldn't survive off Broadway for more than 104 performances tells more about economic conditions in the smaller New York theaters today than all the shows in Papp's theaters put together.

Elsewhere in independent off-Broadway production, Michael Sawyer's *Naomi Court* provided two of the season's most keenly-felt, if abhorrent, experiences in a program of two one-acters tied together by their setting, a soon-to-be-razed apartment building. The first play showed a lonely woman creating an ideal middle-aged lover in her imagination to relieve her intense longing; the second was an episode of sheer menace with a little burglary and a lot of sex perversion thrown in.

Then there were two Tom Eyen amusements which opened off Broadway under individual auspices after having been tried by groups off off Broadway: *Why Hanna's Skirt Won't Stay Down,* a program of linked comedies about a pair of sisters, and *Women Behind Bars,* a takeoff of women's prison movies. The three 1974–75 foreign scripts did less for the off-Broadway season than their counterparts did on Broadway. They were *The Advertisement* (Italian, an emotional tangle in modern Rome); *Bullshot Crummond* (a British lampoon of detective thrillers); plus the one produced institutionally, *The Burnt Flowerbed* (the New York professional premiere at the Roundabout of Ugo Betti's 1952 play about an aging political leader).

Other independent off-Broadway production was more striving than succeeding (and if costs weren't so high, that's the way it ought to be off Broadway; an experimental theater's reach should often exceed its grasp). This was nowhere more apparent than on the musical stages. The year's musicals included *I'll Die if I Can't Live Forever* (a youthful expression of show-biz ambitions), *How to Get Rid of It* (an Eric Blau-Mort Shuman effort to musicalize Ionesco's *Amedée*), *Lovers* (a hymn to homosexuality), *Wings* (an effort to musicalize Aristophanes's *The Birds*), *Be Kind to People Week* (a harmonious chord in these discordant times, in a fable about a girl who wants to unite all the militant groups) and *The Glorious Age* (a Cy Young fantasy of medieval times).

Among the season's best off-Broadway musicals, *Philemon* was produced independently as a work in progress by Tom Jones and Harvey Schmidt in their Portfolio Studio and finally made available for public viewing for a few weeks in the spring. Based on a third-century Christian legend, it is a bloody, tortured tale of a clown who masquerades as a Christian leader in order to spy for the Roman tyrant until he's trapped by his role into real martyrdom. Both musically and dramatically, it was a powerful and memorable show, even if sometimes a little too heavy for its own strength. In contrasting mood, Chelsea Theater Center's *Diamond Studs* provided one of the season's pleasantest diversions with a stylized, folklorish musical about the life and times of Jesse James. *The Prodigal Sister,* a promising musical of the black big-city experience by J.E. Franklin and Micki Grant, was brought uptown by the New Federal Theater but couldn't find a commercial-theater audience. *The $ Value of Man* was yet another of those Byrd Hoffman Foundation (Robert Wilson) "operas" that seem to be offered almost exclusively for the amusement of the performers.

In the area of new playscripts, the institutional producers carried the day off Broadway. After a very slow start, with off Broadway looking about the way Joseph Papp says it does for months and months, the superior scripts came tumbling in on each other's heels. The Negro Ensemble Company can always be depended on to produce at least one very strong play every year; this year's was *The First Breeze of Summer* by Leslie Lee, a reflection on three generations of a black, now middle-class family, as the quarrels of the younger members set their much-admired grandmother to remembering some of the sacrifices and heartaches she had to suffer in order to bring them all this far. With Frances Foster in another of her portrayals of a lovable, indomitable matriarch under Douglas Turner Ward's direction, this was a highlight of the off-Broadway year which, following the present pattern, was set to move to Broadway in July. The NEC 1975 schedule included another "Season-Within-a-Season," a schedule of four programs of new plays by Burial Clay, Don Evans, Rudy Wallace and Samm Williams showcased for one-week runs each. Finally, NEC presented Silas Jones's *Waiting for Mongo,* a reality-fantasy kaleidoscope of the thoughts of a rapist in hiding.

American Place, too, took time to hit its stride this year. An effort to bring back S.J. Perelman's *The Beauty Part* got their season off on the wrong foot, and it didn't recover until April with the arrival of a new Sam Shepard program: *Killer's Head* (a murderer's thoughts in the electric chair just before the current is turned on) and the longer *Action,* produced last year in London by the Royal Court (a symbolic representation of the human condition by four bedraggled souls unable to take hold of themselves or their lives). Challenging as this program was, American place finished its season with an even bigger bang in a May program of two one-acters by an outstanding new playwright, Jonathan Reynolds. The first, *Rubbers,* was a broad satire on the machinations of the New York State Assembly (or any other such body), with an eager-beaver representative from Brooklyn (Laura Esterman) introducing a bill calling for open display of contraceptives in drug stores, over the loud objections of the entrenched, fossilized majority of her colleagues. It was like an erratic fast-ball pitcher, wild but with some great stuff—and that brings us to the second of Reynolds's plays whose title expressed its situation: *Yanks 3 Detroit 0 Top of the Seventh.* It was observed from the point of view of the pitcher's mound, where an over-the-hill Yankee pitcher has a perfect game so far but is slowly losing the confidence to complete it, and consequently his stuff except for a slider which his opponents are beginning to hit. Perfectly played by Tony Lo Bianco, the pitcher treats the audience to a batter-by-batter account of his fears of the moment—which is only a game, after all—and for his future, which is not. He tries to hide his fears from his thin-skinned catcher "Beanie" Maligma (Lou Criscuolo) and his manager, a rubber stamp of sports cliches. Both *Rubbers* and *Yanks 3 Detroit 0* were uneven in style, a problem which the director, Alan Arkin, wasn't able to solve, but they reached peaks of satire (and, in the latter case, of pathos as well) seldom attained in this season's shows. The success of this program caused American Place to suspend its subscriptions-only policy for the first time and open its box office for the sale of tickets to the public on a regular basis.

The name of Gene Feist's Roundabout Theater Company conjures images of bright revivals in its midtown setting, but like the other off-Broadway organizations it too presented a strong new script in its 1974–75 schedule. *James Joyce's Dubliners* was a study of the *Ulysses* author's youth and family life, dominated by his father (played by Stan Watt)—a stubborn, opinionated, courageous but debt- and booze-ridden parent who was surely destined to find a brilliant son among his nine children and bound to clash with him and finally drive him from the Joyces' poor excuse for a home in search of a more fulfilling life. Philip Campanella's original music and lyrics provided a punctuation of Irish ballads expressing the ineffable sweetness within the hard shell of despair, surviving under any and all pressures. *James Joyce's Dubliners* was as episodic as most biographical dramas, but at the same time a colorful and moving show with the sprawling succession of times, places and characters neatly compressed and plainly expressed under Gene Feist's direction. According to the credits, the script was based on James's younger brother Stanislaus's *My Brother's Keeper* and written by one J.W. Riordan whom we might hail as a promising new playwright if we weren't pretty sure that Riordan is none other than that same Gene Feist disguised in an Irish brogue and pseudonym. For whatever reason he may have chosen to adopt this bushel, decidedly there was a light under it.

Diamond Studs was the hit of Chelsea Theater Center's 1974–75 show, but it was only a small segment of Chelsea's energetic and eclectic schedule spread out across the river into both boroughs. In the home base in Brooklyn there were three new scripts and a revival, all of more than routine value: Megan Terry's *Hothouse,* trying for a comic blend by dissolving three generations of man-hungry women in alcohol; *Yentl the Yeshiva Boy*, adapted by Leah Napolin and Isaac Bahevis Singer from Singer's own story, with Tovah Feldshuh playing a 19th-century Polish girl so hungry for learning that she disguises herself as a boy in order to seize the opportunities denied to her sex; *Santa Anita '42,* Allan Knee's drama of Japanese Americans interned at a California racetrack during World War II; and *Polly,* the John Gay sequel to his *The Beggar's Opera,* a beautifully-mounted collector's item if there ever was one. *Yentl* proved to be the hardiest and most appealing element of Chelsea's home program and is to join the parade of off-Broadway hits bound for Broadway next season. In its Manhattan playhouse in the West Forties, Chelsea put on a "World Series" of guest appearances, including San Francisco Mime Troupe and a return engagement of London's *Wild Stunt Show.*

Over at Charles Ludlam's Ridiculous Theatrical Company they mixed and stirred their ingredients as before, with the usual result that Ludlam's fanciful productions came out a bright shade of purple. His *Stage Blood* was a *Hamlet* played by clowns (a group of touring players) using an amateur Ophelia and contriving a happy ending and anything else that might be good for a laugh, onstage or backstage. *Bluebeard* was more of the same special madness. Still another far-out ensemble, the Music-Theater Performing Group under the direction of Richard Foreman (the *Doctor Selavy's Magic Theater* man) tried a musical satire of film melodramas, *Hotel for Criminals,* with mixed results.

Many off-Broadway revues and specialties made bright little corners of entertainment here and there in the huge grey city. *Pretzels* was an assortment of tuneful and witty comments on urban foibles. *The National Lampoon Show* took off where *National Lampoon's Lemmings* left off, in its form of comic commentary. The revue *In Gay Company* provided an outlet for special interest in one direction; the one-man show *The World of Lenny Bruce* with Frank Speiser provided another (and a rare if not unique instance of a replacement in a one-man show when Ted Schwartz substituted for Speiser the last two weeks of the run).

The year's programs also included the Indian epic *The Ramayana* dramatized as a one-woman reading (by Jalabala Vaidya) in English; Paul Shyre's one-man presentation of H.L. Mencken and his works, *Blasts and Bravos;* and the National Theater of the Deaf in *The Dybbuk* and *Priscilla, Princess of Power,* the latter a comic-book-style entertainment based on a James Stevenson script about the prevalence of sugar in the American diet. And for the ninth season the Baird Marionettes offered a diet of delight with their version of *Peter and the Wolf* and a new marionette musical adaptation of *Alice in Wonderland* with book by A.J. Russell, music by Joe Raposo and lyrics by Sheldon Harnick, with Alice portrayed both by a marionette and a live actress.

If off Broadway is indeed d-e-a-d (Joseph Papp spelled it out to make sure the *Times* reporter got it right), then where did these 80-odd shows come from? Some were vanity productions, true. Others were plastic or worse. Still others were sheltered under special umbrellas from the direct, cruel blasts of this year's economic conditions. But there was also a group of a least ten good, solid, entertaining, challenging shows that might never have appeared under today's limited Broadway circumstances, or would almost certainly have passed unnoticed in the seething experimental crucible of off off Broadway's work in progress. True, it's much harder these days—which is to say much, much more expensive —to rare back and defy hubris with a single, independent off-Broadway production; and it must be agonizingly difficult, too, to mount a schedule of productions in a semi-subsidized organization, with the present shrinkage of public and private support for the performing arts. But it's not impossible—not yet, anyway, judging from our perspective on 1974–75 off Broadway. And until it is, if it ever is, never say die.

Offstage

In the strange economic and artistic climate of the 1974-75 season, stage production began to proliferate, even populating a new area: dinner theater so-called, a twofer proposition holding out the promise of dinner (not just a snack or a short-order meal) followed by a program-length live show to be enjoyed without moving from the table, where after-dinner refreshment often continues to be available, especially in the calculatedly long intermissions. The type of show, if not the food, tends to be light. This new development has scarcely touched New York City (possibly because of the many cabaret-style entertainments already available there), though the Belasco on Broadway was adapted for tables instead of aisles for the brief run of the imported musical *The Rocky Horror Show.* Indeed, dinner theater isn't aimed at the regular theatergoer at all, but at a new audience coaxed by the promise of being fed and cosseted into putting its toe into live-theater entertainment. An all-inclusive tab of, say, $13 per person would have about $5 apportioned as the show-biz share and the rest for food. A review of the 1974-75 dinner theater season by Francine L. Trevens appears in "The Season Around the United States" section of this volume.

While dinner theater was creating new audiences across the country, the TKTS cut-rate ticket booths were doing the same right in Manhattan, in the heart of Times Square and down on Wall Street. These booths are a non-profit venture sponsored by the Theater Development Fund and others. Now in its second season, TKTS offers unsold same-day tickets to Broadway and off-Broadway shows at half price plus a $.50 surcharge for the tickets listed at less than $10 and $1 for the more expensive ones. During the 12 months of the season, according to *Variety* estimate, TKTS moved 652,864 tickets (more than half a million Broadway, the rest off Broadway and Lincoln Center) for receipts of $3,239,417. This amounts to somewhere between 4 and 5 per cent of the year's total gross. In the report on its first fiscal year in December, TKTS calculated that of the $2,339,618 taken in at its windows, $2,051,898 went to the theaters and only $287,720 for maintenance. The Wall Street TKTS base was new this season, and business there was disappointing, according to Hugh Sothern, executive director of the Theater Development Fund, but helpful in bringing new audiences into the theaters.

Some of theater subsidy's 1974-75 problems arose inevitably from troublesome economic conditions, and some did not. It was obvious early in the season that with money in increasingly short supply from both private and public sources, the various stage enterprises which rely heavily on subsidy were entering upon hard times, made still harder by pressures on the foundations to direct more and more of their shrinking resources to relieve sociological instead of artistic want. The National Endowment's $6.1 million in theater grants was up $2 million from the previous season but barely covered sharply-rising costs when spread thinly over the whole surface of the American stage. The Endowment roused some resentment with a $250,000 matching grant to the Royal Shakespeare Company for special educational performances and programs at American universities.

Stage groups complained that American companies were more deserving of this American subsidy (it should be noted, however, that this was an education, not an arts, grant from the Endowment; at least the funds didn't come out of the arts pocket). The Federal arts allotment for 1974–75 was $74,750,000 out of $81 million requested by the Endowment. For next season, the White House has asked Congress for $82 million for the arts. New York State's subsidy was pegged at about $34 million to spread around its non-profit performing arts organizations ($21.5 million for basic support, $7.6 million for program funding, $5 million for community arts services), and the same amount has been requested for next year.

Among offstage activities of individuals this season was Neil Simon's decision to give himself a working Sabbatical on the West Coast. The most successful dramatist of the modern era moved from New York to California with his wife, the actress Marsha Mason, for a couple of years or so while his younger daughter goes to school there and while both the elder Simons fulfill movie commitments. Simon isn't turning his back on Broadway, which was alleged in some reports. He still owns the Eugene O'Neill Theater, where his 14th Broadway production, *God's Favorite,* was housed this season, and he hopes to have a new script ready year after next. In his own words, "I need a year off from the theater. Coming up with a play a year for so long a time has been rigorous, and I need a rest. But I certainly plan to be back."

Another distinguished legitimate stage artist, George Abbott, was getting ready to celebrate his 88th birthday and the 117th show with which he's been associated as actor, author, director or producer and sometimes a little of each. (The new Abbott show is *Music Is,* which he'll stage next season after writing the book.) Abbott's 116th show, according to *Variety's* count, was a hit revival of *Life With Father* which he directed this season in Seattle.

In another part of the forest, Tennessee Williams was elected to a three-year term on the governing council of the Dramatists Guild, the professional organization of America's and some of Europe's 2,500 actual and would-be playwrights, librettists, lyricists and composers. This group of authors communicates frankly and regularly with each other in their own publication, the *Dramatists Guild Quarterly;* and theater fans can now audit their dialogue in an anthology entitled *Playwrights/Lyricists/Composers on Theater* published by Dodd, Mead and containing more than 35 articles, plus scores of short comments including one on the function of the dramatist by this same Tennessee Williams.

Among critics, the question of who would follow in Richard Watts Jr.'s large and long-running professional footsteps as drama critic of the New York *Post* was answered when Marton Gottfried switched from *Women's Wear* to the *Post* job. Among press agents, Merle Debuskey was re-elected to the presidency of the Association of Theatrical Press Agents and Managers, with Harvey Sabinson as vice president.

What is often referred to as the "critical fraternity" of those who cover American theater has been anything but fraternal. Unlike their European counterparts, American critics have never banded together in any organization (except for local groups formed solely to give prizes, like the New York Drama Critics Circle). They've never had a spokesman who could represent them officially at international convocations, etc. Now all that is changed. In August 1974, 23 working critics in various media in cities from New York to Los Angeles met under the auspices and roof of the Eugene O'Neill Memorial Theater Center in Waterford, Conn. and formed an American Theater Critics Association with this agreed-upon statement of purposes:

Since the American theater is beginning once again to become a truly national institution, we have formed an American Theater Critics Association in order to pursue the following goals:
1. To make possible greater communication among American theater critics.
2. To encourage absolute freedom of expression in the theater and in theater criticism.
3. To advance the standards of the theater by advancing the standards of theater criticism.
4. To increase public awareness of the theater as an important national resource.
5. To reaffirm the individual critic's right to disagree with his colleagues on all matters, including the above.

The bylaws of this new critics' organization call for an executive committee with staggered terms. Those elected were Henry Hewes (New York, executive secretary), Ernest Scheier (Philadelphia), Elliot Norton (Boston), Dan Sullivan (Los Angeles) and Clara Hieronymus (Nashville). Among other cities represented in the Association's charter membership were Washington, Detroit, Denver, Cincinnati, Indianapolis and Providence. Representatives of national publications included the critics of *Time, The New Yorker* and *Best Plays.*

Along Times Square, the process of theater demolition seemed to have been slowed by economic difficulties attending the announced, grandiose new construction schemes. As of season's end the Morosco and Helen Hayes Theaters still stood where a big hole for a skyscraper office-hotel complex had been planned. The Winter Garden was damaged by fire but soon repaired. The talk about "cleaning up" Times Square and establishing a Broadway pedestrians' mall continued through this season and will probably go on through the next. Forty-second Street is still a zoo and vice is said to thrive behind the neon-colored mask of Broadway; but violent crime in the streets seemed to be stamped out in New York's principal Broadway and off-Broadway theater districts, at least at show time and for a long time before and after.

Lawsuits may be an unhappy means of settling arts controversies, but they often exert a profound influence on the economics and even the esthetics of the theater. A United States Supreme Court ruling in March, overturning lower-court rulings in support of a Chattanooga ban on the musical *Hair,* extended the freedom-of-speech protection of the First Amendment to the theater for the first time. The Authors League filed an *amicus curiae* brief in support of *Hair's* appeal in this case, prepared by Irwin Karp, the League's counsel, who commented as follows on the decision: "The results are not as satisfactory as those the Authors

League and Dramatists Guild would have liked and have been seeking since 1957 —complete First Amendment protection against any restraint on the rights of adults to see any play or read any book they choose to read or view, regardless of its contents. But the. . . . opinion is a first step toward true First Amendment protection for the living stage."

Numerous copyright problems arose and were adjudicated during the year. Many of them arose—and many more will arise—from the new recording devices in both sight and sound, and from lack of clear definitions as to what is "fair use" of copyrighted material by these new duplicating devices. The revised Copyright Act itself, so long in committee, was finally passed by the U.S. Senate, but time ran out before it could get through the House in the 93d Congress. It has been re-introduced in the 94th by Sen. John J. McClellan, chairman of the Senate Judiciary Committee on Patents, Trademarks and Copyrights, and in the House by Rep. Robert W. Kastenmeier. It is expected that this first revision of the national copyright laws since 1909 will have a speedy and uneventful passage through the new Congress.

Alexander H. Cohen, Hildy Parks and their staff surrounded the Tony Awards ceremonies with yet another outstanding TV presentation, this one built around the history of the Winter Garden Theater, where the ceremonies took place. As usual, the Tonys were awarded by vote of theater industry members from a nominations-list prepared by a committee of critics; and as usual, a good deal of controversy arose from the nomination choices. George Rose would have none of his candidacy as a "supporting" player in *My Fat Friend,* claiming that his role was the lead (Frank Langella won in the category, anyway, for his role as the *Seascape* lizard). An even sharper protest was registered by Michael Stewart, nominated for the book of *Mack & Mabel,* whose Jerry Herman score went unnominated. Mr. Stewart bought space in *Variety* to speak his mind about the nominators' "ability to force their prejudices and/or lack of taste on the voting body as a whole," and concluding: "I am a nominee this year, as is the show itself. . . . (God knows why since the score, an integral part of any musical, was judged unqualified to compete). . . . and so help me if I win I'll saw the damned thing in two and give half to the man so unfairly prevented from competing. . . . Jerry Herman." The rules governing the Tony nominating process are to be changed somewhat next year. Among other developments, Isabelle Stevenson, president of the American Theater Wing, which originated the Tony Awards, arranged to have Radie Harris and Richard Weaver represent the Wing on the Tony Adminis-tration Committee of the League of New York Theaters, the producers' organiza-tion which supervises the annual prize-giving process and ceremonies. The Wing also appointed Stuart Little as executive director—its first paid executive—to oversee its activities.

Such were the circumstances of the 1974–75 New York theater season, for better or worse (definitely better), for richer or poorer (definitely richer), in sickness and in health (paradoxically, in some ways more fabulous, in others more of an invalid). The year 1975 will go down in history not only as the one in which the United States of America began to close out its second century, but also—

we ardently hope—as the one in which the theater's pendulum began a long upswing.

As we look forward to the Bicentennial, we can't help noting that no major Bicentennial observation is yet planned on or off Broadway. In line with today's decentralizing trend, the major observances will take place in regional and college theaters which have commissioned and/or held contests for Bicentennial plays. The biggest blast of all will take place, appropriately, at the John F. Kennedy Center for the Performing Arts in Washington, D.C., with a special American Bicentennial Theater season of old and new American plays produced by Roger L. Stevens, the Center's chairman, and Richmond Crinkley. With funding co-sponsorship from Xerox, the Washington theater complex will attempt to mount "a representative selection of American classics and new plays, drawn from the full range and repertory of the American theater."

As of our press time, American Bicentennial Theater had already begun with a production of Thornton Wilder's *The Skin of Our Teeth* (1942) and is to continue with Percy MacKaye's *The Scarecrow* (1909), William Gillette's *Too Much Johnson* (1894), Tennessee Williams's *Sweet Bird of Youth* (1959), George S. Kaufman's and Edna Ferber's *The Royal Family* (1927), Eugene O'Neill's *Long Day's Journey Into Night* (1956), *Rip Van Winkle* (1865) written by Dion Boucicault for Joseph Jefferson, and William Inge's *Bus Stop* (1955). In addition, half a dozen contemporary playwrights have been commissioned to write scripts for possible production by American Bicentennial Theater during the year.

The city of Washington didn't even exist in 1776, but it certainly will be the center of Bicentennial attention in 1975–76, theatrically as well as politically. Still, this American Bicentennial Theater celebration is also a Broadway theater celebration, if only by proxy. New York is where the theater was for those 200 years, and it's still where it's at as far as the majority of new work is concerned. Fly the flags and strike up the band, Washington, but remember your Revolution came from Boston, your Constitution from Philadelphia and your plays from New York and its good old Broadway.

THE 1974–75 SEASON OFF OFF BROADWAY

By Marion Fredi Towbin

Playwright and critic, author of *What! And Leave Bloomingdale's?*

"I NEVER knew off off Broadway was so professional!" This was expressed frequently by students attending *Inside off off Broadway,* a seminar I organized this year at the OOB Joseph Jefferson Theater, housed in the nave of the Little-Church-Around-the-Corner in New York City. The class, comprised of many college students, two lawyers, a receptionist and a marine biologist, attended OOB productions, met actors, producers, directors, foundation executives, New

York *Times* drama critic Mel Gussow and award-winning playwright Edward J. Moore *(The Sea Horse)*. After "intensive exposure" to all aspects of OOB each student realized that OOB is no longer the stepchild of commercial theater, no longer the underdog, the poor relation, the crazy aunt. It's an arena where professionals often *choose* to work. In 1974–75 Tennessee Williams premiered his new play off off; Terrence McNally, with a hit on Broadway, said "I'm not sure I'd want to be a writer if off off Broadway didn't exist"; and La Mama founder Ellen Stewart was awarded the honorary degree Doctor of Humane Letters from Bard College.

The actors working for little or no pay off off Broadway are often between Broadway jobs; they've done Shakespeare in regional theater; often they're "steadies" on the afternoon soap operas, and if they're really lucky they have a commercial running on TV. Many of OOB's directors, designers and, to a lesser extent, playwrights have also worked (and continue to work) in commercial theater. OOB is, and has always been, a place for the young, talented and untried. Increasingly it's becoming a "place to return" for the seasoned artist who wants to experiment—to try out a new play, to interpret a role he'd not find elsewhere, to be challenged—free from commercial pressure.

OOB theaters exist all over the city: in lofts, storefronts, basements, prisons, Y's and church naves. This season I visited Nora and Thorvald in their basement apartment on West 81st Street; witnessed the steady demise of ten murderous English eccentrics in a YMHA on Nagle Avenue in Washington Heights; saw the virile young con man Bill Starbuck sing and create rain in the fleabag Hotel Dixie; and gasped when Frederick Woyzeck was hanged a block south of Luchow's. All this professional theater was happening in a city whose dire financial straits caused the mayor to close schools and hospitals and relegate police and firemen to the unemployment lines. There were so many outstanding shows off off Broadway this year that I wonder if New York will be the only city in history to thrive in the spirit and starve in the flesh. A ticket to any of the Equity Showcases cost considerably less than a hamburger and coke.

Seventeen years ago the late Greenwich Village cafe owner Joe Cino pushed back a table, created a small acting area and invited young unknown playwrights like Lanford Wilson to stage their plays, thus heralding the quiet beginnings of OOB. Today it's an internationally recognized fact that the vitality, spirit and hope of professional American theater exists not on or even off Broadway, but off off. Today off off Broadway is the laboratory where playwrights, directors and actors can sharpen their craft; where showcase productions often replace the old road tour.

1974–75 was an exciting season off off, even though productions didn't move from Equity Showcase to commercial productions with last season's frequency. The Henry Street Settlement Theater provided Joseph Papp with Ed Bullins's *The Taking of Miss Janie* which moved to the Vivian Beaumont at Lincoln Center. Michael Sawyer's *Naomi Court,* two one-act melodramas, went from a $100 reading at the Manhattan Theater Club to a full scale, very well acted $1,200 production in the same complex and was finally scooped up by David Susskind Enterprises for an eventual film. But even given this success, neither *Miss Janie* nor *Naomi Court* was a theatrical event of the magnitude of last season's *The Sea Horse* or, before that, *When You Comin' Back, Red Ryder?*

The Equity Showcase Code, adhered to by all OOB theaters, has undergone some modification now that OOB has become a recognized competitive arena for the professional actor. Since agents, critics, producers and directors attend showcase (or workshop) productions, the exposure for the actor is valuable. The Code permits an Equity actor to appear in a maximum of 12 non-paid performances of a given work within a four week period: thus most OOB theaters play a Thursday-through-Sunday schedule when audience turnout is greatest. 1974–75 was the first full season OOB theaters operated under the revised code allowing them to charge $2.50 admission (vs. soliciting contributions) and to advertise (vs. free listings). OOB was thus more visible than ever and some theaters even had small advertising budgets. Gone forever was the omnipresent plain white envelope which, in the early years of off off, was slipped in the evening's program (if there was money for a program) and was followed by a curtain speech wherein Hamlet or Hedda would arise from the dead, face the audience and "hope you had a good evening and please give whatever you can so we may continue."

This year the Off Off Broadway Alliance (OOBA), a highly successful umbrella organization which secures funds and publicity for the OOB movement, lists 65 member theaters, up from 53 last year. Under the leadership of Virginia Kahn, OOBA makes no artistic judgments on member productions; it is purely administrative and supportive. Theaters are eligible for OOBA membership if they are legally incorporated as a not-for-profit-organization and if they are professional (vocational, not avocational). This year three-year-old OOBA organized a Festival Fortnight with member theaters listed in a special "passport" sold for $5 in Times Square. It was possible—if you had boundless energy—to see 28 productions within the fortnight period. An extra bonus was given to those who saw all 28 shows: two free passes to all OOBA productions for the coming season.

OOB got a boost from the Theater Development Fund which poured $150,000 into its voucher program, an increase of $50,000 over last year, and initiated a separate dance voucher program. Vouchers are purchased by individuals for $1 and are redeemed by the participating theater for $2.50. Peregrine Whittlesey, who organized this subsidized voucher program, notes "this season vouchers were valid for six months rather than a year. Audiences were thereby more eager and selective in choosing productions within the shortened expiration time, and theater turnout was enormous." The New York State Council on the Arts, a major source of OOB funds, granted monies to 56 OOB theaters in 1974–75, a total of $975,000. The Council's three-year theater evaluation noted of OOB that "the infusion of public money has engendered a stability and continuity. . . . instead of being a refuge for the failed . . . . and the bizarre (it) has become primarily a place for artists to work and grow. . . . under modestly professional conditions, subject to the critical evaluation available only in New York City and with audiences who are willing to follow such activity."

As a result of Equity's Showcase ruling, OOB theaters construct a season from a series of plays with limited runs. Generally—though not exclusively—there is no connection between one play at a given theater and the next production at the same theater. Two notable exceptions are the Joseph Jefferson Theater Company and the Octagon Theater. JJTC, now in it's third year, constructed a season around a theme: "Four Decades of American Theater." The presentations were Avery Hopwood's and Wilson Collison's *Getting Gertie's Garter* (1920s), Clifford Odets's *Awake and Sing* (1930s), John van Druten's *I Remember Mama* (1940s) and Lillian Hellman's *The Autumn Garden* (1950s). Each was preceeded by a "Conversation With . . ." theater personalities involved with the original Broadway productions, including Brendan Gill, Harold Clurman, Peggy Wood and Kermit Bloomgarden. JJTC's praiseworthy season was rounded out with a New Play Series and a return engagement of *Rip Van Winkle,* Washington Irving's play (originally starring JJTC's namesake, Joseph Jefferson).

Octagon, the American Musical Theater Company, enlivened the 1974–75 season with a number of new shows and revivals, including *Knickerbocker Holiday, Turkey Salad* (songs from flops) and a glorious *110 in the Shade,* the musical based on *The Rainmaker. 110* proved that a long, narrow stage, one piano instead of an orchestra and the unlikely setting of the Hotel Dixie needn't be obstacles to first-rate musical theater.

Other 1974–75 OOB productions of note included WPA's production of *Craig's Wife,* by George Kelly, *Hamm and Clov's* overly long but interesting political comedy, *Trees in the Wind* by John McGrath and CSC Repertory's *The Tempest.* In addition to consistently outstanding productions, CSC is housed in one of New York's most beautiful theaters, the Abbey, on East 13th Street.

Direct Theater, housed in a former funeral parlor near Hell's Kitchen, presented a "cruel version" of John Whiting's *The Devils,* marked by a spectacular performance by Glynis Bell as a sexually frustrated nun. The tiny, basement-bound West Side Community Theater, devoted to the classics and using actors of many ethnic backgrounds, presented a splendid *A Doll's House* with a Latin Thorvald. At the Manhattan Theater Club a rich and varied season included Jean-Claude van Itallie's translation of *The Seagull,* directed by Joseph Chaikin; the American premiere of Edward Bond's *The Sea,* directed by Robert Mandel; and the haunting *The Morning After Optimism* by Thomas Murphy. The latter, produced originally at the Abbey Theater in Dublin, was enhanced at MTC by two fine performances by Kevin O'Connor and Jill Eikenberry.

Newly ensconced in the former Sheridan Square Playhouse, the Circle Repertory Company, under the artistic direction of Marshall W. Mason, presented Lanford Wilson's *The Mound Builders,* Julie Bovasso's *Down by the River Where Waterlilies Are Disfigured Everyday,* described as "a romp among hypothetical possibilities of the improbable," the New York premiere of Tennessee Williams's *Battle of Angels* and Corinne Jacker's *Harry Outside.* The Circle Repertory Company is one of the few OOB theaters which pays its actors—small salaries, but salaries nonetheless—and already some critics see OOB following in the footsteps of off Broadway and contractualizing itself out of existence. Still, *Ars Gratia Pecuniae* is a sign we'll not see OOB for a long, long while. Let's hope, never.

THE SEASON AROUND THE UNITED STATES

with

A DIRECTORY OF PROFESSIONAL REGIONAL THEATER

Including casts and credits of new plays, selected Canadian programs, selected programs for children and extended coverage of the Los Angeles, Washington and Dinner Theater seasons

INTRODUCTION: THEATER IN NEW ENGLAND

By Elliot Norton

Drama critic of the Boston *Herald American/Sunday Advertiser*

IN the 1930s, 40s and 50s of this troubled century, the professional—or, if you prefer the term the academics use, the "commercial"—theater of New England was confined almost entirely to the playhouses of Boston and New Haven. There were seven such theaters in Boston, all owned or operated by the Shubert organization of New York; and one in New Haven which was also theirs, and still is. These theaters were all dedicated to the testing and perfecting of plays and musicals on their way to Broadway, where the knowing audiences and the big spenders are; or to exhibiting more or less triumphantly those which had made it in New York one, two or even five years earlier and were now to be seen and hopefully to be enjoyed in "national" companies.

This New Haven-Boston-Broadway axis produced for patient showgoers a number of good shows and some memorable ones, from *Our Town* and *The Time*

42

of Your Life to musicals like *Oklahoma!* and *South Pacific* and *Carousel.* It also presented a spate of productions of dubious merit and a good many others which were demonstrably imperfect and were not to be perfected until many of our showgoers had squirmed and suffered through their faulty first, second and sometimes third acts, serving as reluctant guinea pigs.

In the late 1950s, this system began to break down for a number of reasons. First, the Department of Justice moved against the Shuberts as a monopoly, which they most surely were, and required them to sell one Boston theater, the Colonial, and to give up their lease on another, the Wilbur. Going far beyond the consent decree which they accepted rather than face a court confrontation, the New York owners decided at that time to sell off the Boston Opera House and the Copley Theater and to let two other playhouses, the good Plymouth and the deteriorated Majestic, to a movie chain.

The Opera House went to Northeastern University, to be torn down; a dormitory stands in its place now, a questionable replacement. The Massachusetts Turnpike Authority took the Copley, which had long housed stock companies and had occasionally served as the test tube for plays of substance like *Harvey.* In a matter of weeks, the Authority obliterated it; the site is now a patch of green grass over what is called the Turnpike Extension, a noisy, noisome—and withal useful—strip of high-speed highway and a symbol of the kind of progress which continually and grimly challenges the theater and all other forms of art and imagination in our increasingly uncivilized civilization.

Today in Boston we have three of our seven big playhouses still standing and still, for the most part, serving Broadway as tryout theaters. And in New Haven, the Shubert continues. But while these commercial theaters have dwindled in number and in the number of productions they present each season, the regional theaters have come into existence and in some cases are flourishing.

Instead of being centered almost entirely in Boston, with that branch office in New Haven, the theater of New England has expanded to cover Massachusetts, Rhode Island and Connecticut, with some flurries in New Hampshire. And where the Boston/New Haven plays, whether good or bad or indifferent, were designed specifically for New Yorkers and their visitors, the productions of these newer and often livelier theaters are created primarily, and most of the time exclusively, for the showgoers of their own communities.

Significantly, this move to a grass-roots theater began in Boston just at the time that the Shuberts were unloading their playhouses. In 1955, a group of students from the recently-spawned theater division of Boston University, being now graduated and finding that the commercial theater was not yet ready for them, created in an upstairs room over a fish market on Charles Street a curious theater-in-the-long, which is like a theater-in-the-round except for its shape. In this case, the shape was necessary because the upstairs room was long and narrow with space in the middle for actors and places at either end for spectators.

The next year, these young actors and actresses moved their sets and costumes into an old building on Warrenton Street (directly behind the Shubert Theater), turned professional and set up the Charles Playhouse as the first of the "resident regional theaters" of New England. Under Michael Murray, a good director with high ideals and a true vision, the Charles was intended as a resident theater which would produce for Bostonians the best plays, new or old, with the best actors and actresses in productions which would match in excellence the best in the country. It was Mr. Murray's dream, and that of some of his associates, that this theater should achieve the same standing in its field as the Boston Symphony Orchestra has in its.

For a time it seemed possible that this might be more than a dream. There was a period when the Charles had a subscription audience of approximately 14,000 playgoers. But there were always problems, financial, administrative and artistic, and after 14 years the experiment at the Charles Playhouse came to an end. Today, the 500-seat theater is used commercially for productions booked in from off Broadway—*One Flew Over the Cuckoo's Nest, Moonchildren* and the like— for audiences consisting largely of younger playgoers.

While the Charles was getting established as a resident regional theater, another company with comparable aims was inaugurated in Boston. With David Wheeler (who has learned from Jose Quintero at the Circle in the Square) as director, the Theater Company of Boston was dedicated to producing the plays of authors like Harold Pinter, which were novel then and strange enough to scare the daylights, or the nightlights, out of our conventional playgoers. This company still exists, but without a playhouse and with a diminished audience. It has been artistically successful, presenting some extraordinary productions, including a terse drama of Vietnam called *Medal-of-Honor Rag* in the spring of 1975. But it has lost its sense of continuity through a failure to find and maintain a theater and a regular audience.

In the meantime, a new company calling itself by an ancient and honorable name, the Repertory Theater of Boston, has gained a foothold in the city and, as this is written, its actors are converting an old sound studio on Boylston Place, near the Colonial Theater, into a small playhouse. This newest resident troupe began on Cape Cod in the summer of 1971, when a young idealist named Esquire Jauchem and some of his friends from Defiance College of Ohio started a repertory company and introduced it to Boston the following year. In a dingy playhouse at the Boston Center for the Arts and later on a makeshift stage in a church at Marlborough and Clarendon streets in the Back Bay, they began to find an audience for dramas of some originality. As a cooperative, with their twelve actors and actresses as equal partners and trustees, they won the respect and affection of the community. In the spring of 1975 they found a location on Boylston Place for the theater they had always wanted and were able to persuade a Boston bank to give them a mortgage which would make their playhouse possible. Nothing they had done so far was half so dramatic as that; Boston bankers are cool to theatrical ventures.

Once this new playhouse is open, the Boston Repertory Theater will be in a position to take its place as the resident regional theater the city has long needed. But acceptance will not be automatic. The players are young, congenial and earnest, and although they do not yet belong to the Actors Equity Association, professional: they earn their living as actors and technicians. But the quality of their performances so far has been variable, ranging from pleasant to incompetent. In this coming season of 1975–76 they will have to prove themselves on a higher level of professionalism or they must necessarily dwindle into a kind of downtown community playhouse for friendly collegians.

While they are proving themselves, the best regional companies of Providence, Hartford and New Haven have long since found a respected place in their communities, and so, in its way, has the troupe at Springfield, Mass. In all these cities, the successful companies represent to a great extent the driving force of one dedicated director, usually supported and seconded and often rescued by a business manager with a head for figures and finances.

Adrian Hall, who created the Trinity Square Repertory Company in Providence, is a case in point. Mr. Hall is an artist, dedicated to putting on rare plays in good productions and good plays in rare productions. In the background, supporting his enthusiasms and seeing to it that the bills get paid, Marion Simon keeps his company solvent.

As a Texan, Mr. Hall hit Providence with the force of a typhoon. This metropolis of Rhode Island was a theatrical desert when he arrived. He had no available playhouse and no audience. He made both, and although the quality of his productions has varied enormously, he had never put on one which was dull: terrible, yes—occasionally—but dull, no.

For eight years, he produced most of his shows in a church building at Trinity Square or in the auditorium of the Rhode Island School of Design. Season before last, with a gift from a civic-minded devotee, he and his troops took over and made over an old movie theater, the Majestic, into a center with two playhouses: one large, one small and intimate.

In the large theater, the Lederer, Mr. Hall has done some large things, among them a production of *Peer Gynt* which was overelaborate and not well enough acted; and, during the last season, a dynamic and joyous *Tom Jones,* adapted and directed felicitously by Larry Arrick. In the downstairs theater, which is intimate and comfortable and which runs concurrently with the other, he has done such shows as *The Tooth of Crime,* which is venturesome and unconventional, and George M. Cohan's *Seven Keys to Baldpate,* which is fun. The level of performance is unpredictable at Trinity Square, but there is a sense of excitement in almost every show—and that is something to admire.

In Connecticut, the Hartford Stage Company is more modestly housed than Trinity Square, but its small playhouse is comfortable and genuinely intimate, and there is another, newer and grander one on the drawing boards. At this time, as heir to other pioneers, Paul Weidner is the artistic director at Hartford Stage and although—like everyone else—he is not able to direct with full effectiveness all types of plays, he has done some good things and at least a few memorable ones.

Last season, Mr. Weidner won the Margo Jones Award as the director who had done most during the year to follow the Margo Jones lead by presenting new dramas. He deserved it. He earned it for such boldly original plays as Harvey Perr's *Afternoon Tea,* a genuinely experimental and provocative drama of a man and a woman reaching out to one another for fulfillment, which is hard to come by. It took courage to present *Afternoon Tea,* which is more given to hints and innuendoes than to facts and so requires the close attention that some playgoers will not or cannot give. It took a high measure of skill to make it work, as Paul Weidner and his players, Barbara Caruso and Jordan Charney, did.

In New Haven, the Long Wharf Theater, under the direction of Arvin Brown, has developed an admirable acting company and has attracted an almost equally admirable audience, the kind that is willing to listen, a rare and much-to-be-desired kind of congregation. Mr. Brown has certain special advantages. Since his theater is near New York, where most actors and actresses prefer, for some strange reason, to live, he can call on some good ones who might not travel as far as Hartford or Providence. He does. At the same time, he has built up over the years a nucleus of resident players of broad and varied capabilities, able to take part, as they did successfully during 1975, in a pleasant revival of *Pygmalion* (you know, *My Fair Lady* without the songs) or in such other and more exotic works as *The National Health* or, in the previous season, *The Changing Room,* both of which went directly from Long Wharf to Broadway.

That the Long Wharf coexists with the Yale Repertory Theater is interesting and heartening, for both must be drawing on the same audiences and one or the other is probably affecting the box office at the old Shubert Theater, where some of the tryouts still play. Yale, in its ninth season of professional repertory, is obviously the child of Robert Brustein, who scorns the commercial theater but has managed to find room on his stage for at least one Broadway-bound play, in what amounted to a tryout.

In an old church which is far more uncomfortable than any commercial playhouse ever owned by the Shuberts, Mr. Brustein and his associates have generally striven to introduce drama of a kind that Broadway cannot or dare not or will not produce, with some success. During the 1974–75 season they presented in a happy production Brecht's *Happy End* which followed in point of time his *The Threepenny Opera* but failed in Berlin because his wife turned the ending into a political harangue. It was fun at Yale.

At the end of last season, back in the old auditorium of the Yale School of Drama, the Brustein troupers put on what may have been their finest show, a new production of *A Midsummer Night's Dream,* brightly staged by Alvin Epstein, brightly acted by a good company and embellished with the music of Henry Purcell's score from *The Fairy Queen,* a sumptuous show. Yale's old church is to be renovated and restored during summer of 1975 for the comfort of playgoers and the convenience of actors and, in the process, the professional nucleus is being increased from ten to 20 players, a good and hopeful portent.

It remains to discuss the Stage/West Company of Springfield, Mass., which concluded its eighth season in May. Stephen E. Hays, a young man of Boston, was the founder and is the managing director of Stage/West, which is established snugly in a small brick playhouse on the grounds of the Eastern States Exposition in West Springfield. Mr. Hays is one of the wiser regional theater operators. When he found that Springfielders were somewhat more conservative than Bostonians (really!) in their theatrical tastes, he changed his first year's schedule, substituting such comfortable comedies as *Charley's Aunt* for other, more extravagant works of drama. Over the years he has won the confidence and support of a community otherwise distinguished only by its fondness for Ann Corio's dramaturgic flap-

doodle, *This Was Burlesque,* which fills a huge tent theater during the summers.
That Mr. Hays will ever outdraw Ann is unlikely, but his little theater continues to give his city's playgoers dramas of unusual interest and now and then a new one. Last year's most considerable venture was a new play by Paul Foster, *Marcus Brutus,* in its world premiere performances. This proved to be a drama about a writer who can't believe that such an idealist as Brutus would become an assassin and who, thrashing it out in his mind, is visited by the characters of *Julius Caesar.* At Stage/West it was given an interesting production but with some actors who didn't belong in the cast. As it grows, this group must face the need for developing a stronger acting company, to bring its productions up to the level of Trinity Square, Long Wharf and the others which, in New England, are making a big and generally beautiful noise.

A DIRECTORY OF PROFESSIONAL REGIONAL THEATER

Compiled by Ella A. Malin

Professional 1974–75 programs and repertory productions by leading resident companies around the United States, plus selected Canadian programs and major Shakespeare festivals including that of Stratford, Ontario (Canada), are grouped in alphabetical order of their locations and listed in date order from May, 1974 to June, 1975. This list does not include Broadway, off-Broadway or touring New York shows, summer theaters, single productions by commercial producers or college or other non-professional productions. The directory was compiled by Ella A. Malin for *The Best Plays of 1974–75* from information provided by the resident producing organizations at Miss Malin's request. First productions of new plays—American or world premieres—in regional theaters are listed with full cast and credits, as available. Figures in parentheses following title give number of performances and date given is opening date, included whenever a record of these facts was obtainable from the producing managements.

Augmented reports on other than regional theater production in Los Angeles by Rick Talcove and Washington, D.C. by David Richards are included under those cities's headings in this listing. A section on U.S. dinner theater by Francine L. Trevens appears at the end of this Directory.

Summary

This Directory lists 378 productions of 327 plays (including one-acters and workshop productions) presented by 41 groups in 68 theaters in 39 cities (34 in the United States and 5 in Canada) during the 1974–75 season. Of these, 175 were American plays in 151 full productions and 24 workshop productions. 46 were world premieres, 16 were American or North American continental premieres and three were professional premieres. In addition, 15 groups presented 34 children's theater productions of 34 plays, including three world premieres.

Frequency of production of individual scripts was as follows:

   1 play received 5 productions (*Hamlet*)
   6 plays received 4 productions (*Harvey, The Hot l Baltimore, The Real Inspector Hound, That Championship Season, Tobacco Road, Twelfth Night*)
 11 plays received 3 productions (*The Cherry Orchard, The Dybbuk, Frankenstein, Godspell, The Little Foxes, A Midsummer Night's Dream, Macbeth, Me and Bessie, Romeo and Juliet, Richard III, The Taming of the Shrew*)
 37 plays received 2 productions
272 plays received 1 production.

Listed below are the playwrights who received the greatest number of productions. The first figure is the number of productions; the second figure (in parentheses) is the number of plays produced, including one-acters.

Shakespeare	44 (22)	Miller, Arthur	4	(2)
Shaw	10 (8)	Chase, Mary	4	(1)
Coward	9 (8)	Miller, Jason	4	(1)
Stoppard	7 (3)	Hailey	3	(3)
Brecht	6 (5)	Shepard	3	(3)
Feydeau	6 (5)	Albee	3	(2)
Molière	6 (5)	Sheridan	3	(2)
Wilson, Lanford	6 (3)	Hellman	3	(1)
Ibsen	5 (4)	Friel	2	(2)
Simon	5 (3)	Goldoni	2	(2)
Kirkland	5 (2)	Melfi	2	(2)
O'Neill	4 (4)	Miller, Susan	2	(2)
Anouilh	4 (3)	Nichols, Peter	2	(2)
Fugard	4 (3)	O'Casey	2	(2)
Kaufman	4 (3)	Perr	2	(2)
Williams	4 (3)	Pinter	2	(2)
Chekhov	4 (2)	Wilder	2	(2)

ABINGDON, VA.

Barter Theater: Main Stage

(Founder, Robert Porterfield; artistic director-manager, Rex Partington)

THE TORCH-BEARERS (20). By George Kelly. June 4, 1974. Director, Owen Phillips; Lighting, Myron White; costumes, Sigrid Insull. With David Darlow, Barbara Tarbuck, Gwyllum Evans, Joseph Costa, Dale Carter Cooper.

STRAITJACKET (20). By Howard Koch. June 18, 1974 (world premiere). Director, Kenneth Frankel; scenery & lighting, Raymond C. Recht; costumes, Sigrid Insull.

Mary Lamb	Barbara Tarbuck
Charles Lamb	George Hosmer
Samuel Coleridge	Michael Tolaydo
Sarah Coleridge	Nancy Snyder

Fanny Kelly . . . . Marsha Wischhusen
William Hazlitt . . . . David Darlow
Emma Isola . . . . Mary Carney
Thomas Tipp . . . . Gwyllum Evans
Act I, Scene 1: The Lamb residence, winter, 1796. Scene 2: The Lamb residence, spring, fourteen months later. Scene 3: The Lamb residence, several months later. Act II, Scene 1: India House, March 20, fifteen years later. Scene 2: The Lamb residence, later that day. Scene 3: The Lamb residence, winter, eighteen months later.

THE ODD COUPLE. (20) By Neil Simon. July 2, 1974 Director, Kenneth Frankel; scenery and lighting, Raymond C. Recht; costumes, Sigrid Insull. With David Darlow, George Clark Hosmer, Barbara Tarbuck, Dorothy Marie.

PRIVATE LIVES (20). By Noel Coward. July 16, 1974. Director, Rae Allen. Scenery, Bennet Averyt; lighting, Myron White; costumes, Sigrid Insull. With Ann Buckles, James Noble, Barbara Tarbuck, Gwyllum Evans, Nancy Snyder.

BEYOND THE FRINGE (3). By Alan Bennett, Peter Cook, Jonathan Miller and Dudley Moore. July 26, 1974. Director, Dorothy Marie; lighting, Myron White; costumes, Sigrid Insull. With David Darlow, Gwyllum Evans, George Hosmer, Michael Tolaydo.

TEN NIGHTS IN A BARROOM (24). By William W. Pratt; adapted by Fred Carmichael. August 27, 1974. Director, John Olon; scenery, Bennet Averyt, Raymond C. Recht; lighting, Myron White, costumes, Sigrid Insull. With members of the company.

CHAMPAGNE COMPLEX (24). By Leslie Stevens. September 17, 1974. Director, John Olon; scenery, Raymond C. Recht; lighting, Myron White; costumes, Susan Tucker. With Raymond Lynch, Nancy Tribush, John W. Morrow Jr.

SILENT NIGHT, LONELY NIGHT (24). By Robert Anderson. October 8, 1974. Director, Owen Phillips; scenery, Bennet Averyt; lighting, Myron White; costumes, Sigrid Insull. With Cleo Holladay, Carey Connell, John W. Morrow Jr., Nancy Tribush, Raymond Lynch, Andy Heil.

THE DEVIL'S DISCIPLE (32). By George Bernard Shaw. April 7, 1975. Director, Kenneth Frankel; scenery, Bennet Averyt; costumes, Sigrid Insull. With Rex Partington, John Spencer, Tina Cartmell, Amy Nathan, Mary Carney, George Clark Hosmer.

THE DIARY OF ANNE FRANK (32). By Frances Goodrich and Albert Hackett; based on Anne Frank's Diary. May 6, 1975. Director, Owen Phillips; scenery & lighting, Bennet Averyt; costumes, Sigrid Insull. With Mary Carney, Tina Cartmell, John W. Morrow Jr., Raili Helsing, George Clark Hosmer, Pete Edens.

Barter Theater: Playhouse—Children's Theater

WHO AM I? (5). Written and directed by Barbara Tarbuck, June 5, 1974; WINNIE-THE-POOH (5), adapted and directed by Donna Searcy, June 20, 1974; THE BREMEN TOWN MUSICIANS (5). By Pat Hale, directed by Donna Searcy, July 24, 1974. Performed by members of the Barter Intern Ensemble and Apprentices.

Barter Theater: Playhouse—Intern Ensemble

THE NATURE OF COMEDY (3). Created by the Intern Ensemble, directed by Dorothy Marie, June 14, 1974.

COLLISION COURSE (3): CAMERA OBSCURA by Robert Patrick, WANDERING by Lanford Wilson, COWBOYS #2 by Sam Shepard, directed by David Darlow; CHUCK by Jack Larson, JEW! by Harvey Perr, THOUGHTS ON THE INSTANT OF GREETING A FRIEND ON THE STREET by Jean-Claude van Itallie and Sharon Thie, THE UNEXPURGATED MEMOIRS OF BERNARD MERGENDEILER by Jules Feiffer, directed by Dorothy Marie; ANIMAL by Oliver Hailey, MOMMA AS SHE BECAME—BUT NOT AS SHE WAS by John Rechey, STARS AND STRIPES by Leonard Melfi, directed by Owen Phillips, June 21, 1974.

UNDER MILK WOOD (15). By Dylan Thomas, directed by David Darlow, June 28, 1974.

AN EVENING WITH SHAKESPEARE (12). Scenes from nine plays and two sonnets, directed by staff directors. August 2, 1974.

Barter Intern Ensemble: Sarah Buxton, Eric Conger, Pete Edens, Shannon Eubanks, Margaret Lunsford, Katherine Manning, Peggity Price, Bryan Rice, Robert E. Rutland Jr., William Schlueter, Donna Searcy.

Note: Members of the Barter Intern Ensemble were selected by auditions throughout the country to participate in a two-year training/performance program leading to the formation of a resident repertory company.

ASHLAND, ORE.

Oregon Shakespearean Festival: Elizabethan Theater (outdoors)

(Founder, Angus L. Bowmer; producing director, Jerry Turner; general manager, William W. Patton. Designers: scenery, Richard L. Hay; lighting, Steven A. Maze; costumes, Robert Morgan, John David Ridge, Robert Hines.)

TWELFTH NIGHT (19). By William Shakespeare. June 21, 1974. Director, Jim Edmondson. With Michael Kevin Moore, Christine Healy, Margit Moe, Richard Riehle, le Clanché du Rand, Laird Williamson, Jeff Brooks.

TITUS ANDRONICUS (29). By William Shakespeare. June 22, 1974. Director, Laird Williamson. With Denis Arndt, Christine Healy, A.

Bryan Humphrey, Richard Riehle, John Renforth, Mona Lee Fultz.

HAMLET (29). By William Shakespeare. June 23, 1974. Director, Jerry Turner. With Raye Birk, Mary Turner, le Clanché du Rand, Michael Kevin Moore, Cal Winn, Mark D. Murphey, A. Bryan Humphrey.

Oregon Shakespearean Festival: Angus Bowmer Theater (indoors)

THE TWO GENTLEMEN OF VERONA (42). By William Shakespeare. June 22, 1974. Director, Laird Williamson. With Mark D. Murphey, Denis Arndt, Wil Huddleston, le Clanché du Rand, Margit Moe, Diane Salinger, David Q. Combs.

WAITING FOR GODOT (22). By Samuel Beckett. June 23, 1974. Director, Andrew J.

Traister. With Cal Winn, James Edmondson, Jeff Brooks, Richard Riehle, John Mansfield/Kirk Gibson.

THE TIME OF YOUR LIFE (21). By William Saroyan. June 24, 1974. Director, Pat Patton. With James Edmondson, Richard Riehle, Christine Healy, Michael Kevin Moore, Mark D. Murphey, Franklin Brown, Wil Huddleston.

Oregon Shakespearean Festival Stage II: Angus Bowmer Theater

(Designers: scenery, Richard L. Hay; lighting, Steven A. Maze; costumes, Jeannie Davidson.)

THE WINTER'S TALE (15). By William Shakespeare. February 14, 1975. Director, Audrey Stanley. With James Edmondson, le Clanché du Rand, Carmi Boushey, Michael Horton, David L. Boushey, Randi Douglas.

CHARLEY'S AUNT (14). By Brandon Thomas. February 15, 1975 (matinee). Director, Pat Patton. With Mark D. Murphey, Peter Silbert, Judd Parkin, Adrienne Alexander, Shirley Patton, Christine Healy, Joseph De Salvio, Michael Kevin Moore.

OEDIPUS THE KING (15). By Sophocles; translated by Donald Sutherland. February 15, 1975 (evening). Director, Robert Loper. With Ted D'Arms, James Edmondson, le Clanché du Rand, Todd Eleson, Michael Kevin Moore, Nicole Edstrom, Mari Graham.

THE PETRIFIED FOREST (14). By Robert Sherwood. February 16, 1975. Director, Jerry Turner. With Peter Silbert, Adrienne Alexander, Mark D. Murphey, Joseph De Salvio, Philip L. Jones, David L. Boushey, Christine Healy.

BALTIMORE

Center Stage: Whirligig Company—Peabody Institute's Leakin Hall

(Artistic director, Jacques Cartier; managing director, Peter W. Culman.)

THE DOCTOR IN SPITE OF HIMSELF (6). By Molière. December 29, 1974. Director, Stan

Wojewodski Jr. With James Broaddus, Rise Collins, Nicholas Cosco, Edward Hambleton, Mi-

chael Hartman, Kaeren Hawksworth, Jeffrey B.
McLaughlin, Gina McMather, Nancy Hamilton

Spies, Anthony White.

Note: Center Stage's theater was burned out in January 1974. A new 500-seat theater is expected to
be completed by the fall of 1975 and ready for a production season by winter. During the 1974–75
season, Center Stage created the Whirligig Company, consisting of ten professional actors headed by
Stan Wojewodski Jr. to tour programs throughout Baltimore City and Maryland from October 28,
1974 through May, 1975 for students and special adult groups. Center Stage also presented a staged
reading of *Our Father's Failing* by Israel Horovitz and conducted a tuition-free, 20-week student-actor
workshop.

BERKELEY, CALIF.

Berkeley Repertory Theater

(Producing director, Michael Leibert)

THE FRONT PAGE (27). By Ben Hecht and
Charles MacArthur. June 7, 1974. Director, Mi-
chael Leibert; scenery, Jeffer Whitman; lighting,
Joan Liepman; costumes, Diana Smith. With
Douglas Johnson, Ron Vernan, Linda Lee John-
son, Karen Ingenthron.

LONDON ASSURANCE (27). By Dion Boucicault. July 12, 1974. Director, Douglas Johnson;
scenery & costumes, John Raymond Freimann;
lighting, Matthew Cohen. With Paul Laramore,
John Tyson, Michael Leibert, Robert Hirschfeld,
Holly Barron, Linda Lee Johnson, Karen Ingenthron, Ron Vernan.

BLITHE SPIRIT (33). By Noel Coward. September 20, 1974. Director, Angela Paton; scenery & costumes, Warren Travis; lighting, Matthew Cohen. With Julia Odegard, Paul
Laramore, Karen Ingenthron, Holly Barron.

THE LITTLE FOXES (27). By Lillian Hellman.
November 1, 1974. Director, William I. Oliver;
scenery, Ron Pratt; lighting, Joan Liepman; costumes, Diana Smith. With Holly Barron, Ron
Vernan, W. L. Jenkins, Robert Hirschfeld, Barbara Oliver, Sally Livingston, Michael Leibert.

A MIDSUMMER NIGHT'S DREAM (33). By
William Shakespeare. December 6, 1974. Direc-
tor, Douglas Johnson; scenery, Jeffer Whitman;
lighting, Matthew Cohen; costumes, Lesley
Skannal. With Joe ∪pano, Holly Barron, Linda
Lee Johnson, Paul Laramore, W. L. Jenkins,

Karen Ingentron, Robert Hirschfeld.

THE DEVIL'S DISCIPLE (27). By George Bernard Shaw. January 17, 1975. Director, Michael
Leibert; scenery, Ron Pratt; lighting, Joan Liepman; costumes, Diana Smith. With Douglas
Johnson, Holly Barron, Joe Spano, Halcyon Old-
ham, Sally Livingston.

CONTINENTAL DIVIDE (27) By Oliver Hailey. February 21, 1975 (world premiere). Director, Michael Leibert; scenery, Jeffer Whitman;
lighting, Matthew Cohen; costumes, Diana
Smith; sound, Paul Dixon.

Lucille . . . . .Linda Lee Johnson
Cullum . . . . Paul Laramore
Mae Battle . . . . Karen Ingenthron
Mr. John Battle . . . . .Ron Vernan
  Time: Now. Place: Long Island home of Lu-
cille and Cullum. One intermission.

UNCLE VANYA (27). By Anton Chekhov;
translated by Douglas Johnson. March 28, 1975.
Director, Douglas Johnson; scenery, Gene An-
gell, Ron Pratt; lighting, Joan Liepman; costumes, Lesley Skannal. With Michael Leibert,
Ron Vernan, Robert Hirschfeld, Linda Lee
Johnson, Karen Ingenthron.

THE HOSTAGE (26). By Brendan Behan. May
2, 1975. Director, Michael Leibert; scenery,
Jeffer Whitman; costumes, Diana Smith. With
Gerry Wills, Julia Odegard, Paul Dixon, Robert
Hirschfeld, Rick Johnson.

Note: A workshop production of *The Real Inspector Hound* by Tom Stoppard was given 4 performances in August 1974, directed by Gregory Boyd, with the summer apprentice company.

BUFFALO

Studio Arena Theater

(Executive producer, Neal Du Brock)

I GOT A SONG (34). A view of life and times through the lyrics of E. Y. Harburg; music by Harold Arlen, Vernon Duke, Sammy Fain, Burton Lane, Jay Gorney, Earl Robinson; dramatized by E. Y. Harburg and Fred Saidy. September 26, 1974 (world premiere). Director, Harold Stone; choreography, Geoffrey Holder; musical director, Marty Henne; orchestrations, Tony Ragusa; scenery, R. J. Graziano; lighting, Thomas Skelton; costumes, Theoni V. Aldredge. With D. Jamin-Bartlett, Alan Brasington, Norma Donaldson, Bonnie Franklin, Miguel Godreau, Gilbert Price.

Musical Numbers—Act I: "Look to the Rainbow," "I Got a Song," "Great Day Coming Manana," "Brother, Can You Spare a Dime?," "April in Paris," "Let's Take a Walk Around the Block," "Necessity," "The Money Cat," "When the Idle Poor Become the Idle Rich," "Happiness Is a Thing Called Joe," "Silent Spring," "The Eagle and Me," "The Monkey in the Mango Tree," "Jump, Children, Jump," "Noah," "We're off to See the Wizard." Act II —"We're Off to See the Wizard" (Reprise), "Napoleon," "Ain't It de Truth," "Leave de Atom Alone," "We're in the Same Boat, Brother," "If This Isn't Love," "The World is Your Balloon," "Old Devil Moon," "Right as the Rain," "Over the Rainbow," "Eagle Dance," "That Great Come-and-Get-it Day," "It's Only a Paper Moon."

COME BACK, LITTLE SHEBA (32). By William Inge. October 31, 1974. Director, Warren Enters; scenery, Bennet Averyt; lighting, Peter Gill; costumes, Lorena McDonald. With Jan Sterling, Henderson Forsythe, Bruce Detrick, Donald Keyes.

GABRIELLE (35). Book by José Quintero; based on an original idea of Neal Du Brock; music, Gilbert Becaud; original lyrics and adaptations, Jason Darrow; French lyrics by Louis Amade, Pierre Delanoe, Maurice Vidalin. December 9, 1974 (world premiere). Director, José Quintero; choreography, Dania Krupska; musical concepts & orchestrations, Garry Sherman; musical director, William Cox; scenery, Eugene Lee; lighting, Jules Fisher; costumes, Franne Lee.

Madame Gabrielle . . . . Tammy Grimes
Rosy . . . . Marilyn Cooper
Gaston . . . . Laurence Guittard
Swan . . . . Robin Hoff
John . . . . Danny Meehan
Clown . . . . David Sabin

Garcon . . . . Danny Kenefick
Musical Numbers—Act I: (original French titles appear in parentheses) "The Cherry Trees Are Blue" (Les Cerisiers Sont Blancs), "Gilbert Becaud" (L'Orange), "Gabrielle" (Dimanche à Orly), "Don Juan," "Rosy and John," "If I Could Choose One Day" (On Prend Toujours un Train Pour Quelque Part), "Home" (Il Faut Marcher), "Et Maintenant," "Waiting" (Moi Quand Je Serai Gueri). Act II: "Cheer Up, Madame" (Felicitations), "The Little Girl" (Une Petite Fille Entre 9 et 10 Ans), "Seul Sur Son Etoile," "Rosy and John" (Reprise), "The Masquerade" (La Grande Roue), "L'Important C'Est la Rose".

DESIRE UNDER THE ELMS (33). By Eugene O'Neill. January 9, 1975. Director, Warren Enters; scenery, Stephen Hendrickson; lighting, Peter Gill; costumes, Linda Letta. With Roy Cooper, Lawrie Driscoll, Carol May Jenkins, Dermot McNamara, Alvah Stanley.

13 RUE DE L'AMOUR (31). By Georges Feydeau; adapted by Mawby Green and Ed Feilbert. February 6, 1975. Director, Donald Moffat; scenery, Michael Sharp; lighting, Robert Monk; costumes, Clifford Capone. With Donald Moffat, Gwen Arner, Jessica James, David Laundra, Tom Mardirosian, Philip Minor.

P.S. YOUR CAT IS DEAD! (32). By James Kirkwood. March 6, 1975 (world premiere). Scenery, William Ritman; lighting, David Zierk; costumes, Frank J. Boros.

Vito . . . . Tony Musante
Kate . . . . Jennifer Warren
Jimmy . . . . Keir Dullea
Fred . . . . Peter White
Carmine . . . . Antony Ponzini
Janie . . . . Mary Hamill
Wendell . . . . Bill Moor

Place: Jimmy Zoole's loft apartment in New York City. Act I, Scene 1: Late Evening. Scene 2: Thirty minutes later. Act II: Later the same night.

GODSPELL (31). By John-Michael Tebelak, based upon the Gospel According to St. Matthew; music and new lyrics, Stephen Schwartz. April 3, 1975. Directorial supervision, William R. Cox; scenery, Jim Crossley; lighting, David Zierk; costumes, Reet Pell; musical numbers restaged by Maggie Hyatt. With actors from various Godspell productions and local actors.

Anthony Hopkins as Martin Dysart and Peter Firth as Alan Strang in *Equus*

John Kani as John and Winston Ntshona (FAR RIGHT) as Winston in *The Island*

Elizabeth Ashley as Margaret in *Cat on a Hot Tin Roof*

Ann Reinking as Joan of Arc in *Goodtime Charley* (FAR LEFT)

Maggie Smith as Amanda Prynne in *Private Lives*

Kristoffer Tabori as Leeds in *The Wager* (FAR RIGHT)

Tony Lo Bianco as Emil "Duke" Bronkowski in *Yanks 3 Detroit 0*

Estelle Parsons as Mert in *Mert & Phil* (FAR LEFT)

Ellen Burstyn as Doris in *Same Time, Next Year*

John Cullum as Charlie Anderson in *Shenandoah* (FAR RIGHT)

Angela Lansbury as Rose in *Gypsy*

Larry Blyden as Sidney in *Absurd Person Singular* (FAR LEFT)

Rita Moreno as Googie Gomez in *The Ritz*

Donald Sinden as Sir Harcourt Courtly in *London Assurance* (FAR RIGHT)

John Wood as Sherlock Holmes in *Sherlock Holmes*

Liv Ullmann as Nora Helmer in *A Doll's House* (FAR LEFT)

Above, in Peter Shaffer's *Equus,* Peter Firth is the stableboy astride his horse Nugget (Everett McGill), watched by the other horses. *Below,* in Peter Nichols's *The National Health,* Leonard Frey (*foreground*), Rita Moreno (*right*) and other hospital staffers tend their rows of patients

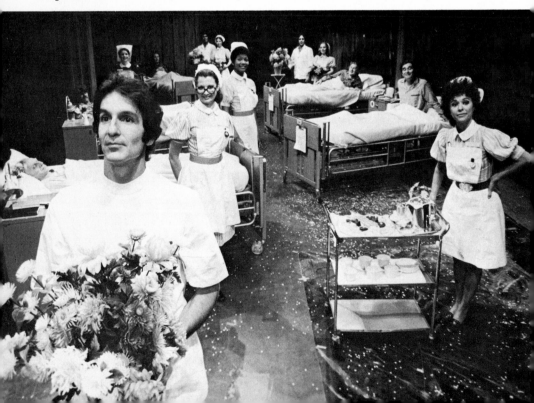

BRITISH PLAYS
ON BROADWAY

Right, Rex Harrison and Julie Harris as husband and wife in Terence Rattigan's *In Praise of Love. Below,* the three couples of Alan Ayckbourn's *Absurd Person Singular*: Larry Blyden and Carole Shelley (*left* and *right*), Sandy Dennis and Tony Roberts (*back row*) and Geraldine Page and Fritz Weaver, who replaced Richard Kiley in the role (*front row*)

THE ISLAND—John Kani and Winston Ntshona (*foreground*) as South African political prisoners playing Creon and Antigone in their own version of the ancient Greek drama, in one of two plays which they devised in collaboration with Athol Fugard

ALL OVER TOWN—*Above,* William LeMassina, Every Hayes, Cleavon Little, Pamela Payton-Wright and Barnard Hughes in Murray Schisgal's comedy

THE RITZ—*Below,* Christopher J. Brown, Jerry Stiller, F. Murray Abraham, John Everson, Ruth Jaroslow and Jack Weston in a scene from the comedy by Terrence McNally set in a men's bathhouse

SEASCAPE — *Above,* the lizards Leslie and Sarah (Frank Langella and Maureen Anderman) frighten Deborah Kerr and Barry Nelson into a submissive pose in the Edward Albee play. Fred Voelpel's lizard costume designs appear at *left* (for Leslie) and at *right* (for Sarah), with a closeup of the sea creatures *below*

SAME TIME, NEXT YEAR — *Right,* Ellen Burstyn and Charles Grodin in the comedy by Bernard Slade

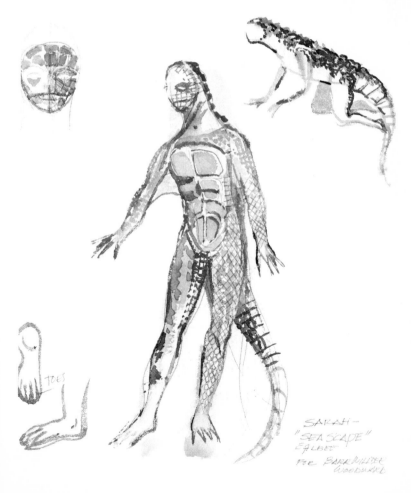

SARAH—
"SEASCAPE"
BALLET
FOR BARBARA MILLER
WOODWARD

GOD'S FAVORITE—*Left,* Charles Nelson Reilly and Vincent Gardenia in Neil Simon's play

FLOWERS—*Below,* Lindsay Kemp as a transvestite in his own pantomime based on a work by Jean Genet

DREYFUS IN REHEARSAL—*Left,* Sam Levene (*at top*) Avery Schreiber and Ruth Gordon in Garson Kanin's adaptation of a French script

MERT & PHIL—Marilyn Roberts, Estelle Parsons (as Mert) and Rhoda Gemignani in the Anne Burr play produced by Joseph Papp at Lincoln Center

P.S. YOUR CAT IS DEAD!—Keir Dullea and Tony Musante in a scene from the play by James Kirkwood

WHO'S WHO IN HELL—
Right, Peter Ustinov (author) as a Russian Chairman, Beau Bridges as an assassin and George S. Irving as a President of the United States

A LETTER FOR QUEEN VICTORIA—*Below,* Robert Wilson in a fanciful concoction of his own unique devising

SHENANDOAH—*Above,* David Russell, Jordan Suffin, Ted Agress, Penelope Milford, Joel Higgins and Robert Rosen as the younger generation in the Civil War era musical. *Right*, a Pearl Somner costume design for *Shenandoah*'s "Freedom" musical number

SHENANDOAH. FREEDOM" SONG Donna Theodore & Chip Ford

THE WIZ—Witches of Oz are pictured here with two of their costumes. *At left,* Dee Dee Bridgewater (*right*) as Glinda; *below, left,* Mabel King as Evillene

Right, on page opposite, Geoffrey Holder's costume design for the dancer portraying *The Wiz*'s tornado

Above, Geoffrey Holder's design for Glinda's costume; *left,* his design for Evillene's

RODGERS & HART—*Above,* the cakewalk number from the revue of show tunes written by Richard Rodgers and Lorenz Hart in the 1920s and 1930s

GOODTIME CHARLEY
—*Left*, Joel Grey as the Dauphin and Ann Reinking as Joan of Arc, in the setting depicted *right*, at top of opposite page, in photo of the model of Rouben Ter-Arutunian's scenery design. Also shown *right* is the same set adapted to the throne-room scene

MACK & MABEL—Robert Preston as Mack Sennett surrounded by bathing beauties in the Michael Stewart-Jerry Herman silent film-era musical

SGT. PEPPER'S LONELY
HEARTS CLUB BAND
ON THE ROAD — *Right*,
Kay Cole is entangled in a
fanciful prop in the spec-
tacle based on the famous
Beatles album

THE NIGHT THAT MADE
AMERICA FAMOUS — De-
lores Hall, Harry Chapin and
Kelly Garrett in a multi-media
show of Chapin songs

MUSICAL REVIVALS
—*Above*, Alice Faye in *Good
News*; *right*, Patricia Gaul and
others in *Dance With Me*, both
shows extensively reworked for
1975 Broadway presentation

THE WAGER—From foreground to background *above*, John Heard (Ron), Kenneth Gilman (Ward), Linda Cook (Honor) and Kristoffer Tabori (Leeds) in the Mark Medoff play directed by Anthony Perkins

NEW YORK SHAKESPEARE FESTIVAL PRESENTS — Joseph Papp's season included Ed Bullins's Critics prizewinning *The Taking of Miss Janie* (*above*, with Adayemi Lithcott and Hilary Jean Beane) at Lincoln Center; and, at the Public Theater, *Kid Champion* (*left*, with Christopher Walken and Anna Levine) and *Fishing* (*below*, with Lindsay Crouse and Kathryn Grody)

PHILEMON—At *left*, Dick Latessa and the company in the Tom Jones-Harvey Schmidt musical drama

FIRST BREEZE OF SUMMER — *Below*, Ethel Ayler, Charles Brown, Moses Gunn and Reyno in the Negro Ensemble Company production of the play by Leslie Lee

CHELSEA THEATER CENTER — The two-borough 1975 production schedule of this Brooklyn-based organization included, in Manhattan, the "saloon musical" *Diamond Studs* (*above*, with Jim Wann as Jesse James, Rick Simpson, Tommy Thompson as Mrs. James, Jim Watson and Bill Hicks); and, at home at the Brooklyn Academy of Music, *Yentl the Yeshiva Boy* based on a story by Isaac Bashevis Singer (*left*, with John Shea and Tovah Feldshuh in the title role)

JAMES JOYCE'S DUBLINERS—*Below*, the Irish author and his family join in song, portrayed by Ty McConnell (Stanislaus Joyce), Martin Cassidy (James), Stan Watt (John Joyce, their father) and Ruby Holbrook (Mary, their mother), in the Roundabout Theater Company production of the biographical drama

RUBBERS—*Above*, Laura Esterman and John Horn in Jonathan Reynolds's play at American Place

PRETZELS — *Left*, Jane Curtin, Judy Kahan and Timothy Jerome in a revue

REVIVALS, BRITISH AND AMERICAN

SHERLOCK HOLMES —
Above, Mel Martin, John
Wood, Nicholas Selby and
Barbara Leigh-Hunt

THE MISANTHROPE —
Right (on opposite page),
Diana Rigg and Alec Mc-
Cowen

LONDON ASSURANCE —
Left, Roger Rees and Polly
Adams

CAT ON A HOT TIN ROOF—*Above*, Joan Pape, Kate Reid, Elizabeth Ashley, Fred Gwynne, Charles Seibert and Michael Zaslow

ALL GOD'S CHILLUN GOT WINGS—*Below*, Robert Christian and Trish Van Devere in Circle in the Square's revival of O'Neill's drama

OF MICE AND MEN— *Right*, Kevin Conway as George and James Earl Jones as Lennie

SUMMERFOLK — *Below*, Estelle Kohler, Ian Richardson, Mike Gwilym, Janet Whiteside and Susan Fleetwood in Royal Shakespeare Company's production of the play by Maxim Gorky

INSTITUTIONAL PRODUCTION

Left, Beatrice Straight and Hugh Marlowe in the Roundabout's *All My Sons*

Above center, Charlotte Moore and Randall Duk Kim in N.Y. Shakespeare's *Pericles* in Central Park; *Above right*, Michael Moriarty in N.Y. Shakespeare's *Richard III* at Lincoln Center

Left, Stephen D. Newman (Macheath) and Richard Ryder in *Polly,* John Gay's musical sequel to *The Beggar's Opera*

Below, Joseph Bova and Peter Kingsley in S.J. Perelman's *The Beauty Part* at American Place

CROSS-COUNTRY
THEATER

WASHINGTON—At *top of page*, a scene from the Soviet play *The Ascent of Mount Fuji* in its English-language premiere at Arena Stage. *Left*, Lauri Peters, Anne Stone and Elizabeth Perry in the Folger Theater production of David Storey's British script, *The Farm*

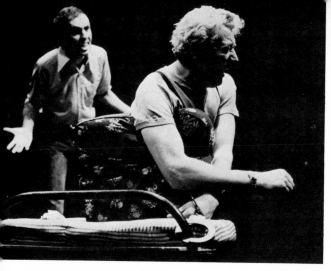

LOS ANGELES—*Above*, Christopher Hampton's *Savages* at Mark Taper Forum, with Michael Ivan Cristofer and Joseph Maher. *Right*, Doris Martin and Arthur Peterson in Frank Salisbury's *The Seagulls of 1933* at Actors' Alley

PROVIDENCE—*Above*, a scene from Trinity Square's *Well Hung*, American premiere of a play by New Zealander Robert Lord

LOUISVILLE — *Above*, Patricia Pearcy and Adale O'Brian in *Female Transport* at the Actors' Theater

SEATTLE—*Right*, John Harkins in Lloyd Gold's *A Grave Undertaking* at Seattle Repertory Theater

SPRINGFIELD, MASS.—*Above*, a scene from Paul Foster's *Marcus Brutus* in its world premiere production at Stage/West

ST. LOUIS — *Above*, Wil Love, Georgia Engel, Henry Strozier and Brendan Burke in Loretto-Hilton production of *Have I Stayed Too Long at the Fair?*

MILWAUKEE — *Right*, Joel Stedman and Rose Herron in Milwaukee Repertory's *Down by the Gravois (Under the Anheuser-Busch)*

NEW HAVEN—*Left*, Stephen Rowe and Christopher Lloyd in the Yale Repertory Theater production of Andrzej Wajda's *The Possessed*, based on a Dostoevsky work

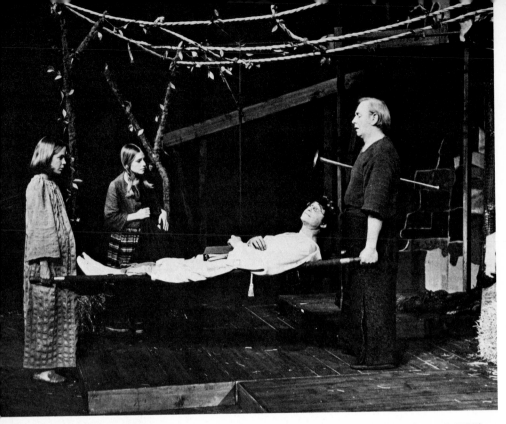

SYRACUSE—*Above*, a scene from the world premiere production of William Gibson's *The Butterfingers Angel* at Syracuse Stage

DINNER THEATER — 1974–75 programs included new work like (*above*) *Red Dawg* with Richard Blair (*foreground*) at Firehouse Dinner Theater, Omaha; and (*left*) *An Evening with WHO?* with Michael Perrier and Pat Carroll at Coachlight Dinner Theater, Warehouse Point, Conn.

THE LEGEND OF WU CHANG (32). Conceived and directed by Tisa Chang; based on a classic Chinese adventure tale. May 15, 1975. Scenery, Stephen Hendrickson; lighting, Robert Monk; costumes, Fredda Slavin; consultant for costumes, makeup and movement, Lu Yu; women's choreography, Sheree Lin; men's choreography, Eddie Chen. With Ernest Abuba, Lori Tan Chinn, Lynette Chun, Alvin Lum, Tom Mardirosian, Tom Matsusaka, Dennis Sakamoto, Atsumi Sakoto, Pamela Tokunga, Peter Yoshida.

BURLINGTON, VT.

Champlain Shakespeare Festival: University of Vermont Arena Theater

(Producer-director, Edward J. Feidner; scenery, W. M. Schenck; lighting, Charles Towers; costumes, Nanalee Raphael)

THE TEMPEST (16). By William Shakespeare. July 24, 1974. Director, Edward J. Feidner. With John Milligan, Andrew Jones, Stephanie Satie, Peter Covette, Robert Rovin.

CYMBELINE (15). By William Shakespeare. July 30, 1974. Director, Nancy Haynes. With John Milligan, Kenneth Gray, Michael Diamond, Glynis Bell, Stephanie Satie.

HAMLET (15). By William Shakespeare. August 6, 1974. Director, Michael Diamond. With Kenneth Gray, Robert Rovin, John Milligan, Dennis Lipscomb, Andrew Jones, Stephanie Satie, Glynis Bell.

CHICAGO

Goodman Theater Center: Professional Series

(Artistic director, William Woodman; managing director, John Economos)

THE CHERRY ORCHARD (44). By Anton Chekhov; translated by Tyrone Guthrie and Leonid Kipnis. October 4, 1974. Director, Brian Murray; scenery, David Mitchell; lighting, Patricia Collins; costumes, Virgil Johnson. With Nancy Marchand, William Roerick, Roger Omar Serbagi, Julie Garfield, Cecilia Hart, Nancy Zala, Edward Herrmann, Maurice D. Copeland, Bruce Kornbluth.

THE SEA (44). By Edward Bond. November 15, 1974 (American premiere). Director, William Woodman; scenery David Jenkins; lighting, F. Michell Dana; costumes, James Edmund Brady.

Willy Carson	Bruce Kornbluth
Evens	Martyn Green
Hatch	Lenny Baker
Louise Rafi	Brenda Forbes
Jessica Tilehouse	Jane MacIver
Hollarcut	Eugene J. Anthony
Thompson	Joe Bell
Carter	Dennis Kennedy
Mafanwy Price	Allison Giglio
Jilly	Judith Ivey
Rachel	Helen Cutting
Vicar	Maurice D. Copeland
Rose Jones	Rebecca Balding
Davis	Brigid Duffy

The action takes place in a small town on the East Coast of England a few years before World War I. The play is in eight scenes with one intermission after Scene 5.

THE PHILANTHROPIST (44). By Christopher Hampton. February 14, 1975. Director, Michael Montel; scenery, Peter Wexler; lighting, Ken Billington; costumes, John David Ridge. With Brian Murray, David H. Leary, Swoosie Kurtz, Veronica Castang, Jarlath Conroy, Richard Clarke, Judith Ivey.

THE RESISTIBLE RISE OF ARTURO UI (45). By Bertolt Brecht; adapted by George Tabori; music by Hans-Dieter Hosalla. March 28, 1975. Director, William Woodman; scenery, Joseph Nieminski; lighting, Gilbert V. Hemsley Jr.; costumes, John David Ridge. With Kenneth Welsh, Paul Larson, George Brengel, Charles Randall, Anthony M. Mockus.

CHEMIN DE FER (45). By Georges Feydeau; translated by Suzanne Grossman and Paxton Whitehead. May 9, 1975. Director, Stuart Gordon; scenery, James E. Maronek; lighting, F. Michell Dana; costumes, James Edmund Brady. With Richard Fire, Eugenie Ross-Leming, Warren Casey, Dennis Franz, Richard Kline, Kathleen Doyle.

Goodman Theater Center: Professional Series—Guest Production

'TIS PITY SHE'S A WHORE (44). By John Ford. January 3, 1975. Director, Michael Kahn. Production of the McCarter Theater, November, 1974.

Goodman Theater Center: Stage 2

WINNEBAGO (6). Written and directed by Frank Galati. November 1, 1974. Scenery and costumes, Paul Appel; lighting, Craig Miller; music and sound, Nick Venden; choreography, Peter Amster. With John Mohrlein, Janice Davies, Rex Troxell, Mary Cobb, Jane MacIver, John-Dennis Johnston.

THE SON (8). By Gert Hofmann; translated by Jon Swan. January 3, 1975. Director, Gregory Mosher; scenery, Beverly Sobieski; lighting, Robert Christen; costumes, Maggie Bodwell. With Beatrice Fredman, Danny Goldring, Charles Berendt, Arnold Coty, Bunny Kacher, Ann Ryerson, Sonja Lanzener.

ONCE AND FOR ALL (6). By Robert Gordon. February 28, 1975. Director, Patrick O'Gara; designer, Michael Merritt. With Shelly Safir, Ronald Koules, Rachel Stephens, Kenneth Karp.

THREE WOMEN (12). Created by Cecil O'Neal and the Company. April 18, 1975. Director, Cecil O'Neal; lighting, Robert Shook. With Cynthia Baker Johnson, Sandy Lipton, Roberta Maguire.

Note: Stage 2 productions are experimental plays, works in progress, or plays considered worthy of production but not suited for the regular series.

Goodman Theater Center: Children's Theater

THE POPCORN MAN (70). Book and lyrics by Dodi Robb and Pat Patterson; music by Pat Patterson. June 24, 1974. Director, Bella Itkin; scenery & costumes, David Emmons; lighting, Daniel Aberson, G. E. Naselius; choreography & musical coordination, Estelle Spector; additional music and lyrics, Errol Pearlman. With Adrian Smith, Sandra Gray, Frederick Schmidt.

THE PRINCE, THE WOLF AND THE FIREBIRD (28). By Jackson Lacey. October 19, 1974. Director, Bella Itkin; scenery, Brad R. Loman; lighting, William C. Fox; costumes, Susan T. Gayford. With Rick Goldman, Timothy Smith, Linda Sue Pieper, William Hollis.

RAGS TO RICHES (29). By Aurand Harris; suggested by two Horatio Alger stories. December 7, 1974. Director, Eleanor Logan; scenery, Eric Fielding; lighting, Steven E. Burgess; costumes, Nancy E. Grabowski. With Daniel Woodard, Gene Schuldt, Richard Babcock, Cathy Karp.

PECK'S BAD BOY (32). By Aurand Harris; based on stories from Peck's Bad Boy. January 25, 1975. Director, Kelly Danford; scenery, Brad R. Loman; lighting, Neal J. Yablong; costumes, Richard Donnelly. With Richard Porter, Susan Monts, Geoffrey Shlaes, William Kenzie, Martin Levy.

THE GREAT CROSS-COUNTRY RACE (32). By Alan Broadhurst; adapted from The Hare and The Tortoise. March 22, 1975. Director, David L. Avcollie; scenery, Eric Fielding; lighting, Terry Jenkins; costumes, Phyllis Hojnacki. With Richard Flegle, Gregory Polcyn.

Note: The Goodman Theater Center again presented a subscription series at the School of Drama Studio Theater: Merton of the Movies by George S. Kaufman and Marc Connelly; adapted and directed by Kelly Danford; music and lyrics by David Coleman, November 1, 1974; Funeral Games by Joe Orton and Vampire by Snoo Wilson, adapted and directed by Joseph Slowik, November 29, 1974; Major Barbara by George Bernard Shaw, directed by John Clingerman, January 31, 1975; Romeo and Juliet by William Shakespeare, directed by Bella Itkin, February 28, 1975; The Hot l Baltimore by Lanford Wilson, directed by Rae Allen, April 4, 1975; The Liar by Carlo Goldoni, translated by Tunc Yalman, directed by Libby Appel, May 2, 1975.

CINCINNATI

Playhouse in the Park: Shelterhouse Theater

(Artistic director, Harold Scott; managing director, Sara O'Connor; director, James Thornton; scenery, Ron Naversen; lighting, Dwight Werle; costumes, Ann Firestone; musical director, Brian Hall; choreography, Ray Miller)

THE FANTASTICKS (22). Book and lyrics by Tom Jones; music by Harvey Schmidt; based on Edmond Rostand's play, *Les Romantiques.* June 20, 1974.

THE APPLE TREE: THE DIARY OF ADAM AND EVE; PASSIONELLA (22). Book, music and lyrics by Sheldon Harnick and Jerry Bock; additional book material by Jerome Cooper-smith; based on stories by Mark Twain and Jules Feiffer. July 11, 1974.

EL GRANDE DE COCA-COLA (22) By Ron House, John Neville-Andrews, Alan Shear-man, Diz White and Sally Willis; from an idea by Ron House and Sally Willis. August 1, 1974.

Shelterhouse Company: Jeffery Bixby, Alex Davis, Rick Henzel, Marge Kotzynski, Wendy Kriss, Anne Lucas, David Prittie, Tom Robins, James Rosenberger.

Playhouse in the Park: Robert S. Marx Theater

(Producing director, Thomas Kelly; associate director, Lani Ball)

TARTUFFE (30). By Molière; English verse translation by Richard Wilbur. October 17, 1974. Director, Daniel Sullivan; scenery, Eric Head; lighting, John Gleason; costumes, Susan Tsu. With Austin Pendleton, Neil Flanagan, Richard Green, Dee Victor, Teri Ralston.

WHO'S AFRAID OF VIRGINIA WOOLF? (30). By Edward Albee. November 21, 1974. Di-rector, Garland Wright; scenery, John Scheffler; lighting, Marc B. Weiss; costumes, Susan Tsu. With Bette Ford, James Ray, Eda Zahl, J. Kenneth Campbell.

ARSENIC AND OLD LACE (30). By Joseph Kesselring. February 20, 1975. Director, An-thony Stimac; scenery, John Scheffler; lighting, John Gleason; costumes, Susan Tsu. With Dee Victor, Gene Wolters, Reid Shelton, Nancy Cushman, Raymond Thorne, William Metzo.

THAT CHAMPIONSHIP SEASON (30). By Jason Miller. March 27, 1975. Director, John Dillon; scenery, John Scheffler; lighting, John Gleason; costumes, Susan Tsu. With James Cook, Eddie Jones, William Metzo, Reid Shel-ton, Raymond Thorne.

THE HOT L BALTIMORE (30). By Lanford Wilson. May 1, 1975. Director, Daniel Sullivan; scenery, Eric Head; lighting, John Gleason; cos-tumes, Susan Tsu. With Jill O'Hara, Joan Pape, Tracy Brooks Swope, Ray Fry, Frank Geraci, Gibby Brand, James Roman, David Lyman.

OH COWARD! (30). Devised by Roderick Cook; words and music by Noel Coward. June 5, 1975. Director, Garland Wright; scenery, Eric Head; lighting, John Gleason; costumes, Susan Tsu; musical director, Worth Gardner; choreog-raphy, Gary Menteer. With Alan Brasington, Bonnie Franklin, Leonard Frey.

CLEVELAND

The Cleveland Play House: Euclid-77th Street Theater

(Managing director, Richard Oberlin)

HAPPY END (22). By Bertolt Brecht and Kurt Weill; adaptation and lyrics by Michael Fein-gold, based on the German play by Dorothy Lane. October 18, 1974. Director-choreogra-pher, Dennis Rosa. With Dan Desmond, Rich-ard Halverson, Robert Allman, Barbara Meek, Charlotte Hare, Dana Hart.

THE FREEDOM OF THE CITY (22). By Brian Friel. November 22, 1974. Director, Larry Tar-rant. With Evie McElroy, Daniel Mooney, Greg-ory Lehane, Paul Lee, Robert Allman, John Buck Jr., Robert Snook.

HAY FEVER (22). By Noel Coward. December 27, 1974. Director, Paul Lee. With June Gib-

bons, Leslie Rapp, Gregory Lehane, Robert All-man, Kerry Slattery, Marjorie Dawe, Daniel Mooney, John Bergstrom.

RICHARD III (2). By William Shakespeare. January 31, 1975. Director, Bill Francisco. With John Buck Jr., Richard Halverson, Jon Peter Benson, Robert Allman, June Gibbons, Brenda Curtis, Marji Dodrill, Jonathan Farwell.

CONFESSION AT NIGHT (22). By Aleksei Arbuzov; translated by Ariadne Nicolaeff. March 7, 1975 (American premiere). Director, Larry Tarrant; scenery, Richard Gould; lighting, Kathleen Vance Tomzic; costumes, Joe Dale Lunday; properties, David Smith.

Maj. Evald Hissling . . . . . Jonathan Farwell
Lt. Heinrich von Halem . . Jon Peter Benson
Nicolay Samarin . . . . Robert Allman
Zinovy Mironetz . . . . William Turner
Pvt. August Sholtz . . . . Allen Leatherman
Boris Glebov . . . . Richard Halverson
Yulya Glebova . . . . Dee Hoty
Andrey Koverga . . . . Dan Desmond
Eduard Koverga . . . . Frederic Serino
Yelena Svetlova . . . . Leslie Rappy
Anatoly Bryansky-Martinelli   Gregory Lehane
Viktor Zaitsev . . . . Tony Campisi
Yevgeny Lastochkin . . . . . . John Buck Jr.

Other Members of German Command:Robert Kneen, Keith Rosenblum, Robert Barnes

Time: The spring of 1944. Place: A small town in South Ukraine, occupied by the Germans; the office of the commandant, and a makeshift cell nearby. One intermission.

THE PRISONER OF SECOND AVENUE (24). By Neil Simon. April 11, 1975. Director, Richard Halverson. With Jonathan Farwell, Stanja Lowe, Norm Berman, Vivienne Stotter, Edith Owen, Jo Farwell.

The Cleveland Play House: Drury Theater

CAT ON A HOT TIN ROOF (22). By Tennessee Williams. November 8, 1974. Director, Jonathan Bolt. With Paula Wagner, Douglas Jones, Richard Oberlin, June Gibbons, Jo Farwell, Jonathan Farwell.

THE COUNT OF MONTE CRISTO (22). By Marshall Borden; based on the novel by Alexandre Dumas. December 13, 1974. Director, William Rhys. With Jonathan Farwell, Ralph Neeley, Brenda Curtis, Dan Desmond, Edmund Lyndeck, Richard Halverson, Jo Farwell.

THE HOT L BALTIMORE (32). By Lanford Wilson. January 17, 1975. Director, Jonathan Bolt. With Dan Desmond, Edith Owen, Evie McElroy, Myrna Kaye.

THE RIVALS (7). By Richard Brinsley Sheridan. March 21, 1975. Director Paul Lee. With Brenda Curtis, Daniel Mooney, June Gibbons, Norm Berman, Dennis M. Romer, Robert Snook, Lora Beth Staley.

The Cleveland Play House: Brooks Theater

THE SEA HORSE (40). By Edward J. Moore. October 25, 1974; reopened March 19, 1975. Director, Paul Lee. With Evie McElroy, John Bergstrom.

COLETTE (18). By Elinor Jones; adapted from

Robert Phelps's *Earthly Paradise;* music and lyrics by Harvey Schmidt and Tom Jones. December 20, 1974. Director, Fran Soeder. With Myrna Kaye, Edith Owen, Robert Snook, Douglas Jones, Norm Berman, Dee Hoty.

The Cleveland Theater: Youth Theater Productions

A CHILD'S CHRISTMAS IN WALES (2). By Dylan Thomas. December 27, 1974. Director, Daniel Morris.

ANDROCLES AND THE LION (2). By Aurand Harris. May 3, 1975. Director, Daniel Morris.

Designers: Scenery, Richard Gould, Tim Zupancic, Barbara Leatherman, David Smith; lighting, David Eisenstat, Kathleen Vance Tomazic, Russell Lowe; costumes, Joe Dale Lunday.

Note: *The Rivals* was performed mainly for student audiences in the spring of 1975. Seven performances were given for the regular audience.

DALLAS

Dallas Theater Center: Kalita Humphreys Theater

(Managing director, Paul Baker)

ARSENIC AND OLD LACE (33). By Joseph Kesselring. June 4, 1974. Director, Randolph Tallman; scenery, John Henson; lighting, Sam Nance; costumes, Celia Karston. With Ella-Mae Brainard, Jacque Thomas, Randy Moore, Gary Moore, Chelcie Ross, Michael Dendy, Daryl Conner.

TOBACCO ROAD (33). By Jack Kirkland; based on a novel by Erskine Caldwell. July 16, 1974. Director, Ken Latimer; scenery, George T. Green; lighting, Randy Moore; costumes, Daryl Conner. With James Crump, Mary Sue Jones, Robyn Flatt, John Logan, Michael Mullen, Cindy Holden, Martha Robinson Goodman.

CHEMIN DE FER (33). By Georges Feydeau; translated and adapted by Suzanne Grossmann and Paxton Whitehead. October 8, 1974. Director, David Pursley; scenery, Peter Wolf; lighting, Sally Netzel; costumes, Irene Corey. With Mona Pursley, Randy Moore, Matt Tracy, Ken Latimer, Synthia Rogers, John Figlmiller.

THE BRADLEYVILLE TRILOGY: THE OLDEST LIVING GRADUATE (world premiere), THE LAST MEETING OF THE KNIGHTS OF THE WHITE MAGNOLIA (revised), LU ANN HAMPTON LAVERTY OBERLANDER (revised) (39). By Preston Jones. November 19, 1974. Director, Paul Baker; scenery, Mary Sue Jones; lighting, Linda Blase; costumes, Kathleen Latimer. With James Crump, John Henson, Ken Latimer, Sallie Laurie, Randy Moore, Mona Pursley, Synthia Rogers.

The Oldest Living Graduate:

Col. J. C. Kinkaid	Randy Moore
Floyd Kinkaid	John Henson
Maureen Kinkaid	Mona Pursley

Clarence Sickenger	Tim Green
Martha Ann Sickenger	Robyn Flatt
Mike Tremaine	William Landry
Maj. LeRoy W. Ketchum	Allen Hibbard
Cadet Whopper Turnbull	Tommy G. Kendrick
Claudine Hampton	Synthia Rogers

Time: Summer 1962. Place: The Kinkaid home. Act I, Scene 1: Afternoon. Scene 2: An hour later. Act II, Scene 1: Four days later. Scene 2: An hour later. Scene 3: 2 A.M. that night. The trilogy was performed each evening with intermissions. Dinner and dessert were served at the first and second intermissions.

INHERIT THE WIND (39). By Jerome Lawrence and Robert E. Lee. January 14, 1975. Director, Jerome Lawrence; scenery, Nancy Levinson; lighting, Sam Nance; costumes, John Henson. With Preston Jones, Barry Hope, John Figlmiller, Nick Dalley, Diana Devereaux, Lynn Trammell.

MISALLIANCE (39). By George Bernard Shaw. March 4, 1975. Director, Linda Daugherty; scenery, Virgil Beavers; lighting, Randy Moore; costumes, Kathleen Latimer. With Chelcie Ross, Norma Moore, Louise Mosley, Steve Lovett, Matt Tracy, Sally Netzel, Steven Mackenroth, Paul Buboltz, Randolph Tallman.

JOURNEY TO JEFFERSON (33). By Robert L. Flynn; adapted from William Faulkner's novel, *As I Lay Dying.* April 22, 1975. Director, Paul Baker; designer, Virgil Beavers; lighting, Robyn Flatt, Randy Moore. With Randy Moore, Mary Sue Jones, Ken Latimer, Drexel H. Riley, Robyn Flatt, John Logan, Tommy G. Kendrick, Paul Porter.

Dallas Theater Center: Down Center Stage

MY DRINKING COUSIN (12). By Frank Jarrett. October 31, 1974 (professional premiere). Director, Rebecca Logan; scenery, Allen Hibbard; lighting, Linda Blase; costumes, Catherine Mackenroth; sound, Patricia Lovell.

Bert Hamilton	Bryant J. Reynolds
Bertram Hamilton	Richard F. Ward
Maudie Hamilton	Cheryl Denson
Ida Morton	Mary Rohde
Bud Freeman	Chelcie Ross
Billie Reed	Norma Moore

Act I, Scene 1: Dallas, March 4, 1933, early Saturday morning. Scene 2: Before supper that same day. Scene 3: Around midnight that evening. Act II, Scene 1: Before sunrise, a week later. Scene 2: After dinner that evening. Scene 3: Later that same evening.

WHY DON'T THEY EVER TALK ABOUT THE FIRST MRS. PHIPPS? (12). By Sue Ann Gunn. December 5, 1974 (world premiere). Director, Lynn Trammell; scenery, Cheryl Denson; lighting, Matt Tracy; costumes, Celia Karston;

Louise	Jacque Thomas
Morton	Chelcie Ross
Sally	Sarah Converse

Place: An apartment in a large city. One intermission.

PUPPY DOESN'T LIVE HERE ANY MORE (12). By Iris Rosofsky. February 13, 1975 (world premiere). Director, Sallie Laurie; scenery, Robert Duffy; lighting, William Smotherman; costumes, Celeste Varricchio,

Jeff . . . . .James Crump
Puppy . . . . Cheryl Denson
Cora . . . . .Elfriede Russell
Chuck . . . . .John Logan
Nettie . . . . Diane Crane
Junior . . . . Ken Kieffer/Matthew Broussard.
   Place: A small cafe-hotel in the Arizona desert. One intermission.

SOURWOOD HONEY (12). By T. Alan Doss. March 27, 1975 (world premiere). Director, Bryant J. Reynolds; designer, Peter Lynch; lighting, Gina Taulane.

Robert C. Johnson . . . . . Herman Wheatley
Jimbo . . . . Paul Dollar
Maybelle . . . . Sue Ann Gunn
Precious Angel . . . . Roselee Blooston
Cat Daniels . . . . Tony Kish
Crab-Bite Charley . . . . .Fred Moore
Myra Lou . . . . Susan A. Haynie
Lamejaw Luther . . . . Robert Duffy
   Time: March, 1951. Place: Rabbit Town city dump overlooking the Coosa River in Northeast Alabama. One intermission.

LA TURISTA (12). By Sam Shepard. May 8, 1975. Director, Tommy G. Kendrick; scenery, Sam Nance; lighting, Carolyn Moon; costumes, Susan A. Haynie. With Jacque Gavin, Rebecca Ramsey, Nick Dalley, Tommy Cantu, Robert Duffy, Randolf Pearson.

Dallas Theater Center: Down Stage Center, Magic Turtle Children's Theater

October 19, 1974–May 24, 1975 (8 performances each). CHI-CHIN-PUI-PUI, adapted by T. Alan Doss from Japanese folk tales by Kyo Ozawa; GRIMM'S FAIRY TALES: HANS

BRINKER AND THE SILVER SKATES, KING MIDAS AND THE GOLDEN TOUCH.

Note: Dallas Theater Center is affiliated with the graduate program of Trinity University. Its resident professional company is augmented by journeymen and apprentices who work from three to four years in a comprehensive professional career program.

HARTFORD, CONN.

Hartford Stage Company

(Producing director, Paul Weidner; managing director, Jessica L. Andrews)

THE HOT L BALTIMORE (44). By Lanford Wilson. September 20, 1974. Director, Paul Weidner; scenery, Marjorie Kellogg; lighting, Larry Crimmins; costumes, Caley Summers. With Seret Scott, Ray Aranha, Vera Lockwood, Victoria Zussin, Tana Hicken, David O. Petersen, Jack Swanson.

SHORT EYES (44). By Miguel Piñero. November 1, 1974. Director, Marvin Felix Camillo; scenery, Hugh Landwehr; lighting, Larry Crimmins; costumes, Paul Martino. With Richard Loder, Hollis Barnes, Eduardo Figueroa, Tito Goya, Ben Jefferson, J. J. Johnson, Chu Chu Malave.

THE CHERRY ORCHARD (44) By Anton Chekhov. December 13, 1974. Director, Paul Weidner; scenery Santo Loquasto; lighting, Larry Crimmins; costumes, Caley Summers. With Anne Jackson, Bernard Frawley, Larry Bryggman, Tana Hicken, Jack Swanson, Brenda Currin, David O. Petersen.

A RAISIN IN THE SUN (44). By Lorraine Hansberry. January 31, 1975. Director, Irene Lewis; scenery, Hugh Landwehr; lighting, Larry Crimmins; costumes, Linda Fisher. With Claudia McNeil, William Jay, Deloris Gaskins, Seret Scott, Hannibal Penney Jr./David Downing.

AFTERNOON TEA (44). By Harvey Perr. March 21, 1975 (world premiere). Director, Paul Weidner; scenery, Marjorie Kellogg; lighting, Larry Crimmins; costumes, Linda Fisher.
Rachel . . . . .Barbara Caruso
Aaron . . . . .Jordan Charney
   Time: A Sunday afternoon in autumn. Place: Rachel's house in the country. No intermission.

ROOM SERVICE (44). By John Murray and Allen Boretz. May 9, 1975. Director, Paul Weidner; scenery, John Conklin; lighting, Peter Hunt; costumes, Caley Summers. With Robert Moberly, Ted Graeber, Bernard Frawley, Richard Loder, Tana Hicken, Louis Beachner.

Note: Stage 2, directed and coordinated by Hartford Stage Company's Irene Lewis, presented a series of Monday performances, October 1974 through June, 1975. Those marked with * toured throughout New England. *Annelies Marie Frank: Witness*;* El Teatro Campesino, *The Family—"Street Sounds"*; *A Clown's Corner Concert;** *Spoon River*;* *In Performance—Gretchen Cryer and Nancy Ford; The Collected Works of Billy the Kid: The Poetry of Michael Ondaatje;* The Hartford Stage Studio, directed by Henry Thomas.

HOUSTON

Arena Theater: Large Stage

(Producer-director, Nina Vance)

WILSON (32). By George Greanias. October 17, 1974 (world premiere). Director, Nina Vance; assistant director, Beth Sanford; scenery, William Trotman; lighting, Jonathan Duff; costumes, Barbara C. Cox; musical director, Paul Dupree; technical director, William C. Lindstrom; music, George Greanias, Paul Dupree; lyrics, George Greanias; additional music, John Philip Sousa, George M. Cohan.

Woodrow Wilson	Shepperd Strudwick
Edward M. "Colonel" House	Tony Russel
Sen. Henry Cabot Lodge	William Trotman
Cary T. Grayson	Philip Davidson
Edith Bolling Galt Wilson	Darlene Conley
Joseph P. Tumulty	Roger Baron
Clemenceau	E. A. Sirianni
Orlando	Sidney Armus
Lloyd George	Joseph Costa
Sen. Albert Fall	Ronald Bishop

Reporters, Photographers: Christopher Fazel, Mark Keeler, Mike Kiibler, Simon L. Levy, David Okarski, Ed Wittner.

The play concerns events in the life of Woodrow Wilson and in the history of the United States just before, during, and immediately after World War I. Place: Washington, D. C., Paris, and various towns and cities throughout the western United States. Two intermissions.

THE MAN WHO CAME TO DINNER (44). By George S. Kaufman and Moss Hart. November 28, 1974. Director, Robert E. Leonard; scenery, John Kenny; lighting, Paul Gregory; costumes, Barbara C. Cox. With Ronald Bishop, Darlene Conley, Tony Russel, Mimi Carr, Joseph Costa, Lillian Evans.

TWELFTH NIGHT (46). By William Shakespeare. January 16, 1975. Director, Robert E. Leonard; scenery, John Kenny; lighting, Jonathan Duff; costumes, Barbara C. Cox. With

Sharon Swink, Tony Russel, Lillian Evans, Cal Bedford, Ronald Bishop, E. A. Sirianni, Mimi Carr, David Wurst, Sheldon Epps.

A STREETCAR NAMED DESIRE (38). By Tennessee Williams, February 27, 1975. Director, Beth Sanford; scenery, William Trotman; lighting, Jonathan Duff; costumes, Barbara C. Cox. With Tony Russel, Bettye Fitzpatrick, Lillian Evans, William Trotman.

TOBACCO ROAD (38). By Jack Kirkland. April 10, 1975. Director, William Trotman; scenery, John Kenny; lighting, Jonathan Duff; costumes, Barbara C. Cox. With John Newton, Lillian Evans, Mimi Carr, Donna O'Connor, David Wurst, Rutherford Cravens, Susan Slater.

THE CONTEST (38). By Shirley Mezvinsky Lauro. May 22, 1975 (world premiere). Director, Nina Vance; assistant director, Beth Sanford; scenery, William Trotman; lighting, Jonathan Duff; costumes, Barbara C. Cox; musical director, Paul Dupree; technical director, William C. Lindstrom.

Lily Green	Jo Allessandro Marks
Beverly Green	Cristine Rose
Joe Green	Sidney Armus
Gert Kramer	Marji Bank
Louie Kramer	Joe Finkelstein
Marilyn Kramer	Amy Konig
Mamie Abrams	Victoria Zussin
Irma Jean	Kathryn Mosbacher
Grocery Boy	Richard Holloman

Place: A small city in the midwest. Time: January, 1943. Act I, Scene 1: Early Sunday evening. Scene 2: Three weeks later, a Sunday night. Act II: One month later, a Tuesday afternoon. Act III, Scene 1: Five weeks later, a Wednesday afternoon. Scene 2: Seven months later, a Saturday night.

Alley Theater: Arena Stage

A CHRISTMAS CAROL (6) By Charles Dickens; adapted from the novel, by Frederick Koch.

December 13, 1974. With William Trotman.

Note: Alley Theater's children's theater production, *The Yellow Brick Road,* adapted and directed by Iris Siff from *The Wizard Of Oz,* was presented in February and May, 1975. Original music by George Morgenstern.

INDIANAPOLIS

Indiana Repertory Theater

(Artistic director, Edward Stern; producing director, Benjamin Mordecai)

HARVEY (21). By Mary Chase. October 24, 1974. Director, Edward Stern; scenery, Richard Ferguson-Wagstaffe; lighting, Jody Boese; costumes, Joan Thiel. With Dorothy Blackburn, James Noble, Priscilla Lindsay, Steven Ryan, Max Gulack.

THE LITTLE FOXES (21) By Lillian Hellman. November 21, 1974. Director, John Going; scenery & lighting, Richard Ferguson-Wagstaffe; costumes, Joan Thiel. With Carolyn Coates, James Noble, Bernard Kates, Margaret Phillips.

ONE FLEW OVER THE CUCKOO'S NEST (22). By Dale Wasserman; based on the novel by Ken Kesey. December 19, 1974. Director, Edward Stern, scenery & lighting, Richard Ferguson-Wagstaffe; costumes, Sherry Mordecai. With Mel Cobb, Laurinda Barrett, John Abajian, Bernard Kates, Robert Scogin.

THE TAMING OF THE SHREW (21) By William Shakespeare. January 23, 1975. Director, Garland Wright; scenery & costumes, William E. Schroder; lighting, Jody Boese. With Michael

Parish, Linda Carlson, Gun-Marie Nilsson, Russell Gold.

THE RAINMAKER (21). By N. Richard Nash. February 20, 1975. Director, Edward Stern; scenery, Richard Ferguson-Wagstaffe; lighting, Jody Boese; costumes, Sherry Mordecai. With Katharine Houghton, Ken Jenkins, Robert Scogin, Russell Gold.

A BIRD IN THE HAND (21) By Georges Feydeau; translated and adapted by Edward and Anne Ward Stern. March 20, 1975 (American premiere). Director, Benjamin Mordecai; scenery, Richard Ferguson-Wagstaffe; lighting, Jody Boese; costumes, Thom Schmunk.

Monsieur Parcarel . . . . . . Bernard Kates
Dufausset . . . . Collis White
Dr. Landernau . . . . Russell Gold
Lanoix de Vaux . . . . John Abajian
Tiburce . . . . .Robert Scogin
Martha . . . . Elaine Kilden
Amardine . . . . .Leta Bonynge
Julie . . . . .K. T. Baumann

KANSAS CITY, MO.

Missouri Repertory Theater: University of Missouri

(Director, Patricia McIlrath.)

THE RIVALS (16). By Richard Brinsley Sheridan. June 27, 1974. Director, John O'Shaughnessy; scenery, J. Morton Walker; lighting, Marc Schlackman; costumes, Vincent Scassellati. With Steven Ryan, Ken Graham, Robert Elliott, Vincent Dowling, Robert Scogin, Harriet Levitt, Susan Borneman.

PEG O' MY HEART (16). By J. Hartley Manners. July 4, 1974. Director, Vincent Dowling; scenery, John Ezell; lighting, Marc Schlackman; costumes, Douglas A. Russell. With Jeannine Weeks, Harriet Levitt, Art Ellison, Mary-Linda Rapelye, John Q. Bruce, Jr., Robert Scogin.

THAT CHAMPIONSHIP SEASON (17). By Jason Miller. July 11, 1974. Director, John O'Shaughnessy; scenery, Max A. Beatty; lighting, Marc Schlackman; costumes, Vincent Scassellati. With Steven Ryan, Robert Elliott, Ken

Graham, Walter W. Atamaniuk, Al Christy.

A MIDSUMMER NIGHT'S DREAM (16). By William Shakespeare. July 18, 1974. Director, Thomas Gruenewald; scenery, Max A. Beatty; lighting, Marc Schlackman; costumes, Douglas A. Russell. With Robert Scogin, Ronetta Wallman, Steven Ryan, Walter W. Atamaniuk, Michele Garrison, Mary-Linda Rapelye, Al Christy, Robert Elliott.

THE EFFECT OF GAMMA RAYS ON MAN-IN-THE-MOON MARIGOLDS (16). By Paul Zindel. August 1, 1974. Director, Patricia McIlrath; scenery, J. Morton Walker; lighting, Marc Schlackman; costumes, Vincent Scassellati. With Ronetta Wallman, Mindy McCrary, Valli Hanley, Harriet Levitt, Michele Garrison.

PEER GYNT (15). By Henrik Ibsen; a play with

music adapted by Adrian Hall and Richard Cumming, based on the Christopher Fry adaptation of Johann Fillinger's translation; music and lyrics by Richard Cumming. August 8, 1974 (American premiere). Director, Adrian Hall; scenery, John Ezell; lighting, Marc Schlackman; costumes, Douglas A. Russell; properties, John Ezell, Karen Schulz, Judy Juracek; choreography, Gladys Hannay.

Peer Gynt . . . . .Robert Elliott
Peer Gynt (middle aged) . . . . . .Al Christy
Peer Gynt (youth) . . . . George Ward Byers
Aase . . . . Frances Peter
Buttonmoulder;
   Strange passenger . . . . Steven Ryan
Thin Man; Captain . . . . . . .Robert Scogin
Bo'sun . . . . Michael Matthews
Cabin Boy . . . . Henry Stram
Priest . . . . Vincent Dowling
Solveig . . . . .Carol Pfander
Helga . . . . Gabrielle Weeks
Solveig's Father;
   English Plutocrat . . . . Ken Graham
Solveig's Mother . . . . . . .Carolyn Selberg
Aslak . . . . Howard Renensland
Mott Moen . . . . .Michael LaGue
Ingrid . . . . Loren Beth Brown
Bridegroom's Father;
   English plutocrat . . . . . George C. Berry
Bridegroom's Mother . . . . .Gladys Hannay
Old Woman . . . . Alison Bowyer
Mountain King . . . . . . Martin Marinaro
Old Troll Courtier . . . . Art Ellison
Woman in Green . . . . . Susan Borneman
Pig Pusher . . . . .David Duncan
Troll Musician . . . . Glenda Williams
German Plutocrat . . . Walter W. Atamaniuk
French Plutocrat . . . . . . John Q. Bruce, Jr.
Slave . . . . .David Peter Lauria
Anitra . . . . .Jeannine Weeks

Fence . . . . .Steve Searcy
Thief . . . . Douglas Huff
Begriffenfeldt . . . . .John Maddison
Huhu . . . . Paul Casey
I.R.A. Man . . . . Roger Atwell
   Sailors, Girls at wedding, Harem dancers: Steve Searcy, Nicholas Jacquez, Brian Klinknett, Frederic-Winslow Oram, Gary Groner, David Peter Lauria, Stuart Brooks, Caroline Campbell, Susan Scott Graves, Joni Wadtke, Evie Gould, Catherine Corum, Sheila Olson, Anastasia Ramos, Terri L. Treas, Michele Garrison. Actor Musicians: Henry Stram, Brian Klinknett, Roger Atwell, David Peter Lauria, Valli Hanley, David Duncan.

Time: The play moves backward and forward from 1857 to the present. Act I begins on board a ship returning to Norway; the action moves from Peer Gynt's imagination, to a country churchyard, all within the area of the Rhone Mountains. Act II begins in the churchyard and moves to the coast of Morocco, to the desert, to an asylum in Cairo and back to the Rhone Mountains.

Musical numbers: "God of Our Fathers," "Crazy Peer Gynt Has Done It Again," "I'll Be King of the World," "This Time You've Gone Too Far, Peer Gynt," Aase's Song: "Either You Take to the Bottle or Lies," "Opposites," "Banish the Outside World," "Self-Sufficient," "Sleep Between Our Thighs Tonight," "No Advice to Be Had," Plutocrats Quartet: "You're Wonderful Peer Gynt," "Of Royal Blood," "Mammy's Little Baby Loves Peer Gynt," "Liberty and Money," Thief and Fence duet, "The Prophet Is Come," Peer's Serenade, Solveig's Song: "The Winters Pass," "Final Solution," Song of the Wandering Jew, I.R.A. Revolutionary Song, "Where Did It Go?" The Return of Peer Gynt.

Note: Missouri Repertory Theater also has a touring unit, Missouri Vanguard Theater, which takes major productions and children's programs throughout the state. *Peg O' My Heart,* and two children's programs (*Story Caravan,* director, James Assad; scenery & lighting, Joseph Appelt; costumes, Barbara Medicott, with a cast of six professional actors, and *Hansel And Gretel* in a puppet theater version written and directed by Leslie Robinson, with puppets by Robert Finch and Gayla Pryor) were on the 1974–1975 touring program.

LAKEWOOD, OHIO

Great Lakes Shakespeare Festival: Lakewood Civic Auditorium

(Producer-director, Lawrence Carra; designers, Mark Pirolo, Frederic Youens, William French)

KING LEAR (22). By William Shakespeare. July 6, 1974. With Wesley Addy, Kendall March, Edith Owen, Janet Hayes, John Newton, Richard Yarnell, Gregory Lehane.

THE PLAYBOY OF THE WESTERN WORLD (18). By John Millington Synge. July 11, 1974. With Kendall March, Keith Mackey,

Janet Hayes, Gregory Lehane, Robert Allman.

MEASURE FOR MEASURE (12). By William Shakespeare. August 1, 1974. Guest director, Henry Hewes. With Robert Allman, Richard Yarnell, Tom Fucello, Carol Emshoff, Dee Hoty, Edith Owen.

UNDER THE GASLIGHT (14). By Augustin Daly. August 15, 1974. With Jonathan Steele, Keith Mackey, Wesley Addy, Kendall March, Christine Wiedemann.

THE COMEDY OF ERRORS (9). By William Shakespeare. August 29, 1974. Lyrics, Mary Fournier Bill; music, Frederick Koch. With Nathaniel Fuller, Christopher Holder, Gregory Lehane, Tom Fucello, Carol Emshoff, Kendall March.

LOS ANGELES

Center Theater Group: Ahmanson Theater

(Managing director, Robert Fryer.)

PRIVATE LIVES (47). By Noel Coward. October 8, 1974. Director, John Gielgud; scenery, Anthony Powell; lighting, H. R. Poindexter; costumes, Germinal Rangel. With Maggie Smith, John Standing, Remak Ramsay, Niki Flacks, Marie Tommon.

A MOON FOR THE MISBEGOTTEN (55). By Eugene O'Neill. November 26, 1974. Director, José Quintero; scenery & lighting, Ben Edwards; costumes, Jane Greenwood. With Colleen Dewhurst, Jason Robards, Tom Clancy, John O'-Leary, Edwin J. McDonough.

MACBETH (47). By William Shakespeare. January 28, 1975. Director, Peter Wood; scenery & lighting, H. R. Poindexter; costumes, Sam Kirkpatrick. With Vanessa Redgrave, Charlton Heston, Richard Jordan, John Devlin, John Ireland, Patrecia Wynand.

RING ROUND THE MOON (47). By Jean Anouilh; adapted by Christopher Fry. April 1, 1975. Director, Joseph Hardy; designer, Anthony Powell; lighting, H. R. Poindexter. With Michael York, Glynis Johns, Kitty Winn, Kurt Kasznar, Rosemary Murphy, Joan Van Ark.

Center Theater Group: Mark Taper Forum

(Artistic Director, Gordon Davidson; director, New Theater For Now, Edward Parone; director, Forum/Laboratory, Robert Greenwald.)

SAVAGES (54). By Christopher Hampton. August 15, 1974 (American premiere). Director, Gordon Davidson; scenery & costumes, Sally Jacobs; lighting, John Gleason.

Alan West	Joseph Maher
Mark Crawford	Ben Piazza
Mrs. West	Susan Brown
Carlos Esquerdo	Michael Ivan Cristofer
Maj. Brigg	Martyn Green
Bert	David Villa
Rev. Elmer Penn	David White
Kumai	Robert Huerta
Investigator	Daniel Sullivan
Ataide Pereira	Vito Scotti

The Tribe: Soledad de Oram, Ken R. Ganado, Frank Michael Liu, Fredd Morgan, Nilak, Mauricio Palma, Milcha C. Scott, Muni Zano. The Integradoes: Erik Arbiso, Robert Huerta, Ruth Pinedo, Fred Sannoya, Henry Santillan, David Villa, Ronald Yates Warden. Members of the M.R.B.: Erik Arbiso, Ronald Yates Warden.

The bombing of the Cintas Largas tribe during the performance of their funeral ritual took place in 1963; and the confession of Ataide Pereira was recorded shortly after this. The rest of the play is set in Brazil in 1970–71. One intermission.

JUNO AND THE PAYCOCK (54). By Sean O'Casey. November 7, 1974. Director George Seaton; scenery, John Conklin; lighting, Donald Harris; costumes, Dorothy Jeakins. With Maureen Stapleton, Walter Matthau, Jack Lemmon, Laurie Prange, John Glover, Dennis Robertson, Nicholas Hammond, Mary Wickes.

THE DYBBUK: BETWEEN TWO WORLDS (54). By S. Ansky; adapted by John Hirsch. January 30, 1975 (American premiere). Director-choreographer, John Hirsch; scenery, Maxine Graham; lighting, Pat Collins; costumes, Mark Negin, Maxine Graham; music, Alan Laing; musical supervision, John Berkman.

Henak	Don Samuels
Messenger	George Sperdakos
Pinye	Herb Foster
Shimon	Michael Strong
Meyer	Marvin Kaplan
Chanon	Jean-Paul Mustone
Hanna-Esther	Adrienne Marden
Faigele	Cindi Haynie
Leah	Marilyn Lightstone/Melora Marshall
Frade	Helene Winston
Gittle	Lisa Donaldson

WALTER MATTHAU, MAUREEN STAPLETON AND JACK LEMMON IN THE REVIVAL
OF SEAN O'CASEY'S "JUNO AND THE PAYCOCK" AT THE MARK TAPER FORUM

Ashe	Lou Wagner
Sender	Bert Freed
Yashka	Steven Rotblatt
Nemad	John La Motta
Razle	V. Phipps-Wilson
Rifke	Anne Turner
Batye	Constance Sawyer
Basia	Stephanie Liss
Yontel	John Hesley
Isaac	Robert Corff
Schmulke	Gene Castle
Nachman	Alfred Dennis
Rabbi Mendel	Jo Davidson
Menashe	Charles Briscoe
Rabbi Azrielke	Nehemiah Persoff
Rabbi Shimson	Alan Bergmann

Scholars, Beggars, Members of the Wedding Party, Rabbi's Court: Charles Briscoe, Gene Castle, Robert Corff, Stefan Fischer, Harvey Gold, John Hesley, Steven Rotblatt.

Time: 1880. Place: Poland. Act I, Scene 1: Synagogue at Brinitz. Scene 2: Sender's courtyard at Brinitz. Act II: Azrielke's house in Miropol.

ME AND BESSIE (35). By Will Holt and Linda Hopkins. April 4, 1975. Director, Robert Greenwald; scenery and lighting, Donald Harris; costumes, Pete Menefee; musical director, Tony Berg; special dance sequences, Lester Wilson. With Linda Hopkins, Lester Wilson, Gerri Dean.

CHARLTON HESTON AS MACBETH

Center Theater Group: Mark Taper Forum—New Theater For Now

THE DEATH AND LIFE OF JESSE JAMES
(13). By Len Jenkin. July 19, 1974 (world premiere). Director, Jeff Bleckner; scenery & costumes, Robert Clair La Vigne; lighting, Marilyn
Rennagel; musical director, Richie Jenkin

Cole Younger	Scott Hylands
Frank James	Arthur Metrano
Jesse James	Andy Robinson
Bob Ford	David Dukes
Huey Dalton	Gerrit Graham
Dewey Dalton	Herman Poppe
Louie Dalton	Frederick Neumann
Mrs. James; Wife; Mamacita	Claudette Nevins
Mom Ford	Susan Tyrrell
Reverend; President; Man; Sheriff	Robert Symonds
Deacon Smith; Commissioner; Interviewer	James Greene
Speedy Gonzales; Priest; Chief Iron Porcupine	James Victor
Little Girl; Daughter, Rosita	Edith Diaz
Bartender; Man in Derby #1	Michael Mc Neilly
Conchita	Lupe Ontiveros
Pepita	Karmin Murcelo

Victim; Man in Derby #2 . . Paul Rubenfeld
The Band—Country Space: Richie Jenkin,
Tom Child, Bob Stern, George Stavis
Two intermissions.

ME AND BESSIE (8). By Will Holt and Linda
Hopkins. October 3, 1974 (world premiere). Director, Robert Greenwald; scenery & lighting,
Donald Harris; costumes, Terence Tam Soon;
musical coordinator, Tony Berg.

Bessie	Linda Hopkins
Man	Lester Wilson
Woman	Gerri Dean

The Band: Howlett Smith piano; Monte Bud-
wig bass; Lowell E. McPowell drums; Joe Roc-
cisano saxophone.
One intermission.

LA GRANDE CARPA DE LOS RASQUA-
CHIS (8). Written, directed and produced by El
Teatro Campesino. October 12, 1974. Designer,
Donald Harris; music, El Teatro Campesino.
With Felix Alvarez, Lily Alverez, Socorro Cruz,
Jose Delgado and the La Familia Rasquachi
Company

Note: Mark Taper Forum again presented an improvisation theater project in the winter of 1974 and the spring of 1975 and a Forum/Laboratory which presented *Spin 411*, conceived and directed by Ron Rudolph (June 11, 1974); *Lady Lazarus*, directed by Vickie Rue (July 12, 1974); The Improvisational Workshop, directed by John Dennis (August 12, 1974); *Miller in Pieces* by Susan Miller, directed by Jeremy Blahnik (August 20, 1974): *President Wilson in Paris* by Ron Blair, directed by Gordon Hunt (January 14, 1975); *A Witness to the Confession* conceived by Jack Voorhies and Robert Ravan, music by Laura Nyro, directed by Robert Ravan (February 4, 1975); *Cross Country* by Susan Miller, directed by Vickie Rue (February 11, 1975); *Signals* by John O'Brien, conceived and directed by Michael Griggs (February 24, 1975); *The Amazing Flight of the Gooney Bird*, music and lyrics by Dory Previn, directed by Robert Greenwald (March 13, 1975); *The Mother Jones and Mollie Bailey Family Circus* by Megan Terry, directed by Jeremy Blahnik and Vickie Rue (April 11, 1975); *Upon A Dying Lady* by William Butler Yeats, directed by Susan Burkhalter (April 25, 1975); *The Killing of Yablonski* by Richard Nelson, directed by John Dennis (June 5, 1975).

The Season Elsewhere in Los Angeles
By Rick Talcove

Theatre Critic of the Van Nuys, Calif. *Valley News.*

Los Angeles theater production in 1974–75 was one of extremes. The good productions were generally *very* good; that is, extremely finished presentations not unlike a good off-Broadway production. The bad entries were either artistically misguided or just plain "vanity" showcases, which usually expired within a few performances.

Several interesting scripts emerged during the year. Frank Salisbury's *The Seagulls of 1933* sounds like a nostalgic comedy of the depression years. In fact, it is a highly sophisticated work of considerable merit, a kind of raunchy *Philadelphia Story* about a group of sexually-oriented Americans on the Riviera all trying to justify their need to exist by exploiting their carnal desires. The wit is real here and the writing borders on the poetic without being pretentious. Some critics faulted the play for not having likeable characters; a rather limited view of theater, to say the least. Margaretta Ramsey stood out in an exceptional cast.

Another comedy of somewhat lesser merit but equal fascination is John Allison and Ray Scantlin's *Stand By Your Beds Boys*. This wild farce about two gay roommates—an English professor from London and an American pro football player—whose lives are invaded by a kook and her black offspring threw in every *in*conceivable situation in the book, and somehow it worked. Despite mixed reviews, an audience discovered the show and kept it running for seven months, closing only when the production found itself without a cast after putting in an entirely new company each time the writers revised their work. The idea of improving your production during the run is almost unheard of in Los Angeles, but Allison and Scantlin did it, even if it meant closing their own show to achieve what they set out to do. In any event, *Boys* was a crazy venture that Los Angeles desperately needs more of.

Three production groups did much to raise the level of small theater craftsmanship in Los Angeles. Lonny Chapman's Group Theater moved from its small

Hollywood quarters to considerably larger North Hollywood facilities. The premiere production at the new address, Chapman's *Happy Days Are Here Again Blues* from Gorky's *The Lower Depths,* proved to be a well-written, exceptionally acted drama. Producers Joseph Stern, Allan Miller and Kathleen Johnson sponsored a superb production of Eric Bentley's *Are You Now or Have You Ever Been* in its local premiere under actor William Devane's masterful direction. (Devane had already scored a success as the lead in *One Flew Over the Cuckoo's Nest* at the Huntington Hartford earlier this same season.) *Are You Now* began in the 50-seat Cast Theater and moved into the Hollywood Center Theater, at five times the capacity, to sellout business. Another actor of note, Ralph Waite (best known as the father on television's *The Waltons*) decided to bankroll a two-play season at the Oxford Playhouse. The first production, O'Neill's *The Hairy Ape* with Mitch Ryan, fared poorly under Waite's own unsure direction. Calling in actress Gwen Arner to stage the second production—Arnold Wesker's *The Kitchen*—gave the group an unqualified success.

It was not a good year for the smaller, critically encouraged experimental groups. The Company Theater offered two mediocre scripts—Michael McClure's *The Derby* and John Osborne's *A Sense of Detachment*—with dismal results. The ProVisional Theater, which last season offered the spectacular *Dominus Marlowe,* wasted a great deal of time and grant money in assembling *America Piece,* a nadir of theatrical imagination.

The following is a selection of the most noteworthy Los Angeles productions of the year. The list does not include the numerous touring shows nor the Center Theater Group productions at the Ahmanson and the Mark Taper (see the Regional Theater listing above). A plus sign (+) with the performance number indicates the show was still running on June 1, 1975.

GREEN JULIA (21). By Paul Ableman. June 6, 1974. Director, Rick Talcove; scenery & lighting, Robert W. Zentis. With Richard Cottrell, Mark York. Produced by William S. Bartman Jr. at the Merle Oberon Playhouse.

THE DREAM CRUST (47). By Roger Karshner. December 20, 1974 (world premiere). Director, Alan Vint; scenery, Keith Hein; costumes, Jac McAnnelley; lighting, Stephen Whittaker and Michael Hunter. At the MET Theater.

Frank	James Gammon
Pearl	Viola Kates Stimpson
Galen	Bill Cross
Bobby	Kirby Furlong
Merteen	Kiva Lawrence
Helen	Aileen Fitzpatrick
Dude	Timothy Scott

Two intermissions.

LUMPKIN (27). Musical with book by William Glover; music and lyrics by Jill Williams; based on Oliver Goldsmith's *She Stoops to Conquer.* September 20, 1974 (world premiere). Director,

William Glover; costumes, Ivy Trent; lighting, Bob Ballinger. At the Shakespeare Society of America-Globe Theater.

Tony Lumpkin	Jeff Redford
Mrs. Hardcastle	Beth Peters
Mr. Hardcastle	William Glover
Kate Hardcastle	Carol Kristy
Marlow	John Fink

One intermission.

PETRIFIED MAN by Eudora Welty and DEATH OF A DOLL by Robert Houston (8). September 26, 1974. Directors, Peter Maloney, Anthony Carbone; scenery & lighting, Peter Clemens; costumes, Mary Taylor. With Marian Mercer, Jacque Lynn Colton. Produced by La Mama Hollywood at Theater Vanguard.

ONE FLEW OVER THE CUCKOO'S NEST (97). By Dale Wasserman; from the novel by Ken Kesey. November 1, 1974. Director, Harvey Medlinsky; scenery & lighting, Neil Peter Jampolis. With William Devane, Salome Jens, Rockne Tarkington, John Savage, Val Bisoglio.

Produced by David Lonn at the Huntington Hartford Theater.

STAND BY YOUR BEDS BOYS (105). By John Allison and Ray Scantlin. October 24, 1974 (world premiere). Director, the authors and Mike Pippi; scenery & lighting, Brian Eatwell; costumes, May Routh. Produced by Lee Scott at the Callboard Theater.

Alice	Pamela Fife
Goliath	Jarrod Johnson
Miss Wilt	Betty Huckabee
David	Rod Haase
Mr. Whittlebom	Charles Sladen
Ned	John Allison
Mrs. Schuman	Billie Bird

One intermission.

THE SEAGULLS OF 1933 (59). By Frank Salisbury; score by William Scherer. February 15, 1975 (world premiere). Director, Logan Ramsey; designer, John Griffith; lighting, Sy Marcus. Produced by Actors' Alley at the Sherman Oaks Playhouse.

Colonel Gore	Arthur Peterson
Margaret Beaumont	Doris Martin
Velma Darcy	Vivian Tann
Francesca	Margaretta Ramsey
Lillian Monroe	Ruth Marcus
Van Thomas	George Cederberg
Ann Beaumont	Carrie Dieterich
Count Vagram	Sandy Ignon

One intermission.

ARE YOU NOW OR HAVE YOU EVER BEEN (47+). By Eric Bentley. February 15, 1975. Director, William Devane; scenery, Barry Robison; lighting, Allen Williams. With Phillip R. Allen, Allen Garfield, Allan Miller, David Spielberg. At the Cast Theater.

HAPPY DAYS ARE HERE AGAIN BLUES (12+). By Lonny Chapman; based on Maxim Gorky's The Lower Depths. April 17, 1975 (world premiere). Director, Victor French; scenery, Ruth Wald; costumes, John Petlock; lighting, Mike Hunter. At the Group Theater.

Countess	Margaret Fairchild
Ike	Hal England
Clyde	Vincent Cobb
Kate	Teda Bracci
Anne	Sarah Zitin
Naomi	Hazel Medina
Slick	Russ Marin
Mae	Jennifer Billingsley
Hogan	Robert Broyles
Victor	Bert Kramer
Percy	William Lanteau
Ellie	Lisa Buck
Alvin	Joe Anderson
Maggie	Suzanne Charney
Jake	John Petlock

Two intermissions.

THE KITCHEN (27). By Arnold Wesker. April 10, 1975. Director, Gwen Arner; scenery, Robert W. Zentis; costumes, Teresa Kelley; lighting, Peter Parkin. With Ralph Waite, Joyce Van Patten, Donald Moffat, Mary Jackson, Dennis Dugan, Marilynn Lovell, Bert Conway, Pearl Shear, Dan Priest. Produced by Los Angeles Actors' Theater at the Oxford Playhouse.

LOUISVILLE, KY.

Actors' Theater of Louisville: Pamela Brown Auditorium

(Producing director, Jon Jory.)

THAT CHAMPIONSHIP SEASON (28). By Jason Miller. October 10, 1974. Director, Israel Hicks; scenery, Paul Owen; lighting, Geoffrey T. Cunningham; costumes, Kurt Wilhelm. With Michael Gross, G. W. Bailey, Bob Burrus, Ric Mancini, Alfred Hinckley.

FRANKENSTEIN (19) based on a story by Mary Shelley and COUNTESS DRACULA (14) based on Sheridan Le Fanu's *Carmilla*. By David Campton. November 7, 1974, in repertory (American premieres). Director, Charles Kerr; scenery, Paul Owen; lighting, Geoffrey T. Cunningham; costumes, Kurt Wilhelm; properties, Linus M. Carleton.

Frankenstein:

Victor Frankenstein	Jeffrey Duncan Jones
Henri Clerval	Scott Porter
Elizabeth	Patricia Pearcy
Justine	Wanda Bimson
William	John William Miller, IV
Mme. Couper	Adale O'Brien
Clerval Sr.	Bob Burrus
The Creature	Michael Gross

Time: 1817. Place: In Doctor Frankenstein's laboratory and Monsieur Clerval's home in a remote part of the Bavarian forests. One intermission.

Countess Dracula:

Capt. Field	Scott Porter
Ivan	Jeffrey Duncan Jones
Laura	Patricia Pearcy
Mme. Perrodon	Adale O'Brien
Col. Smithson	Bob Burrus
Countess Dracula	Wanda Bimson
Dr. Spielsberg	Michael Gross

Time: 1872: Place: In and about Colonel Smithson's schloss and the ruins of a nearby castle in Styria. One intermission.

THE REAL INSPECTOR HOUND BY Tom Stoppard; SWAN SONG by Anton Chekhov; RED PEPPERS by Noel Coward (27). December 12, 1974. Director, Jon Jory; scenery, Anne A. Gibson; lighting, Geoffrey T. Cunningham; costumes, Paul Owen; musical director, Eileen La Grange; choreography, Janet Kerr. With Victor Jory, Jean Inness, Ray Fry, Adale O'Brien, Scott Porter, Jim Baker, Michael Gross, Teri Ralston, Patricia Pearcy, Bob Burrus, Jeffrey Duncan Jones.

THE THREEPENNY OPERA (33). By Bertolt Brecht and Kurt Weill; adapted by Marc Blitzstein. January 9, 1975. Director, Jon Jory; scenery, Paul Owen; lighting, Geoffrey T. Cunningham; costumes, Kurt Wilhelm; musical director, Eileen LaGrange; choreography, Patty Simmonds-Corcoran. With Haskell Gordon, Adale O'Brien, Teri Ralston, Stephen Pearlman, Margaret Gathright.

A FLEA IN HER EAR (28). By Georges Feydeau. February 13, 1975. Director, Jon Jory; scenery, Raymond C. Recht; lighting, James Stephens; costumes, Kurt Wilhelm. With Ray Fry, Vinnie Holman, Vaughn McBride, Haskell Gordon, Mary Ed Porter.

THE BALLAD OF THE SAD CAFE (27). Adapted by Edward Albee from Carson McCullers's novel. March 13, 1975. Director, Jon Jory; scenery, Paul Owen; lighting, Geoffrey T. Cunningham; costumes, Kurt Wilhelm. With William Cain, Scott Porter, Bob Burrus, Jim Baker, Adale O'Brien, John Pielmeier.

RELATIVELY SPEAKING (27). By Alan Ayckbourn. April 10, 1975. Director, Christopher Murney; scenery, Richard Gould; lighting, Geoffrey T. Cunningham; costumes, Kurt Wilhelm. With Michael Gross, Barrie Youngfellow, William Cain, Adale O'Brien.

SLEUTH (12). By Anthony Shaffer. May 8, 1975. Director, Adale O'Brien; scenery, Paul Owen; lighting, Geoffrey T. Cunningham; costumes, Kurt Wilhelm. With William Cain, Michael Gross, Stanley Rushton, Harold Newman, Roger Purnell.

Actors' Theater of Louisville: Victor Jory Theater

FEMALE TRANSPORT (17). By Steve Gooch. October 15, 1974 (American premiere). Director, Jon Jory; scenery, Paul Owen; lighting, Geoffrey T. Cunningham; costumes, Kurt Wilhelm.

Winnie	Mary Ed Porter
Nance	Susan Cardwell Kingsley
Madge	Gail Kellstrom
Pitty	Jadeen Barbor
Charlotte	Adale O'Brien
Sarah	Patricia Pearcy
Sarge	Jeffrey Duncan Jones
Tommy	John Pielmeier
Captain	Vaughn McBride
Surgeon	Scott Porter

LUV (17). By Murray Schisgal. January 21, 1975. Director, Elizabeth Ives; scenery, Geoffrey T. Cunningham; lighting, James Stephens; costumes, Kurt Wilhelm. With Gary L. Carlson, Vaughn McBride, Kay Erin Thompson.

JACQUES BREL IS ALIVE AND WELL AND LIVING IN PARIS (37). By Eric Blau and Mort Shuman; based on Brel's lyrics and commentary; music by Jacques Brel. March 2, 1975. Director, Teri Ralston; scenery, Paul Owen; lighting, Geoffrey T. Cunningham; costumes, Kurt Wilhelm; musical director, Eileen LaGrange. With David Canary, Steve James, Andrea Levine, Teri Ralston.

NOON by Terrence McNally and WELCOME TO ANDROMEDA by Ron Whyte (12). April 9, 1975. Director, Charles Kerr; scenery, Paul Owen; lighting, James Stephens; costumes, Kurt Wilhelm. With Jeffrey Duncan Jones, Scott Porter, Mary Ed Porter, Beverly May, Bob Burrus, John Pielmeier.

MILWAUKEE

Milwaukee Repertory Theater Company: Todd Wehr Theater

(Artistic director, Nagle Jackson; managing directors, Charles Ray McCallum, Sara O'Connor)

DOWN BY THE GRAVOIS (UNDER THE ANHEUSER-BUSCH) (50). By James Nicholson. September 13, 1974 (world premiere). Director, Nagle Jackson; associate director, Fredric H. Orner; scenery & lighting, Christopher M. Idoine; costumes, Ellen Kozak.

Dan O'Grady	Durward McDonald
Mary O'Grady	Ruth Schudson
Jimmie O'Grady	Joel Stedman
Sharon O'Grady	Rose Herron

Moose . . . . Michael Duncan
Carrie . . . . Penelope Reed
Benjamin . . . . Robert Dawson
Mike . . . . James Pickering
Kitty . . . . Leslie Geraci
Terry . . . . Andrew Miner
Trudy . . . . Tracy Friedman
Rosie . . . . Cheryl Anderson
Otto . . . . Jeffrey Tambor
Bryan . . . . Robert Ingham
Kathleen . . . . Susan Schoenfeld.
The action takes place in the O'Grady home, St. Louis, Missouri. Two intermissions.

THE REHEARSAL (50). By Jean Anouilh. November 1, 1974. Director, William McKereghan; scenery & lighting, Christopher M. Idoine; costumes, Elizabeth Covey. With William Cain, Margaret Hilton, Leslie Geraci, Robert Lanchester, Tracy Friedman.

ANDROCLES AND THE LION (50). By George Bernard Shaw. December 20, 1974. Director, Robert Lanchester; scenery, Richard H. Graham; lighting, Duane Schuler; costumes, Elizabeth Covey. With Michael Pierce, John Hancock, John Mansfield, Cheryl Anderson, Rose Herron, Robert Dawson, Jeffrey Tambor.

RICHARD II (50). By William Shakespeare. February 7, 1975. Director, Nagle Jackson; scenery and lighting, Christopher M. Idoine; costumes, Elizabeth Covey. With Robert Lanchester, John Mansfield, Jeffrey Tambor, William McKereghan, Leslie Geraci, Rose Herron.

BIG FISH, LITTLE FISH (50). By Hugh Wheeler. March 28, 1975. Director, Jeffrey Tambor; scenery and lighting, Richard H. Graham; costumes, Ellen Kozak. With Robert Ingham, Robert Lanchester, Janice Davis, William McKereghan, Penelope Reed, Owen Sullivan, Durward McDonald.

A DAY IN THE DEATH OF JOE EGG (50). By Peter Nichols, May 16, 1975. Director, Nagle Jackson; scenery & lighting, Christopher M. Idoine; costumes, Ellen Kozak. With Woody Eney, Peggy Cowles, Jeffrey Tambor, Rose Herron, Jody Lieberman.

Milwaukee Repertory Theater Company: Court Street Theater

CLOCKS by Carl Larsen, directed by Nagle Jackson; CHAMBER PIECE (variations on a theme by Dante Alighieri) written and directed by Nagle Jackson; COMMITMENTS AND OTHER ALTERNATIVES by Norman Kline, directed by Fredric H. Orner (17). April 3, 1975. Scenery and lighting, Ernest Foster; costumes, Joanne Karaska, Rita LaDoux, Jean Steinbrecher. With Cheryl Anderson, Robert Dawson, Leslie Geraci, John Hancock, Rose Herron, John Mansfield, James Pickering, Stephen Stout.

THE GREAT NEBULA IN ORION by Lanford Wilson, directed by Nagle Jackson; THE DUMB WAITER by Harold Pinter, directed by Fredric H. Orner (17). April 24, 1975. Scenery & lighting, Ernest Foster; costumes, Ellen Kozak, Catherine Cerny. With Cheryl Anderson, Rose Herron, James Pickering, Jeffrey Tambor.

THE REID GILBERT MIME SHOW (2). April 8, 1975. Director, Reid Gilbert. With Reid Gilbert, Terry Kerr, John Aden, Kaye Dubie Potter.

Note: Milwaukee Repertory Theater Company toured The English Mystery Plays: The Creation, The Story of Adam and Eve, Cain and Abel, The Play of Noah, Abraham's Story to churches throughout Wisconsin from November 3, 1974 through December 15, 1974. Director, Penelope Reed; designer, Richard H. Graham. MRT also presented a program including Clocks and three vignettes from Commitments and Other Alternatives, at a major shopping mall on April 6, for two performances. And climaxing the season, an original children's production Once Upon the River, by Nagle Jackson and Penelope Reed, was presented on 20 playgrounds throughout Milwaukee as part of the summer playground arts program. Directed by Nagle Jackson, with Penelope Reed, John Hancock, Leslie Geraci, Jack Swanson.

MINNEAPOLIS

The Guthrie Theater Company: Guthrie Theater

(Artistic director, Michael Langham; managing director, Donald Schoenbaum)

KING LEAR (47). By William Shakespeare. July 1, 1974. Director, Michael Langham; scenery, John Jensen; lighting, Gilbert V. Hemsley Jr.; costumes, Desmond Heeley. With Len Cariou, Barbara Bryne, Maureen Anderman, Blair Brown, Mark Lamos, Kenneth Welsh, Nicholas Kepros, Paul Ballantyne, James Blendick, Peter Michael Goetz, August Schellenberg.

LOVE'S LABOUR'S LOST (42). By William Shakespeare. July 3, 1974. Director, Michael Langham; scenery, John Jensen; lighting, Duane Schuler; costumes, Desmond Heeley. With Nicholas Kepros, Patricia Conolly, Lance Davis, Katherine Ferrand, Ken Ruta, Sheriden Thomas, Ivar Brogger.

THE CRUCIBLE (49). By Arthur Miller. August 20, 1974. Director, Len Cariou; scenery & costumes, John Jensen; lighting, Robert Scales. With James Blendick, Patricia Conolly, Katherine Ferrand, Sheriden Thomas, Eda Reiss Merin, Ken Ruta, Paul Ballantyne, Fran Bennett.

TARTUFFE (39). By Molière; English verse translation by Richard Wilbur. October 1, 1974. Director, Michael Bawtree; scenery, Lowell Detweiler; lighting, Richard William Tidwell; costumes, Sam Kirkpatrick. With Ken Ruta, Larry Gates, Ivar Brogger, Peter Michael Goetz, Mark Lamos, Barbara Bryne, Katherine Ferrand.

SCHOOL FOR SCANDAL (39). By Richard Brinsley Sheridan. November 19, 1974. Director, Michael Langham; scenery, Jack Barkla; lighting, Duane Schuler; costumes, Sam Kirkpatrick. With Bernard Behrens, Blair Brown, Sheriden Thomas, Nicholas Kepros, Kenneth Welsh, Larry Gates, Barbara Bryne, Patricia Conolly, Macon McCalman.

EVERYMAN (17). Abridged version of the original medieval allegory. December 26, 1974. Director, Robert Benedetti; designer, Bruce Cana Fox; lighting, Richard Borgen; costumes, Jack Edwards, Ching Ho Chen. With Fran Bennett, Drew Birns, Jeff Chandler, Valery Daemke, Robert Engels, James Harris, Henry J. Jordan, Macon McCalman, Gary Martinez, William Schoppert, Sheriden Thomas.

Note: *Everyman* toured for 17 weeks, January-June, 1975 through Minnesota, Iowa, Wisconsin, North and South Dakota, Montana, Wyoming, Idaho, Utah, Colorado, New Mexico. The Guthrie Theater, working with the New Focus Arts and Corrections Program (Minnesota Department of Corrections), started a one-year pilot theater project in three Minnesota prisons with the following goals: To operate ongoing workshops in all phases of production, including acting and playwriting; develop theater departments in the three prisons; utilize the resources of the professional staff and available touring productions; develop tours by the institutions to other prisons and the community; train inmate coordinators to manage productions, companies and classes.

NEW HAVEN

Long Wharf Theater

(Artistic director, Arvin Brown; executive director, M. Edgar Rosenblum.)

SIZWE BANSI IS DEAD and THE ISLAND (33). Conceived and devised by John Kani, Winston Ntshona and Athol Fugard. October 11, 1974 (American premiere). Director, Athol Fugard, With John Kani, Winston Ntshona.

THE SOLDIER'S TALE by Igor Stravinsky, text by C. F. Ramuz, translation by Michael Flanders and Kitty Black; and THE KNIGHT OF THE BURNING PESTLE adapted by

Brooks Jones from the play by Beaumont and Fletcher, additional lyrics by Brooks Jones and Peter Schickele, music by Peter Schickele (33). November 15, 1974. Director, Brooks Jones; choreography, Martha Clarke; musical directors, Thomas Fay, Daniel Stepner. With Teresa Wright, David Byrd, Victor Garber, Robin Gammell, Linda Hunt.

AH, WILDERNESS! (33). By Eugene O'Neill.

December 20, 1974. Director, Arvin Brown. With Geraldine Fitzgerald, Teresa Wright, William Swetland, Richard Backus, Emery Battis, Susan Sharkey.

PYGMALION (33). By George Bernard Shaw. January 24, 1975. Director, Robin Gammell. With Rex Robbins, Suzanne Lederer, Emery Battis, William Swetland, Carmen Mathews, Shirley Bryan.

YOU'RE TOO TALL, BUT COME BACK IN TWO WEEKS (33). By Richard Venture. February 28, 1975 (premiere of revision). Director, Arvin Brown; scenery & costumes, Elmon Webb, Virginia Dancy; lighting, Ronald Wallace; costumes, Bill Walker.

Guido Ferrara . . . . Richard Venture
Ruth Ferrara . . . . Joyce Ebert
Sterling . . . . Hannibal Penney Jr.
Dee . . . . Mary Alice
Big Mama . . . . Beatrice Winde
Place: Dee's New York City apartment and Ruth's home in Connecticut. One intermission.

AFORE NIGHT COME (33). By David Rudkin. April 4, 1975 (American premiere). Director,

Ron Daniels; scenery, David Jenkins; lighting, Ronald Wallace; costumes, Jania Szatanski.

Jeff . . . . Stephen McHattie
Larry . . . . David Huffman
Spens . . . . Emery Battis
Mrs. Trevis . . . . .Mary Fogarty
Jumbo . . . . .John Tillinger
Ginger . . . . Sean G. Griffin
Albert . . . . .William Swetland
Jim . . . . .Stephen Mendillo
Taffy Hughes . . . . George Taylor
Roche . . . . .Joseph Maher
Johnny "Hobnails" Carter . .Frank Converse
Tiny . . . . Rex Robbins
Mrs. Hawkes . . . . .Don Gantry
Gloria . . . . Christina Whitmore
One intermission.

RICHARD III (33). By William Shakespeare. May 9, 1975. Director, Barry Davis. With Robin Gammell, Nancy Kelly, Lynn Milgrim, Joseph Maher, Richard Venture, Josef Sommer, Carolyn Coates.

Designers: scenery, Steven Rubin, Paul Zalon, John Conklin; lighting, Ronald Wallace, Judy Rasmuson, Jamie Gallagher, John Conklin; costumes, Steve Walker.

Long Wharf Theater: Young People's Theater

TROUBADOURS' CARNIVAL (5). Created by the Company; director Bill Carpenter. October 19, 1974.

FROLICKS (5). Created and directed by Terrence Sherman and the Company. November 30, 1974.

CREATIONS MYTHS (5). January 11, 1975.

TICKET TO TOMORROW (5). Written and directed by Terrence Sherman. March 8, 1975.

THE HOUR OF NEED (5). By Carl Schurr; music and lyrics by Terrence Sherman and Carl Schurr. April 19, 1975. Director, Terrence Sherman.

Nellie Fairfield . . . . January Eckert
Jerry Fairfield . . . . Michaelin Sisti
Noble Trueblood . . . . Jack Hoffman
Silas Macgruder . . . . . .Antonino Pandolfo
Dora . . . . Barbara MacKenzie
Dan . . . . Terrence Sherman

Designers: Wilton Duckworth, Wayne Durst, Rachel Kurland, Jania Szatanski.

Note: The Long Wharf Theater presented a series of Monday Night New Playwright's staged readings with members of the company, selected and staged by John Tillinger. *Memento Mori,* adapted by Eleanor Perry from Muriel Spark's novel, April 21, 1975; *Pledges* by Edward Snowden, April 28, 1975; *Going Away* by Tom Dulac, May 12, 1975; *On the Inside, on the Outside,* Brian Murray, May 19, 1975.

Yale Repertory Theater

(Artistic director, Robert Brustein; associate director, Alvin Epstein)

THE POSSESSED (24). By Andrzej Wajda; based on Fyodor Dostoevsky's novel; from an adaptation by Albert Camus translated by Justin O'Brien. October 3, 1974 (American premiere). Director, Andrzej Wajda; scenery, costumes & lighting, Krystyna Zachwatowicz and Michael H. Yeargan, William B. Warfel, Gerda Proctor;

composer, Zygmunt Konieczny; assistant director, Jaroslaw Strzemien.

Nicholas Stavrogin . . . . . Christopher Lloyd
Matriosha . . . . Landon Storrs
Tikhon . . . . .Robert Brustein
Grigoriev . . . . .Charles Levin
Alexey Kirilov . . . . .Alvin Epstein

Ivan Shatov . . . . Steven Nowicki
Lisa Drozdov . . . . Meryl Streep
Maria Lebyatkin . . . . . Elzbieta Czyzewska
Captain Lebyatkin . . . . Jeremy Geidt
Varvara . . . . Norma Brustein
Prascovya . . . . Mary Van Dyke
Daria (Dasha) . . . . Kay Tornborg
Stepan . . . . Jerome Dempsey
Liputin . . . . Joseph Capone
Shigalov . . . . Ralph Drischell
Virgininsky . . . . John Rothman
Student . . . . Christopher Durang
Lyamshin . . . . Michael Lassell
Alexey Yegorovich . . . . . . Ralph Redpath
Maurice Nicolaevich . . . . R. Neresian
Peter . . . . Stephen Rowe
Fedka . . . . Paul Schierhorn
Virginska . . . . . . .Franchelle Stewart Dorn
Schoolgirl . . . . Linda Atkinson
Captain; Priest . . . . Barry E. Marshall
Maria Shatov . . . . . Kate McGregor-Stewart
   The Demons: Coleman Allen, Peter Blanc,
Michael Cadden, Paul Cooper, Peter C. Craw-
ford, Charles Gunn, Thomas Holaday, Stephen
J. Miklos, Tony Schlaff, Richard Taus.
   One intermission.

THE IDIOTS KARAMAZOV (25). By Christo-
pher Durang and Albert F. Innaurato. October
31, 1974 (world premiere). Director, William
Peters; scenery, Michael H. Yeargan; lighting,
Lloyd S. Riford III; costumes, William Ivey
Long; composer, Jack Feldman; musical direc-
tors, Paul Schierhorn, Carol Lees.
Alyosha Karamazov . . . Christopher Durang
Fyodor Karamazov . . . . . . John Rothman
Constance Garnett . . . . Meryl Streep
Ernest . . . . Ralph Redpath
Ivan Karamazov . . . . Charles Levin
Gruchenka . . . . . .Franchelle Stewart Dorn
Dmitri Karamazov . . . . R. Neresian
Smerdyakov Karamazov . . . Stephen Rowe
Father Zossima . . . . Jeremy Geidt
Mary Tyrone Karamazov . . .Linda Atkinson
Djuna Barnes . . . . . . Christine Estabrook/
                                    Lizbeth Mackay
Anais Pnin . . . . . Kate McGregor-Stewart
Joaquin Pnin . . . . Peter Blanc
   Altar Boys, Leather Girls: Danny Brustein,
Evan Drutman, Margot Lovecraft, Dawn For-
rest.
   One intermission.

VICTORY (24). By Walt Jones and Alvin Ep-
stein; a story theater version based on Joseph
Conrad's novel. November 14, 1974 (world pre-
miere). Director, Alvin Epstein; scenery, Tony
Straiges; lighting; Stephen R. Woody; costumes,
Vittorio Capecce.
Heyst . . . . Jerome Dempsey
Davidson . . . . Walt Jones
Schomberg; Wang . . . . . . .Ralph Drischell

Mrs. Schomberg . . . . . Elzbieta Czyzewska
Jones . . . . .Hurd Hatfield
Ricardo . . . . Joseph Grifasi
Pedro . . . . Paul Schierhorn
Lena . . . . Carmen de Lavallade
His Excellency . . . . .Ralph Redpath.
   One intermission.

HAPPY END (29). By Bertolt Brecht and Kurt
Weill; from the original German play by Dorothy Lane; American adaptation and lyrics by Michael Feingold. February 6, 1975. Director, Michael Posnick; scenery and costumes, Michael H.
Yeargan; lighting and projections, Stephen R.
Woody; musical direction, Otto-Werner Mueller.
With Jeremy Geidt, Alvin Epstein, Charles Levin, Jerome Dempsey, Paul Schierhorn, Ralph
Drischell, Elizabeth Parrish, Stephanie Cot-
sirilos.

THE FATHER (24). By August Strindberg.
February 21, 1975. Director, Jeff Bleckner; sce-
nery, Michael H. Yeargan; lighting, William B.
Warfel; costumes, Jeanne Button. With Rip Torn,
Frederic Warriner, Elzbieta Czyzewska, Ralph
Drischell, Elizabeth Parrish.

THE SHAFT OF LOVE (24). By Charles
Dizenzo. March 28, 1975 (world premiere). Di-
rector, David Schweizer; scenery & costumes,
Atkin Pace; lighting, James F. Ingalls; music,
Walt Jones, Paul Schierhorn.
Jean . . . . Meryl Streep
Mary Burns . . . . .Elizabeth Parrish
Dr. John Burns . . . . . . .Jerome Dempsey
Nurse Black; Missie . . . . . .Linda Atkinson
Nurse Norse . . . . Alma Cuervo
Tess . . . . Julie Haber
Maxine . . . . . Kate McGregor-Stewart
Brad . . . . Joe Grifasi
Doug . . . . .Charles Levin
Hank . . . . Barry E. Marshall
Dr. Joyce . . . . Norma Brustein
Bailiff . . . . Ted Tally
Prosecutor . . . . Joseph Capone
Judge . . . . Frederic Warriner/Jeremy Geidt
Keyboards . . . .Paul Schierhorn, Carol Lees
   Time: The televised present. One intermission.

A MIDSUMMER NIGHT'S DREAM (27). By
William Shakespeare; music from The Fairy
Queen by Henry Purcell. May 9, 1975. Director,
Alvin Epstein; scenery, Tony Straiges; lighting,
William B. Warfel; costumes, Zack Brown; mu-
sic adapted and conducted by Otto-Werner
Mueller; associate musical director, Gary Fagin;
choreography, Carmen de Lavallade. With
Jeremy Geidt, Franchelle Stewart Dorn, Kate
McGregor-Stewart, Stephen Rowe, Peter
Schifter, Meryl Streep, Charles Levin, Linda At-
kinson, Christopher Lloyd, Carmen de Lavallade.

Note: Purcell's, *The Fairy Queen* has been incorporated in a production of *A Midsummer Night's Dream* for the first time. Yale Repertory and Drama School also presented Yale Cabaret, Experimental Theater, Studio projects and Main Stage productions with students, members of the Repertory Theater and faculty members. The major productions presented by the University Theater Drama School were Ben Jonson's *Bartholomew Fair* and Sam Shepard's *The Tooth of Crime;* at the Experimental Theater, Frank Wedekind's *Lulu* and Christopher Durang's *Death Comes To Us All, Mary Agnes.*

PRINCETON, N.J.

McCarter Theater Company: McCarter Theater

(President, Daniel Seltzer; producing director, Michael Kahn)

BEYOND THE HORIZON (10). By Eugene O'Neill. October 10, 1974 (professional premiere). Director, Michael Kahn; scenery, Robert U. Taylor; lighting, David F. Segal; costumes, Jane Greenwood.

Robert Mayo	Richard Backus
Andrew Mayo	Edward J. Moore
James Mayo	Hugh Reilly
Ruth Atkins	Maria Tucci
Kate Mayo	Laurinda Barrett
Capt. Dick Scott	Paul Larson
Mrs. Atkins	Camilla Ashland
Mary	Sharon Chazin
Ben	Michael Houlihan
Dr. Fawcett	Daniel Seltzer

Act I, Scene 1: The top of a hill on a Connecticut farm overlooking the sea; sunset of a day in Spring, 1912. Scene 2: The farm house the same night. Act II, Scene 1: Several years later, the farm house, noon of a summer day. Scene 2: The hill, the following day. Act III, Scene 1: Five years later, the farm house, dawn of a day in late fall. Scene 2: The hill, sunrise. The acting script for this production is based on the first version of the play, published in 1920, now performed for the first time.

'TIS PITY SHE'S A WHORE (10). By John Ford. November 14, 1974. Director, Michael Kahn; scenery, Robert U. Taylor; lighting, John McLain; costumes, Lawrence Casey. With Franklyn Seales, Christine Varanski, Hugh Reilly, Charlotte Jones, Theodore Sorel, Ellen Holly, Michael Levin, Al Freeman Jr., Frank Borgman, John Tillinger, Michael Houlihan.

MOTHER COURAGE AND HER CHILDREN (10). By Bertolt Brecht; English version by Eric Bentley. February 13, 1975. Director, Michael Kahn; scenery, David Jenkins; lighting, John McLain; costumes, Lawrence Casey. With Eileen Heckart, Maria Tucci, Charles Sweigart, Philip Yankee, Rod Loomis, Ronald C. Frazier, Lee Richardson, Patrick Hines, Tom Poston, Ron Siebert, Michele Shay, John Seidman.

KINGDOM OF EARTH (10). By Tennessee Williams. March 6, 1975. Director, Garland Wright; scenery, Paul Zalon; lighting, Marc B. Weiss; costumes, David James. With David Pendleton, Marilyn Chris, Courtney Burr.

ROMEO AND JULIET (10). By William Shakespeare. March 27, 1975. Director, Michael Kahn; scenery, John Conklin; lighting, Marc B. Weiss; costumes, Jane Greenwood. With Richard Backus, Maria Tucci, Charlotte Jones, Tom Poston, Briain Petchey, Jack Ryland, William Larsen, Laurinda Barrett, Wyman Pendleton, Grayce Grant.

PROVIDENCE, R.I.

Trinity Square Repertory Company: Lederer Theater—Downstairs

(Producing director, Adrian Hall)

WELL HUNG (38). By Robert Lord. October 31, 1974 (American premiere). Director, Adrian Hall; scenery, Eugene Lee; costumes, Betsey Potter; properties, Sandra Nathanson; production stage manager, William Radka; stage manager, Beverly Andreozzi.

Sgt. Bert Donelly	Robert Black
Constable Trev Brown	Richard Jenkins
Detective Jasper Smart	George Martin
Mrs. Lynette Donelly	Mina Manente
Mrs. Hawkins	Marguerite Lenert
Wally	Tom Griffin
Adam Turner	William Damkoehler

Place: The police station of Pukekawa, a small country town about 40 miles from Auckland (the largest city in New Zealand). Serving a sheep farming community, the town's major annual event is a Blossom Festival. The action of the play spans a single day. One intermission.

JUMPERS (54). By Tom Stoppard. December 12, 1974. Director, Word Baker; scenery, Robert D. Soule; lighting, John McLain; costumes, James Berton Harris; musical director, Richard Cumming; gymnastic trainer, Bill Finlay. With Margo Skinner, Mina Manente, Daniel Von Bargen, Richard Kneeland, David Jones, George Martin, John D. Garrick and the Jumpers.

EMPEROR HENRY IV (40). By Luigi Pirandello; English version by Eric Bentley. February 25, 1975. Director, Brooks Jones; scenery, Robert D. Soule; lighting, John McLain; costumes, James Berton Harris. With Richard Kneeland, Ed Hall, Richard Kavanaugh, Jan Farrand, Margo Skinner.

SEVEN KEYS TO BALDPATE (64). By George M. Cohan. April 22, 1975. Director, Adrian Hall; scenery and lighting, Eugene Lee; costumes, James Berton Harris. With Richard Kneeland, Barbara Orson, Richard Kavanaugh, Mina Manente.

Trinity Square Repertory Company: Lederer Theater—Upstairs

PEER GYNT (47). By Henrik Ibsen; adapted by Adrian Hall and Richard Cumming. January 7, 1975. Director, Adrian Hall; music and lyrics composed and directed by Richard Cumming; scenery & lighting, Eugene Lee; costumes, James Berton Harris. With Richard Kavanaugh, Marguerite Lenert, Barbara Meek, Lila Daniels, Robert J. Colonna, Ed Hall.

TOM JONES (63). By Henry Fielding; adapted by Larry Arrick; songs and music by Barbara Damashek; lyrics by Barbara Damashek and Larry Arrick, March 4, 1975. Directors, Larry Arrick, Barbara Damashek; scenery & lighting, Eugene Lee; costumes, James Berton Harris. With Robert Bruce, William Damkoehler, Mina Manente, Barbara Orson, George Martin, Lila Daniels.

RICHMOND, VA.

The Repertory Company of the Virginia Museum Theater

PURLIE (21). Book by Ossie Davis, Philip Rose, Peter Udell; based on Purlie Victorious by Mr. Davis; music by Gary Geld; lyrics by Peter Udell. November 8, 1974. Director, Albert B. Reyes; scenery, deTeel Patterson Tiller; lighting, Michael Watson; costumes, Frederick N. Brown; musical director, William Marion Smith; choreography, Nat Horne. With Milledge Mosley, Monty Cones, Marie Goodman Hunter, Jim Cyrus, James Kirkland, Birdie M. Hale, Walter Rhodes, Ted Goodridge.

OUR TOWN (21). By Thornton Wilder. November 29, 1974. Director, R. S. Cohen; scenery, Richard Norgard; lighting, Cameron Grainger; costumes, Frederick N. Brown. With Keith Fowler, Gene Snow, Margaret Thomson, Kathy O'Callaghan, James Kirkland, K. Lype O'Dell, Marie Goodman Hunter, Frank Geraci, William Pitts, Mark Hattan.

KASPAR (18). By Peter Handke. December 27, 1974. Director, Gene Snow; scenery, deTeel Patterson Tiller; lighting, Cameron Grainger; costumes, Frederick N. Brown. With Frank Geraci, Rachael Lindhart, Kathy O'Callaghan, William Marion Smith, Mark Hattan, James Kirkland, William Pitts.

THE MISER (20). By Molière; English adaptation by Miles Malleson. January 17, 1975. Director, Keith Fowler; scenery, Richard Norgard; lighting, deTeel Patterson Tiller; costumes, Frederick N. Brown. With Mark Hattan, Janet Bell, James Kirkland, Ken Letner, Frank Geraci, Gene Snow, Leigh Burch.

OUR FATHER (20). By Maxim Gorky; translated by William Marion Smith. February 7, 1975 (American premiere). Director, Keith Fowler; scenery, deTeel Patterson Tiller; lighting, Michael Watson; costumes, Frederick N. Brown.

Ivan	Irwin Atkins
Sofya	Kathy O'Callaghan
Jakov	Ken Letner
Nadya	Lynda Myles
Sasha	James Kirkland
Luba	Nona Pipes
Pyotr	Mark Hattan
Vera	Janet Bell
Dr. Lesch	K. Lype O'Dell
Officer Jakorjev	Mel Cobb
Fedosya	Katherine Johnson
Maid	Compton O'Shaughnessy
Sokolova	Margaret Thomson

MUCH ADO ABOUT NOTHING (26). By William Shakespeare. February 28, 1975. Director, Ken Letner; scenery, Richard Norgard;

lighting, Cameron Grainger, Glenna Handley; costumes, Frederick N. Brown. With Walter Rhodes, Lynda Myles, K. Lype O'Dell, Pamela Costello, James Kirkland, Margaret Thomson.

TOBACCO ROAD (20). By Jack Kirkland, adapted from Erskine Caldwell's novel. March 28, 1975. Director, James Kirkland; scenery, de-Teel Patterson Tiller; lighting, Cameron Grainger, Frederic Brumbach; costumes, Frederick N. Brown. With Walter Rhodes, Mark Hattan, Kathy O'Callaghan, Nona Pipes, Margaret Thomson, Gene Snow.

ROCHESTER, MICH.

Oakland University Professional Theater Program: Meadow Brook Theater

(Artistic director, Terence Kilburn; managing director, David Robert Kanter)

TONIGHT AT 8:30: *Ways and Means, Fumed Oak, Family Album* (29). By Noel Coward. October 10, 1974. Director, Terence Kilburn; scenery, David Weber; lighting, Jeffrey M. Schissler; costumes, Mary Lynn Bonnell. With Jonathan Alper, John Bayliss, Patricia Collins, Donald Ewer, Jayne Houdyshell, Marianne Muellerleile, Elisabeth Orion, Dennis Romer, Fred Thompson.

TWELFTH NIGHT (29). By William Shakespeare. November 7, 1974. Director, Terence Kilburn; scenery, Peter Hicks; lighting, Dan File; costumes, Mary Lynn Bonnell. With Donald Ewer, Diana Barrington, John Bayliss, John Crawford, Marianne Muellerleile, Patricia Collins, Dennis Romer.

HARVEY (29). By Mary Chase. December 5, 1974. Director, Donald Ewer; scenery, Susan Zsidisin; lighting, Lawrence Reed; costumes, Mary Lynn Bonnell. With Edgar Meyer, Dorothy Blackburn, Harry Ellerbe, Marianne Muellerleile, Stephanie Lewis, Dennis Romer.

DEATH OF A SALESMAN (28). By Arthur Miller. January 2, 1975. Director, Charles M. Nolte; scenery, Lee Adey; lighting, Jean Montgomery; costumes, Mary Lynn Bonnell. With Booth Colman, Josephine Nichols, David Himes, Douglas Travis, Robert Grossman.

THE MISANTHROPE (29). By Molière; English verse translation by Richard Wilbur. January 30, 1975. Director, Terence Kilburn; scenery, Nancy Thompson; lighting, Robert Neu; costumes, Mary Lynn Bonnell. With Guy Stockwell, David Combs, Joseph Shaw, Susanne Peters, Cheryl Giannini.

SEE HOW THEY RUN (29). By Phillip King. February 27, 1975. Director, Donald Ewer; scenery, Susan Zsidisin; lighting, Jeffrey M. Schissler; costumes, Mary Lynn Bonnell. With Cheryl Giannini, Elisabeth Orion, Briain Petchey, Barbara Tarbuck, David Combs/James Corrigan.

COME BACK, LITTLE SHEBA (29). By William Inge. March 27, 1975. Director, Terence Kilburn; scenery, Thomas A. Aston; lighting, Jean Montgomery; costumes, Mary Lynn Bonnell. With Priscilla Morrill, Guy Stockwell, David Combs.

THE DRUNKARD (29). By Bro Herrod; adapted from the melodrama by W. H. S. Smith; music and lyrics by Barry Manilow. April 24, 1975. Director, John Ulmer; scenery, Peter Hicks; lighting, Larry Reed; costumes, Mary Lynn Bonnell; musical director, Richard Sharp; choreography, James Tompkins. With Michelle Mullen, Eric Tavaris, Curt Williams, Evalyn Baron.

Note: *See How They Run* toured for three weeks to 11 cities.

ST. LOUIS

Loretto-Hilton Repertory Theater

(Managing director, David Frank; consulting director, Davey Marlin-Jones)

INDIANS (27). By Arthur Kopit. October 25, 1974. Director, Davey Marlin-Jones; scenery, Grady Larkins; lighting, Peter E. Sargent; costumes, Sigrid Insull. With Joneal Joplin, Robert Darnell, Brendan Burke, Arthur A. Rosenberg, Margaret Winn, Vance Sorrells.

CAESAR AND CLEOPATRA (27). By George Bernard Shaw. November 29, 1974. Director, Davey Marlin-Jones; scenery, John Kavelin; lighting, Vance Sorrells; costumes, Sigrid Insull. With Brendan Burke, Francesca James, Kevin Lorin Pawley, Henry Strozier, Ellen Spier.

THE CRUCIBLE (27). By Arthur Miller. January 3, 1975. Director, Gene Lesser; scenery, Grady Larkins; lighting, Peter E. Sargent; costumes, John David Ridge. With Robert Darnell, Margaret Winn, Wil Love, Louise Jenkins, Judy Meyer, Arthur A. Rosenberg.

TREVOR By John Bowen and THE REAL INSPECTOR HOUND by Tom Stoppard (27). February 7, 1975. Director, John Dillon; scenery, John Kavelin; lighting, Peter E. Sargent; costumes, Sigrid Insull, Mary Strieff. With Margaret Winn, Renee Tadlock, Arthur A. Rosenberg, Trinity Thompson, Wil Love, Barbara Lester, Henry Strozier, Brendan Burke.

HAVE I STAYED TOO LONG AT THE FAIR? (27). Assembled from and inspired by the songs, newspapers, magazines, diaries and books of the 1904 era by the Loretto-Hilton Repertory Theater Company and Staff (27). March 15, 1975 (world premiere). Director, Davey Marlin-Jones; musical director, Tony Zito; scenery, Grady Larkins; lighting, Peter E. Sargent; costumes, Sigrid Insull; choreography, Darwin Knight; movement, Bob DeFrank; research, Barbara Frank.

Cast: Joseph Folk the Giraffe, Boy Boer—Lewis Arlt; Rat Paste Salesman, Police Commissioner, 1st Narrator—Brendan Burke; Handsome Harry Horse, Barker, Smiley—Robert Darnell; Carrie Nation, Gertrude Trusty, Liberated Woman, Nella, Bumblebee—Georgia Engel; Mama Lou, China, Little Boy—Asa Harris; David Francis—Joneal Joplin; Teddy Roosevelt, Kingsley, Rev. Mr. Buck,—Wil Love; Mayor, Edward Butler the Bear, Chef,—Arthur A. Rosenberg; Mars W. Bailey, Poker Players, Col. Cummins—Vance Sorrells; Ruben Jasper, Esq., Frank Fenster the Pikeman, Felix Carvajal—Robert Spencer; John A. Leeper, Announcer, 2d Narrator—Henry Strozier; Madame, Babe Connors, Maud, Widow—Renee Tadlock; Musicians—Ben Pocost, Herb Oberlag, Artie Schieler, Tony Zito.

One intermission.

Loretto-Hilton Repertory Theater: Children's Theater

STORY THEATER (10). Adapted and directed by Bob DeFrank, David Frank, Dwight Schultz and Stephen Walker from a collection of stories based on American heritage. February 28, 1975. With Gregg Berger, James Anthony, Richard McGougan, Jessica Richman, Stephen Walker.

CHILDREN'S THEATER MIME SHOW (4). Created and performed by Bob DeFrank and Dwight Schultz.

Note: *Story Theater* toured 30 schools throughout Missouri, February-March 1975. Also sent on tour, Bert Houle and Sophie Wibaux in a program of mime. This program went to 22 cities in four states (Kansas, Missouri, Nebraska, Oklahoma). It was produced by the Loretto-Hilton Repertory Theater in cooperation with the arts councils of these states.

SAN FRANCISCO

American Conservatory Theater: Geary Theater

(General director, William Ball)

THE SUNSHINE BOYS (56). By Neil Simon. May 21, 1974. Director, Jeremiah Morris; scenery, Kert Lundell; lighting, Fred Kopp; costumes, Walter Watson. With José Ferrer, Phil Leeds, Henry Hoffman, Vivian Bonnell.

RICHARD III (33). By William Shakespeare. October 3, 1974. Director, William Ball. With Randall Duk Kim, Daniel Davis, William Paterson, Randall Smith, Andy Backer, Raye Birk, Hope Alexander-Willis, Elizabeth Cole, Fredi Olster

PILLARS OF THE COMMUNITY (30). By Henrik Ibsen; translated and directed by Allen Fletcher. October 9, 1974 With Earl Boen, Joy Carlin, David Darling, Sydney Walker, Elizabeth Huddle, David Darling, Anne Lawder.

CYRANO DE BERGERAC (31). By Edmond Rostand; translated by Brian Hooker; adapted by Dennis Powers. October 24, 1974. With Ray Reinhardt, Stephen Schnetzer, Laird Williamson, Deborah May, Elizabeth Huddle.

HORATIO (28). By Ron Whyte. November 20, 1974. Director, James Dunn; music, Mel Marvin; conductor, Fae McNally. With Sydney Walker, Patrick Treadway, Daniel Davis, Joy Carlin, Marrian Walters, Candace Barrett.

JUMPERS (35). By Tom Stoppard. December 11, 1974. Director, William Ball. With William Paterson, Hope Alexander-Willis, Ray Reinhardt, Earl Boen, Joseph Bird, Barbara Dirickson, Randall Smith and the Jumpers.

THE TAMING OF THE SHREW (32). By William Shakespeare. January 9, 1975. Director, William Ball; music, Lee Hoiby. With Anthony S. Teague, Fredi Olster, William Paterson, Stephen Schnetzer, Sandra Shotwell.

STREET SCENE (28). By Elmer Rice. January 29, 1975. Director, Edward Hastings. With Joseph Bird, Ruth Kobart, Elizabeth Huddle, Alan Lyons, Charles Hallahan, Megan Cole, Ronald Boussom.

THE RULING CLASS (34). By Peter Barnes. March 12, 1975. Director, Allen Fletcher. With

Rene Auberjonois, William Paterson, Sydney Walker, Earl Boen, James R. Winker, Eve Roberts, Raye Birk, Laird Williamson, E. Kerrigan Prescott, Joy Carlin, Fredi Olster.

THE THREEPENNY OPERA (33). By Bertolt Brecht and Kurt Weill; English adaptation by Marc Blitzstein. April 2, 1975. With Randall Duk Kim, Ray Reinhardt, Ronald Boussom, Ruth Kobart, Anthony S. Teague, Deborah May, Charles Hallahan, Elizabeth Huddle, Hope Alexander-Willis.

Designers: scenery, Robert Blackman, Ralph Funicello, John Jensen; lighting, E. Mitchell Dana; costumes, Robert Fletcher, Robert Morgan, J. Allen Highfill, Dirk Epperson.

American Conservatory Theater: Geary Theater—Guest Productions

AS YOU LIKE IT (18). By William Shakespeare. July 13, 1974. National Theater of Great Britain production, all-male cast, directed by Clifford Williams.

GREASE (48). Book, music and lyrics by Jim

Jacobs and Warren Casey. August 6, 1974. Director, Tom Moore; choreography, Patricia Birch; scenery, Douglas W. Schmidt; lighting, Karl Eigsti; costumes, Carrie F. Robbins. Kenneth Waissman-Maxine Fox production.

American Conservatory Theater: Marines' Memorial Theater

GODSPELL (103). By John-Michael Tebelak; based upon the Gospel According to St. Matthew; music and new lyrics by Stephen Schwartz. June 18, 1974. Director, Larry Whiteley; lighting, Fred Kopp; costumes, Reet Pell; musical director, Joe Speck. With the Godspell Company.

SOMETHING'S AFOOT (70). Book, music and lyrics by James McDonald, David Vos and Robert Gerlach; additional music and musical consultation by Ed Linderman. November 5, 1974.

Director, Tony Tanner; scenery, Richard Seger; lighting, Fred Kopp; costumes, Walter Watson; musical director, John Price. With Gary Beach, Willard Beckham, Douglas Broyles, Darryl Ferrera, Gary Gage, Barbara Heuman, Lu Leonard, Pamela Myers, Jack Schmidt, Liz Sheridan.

FATHER'S DAY (79). By Oliver Hailey. February 25, 1975. Director, Tom Troupe; scenery, Dale Hennesy; lighting, Conrad Penrod. With Carole Cook, Barbara Rush, Laura Wallace, Jordan Rhodes, Paul Kent, Tom Troupe.

American Conservatory Theater: Marines' Memorial Theater—Guest Productions

GIVE 'EM HELL HARRY! by Samuel Gallu; based on the life and times of President Harry S. Truman. May, 1975. Director, Peter H. Hunt; designer, James Hamilton. With James Whitmore.

ME AND BESSIE by Will Holt and Linda Hopkins. June, 1975. Directed by Robert Greenwald. With Linda Hopkins, Gerri Dean, Lester Wilson.

American Conservatory Theater: Playroom Studio—Plays In Progress

BAM! NEBRASKAN BARBARIAN #1 by Andy Backer. Director, Robert Bonaventura; scenery & lighting, Michael Garrett; costumes, Cathy Edwards.

GEE, POP! by Frank Chin. Director, Edward

Hastings; scenery & lighting, Michael Garrett; costumes, Cathy Edwards; sound, Joseph Broido; videotape, Blake Torney, Joseph Broido.

DAVID DANCES by Stephen Hanan. Director, Paul Blake; scenery & lighting, Gregory Bolton;

costumes, Cathy Edwards; sound, Gamble Wetherby.

QUARTET: OMENS by Donald Alexander, directed by Sandra L. Richards; ROUTE 66 by Mark Berman, directed by Sabin Epstein; THE BAR by Thomas Bellin, directed by Joseph Broido; WHERE DO THE ELEPHANTS GO? by Ralph Bourne, directed by David Hammond. Scenery & lighting, Michael Garrett; costumes, Cathy Edwards, Barbara Hartman.

DOUGH-NUTZ! written and directed by Ronald Boussom; music by Bruce Bitkoff; scenery & lighting, Michael Garrett; costumes, Kim Dennis; sound, Joseph Broido; finale dance, Linda Kostalik.

Plays in Progress are performed by regular members of A.C.T. Company and workshop actors and were presented November 1974-June 1975 for 15 performances each.

Note: American Conservatory Theater toured two productions in Hawaii, for 7 performances each; *Cyrano de Bergerac* (May 27, 1975), and *The Taming of the Shrew* (June 3, 1975).

SARASOTA, FLA.

Asolo Theater Festival: The State Theater Company

(Artistic director, Robert Strane; managing director, Howard J. Millman; executive director, Richard G. Fallon)

RING ROUND THE MOON (14). By Jean Anouilh; adapted by Christopher Fry. June 28, 1974. Director, Jim Hoskins.

MACBETH (15). By William Shakespeare. July 27, 1974. Director, Robert Strane.

THERE'S ONE IN EVERY MARRIAGE (32). By Georges Feydeau; translated and adapted by Paxton Whitehead and Suzanne Grossmann from *Le Dindon*. February 13, 1975. Director, Howard J. Millman.

THE MISTRESS OF THE INN (26). By Carlo Goldoni; translated and adapted by Robert Strane. February 15, 1975. Director, Bradford Wallace.

THE PLOUGH AND THE STARS (23). By Sean O'Casey. February 21, 1975. Director, Robert Strane.

TOBACCO ROAD (30). By Erskine Caldwell and Jack Kirkland; based on Mr. Caldwell's

novel. February 28, 1975. Director, S. C. Hastie.

HEARTBREAK HOUSE (26). By George Bernard Shaw. April 4, 1975. Director, Paxton Whitehead.

THE SEA (19). By Edward Bond. May 2, 1975. Director, John Dillon.

GUYS AND DOLLS (31). Book by Jo Swerling and Abe Burrows; music by Frank Loesser; adapted from stories by Damon Runyon. May 30, 1975. Director, Howard J. Millman.

Designers: Scenery, Rick Pike; lighting, Martin Petlock; costumes, Catherine King, Flozanne John. Acting Company (summer 1974; wintersummer, 1975): Martha J. Brown, Burton Clarke, Bernerd Engel, Max Gulack, Stephen Johnson, Henson Keys, William Leach, Jillian Lindig, Philip LeStrange, Barbara Reid McIntyre, Robert Murch, Ellen Novack, Bette Oliver, Nona Pipes, Walter Rhodes, Joan Rue, Robert Strane, Isa Thomas, Bradford Wallace.

Asolo Theater Festival: Children's Theater

DON QUIXOTE OF LA MANCHA (14). By Arthur Fauquez; based on the novel by Cervantes. March 17, 1974.

STORY THEATER (13). By Paul Sills; adapted from various fairy story collections. August 4, 1974.

Note: Asolo Theater Festival's company toured throughout the state of Florida with its production of *The Mistress of the Inn* from October, 1974 through mid-January 1975, at which time the play joined the regular repertory season. Asolo also has an MFA program which permits those studying for their Master's degree to perform as well, with the regular professional company.

SEATTLE

Seattle Repertory Theater: Main Stage

(Artistic director, Duncan Ross; producing director, Peter Donnelly; assistant artistic director, Arne Zaslove)

HAMLET (25). By William Shakespeare. October 16, 1974. Director, Duncan Ross; scenery, Eldon Elder; lighting, Richard Nelson; costumes, Lewis D. Rampino. With Christopher Walken, Marsha Wischhusen, Jeannie Carson, Ted D'Arms, Clayton Corzatte, Mark Metcalf.

A GRAVE UNDERTAKING (25). By Lloyd Gold. November 13, 1974 (premiere of revision). Director, Duncan Ross; scenery, John Wright Stevens; lighting, Richard Nelson; costumes, Lewis D. Rampino; technical director, Floyd Hart.

Dominic Savio Paquette . . .	Gastone Rossilli
Louis Hogshead	William Preston
The Man	Loren Foss
The Woman	Zoaunne Le Roy
Herman Starr	John Harkins
Doctor Suit	Jay Garner
Monica Starr	Deborah Offner
Mr. Waddy	Gardner Hayes
The Sheriff	Adrian Sparks

The action takes place in a home located in the run-down fringes of the Garden District in New Orleans. Act I, Scene 1: A Friday. Scene 2: That evening. Act II, Scene 1: The next day, Saturday. Scene 2: the following night, Sunday. Scene 3: The next day, Monday. Act III, Scene 1: The next day, the day of the Mardi Gras. Scene 2: That evening. Scene 3: The same evening, after midnight.

LIFE WITH FATHER (24). By Howard Lindsay and Russel Crouse. December 11, 1974. Director, George Abbott; scenery, John Wright Stevens, Steven A. Maze; costumes, Lewis D. Rampino. With Biff McGuire, Jeannie Carson, Gerald Burgess, Jan Devereaux, Judith Drake, C. K. Alexander.

THE WALTZ OF THE TOREADORS (25). By Jean Anouilh. January 8, 1975. Director, Harold Scott; scenery, Robert Dahlstrom; lighting, Richard Nelson; costumes, Lewis D. Rampino. With Shirl Conway, David Hurst, Clayton Corzatte, Marian Mercer, Zoaunne Le Roy.

A DOLL'S HOUSE (25). By Henrik Ibsen; translated by Eva Le Gallienne. February 5, 1975. Director, Eva Le Gallienne; scenery, Eldon Elder; lighting, Richard Nelson; costumes, Lewis D. Rampino. With Jeannie Carson, Curt Dawson, Hurd Hatfield, Margaret Hilton, David Hurst.

THE MATCHMAKER (25). By Thornton Wilder. March 5, 1975. Director, Word Baker; scenery, John Naccarato; lighting, Steven A. Maze; costumes, Lewis D. Rampino. With Shirl Conway, Donald Woods, Jean-Pierre Stewart, Gerald Burgess, Jo Henderson.

Seattle Repertory Theater: Second Stage

BIOGRAPHY (16). By Max Frisch. March 11, 1975. Director, Arne Zaslove; scenery & lighting, Phil Schermer; costumes, Lewis D. Rampino. With George Morfogen, Duncan Ross, Pamella Burrell, Paul Vela, John Brandon, Robert Davidson, Larry Swansen, Adrian Sparks, Marjorie Nelson, Sally Kniest, Maria Mayenzet.

AFTER MAGRITTE and THE REAL INSPECTOR HOUND (16). By Tom Stoppard. April 1, 1975. Director, William Glover; scenery, W. Scott Robinson; lighting, D. Edmund Thomas; costumes, Lewis D. Rampino. With Robbyn Stuart, Pamela Burrell, Marjorie Nelson, Edwin Bordo, John Brandon, John Gilbert, Amelia Lauren, Robert Doyle.

LUNCHTIME, directed by Duncan Ross and HALLOWEEN directed by Assad Kelada (22).

By Leonard Melfi. May 11, 1975. Scenery, W. Scott Robinson; lighting, Cynthia J. Hawkins; costumes, Lewis D. Rampino. With Valerie Harper, Anthony Zerbe.

THE ARCHITECT AND THE EMPEROR OF ASSYRIA (13). By Fernando Arrabal; translated by Everard D'Harnoncourt and Adele Shank. May 15, 1975. Director, Arne Zaslove; scenery & lighting, Phil Schermer; costumes, Lewis D. Rampino. With Michael Christensen, Adrian Sparks.

A LOOK AT THE FIFTIES (14). By Al Carmines. June 3, 1975. Director, Arne Zaslove; scenery, W. Scott Robinson; lighting, D. Edmund Thomas; costumes, Ethel Anderson; musical director, Howard Crook. With members of the company and local actors.

STRATFORD, CONN.

American Shakespeare Festival

(Artistic director, Michael Kahn; managing director, William Stewart)

TWELFTH NIGHT (35). By William Shakespeare. June 15, 1974. Director, David William. With Carole Shelley, Caroline McWilliams, Larry Carpenter, Fred Gwynne, Philip Kerr, Roberta Maxwell, Donald Warfield, David Rounds.

ROMEO AND JULIET (34). By William Shakespeare. June 16, 1974. Director, Michael Kahn. With David Birney, Roberta Maxwell,

Kate Reid, Jack Gwillim, Michael Levin, David Rounds.

CAT ON A HOT TIN ROOF (26). By Tennessee Williams. July 10, 1974. Director, Michael Kahn. With Elizabeth Ashley, Keir Dullea, Fred Gwynne, Kate Reid.

Designers: Scenery, John Conklin; lighting, Marc B. Weiss; costumes, Jane Greenwood.

American Shakespeare Festival: New Playwrights Series

FELIX CULPA by Anita Gustafson. July 4, 1974. YANKS 3 DETROIT 0 TOP OF THE SEVENTH by Jonathan Reynolds. July 25, 1974. DUEL by Bruce Feld. August 8, 1974.

GOING OVER by Robert Gordon. August 22, 1974. 3 performances each; directed and performed by members of the regular company.

Note: American Shakespeare Festival has an extensive student audience program. From April 4, 1975-June 6, 1975, *Romeo and Juliet* and *King Lear* were performed in repertory for students.

SYRACUSE

Syracuse Stage

(Artistic Director, Arthur Storch; general manager, Karl Gevecker)

LA RONDE (27). By Arthur Schnitzler; adapted and directed by Arthur Storch. October 25, 1974. Scenery, John Doepp; lighting, Judy Rasmuson; costumes, James Berton Harris; choreography, Frances Barbour. With Kelly Wood, David Kagen, Jacqueline Bertrand, Mitchell McGuire, Earl Sydnor.

HEDDA GABLER (27). By Henrik Ibsen; adapted and directed by John Dillon. November 22, 1974. Scenery, David Chapman; lighting, Arden Fingerhut; costumes, Randy Barcelo. With Sara Croft, James Secrest, Virginia Kiser, Merwin Goldsmith, Paul Collins.

THE BUTTERFINGERS ANGEL, MARY AND JOSEPH, HEROD THE NUT and THE SLAUGHTER OF 12 HIT CAROLS IN A PEAR TREE (27). By William Gibson. December 20, 1974 (world premiere). Director, Arthur Storch; scenery, John Doepp; lighting, Judy Rasmuson; costumes, Lowell Detweiler; musical director, Julie Arenal; vocal director, Louis Lemos; production stage manager, Robert Colson; technical director, Mark Luking.

Angel	Steve Vinovich
Joseph	John Carpenter
Tree	Kelly Wood
Mary	Faith Catlin
1st Woman; Harem Lady	Mary Carter
2d Woman; Harem Lady	Sally Sockwell
Sheep	J. Thomas Wierney
Rebecca	Rachael Potash
Miriam	Haley Alpiar
Sherman	Walter White
Man in Grey; Herod; Courier	Thomas MacGreevy
1st Brute; 1st King	Merwin Goldsmith
2d Brute; 2d King	Fred Stuthman
3d Brute; 3d King	Mitchell McGuire
Cow	Barbara Kudan
Donkey	Ben Kapen

Girls at the Inn, Soldiers, Roustabouts: Sharon Ganjoian, Brad Videki, Kevin Meikleham, Nancy Hahn, Barbara White. Troubadour: Robert Stabile.

Time: Many years ago. Place: In and around Galilee. One intermission.

THE IMPORTANCE OF BEING EARNEST (27). By Oscar Wilde. January 17, 1975. Director, Pirie MacDonald; scenery, Philip Gilliam; lighting, Arden Fingerhut; costumes, James Berton Harris. With Anne Francine, Robert Moberly, Virginia Kiser, Eren Ozker, Thomas MacGreevy.

ARMS AND THE MAN (27). By George Bernard Shaw. February 14, 1975. Director, Thomas Gruenewald; scenery, David Chapman; lighting, Jeff Davis; costumes, Jerry Pannozzo. With Eren Ozker, Robert Moberly, Ben Kapen, Kelly Wood, Patricia O'Connell, Merwin Goldsmith.

THE LITTLE FOXES (27). By Lillian Hellman. March 14, 1975. Director, John Going; scenery, Stuart Wurtzel; lighting, William Lyons; costumes, Whitney Blausen, Nanzi Adzima. With Virginia Kiser, Robert Blackburn, Margaret Phillips, Robert Nichols, John Carpenter.

WALTHAM, MASS.

Brandeis University:

Spingold Theater

(Chairman, Theater Arts Department, Martin Halpern)

YOU CAN'T TAKE IT WITH YOU (9). By Moss Hart and George S. Kaufman. October 9, 1974. Director, Peter Sander; scenery, Theodore Cohen; lighting, Hank Sparks; costumes, Diana Greenwood. With David Palmer, Barbara Bolton, Terrence Beasor, Alexander Sokoloff.

MACBETH (5). By William Shakespeare. December 3, 1974. Director, Ted Kazanoff; scenery, J. Barnett Howard; lighting, John A. Olbrych Jr.; costumes, Wendy Pierson. With David Palmer, W. G. McMillan, Jay Alan Ginsberg, Barbara Bolton, Nancy Mette.

HEDDA GABLER (8). By Henrik Ibsen. March 4, 1975. Director, Ted Kazanoff; scenery, Robert Murphy; lighting, J. Barnett Howard; costumes, Diana Greenwood. With David Palmer, Susan Davis, Nancy Mette, Terrence Beasor.

LORD SCARECROW (8). Book and lyrics by Charles Kondek, based on Percy MacKaye's The Scarecrow; music by Gregg Saeger. April 22, 1975 (world premiere). Director, Charles Werner Moore; dances & musical numbers staged by Ed Nolfi; musical director, James Stenborg; orchestrations, Don Sturrock; scenery, Michael-John Zolli; lighting, Steven Berkowitz; costumes, Anna Belle Kaufman.

Goody Rickby . . . . Carol Glassman
Dickon . . . . David S. Howard

Rachel . . . . Kathie Irving
Richard . . . . Rick Porter
Scarecrow . . . . Christopher Josephs
Lord Ravensbane . . . . . . Randall Forsythe
Prudence . . . . Sharon Asro
Patience . . . . Diane Simmons
Justice Gilead Merton . . . . . . David Palmer
Myrtle . . . . Jean Trounstine
Capt. Bugby . . . . David Cohen
Rev. Todd . . . . Alan G. Kobritz
Rev. Rand . . . . Jim Kenney
Minister Dodge . . . . . . David Krentzman
Tavernkeeper . . . . . . Spencer Cherashore
Mistress Dodge . . . . Kat Krone
Townspeople, Crows: Gregg Bedol, Lisa Giles, Barbara Nachman, Mina Vanderberg, Pat Zadok, Susan Gellman, Jill Goodman, Marta Kauffman, Casey Kramer.

The action takes place on a day in New England in the late 17th Century.

Musical numbers: Act I—"I'll Build Me A Scarecrow," "Necessary Evil," "Lullaby," "I'll Build Me a Scarecrow" (Reprise), "Who Is That?", "Sparks! Bright Coals! Flames!", "Be A Little Different," "I Don't Know You," "Happy Father! Happy Son!", "Lines of Love," "Flip-Flop," "What Does She See In Him?", "I Will Examine The World Again!" Act II—"Isn't He Just!", "The Mirror," "Be A Little Different" (Reprise), "What Do You Do When You've Wasted Your Life?", "Rachel Is," "The Prognostication of the Crows," "Lullaby" (Reprise).

Brandeis University: Spingold Theater; Guest Productions

MUCH ADO ABOUT NOTHING (8). By William Shakespeare. December 16, 1974. Oxford and Cambridge Shakespeare Company. PRUDENCE & JURISPRUDENCE (1). Conceived by Babette R. Milunsky and improvised by members of the Brandeis Company. May 17, 1975. Auspices of the Greater Boston Chapter of the National Genetics Foundation.

Brandeis University: Laurie Theater

MAJOR BARBARA (5). By George Bernard Shaw. October 23, 1974. Director, Will Maitland Weiss; scenery & lighting, Robert Murphy; costumes, David Potts. With Janet Rodgers, Jay Alan Ginsberg, Donna Charron, Randall Forsythe, Christopher Josephs.

THE HOSTAGE (5). By Brendan Behan. November 20, 1974. Director, James Foster Kenney Jr.; scenery, David Potts; lighting, Steven Berkowitz; costumes, Anna Belle Kaufman. With Annette Miller, Terrence Beasor, Randall Forsythe, Renee Hariton.

THE HOMESICKNESS OF CAPTAIN RAPAPORT (5). By William S. Weshta. February 26, 1975 (world premiere). Director, Will Maitland Weiss; scenery, Delmadean Bryant; lighting, Michael-John Zolli; costumes, David Potts.

Robert Rapaport . . . . . Charles A. Stransky
Andrea Rapaport . . . . . . .Donna Charron
Saul Kushner . . . . Peter Sander
Donald Rapaport . . . . Christopher Josephs
Morris Rapaport . . . . . . David Krentzman
Rose Rapaport . . . . Lisa Kaufman
Moe Pittman . . . . Kerry Ruff
    One intermission.

TO SKIN A CAT by Liz Coe, directed by Debra Lee Garren, and TANGLEWOOD by David Cohen, directed by Lee Rachman (3). April 9, 1975 (world premiere). Scenery, Mark Daniel Berger; lighting, John Olbrych Jr.; musical director, David Krentzman.

To Skin a Cat:
Montgomery Duncan . . . . Tim Wise
Ethan Cantor . . . . .Aaron Speiser
Stacey . . . . .Susan Davis
    Place: A cabin in western Vermont.

Tanglewood:
Paul Reichman . . . . .Darrell Hayden
Don Spinelli . . . . Charles A. Stransky
Norman Kerry . . . . Andrew Traines
    Time: July. Place: Paul's room at the Berkshire Music Festival, Tanglewood.

SWING/SLIDE by Patricia Gibson, directed by Nancy Alexander, and THE MAN ON THE MONKEY BARS by Janet L. Neipris, directed by Will Maitland Weiss (4). April 10, 1975 (world premiere). Scenery, Mark Daniel Berger; lighting, John Olbrych Jr.; musical director, David Krentzman.

Swing/Slide:
Thelli . . . . Loretta Devine
Salina . . . . Lisa Kaufman
Earlton . . . . Kerry Ruff
    Time: The present. Place: A small playground in an urban community.
The Man on the Monkey Bars:
Katy Valentine . . . . .Marcheta Gillam
Alex Ainbinder . . . . . .Alexander Sokoloff
Harry Burns . . . . Terrence Beasor

THE BRIDGE AT BELHARBOUR by Janet Neipris, directed by James H. Clay, and THE PRIMARY ENGLISH CLASS by Israel Horovitz, directed by Stephen Drewes (3). May 7, 1975. Scenery, Wendy Pierson; lighting, Barbara Alpert; costumes, Jeff Howard. With Katie McDonough, Charles A. Stransky, Jay Alan Ginsberg, Andrew Traines, Terrence Beasor, Edith Agnew, Casey Kramer, Annette Miller, Donna Charron, Will Maitland Weiss.

WASHINGTON, D. C.

Arena Stage: Arena Theater

(Producing director, Zelda Fichandler; associate producer, George Touliatos; executive director, Thomas C. Fichandler)

DEATH OF A SALESMAN (42). By Arthur Miller. October 18, 1974. Director, Zelda Fichandler; scenery, Karl Eigsti; lighting, Hugh Lester; costumes, Marjorie Slaiman. With Robert Prosky, Dorothea Hammond, Bruce Weitz, Stanley Anderson, Mark Hammer.

WHO'S AFRAID OF VIRGINIA WOOLF? (39). By Edward Albee. October 25, 1974. Director, John Dillon; scenery, Karl Eigsti; lighting, Hugh Lester; costumes, Gwynne Clark. With Peg Murray, Richard Bauer, Dianne Wiest, Gary Bayer.

THE FRONT PAGE (41). By Ben Hecht and Charles MacArthur. December 6, 1974. Director, Edward Payson Call; scenery, Karl Eigsti;

lighting, Hugh Lester; costumes, Marjorie Slaiman. With Gary Bayer, Halo Wines, Dianne Wiest, Howard Witt.

JULIUS CAESAR (45). By William Shakespeare. February 26, 1975. Director, Carl Weber; scenery, Ming Cho Lee; lighting, William Mintzer; costumes, Marjorie Slaiman. With Robert Prosky, Stanley Anderson, James Blendick, Richard Bauer, Leslie Cass, Dianne Wiest.

THE DYBBUK (40). By S. Ansky; adaptation by John Hirsch. April 11, 1975. Director, Gene Lesser; scenery, Karl Eigsti; lighting, William Mintzer; costumes, Marjorie Slaiman. With Terrence Currier, Carl Don, Leonardo Cimino, Richard Bauer, Michael Mertz, Dianne Wiest.

Arena Stage: Kreeger Theater

BOCCACCIO (67). By Kenneth Cavander, dramatized from *The Decameron;* music by Richard Peaslee. November 15, 1974. Director, Gene Lesser; scenery, David Jenkins; lighting, William Mintzer; costumes, Linda Fisher. With Peggy Atkinson, Michael Burg, Ralph Byers, Jill Choder, David Eric, Caroline Kava, Lynn Ann Leveridge, Robert LuPone, J. Zakkai.

THE LAST MEETING OF THE KNIGHTS OF THE WHITE MAGNOLIA (46). By Preston Jones. March 21, 1975. Director, Alan Schneider, scenery, Karl Eigsti; lighting, William Mintzer; costumes, Gwynne Clarke. With John Marriott, Walter Flanagan, Macon McCalman, Patrick Hines, Henderson Forsythe, Paul Rudd, Roberts Blossom, Ken Zimmerman, Wayne Maxwell.

THE ASCENT OF MOUNT FUJI (42). By Chingiz Aitmatov and Kaltai Mukhamedzhanov; translated by Nicholas Bethell. May 27, 1975 (American premiere). Director, Zelda Fichandler; scenery, Ming Cho Lee; lighting, Hugh Lester; costumes, Marjorie Slaiman; technical director, Henry R. Gorfein.

Mambet Abayev	Max Wright
Osipbay Tatayev	Mark Hammer
Dosbergen Mustafayev	Howard Witt
Isabek Mergenov	Richard Bauer
Gulzhan Mergenov	Dianne Wiest
Anvar Abayev	Leslie Cass
Almagul Mustafayev	Halo Wines
Aysha-Apa	Vivian Nathan
Driver	Bob Harper
Forestry worker	Stanley Anderson

Time: Summer, about 1970. Place: On a mountaintop in Kirghisia, a Republic of the Soviet Union in central Asia. Two intermissions.

Arena Stage: Kreeger Theater Guest Production

OBA KOSO (14). The Yoruba Folk Festival, written and directed by Duro Ladipo; Nigerian National Theater. February 16, 1975.

The Season Elsewhere in Washington

By David Richards

Drama critic of the Washington *Star*

Despite some bravura performances and eye-opening premieres, the most significant event of the 1974–75 theatrical season in Washington took place behind closed doors. In November, the Kennedy Center assumed the long-term lease on the venerable National Theater, once the city's prime tryout house.

For three seasons, the Nederlander family had waged battle with the marble monolith on the Potomac, but the prestigious bookings had inevitably gone to the Kennedy Center, leaving the National with second best and dwindling audiences.

Although a non-profit organization with its own slate of officers, New National Theater, Inc., was set up to run the National, for all practical purposes the theater passed under the control of the Center's omnipotent chairman, Roger L. Stevens. Ironically, the take-over came at a time when Stevens was formulating plans for an American Bicentennial Theater, a schedule of revivals and commissioned new works to be produced by Kennedy Center Productions, to occupy the Eisenhower Theater for the full 1975–76 season. That meant that the choice commercial bookings would probably once again end up at the National—this time, however, with the Center's blessing.

There were, of course, the usual cries of monopoly and unfair play, but the move did seem to guarantee the National a future somewhat commensurate with its long and rich past. It also gave Stevens, with three of the city's major theaters at his disposal (the Eisenhower, the Opera House and the National) awesome leverage in his dealings with the New York establishment.

Elsewhere, the American Theater in L'Enfant Plaza folded after four shows and further attempts to keep it alive under new management seemed equally doomed. Likewise, the Washington Theater Club, faced with mounting mortgage payments, gave up the ghost and was sold at public auction, thus chastening those hardy optimists who had been predicting that Washington was on the verge of overtaking New York as the theatrical center of the nation. Cultural hubris, like its political counterpart, seems to thrive in the local climate.

The strongest creative impulses continued to emanate from Arena Stage, which beat everyone to the Bicentennial punch with impeccable revivals of *Death of a Salesman, The Front Page* and *Who's Afraid of Virginia Woolf?* and then went on to a new piece of Americana, Preston Jones's *The Last Meeting of the Knights of the White Magnolia.* A rowdy, pungent account of small-town Texas lodge brothers trying with comic ineffectuality to carry on the tradition of the white sheet and the blazing cross, *Magnolia* was first produced last season in Dallas and was easily the most interesting new American work Washington saw all season. Arena, at its best in plays of a realistic nature, gave it a flawless production.

Notable, too, was Olney Theater's world premiere of *Summer,* a moody but often startlingly funny study of middle-aged discontent. Had Chekhov been an Irishman, he might have written this play. Actually, it was the work of Hugh Leonard, who seems to have found an American home at Olney. (The alliance is already five plays old.) Virtually plotless, *Summer* charted the erosion of aspirations and the slippage of time, as experienced by three married couples in the course of two summer picnics. Always a clever writer, Leonard is becoming a reflective one as well, and *Summer* seemed to emphasize the deepening of his comedies that began two seasons ago at Olney with *Da.*

Ford's Theater had a generally limp year, although it scored a big coup with *Give 'em Hell, Harry,* Samuel Gallu's one-man show detailing the life and times of Harry S. Truman (in the person of actor James Whitmore). Both a feisty portrait and a generous statement of pre-Watergate principles, the show undid one local superstition when President Ford dropped in to see it and thereby became the first chief executive to set foot in the historic theater since Lincoln's assassination. And there were real, if unpretentious, joys to be found in *The Portable Pioneer and Prairie Show,* the musical saga of a family of Swedish entertainers in the Upper Midwest a century ago.

The Folger Theater Group devoted half of its season to lackluster Shakespeare; of its new works, only David Storey's *The Farm,* a female version of his *In Celebration,* was intriguing. The D. C. Black Repertory Company's *Owen's Song* turned out to be an overly murky collage of dance and poetry, celebrating the writings of former Howard University professor Owen Dodson. But the company had a big popular success, and deservedly so, with a spunky revival of *Day of Absence,* played with incisive flair.

Still, the city's greatest attention-getter remained the Kennedy Center which hovered at capacity levels all season long with such tryouts as *Absurd Person*

Singular, Sherlock Holmes, Seascape and such post-Broadway engagements as *Of Mice and Men* and *Cat on a Hot Tin Roof.* The glittery names (Yul Brynner in a disastrous musicalization of the *Odyssey,* Ingrid Bergman in *The Constant Wife,* Diana Rigg and Alec McCowen in *The Misanthrope*), coupled with the comfort and the glamor of the Center itself, had the public acting like lemmings.

Some of the city's smaller theaters trembled in the Center's shadow and occasionally suffered directly from its enormous clout. There was no question that Stevens had a monumental attraction on his hands, seemingly incapable of housing a box-office bust. "He could sell out that place with a dancing flea," commented one wag, although Stevens wasn't risking it yet.

The following is a selection of the most noteworthy Washington productions of the year. The list does not include details of the numerous touring shows nor the Arena Stage productions (see the Regional Theater listing above). A plus sign (+) with the performance number indicates the show was still running on June 1, 1975.

D.C. Black Repertory Company

OWEN'S SONG (25). A musical conceived by Mike Malone and Glenda Dickerson; based on the writings of Owen Dodson; music by Clyde-Jacques Barrett and Dennis Wiley. October 24, 1974 (world premiere). Directed & choreographed by Mike Malone and Glenda Dickerson; scenery, Ron Anderson; lighting, Ron Truitt; costumes, Quai Barnes Truitt.

Reve Grant	David Cameron
Sophie-Louise; Bird of Freedom	Amii
Maude Grant	Lynda Gravatt
Mrs. Candy Mayme	Carol Maillard
Bettysue	Lisa Sneed
Apocalypse	Robert MacFadden
Yancey	Carlton Poles
Troy	Skipper Driscoll
Naomi	Loretta Rucker
Judas	Kenneth Daugherty
Clove	Janifer Baker
Oleander	Kiki
Tulip	Alva Petway
Hethabella	Lynn Whitfield
Jackleg Preacher	Bernie Gibson
Willie Silvers	Ed DeShae
The Ruler	Charles Augins
Mother with Child	Carol Maillard
Black Mothers Praying	Mie; Lynda Gravatt
Crazy Woman	Alva Petway
Blind Man	Moon

An abstract musical collage, the work depicts the struggle for freedom, as reflected in excerpts from the writings of black poet and playwright Owen Dodson. (Production transferred to the Eisenhower Theater, John F. Kennedy Center for the Performing Arts on December 31, 1974 for 16 additional performances.)

Musical Numbers: Act I—"Reve's Theme," "Prologue," "Townspeople's Theme," "Mourn Your Mourn," "Clove, Oleander and Tulip's Theme," "Wedding Dance," "Wedding March," "Maud's Theme and Revival," "Reve's Descent." Act II—"Theme of Oppression," "Winter Chorus' Theme," "Lullaby," "Sorrow," "Black Mother Praying," "Bird of Freedom," "Owen's Song."

DAY OF ABSENCE (45). By Douglas Turner Ward. January 8, 1975. Directed by Robert Hooks; scenery, Jimmy Hooks; lighting, Motojicho; costumes, Quai Barnes Truitt; music, Jackie McLean; sound, Robert Daughtry. With Smokey, Jim Vance, Rosie Lee Horn, Chester Sims, Luzern Washington, Cynthia Warfied, Ida Pinkney, Sugarbear. And SISTER SELENA GOT THE GIFT. By Joann Bruno. Directed by Motojicho; scenery, Jimmy Hooks; lighting, Motojicho; costumes, Victoria Peyton; music, Jackie McLean. With Nadyne Spratt, Robert Whitson, Francis Mann, Gloria Hill, Sugarbear.

Folger Theater Group

THE FARM (35). By David Storey. October 8, 1974 (American premiere). Directed by Louis W. Scheeder; scenery, David Chapman; lighting, Hugh Lester; costumes, Bob Wojewodski; vocal consultant, Robert Neff Williams.

Wendy	Elizabeth Perry
Jennifer	Lauri Peters
Brenda	Anne Stone
Slattery	Roy Cooper
Mrs. Slattery	Kate Wilkinson
Albert	John Calkins
Arthur	Allan Carlsen

Time: The present. Place: A farmhouse in Yorkshire. The rifts and misunderstandings between a rugged farmer and his wife and their three more educated daughters. Two intermissions.

HENRY IV, Part 1 (35). By William Shakespeare. November 26, 1974. Directed by Paul Schneider; scenery, William Mickley; lighting, Arden Fingerhut; costumes, Joan E. Thiel; stagefights, Ron Mangravite. With Earl Hindman, John Christopher Jones, James Cahill, Clement Fowler, Donald C. Moore, Anne Stone.

HE'S GOT A JONES (28). By G. Tito Shaw. February 4, 1975 (Professional premiere). Directed by Harold Scott; scenery, Stuart Wurtzel; lighting, Betsy Toth; costumes, Joan E. Thiel;

music, E.L. James and Hilton Felton.

Joe Willie . . . . Terry Alexander
Gladys . . . . .Cecelia Norfleet
Joffrey Leeroy . . . . Count Stovall
Margaret . . . . Cara Duff-MacCormick

Time: The 1930s. Place: A decayed Southern plantation. Two black sharecroppers dream about fleeing north to escape the Depression. Two intermissions

THE TEMPEST (55). By William Shakespeare. April 8, 1975. Directed by Paul Schneider; scenery, Paul Zalon; lighting, Arden Fingerhut; costumes, Bob Wojewodski; choreography, Virginia Freeman. With Steve Gilborn, Terry Hinz, Charles Morey, Seret Scott, Ron Seibert, Peter Vogt.

Ford's Theater

THE PORTABLE PIONEER AND PRAIRIE SHOW (40). Musical by David Chambers; music by Mel Marvin; lyrics by David Chambers and Mel Marvin. February 11, 1975. Directed by David Chambers; scenery, James Bakkom; Lighting, Spencer Mosse; costumes, William Henry; choreography, Dennis Nahat; musical direction, Mel Marvin. With Mary Wright, Terry Hinz, Lyle Swedeen, John Long, Ingrid Helga Son-

nichsen, Donovan Sylvest, Prudence Wright Holmes, Diane Sherman.

GIVE 'EM HELL, HARRY (24). By Samuel Gallu. April 15, 1975. Directed by Peter H. Hunt; scenery, James Hamilton. With James Whitmore. One-man show based on the life and times of President Harry S. Truman. One intermission.

Note: The season at Ford's also included guest productions of *Me and Bessie* and *A Tribute to Rosalind Russell* and touring productions of *Love's Labour's Lost* (The City Center Acting Company), *Nash at Nine, Gabrielle, Light Up the Sky* and *Diamond Studs.*

National Theater

BIG BAD MOUSE (32). By Philip King and Falkland Cary. February 17, 1975. Directed by Paul Elliott. With Eric Sykes, Jimmy Edwards, Sheila Haney, Patrick Brymer, Judy Johnson, Anne-Francis Thom, Joyce Campion.

HEDDA GABLER (16). By Henrik Ibsen. April 22, 1975. Directed by Trevor Nunn. Scenery &

costumes, John Napier; lighting, Andy Phillips. With Glenda Jackson, Timothy West, Peter Eyre, Patrick Stewart, Constance Chapman, Pam St. Clement, Jennie Linden. A Royal Shakespeare Company production, presented by Paul Elliott and Duncan C. Weldon for Triumph Theater Productions.

Note: The National season also included pre-Broadway productions of *All Over Town* and *The Ritz* and touring productions of *What the Wine-Sellers Buy, Good Evening, The Philanthropist* (Goodman Theater), and *The Magic Show.*

John F. Kennedy Center: Eisenhower Theater

LLOYD GEORGE KNEW MY FATHER (33). By William Douglas Home. July 2, 1974. Directed by Robin Midgley; designed by Anthony Holland. With Ralph Richardson, Meriel Forbes, Simon Merrick, David Stoll, Daphne Anderson, Carolyn Lagerfelt, Christopher Bernau, Norman Barrs. Produced in association with Paul Elliott and Duncan C. Weldon.

DESIRE UNDER THE ELMS (31). By Eugene O'Neill. July 30, 1974. Directed by Jeffrey Hay-

den; scenery, Milton Duke; lighting & costumes, James Riley. With Eva Marie Saint, James Broderick, John Ritter, Jerry Harden, John McKinney. Produced in association with Leonard Blair and Jeffrey Hayden.

THE AMERICAN COLLEGE THEATER FESTIVAL. Seventh annual two-week festival of representative college productions, selected from across the country. April 7–20, 1975. Held in the Eisenhower Theater and George Washington

University's Marvin Theater. Produced in cooperation with the Alliance for Arts Education, the Smithsonian Institution, the American Theater Association and Amoco Oil Company. MEDEA: A NOH CYCLE BASED ON THE GREEK MYTH (3). By Carol Sorgenfrei. April 19, 1975. Scenery, Paulette Brimie; lighting, Steve Hirsh; costumes, Alan Armstrong; choreography, Susan Speers. Produced by the University of California at Santa Barbara. Winner of the ACTF Playwrighting Award.

Medea	Lorraine Devivian
Jason	Tony Acierto
Nurse	Jeanne Reynolds
Cruesa	Lisa Amy Silver

Chorus: Peter Davies, Stephen James Goodwin, Eric Larson, Debra Loomis, Deborah St. George. Dancers: Reenie Matthes, Cynthia Richards. Stage assistants: Nancy Collinge, Terry Jo. Johnson.

Time: Mythological times. Place: A mountaintop in Greece; Colchis; the palace of Jason and Medea. Five scenes. A retelling of the Greek myth in the style and conventions of the Japanese Noh Theater, in which Medea is exonerated as an early feminist.

The Festival also included: *H.M.S. Pinafore* (3), California State University, Sacramento; *Juno and the Paycock* (2), Louisiana State University; *One Flew Over the Cuckoo's Nest* (2), Illinois State University; *The Scarlet Princess of Edo* (3), University of Hawaii at Manoa; *Fashion! Or Life in New York* (3), University of Missouri; *You're a Good Man, Charlie Brown* (3), University of Maryland, Baltimore County; *Our Town* (4), University of Oregon; *The House of Bernarda Alba* (2), University of Nevada, Las Vegas.

PRESENT LAUGHTER (63+). By Noel Coward. April 29, 1975. Directed by Stephen Porter; scenery, Oliver Smith; lighting, John Gleason; costumes, Nancy Potts. With Douglas Fairbanks Jr., Jane Alexander, Ilka Chase, Diana Van Der Vlis, Lindsay Crouse, Roy Cooper, George Pentecost. Produced by Roger L. Stevens and Richmond Crinkley for Kennedy Center Productions, Inc.

Note: The Eisenhower season also included pre-Broadway or touring productions of *Absurd Person Singular*, *Sherlock Holmes*, *London Assurance*, *Seascape*, *The Member of the Wedding* (The New Phoenix Repertory Company), *The Misanthrope*, and *Of Mice and Men*.

John F. Kennedy Center: Opera House

ODYSSEY (45). Musical play by Erich Segal; music by Mitch Leigh; lyrics by Erich Segal. December 29, 1974. Directed by Albert Marre; scenery & lighting, Howard Bay; costumes, Howard Bay; Ray Diffen; choreography, Billy Wilson; musical direction, Ross Reimueller; orchestrations, Buryl Red; dance arrangements, Danny Holgate. Produced for Kennedy Center Productions, Inc., by Roger L. Stevens, Martin Feinstein and Alexander Morr.

Antinous	Martin Vidnovic
Agelaos	Greg Bell
Ktesippos	Bill Mackey
Eurymachus	Michael Mann
Leokritos	Brian Destazio
Pimteus	John Gorrin
Mulios	Jeff Phillips
Polybos	Derrick Bell
Penelope	Joan Diener
Telemachus	Russ Thacker
Odysseus	Yul Brynner
Kalypso	Catherine Lee Smith
Nausikaa	Diana Davila
Therapina	Christine Uchida
Melantho	Cecile Santos
Hippodameia	P.J. Mann
King Alkinoos	Shev Rodgers
Kerux	Garon Douglass
Polyphemus	Ian Sullivan

Time: Nine years after the Trojan War. Place: Odysseus's Palace at Ithaca and various islands on Odysseus' travels. One intermission. No musical numbers listed.

Note: The Opera House season also included touring productions of *I Do, I Do, Seesaw,* and *Cat on a Hot Tin Roof* and pre-Broadway engagements of *Gypsy, Mack & Mabel, In Praise of Love* and *The Constant Wife*.

Olney Theater

TONIGHT AT 8:30 (*We Were Dancing, Family Album, Red Peppers*) (21). By Noel Coward. June 4, 1974. Directed by John Going; scenery & lighting, James D. Waring; costumes, Joan E. Thiel. With Jane Summerhays, Tom Urich, John Wylie, Kathleen O'Meara Noone, June Gibbons.

HAPPY END (21). By Bertolt Brecht and Kurt Weill; adapted by Michael Feingold. June 25, 1974. Directed By James D. Waring; scenery & lighting, James D. Waring; costumes, Jo Ellen LaRue. With Stephen Joyce, Sydney Walker, Kathleen O'Meara Noone, David Snell, Anne Chodoff, Paul Schierhorn.

THE MISER (21). By Molière; adapted by Miles Malleson. July 16, 1974. Directed by Leo Brady; scenery & lighting, James D. Waring; costumes, Roberta Pioli. With Sydney Walker, Pauline Flanagan, David Snell, Jane Summerhays, George Vogel, John Wylie.

SUMMER (21). By Hugh Leonard. August 6, 1974 (world premiere). Directed by James D. Waring; scenery & lighting, James D. Waring; costumes, Meg Hamilton Patterson.

Richard Halvey . . . . .Stephen Joyce
Trina Halvey . . . . Lois Smith
Stormy Loftus . . . . Sydney Walker
Jan Loftus . . . . .Lois Markle
Jess White . . . . John Wylie
Myra White . . . . Pauline Flanagan
Michael Halvey . . . . Davis Hall
Lou Loftus . . . . .Harriet Hall
    Time: Sunday, summer of 1968; and Sunday, summer of 1974. Place: A hillside overlooking Dublin. One intermission. Leonard explores the disintegration and disenchantment of three married couples who gather for two summer picnics, six years apart. (Production transferred to the Eisenhower Theater, John F. Kennedy Center

for the Performing Arts on August 27, 1974 for an additional 8 performances.)

CRIME AND PUNISHMENT (21). An adaptation of Dostoevsky's novel by Leo Brady. August 27, 1974 (world premiere). Directed by William H. Graham; scenery & lighting, James D. Waring; costumes, Marguerite Mayo.

Raskolnikov . . . . David Snell
Nastasya . . . . Joyce Audley
Alyona . . . . Geralyn Lutty
Lizaveta . . . . Jean Fish
Razumikin . . . . .Jordan Clarke
Sonia . . . . Kathleen O'Meara Noone
Marmeladov . . . . .Al Corbin
Pulcheria . . . . Dorothea Hammond
Dunya . . . . Esther Koslow
Svidrigailov . . . . Dalton Dearborn
Porfiry . . . . Herb Voland
Organ Grinder . . . . .Bernie Passeltiner
Nicolai . . . . Stanley Wojewodski Jr.
Policeman . . . . Tom Marcellino
Tavern Keeper . . . . .Jim Singer
Clerk . . . . .Philip Cunningham
    Time: 1865. Place: St. Petersburg. One intermission.

Summer Shakespeare Festival

TWELFTH NIGHT (34). By William Shakespeare. July 2, 1974. Directed by Tony Tanner; scenery, Richard Ferrer; lighting, Larry Metzler. With Susan Watson, Maureen Maloney, Donna Curtis, Albert Verdesca, Danny Sewell, Dennis McGovern, Richard Bowden, Henry Victor, Josef Warik, Alfred Karl. Produced by Ellie Chamberlain in association with National Capital Parks.

THE IMPORTANCE OF BEING EARNEST (5). By Oscar Wilde. August 6, 1974. Directed by Tony Tanner; scenery, Richard Ferrer; lighting, Jack Carr; costumes, Jean Teuteberg. With Josef Warik, Henry Victor, Albert Verdesca, Richard Bowden, Maureen Maloney, Donna Curtis, Susan Watson, Danny Sewell. Produced by Ellie Chamberlain in association with National Capital Parks.

WATERFORD, CONN.

Eugene O'Neill Theater Center: National Playwrights Conference

(President, George C. White; artistic director, Lloyd Richards; designers, Peter Larkin, Fred Voelpel, Arden Fingerhut. All programs new works in progress)

Barn Theater (outdoors)

THE MIGHTY GENTS (2). By Richard Wesley. July 18, 1974. Director, James Hammerstein; dramaturg, Arthur Ballet.

Frankie . . . . Robert Christian
Figure; Tyson; Shadow Man   .David Downing
Lucky . . . . Hannibal Penney
Tiny . . . . Sam Harris
Eldridge . . . . Brent Jennings
Zeke . . . . .Bill Cobbs

YOU'RE TOO TALL, BUT COME BACK IN TWO WEEKS (2). By Richard Venture. July 20,

1974. Director, Hal Scott; dramaturg, Edith Oliver.

Guido Ferrara . . . . .Victor Arnold
Ruth Ferrara . . . . . . Rosemary De Angelis
Sterling Simmons . . . . . . Hannibal Penney
Dee Holden . . . .·Mary Alice
Big Mama . . . . Jay Vanleer
Priest . . . . Edward Zang
    Two intermissions.

FOUNDING FATHER (2). By Amlin Gray. August 1, 1974. Director, Ed Hastings; dramaturgs, Martin Esslin, Edith Oliver.

Leeroy	Michael Sacks
Margaret Blennerhasset	Geraldine Sherman
Robinson; John Marshall	Peter Turgeon
Aaron Burr	Kevin O'Connor
Harman Blennerhasset	Brian Syron
James Wilkinson	Richard Venture
Theodosia Burr	Jill Eikenberry
Gideon Sloat	Tom Costello
Marques De Casa Yrujo	Gene Gross
Luther Wickham	Victor Arnold
George Hay	Edward Zang

Act I, Scene 1: Blennerhasset Island. Scene 2: U. S. Senate. Scene 3: Blennerhasset Island. Scene 4: A barge on the Ohio River. Scene 5: Yrujo's house, Washington. Scene 6: Blennerhasset Island. Scene 7: Wilkinson's quarters. Act II, Scene 1: The barge. Scene 2: Blennerhasset Island. Scene 3: The barge. Scene 4: A tavern. Scene 5: A courtroom. Scene 6: Burr's bedroom. Scene 7: The courtroom. Scene 8: Yrujo's house. Scene 9: Somewhere in Sweden.

SHE'S BAD TODAY (2) By A.E.O. Goldman. August 7, 1974. Director, Tony Giordano; dramaturg, Edith Oliver.

Mr. Janson	Gene Gross
Marc	Kevin O'Connor
Edna	Geraldine Sherman
Old Man	Peter Turgeon

One intermission.

Barn El (indoors)

THE JUICE PROBLEM (AN EROTIC LOVE CHARTUNE) (2). By Oyamo. July 26, 1974. Director, Ed Hastings; dramaturg, Arthur Ballet.

Bethea	Mary Alice
Bohannon	Bill Cobbs
Mama Nigga	Jay Van Leer
Sadie Mae	Michele Shay
Vicky	Caroline Godfrey
Malcom	Hannibal Penney

Offstage Voices: Caroline Godfrey, Geraldine Sherman, Samuel Harris. One intermission.

THE PRAGUE SPRING (2). By Lee Kalcheim.

August 5, 1974. Director, James Hammerstein; dramaturg, Dale Wasserman; musical director, Barbara Damashek; composer, Joe Raposo; guitarist, Bill Partlan.

Dubcek	John Harkins
Player #1	Ben Masters
Player #2	Edward Zang
Player #3	Tom Fitzsimmons
Player #4	James Gallery
Player #5	Victor Arnold
Player #6	Carolyn Coates

One intermission.

Amphitheater (outdoors)

A GRAVE UNDERTAKING (2) By Lloyd Gold. July 24, 1974. Director, James Hammerstein; dramaturg, Arthur Ballet.

Dominic Savio Paquette	Michael Sacks
Louis Hogshead	Gene Gross
Mrs. O'Brien	Carolyn Coates
Mr. Ryan	Kevin O'Connor
Herman Starr	John Harkins
Dr. Suit	Edward Zang
Monica Starr	Jill Eikenberry
Mr. Waddy	James Gallery
Sheriff	Victor Arnold

Two intermissions.

ONCE AND FOR ALL (2). By Robert Gordon. July 27, 1974. Director, Harold Scott; dramaturgs, Edith Oliver, Martin Esslin.

Mister	Ben Masters
Al	Robert Christian
Ruth	Carolyn Coates
Charlie	Gene Gross

Scene 1: Once. Scene 2: And. Scene 3: For all.

EVERY NIGHT WHEN THE SUN GOES DOWN (2). By Phillip Hayes Dean. August 2, 1974. Director, Hal Scott.

Sneaky Pete	Bill Cobbs
Phoenix	Robert Christian
Caledonia	Mary Alice
Ballerina	Michele Shay
Queen Sam	David Downing
Jericho	Hannibal Penny
Cockeyed Rose	Jay Vanleer
Pretty Eddie	Brent Jennings

Place: Moloch, Michigan.

EARTH WORMS (2). By Albert F. Innaurato. August 9, 1974. Director, James Hammerstein; dramaturg, Arthur Ballet.

Mary	Jill Eikenberry
Arnold	Ben Masters
Scodge	Michael Sacks
Bucky	Victor Arnold
Marge	Mary Alice
Mother Superior	Carolyn Coates
Nuns	James Gallery, Michele Shay
Michael	Robert Christian
Boy	Tom Fitzsimmons
Bernard	John Harkins
Edith	Rosemary De Angelis
Bartender	Tom Costello

Two intermissions.

Instant Theater (outdoors)

TAKING CARE OF HARRY (2) By Corinne Jacker. July 18, 1974. Director, Ed Hastings, Dale Wasserman.

Irene . . . . .Geraldine Sherman
Susan . . . . Michele Shay
George . . . . .Ben Masters
Harry . . . . John Harkins
Marsha . . . . Jill Eikenberry
Gabby . . . . Carolyn Coates
Mr. Crosley . . . . Gene Gross
     Place: A clearing in the woods, Berkshire, Mass. Act I, Scene 1: Noon, late August. Scene

2: Later that afternoon. Scene 3: The same night. Act II, Scene 1: Dawn the next morning. Scene 2: Late morning the same day. Scene 3: A night in late November.

FALLING APART (2). By Monte Merrick. July 30, 1974. Director, Tony Giordano; dramaturgs, Arthur Ballet, Martin Esslin. With Jo Anne Belanger, Robert Christian, Rosemary De Angelis, James Galley, Deloris Gaskins, Edward Zang. One intermission.

Special Productions

(In cooperation with Theater Communications Group and Connecticut College American Dance Festival)

Section Ten in New York Monster Show (2). July 21, 1974. Directors, Andrea Balis, Omar Shapli; designer, Theodora Skipitares. With Abigail Costello, Lee De Ross, Stephannie Howard, Ste-

phan Hymes, Cecil Mackinnon, Ron Van lieu.

Mabou Mines in The B-Beaver Animation and *The Red Horse Animation* (1). Text/director, Lee Breuer. July 30, 1974. Music, Philip Glass; designer, Tina Girouard. With Fred Neumann, Dawn Gray, David Warrilow, Ruth Maleczech, Joanne Akalaitis.

WEST SPRINGFIELD, MASS.

Stage/West

(Artistic director, John Ulmer; managing director, Stephen E. Hays)

THAT CHAMPIONSHIP SEASON (28). By Jason Miller. November 2, 1974. Director, John Ulmer. With John Towey, Eddie Jones, John Hallow, Ed Rombola, Joseph Warren.

MASQUERADE (27). Book by John Ulmer; music and lyrics by Thomas Babbitt; based on Carlo Goldini's *The Servant of Two Masters.* December 7, 1974 (world premiere). Director, John Ulmer; designer, Charles G. Stockton; costumes, Clifford Capone; choreography and musical numbers, Judith Haskell; musical director, Thomas Babbitt.

Truffaldino . . . . .Eric Tavaris
Federigo; Pasqual; Porter . . . . . Chip Lucia
Bernice . . . . Vinnie Holman
Florindo . . . . .Ray Gill
Pantalone . . . . Stephen Daley
Dr. Lombardi . . . . Roy Brocksmith
Silvio . . . . .Michael Forella
Clarice . . . . .Heidi Mefford
Brighella . . . . Louis Turenne
Smeraldina . . . . Maryin Brasch
     Time: 1743. Prologue: Turin, Italy. Act I: Courtyard of an Inn, Venice. Act II: The same. One intermission.

MARCUS BRUTUS (22). By Paul Foster. January 11, 1975 (world premiere). Director, John Ulmer; scenery and lighting, Charles G. Stockton; costumes, Clifford Capone; original score, Randall McClellan.

Cat . . . . Ed Rombola
Marcus Brutus . . . . .Eric Tavaris
Memphis; Cleopatra . . . . Lea Scott
Casca . . . . Edward Holmes
Cassius . . . . Stephen Daley
Metellus Cimber . . . . Ralph Levy
Cinna . . . . .Michael Forella
Julius Casesar . . . . Louis Turenne
Marc Antony; Doctor . . . . Chip Lucia
Soothsayer; Orderly;
     Secretary . . . . Armin Shimerman
Porcia . . . . Maryin Brasch
Servilia . . . . Kate Williamson
Calpurnia . . . . .Heidi Mefford
Stahr . . . . Roy Brocksmith
     Time: The present, during a single day. Place: A tenement in New York. One intermission.

PROMENADE, ALL! (22). By David V. Robison. February 15, 1975. Director, Harry Ellerbe. With Michael Forella, Lori March, Piri MacDonald, Stephen Daley.

THE GUARDSMAN (22). By Ferenc Molnar; English version by Grace I. Colbron and Hans Bartsch; acting version by Philip Moeller. March 22, 1975. Director, John Ulmer; choreography, Shirley Jean Measures. With Jean DeBaer, Richard Jamieson, Stephen Daley, Heidi Mefford, Betty Williams, Harry Ellerbe, Jean Burns.

ONE FLEW OVER THE CUCKOO'S NEST (37). By Dale Wasserman; based on the novel by

Ken Kesey. April 19, 1975. Director Peter J. Hajduk. With Ralph Roberts, Anthony White, Ron Recasner, Maryin Brasch, Michael Connolly, Bruce Bouchard, James Sutorius, Peter Boyden, Mary Gallagher.

Designers: Scenery, Charles G. Stockton; lighting, James R. Riggs, Charles G. Stockton; costumes, Peg McMaster, Clifford Capone, William E. Schroder.

Stage/West: Children's Theater

THE MISCHIEF ON MERRY MOUNTAIN (2). By Lionel Wilson. March 11, 1975 (world premiere). Director, Peter J. Hajduk.

Regina Clammer . . . . Susan Genis
Addie Honker . . . . Terri McRay
Busby Bumble; Weasel . . . . . . Steve Cole
Brewster Doodle . . . . John O'Creagh

Roscoe Ripoff;
Dimwit DePew . . . . . . Maury Covington
Snouter Spotless . . . . Walter Wood
Scene 1: The conniving Caboodle. Scene 2: The dog who lost his bark. Scene 3: The unmaking of murky mountain. No intermission. This production toured statewide from March 3-March 27, 1975.

CANADA

HALIFAX, NOVA SCOTIA

The Neptune Theater Company: Sackville Street Theater

(Artistic director, John Wood)

In repertory, July 8-August 24, 1974 (total of 56 performances).

THE GOOD SOLDIER SCHWEIK. Adapted and directed by Keith Turnbull from the novel by Jaroslav Hasek. July 8, 1974. Designer, Peter Wingate; lighting, Robert C. Reinholdt; original music and lyrics, Phillip Schreibman.

HARVEY. By Mary Chase. July 16, 1974. Director, Michael Mawson; designer, Peter Wingate; lighting, Robert C. Reinholdt.

Summer 1974 Acting Company: Nancy Beatty, John Bird, Jay Bowen, Tom Carew, David Ferry, Jerry Franken, Michael Hogan, James Hurdle, Nicola Lipman, Patricia Ludwick, Don MacQuarrie, Michael Mawson, Mina Erian Mina, Cecile O'Connor, Joan Orenstein, David Renton, John Roby, Jocelyne St. Denis, Phillip Schreibman, Suzanne Turnbull, Dee Victor.

GODSPELL (32). By John-Michael Tebelak, based upon the Gospel according to St. Matthew; music and lyrics by Stephen Schwartz. November 11, 1974. Director, John Wood; designer, David Dague; lighting, Robert C. Reinholdt; musical director, Alan Laing, conductor, Bob

Quinn. With Marc Connors, P. M. Howard and members of the company.

HAMLET (24). By William Shakespeare. February 3, 1975. Director, John Wood; designer, John Ferguson; lighting, Robert C. Reinholdt. With Neil Munro, Marti Maraden, Denise Fergusson, Michael Ball, Joseph Rutten, Brian McKay.

YOU CAN'T TAKE IT WITH YOU (24). By George S. Kaufman and Moss Hart. March 3, 1975. Director, Donald Davis; scenery, John Ferguson; lighting, Robert C. Reinholdt; costumes, Judy Peyton Ward. With Jack Creley, Rita Howell, David Renton, Rosemary Dunsmore, Jonathan Welsh, Florence Paterson.

JACQUES BREL IS ALIVE AND WELL AND LIVING IN PARIS (16), By Eric Blau and Mort Shuman; based on Brel's lyrics and commentary; music by Jacques Brel. March 24, 1975. Directors, John Wood, Alan Laing; designer, John Ferguson; lighting, Robert C. Reinholdt; musical director, Alan Laing; choreography, Lynn McKay. With Rory Dodd, P.M. Howard, Rita Howell, Nicola Lipman, Brian McKay, Mary McMurray, Sharon Lyse Timmins.

Neptune Theater Company: Rebecca Cohn Auditorium

(In association with Dalhousie Cultural Activities)

THE ADVENTURES OF PINOCCHIO (20). Adapted and directed by John Wood from the story by Carlo Collodi; music composed and conducted by Alan Laing. December 16, 1974. Designer, John Ferguson; lighting, Robert C. Rein- holdt. With Michael Burgess, Iris Lyn Angus, Gordon Clapp, Paul Davis, Brian McKay, Jack Medley, David Renton, Joel Sapp, Muggsy Sweeny, Jonathan Welsh.

Note: The Neptune Theater Company, toured GODSPELL throughout Nova Scotia from October 14, 1974 until it opened at the Sackville Street Theater in November.

MONTREAL

Centaur Theater: Centaur 2 (large stage)

(Artistic director, Maurice Podbrey)

SUMMER (32). By Hugh Leonard. November 20, 1974. Director, Maurice Podbrey; scenery & costumes, Michael Eagan; lighting, Phil Phelan. With Ken James, Angela Clare, Peter Biermann, Antony Parr, Scotty Bloch, Linda Huffman, Les Carlson, Felixe Fitzgerald.

THE DAUGHTER-IN-LAW (32). By D. H. Lawrence. January 2, 1975. Director, Elsa Bolam; designer, Barbra Matis; lighting, Tim Williamson. With Lynne Gorman, Peter Biermann, Joy Coghill, B. J. Gordon, John Peters, Carlo Verdicchio.

BETHUNE (32). By Rod Langley. February 6, 1975 (world premiere). Director, George Plawski; designer, Marti Wright; lighting, Tim Williamson.

Dr. Norman Bethune . . . . . . .Neil Vipond
Frances Bethune . . . . B. J. Gordon
Porter; Montreal Director; Colonel;
    Gen. Neigh . . . . Bob Aarron
Detroit Asst. Director;
    Sorenson . . . . .Martin Kevan
Matron; Detroit Director's Wife;
    Mrs. Penney . . . . Ann Wickham
Miss Scarlet; Trudeau Nurse; Brigit;
    Prostitute . . . . Wenna Shaw
Greely; R. E. Coleman . . . . .Roger Stevens
Detroit Director; Dr. Archibald;
    Gen. Calabras . . . . Patrick Boxill
Detroit Nurse;
    Montreal Matron; Ma . . . . . Joy Coghill

McKenna; Mr. Penney; Kon; Japanese
    Casualty . . . . Walter Massey
Accountant . . . . John Peters
Spanish Guard; Tung . . . . .Chris Li
    Members of Spanish Unit, Press, Soldiers, Medical Assistants: Michael Meagher, Walter Massey, Wenna Shaw, Ann Wickham, Roger Stevens, John Peters.
    The journey of Dr. Norman Bethune ranges over his professional lifetime in Detroit, Trudeau, Edinburgh, Montreal, Spain, China. Two intermissions.

HAMLET (32). By William Shakespeare. March 14, 1975. Director, Barry Boys; scenery & costumes, Michael Eagan; lighting, Vladimir Svetlovsky. With Alan Scarfe, Sara Botsford, William Webster, Dawn Greenhalgh, Patrick Boxill, Jack Wetherall, James Hurdle.

FRANKENSTEIN (32). By Alden Nowlan and Walter Learning; based on Mary Shelley's novel. April 17, 1975. Director, Walter Learning; scenery & costumes, Michael Eagan; lighting, Vladimir Svetlovsky. With Jack Wetherall, David Calderisi, John Peters, Wenna Shaw, Gary Chipps, Antony Parr.

PEOPLE ARE LIVING THERE (32). By Athol Fugard. May 22, 1975. Director, Ted Follows; designer, Barbra Matis; lighting, Tim Williamson. With Joan Orenstein, Steve Whistance-Smith, Douglas Stratton, Wenna Shaw.

Centaur Theater du Maurier Festival of New Plays: Centaur 1 (small stage)

ON THE JOB (32). By David Fennario. January 29, 1975 (world premiere). Director, David Calderisi; scenery & overall design, Felix Mirbt; lighting, Tim Williamson; costumes, Diane Johnston.

Billy . . . . Griffith Brewer
Union Boss . . . . .Alex Bruhanski
Rene . . . . .Edmond Grignon
Jacky . . . . Terry Haig

Gary . . . . Jorma Lindqvist
Jerome . . . . Denis Payne
Shaw . . . . R.D. Reid
Mike . . . . Michael Rudder
Time: The present. Place: A garment factory in Montreal. No intermission.

WOYZECK (32). By Georg Buechner; translated by Henry J. Schmidt. March 12, 1975. Directors, Jean Herbiet, Felix Mirbt; scenery, Michael Eagan; lighting, Pierre-Rene Goupil; costumes, Janet Logan; puppets created by Felix Mirbt. With actors—Janet Barkhouse, Gary Chipps, Dominique Phillmore, John Reymont, Jerome Tiberghien, Vlasta Vrana; puppeteers—Felix Mirbt, David Brewer, Louis Di Bianco, Richard Pochinko, Evan Roper, Michael Rudder.

LENZ (32). By Mike Stott, based on a short story by Georg Buechner. April 9, 1975 (North American premiere). Director, Neil Vipond; designer, Hugh Jones, lighting, Tim Williamson; costumes, Connie Chalke.
Lenz . . . . Domeric Awhile
Oberlin . . . . Jerome Tiberghien

Frau Oberlin . . . . Janet Barkhouse
Scheidecker . . . . Vlasta Vrana
Magda . . . . Dominique Phillimore
Kaufmann . . . . John Reymont
One intermission.

RIVERLISP: BLACK MEMORIES (32). By Frederick Ward; adapted by Jeff Henry and Frederick Ward from Mr. Ward's book. May 8, 1975 (world premiere). Director, Jeff Henry; scenery and costumes, Michael Eagan; lighting, Tim Williamson; original music, Frederick Ward; Negro National Anthem written in 1900 in Jacksonville, Fla., lyrics by James Weldon Johnson, music by Rasomon Johnson.
Purella . . . . Alma Brooks
John Slaughter . . . . Richard Martineau
Musician . . . . Badja Medu
Jimmie Lee . . . . Ronald Salley
Rev. Melvin Mores . . . . Errol Slue
Micah Koch . . . . Martin Swerdlow
Martha . . . . Dietrah Thomas
A play of words, movement and music of life in a black suburb that could be Halifax, Montreal or Louisiana. No intermission.

STRATFORD, ONT.

Stratford Festival: Festival Theater

(Artistic director, Jean Gascon; artistic director designate, Robin Phillips)

THE IMAGINARY INVALID (44). By Molière; translated by Donald M. Frame. June 3, 1974. Director, Jean Gascon; designer, Tanya Moiseiwitsch; lighting, Gil Wechsler; music, Gabriel Charpentier. With William Hutt, Mervyn Blake, Pat Galloway, Pamela Brook, Dawn Greenhalgh, Gordon Thomson, Nicholas Pennell.

PERICLES, PRINCE OF TYRE (21). By William Shakespeare. June 4, 1974. Director, Jean Gascon; designer, Leslie Hurry; lighting, Gil Wechsler; music, Gabriel Charpentier. With Nicholas Pennell, Kenneth Pogue, Edward Atienza, Pamela Brook, William Needles, Martha Henry.

LOVE'S LABOUR'S LOST (41). By William Shakespeare. June 5, 1974. Director, Michael Bawtree; designer, Sam Kirkpatrick; lighting, Gil Wechsler; music, Alan Laing. With Briain Petchey, Nicholas Pennell, Edward Atienza, William Hutt, Dawn Greenhalgh, Pat Galloway, Pam Rogers, Marti Maraden, Pat Bentley-Fisher.

KING JOHN (20). By William Shakespeare. July 23, 1974. Director, Peter Dews; designer, Brian Jackson; lighting, Gil Wechsler; music, Louis Applebaum. With Edward Atienza, Douglas Rain, William Needles, Ian MacDonald, Martha Henry, Powys Thomas.

Stratford Festival: Avon Theater

LA VIE PARISIENNE (77). By Jacques Offenbach; libretto and lyrics by Meilhac and Halévy; translated by Jeremy Gibson. June 27, 1974. Director, Jean Gascon; music director, Raffi Armenian; scenery, Robert Prevost; lighting, Gil Wechsler; costumes, Francois Barbeau. With Gabriel Gascon, Jack Creley, Douglas Campbell, Marilyn Gardner, Denise Fergusson, Barry MacGregor.

Stratford Festival: Third Stage

THE SUMMONING OF EVERYMAN (5). Libretto by Eugene Benson, based on a 16th-century Morality Play; music by Charles Wilson. July 10, 1974. (professional world premiere). Director, Michael Bawtree; designer, Susan Benson; lighting, Michael J. Whitfield; musical director, Raffi Armenian.

Doctor of Theology/Fellowship	George Reinke
God/Goods	Alvin Reimer
Death	Philip May
Devil	Phil Stark
Steward/Monk	Keith Batten
Servants/Monks	Darryl Beschell, Larry Zacharko
Monk/Kindred	Dan Lichti
Cousin	Eleanor Calbes
Paramour	Phyllis Mailing
Everyman	Garnet Brooks
Good Deed	Lynda Neufeld
Faith	Sister Barbara Ianni

One intermission.

THE MEDIUM (5). By Gian Carlo Menotti. July 11, 1974. Director, Michael Bawtree; designer, Susan Benson; lighting, Micháel J. Whitfield; musical director, Raffi Armenian. With Maureen Forrester, Janis Orenstein, Sebastien Dhavernas, Lynda Neufeld, Dan Lichti, Sister Barbara Ianni.

WALSH (21). By Sharon Pollock. July 24, 1974. Director, John Wood; designer, John Ferguson; music & sound, Alan Laing. With Michael Ball, Donna Farron, J. Kenneth Campbell, John Stewart, David Hemblen, Derek Ralston.

READY STEADY GO (22). Play and lyrics by Sandra Jones; music by Berthold Carriere. August 14, 1974. Director, Arif Hasnain; designer, Grant Guy; lighting, Michael J. Whitfield. With Susan Hogan, Robert Thomson, Diane D'Aquila, Hardee T. Lineham, John Bayliss, Terry Judd, J. Kenneth Campbell.

VANCOUVER

The Playhouse Theater Center of British Columbia: Queen Elizabeth Theater

(Artistic director, Christopher Newton)

THE TAMING OF THE SHREW (18). October 7, 1974. Director, Christopher Newton; designer, Cameron Porteous; lighting, Graham Cook. With A. E. Holland, Denise Fergusson, Michael Ball, Janis Nickleson, Eric Donkin, Bernard Hopkins.

HARVEY (18). By Mary Chase. November 11, 1974. Director, Bernard Hopkins; designer, Jack Simon; lighting, Graham Cook. With Denise Fergusson, Leslie Yeo, Doris Chillcott, Janis Nickleson, Guy Robinson, Eric Donkin.

OF THE FIELDS, LATELY (18). By David French. January 13, 1975. Director, Jace van der Veen; designer, Cameron Porteous; lighting, Graham Cook. With Powys Thomas, Florence Paterson, Kenneth Farrell, Barney O'Sullivan.

THE CAUCASION CHALK CIRCLE (18). By Bertolt Brecht. February 17, 1975. Director, Stephen Katz; designer, Mary Keir; lighting, Graham Cook. With Jane Buss, Lally Cadeau, Alex Diakun, Kenneth Farrell, Michael Fletcher, Paul Emile Frappier, Daphne Goldrick, Robert Graham, Terence Kelly, Al Kozlik, Anna-May McKellar, Janis Nickleson.

AND OUT GOES YOU? (18). By Sharon Pollock. March 24, 1975 (world premiere). Director, Christopher Newton; designer, Jack Simon; lighting, Graham Cook.

Goose	Irene Hogan
George	John Gardiner
Premier	Owen Foran
Chairman	Michael Ball
Elizabeth	Lally Cadeau
Frankie	Alex Diakun
Richard	Kenneth Farrell
Bob Handle	Norman Browning

Time and place: Dominion Day, 1935, in Regina. One intermission.

FRANKENSTEIN (18). By Alden Nowlan and Walter Learning. April 21, 1975. Director, Christopher Newton; designer, Cameron Porteous; lighting, Graham Cook. With Norman Browning, Derek Ralston, Jean-Pierre Fournier, B. J. Gordon, Susan Ferley, David Schurmann.

Playhouse Theater Center of British Columbia: Guest Production

TEN LOST YEARS (8). By Jack Winter and Cedric Smith; dramatized from Barry Broadfoot's book: original songs by Cedric Smith. October 28, 1974. Director, George Luscombe. A Toronto Workshop Production.

Playhouse Theater Center of British Columbia: Children's Theater

THE ADVENTURES OF PINOCCHIO (18). Adapted and directed by Alan Laing from the story by Carlo Collodi; music by Alan Laing. December 9, 1974. Designer, Jack Simon. With Tom Wood, Barney O'Sullivan, Denise Fergusson, Christopher Newton, Pat Armstrong, Des Smiley.

Note: Playhouse Holiday toured three productions to schools throughout the province during the fall and spring of 1974–1975. *Waterfall* by Larry Fineberg with music by William Skolnick; directed by David Latham. *Paraphranalia*, directed by Gloria Shapiro-Latham. *Winners* by Brian Friel, directed by Jace van der Veen and Christopher Newton. Scenery and costumes were designed by Glenn MacDonald.

WINNIPEG

Manitoba Theater Center: Main Stage

(Artistic director, Edward Gilbert)

THE SUNSHINE BOYS (27). By Neil Simon. October 18, 1974. Director, John Going; scenery & costumes, Peter Wingate; lighting, Christopher Lester. With Milton Selzer, Tom Pedi, Richard Kline, Max Tapper, Juanita Bethea.

THE CHERRY ORCHARD (27). By Anton Chekhov. November 22, 1974. Director, Edward Gilbert; scenery & costumes, Peter Wingate; lighting, Christopher Lester. With Pat Galloway, William Needles, George Morfogen, Mia Anderson, James Hurdle.

THE BOY FRIEND (27). By Sandy Wilson. January 10, 1975. Director & choreographer, Alan Lund; scenery & costumes, Alistair MacRae; lighting, Christopher Lester; musical director, Victor Davies. With Edda Gburek, Pamela MacDonald, Evelyne Anderson, Barrie Wood, Jack Northmore, Edward Greenhalgh, Janis Dunning.

FORGET-ME-NOT LANE (27). By Peter Nichols. February 14, 1975. Director, Arif Hasnain; scenery & costumes, Peter Wingate; lighting, Kent McKay. With Derek Godfrey, Budd Knapp, Mary Savidge, Irena Mayeska, Brian Tree, Susan Hogan.

RED EMMA, QUEEN OF THE ANARCHISTS (31). By Carol Bolt. March 21, 1975. Director, Edward Gilbert; scenery & costumes, Mark Negin; lighting, Christopher Lester; music composed & directed by Phillip Schreibman. With, Carole Zorro, Francine Baughman, Leon Fermanian, Dixie Seatle.

TRELAWNY OF THE "WELLS" (27). By Arthur Wing Pinero. April 25, 1975. Director, Leon Major; scenery, Murray Laufer; lighting, Donald Acaster; costumes, Hilary Corbett. With Betty Leighton, Domini Blythe, Gerard Parkes, Jennifer Phipps, Claude Bede.

Manitoba Theater Center: Warehouse Theater

OLD TIMES (10). By Harold Pinter. October 30, 1974. Director, Frances Hyland; scenery, lighting & costumes under supervision of staff designers. With W. B. Brydon, Toby Brydon, Zoe Alexander.

ALMIGHTY VOICES (4). Conceived and directed by Clarke Rogers. February 6, 1975. With Judith Elizabeth, Thomas Hauff, Hardee T.

Lineham, Richard Moffatt.

HOSANNA (14). By Michel Tremblay; English translation by John Van Burek and Bill Glassco. February 24, 1975. Director, Michael Mawson; staff designers. With David Calderisi, Michael Hogan.

THE KNACK (12). By Ann Jellicoe. April 23,

1975. Director, Arif Hasnain; designer, Doug McLean. With Rosemary Dunsmore, Clive Endersby, Jan Muszynski, Robert Thomson.

CRABDANCE (12). By Beverley Simons. May

14, 1975. Director, Jeremy Gibson; scenery & costumes, Doug McLean; lighting, Bill Williams. With Helene Winston, Jim Mezon, Dennis Thatcher, Roland Hewgill.

Manitoba Theater Center: Children's Theater

ANDROCLES AND THE LION (40). By Aurand Harris. November 18, 1974. Director, Powys Thomas; designers, Eric Scott, Christopher Lester. With Powys Thomas, Sam Moses, Lewis Gordon, Pam Rogers, Jack Roberts, Don Allison.

THE BRAVE LITTLE TAILOR (16). By Aurand Harris. December 23, 1974. Director, Hutchison Shandro; designer, C. Zak. With Francine Boughman, Brenda Devine, Raymond O'Neill, Duncan Regehr, Pam Rogers and James Timmins.

Note: Manitoba Theater Center also presented a guest production on their main stage of *Ten Lost Years* (6 performances, November 14, 1974) from the book by Barry Broadfoot; dramatized by Jack Winter and Cedric Smith; music by Cedric Smith; director, George Luscombe. Two previous productions of the Theater Center, *Jubalay* and *The Dybbuk* toured Toronto, Waterloo, Niagara-on-the-Lake, Ottawa, Calgary and Montreal from September through November 1974.

DINNER THEATER

Many new establishments and a few new plays

By Francine L. Trevens

Playwright and co-founder of Reader's and Playwright's Theater, Springfield, Mass.

More surely than love, dinner theater is sweeping the country, to the tune of 169 professional theaters (though only 71 are Equity) by the end of the 1974–75 season. This two-scale entertainment—dinner and a show—often has other notes of interest to audiences, such as pre-show singing (and sometimes, pre-show shows!) and/or after-show dancing or revues.

In most dinner theaters you sit at tables set in tiers, like old Roman theaters, to dine and see the show while imbibing beverages served pre-show and during long intermissions. A few dinner theaters have a separate bar room, such as the new-this-year Parkway Casino in Tuckahoe, N.Y. One, the Showboat in Tampa, Fla. allows you to buzz for drinks right from your table.

The dinner theater movement began with Meadowbrook Dinner Theater in Cedar Grove, N.J. a lucky 13 years ago. It then jumped to Virginia, with the original Barn Dinner Theater, a non-Equity house which eventually franchised other dinner theaters (which is why there are so many Barns in the country) in North Carolina, Tennessee, Missouri, Virginia, Georgia and Kentucky.

Meadowbrook sank under the economic crunch this year, and one of the Texas Windmill Dinner Theater chain sank, literally. Built on land fill, in Fort Worth, it just kept settling. There are plans to rebuild another Fort Worth Windmill in the near future. For every dinner theater that closes or goes nonprofessional (such as Four Seasons in Higganum, Conn.) two more Equity houses spring up, such as Sardi's and the Parkway Casino, both in New York State.

The American Dinner Theater Institute was formed in 1972 and gives professional dinner theaters collective bargaining power with unions such as Equity. It holds semi-annual meetings enabling owners and managers to exchange ideas, air grievances and discuss problems. Forty-seven theaters belonged as of May, 1975. Last September, the A.D.T.I. meeting was hosted by Coachlight Dinner Theater in Warehouse Point, Conn. and guests saw a world premiere production with Pat Carroll called *An Evening With Who?* (More new scripts are sought by dinner theaters which, after several years of year-round presentation of comedies and musicals, are running short of plays.) The spring convention was held in Florida, cohosted by Sarasota's Golden Apple and Tampa's Showboat.

Most dinner theaters offer a buffet. The new Harlequin in Santa Ana, Calif. and the Canterbury Dinner Playhouse in Baltimore opt for sit-down dinners. The Chateau de Ville chain in New England fluctuates between buffets and table service.

As for the stage fare, Ray Carlson of the Colorado Music Hall and the Minnesota Music Hall spoke for most dinner theater operators when he said, "Audiences want light and funny shows—no message. They're here to be entertained." Frank Matthews of the very popular Hayloft Dinner Theater in Manassas, Va. reports great success with *The Lion in Winter,* however.

The most popular shows last season, according to other dinner theater owners, included *Never Too Late, Plaza Suite, South Pacific* (a huge success in the South Pacific Dinner Theater in Honolulu) *The Sound of Music, Harvey, Play It Again, Sam* (winner at Firehouse in Nebraska, Limestone Valley in Maryland, and Tiffany's Attic and Waldo Astoria, both in Missouri).

Bob Cummings, Phyllis Diller, Van Johnson, Dorothy Collins, Gig Young, Theodore Bikel and Nanette Fabray were named favorites with the audiences.

Most dinner theaters have about 300 seats, with Grendel's Lair Cafe in Philadelphia the smallest Equity house, reporting in with 200 seats, and Seattle's new-this-season Cirque Dinner Theater (550) and three-year-old Coachlight Dinner Theater in Warehouse Point, Conn. (600) reporting top seating capacities.

Most dinner theaters are converted buildings, ranging from laundries, gambling casinos, and old firehouses, to old theaters. A few new ones have been built specifically as dinner theaters. Most have small stages, thrust or in the round. Some have fanciful names, such as Florida's Once Upon a Stage, New York's An Evening and Oklahoma's Inn of Four Falls. There are package shows booked into some dinner theaters, but most Equity houses have their own producing teams. It is not unusual for directors to leave one company for another, as Cash Baxter, who began with Windmill and now produces for Coachlight and Parkway Casino.

Following are premiere productions which first saw the light of stage in dinner theaters during the 1974–75 season.

SEPARATE CHECKS, PLEASE (8 wks.) Book by Harry Cauley and Sally Jane Heit; music and lyrics by Shirley Grossman. November 5, 1974. Directed by Harry Cauley; scenery, Jay Scott; lighting, Judy Hashagen; musical direction, Michael Howe. With Harry Cauley, Sally Jane Heit.

Limestone Valley Dinner Theater, Cockeysville, Md. and Canterbury Dinner Playhouse, Baltimore.

AN EVENING WITH WHO? (9 wks.) Script co-ordination by Frank Giordano; music by Michael Brown, Peter Tchaikovsky, Nancy Pope and David Heefner. July 16, 1974. Directed by Cash Baxter; scenery, Cash Baxter, David Guthrie; lighting, Claire Carter; costumes, David Guthrie; musical direction, Susan Romann; choreography, John Montgomery. With Pat Carroll, Mary Jo Catlett, Rick Atwell, Connie Shafer, Michael Perrier, Joan Bell, Barbara Hyslop, Sean Nolan, Dan Brown. Coachlight Dinner Theater, Warehouse Pt., Conn.

RED DAWG (10 wks.) Book and lyrics by Leland Ball; music by Arthur B. Rubinstein. May 21, 1975. Directed by Leland Ball; scenery, Wayne Madison; lighting, Tom Truax; costumes, Chris Vesper; musical direction, Milt Bailey; choreography, Leland Ball. Firehouse Dinner Theater, Omaha, Neb.

Sneaky Fitch . . . . Richard Blair
Maroon . . . . Louisa Flaningan
Rakham . . . . Ralph Wainwright
Doc Burch . . . . Dick Solowicz
Mervyn Vale . . . . Thomas Lee Sinclair
Mrs Vale . . . . Justine Johnston
Reverend . . . . Jeff England
Mrs Blackwood . . . . Jean Palmerton
Sheriff . . . . Dick Bonelle

THE SEASON IN LONDON

By Ossia Trilling

Author, critic, lecturer, broadcaster; member of the council of the Critics Circle; vice president of the International Association of Theater Critics; European Editor of *Best Plays*

THIS season the press has been interested less than usual in the excellence or otherwise of the theatrical fare, and more than usual in the threat to the financial stability of the arts as a whole and of the theater in particular, at a time of soaring inflation, mounting production costs, steep rises in the price of materials (though ironically by no means in the level of actors' salaries) and, last but not least, the wayward manipulations of the property developers. Trevor Nunn, managing director of the Royal Shakespeare Company, launched a world-wide appeal for money to save the theater he had taken over from Peter Hall six years before. Later the R.S.C.'s new p.r.o., the New Zealander Des Wilson, let it be known that without a fresh government grant to make up the shortfall in income caused by the 25 per cent rise in costs (in spite of increased box office takings all round), their London home, the Aldwych, would have to be closed, the new theater in the Barbican abandoned, the company disbanded and the tryout seasons at London's The Place cut short—all this at a time when the R.S.C. were gaining new reputations with their foreign tours in Europe, the Americas and other parts of the globe.

Peter Hall himself had found that rising costs and building delays had torpedoed his plans for a gala opening of the National Theater's new complex on Shakespeare's birthday in the presence of Queen Elizabeth II. Even if the National were brought into use piecemeal, as has been suggested, and despite a government guarantee for building costs, the finance for operating costs was as far away as ever. Several regional theaters, even some whose box-office records were being broken, were faced with bankruptcy and closure. The small stage of the Royal Court Theater, the Theater Upstairs, home of much dramatic experiment, was due to be closed for good, in an effort to help clear the outstanding deficit. The incidence of the new Value Added Tax, which anomalously applied to the spoken but not to the written word, had been crippling the theater. In many cases the tax paid was the exact equivalent of the annual loss. Though the Shaftesbury Theater, for instance, had been saved from demolition by property

99

developers and so provided a new home for a revival of *West Side Story,* other theaters still had a threat hanging over them. The campaign to save the Criterion in Piccadilly Circus seems at this writing to have staved off the danger of destruction for the time being only. As the news grows progressively gloomier, so speculation rises as to where to seek the remedy. Hugh Jenkins, Arts Minister in the Labor government, has given a sympathetic hearing to the stories of woe. The administration, he has said, will not allow one of Britain's finest assets and best dollar-earning exports—the theater—to go to the wall. The will, at least, is there. One can only hope that Philistine decisions will not prevail.

Meantime the critic returns to his allotted task of commenting on the theatrical scene without fear or favor, fully aware, as he must be, that too strict a judgement might often make all the difference between the continuing existence of an enterprise and its sudden failure. Fortunately my present task is not as heartbreaking as that of the daily newspaper or radio critics, who often have to rush into snap judgements to satisfy readers or listeners, little caring how their words might affect an artistic endeavor or a financial investment. Nevertheless, I confess myself once again reluctant (even though I have had to comply in the end) to join in the accepted American practise of making critical awards by selecting the best this, the best that, and so forth. I bow to the wishes of the *Best Plays* editor in making my annual list of Trilling's Top Twenty (as they are this year), but I cannot honestly profess any faith in this, or any other, system of priorities. How can I possibly justify the present choice of the three best directors? Still, I suppose that the practise of giving expanded entries to my 20 first choices is one way of pointing to varieties of artistic merit in different theatrical disciplines.

Let me begin, then, with the R.S.C. The repertory system practised since the Aldwych was taken over in 1959 and a permanent company engaged to act in both classical and modern plays at one and the same time has had to be dropped midway through the season for reasons of economy. Previously, Londoners could go to see the remarkable Ian Richardson and compare his very different performances in David Jones's truthfully realistic production of Gorky's *Summerfolk* and in Ronald Eyre's artfully stylized version of Wedekind's *The Marquis of Keith.* This pleasure was denied when Richardson returned from New York in David Jones's poetical rendering of *Love's Labour's Lost.* From then on the R.S.C. joined the ranks of the commercial theaters and the advantage of the repertory system to the actor and to the spectator was denied them both. This may sound like a trivial loss, but by comparison with the R.S.C.'s rival on the South Bank, the National Theater Company at the Old Vic, which has retained the system, the loss seems rather unfair, to say the least.

At the outset it was all hilarity at the Aldwych. This was most notable in Tom Stoppard's latest extravaganza, *Travesties.* Here Peter Wood was able to squeeze every ounce of fun out of the comical situations and out of the witty dialogue; and the chameleon-like performance of John Wood, switching ages from young man to dotard and back to suit the changing time-scale, alone earned universal admiration. Strongest in the Gorky, no doubt, was the teamwork, but in the very large cast I remember with special delight the blend of humor and earnestness in Susan Fleetwood's performance, a mixture that she repeated even more insistently in the role of the man-eating Bertha in Strindberg's *Comrades* at the R.S.C. experimental season at The Place. It was at The Place that one could savor the unique directing talent of the ill-fated Buzz Goodbody when her truncated *Lear* was transferred from The Other Place, the R.S.C.'s tryout stage alongside their regular playhouse in Stratford. Within a few months the 26-year-old director, so full of brilliant promise, was inexplicably to take her own life.

How different, too, were the two performances, both vocally and physically, of Ian McKellen, first as the egregious con-man of the title role in Wedekind's socio-critical satire, and then as the inquiring agnostic in Marlowe's, or rather John Barton's, *Dr. Faustus!*—and again as the weak-willed monarch in Barton's well-judged production of *King John.* The classical plays, transferred with minor changes from Stratford for reasons of economy, showed that the company had lost nothing in the move, even when, as in Trevor Nunn's 110-minute-long production of *Macbeth* without intermission, with Nicol Williamson and Helen Mirren as the sexiest Lady Macbeth I have ever seen, the scenic trappings designed by the R.S.C.'s new associate designer, John Napier, had to be scrapped. No less stimulating was Peter Gill's *Twelfth Night,* with Jane Lapotaire's ravishing Viola, and a self-loving arch-puritan Malvolio in Nicol Williamson, veering uncertainly between a Welsh and a Scottish accent.

The National had two honorable directing failures to its discredit: by Jonathan Miller in both cases. First in *The Marriage of Figaro,* in which his jejune innovations and unmotivated stage business contrasted awkwardly with Patrick Robertson's decor, in which projections switched the venue enchantingly from one exterior to another, as required. The disappointing socio-critical *The Freeway,* a futuristic comedy by Peter Nichols, would probably have thrown an even more inventive director just as badly. Incidentally, Miller scored another low when staging *The Importance of Being Earnest* at Greenwich, with a Lady Bracknell with a strong German accent (!). Shortly afterwards, a press report announced his resignation from the National and his imminent return to full-time medical work.

Thereafter the National went from strength to strength. First came A.E. Ellis's *Grand Manoeuvres,* a witty, sometimes painfully witty, strip-cartoon version of the lamentable Dreyfus scandal, which to me, for one, carried uncomfortable though no doubt unintended echoes of the Watergate affair, and to which Michael Blakemore gave the full theatrical treatment, in the best tradition of the Brechtian parable drama. Then followed one artistic peak after another: Peter Hall's directing triplet, comprising *Happy Days,* by Samuel Beckett, *John Gabriel Borkman* (in each of which Peggy Ashcroft gave a sparklingly fresh and distinctive performance) and Pinter's latest foray into Pirandellian dichotomy, *No Man's Land,* in which every incident seemed equally plausible when witnessed or related, but invariably called in question both the veracity of the teller and the verisimilitude of the action. Ralph Richardson towered like some theatrical giant in each of the last-named, but in the Pinter he was overshadowed by John Gielgud, who managed to disguise his appearance and mien so skilfully that I failed to recognize the actor for a long time after his first entry.

No Man's Land, in a claustrophobic setting designed by John Bury, poses as many puzzles as any Pinter play, but the combination of Gielgud and Richardson —renewing a stage partnership that blossomed so finely in David Storey's *Home* —seems to suggest that there are unplumbed existentialist depths in a rather simple confrontation between two elderly intellectuals with a past to hide and a forbidding future staring each in the face. John Schlesinger's directing debut since becoming associate director at the National was another *tour de force,* since he gave Shaw's *Heartbreak House* a much-needed feeling of nostalgia in the shadow of impending doom and obtained a series of first-rate performances from his company. The Young Vic, taking a leaf out of R.S.C.'s book by helping to fill its depleted coffers from its foreign tours, finally cut the umbilical cord connecting it to the parent theater. Its regular patrons, largely drawn from local audiences, were able to enjoy a long-forgotten farcical comedy by Henry Fielding, nothing less than *Tom Thumb,* played with the high-camp panache that has become the company's signature tune. I only wish the National would employ Ralph Koltai, one of England's foremost stage designers as was made clear by his brilliant set for an otherwise ill-starred version of Schiller's *Die Räuber,* staged at the Round House and partly financed by the Goethe Institute.

Oscar Lewenstein, artistic director and a leading light of the Royal Court Theater's artistic board from the earliest days of the late George Devine's regime, was taken to task, unjustly in my view, by some critics who complained that the repertory he was responsible for had ceased to be adventurous. The same critics seemed to welcome with undue haste his imminent departure to make room for a younger directing team. Nevertheless, the plays put on the Royal Court's two stages confirm that Lewenstein never wavered in his efforts to foster new drama. Examples of this include Mustapha Matura's *Play Mas,* a satire on West Indian mores, which transferred to a commercial theater and even went across famously in a radio version; Edward Bond's *Bingo,* a many-layered drama about the lack of conscience of our society in terms of a fictitious reconstruction of a slice of history, with Gielgud as Shakespeare chopping logic with with Arthur Lowe as Ben Jonson, in a pregnantly written and unforgettably acted duologue; a second play by Caryl Churchill which was also the welcome stage directing debut of John Tydeman from the BBC Drama Department; the British premiere (entitled *Don's Party*) of Australia's foremost young dramatist David Williamson whose later play *What If You Died Tomorrow?,* also about failed Australian eggheads, had been presented for a short West End run by its original Australian troupe earlier in the season; and many other unusually thoughtful new plays by various authors at the Theater Upstairs.

Miller's fiasco at the Greenwich Theater has already been mentioned. An Osborne season there proved almost as frustrating. His own self-indulgent production of *The Entertainer,* with the prodigious comedian Max Wall as Archie Rice, might have improved in the hands of a less self-centered director. His 24th and latest play *The End of Me Old Cigar* meandered wilfully between sex and love without any visible aim in mind. Only Clive Donner's skilled direction of Osborne's faithful stage version of Oscar Wilde's story of hedonism run riot, *The Picture of Dorian Gray,* was at all acceptable. Michael Frayn's topical comedy

Alphabetical Order, about the vagaries of life in the newspaper world, was Hampstead's main contribution to the gaiety of the season and earned a transfer to the West End. The other subsidized stages, like Charles Marowitz's Open Space and Joan Littlewood's Theater Workshop, offered much the same mixture as before. In the former the accent was on German drama; in the latter Gerry Raffles (who died dramatically while on a holiday in France) had stepped down as a protest against inadequate state subsidy, and his place was taken by Ken Hill, prolific author of an unending series of musical entertainments geared to local tastes.

The fringe really came into its own this time. Stephen Poliakoff, a young writer who left his university without graduating in order to write full time, had three new plays staged, two of which, *The Carnation Gang,* about the drug scene, and *Hitting Town,* about an incestuous relationship, left indelible impressions of integrity and skill. Robert Patrick's *Kennedy's Children,* a series of monologues about the dismal post-Kennedy era, effectively staged by Clive Donner at a "pub-theater", was the first fringe production to be promoted to the West End. At one time Patrick had four plays in town. David Hare's adaptation of William Hilton's novel about the Communist revolution in peasant China, *Fanshen,* was given an impressive airing in a collective staging supervised by William Gaskill at the new open-stage theater of the Institute of Contemporary Arts. Here, too, the R.S.C. transferred a collectively-organized drama, supervised by Mike Leigh, from Stratford's The Other Place. Before concluding with a note on the commercial stage, I should briefly mention the travelling productions of Shakespeare's first three Henry plays done on the open stage of the Round House by Prospect Theater; the Brazilian troupe, on the same stage, of 15 stark naked players in Victor Garcia's idiosyncratic synthesis of The Creation and The Fall, using texts by Calderon translated into Portuguese (called *Autos Sacramentales*); and the four-week-long World Theater Season, which, if it did nothing else, no doubt wakened some uninformed British theatergoers out of a needlessly complacent state of artistic insularity.

And so to the commercials: musicals that included *Cole* (at the Mermaid, commercial not in form or intent, but *de facto*), the sad story of the Beatles, *The Black Mikado, The Good Companions, Jack The Ripper, A Little Night Music, Hans Andersen, Cinderella* (with the cluelessly sweet Twiggy miscast in the title role) and *Jeeves,* all box-office hits except the last two. Straight plays with memorable acting performances included the inhuman *A Family and a Fortune,* with Alec Guinness playing an Edwardian Englishman with a gentleman's exterior but a heart of inexorable cruelty, and with Rachel Kempson playing a scatterbrained matron with a touching deathbed scene to give her humanity; Barrie's civilized turn-of-the-century drama of politics and women's secret emancipation, *What Every Woman Knows,* starring Dorothy Tutin; *The Dame of Sark,* as contrived a political thriller as only William Douglas Home knows how to write, with first Celia Johnson and then Anna Neagle lording it with equal imperturbability over the servants and the nasty Nazis; Alan Ayckbourn's *The Norman Conquests,* a box-office "smasheroo" thanks to the ingenuity of the trilogy, the genuineness of the characterizations of suburban types, and the directing mastery of Eric Thompson; *The Tempest,* in an indifferent production from the regions, but ennobled by Paul Scofield's magisterial Prospero; Anthony Shaffer's teasing thriller *Murderer,* a tailor-made vehicle for Robert Stephens's histrionic versatility; and a whole series of slick English and American trivia as shop-window displays for the talents of Alfred Marks, Elaine Stritch, Edward Woodward, Hayley Mills, Brian Rix, Ray Cooney, you name 'em, we have 'em.

Highlights of the London Season

Selected and compiled by Ossia Trilling, who has designated his choice of the 20 best productions of the 1974–75 season. These 20 appear within the listing in expanded entries, with full casts and credits.

TRILLING'S TOP TWENTY
(listed from left to right in the order of their opening dates)

Travesties	*Play Mas*	*The Norman Conquests*
Bingo	*John, Paul, George,*	*Summerfolk*
	Ringo . . . And Bert	
Dr. Faustus	*Kennedy's Children*	*The Marquis of Keith*
Grand Manoeuvres	*Hans Andersen*	*John Gabriel Borkman*
Twelfth Night	*Heartbreak House*	*Alphabetical Order*
Murderer	*Hitting Town*	*A Little Night Music*
No Man's Land	*Love's Labour's Lost*	

OUTSTANDING PERFORMANCES

JOHN WOOD as Henry Carr in *Travesties*	TOM COURTENAY as Norman in *The Norman Conquests*	IAN MC KELLEN as Dr. Faustus in *Dr. Faustus*
JOHN GIELGUD as Shakespeare in *Bingo*	PAUL SCOFIELD as Prospero in *The Tempest*	PAUL ROGERS as Major Henry in *Grand Manoeuvres*
PEGGY ASHCROFT as Ella Rentheim in *John Gabriel Borkman*	RALPH RICHARDSON as John Gabriel Borkman in *John Gabriel Borkman*	COLIN BLAKELY as Captain Shotover in *Heartbreak House*
NICOL WILLIAMSON as Macbeth in *Macbeth*	DINSDALE LANDEN as John in *Alphabetical Order*	ROBERT STEPHENS as Norman in *Murderer*
ALEC GUINNESS as Dudley in *A Family and a Fortune*	JOHN GIELGUD as Spooner in *No Man's Land*	IAN RICHARDSON as Berowne in *Love's Labour's Lost*

OUTSTANDING DIRECTORS

DAVID JONES *Summerfolk*	MICHAEL BLAKEMORE *Grand Manoeuvres*	PETER HALL *John Gabriel Borkman*

OUTSTANDING DESIGNERS

PATRICK ROBERTSON *The Marriage of Figaro*	RALPH KOLTAI *The Highwaymen*	JOHN BURY *No Man's Land*

OUTSTANDING NEW BRITISH PLAYS

(D)—Playwright's London debut. Figure in parentheses is number of performances; plus sign (+) indicates play was still running on June 1, 1975.

TRAVESTIES by Tom Stoppard. Produced by the Royal Shakespeare Company at the Aldwych Theater. Opened June 10, 1974. (39+ in repertory)

Henry Carr	John Wood
Tristan Tzara	John Hurt
James Joyce	Tom Bell
Vladimir Ilyich Ulyanov (Lenin)	Frank Windsor
Bennett	John Bott
Gwendolen Carr	Maria Aitken
Cecily Carruthers	Beth Morris
Nadezhda Krupskaya	Barbara Leigh-Hunt

Directed by Peter Wood; design, Carl Toms; musical numbers staged by William Chappell; music arranged & composed by Grant Hossack.

An allusive comedy, crammed with musical gags, verbal jokes, and literary, political, pseudo-historical, and philosophical ideas, about the none too reliable reminiscences of a retired British diplomat who ostensibly rubbed shoulders in Zurich during World War I with Lenin, Joyce and Tzara. One intermission. Won the *Evening Standard* best comedy award.

Robert Powell replaced John Hurt, John Quentin replaced Tom Bell, Harry Towb replaced Frank Windsor, Meg Wynn replaced Maria Aitken, Frances Cuka replaced Barbara Leigh-Hunt 5/29/75.

THE SEA ANCHOR by E. A. Whitehead. A Dublin foursome on the quayside reveal the sexual violence below the surface. With Peter Armitage, Marjorie Yates, Alison Steadman, David Daker. (21)

PLAY MAS by Mustapha Matura. Produced by the Royal Court Theater at the Royal Court Theater. Opened July 16, 1974. (Closed August 3, 1974) (19) Later produced by Eddie Kulukundis, Michael White and the English Stage Company in association with Veronica Flint-Shipman and transferred to the Phoenix Theater. Opened August 21, 1974. (Closed September 14, 1974) (48)

Ramjohn Gokool	Stefan Kalipha
Samuel	Rudolph Walker
Miss Gokool	Mercia Mansfield
Frank	Norman Beaton
Mr. McKay	Charles Pemberton
Doctor	Tommy Eytle
Mrs. Banks	Lucita Lijertwood
Mr. Tate	Frank Singuineau
Mr. Lyle	Robert La Bassiere
Sergeant	Trevor Thomas
Mrs. Samuel	Mona Hammond
Chuck Reynolds	Ed Bishop

Directed by Donald Howarth; design, Douglas Heap; costume design, Peter Minshall; lighting, Nick Chelton.

Act I: The Gokools' tailor shop in Port-of-Spain, Trinidad. Act II: The office of the Chief of Police, some years later.

A colorful, bitter comedy in a Trinidadian setting about life in a multi-racial society before independence and the awful turn it takes after power has fallen into the hands of the semi-educated natives who have been freed from colonialism. Won the 1974 *Evening Standard* award for the most promising playwright.

THE NORMAN CONQUESTS by Alan Ayckbourn, comprising *Table Manners, Living Together,* and *Round and Round the Garden.* Produced by Michael Codron at the Globe Theater. Opened August 1, 1974. (each play 116+ in repertory)

Norman	Tom Courtenay
Tom	Michael Gambon
Sarah	Penelope Keith
Annie	Felicity Kendal
Reg	Mark Kingston
Ruth	Bridget Turner

Directed by Eric Thompson; design, Alan Pickford; lighting, Nick Chelton.

Table Manners, The Dining Room—Act I, Scene 1: Saturday, 6 P.M. Scene 2: Sunday, 9 A.M. Act II, Scene 1: Sunday, 8 P.M. Scene 2: Monday, 8 A.M. *Living Together,* The Sitting Room—Act I, Scene 1: Saturday, 6.30 P.M. Scene 2: Saturday, 8 P.M. Act II, Scene 1: Sunday, 9 P.M. Scene 2: Monday, 8 A.M. *Round and Round the Garden,* The Garden—Act I, Scene 1: Saturday, 5.30 P.M. Scene 2: Saturday, 9 P.M. Act II, Scene 1: Sunday, 11 A.M. Scene 2: Monday, 9 A.M.

Trilogy about the affairs of the heart of the eponymous hero, seen from simultaneous but different viewpoints, and his womanizing ways with his two sisters-in-law Annie and Sarah and his wife Ruth. Each play is "seen as the off-stage of another" in the trilogy. Plans for a dirty weekend with Annie are thwarted by Sarah, who unexpectedly prepares to take her place, as Norman wheedles his way back into Ruth's favor, only to be denounced by all three at the end.

Originally performed at the Library Theater, Scarborough, 6/16/73 in alternating repertory and then at the Greenwich Theater, London, 5/8/74, 5/20/74 and 6/5/74, closing 6/29/74. The three plays re-opened in the West End 8/1/74 at the Globe Theater and won both the *Plays and Players* best new play and the *Evening Standard* best play awards.

BINGO by Edward Bond. Produced by the Royal Court Theater and Eddie Kulukundis at the Royal Court Theater. Opened August 14, 1974. (Closed October 5, 1974) (53)

Shakespeare . . . . John Gielgud
Old man . . . . John Barrett
Judith . . . . Gillian Martell
Young woman . . . . Yvonne Edgell
Old woman . . . . Hilda Barry
William Combe . . . . Ewan Hooper
Son . . . . Oliver Cotton
Joan . . . . Joanna Tope
Jerome . . . . Derek Fuke
Wally . . . . Paul Jesson
Ben Jonson . . . . Arthur Lowe
    Directed by Jane Howell and John Dove; design, Hayden Griffin; lighting, Nick Chelton.
    Part One—One: Garden. Two: Garden. Three: Hill. Part Two—Four: Inn. Five: Fields. Six: Room. Setting: Warwickshire 1615 & 1616.
    Dramatic parable about the cruelty and apathy of human beings and the responsibility of the artist in society in the guise of a dramatic portrait of Shakespeare towards the end of his growingly disillusioned days, when the greed and injustice that drove him from London follow him to Stratford and precipitate his suicide.
    Bingo, with a different cast, was originally premiered in the same production at the Northcott Theater, Exeter, 11/14/73.

GRAND MANOEUVRES by A. E. Ellis (D). Produced by The National Theater at the Old Vic. Opened December 3, 1974. (Closed February 13, 1975) (24 in repertory)
Maj. Henry . . . . Paul Rogers
Capt. Lauth . . . . Malcolm Reid
Capt. Matton; Cousin Gustave . Harry Waters
Maj. du Paty de Clam . . . . Roland Curram
Maj. Picquart . . . . Edward de Souza
Gen. Mercier . . . . Mark Dignam
Gen. Saussier; Cavaignac . . . Antony Brown
Gen. de Boisdeffre . . . . . Edward Jewesbury
Gen. Gonse . . . . Lionel Murton
Col. Maurel . . . . John Bown
Lt. Col. Echemann . . . . Bill Bailey
Maj. Florentin . . . . Philip Trewinnard
Deniel; Dupuy; Steevens . . Alex McCrindle
Col. Jouast; Uncle Jules . . . . Harry Lomax
Maj. de Breon . . . . Malcolm Reid
Member of 1899 Court Martial   Ray Edwards
Capt. Dreyfus . . . . . . Alan MacNaughtan
Lucie Dreyfus . . . . Dona Martyn
Jeanne Dreyfus . . . . Nicola Cave
Pierre Dreyfus . . . . John Relevy
Bertulus; Barrès . . . . David Graham
Demange . . . . James Hayes
Labori; Anti-Drefusard . . . . David Bradley
Juarès; Maj. Esterhazy . . . Peter Whitbread
Minister; Lemercier Picard . . . . . Alan Hay
Colonel von Schwartzkoppen . . . Alan Brown
Aide . . . . Robert O'Mahoney
Mme. Bastian . . . . Freda Jeffries
Aunt Louise . . . . Jennifer Tudor
Cousin Emile; Bertillon . . . . Michael Stroud
Eugenie . . . . Mel Churcher
Dreyfusard . . . . Pip Miller

Jean Paul . . . . Stuart Knee
Maids . . . Veronica Sowerby, Sara van Beers
M. Lagrange . . . . Michael Mara
Court Official . . . . Chris Tranchell
Assassin . . . . Martin Bax
Gribelin; Innkeeper . . . . . . Peter Schofield
Wife . . . . Catherine Harding
Son . . . . Andrew Dunford
Drummers . Laurie Morgan, Lennie Bresslaw
Flautist . . . . Geoffrey Young
Trumpeter . . . . Norman Wells
    Directed by Michael Blakemore; scenery & lighting, John Bury; costumes, Deirdre Clancy; movement, Sue Lefton; music, Marc Wilkinson.
    A neo-Brechtian, epic treatment of the story of the notorious scandal in which the French Army and the French establishment conspired to implicate an innocent Army officer of the Jewish faith in an espionage plot in an effort to cover up the crimes and misdemeanors of which high-ranking officials and others were in fact guilty, and their continual efforts to exploit anti-semitic prejudice and chauvinist hatred in pursuit of their cover-up schemes. Two intermissions.

ALPHABETICAL ORDER by Michael Frayn. Produced by Michael Codron by arrangement with the Hampstead Theater Club at the May Fair Theater. First presented at the Hampstead Theater Club on March 11, 1975. (Closed April 5, 1975) (34) Opened at the May Fair Theater April 8, 1975. (89+)
Leslie . . . . Barbara Ferris
Geoffrey . . . . A. J. Brown
Arnold . . . . James Cossins
John . . . . Dinsdale Landen
Lucy . . . . Billie Whitelaw
Nora . . . . June Ellis
Wally . . . . Bernard Gallagher
    Directed by Michael Rudman; design, Alan Tagg; costumes, Frances Haggett; lighting, Howard Eldridge.
    The play is set in the library of a provincial newspaper office. Two girls, the librarian and her newly-arrived assistant, tackle the threatening crisis in their private and professional lives each in her own way. The newcomer takes command and looks like saving the situation. One intermission.

HITTING TOWN by Stephen Poliakoff. Produced by the Bush Theater at the Bush Theater. Opened March 27, 1975. (Closed May 4, 1975) (33)
Clare . . . . Judy Monahan
Ralph . . . . James Aubrey
Waitress . . . . Lynne Miller
    Directed by Tim Fywell; design, Angela Pascoe.
    Long one-acter about an uprooted provincial student of architecture who calls on his lonely sister in a big city and how the bleakness and seeming pointlessness of their lives throws them

together into an unprepared-for incestuous relationship.

FANSHEN by David Hare. Adapted from William Hinton's book about the impact of the Revolution on a Chinese village. With the Joint Stock Theater Group. (18)

NO MAN'S LAND by Harold Pinter. Produced by the National Theater at the Old Vic. Opened April 23, 1975. (18+ in repertory)
Hirst . . . . Ralph Richardson
Spooner . . . . John Gielgud
Foster . . . . .Michael Feast
Briggs . . . . Terence Rigby
Directed by Peter Hall; design & lighting, John Bury.

A typically Pinterish comedy of menace, intrusion of privacy, and the illusory frontier between appearance and reality, in which an elderly, rich, and alcoholic writer, looked after by two young, ill-mannered ruffians, entertains, somewhat against his will, an equally elderly, but shabby, minor poet, with a gift of the gab, and a persuasive manner, who overstays his welcome but appears unable either to tear himself away or to be sent packing. One intermission.

POPULAR ATTRACTIONS

THE NATURAL CAUSE by Robert Holman (D). The tragic downfall of a newly-married working-class lad. With Natasha Pyne. (24)

A MIDSUMMER NIGHT'S DREAM by William Shakespeare. Open Air Theater production. With Nicky Henson, Linda Thorson. (64)

THE TOOTH OF CRIME by Sam Shepard. New rock version of American Londoner's drama of gangsterland where pop culture holds sway. With Mike Pratt, Richard O'Brien, Diane Langton. (37)

THE ODDITY by Clive Stuart. A Musical loosely based on Homer's *Odyssey*. With Vicky Silva, Sally Bentley. (21)

LENZ by Mike Stott. Adapted by the author and his cast from Georg Buechner's story of the German writer. With Simon Rouse, Peter Tilbury. (25)

UNDER MILK WOOD by Dylan Thomas. Dolphin Theater Company revival of stage adaptation of famous radio play. With Frances Cuka, Roy Holder. (42)

HAIR by Gerome Ragni and James Rado. Revival of long-running British version of American folk musical. With Gary Hamilton, Sonja Kristina. (110)

JACK THE RIPPER by Ron Pember and Denis de Marne. A pseudo-Victorian melodrama, in a simulated music-hall setting, purporting to identify the mysterious murderer of history. With Terese Stevens, Howard Southern. (251)

THE MAN WHO KNEW HE WAS JESUS CHRIST by Michael G. Jackson. A send-up of modern Britain in pastiche New Testament terms. With Linda Polan, Tony Doyle. (25)

OTHER PEOPLE by Mike Stott. A farcical skit

on the domestic life and sexual mores of middle-class English people. With Ian Holm, Julian Curry. (28)

THE 3p OFF OPERA by Billy Colvill, with songs and music by Murray Head. An old theme updated to the 1970's acquisitive society in London's East End. With Pamela Moiseiwitsch, the author. (52)

COLE, an entertainment based on the words and music of Cole Porter, devised by Benny Green and Alan Strachan. With Una Stubbs, Bill Kerr. (326)

BLOOMSBURY by Peter Luke. The private life of Virginia Woolf, Lytton Strachey and the famous Bloomsbury set. With Daniel Massey, Yvonne Mitchell, Moyra Fraser. (53)

THE GOOD COMPANIONS by André Previn, Johnny Mercer and Ronald Harwood. Musical version of J. B. Priestley's 1930s novel about a concert-party tour. With Judi Dench, John Mills. (261)

HEIDI by Robert Keane. Children's musical based on Johanna Spyri's original story. With Margaret O'Leary, Philip Doghan, Jacob Witkin. (86)

THE GOLDEN PATHWAY by John Harding and John Burrows. Sheffield Crucible Studio Theater production about the post-war generation growing up. With Mark Wing-Davey, Maggie McCarthy, the authors. (45)

SHERLOCK'S LAST CASE by Matthew Lang. A new view of the old detective. With Julian Glover, Peter Bayliss, Kate O'Mara. (34)

THE SACK RACE by George Ross and Campbell Singer. A comedy-thriller set in the world of big business. With Michael Denison, Dulcie Gray, Terence Langdon, Anthony Nicholls. (20)

THE TWO NOBLE KINSMEN by William Shakespeare and John Fletcher. An Open Air Theater production; first London revival since 1928. With David Dodimead, Martin Potter, Frances Viner. (45)

THE COUNT OF MONTE CRISTO by Ken Hill. Adapted from the Alexandre Dumas classic, with music, by Ian Armit, based on contemporary French folk songs. With Toni Palmer, Bill Zappa. (28)

BULLSHOT CRUMMOND by Derek Cunningham and the company. A satire on the famous 1920s thriller series by Sapper. With the Low Moan Spectacular Company. (27)

"X" by Barry Reckord. A professor and his daughter talk and do sex. With Terence Frisby, Libba Davies. (48)

JOHN, PAUL, GEORGE, RINGO . . . AND BERT by Willy Russell (D). Produced by Robert Stigwood and Michael Codron at the Lyric Theater. Opened August 15, 1974. (332+)

Bert	George Costigan
John Lennon	Bernard Hill
Paul McCartney	Trevor Eve
George Harrison	Phillip Joseph
Ringo Starr	Anthony Sher

Brian Epstein;
    1st Ballroom Manager . . . Robin Hooper
Porter, Hitler, Party Guest, London Theater Manager, Foreman, Allan Klein, Phone Man—Nick Stringer; Sam Platt, Teddy Boy, Cavern Bouncer, Party Guest, Photographer, Diplomat, Apple Bouncer, Promoter—Barry Woolger; Bandsman, Milk Float Driver, Teddy Boy, Party Guest, Photographer, Waiter, TV Electrician—Dick Haydon; Bandsman, Teddy Boy, Party Guest, Photographer, Embassy Aide, TV Electrician—Ian Jentle; Tiny Tina, Ballroom Chick, Party Guest, Embassy Debutante, Linda McCartney, Agent—Luan Peters; Titular 1, Alice, Party Guest, Embassy Guest, Makeup Girl—Elizabeth Estensen; Titular 2, Ballroom Chick, Party Guest, Kid, American Woman in Embassy, Yoko, Film Lady—Linda Beckett; Titular 3, Ballroom Chick, Mrs. Starkey, Cafe Washer-Up, Party Guest, Diplomat's Wife, TV Reporter—Valerie Lilley; Musicians—Barbara Dickson (singer and pianist), Robert Ash, Terry Canning.
    Directed by Alan Dossor; design, Graham Barkworth; sound, David Collison; lighting, Mick Hughes.
    Musical documentary in flashback form and with the use mostly of original recordings of the Beatles' music that tells the story of the rise and fall of the legendary group and how their partnership was soured and destroyed by the commercial pressures of the pop-music world. Originally performed at the Everyman Theater,

Liverpool, 5/15/74, it won both the *Plays and Players* best new musical play and the *Evening Standard* best musical play awards. One intermission.

MAGNIFYCENCE by Thomas Skelton, adapted by John Duncan. Jazzed-up musical version of 16th century morality. With the National Youth Theater Company. (17)

ROMEO AND JULIET by William Shakespeare. National Theater's Mobile Production. With Veronica Quilligan, Peter Firth (later Michael Kitchen). (6+ in repertory)

LET'S GET LAID by Sam Cree. Revised version of Paul Raymond's pornographic titillater, The Bed. With John Inman, Jack Haig, Jenny Kenna, Fiona Richmond. (468+)

THE BEDWINNER by Tony Lesser. The domestic and professional roles of a married couple exchanged. With Roland Culver, John Pertwee, Lynda Baron. (45)

DR. FAUSTUS by Christopher Marlowe. Adapted by John Barton with the cast. Produced by the Royal Shakespeare Company at the Aldwych Theater. Opened September 5, 1974. (Closed January 1, 1975) (37 in repertory)

Lucifer	Clement McCallin
Beelzebub	Richard Mayes
Mephistophilis	Emrys James
Faustus	Ian McKellen
Wagner	Terence Wilton

1st Scholar; Frederick;
    Duke of Vanholt . . . Malcolm Armstrong
2d Scholar; Charles V . . . . . . Leon Tanner
3d Scholar; Benvolio . . . . . Julian Barnes
Old Man; Duke of Saxony . . . John Boswell
Duchess of Vanholt . . . . Jean Gilpin
Countess . . . . Meriel Brook
Horse-dealer . . . . Denis Holmes
Musician . . . . John Riley
    Directed by John Barton; design, Michael Annals; puppets designed & made by Jennifer Carey; music, Guy Woolfenden; lighting, Michael Murray.
    The present version of *Dr. Faustus*, based on an earlier version adapted by John Barton and performed at Stratford-upon-Avon in 1974, contains many cuts and some 550 lines taken from the English translation, printed in 1592, of the German "Faust-Book", called *The History of the Damnable Life and Deserved Death of Dr. Faustus*, the so-called "English Faust-Book". First seen in Nottingham, Newcastle and at the Edinburgh Festival, 1974. One intermission.
    Jeffery Dench replaced Clement McCallin 9/7/74.

USHER by David Campton Adapted from Edgar Allen Poe's *The Fall of the House of*

Usher. With Andrew Hawkins, Barbara Berkery. (20)

HENRY IV, Part 1 by William Shakespeare. New production by the Prospect Theater Company. With Edgar Wreford, Paul Hardwick, Tim Hardy, Timothy Dalton. (14+ in repertory)

HENRY IV, Part 2 by William Shakespeare. New production by the Prospect Theater Company. With Timothy Dalton, Sylvia Coleridge, Helen Cotterill, John Warner, Paul Hardwick. (11+ in repertory)

A BIT BETWEEN THE TEETH by Michael Pertwee. A bachelor jeweller and his horny partner get into a marital entanglement. With Brian Rix, Jimmy Cogan, Vivienne Johnson, Donna Reading. (156)

ACTION by Sam Shepard. World premiere of American's 55-minute-long Beckettian one-acter on the purpose of life as seen by an odd mid-American foursome at their sparse Christmas dinner. With Stephen Rea, Stephen Moore, Jennie Stoller, Jill Richards. (24)

RICHARD II by William Shakespeare. 1974 Stratford Festival production with alternating actors in the title role. With Ian Richardson, Richard Pascoe, Denis Holmes, Julian Barnes, Tony Church. (36 in repertory)

KONG LIVES by George Byatt (D). The revenge of a lonely woman in a Glasgow slum. With Douglas Heard, Cherie Lunghi, Irene Sunters. (22)

THE FREEWAY by Peter Nichols. A jam on the Freeway of the future symbolizes the mess Britain is in today. With Irene Handl, Joan Hickson, Rachel Kempson, Paul Rogers, Graham Crowden. (30 in repertory)

YEAR ONE by Keith Dorland (D). Disaster overtakes a group of exiles from a tyranny. With Maggie Stride, Vass Anderson. (On a double-bill with THE PICTURE—originally titled *The Portrait*—by Eugene Ionesco. With Andrew Hawkins, R. J. Bell.) (23)

THE LAND OF THE DINOSAURS by Ken Hill, with music by Ian Armit. A satire on present-day civilization for children of all ages. With Geoffrey Freshwater, Larry Dann, Eamon Boland. (58)

THE TAMING OF THE SHREW by William Shakespeare. James Roose-Evans's production for the Dolphin Theater Company. With Nicky Henson, Susan Hampshire, Susan Penhaligon, Peter Bayliss, Barrie Rutter. (48)

THERE GOES THE BRIDE by Ray Cooney and John Chapman. A knock on the head sends the father of a bride into a Walter Mitty world. With Bernard Cribbins, (later Ray Cooney), Peggy Mount (later Joyce Heron), Trudi van Doorn (later Helen Gill). (287+)

THE HAMMERS by Alan Plater, adapted by Billy Colvill. The story of Ray and West Ham, his favorite football club. With Mary Sheen, Maurice Colbourne. (35)

THE TRAGEDY OF TRAGEDIES, OR THE LIFE AND DEATH OF TOM THUMB THE GREAT by Henry Fielding. Young Vic revival of 18th century classical satire in its first professional viewing since 1745. With Peter O'Farrell, Alfred Lynch, Christopher Timothy, Jennifer Guy, Zoë Wanamaker. (17 in repertory)

THE GREAT CAPER by Ken Campbell. A visionary science-fiction drama of the world's plight. With Warren Mitchell, Richard O'Callaghan, Lisa Harrow, the author. (43)

THE LOONEYS by John Antrobus. Who is normal, the seemingly mad or the patently sane? With Leonard Rossiter, Colin Welland. (26)

THE TAMING OF THE SHREW by William Shakespeare, adapted by Caroline Eves. Theater Workshop Production for Young People. With Robert McIntosh, Yvonne Edgell, Marcia King, Geoffrey Freshwater. (20)

LORD NELSON LIVES IN LIVERPOOL, 8 by Philip Martin (D). An English-born West Indian boy's brush with the law and English society. With Richard Forde, Jane Antony, Alan Igbon. (21)

THE DAME OF SARK by William Douglas Home. Drama of a British ruler under Nazi occupation. With Celia Johnson (later Anna Neagle), Tony Britton, Alan Gifford. (281)

RIALTO PROM by Angela Wye (D). The revenge of the female victims of sexual inequality. With Ann Mitchell, Jacquie Cook. (29)

THE MALE OF THE SPECIES by Alun Owen. The love life of a girl with three suitors, all played by the same actor. With Edward Woodward, Donald Pickering, Michele Dotrice. (62)

LEAR by William Shakespeare. London transfer of Buzz Goodbody's shortened version of KING LEAR for the Royal Shakespeare Company's The Other Place in Stratford. With Tony Church, Sheila Allen, Lynette Davies, Louise Jameson, David Suchet. (12 in repertory)

MARCHING SONG by John Whiting. Greenwich Theater revival of late dramatist's early play. With Kenneth Haigh, Tony Sibbald, John Welsh, Gwen Watford, Cleo Sylvestre. (25)

THE PAY OFF by William Fairchild. Blackmailing gang upsets the well-laid tax-evasion plans of a well-heeled foursome, if appearances can be trusted. With Nigel Patrick, Dulcie Grey, Peter Sallis. (222+)

CRETE AND SERGEANT PEPPER by John Antrobus. Young Vic revival of absurdist comedy about British army behavior, first seen at the Royal Court Theater. With Jimmy Thompson, Alfred Lynch, Harold Innocent. (14 in repertory)

WHAT EVERY WOMAN KNOWS by James M. Barrie. Revival of famous 1908 Scottish drama of a politician's ambitious wife. With Dorothy Tutin, Peter Egan, Dorothy Reynolds, Clive Morton, Andrew Crawford. (212)

CLEVER SOLDIERS by Stephen Poliakoff. The fortunes of a pre-World War I schoolboy at school and on the battlefield. With Simon Ward, Michael Feast, Sheila Ruskin. (30)

HENRY V by William Shakespeare. Prospect Theater Company production. In repertory with HENRY IV, Parts 1 & 2. (10+ in repertory)

AN EVENING WITH HINGE AND BRACKET. Hilda Bracket and Dr. Evadne Hinge perform their favorite songs from Gilbert & Sullivan. With Perri St. Claire, George Logan, Edward Brayshaw. (174+)

DRACULA by Bram Stoker, adapted by Ken Hill. English milieu and setting for the Theater Workshop version of the famous melodrama. With Derek Fuke (later Sylvester McCoy), Toni Palmer, Valerie Walsh, Larry Dann, Kent Baker. (59)

THE ENTERTAINER by John Osborne. Greenwich Theater revival of successful backstage comedy directed by the author. With Max Wall in the role created by Laurence Olivier. (25)

REMEMBER THE TRUTH DENTIST by Heathcote Williams. A revue that takes a sidelong glance at man's frivolities today. With Paola Dionisotti, Philip Donaghy, David Hill. (45)

SEVEN DAYS TO DOOMSDAY by Terrance Dicks. Science-fiction thriller based on the BBC-TV series about Dr. Who and the Daleks, in which the heroes do battle with the deadly enemy on the mysterious planet Karn. With Trevor Martin (Dr. Who), Wendy Padbury, Patsy Dermott, James Mathews. (46)

HANS ANDERSEN, music and lyrics by Frank Loesser and Marvin Laird, book by Beverley Cross, based on the production of Samuel Goldwyn. Produced by Harold Fielding in association with Louis Benjamin at the London Palladium. Opened December 19, 1974. (190+)

Hans Andersen	Tommy Steele
Schoolmaster Meisling	Bob Todd
Louise Meisling	Lila Kaye
Eva	Sarah Bennett
Otto Pedersen	Milo O'Shea
Colonel Guldberg	Willoughby Goddard
Max Klaus	Geoffrey Toone
Jenny Lind	Colette Gleeson
Ballet Master	Paddy McIntyre
1st Dresser	Carolyn Gray
2d Dresser	Jean Morton
Midshipman	Christopher Hall/ Joshua Le Touzel/Christopher Morris
Coachman	Geoffrey Saunders
Lucy	Geraldine Long
King Christian	Wallace Stephenson
Queen	Janet Nelson
Swindler	Gary Downie
Player King	Albin Pahernik
Player Queen	Francesca Lucy

Dancers: Marc Arnall, John Asquith, Maria Baxter, Sarah Bennett, Gary Downie, Terry Etheridge, Miranda Fellows, Karin Gaeng, Garry Ginivan, Rita Henderson, Suzanne Hywel, Geraldine Long, Francesca Lucy, Dawn MacDonald, Paddy McIntyre, Albin Pahernik, Melanie Parr, Graham Tudor Phillips, Trevor Willis, Kay Zimmerman.

Singers: Richard Ashley, Angela Belair, Rosemary Butler, Norma Dunbar, Chris Dyson, Kurt Ganzl, Russell Grant, Carolyn Gray, Patricia Hall, Thomas Kingsley, Shirley Anne Lewis, Jean Morton, Janet Nelson, Geoffrey Saunders, Wallace Stephenson, Geoff Thomas.

Children: Karen Baker, Kathleen Barnett, Diane Gould, Tracy Grant, Clive Griffin, Suzanne Hart, Michelle Julien, Dawn Marvier, Mark Praid, Joanne Willcocks, Nicola Wildman.

Directed by Freddie Carpenter; design, Tim Goodchild; choreography, Gillian Lynne; lighting, Nick Chelton.

Place: Denmark in the 1830s.

A popular reconstruction, sentimentally interpreted with little regard for history, and with the use of several of the songs immortalized by the Danny Kaye movie on the subject, of the life of the Danish carpenter's apprentice who took the traditional "rags to riches" road to fame as Denmark's world-famous story-teller, but failed to win the hand of Jenny Lind, the Swedish singer who befriended him and helped him on his way. One intermission.

THREE FARCES by George Bernard Shaw. (*The Dark Lady of the Sonnets*; *The Music Cure*; *Passion, Poison and Petrifaction*) Misha Williams's revival at the New End Theater. With Sandra Freeman, David Soames, David Delve, Eliza Ward. (26)

CINDERELLA by Frank Hauser. Enlarged version of pantomime first staged at Oxford Playhouse in 1973. With Twiggy, Wilfred Bramwell, Harry H. Corbett, Nicky Henson. (91)

PETER PAN by James M. Barrie. 1974 revival of popular annual Christmas show. With Susan Hampshire, Michael Denison, Marion Grimaldi, Tony Sympson, Stacey Dorning. (24)

CYMBELINE by William Shakespeare. The Royal Shakespeare Company's 1974 Stratford production. With Ian Richardson, Sebastian Shaw, Susan Fleetwood, Sheila Allen. (12 in repertory)

THE GENTLE HOOK by Francis Durbridge. Murder irrupts an affluent Belgravia circle. With Dinah Sheridan, Jack Watling, Raymond Francis. (145)

SAWDUST CAESAR, OR THE STORY OF ALLADDIN D. TWANKY, INCLUDING THE ASSASSINATION TO DEATH OF JULIUS CAESAR by Andy Smith. 1972 Socialist pantomime revived at the Bush Theater for 1974. With Ken Morley, Yvonne Gill, Mary Sheen. (28)

ANANSI AND THE STRAWBERRY QUEEN by Manley Young. Music by Ilona Sekacz. A folk-rock fairy-tale musical about the adventures of black and white allegorical characters. With Eddie Grant, Paul Carter, Grace Hutchinson, Janet Wilson. (19)

HARDING'S LUCK by Peter Nichols. Adapted from the novel by E. Nesbit about an Edwardian lad's adventures in time. With Doreen Mantle, Nicholas Lyndhurst, Stanley Meadows. (26)

DÉJÀ REVUE by Olav Wyper and Alan Melville. A revue of revue items from the past 4 decades. With Sheila Hancock, George Cole. (163+)

OBJECTIONS TO SEX AND VIOLENCE by Caryl Churchill. How sexual misfits and social rebels are made and what makes them tick. With Rosemary McHale, Anna Calder-Marshall, Stephen Moore. (25)

CINDY-ELLA by Johnny Clarke. An East End girl is helped by her godmother to fame and fortune in the movies. With June Page, Harry Meacher, Sam Dale. (27)

THE PETER PAN MAN by Jon Plowman. The life and work of James M. Barrie; the Edinburgh Festival fringe production. With Matthew Francis, the author (later with Scott Anthony, Belinda Carroll). (27)

THE SASH by Hector MacMillan. Religious and political bigotry in a Scottish-Irish community near Glasgow. With the Pool Lunch Hour Theater Club Company of Edinburgh. (24)

THE BIRTHDAY PARTY by Harold Pinter. First professional revival, by the Dolphin Theater Company after ten years. With Sidney Tafler, John Alderton, Anna Wing. (40).

KING JOHN by William Shakespeare. John Barton's Royal Shakespeare Company production from Stratford. With Emrys Jones, Ian McKellen, Sheila Allen. (8 in repertory)

LAURA by Steven Dartnell. Updated, Anglicized version of Strindberg's The Father. With Julia Blalock, Angela Chadfield, Patrick Collingham. (26)

MACBETH by William Shakespeare. Frank Dunlop's production for the Young Vic using two Lady Macbeths and three actors for the title role. With James Bolan, Derek Fowlds, Alfred Lynch, Joanna McCallum, Judy Wilson, Cleo Sylvestre. (27 in repertory)

GO TO THE DEVIL by Marcus Crippen. A widow tries to get her late husband's missing wealth. With Ken Herbert. (24)

THE END OF ME OLD CIGAR by John Osborne. A British society hostess plans the insidious overthrow of the male-dominated social order. With Jill Bennett, Rachel Roberts, Marty Cruikshank, Keith Barron, Sheila Ballantine. (25)

NOT I by Samuel Beckett, revival of Royal Court production with Billie Whitelaw; and STATEMENTS AFTER AN ARREST UNDER THE IMMORALITY ACT by Athol Fugard, revival of 1973 Royal Court production. With Yvonne Bryceland, Ben Kingsley, Wilson Dunster. (26)

CLAW by Howard Barker. A jumped-up blackmailing working-class pimp fights a losing battle against a corrupt establishment. With Billy Hamon, Isabel Dean, William Russell, June Brown, Natasha Pyne. (33)

BABIES GROW OLD by Mike Leigh. Royal Shakespeare Company 1974 production (from The Other Place, Stratford) of group-written drama about egotism and the generation gap. With Anne Dyson, Matthew Guinness, Eric Allan. (28)

THE FALL OF THE HOUSE OF USHER by Steven Berkoff and Terry James. Adaptation of the Edgar Allan Poe story. With Shelley Lee, Alfred Michelson, Steven Berkoff. (26)

TWELFTH NIGHT by William Shakespeare. Produced by the Royal Shakespeare Company at the Aldwych Theater. Opened February 5, 1975. (Closed March 1, 1975) (28)

Orsino	John Price
Curio	Louis Sheldon
Valentine	Philip York
Gentleman	George Fenton
Viola	Jane Lapotaire
Sebastian	Robert Lloyd
Olivia	Mary Rutherford
Sir Toby Belch	David Waller
Sir Andrew Aguecheek	Frank Thornton
Malvolio	Nicol Williamson
Maria	Patricia Hayes
Feste	Ron Pember
Fabian; Sailor	Brian Hall
Priest; Sea Captain	Mark Dowse
Ladies	Mary Duddy, Angela Phillips
Antonio	Paul Moriarty
Sailors; Officers	Richard Griffiths, Anthony O'Donnell

Directed by Peter Gill; staged for the Aldwych by Colin Cook; design, William Dudley; costumes, Deirdre Clancy; music, George Fenton; lighting, Rory Dempster.

The present production was first given in Stratford-upon-Avon in 1974. One intermission.

MRS. GRABOWSKI'S ACADEMY by John Antrobus. Surrealistic prophetic view of a debased world as seen by the inmates of a former army college. With Beth Morris, Philip Stone. (17)

THE PICTURE OF DORIAN GRAY by John Osborne, adapted from the Oscar Wilde short story. With Michael Kitchen, John McEnery, Anton Rodgers, Angharad Rees. (32)

TWO GENTLEMEN OF VERONA by William Shakespeare. Jeremy James Taylor's first major Young Vic production. With Judy Geeson, Pip Miller, Michael Walker, Joanna McCallum. (27 in repertory)

THE TEMPEST by William Shakespeare. John Harrison's Leeds Playhouse production. With Paul Scofield. (116+)

HEARTBREAK HOUSE by George Bernard Shaw. Produced by the National Theater at the Old Vic Theater. Opened February 25, 1975. (41+ in repertory)

Nurse Guinness	Patience Collier
Ellie Dunn	Kate Nelligan
Captain Shotover	Colin Blakely
Ariadne Utterword	Anna Massey
Hesione Hushabye	Eileen Atkins
Mazzini Dunn	Alan MacNaughtan
Hector Hushabye	Graham Crowden
Boss Mangan	Paul Rogers
Randall Utterword	Edward de Souza

Burglar	Harry Lomax

Directed by John Schlesinger; design, Michael Annals; lighting, Richard Pibrow.

Three interesting post-World War II productions of Shaw's 36th play were those at the Arts Theater, London, 7/5/50, directed by John Fernald; at the Wyndham's Theater, 11/1/61, directed by Frank Hauser; and at the Lyric Theater, 11/8/67, directed by John Clements. Two intermissions.

OH, IF EVER A MAN SUFFERED by Mary O'Malley. An Irish mum returns to her family home after 17 years' absence in a mental home. With Eve Belton, Dick Sullivan, Paddy Ward, the author. (28)

MACBETH by William Shakespeare. Trevor Nunn's Royal Shakespeare Company production transferred from Stratford. With Nicol Williamson, Helen Mirren. (28)

LOUD REPORTS by and with John Burrows and John Harding, with songs by Peter Skeltern. The story of British imperialism. With the authors. (40)

THE CASE IN QUESTION by Ronald Millar. Drama of a disputed will adapted from C. P. Snow's In Their Wisdom. With Zena Walker, John Clements, Ronald Pickering. (95+)

THINKING STRAIGHT by Laurence Collinson. Should a gay writer hide his true feelings in his work? With Anthony Sher, Peter Small, Linda Beckett. (15+)

MURDERER by Anthony Shaffer. Produced by Michael White at the Garrick Theater. Opened March 12, 1975. (93+)

Cast: Robert Stephens, Caroline Blakiston, Warren Clarke, Patricia Quinn.

Directed by Clifford Williams; design, Carl Toms; lighting, John B. Read.

The play takes place in the living quarters of a country antique shop. A few hours elapse between Acts I and II.

Psychological thriller that exploits the theatrical game some people love to play, about a would-be wife-murderer, egged on by his mistress, who disastrously bungles what should have been his first, perfect murder.

NIGHT MUST FALL by Emlyn Williams. The first London revival of famous psychological thriller since 1935. With Hywel Bennett, Ruth Dunning. (55)

PADDY by Brian Phelan. Corruption in a racial ambiance. With George Innes, Alan Devlin. (29)

THE IMPORTANCE OF BEING EARNEST by Oscar Wilde. Jonathan Miller's anti-traditional revival at Greenwich. With Irene Handl, David Horovitch, Joan Sanderson. (39)

SHIPS by Alan Wakeman. Chance encounters in a gay city. With Andrew Tourell, Anthony Smee, Elaine Ives-Cameron. (35)

THE EXORCISM by Don Taylor. Stage version of supernatural, socio-critical TV-thriller. With Mary Ure (later Anna Cropper), Honor Blackman, Brian Blessed. (36)

THE TWO OF ME by Stanley Price. Two conflicting aspects of a frustrated TV playwright come to blows. With Clive and David Swift, Rosemary Martin. (28)

BLOODY MARY by Ken Hill. The story of Mary Read, the 18th-century pirate. With Toni Palmer, Valerie Walsh, Stephen McKenna, Larry Dann. (41)

A FAMILY AND A FORTUNE by Julian Mitchell. Stage adaptation of Ivy Compton-Burnett's novel about incidents in the life of an egotistical Edwardian family. With Margaret Leighton, Alec Guinness, Nicola Pagett, Rachel Kempson, Anthony Nicholls. (60+)

MURDER ON THE METROPOLITAN LINE by Chris Woods. A drag skit on the Agatha Christie movie. With Dermot Wynbery, the author. (20)

ENTERTAINING MR. SLOANE by Joe Orton. First black farce in a three-part retrospective Orton season, to be followed by Loot in June, and What the Butler Saw in July. With Beryl Reid, Malcolm McDowell, Ronald Fraser, James Ottaway. (39)

JUMBIE STREET MARCH by T-Bone Wilson. A new life comes to Guyana. With Kay Harrison, the author. (24)

THE DOCTOR'S DILEMMA by George Bernard Shaw. Mermaid Theater's revival of 1906 medical satire. With James Cairncross, Derek Godfrey, Lynn Farleigh, Ken Cranham. (56+)

JEEVES by Alan Ayckbourn, music by Andrew Lloyd Webber. Musical based on the Jeeves stories by P.G. Wodehouse. With David Hemmings, Michael Aldridge, John Turner, Bill Wallis, Angela Easterling. (47)

THE DUMBWAITER by Harold Pinter. Sheffield Crucible actors in a revival of the one-acter. With Neil Dickson, David Stockton. (10)

THE BLACK MIKADO by W. S. Gilbert and Arthur Sullivan. The famous operetta transposed to a Caribbean setting with a Caribbean orchestra and with black performers for all the roles except Pooh-Bah. With Michael Denison (as Pooh-bah), Norman Beaton, Val Pringle, Derek Griffiths. (44+)

PARADISE by David Lan. South African Londoner's drama of life and politics in an imaginary 19th-century Spain. With Jean Boht, Roger Rees. (18)

THE CLANDESTINE MARRIAGE by George Coleman and David Garrick. Transfer of Royal Lyceum Theater, Edinburgh production of 18th-century comedy. With Alistair Sim, Ron Moody, Dandy Nichols, Timothy Bateson. (47+)

SMALL AND BRASSY by Neville Phillips and Robb Stewart. A new nostalgic revue. With Mary Millar, Christine Edmonds, Royce Mills, Christopher Benjamin. (22)

JOURNEY TO LONDON by James Saunders. Adapted from Sir John Vanbrugh's uncompleted play of that name, the first in a series entitled Charades. With Linda Marlowe, Prunella Scales, Barry Foster. (11+ in repertory)

LOVE'S LABOUR'S LOST by William Shakespeare. Produced by the Royal Shakespeare Company at the Aldwych Theater. Opened May 1, 1975. (28)

Ferdinand	David Suchet
Longaville	Robert Ashby
Dumaine	Michael Ensign
Berowne	Ian Richardson
Don Adriano	Tony Church
Moth	Martin Lev
Princess of France	Susan Fleetwood
Boyet	Patrick Godfrey
Maria	Lynette Davies
Katharine	Janet Chappell
Rosaline	Estelle Kohler
French Lord	Wilfred Grove
Marcade	John Labanowski
Dull	Denis Holmes
Costard	Mike Gwilym
Jaquenetta	Louise Jameson
Forester	Gavin Campbell
Holofernes	Norman Rodway
Sir Nathaniel	Jeffrey Dench

Navarre Lords, Foresters, Villagers: Annette Bedland Doyne Byrd Gavin Campbell John Labanowski

Directed by David Jones; design, Timothy O'Brien, Tazeena Firth; music, William Southgate; lighting, Stewart Leviton.

The present production was first given in Stratford-upon-Avon in 1973. One intermission.

DEAR JANET ROSENBERG, DEAR MR. KOONING by Stanley Eveling. Hampstead

Theater Club revival of Scottish author's drama. With Anna Calder-Marshall, Freddie Jones. (20)

OVERRULED by George Bernard Shaw. National Theater Company's lunchtime season: opening play about polygamy and adultery. With Elizabeth Hughes, Michael Keating, Dona Martyn, Michael Stroud. (7 in repertory)

SNATCH-69 by Brian Blackburn. Sexual highjinks on a sex-health-farm. With Chubby Oates, Bryan Burden, Jackie Skarvellis. (24+)

SOFT OR A GIRL? by John McGrath, adapted by Billy Colvill. The story of a strange lad reset in London's East End. With Kate Gielgud, the adaptor. (18+)

LOVE STORY by Colin Bennett. Manipulating the facts. With the Gate Theater Company. (19)

THE BORAGE PIGEON AFFAIR by James Saunders. First professional production of play about municipal corruption; part of season entitled *Charades*. With Petra Markham, Prunella Scales, Barry Foster. (13+ in repertory)

ECHOES FROM A CONCRETE CANYON by John Haire. A London Jewess's trials in her mixed marriage. With Judy Parfitt, Nicholas Ball. (4+)

MEASURE FOR MEASURE by William Shakespeare. Charles Marowitz's 90-minute-long adaptation. With Nikolas Simmonds, Ciaran Madden, Richard Mayes. (5+)

WHAT A CRAZY WORLD by Alan Klein. Theater Workshop's revival of 1962 Cockney musical, with up-dated script and songs. With Kim Smith, Jenny Logan. (5+)

LIMITED RUNS OF INTERESTING NEW BRITISH PLAYS

THE SNOWDROPPERS by Alun Richards. The idealism of a Welsh guerrilla-girl is severely tested by the unexpected intrusion of a shifty cockney petty crook. With Ronald Lewis, Fiona Walker, Roger Gartland. (13)

A WORTHY GUEST by Paul Bailey. A jailbird comes to an understanding of what led him to be convicted. With Martin Ask, Robin Summers. (17)

GO WEST, YOUNG WOMAN by Pam Gems. A play, with music, about the enslavement of women and other instances of man's tyranny as the West is opened up. With the Women's Company. (7)

MR. PRUFROCK'S SONGS by Steven Berkoff. A poetic courtship two-hander echoing T.S. Eliot. With Ian Kellgren, Patricia Trueman. (6)

OUR SORT OF PEOPLE by Jeremy Seabrook and Michael O'Neill. A family gathering of provincial morons and their guests. With Richard Durden, Delia Lindsay. (12)

SECRETS by Richard Crane. A crazy novelist's encounter with her no-good illegitimate son and his feckless dad. With Natasha Parry, Edward Judd. (14)

OLD MAN AESOP: HE KNEW THE GAME by Edwin Turner. A leopard can't change his spots. With Major Wiley, David Adam, Joan Ann Maynard. (12)

SOMEONE ELSE IS STILL SOMEONE by Bernard Pomerance. American-born Londoner's

hour-long drama about the problems of two married couples. With Diane Fletcher, Tony Mathews, Katherine Schofield, Philip Doneghy. (12)

THE RAPIST by James Duke. The analysis of a sexual assault. With Timothy Munro, Maureen O'Brien. (12)

HELL'S BELLS by Tony Perrin. The fantasy world of an electrician. With Sam Kelly, Hilary Labow, Paddy Ward. (12)

FIVE TILL FIVE-THIRTY by John Antiss. The confessions of a lady alcoholic. With Pat Lindsay. (10)

THE ATHLETE by Derek Smith. A fanatical coach's dream ends in near-disaster. With Michael Deacon, Timothy Munro, John Lyons. (12)

KILL-DE-SAC by Frank Long. Black comedy about mayhem in a theater dressing-room. With Anne Clune, Sidney Kean. (14)

THEATER LUNCHTIME by Andrew Dallmeyer. Improvisational drama about the loss of a king's head. With Paul Arlington, Jacqueline Delhaye, Neil Cunningham, John Nightingale. (12)

SAM SLADE IS MISSING by Bill Morrison. A journalist's marital catastrophe. With James Ellis, Joe Melia, Joanna Van Gyseghem. (10)

ALL FOR THE NATION by Bob Hoskins. The dream of a latter-day Frankenstein. With John English, Francis Mortimer. (6)

ASIDES by Alan Drury. Two men and a girl struggle to find a way out of a sexual maze. With Gilliam Rhind, Michael Feast. (18)

LUNATICS TAKE OVER AT THE ALDWYCH by Ronald Graham. The frontiers between illusion and reality all over again. With the Paradise Foundry Company. (10)

THE TRIP TO FLORENCE by Peter Terson. An educational visit by six schoolboys to Italy. With the National Youth Theater Company. (12)

THE CONVERSION OF THE ANGLO-SAXONS by David Shellan. A slice of British history as seen by two dreamers. With Stephen Bateman, Richard Gardner. (12)

BAR-B-Q by John Anthony West. New drama by American-born writer domiciled in Wales about the absurdity of the parvenus. With Richard Durnden, Simon MacCorkindale. (11)

THE IRON HARP by Joseph O'Conor. A plea for reconciliation in Ireland. With John Castle, Maureen O'Brien. (12)

THE CARNATION GANG by Stephen Poliakoff. The world of two upper-class drug-pushers is invaded by lower-class roughnecks. With Michael Feast, Adrian Shergold, Celia Quicke, Simon Jones, David Van-Day. (16)

AWAY FROM IT ALL by Peter King. The rivalry of two married brothers and the comeuppance they get from Dad. With Ann Bell, Colin Douglas, Zena Walker. (13)

DESMONDE THE MIGHTY COSMIC FLEA AND THE SECRET OF THE UNIVERSE by and with the Exploding Trouser Company. A revue based on the comic implications of the fart. (8)

STANDARDS by Chris Allen (D). Two couples take a look at the world collapsing around them. With Katherine Schofield, Ray Armstrong. (12)

THE TIGERS ARE COMING, O.K.? by Alan Plater. The life-story of a famous provincial football-club supporter through thick and thin. With Brian J. Twiddy, Gillian Hudspeth, Raymond Cross, Barry Jones. (19)

MARBLES by John Chapman, Tim Fywell and Nigel Williams. Boy meets girl. Girl leaves boy. With Libba Davies, Adrian Shergold. (15)

THE SILENT MAJORITY by Mike Leigh. The frustrations of an inarticulate married couple at loggerheads. With Stephen Bill, Julia North. (15)

FOURTH DAY LIKE FOUR LONG

MONTHS OF ABSENCE by Colin Bennett. A zany view of life today and in ages past through the eyes of a would-be TV-writer. With Carole Hayman, Toby Salaman, Tony Rohr, Caroline Hutchinson. (16)

THE SCARLET BLADE by John Kane. The marital battlefield is invaded by an unexpected intruder. With Rayner Burton, Juliet Aykroyd, the author. (18)

THE KNOWLEDGE by and with the "Hull Truck". Two freaks reflected in the contemporary life-style. With Linda Bell, Mike Bradwell. (18)

THE BEAST by Snoo Wilson. Royal Shakespeare Company production of a documentary about Aleister Crowley, the dabbler in magic, who died in 1947. With Richard Pascoe, Patrick Godfrey, Tony Church. (12 in repertory)

STAKE-OUT by Johnnie Quarrel. See *Homeworker* under "Foreign Plays."

MR. POE by Robert Nye. Surrealistic exploration of the U.S. writer. With the Edinburgh Pool Theater Company. (17)

A BAD EGG by Marion Jenkins King (D). Newly-formed immigrant Cypriot theater's production of play about immigrants' problems. With Kate Kelly, Joe Goodman. (12)

THE END OF THE WORLD SHOW by Derek Smith and Ian Burnett. Science-fiction satirical rock-musical. With the Wakefield Tricycle Company. (6)

BLACK SLAVES, WHITE CHAINS by Mustapha Matura. A new view of the color bar. With the Keskidee Theater Company. (12)

THE ONLY WAY OUT by George Thatcher. The author's second drama about a convict facing a death sentence, written inside. With Michael Elphick. (12)

FISH IN THE SEA by John McGrath. Politico-social musical of life in present-day Liverpool. With Caroline Hutchinson, Howell Evans. (11)

LIMITATIONS by John Roman Baker. Design for living, or can a *menage à trois* fit in with the needs of a gay couple? With Margaret Ford, William Hayland, Jeremy Arnold. (17)

MURDERS by Robert Siddons. A sado-masochistic couple's murderous fantasies. With Tricia Fine, Tony Meyer. (15)

LADY CHE—A POLITICAL LOVE STORY by and with the Action Theater Company. A hilarious send-up of the didactic drama convention. (18)

STRINDBERG by Colin Wilson. First London production of author's idiosyncratic view of the Swedish writer. With Alec Linstead, Amanda Knott. (12)

PERFECT HAPPINESS by Caryl Churchill. A wife's curiosity about her husband's two girl friends. With Eleanor Bron, Catherine Kessler, Jennie Stoller. (12)

NUMBER 3 by John Grillo. A madman and his even madder keeper. With Peter Ashley, Don Weinstein. (6)

EVENTS IN AN UPPER ROOM, collectively authored. A modern-dress treatment of the Crucifixion by Rony Robinson and the actors of the Coventry Belgrade Theater where it was first staged in January 1975. With Michael Gough, David Calder, Diana Waller. (11)

I RODE WITH JOHNNY SAVAGE by Mark Milstein. A view into a mental hospital ward. With Martin Skinner, Hugh Armstrong. (12)

POST MORTEM by Brian Clark. A lady business tycoon takes a few tumbles but also leaps a few hurdles. With Alison Fiske. (16)

THE DOOMDUCKERS BALL by and with Carole Hayman, Neil Johnston, Mary Maddox, Dinah Stabb. A revue for all and sundry. (11)

THE POLYNESIAN PRIME MINISTER by Frank Long. U.S.A.-U.S.S.R. rivalry in the Pacific. With Jonathan Burn, Vikki Richards. (14)

COMPANY POT by Patience Addo. A Ghanaian girl encounters city life. With Elizabeth Adare, Gordon Tialobi. (15)

ALL GOOD MEN by Trevor Griffiths. National Theater lunchtime play about a Labor peer's angry son. With John Gill, Oliver Cotton, David Firth, Jennifer Piercey. (8 in repertory)

FAMILY SPEAR by Elvania Zirimu. Drama of clash between town and country interests by Ugandan author. With Yemi Adibadi, Gordon Tialobi. (10)

DIARY OF A MADAME by Frederick Bradnum, based on Maria Kroll's *Letters From Liselotte*. With Miriam Karlin. (6+)

CHOCOLATE CAKE by Nicholas Wood. Self-knowledge through adversity. With John Warner, Diane Fairfax, the author. (5+)

SOME AMERICAN PLAYS PRODUCED IN LONDON

THE EFFECT OF GAMMA RAYS ON MAN-IN-THE-MOON MARIGOLDS by Paul Zindel. With Suzanna Williams, Elizabeth Stewart. (17)

THE WALL IS MAMA by Rick Cluchey. With the St. Quentin Workshop. (40)

THE NIGHT OF THE IGUANA by Tennessee Williams. With James Donnelly, Phyllis McMahon, Lisa Fabian. (15)

INFANCY AND CHILDHOOD by Thornton Wilder. With Julie Somers, George Kandelaft. (21)

LET MY PEOPLE COME by Earl Wilson Jr. and Phil Oesterman. With Gil Beresford, Michael Cowie. (316+)

THE CONNECTION by Jack Gelber. With Richard Moore, Mark Heath, Michael Keating. (28)

MORE STATELY MANSIONS by Eugene O'Neill. With Dorothy Reynolds, Frances Cuka, Gary Bond, David Dodimead. (25)

KENNEDY'S CHILDREN by Robert Patrick (D). Produced by Henry Sherwood Productions, Ltd. and Simon Clarke Productions, Ltd. in association with Don Parker and with Dan Crawford. First presented at the King's Head Theater Club. Opened October 22, 1974. (Closed March 29, 1975) (137) Opened at the Arts Theater Club on April 17, 1975. (176+)

Wanda	Vivian Pickles/Pat Starr
Sparger	Don Parker
Rona	Deborah Norton
Mark	Richard Oldfield
Carla	Jan Waters/Shirley Anne Field
Barman	Ray Harding

Directed by Clive Donner; design, Geoff Stephens, John Scully; costumes, Maggi Smith; lighting, D.O. Fitz Moran.

The action of the play takes place in a bar on the Lower East Side of New York, on a rainy February afternoon in 1974. One intermission.

A series of unrelated barroom monologues spoken by five Americans of different social origins and occupations, which echo their several hopes and their growing despair as the promising Kennedy era gives way to growing disillusionment and frustration.

First performed in New York at the Clark

Center for the Performing Arts (Playwrights' Horizons) 5/30/73, it won the first prize in the 1974 Glasgow Citizens' Theater World Playwriting Contest and was the first "Fringe" production to transfer to a West End London Theater.

THE GINGERBREAD LADY by Neil Simon. With Elaine Stritch, Jenny Quayle. (189)

THE GLASS MENAGERIE by Tennessee Williams. With David Delve, Sandra Freeman, David Soames, Eliza Ward. (24)

IN THE BAR OF A TOKYO HOTEL by Tennessee Williams. With Christine Schofield, David Kinsey, Richard Pavell. (12)

WEST SIDE STORY by Arthur Laurents, lyrics by Stephen Sondheim, music by Leonard Bernstein. A revival notable for being the show that reopened the Shaftesbury Theater, saved from demolition by property developers. With Christina Matthews, Lionel Morton, Petra Siniawski, Nicki Adrian. (188+)

THAT'S AMUSING incorporating THE STILL ALARM by George S. Kaufman and DEATH KNOCKS by Woody Allen. With Judith Ellis-Jones, Peter Small, Kelly Robinson. (26)

THIS PROPERTY IS CONDEMNED by Tennessee Williams. With Nicolette Marvin, Gavin Asher. (23)

PERIOD OF ADJUSTMENT by Tennessee Williams, with Kasik Michalski, Anne Vintner; in a double bill with LAUGHS ETC. by Leo Herlihy, with Monica Buferd. (13)

GNOMES by Gordon Porterfield. With Kate Harper, Vicki Ireland. (10)

HARVEY by Mary Chase. With James Stewart, Geoffrey Lumsden, Mona Washbourne. (61+)

LENNY by Julian Barry. With Marty Brill, Harold Kasket, Tessa Bill-Yeald. (58)

A LITTLE NIGHT MUSIC by Hugh Wheeler, music and lyrics by Stephen Sondheim. Produced by Harold Prince, Ruth Mitchell, Frank Milton, Eddie Kulukundis and Richard Pilbrow in association with Bernard Delfont at the Adel-

phi Theater. Opened April 15, 1975. (61+)

Mr. Lindquist	John J. Moore
Mrs. Nordstrom	Chris Melville
Mrs. Anderssen	Liz Robertson
Mr. Erlanson	David Bexon
Mrs. Segstrom	Jacquey Chappell
Fredrika Armfeldt	Christine McKenna
Madame Armfeldt	Hermione Gingold
Frid	Michael Harbour
Henrik Egerman	Terry Mitchell
Anne Egerman	Veronica Page
Fredrik Egerman	Joss Ackland
Petra	Diane Langton
Desirée Armfeldt	Jean Simmons
Bertrand	Christopher Beeching
Count Carl-Magnus Malcolm	David Kernan
Countess Charlotte Malcolm	Maria Aitken
Osa	Penelope Potter

Directed by Harold Prince; choreography, Patricia Birch; scenery, Boris Aronson; costumes, Florence Klotz; lighting, Tharon Musser.

Time: Turn of the Century. Place: Sweden.

Suggested by the Ingmar Bergman movie *Smiles of a Summer Night,* this American musical was first performed at the Shubert Theater, New York, 2/25/73. The London production, with the single exception of Hermione Gingold, had an entirely new, English cast and was otherwise a carbon-copy of the original. One intermission.

NORMAN, IS THAT YOU? by Ronald Clark and Sam Bobrick. American comedy adapted to an English setting. With Harry Worth, Avril Angers, Paul Seed, Freddie Lees. (52)

DIARIES by Robert Coleman. With Heather Chasen, John Hughes. (18)

THE SUNSHINE BOYS by Neil Simon. With Jimmy Jewel, Alfred Marks. (29+)

ONE PERSON in a double-bill with FRED AND HAROLD by Robert Patrick. With Barry McCarthy, Peter Whitman, Michael Deacon. (17+)

A TOUCH OF SPRING (Avanti!) by Samuel Taylor. With Hayley Mills, Peter Donat, Leigh Lawson. (18+)

THE HAUNTED HOST by Robert Patrick. With Ned Van Zendt, Joe Pritchett. (11+)

SOME FOREIGN PLAYS PRODUCED IN LONDON

THE JOSS ADAMS SHOW by Alma De Groen. With John Turnbull, Bridget Armstrong. (30)

BIRDS OF PARADISE (La Maison de Zaza) by Gaby Bruyère, adapted by Michael Pertwee.

With Moira Lister, Robert Coote. (253)

IONESCO QUARTET comprising SALUTATIONS, THE LEADER, THE MOTORSHOW, and FOURSOME by Eugene Ionesco. With

Elizabeth Romilly, Charles Rogers, David Whitworth, Frances Jean Viner. (9)

CRIPPLE PLAY by Max B. Richards. With Nicolette McKenzie. (14)

THE MARRIAGE OF FIGARO by Beaumarchais, translated by John Wells. With Gawn Grainger, Gemma Jones, Derek Godfrey, Nicola Pagett. (28)

THE LABYRINTH by Fernando Arrabal. With Sandra Freeman, Brian Jackson, Iain Reid, Chris Hunter. (12)

ZIMA JUNCTION by Yevgeni Yevtushenko, adapted by David Rodigan. With the adapter. (6)

STALLERHOF by Franz Xaver Kroetz. With Penelope Lee, Celia Quicke, Bill Stewart, John Woodvine. (38)

SUMMERFOLK by Maxim Gorky, English version by Jeremy Brooks and Kitty Hunter Blair. Produced by the Royal Shakespeare Company at the Aldwych Theater. Opened August 27, 1974. (Closed December 11, 1974) (32 in repertory)

Bassov	Norman Rodway
Varvara	Estelle Kohler
Vlass	Mike Gwilym
Zamislov	David Suchet
Kaleria	Susan Fleetwood
Sasha	Annette Badland
Suslov	Tony Church
Yulia	Lynette Davies
Dudakov	Patrick Godfrey
Olga	Janet Whiteside
Ryumin	Robert Ashby
Maria	Margaret Tyzack
Sonya	Louise Jameson
Zimin	Michael Ensign
Pustobaika	Norman Tyrrell
Kropilkin	Gavin Campbell
Woman with bandaged cheek	Maroussia Frank
Shalimov	Ian Richardson
Dvoetochie	Sebastian Shaw
1st Beggar	Doyne Byrd
2d Beggar	John Labanowski
Lady in yellow dress	Janet Chappell
Man in check suit	Wilfred Grove
Gentleman in a top hat	Roger Bizley
Semyonov	Albert Welling
Cadet	Mark Cooper
Young Lady in pink	Deborah Fairfax

Directed by David Jones; design, Timothy O'Brien, Tazeena Firth; music, Carl Davis; lighting, Stewart Leviton.

Act I: The Bassovs' summer villa, evening. Act II, Scene 1: Outside the Bassovs' villa, the next day, early evening. Act II, Scene 2: A picnic in the woods, a few days later. Act III: Outside the Bassovs' villa, some weeks later. Two intermissions.

Summerfolk (Dachniki) was written between 1901 and 1904 as the first part of a dramatic trilogy about the Russian intelligentsia. It was first performed in St. Petersburg 11/4/04 at Vera Kommissarzhevskaya's Theater and banned two months later after the "Bloody Sunday" massacre of 1/9/05, when its author was arrested and thrown into prison. A comedy about the futile intellectuals who live in idleness in their summer retreats, the present version, for the first professional production in England, was specially commissioned by the Royal Shakespeare Company. The most recent production of a radically revised version of the play, directed by Peter Stein, opened at the Schaubühne an Halleschen Ufer in West Berlin 12/22/74 and was selected as one of the entries for the 1975 Berlin Theater Festival by an all-German jury.

WHO'LL BE NEXT, AND WHO'LL BE LUCKY by John Mackendrick. With John Duttine, Chas Bryer. (12)

WHAT IF YOU DIED TOMORROW? by David Williamson. With the Old Tote Theater Company from Australia. (31)

WIDE OPEN SPACES by René de Obaldia. With Kate David, Shaughan Seymour. (11)

THE BLOOD KNOT by Athol Fugard. With Niall Buggy, Alton Kumalo. (23)

EVA PERON and THE FOUR TWINS by Copi. with the Close Theater Club Company. (16)

THE TURNING POINT by Françoise Dorin, adapted by David Crosse and Cornelius Conyn. With David Tomlinson, Helen Christie. (20)

SATURDAY SUNDAY MONDAY by Eduardo de Filippo. West End transfer of Franco Zeffirelli's National Theater production. With Joan Plowright, Frank Finlay, Richard Vernon replacing Laurence Olivier. (260)

COMRADES by August Strindberg. With Brenda Bruce, Peter Eyre, Susan Fleetwood, Rosemary McHale. (16 in repertory)

120 DAYS OF SODOM by the Marquis de Sade, adapted by Guiliano Vasilico. With the Beat 72 Company of Rome. (24)

THE SOLDIERS ARE COMING by George Astalos. With George Bryson, David Jagger Minty, Emma Jean Richards. (9)

THE LITTLE HUT by André Roussin. French comedy, originally staged in London in the 1950s by Peter Brook. With Geraldine McEwan, Gerald Harper, James Villiers. (78)

THE CAN OPENER by Victor Lanoux, adapted by Charles Wood. With Roy Kinnear, Joe Melia. (18 in repertory)

SCHIPPEL by Carl Sternheim. With the Traverse Theater Club Company from Edinburgh. (22)

NIGHT PIECE by Wolfgang Hildesheimer. With Brendan Ellis, Danny Lonergan. (12)

THE VALEDICTORIANS by Charles Smiley. With Toby Byrne, Susannah Page, Kevin D'Arcy. (10)

THE HORTICULTURIST by Charles Smiley. With Toby Byrne, Susannah Page, Kevin D'Arcy. (10)

PLAYING WITH FIRE by August Strindberg. With Juliet Robyns, Saul Rechlin, David MacArthur. (6)

THE HIGHWAYMEN (Die Rauber) by Friedrich Schiller, translated and adapted by Gail Rademacher. With Derren Nesbitt, Jenny Runacre, Richard Huggett. (15)

THE CITY by Yutaka Higashi, with music by Itsuro Shimodo. With the Tokyo Kid Brothers from Japan. (34)

THE COCK-ARTIST by Rainer Werner Fassbinder. With Peter Piccolo, Alan Hulse, Fleur Chandler. (16)

ANNA LAUB by Jacov Lind. With Patricia Leventon, Gary Brooking, Paul Davidson, Andrew Hawkins. (12)

RHINOCEROS by Eugene Ionesco. With Joolia Coppleman, Mike Leigh, David Halliwell. (13)

THE MARQUIS OF KEITH by Frank Wedekind, English version by Ronald Eyre and Alan Best. Produced by the Royal Shakespeare Company at the Aldwych Theater. Opened November 19, 1974. (Closed January 21, 1975) (17 in repertory)

Consul Casimir	Charles Keating
Hermann Casimir	Catherine Kessler
Marquis of Keith	Ian McKellan
Ernst Scholz	Ian Richardson
Molly Griesinger	Louise Jameson
Countess Werdenfels	Sara Kestelman
Saranieff	Jeffrey Dench
Zamriaki	Trevor T. Smith
Sommersberg	Malcolm Armstrong
Raspe	Mike Gwilym
Ostermeier	Norman Tyrrell

Krenzl	Roger Bizley
Grandauer	John Boswall
Frau Ostermeier	Maroussia Frank
Frau Krenzl	Meriel Brook
Baroness von Rosenkron	John Labanowski
Baroness von Totleben	Mark Cooper
Sasha	Emma Williams/Deborah Fairfax
Simba	Patti Love
Bakery Woman	Annette Badland
Butcher's Boy; Photographer	Albert Welling
Chauffeur	Wilfred Grove
Photographer	Doyne Byrd

Patrons of the Hofbrauhaus: Meriel Brook, Doyne Byrd, Mark Cooper, Maroussia Frank, Wilfred Grove, John Labanowski.

Directed by Ronald Eyre; design, Voytek; choreography, David Toguri; music, Carl Davis; lighting, Robert Ornbo.

The action takes place in Munich, in the late summer of 1899.

A new English adaptation of the 1899 black comedy, with pastiche period jazz and Brechtian songs added, in which a social-climbing confidence-trickster plans a mammoth Fun Palace in Munich with the money of a group of rich industrialists but ends up by being exposed and discarded by them. First performed in Berlin 10/11/01. One intermission.

THE LESSON by Eugene Ionesco. With Robert Eddison, Jane Wymark, Astrid Anderson. (10)

HOMEWORKER by Franz Xaver Kroetz, an examination of violence in a working-class milieu transposed to a new English town setting, with Maurice Colbourne, Pam Brighton; and STAKE-OUT by Johnnie Quarrel, specially written short play on the theme of violence to go with Kroetz's play, with Maurice Colbourne, Pam Brighton. (17)

THE SNOB by Carl Sternheim. With Peter Eyre, Madeline Smith, Lucy Griffiths, Patrick Connor. (10)

AUTOSACRAMENTALES adapted by Victor Garcia from Calderon. With the Ruth Escobar Company from Brazil. (19)

JOHN GABRIEL BORKMAN by Henrik Ibsen. English version by Inga-Stina Ewbank and Peter Hall. Produced by the National Theater at the Old Vic Theater. Opened January 28, 1975. (45+ in repertory)

Gunhild Borkman	Wendy Hiller
Maid	Barbara Keogh
Ella Rentheim	Peggy Ashcroft
Erhart Borkman	Frank Grimes
Fanny Wilton	Anna Carteret
John Gabriel Borkman	Ralph Richardson
Frida Foldal	Cheryl Campbell
William Foldal	Alan Webb

Directed by Peter Hall; scenery and costumes,

Timothy O'Brien, Tazeena Firth; lighting, David Hersey.

The action is continuous, starting late afternoon and ending about midnight.

Written in 1896, Ibsen's penultimate parable-drama about a failed tycoon was first performed simultaneously 1/10/97 in Finnish at the Finnish National and in Swedish at the Swedish National theaters in Helsinki. One intermission.

AN ITALIAN STRAW HAT by Eugene Labiche and Marc-Michel. With Sylvester McCoy, Toni Palmer, Stephen McKenna, Valerie Walsh. (35)

DON'S PARTY by David Williamson. With Ray Barrett, Barbara Ewing. (41)

SON OF OBLOMOV (Phlegm) by Ricardo Talesnik. With Bernard Bresslaw, Denise Coffey. (7)

KASPAR by Peter Handke. With Richard Ireson, Royce Hollingworth, Alan Lyddiard, Nigel Nevinson. (20)

HAPPY DAYS by Samuel Beckett. With Peggy Ashcroft, Alan Webb. (17+ in repertory)

WORLD THEATER SEASON: NOVEMBER NIGHT by Stanislaw Wyspianski (8), and FOREFATHERS' EVE by Adam Mickiewicz (7), with the Cracow Stary Theater; GUSTAV III by August Strindberg, with the Gothenburg Stradsteater (8); REGENERATION by Italo Svevo (5), and ENEMY OF THE PEOPLE by Henrik Ibsen (3), with the Compagnia di Prosa Tino Buazzelli, from Italy; and RENGA MOI by Robert Serumaga, with the Abafuma Company of Kampala, from Uganda (8).

THE NUNS by Eduardo Manet. With Michael Blackham, Anthony May. (12)

CREDITORS by August Strindberg. With Laura Graham, Frank Moorey, Richard Cornish. (8)

THE SEASON ELSEWHERE IN EUROPE

By Ossia Trilling

THE financial crisis has, of course, hit even those European countries where inflation has been kept down to a minimum. In Western Germany the talk was all of rationalization and mergers and reduced subsidies. A recent feature has been the enormous spread of touring companies, some of them run entirely for commercial profit. Many of their dates were in subsidized theaters, however, which put them in indirectly subsidized and stiff competition with their host theaters. No remedy has so far been found for this anomaly. Meanwhile, artistic merit seems to be proving lucrative, even in the light of the yearly subsidy per theater ticket, which last year worked out to about $3.

Peter Zadek and his theater in Bochum stole much of the thunder this season, what with several world premieres and two more invitations to the annual German Theater Review in Berlin in May, thus breaking all records both for a theater and an individual director. In his case, he was even represented in Berlin by an iconoclastic guest production, which he had done at the Hamburg Schauspielhaus, of Ibsen's *The Wild Duck,* staged as a rip-roaring comedy on a vast empty stage, uncluttered except for the necessary furniture and obstacles on which the clumsy Gregers Werle kept symbolically bumping his head. The novelties in Bochum itself included Willy Russell's Beatles play; Georg Buechner's translation of *Lucretia Borgia* by Victor Hugo; and a stage version of Heinrich Mann's 1905 novel, *Professor Unrath,* which Carl Zuckmayer used for the film of *The Blue Angel.* Hannelore Hoger plays the part of the whore, Rose Froehlich, immortalized in celluloid by Marlene Dietrich, but by contrast Zadek stuck faithfully to the novel's original anti-bourgeois message. The Argentinian Augusto Fernandes was responsible for two outstanding productions: Lorca's *Dona Rosita,* possibly the most disputed version of this poetic drama to be seen in recent years, and an overlong but fascinating example of traditional "baroque" theater, the spectacular *The Great Zenobia* by Calderon.

In Hamburg, Rudolf Noelte, considered by some critics to be Germany's finest director, staged two plays in virtually the same basic decor and with identical principals: Molière's *The Misanthrope,* which was Hamburg's second entry in the Berlin Theater Review, and a shortened version of *Long Day's Journey Into*

Night. Will Quadflieg excelled himself as the pessimistic hero of each.

Unusual at the Berlin Festival was Hans-Jorg Utzerath's witty version of *The Threepenny Opera,* acted by the Dusseldorf Schauspielhaus Company on the very Volksbuhne stage where the director had suffered so many setbacks as manager in the past. This time the gag-filled production was a triumph. It used a politically loaded text, made topical by adding extracts from Brecht's novel, and staged in the round with the actors discreetly concealed among the surrounding spectators when not on stage, thus critically identifying themselves, socially and politically, with the audience.

Among the new German dramas this season, some were first efforts like *The Marathon Piano Player* by 34-year-old Horst Laube at the Frankfurt City Theater; others were by more expert hands, like Yaak Karsunka's *Germinal* at the Frankfurt TAT (or Theater am Turm). The first, directed by the Swiss *wunderkind* Luc Bondy, and covering the period 1928 to the present, exposed to ridicule the lethargy and egoism of the author's irresponsible countrymen in Hitler times and later. *Germinal,* like Zola's novel, dealt with the miners' strike of 1870 but was given a contemporary political slant in its didactic approach. In Bremen, Peter Weiss's adaptation of Franz Kafka's *The Trial* (originally intended for Ingmar Bergman in Stockholm) was world-premiered in a faithful and technically ambitious version staged by Helm Bindseil. Wolfgang Schwenck was Josef K, the ill-fated bank clerk doomed to destruction by his inability to see, let alone sever, the bonds that tied him fatally to his petty-bourgeois class roots.

In Stuttgart, a theatrical scandal of major proportions was narrowly averted when the publication of a frank (and heavily annotated) theater program to go with a new production of Wedekind's controversial *Spring Awakening* provoked official censure—thereby proving that the author's message regarding sexual obscurantism was as topical as ever. Niels-Peter Rudolph's revival of Friedrich Wolf's pre-war didactic drama *Cyankali,* about the narrow-minded attitude towards abortion in the Weimar Republic, was clearly selected for production as a follow-on to this. Two other novelties were a shade less disturbing: Gerlind Reinshagen's study of the experience of death, *Heaven and Earth,* and Alfred Kirchner's fantastic elaboration of Ionesco's *The Bald Prima Donna,* which gave the ensemble ample opportunities for some inspired fooling in the added clowning numbers and earned the production an invitation to the Berlin Theater Review.

Elsewhere, one must note the success both in Dusseldorf, and in numerous other theaters that followed suit, of the Dutch four-part drama *The Family;* the European premiere in Essen of Solzhenitsyn's *Republic of Labor,* the play about life in a Stalinist camp which has been published in England as *The Love-Girl and the Innocent* and was world premiered in Minneapolis on October 13, 1970 as *A Play by Solzhenitisyn;* and, in the same city, Karl Otto Muehl's second drama, about the drudgery of work, called *Carnival Monday.*

West Berlin

The Schaubuhne am Halleschen Ufer, often referred to as West Germany's finest theater, under Peter Stein, chalked up three triumphs: Heiner Mueller's *The Blackleg*, written in East Germany in 1956, about the hardships of post-war reconstruction in a budding socialist state and ably directed by Frank-Patrick Steckel; Handke's *The Unreasonable Ones Die Out*, world-premiered in Zurich last season, out of which, for all its impenetrable symbolism, Stein made an irresistably eye-catching spectacle; and *Summerfolk*, described in the program as "based on Gorky," a version for which Stein utilized material intended originally for a film. Karl Ernst Hermann designed a superb setting in depth, in which the talk of the characters, all visible on stage throughout, was meshed into an ingenious program of verbal and visual orchestration. Two of the highlights at the Schiller Theater were Hans Lietzau's production of Chekhov's *Ivanov*, starring Martin Benrath, with an exciting symbolical set devised by Achim Freyer, and Samuel Beckett's fourth attempt to stage a play of his own in German, this time *Waiting for Godot*, in which the two main clowns Horst Bollmann and Stefan Wigger as Didi and Gogo switched the roles they had appeared in ten years back. Dieter Dorn's swan-song production at the smaller Schlosspark was Tankred Dorst's *On Mount Chimborazo*, a so-called "epilogue of bourgeois existence," in which a group of five climbers of the symbolic mountain, situated somewhere on the border of the two Germanies, learns to appreciate the drawbacks of the "life lie"; while Ernst Wendt's was a horror-comic double bill by Harold Mueller called *Silent Night* and *Jetsam*.

East Berlin

The Berliner Ensemble's efforts to open up a new tradition were crowned with a remarkably inventive, parodistic production, directed by B.K. Tragelehn and Einar Schleef, on a virtually empty stage, of Strindberg's *Miss Julie*, featuring Jutta Hoffmann and Jurgen Holtz, who both play-act their way through the text with next to no sexual inhibitions, no doubt to the chagrin of the puritanically minded but to the huge delight of an audience that is regaled with a balletic interlude (as required by the author), danced to pop-music. The production of Brecht's *Edward II*, entrusted to Ekkehard Schall and his wife, Barbara Berg, alias Brecht's daughter, was more traditionally Brechtian in concept, but Ruth Berghaus's revision of *Mother*, with Felicitas Ritsch in the role created by Helene Weigel, was stylistically far removed from earlier models. Benno Besson, appointed head of the Volksbuhne, where he had previously been only principal director of plays, went from strength to strength, with a marathon production by a team of different directors, as their contribution to the Berliner Festtage (or East Berlin Arts Festival) of the so-called *Spektakel 2*, consisting of a dozen plays and sketches acted out in various parts of the theater more or less together, and Besson's own colorful production of *As You Like It*, in a new translation by Heiner

Mueller. Another new translation was Maik Hamburger's of *The Tempest,* which Friedo Solter directed at the Deutsches Theater, with a youngish Prospero and Ferdinand and Miranda appropriately straight out of drama school.

Switzerland and Austria

Harry Buckwitz's last years as Director of the Zurich Schauspielhaus, where he is due to stand down next year in favor of Gerhard Klingenberg (currently head of the Vienna Burg Theater), show no sign of a deterioration of quality. His own production of *Mother Courage,* on the same stage as that where Brecht's chronicle-drama was world-premiered in 1941, had non-Brechtian sets and costumes by Hubert Monloup, of France, and a Courage (Heidemarie Hatheyer) who went against the epic tradition, but was none the worse for that. Manfred Wekwerth returned from East Berlin to stage his *Richard III* (with Helmut Lohner as a comic medieval monarch) in Zurich in much the same way as in his home town, and Friedrich Duerrenmatt fulfilled his ambition of directing yet another classic in a new way with Lessing's bourgeois tragedy of *Emilia Galotti.* The greatest excitement was created by the world premier of Carl Zuckmayer's latest drama, the fifth to be world-premiered in Zurich. This was a modern version, though set in medieval times in Leopold Lindtberg's epic production handsomely designed by Zbynek and Radova Kolarova, of the "Pied Piper of Hamelin" legend, called *The Rat Catcher,* to music by Gottfried von Einem. The nearest the septuagenarian playwright has come to the theatrical genre perfected by Brecht, his former fellow-dramaturg of the 1920s in Berlin, Zuckmayer's play, with pointed crowd-scenes and epic songs, unashamedly sides with rebellious youth in the war of the generations. Karl Kraus's unacted and probably unactable mammoth-drama, *The Last Days of Mankind,* a virulent attack on warmongers, political hypocrisy and a sycophantic press, among other targets still valid today, that would take ten consecutive nights to play in full, was given a resplendent two-evening production by Hans Hollmann, at the new, as yet unfinished, City Theater in Basle. Nineteen players shared the hundreds of different roles of Kraus's epic anti-war drama by performing among the 350 spectators, grouped or deployed in various sectors of the theater's staircases and foyers. This fabulous panoramic production, lasting eight hours in all, yielded only a sampling of the original, yet a characteristic one, and earned Hollmann an invitation to Berlin, which had to be refused on logistic grounds, and his appointment as the theater's new head.

In Austria, Thomas Bernhardt was represented by two new plays, *Force of Habit,* a comedy of human foibles in a circus-setting, staged by Dieter Dorn at the Salzburg Festival, and *The President,* staged by Ernst Wendt on the Vienna Burg's small stage, about a republican ruler (Kurt Beck) who escapes an attempt on his life by a gang of anarchists to which his own son belongs and seeks refuge in Portugal with his mistress—a highly charged, topical political drama, written in the author's typically verbose vein. On the large stage, Giorgio Strehler, finally lured out of his native Italy, put on Goldoni's *Countryside Trilogy* in Ezio

Frigerio's familiar setting, while Klingenberg, with the help of John Napier, the English designer, on loan from the R.S.C., gave heraldic authenticity to *Richard II,* starring Michael Heltau. Edward Albee's *Seascape,* starring Peter Luehr and Hilde Krahl, was directed by its translator Pinkas Braun. Klingenberg's revival of Schnitzler's *Anatol* was notable for the inclusion of the sketch *Das Susse Madl,* never before staged. Two other Schnitzler dramas were *Professor Bernhardi,* staged by Hans Jaray at the Josefstadt Theater, and *Wild and Free,* staged by Gustav Manker at the Volkstheater.

Belgium and Holland

A relatively unadventurous policy, relying largely on revivals, characterized Belgian and Dutch repertories this past year. Exceptions were Peter Shaffer's *Equus,* a French-language premiere at the Belgian National; and Christopher Hampton's *Savages,* a similar first, a the Théâtre du Rideau, in Brussels. In Amsterdam an exception was a sequel by Lodewijk de Boer to his successful four-part TV satire entitled *The Family in Heaven;* and in Rotterdam a nightmarish evocation by the English director Pip Simmons entitled *An die Musik* of the Nazi genocide of the Jews.

France

The Comédie Française took a two-year lease on the Marigny while their main building was being redone and opened it with Jean Poiret's *Impromptu a Marigny,* a nostalgic, swift-moving revue of the company's past and present splendors, wittily directed by Jacques Charon, who appears in various guises, notably as Elvis Presley. The other items in the season's repertory included Rojas's *La Celestina,* adapted by Pierre Laville, Hugo's *Ernani,* directed by Robert Hossein, *The Idiot* by Gabriel Arout, based on Dostoevsky, and revivals of Racine's *Iphigénie,* Marivaux's *L'Ile de la Raison,* and Romains's *Monsieur Trouhadec Saisi par la Débauche.*

At the Odéon's two stages, the company was seen in Jean-Claude Grumberg's evocation of a bygone age, *En Revenant de l'Expo,* stylishly staged by Jean-Pierre Vincent, Hossein's production of Lorca's *The House of Bernarda Alba,* and new works by Billetdoux, Ganzl, and Louis Calaferte. At the Théâtre de l'Est Parisien the first smash hit was a musical collage of five of Jarry's plays called *Les Ubs,* staged by Georges Wilson, who, together with the remaining dozen players, acted, danced, sang and performed on the saxophone as to the manner born. The other was Guy Rétoré's delightfully comical production of Shaw's *Androcles and the Lion.*

At Jean Mercure's Théâtre de la Ville, Arthur Miller's *The Creation of the World and Other Business* was followed by Alain-René Lesage's 18th-century satire on the corrupting power of money, *Turcaret,* neatly staged by Serge Peyrat. Jean-Louis Barrault, now permanently ensconced in his new Théâtre d'Orsay, succeeded in amortizing building costs with a number of box-office draws including a two-hour-long, joyous, beautifully designed, kaleidoscopic stage adaptation of Nietzsche's *Thus Spake Zarathustra* (decor by Matias), a revival of *Christophe Colombe,* and of Colin Higgins' *Harold and Maude,* and, on the small stage, the world premiere of Mrozek's tragi-comic *The Emigrants,* that only an emigre like himself could have conceived.

The Théâtre de Chaillot, still building, remained closed but other venues for exciting new experiments were found. Foremost among them was the partly redecorated Théâtre des Bouffes du Nord, of which a five-year lease was granted by the state to Peter Brook and his international arts lab. Here, assisted by Jean-Pierre Vincent and a leavening of French actors, Brook and his mixed bag of players presented a new version, by Jean-Claude Carrière, of *Timon of Athens,* in the stalls area of a gutted audititorium, overlooking a gaping void of what had once been the stage. In Michel Launay's costumes, drawn from every period and clime, and with non-European musical sounds and chanting, the actors combined to give the obscure text of a drama about the corrupting power of money and the fickleness of friendship an entirely new meaning and orientation. The revolutionary disposition helped to create an unprecedented atmosphere of intimacy alternating with dramatic distancing. Their second production, equally collectively conceived under Brook's guiding hand, was a dramatization, by Carrière, Higgins, and the English playwright Dennis Cannan, of the American anthropologist Colin Turnbull's documentary book *The Mountain People,* called in Paris *The Iks,* after the central African tribe which had virtually been forced into self-genocide by the policies of successive British and native governments. A cast of eight (and a handful of children) of mixed nationality play the villagers, irrespective of age or sex, in the identical setting in which previously they had done *Timon.* It is a sad story, acted with such skill and inner conviction that it will bring a blush of shame at the reenactment of the cruelty of man to his own kind to anyone who goes to see it.

Not all was sadness on the French scene during the autumn festival, which sponsored Brook's efforts. *The Magic Circus* under Jerome Savary returned to Paris with a new crazy entertainment called *Goodbye, Mr. Freud,* which poked fun at everything under the sun, from psychoanalysis to all kinds of theatrical genres, from sex to romantic love, from outrageous costuming to sheer nudity. Equally stimulating was Ariane Mnouchkine's return to the Cartoucherie in Vincennes in a collectively-mounted politically-slanted show called *The Golden Age,* which seriously decried, when it did not wittily poke fun at, everything in our farcically organized world and had the audience (as always with her *Théâtre du Soleil* company) moving with the actors from one field of action to another.

Another familiar directing name was that of Antoine Bourseiller, newly established in his own Parisian home, the Récamier, which he launched with an outrageous version of Genet's *The Balcony,* designed by the Rumanian team of Radu and Miruna Boruzescu, and Sylvia Plath's *Three Women,* starring Garance. Roger Planchon's Lyons-based *Théâtre National Populaire* did not fulfil its promise to stop off in Paris during its current tour, so enthusiasts had to make the long journey south to see his tribute to the drama of the late Arthur Adamov (called

A.A.), Patrice Chéreau's production of Bond's *Lear,* and his own collage, called *Bourgeois Follies,* of extracts from some 25 plays staged in Paris before World War I and published in the magazine *La Petite Illustration,* to prove that the trivial TV world of today is much the same as the one that went before.

The private sector seemed to feel the financial pinch less than the subsidized theaters, who not only complained of inadequate subsidy but also criticized the seemingly arbitrary dispositions of the new Cultural Minister, Michel Guy, both as to the allocation of funds and the appointment of heads of theaters and cultural centers. There were, as usual, several money-spinning plays on the boulevard, enjoying both long runs and enthusiastic popular support. Among them were Françoise Dorin's *The Hit Tune,* in which François Perier played the hard-working father of a teenage pop musician who strikes gold the easy way; Jacques Fabbri's hilarious 19th-century backstage comedy *The Glouton Band;* a humorous two-hander by Roland Dubillard, with the untranslatable title of *Diablogues,* a series of quaint sketches for himself and Roland Piéplu; revivals of plays by Anouilh *(Colombe),* Roussin *(L'Amour Fou,)* and Giraudoux *(The Madwoman of Chaillot,* starring Edwige Feuillère); and on the more serious side, the Brazilian author Roberto Athayde's *Madame Marguerite,* a monodrama about a school teacher, performed first by Annie Girardot and then by Madeleine Robinson; and, finally, Arrabal's latest essay in scatology and blasphemy, in the shape of a skit on cycle racing, called *Young Barbarians of Today.*

A particularly large number of foreign plays were done this season. They ranged from Elie Wiesel's drama of the Jews in Soviet Russia, *Zalmen, or the Madness of God,* to Robert Hossein's revival of the Gaston Baty version of *Crime and Punishment.* They included plays by Goethe, Hartmut Lange, Peter Handke, Martin Walser, Wedekind, Buechner and Brecht from Germany; Trevor Griffiths, Peter Terson, Alan Ayckbourn, Richard O'Brien and Shakespeare from England; Tom Eyen, Frank D. Gilroy, Paul Zindel, Israel Horovitz, Tennessee Williams, Lanford Wilson and O'Neill from the U.S.; Pirandello and Aldo Nicolaj from Italy; Chekhov and Babel from Russia; Orkeny from Hungary, Holberg from Denmark and Joao Bethencourt from Brazil. And, last but not least, I must not overlook a hitherto unperformed drama by Henry de Montherlant, *Exile,* his first, written in 1915, at the age of 18, about a wartime lad's tragic relationship with a doting and domineering mother.

Italy

The first new play for seven years by Franco Brusati, *The Roses of the Lake,* brought the team of Rina Morelli and Paolo Stoppa back to the Roman stage, where Franco Enriquez revived a ten-year-old production of *The Taming of the Shrew,* featuring Valeria Moriconi's Katharine. Mario Missiroli directed a new *Tartuffe,* played by Ugo Tognazzi. Another welcome return visit was paid by Giorgio de Lullo, who teamed up with Romolo Valli once more to stage Pirandello's *Tutto per Bene* in Pier Luigi Pizzi's decors. At Turin's City Theater, Aldo Trionfo scored a world first by staging Carl Dreyer's unique film script of *Jesus,* which the Dane did not live to shoot, as a play. In Genoa Luigi Squarzin's version of *Long Day's Journey Into Night* marked a new departure for a director who until then had specialized in Pirandello and Brecht, and, at the same theater, Giorgio Albertozzi was given the task of staging Pirandello's *The Late Matthew Pascal* in his stead. Edmo Fenoglio followed up the previous year's sensational Svevo comedy of *Regeneration* with a satirically stylized version of Ibsen's *An Enemy of the People,* again with Tino Buazzelli in the lead, and both plays attracted considerable attention when visiting the World Theater Season in London. Finally, in Milan Strehler staged a new Chekhov and a new Goldoni: *The Cherry Orchard* was given a thoroughly new look in Luciano Damiani's billowing white-sheeted setting, and *The Town Square* approximated more to the familiar, veristic Goldoni preferred by this inspired director.

Scandinavia

Once again the two pillars of the directing establishment in Stockholm claimed most of the attention: Alf Sjoberg with *Galilei,* starring the monumental Toivo Pawlo in an otherwise well-thought-out production that tended to sink somewhat beneath the weight of its changing scenery; and Ingmar Bergman, whose *Twelfth Night* was his second attempt to tackle Shakespeare. In a simulated Elizabethan theatrical set, designed by Gunilla Palmstjerna-Weiss, Bergman tried to reproduce something of the 16th-century atmosphere of the original by having Antonio, made up like the Bard, presenting his company as players within a play, while an orchestra performed throughout on a balcony in full view of the audience. Bibi Andersson made a delightfully tomboyish Viola and Lil Terselius looked ravishing as Olivia. But the main intention, that of stressing the unrequited love of the young and the absurdity of the sexual longings of the elderly, was nicely realized by having the clownish principals played as balding, sexually impotent dreamers, with the puritanical, but sexually uncontrollable Malvolio (Jan-Olof Strandberg) somewhere halfway in between them and the young ones. The City Theater's sellout, a native revue called *Girls, by Jove,* traced the story of Sweden's fight for women's emancipation over the past 50 years, in a series of witty and ironic sketches with music that had the teenagers collapsing in the aisles for months on end. In Gothenburg, whose earlier production of *Gustav III* at the City Theater had graced both the Edinburgh Festival and the World Theater Season, the actor of the title role, Sven Wollter, made his directing debut with the European premiere of the Turkish novelist's Yasar Kemal's *The Drums,* a play that dealt with the exploitation of Anatolian cotton-growing peasants by rapacious landlords, while the theater's resident dramatist, Kent Andersson, appeared in his own play, *The Hole in the Ground,* a touching slice of Gothenburg working-class history laced with social criticism.

Two outstanding offerings at Oslo's National Theater were Kirsten Sorlie's sprightly production of *The Taming of the Shrew,* with Kari Simonsen as Katharina, and Edith Roger's of *Peer Gynt,* designed by Czech guest-artist Lubos Hruza, and with three separate actors playing Peer in three stages of his life, as boy, as adult, and as old man. This compared interestingly with Keve Hjelm's version of the same play at Stockholm's City Theater (in a new translation by Lars Forssell), which was spread over two evenings with two different actors each night.

Eastern Europe

Two plays by Rustam Ibrahimbekov were added to the repertories of Moscow Theaters this season: at the Mayakovski Theater, in *Unpublished Report,* an oil-prospecting engineer takes on single-handed an army of bureaucrats, whose instructions to dig for his oil in a different part of Siberia cannot be lightly disobeyed; at the Moscow Art Theater, in the farcical melodrama *With the Looks of a Lion,* a social rebel, whose wife "misunderstands" him, kicks over the traces. Oleg Yefremov, at the last-named, staged a sentimental comedy, with a moral message, entitled *The Old New Year,* by Mikhail Roshchin, and Leonid Zorin's elegiac comedy, *The Pokrovsky Gate* was Anatoli Efros's contribution to the Drama Theater (on the Malya Bronnaya), while the Satiric Theater celebrated its 50th anniversary with a new production by Valentin Pluchek of Mayakovsky's hoary satirical fantasy, *The Bed Bug.* A curiosity at the Gogol Theater was *Rock-'n-Roll at Dawn,* a musical by Thomas Kolesnichenko and Vadim Nekrassov, which purported to give an authentic picture of the American drug scene with the use of taped extracts from the score of *Jesus Christ Superstar. Wooden Horses,* a tragedy of village life, based on two stories by Fyodor Abramov, was staged by Yuri Liubimov at the Taganka Theater.

The Annual Polish Theater Review in Warsaw had two outstanding entries, both from the previous season in Krakow, whose Stary deserves to be called Poland's leading theater. The first was a verse play, *November Night,* by Stanislaw Wyspianski, staged by Andrzej Wajda and designed by Krystyna Zachwatowicz. It deals with the abortive officers' uprising against the Russian occupying power in 1830. Wajda uses a musical score to separate the historical from the mythological characters that people the drama, and, as always, he created his own stage designs for it. The other entry, by the same author, was *Liberation,* staged by Konrad Swinarski, with both Pirandellian and Brechtian elements in it. It deals with the subjugation of Polish nationalism in terms of a play within a play, supposedly enacted on the stage of a Krakow theater. Wajda's subsequent contribution to the Warsaw scene was at the capital's newest, rebuilt People's Theater, where he staged Stanislawa Przybyszewska's version of a slice of French political history, called *The Danton Affair,* in the round. At the National Theater Adam Hanuszkewicz once again scandalized orthodox tastes by his irreverent treatment of such classics as Slowacki's pseudo-Shakespearean *Balladyna,* a revival of Wyspianski's *The Wedding,* and at his small arena stage Turgenev's *A Month in the Country,* all popular with his largely youthful audiences despite everything said against him. Warsaw's second newest theater, the Kwadrat (The Square), operated by

Polish TV and devoted to lighter fare, opened with Thurber's *The Male Animal,* staged by Edward Dziewonski. At Janusz Warminski's Ateneum Theater, the revival of *The Mannequins' Ball,* an inter-war satire on Parisian middle-class mores by Bruno Jasienski, who perished in a Stalinist camp, was the talking-point of a very fruitful year.

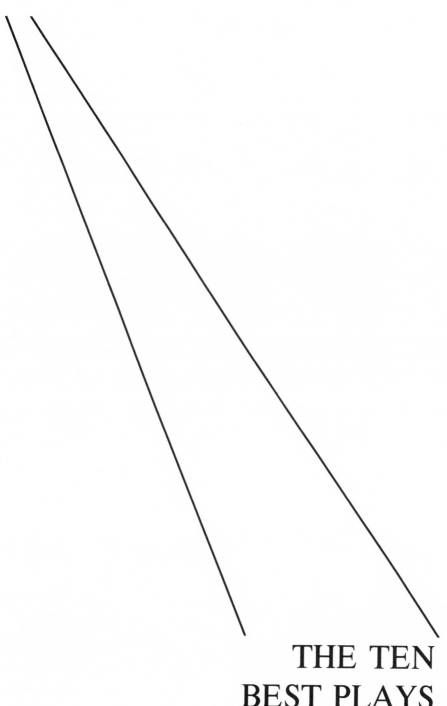

THE TEN
BEST PLAYS

Here are the synopses of 1974–75's ten Best Plays. By permission of the publishing companies which own the exclusive rights to publish these scripts in full in the United States, our continuities include many substantial quotations from crucial/pivotal scenes in order to provide a permanent reference to the style and quality of each play as well as its theme, structure and story line.

Scenes and lines of dialogue, stage directions and description quoted in the synopses appear *exactly* as in the stage version unless (in a very few instances, for technical reasons) an abridgement is indicated by five dots (. . . . .). The appearance of three dots (. . .) is the script's own punctuation to denote the timing of a spoken line.

EQUUS

A Play in Two Acts

BY PETER SHAFFER

Cast and credits appear on page 324

PETER SHAFFER was born in England, at Liverpool, in 1926 (Anthony Shaffer, author of Sleuth, *is his twin). He attended St. Paul's School in London and spent three years at Trinity College, Cambridge (and three years working in English coal mines as a "Bevin Boy" in World War II). In 1951, aged 25, he came to the United States where for still another three years he worked in New York City at Doubleday Book Shop and in the Acquisitions Department of the New York Public Library. He also worked as editor in the Symphonic Department of a London music publishing firm, all the while pursuing a writing career which began to take shape with the production of his* The Salt Land, The Prodigal Father *and* Balance of Terror *on British television. In 1958 his play* Five Finger Exercise *was a success in London. In December, 1959 it was presented in New York at the Music Box and was named a Best Play of its season and the New York Drama Critics choice for Best Foreign Play.*

A pair of Peter Shaffer one-actors, The Private Ear *and* The Public Eye, *were produced in 1963 at the Morosco after a London production that ran 18 months. In 1964 his* The Royal Hunt of the Sun *was the first work by a contemporary playwright to be done by England's National Theater. The following season, in 1965, it was produced on Broadway for 261 performances and was named a Best Play of 1965–66. His next play,* Black Comedy, *was commissioned by the National Theater and produced in 1965. It came to Broadway in 1967 for 337 performances*

Shaffer one-actor, White Lies, *written especially for this tandem production. His next,* The Battle of Shrivings, *was produced in London for 73 performances in the 1970 season.*

Peter Shaffer's third National Theater presentation (in July, 1973) was Equus, *which arrived on Broadway this season to become his fourth Best Play. In life as well as in art, its author is trans-Atlantically active, residing in London but spending a considerable portion of each year in New York.*

The following synopsis of Equus *was prepared by Jeff Sweet.*

Time: The present

Place: In and near Rokeby Psychiatric Hospital in Southern England

SYNOPSIS: The setting is a square of wood set on a circle of wood. The play is divided into numbered scenes, indicating a change of time or locale or mood, but the action is continuous. The published version of the script includes the following author's specifications for his play's physical and stylistic character:

"The square resembles a railed boxing ring. The rail, also of wood, encloses three sides. It is perforated on each side by an opening. Under the rail are a few vertical slats, as if in a fence. On the downstage side, there is no rail. The whole square is set on ball bearings, so that by slight pressure from actors standing round it on the circle, it can be made to turn round smoothly by hand.

"On the square are set three little plain benches, also of wood. They are placed parallel with the rail, against the slats, but can be moved out by the actors to stand at right angles to them.

"Set into the floor of the square, and flush with it, is a thin metal pole, about a yard high. This can be raised out of the floor, to stand upright. It acts as a support for the actor playing the horse Nugget, when he is ridden.

"In the area outside the circle stand benches. Two downstage left and right are curved to accord with the circle. . . . . Further benches stand upstage, and accommodate the actors. All the cast of *Equus* sits on stage the entire evening. They get up to perform their scenes and return when they are done to their places around the set. They are witnesses, assistants—and especially a Chorus.

"Upstage, forming a backdrop to the whole, are tiers of seats in the fashion of a dissecting theater, formed into two railed-off blocks, pierced by a central tunnel. In these blocks sit members of the audience. During the play, the actor playing Dysart addresses them directly from time to time, as he addresses the main body of the theater. No other actor ever refers to them. To left and right, downstage, stand two ladders on which are suspended horse masks. The color of all benches is olive green.

"The Horses: The actors wear track-suits of chestnut velvet. On their feet are light strutted hooves, about four inches high, set on metal horseshoes. On their hands are gloves of the same color. On their heads are tough masks made of alternating bands of silver wire and leather: their eyes are outlined by leather blinkers. The actors' own heads are seen beneath them: no attempt should be made to conceal them.

"Any literalism which could suggest the cosy familiarity of a domestic animal —or worse, a pantomime horse—should be avoided. The actors should never crouch on all fours, or even bend forward. They must always—except on the one occasion where Nugget is ridden—stand upright, as if the body of the horse extended invisibly behind them. Animal effect must be created entirely mimetically, through the use of legs, knees, neck, face, and the turn of the head which can move the mask above it through all the gestures of equine wariness and pride. Great care must also be taken that the masks are put on before the audience with very precise timing—the actors watching each other, so that the masking has an exact and ceremonial effect.

"The Chorus: References are made in the text to the Equus Noise. I have in mind a choric effect, made by all the actors sitting around upstage, and composed of humming, thumping, and stamping—though never of neighing or whinnying. This Noise heralds or illustrates the presence of Equus the God."

ACT I

Scene 1

> *Darkness. Silence. Dim light up on the square. In a spotlight stands Alan Strang, a lean boy of 17, in sweater and jeans; in front of him, the horse Nugget. Alan's pose represents a contour of great tenderness: his head is pressed against the shoulder of the horse, his hands stretching up to fondle its head. The horse in turn nuzzles his neck. The flame of a cigarette lighter jumps in the dark. Lights come up slowly on the circle. On the left bench, downstage, is Martin Dysart, a man in his mid-40s. He is smoking.*

DYSART: With one particular horse, called Nugget, he embraces. The animal digs its sweaty brow into his cheek, and they stand in the dark for an hour—like a necking couple. And of all nonsensical things—I keep thinking about the *horse!* Not the boy: the horse, and what it may be trying to do. I keep seeing that huge head kissing him with its chained mouth. Nudging through the metal some desire absolutely irrelevant to filling its belly or propagating its own kind. What desire could that be? Not to stay a horse any longer? Not to remain reined up forever in those particular genetic strings? Is it possible, at certain moments we cannot imagine, a horse can add its sufferings together—the non-stop jerks and jabs that are its daily life—and turn them into grief? What use is grief to a horse?

> *Alan leads Nugget out of the square and they disappear together up the tunnel, the horse's hooves scraping delicately on the wood. Dysart rises and addresses both the large audience in the theater and the smaller one on stage.*

You see, I'm lost. What use, I should be asking, are questions like these to an overworked psychiatrist in a provincial hospital? They're worse than useless: they are, in fact, subversive.

He enters the square. The light grows brighter.

The thing is, I'm desperate. You see, I'm wearing that horse's head myself. That's the feeling. All reined up in old language and old assumptions, straining to jump clean-hoofed on to a whole new track of being I only suspect is there. I can't see it, because my educated, average head is being held at the wrong angle. I can't jump because the bit forbids it, and my own basic force—my horsepower, if you like—is too little. The only thing I know for sure is this: a horse's head is finally unknowable to me, yet I handle children's heads and try to alter them. After a while, presumption begins to leave a taste, even in the most confident mouth . . . In a way, it has nothing to do with this boy. The doubts have been there for years, piling up steadily in this dreary place. It's only the extremity of this case that's made them active. I know that. The *extremity* is the point! All the same, whatever the reason, they are now, these doubts, not just vaguely worrying—but intolerable . . . I'm sorry. I'm not making much sense. Let me start properly: in order. It began one Monday last month, with Hester's visit.

Scene 2

Hester, *"a woman in her mid-40s,"* comes to Dysart with a special problem. She is a magistrate dealing with juvenile offenses, and she feels that one of her cases needs Dysart's special attention. Dysart objects that his work load is too full already, but she insists that he is the only one who can help as the case is so shocking that she is afraid others would be too revolted to have sufficient sympathy to help the boy in question. "Why? What's he done?" asks Dysart. "He blinded six horses with a metal spike," she replies. The blindings took place one night in the stables near Winchester in which the boy worked weekends. Dysart relents and agrees to see him.

Scene 3

Alan Strang is brought to Dysart's office for the first time. Referring to his file, Dysart tries to make contact with the boy with trivial conversation, but Alan refuses to answer directly, instead singing advertising jingles. Dysart tries to relate to him through the jingles, but the boy petulantly refuses to respond. Dysart tells the boy he will be put in a private room with access to a television set, more pleasant than staying in a ward. "By the way, which parent is it who won't allow you to watch television? Mother or father? Or is it both?" Alan, staring at him, doesn't answer the question. The nurse arrives to take him away. Fascinated, Dysart watches him go.

Scene 4

The nurse shows Alan to his room. Alan again responds by singing. She tells him, "I hope you're not going to make a nuisance of yourself. You'll have a much better time of it here, you know, if you behave yourself." For the first time, Alan responds without a jingle, saying, "Fuck off." She leaves.

PETER FIRTH IN "EQUUS"

Scene 5

Dysart describes to the audience a dream he had that night in which he saw himself as a chief priest, wearing a mask resembling the Mask of Agamemnon. He held a sharp knife and stood by "a thick round stone" and, with the help of two masked assistant priests, was in the process of sacrificing, one by one, the children of Argos.

DYSART: . . . . . They are enormously strong, these other priests, and absolutely tireless. As each child steps forward, they grab it from behind and throw it over the stone. Then, with a surgical skill which amazes even me, I fit in the knife and slice elegantly down to the navel, just like a seamstress following a pattern. I part the flaps, sever the inner tubes, yank them out and throw them hot and steaming on to the floor. The other two then study the pattern they make, as if they were reading hieroglyphics. It's obvious to me that I'm tops as chief priest. It's this unique talent for carving that has got me where I am. The only thing is, unknown to them, I've started to feel distinctly nauseous. And with each victim it's getting worse. My face is going green behind the mask. Of course, I redouble my efforts to look professional—cutting and snipping for all I'm worth: mainly because I know that if ever those two assistants so much as glimpse my distress—and the implied doubt that this repetitive and smelly work is doing any social good at all —I will be the next across the stone. And then, of course—the damn mask begins to slip. The priests both turn and look at it—it slips some more—they see the green sweat running down my face—their gold pop-eyes suddenly fill up with blood—they tear the knife out of my hand . . . and I wake up.

Scene 6

    Hester enters the square. Light grows warmer.
HESTER: That's the most indulgent thing I ever heard.
DYSART: You think?
HESTER: Please don't be ridiculous. You've done the most superb work with children. You must know that.
DYSART: Yes, but do the children?
HESTER: Really!
DYSART: I'm sorry.
HESTER: So you should be.
DYSART: I don't know why you listen. It's just professional menopause. Everyone gets it sooner or later. Except you.
 HESTER: Oh, of course. I feel totally fit to be a magistrate all the time.
 DYSART: No, you don't—but then that's you feeling unworthy to fill a job. I feel the job is unworthy to fill me.
HESTER: Do you seriously?
DYSART: More and more. I'd like to spend the next ten years wandering very slowly around the *real* Greece . . . Anyway, all this dream nonsense is your fault.
HESTER: Mine?
DYSART: It's that lad of yours who started it off. Do you know it's his face I saw on every victim across the stone?
HESTER: Strang?
DYSART: He has the strangest stare I ever met.
HESTER: Yes.
DYSART: It's exactly like being accused. Violently accused. But what of? . . . Treating him is going to be unsettling. Especially in my present state . . .

The scene with Hester continues, running concurrently with a reenactment of what Dysart is describing. The nurse, he says, has told him that Alan too has been having nightmares, screaming out the word "Ek!" in his sleep over and over. Now a session with Alan is re-enacted. The boy bursts in on Dysart unannounced and tells him that his father, Frank, was the one who prohibited television at home.
 A further flashback between Alan and his middle-aged father and mother, Dora, is staged. Dora has brought television into the house and Frank, an old-style socialist, tells his wife and son that the set will have to be returned

to the shop. "You sit in front of that thing long enough, you'll become stupid for life—like most of the population," he asserts. Frank is a printer, and he is particularly disturbed that Alan does virtually no reading. Dora tries to get Frank to change his mind about the set, to no avail. Frank and Dora return to their seats.

The focus of the flashback returns to the session between Dysart and Alan. Alan is especially proud of the fact that his mother was a schoolteacher.

ALAN (belligerently, standing up): She knows more than you.

> Hester crosses and sits by Dysart. During the following, the boy walks round the circle, speaking to Dysart but not looking at him. Dysart replies in the same manner.

DYSART (to Alan): Does she?

ALAN: I bet I do too. I bet I know more history than you.

DYSART (to Alan): Well, I bet you don't.

ALAN: All right: who was the Hammer of the Scots?

DYSART (to Alan): I don't know: who?

ALAN: Edward the First. Who never smiled again?

DYSART (to Alan): I don't know: who?

ALAN: You don't know anything, do you? It was Henry the First. I know all the kings.

DYSART (to Alan): And who's your favorite?

ALAN: John.

DYSART (to Alan): Why?

ALAN: Because he put out the eyes of that smarty little—(Pause; sensing he has said something wrong.) Well, he didn't really. He was prevented, because the jailer was merciful!

HESTER: Oh dear.

ALAN: He was prevented!

DYSART: Something odder was to follow.

ALAN: Who said "Religion is the opium of the people"?

HESTER: Good Lord!

> Alan giggles.

DYSART: The odd thing was, he said it with a sort of a guilty snigger. The sentence is obviously associated with some kind of tension.

HESTER: What did you say?

DYSART: I gave him the right answer. (To Alan.) Karl Marx.

ALAN: No.

DYSART (to Alan): Then who?

ALAN: Mind your own beeswax.

DYSART: It's probably his dad. He may say it to provoke his wife.

HESTER: And you mean she's religious?

DYSART: She could be. I tried to discover—none too successfuly.

ALAN: Mind your own beeswax!

> Alan goes back to bed and lies down in the dark.

DYSART: However, I shall find out on Sunday.

HESTER: What do you mean?

DYSART *(getting up):* I want to have a look at his home, so I invited myself over.

HESTER: Did you?

DYSART: If there's any tension over religion, it should be evident on Sabbath evening! I'll let you know.

Scene 7

Hester returns to her seat as Dora enters the square, which now represents the Strangs' home. Frank is still at work, not setting much store by Sundays. Dysart proposes to Dora that they talk. Dora is bewildered by the turn of events, as Alan had always shown a great love of animals, particularly horses.

DORA: . . . . . He even has a photograph of one up in his bedroom. A beautiful white one, looking over a gate. His father gave it to him a few years ago, off a calendar he'd printed—and he's never taken it down . . . And when he was seven or eight, I used to have to read him the same book over and over, all *about* a horse.

DYSART: Really?

DORA: Yes: it was called Prince, and no one could ride him.

Alan calls from his bed, not looking at his mother . . .

ALAN *(excited, younger voice):* Why not? . . . Why not? . . . Say it! In his voice!

DORA: He loved the idea of animals talking.

DYSART: Did he?

ALAN: *Say it! Say it! . . . Use his voice!*

DORA *("proud" voice):* "Because I am faithful!"

Alan giggles.

"My name is Prince, and I'm a Prince among horses! Only my young Master can ride me! Anyone else—I'll *throw off!*"

Alan giggles louder.

And then I remember I used to tell him a funny thing about falling off horses. Did you know that when Christian cavalry first appeared in the New World, the pagans thought horse and rider was one person?

DYSART: Really?

ALAN *(sitting up, amazed):* One person?

DORA: Actually, they thought it must be a god.

ALAN: *A god!*

DORA: It was only when one rider fell off, they realized the truth.

DYSART: That's fascinating. I never heard that before. . . . Can you remember anything else like that you may have told him about horses?

DORA: Well, not really. They're in the Bible, of course. "He saith among the trumpets, Ha, ha."

DYSART: Ha, ha?

DORA: The Book of Job. Such a noble passage. *You* know—*(Quoting.)* "Hast thou given the horse strength?"

ALAN *(responding):* "Hast thou clothed his neck with thunder?"

DORA *(to Alan):* "The glory of his nostrils is terrible!"
ALAN: "He swallows the ground with fierceness and rage!"
DORA: "He saith among the trumpets—"
ALAN *(trumpeting):* "Ha! Ha!"
DORA *(to Dysart):* Isn't that splendid?
DYSART: It certainly is.
ALAN *(trumpeting):* Ha! Ha!

Dora also tells Dysart that she used to allow Alan to go to a neighbor's to watch the horses in Westerns on TV. Frank returns as Dora continues to tell Dysart about the boy's interest in the word *equus,* Latin for horse, and the curious fact that, despite his love for horses and his weekend job at the stables, he never rode them.

At Frank's suggestion, Dora leaves, ostensibly to make some tea for Dysart, but instead she eavesdrops as Frank tells Dysart that Alan was always closer to her than to himself. Frank is an atheist, and he tells of his disapproval of her habit of reading the Bible to Alan hours at a time. He believes the Bible is to blame for Alan's situation, what with his head having been filled night after night with gruesome scenes like the crucifixion. "It can mark anyone for life, that kind of thing."

Unable to stand any more, Dora comes in again.
DORA *(pleasantly):* You must excuse my husband, Doctor. This one subject is something of an obsession with him, isn't it dear? You must admit.
FRANK: Call it what you like. All that stuff to me is just bad sex.
DORA: And what has that got to do with Alan?
FRANK: Everything! . . . *(Seriously.)* Everything, Dora!
DORA: I don't understand. What are you saying?
He turns away from her.

Dysart seizes the opportunity to ask about Alan's sexual instruction. Dora says she tried to teach him a little, not only the biological facts, but also her beliefs regarding the spiritual side of love. She suddenly breaks into tears. Frank goes to comfort her. They leave the square together.

Scene 8

Alan is having a nightmare, crying out "Ek!" in his sleep as he turns and twists in bed. Dysart enters his room. The boy suddenly wakes. They look at each other and Dysart leaves, returning to the square.

Scene 9

The next day, Alan comes into the office, agreeing to answer Dysart's questions only if Dysart answers his. They will take turns. Dysart wants to know about Alan's dream. Alan denies remembering the dream and in turn asks Dysart what his dreams are about. "Carving up children," the doctor replies. Dysart now tries to get Alan to talk about the first time he saw a horse and the meaning of "Ek." Alan starts singing a commercial jingle. Dysart calls an end to their session. Alan is furious, but he wants to continue the session, so he begins to answer Dysart's questions about his first encounter with a horse.

Scene 10

A flashback is performed to Alan's narration. He is 6 and on a beach. A horseman comes by and offers him a ride. Alan accepts and climbs on. His parents see him riding and are alarmed. Frank yanks the boy off the horse and berates the horseman for endangering the boy. The horseman calls Frank "a stupid fart" and, saying goodbye to Alan, rides off, the horse kicking sand and water all over the family in the process. Dora is somewhat amused by Frank's appearance, but her husband is incensed.

Frank and Dora leave the square as the flashback ends. Alan tells Dysart that he hasn't ridden a horse since then. Dysart tries to get his reason, but Alan's only answer is that he simply doesn't care to.

Dysart tells him that sometimes his patients are ashamed to tell him certain things to his face and that, in such cases, he gives them a tape recorder to record what they want to say. They don't have to be present when he listens to the tape. Alan ridicules this procedure, but at the end of the session, he takes the machine with him.

Scene 11

That evening, Dora comes to visit the doctor. She and her husband have remembered something which might be important. The picture of the horse over Alan's bed had replaced a somewhat gruesome religious picture of Christ on his way to Calvary, full of chains and lashing. Alan had bought it when he was 12 and had loved it. One day, during an argument with his wife on religion, Frank had ripped the picture off the wall and disposed of it. Alan cried for a long time until his father gave him the picture of the horse, which Alan put up in the other picture's old spot. The photo in question is of a horse looking at the camera head on, with huge eyes staring out. It's an uncomfortable moment for her. She tells Dysart that she will look in on Alan sometime soon, then she leaves.

"It was then—that moment—I felt real alarm," Dysart tells the audience. "What was it? The shadow of a giant head across my desk?"

Scene 12

Dalton, owner of the stable, *"heavy set: mid-50s,"* comes to visit Dysart. He feels Alan should be put into prison. He tells Dysart that Jill, a girl who had worked for him and had introduced the boy to him, has had a nervous breakdown because of what has happened. Dalton tells Dysart that Alan had been a very good stable hand, but that he had had the suspicion, never proved, that the boy had taken the horses out at night. Dalton leaves.

Scene 13

Dysart plays the tape Alan has recorded and sent him. We hear Alan's voice not from the machine but as he sits in his room talking. Alan says that riding the horse that time on the beach was "sexy."

ALAN: . . . . . I was pushed forward on the horse. There was sweat on my legs from his neck. The fellow held me tight, and let me turn the horse which way I wanted. All that power going any way you wanted . . . His sides were all warm, and the smell . . . Then suddenly I was on the ground, where Dad pulled me. I could have bashed him . . .
        Pause.
Something else. When the horse first appeared, I looked up into his mouth. It was huge. There was this chain in it. The fellow pulled it, and cream dripped out. I said, "Does it hurt?" And he said—the horse said—said—
        He stops, in anguish. Dysart makes a note in his file.

Thereafter, Alan's fascination with horses grew. He loved to watch them and became deeply empathetic with them. He never told anyone.

ALAN: . . . . . Mum wouldn't understand. She likes "Equitation". Bowler hats and jodhpurs! "My grandfather dressed for the horse," she says. What does that mean? The horse isn't dressed. It's the most naked thing you ever saw! More than a dog or a cat or anything. Even the most broken down old nag has got its *life!* To put a bowler on it is *filthy!* . . . Putting them through their paces! Bloody gymkhanas! . . . No one understands! . . . Except cowboys. They do. I wish I was a cowboy. They're free. They just swing up and then it's miles of grass . . . I bet all cowboys are *orphans!* . . . I bet they are!

The recording turns into a bitter tirade against his parents. Then, abruptly, he turns off the machine, ending the scene.

Scene 14

Frank visits Dysart, eliciting the doctor's promise not to tell his wife about anything he says. Eighteen months before, he confides, he'd accidentally over-heard Alan chanting in the middle of the night.

FRANK: Like the Bible. One of those lists his mother's always reading to him.
DYSART: What kind of list?
FRANK: Those begats. So-and-so begat, you know. Genealogy.
DYSART: Can you remember what Alan's list sounded like?
FRANK: Well, the *sort* of thing. I stood there absolutely astonished. The first word I heard was . . .
ALAN *(rising and chanting):* Prince!
DYSART: Prince?

FRANK: Prince begat Prance. That sort of nonsense.
> *Alan moves slowly to the center of the circle, downstage.*

ALAN: And Prance begat Prankus! And Prankus begat Flankus!

FRANK: I looked through the door, and he was standing in the moonlight in his pyjamas, right in front of that big photograph.

DYSART: The horse with the huge eyes?

FRANK: Right.

ALAN: Flankus begat Spankus. And Spankus begat Spunkus the Great, who lived three score years!

FRANK: It was all like that. I can't remember the exact names, of course. Then suddenly he knelt down.

DYSART: In front of the photograph?

FRANK: Yes. Right there at the foot of his bed.

ALAN *(kneeling)*: And Legwus begat Neckwus. And Neckwus begat Fleckwus, the King of Spit. And Fleckwus spoke out of his chinkle-chankle!
> *He bows himself to the ground.*

DYSART: What?

FRANK: I'm sure that was the word. I've never forgotten it. Chinkle-chankle.
> *Alan raises his head and extends his hands up in glory.*

ALAN: And he said "Behold—I give you Equus, my only begotten son!"

DYSART: Equus?

FRANK: Yes. No doubt of that. He repeated that word several times. "Equus my only begotten son."

ALAN *(reverently)*: Ek . . . wus!

DYSART *(suddenly understanding; almost aside)*: Ek . . . Ek . . .

FRANK *(embarrassed)*: And then . . .

DYSART: Yes: what?

FRANK: He took a piece of string out of his pocket. Made up into a noose. And put it in his mouth.
> *Alan bridles himself with invisible string and pulls it back.*

And then with his other hand he picked up a coat hanger. A wooden coat hanger, and—and—

DYSART: Began to beat himself?
> *Alan, in mime, begins to thrash himself, increasing the strokes in speed and viciousness. Pause.*

FRANK: You see why I couldn't tell his mother. . . . Religion. Religion's at the bottom of all this!

DYSART: What did you do?

FRANK: Nothing. I coughed—and went back downstairs.
> *The boy starts guiltily—tears the string from his mouth—and scrambles back to bed.*

DYSART: Did you ever speak to him about it later? Even obliquely?

FRANK *(unhappily)*: I can't speak of things like that, Doctor. It's not in my nature.

DYSART *(kindly)*: No. I see that.

Frank also informs Dysart that, though he cannot tell the circumstances under which he found out, he knows that the night of the blindings Alan was out with a girl. He exits.

Scene 15

Alan comes in for a session. Dysart brings up the subject of the tape. "One thing I didn't quite understand," he says. "You began to say something about the horse on the beach talking to you." "That's stupid," Alan replies. "Horses don't talk."

Dysart asks him how he found work at the stables. Alan tells him his father had gotten him a job at an electrical supply shop. A flashback in the shop is enacted with Alan scurrying to try to satisfy demanding customers. Then Jill, *"a girl in her early 20s, pretty and middle class,"* enters to buy blades for a machine to clip horses. He recognizes her as the girl who works at Dalton's stables. She recognizes him as the boy who keeps looking into the stables around lunch time. He initially denies this, until he learns there is a possibility of getting a weekend job there.

Scene 16

Jill introduces Alan to Dalton, who hires him. Dalton begins to instruct Alan in stable care, showing him how to use a hoof-pick to get stones out of the hooves. He leaves Alan in Jill's care. She shows him how to use the body brush and curry comb, demonstrating by grooming Nugget. She leaves him alone with the horses. Alan obviously has a natural touch with them. Dysart asks him what he thought about the girl and whether he took her out. The boy resists answering, then explodes into a rage, accusing Dysart of being like his father. The flashback dissolves.

Scene 17

Dysart apologizes. Alan, in a hostile mood, turns the tables on the doctor, baiting him about his childless and loveless marriage. This gets to Dysart, and he orders Alan out of the room. Addressing the audience, Dysart wryly observes that Alan had made enquiries around the hospital about his wife to dig up information to use as ammunition. "Advanced neurotics can be dazzling at that game. They aim unswervingly at your area of maximum vulnerability . . . Which is as good a way as any of describing Margaret."

Scene 18

Hester is in the office. Dysart opens his heart to her about his unsatisfying marriage. His wife is "a Scottish lady dentist," a very "brisk" and severely sensible woman. "We were very brisk in our wooing, brisk in our wedding, brisk in our disappointment," he confides. "We turned from each other briskly into our separate surgeries: and now there's damn all." Their home life consists of her knitting for orphans and his trying to recapture the glory of mythic Greece in art books. He wishes there were someone in his life with whom he could share this world of gods. Also he wishes there were gods he could truly worship in the here and now.

Hester excuses herself, thanking Dysart for what he is trying to do. What is that? he wonders. Restore the boy to a normal life, the magistrate replies. "Normal?" he says. "It still means something, you know," she insists. "Even though you can't exactly define it." She leaves.

Scene 19

Alan is in Dysart's office again, somewhat apologetic for the day before. Dysart suggests they play a game called "Blink," the purpose of which is to hypnotize Alan. As the process begins, Dysart turns to the audience again. The word "normal" is haunting him: "The Normal is a Holy Ghost. He is attended by Bad Angels and Good. But the Good, like Hester, really understand no more than the Bad, like Margaret! The Normal is a murderous, non-existing phantom. And I am his priest! My tools are very delicate. My compassion is honest. I have honestly assisted children in this room. I've talked away terrors. I've relieved many agonies. But also—beyond question—I have cut from them parts of individuality repugnant to this God . . . Sacrifices to Zeus took at the most, surely, sixty seconds each. Sacrifices to the Normal can take as long as sixty months."

In a trance now, the boy answers Dysart's questions. Out of the conversation it becomes apparent that Alan has evolved an elaborate personal religion around horses wherein Equus, the god he worships, is a chained spirit living in all horses. He talks with Equus.

DYSART: . . . . . Now tell me. Why is Equus in chains?
ALAN: For the sins of the world.
DYSART: What does he say to you?
ALAN: "I see you." "I will save you."
DYSART: How?
ALAN: "Bear you away. Two shall be one."
DYSART: Horse and rider shall be one beast?
ALAN: One person!
DYSART: Go on.
ALAN: "And my chinkle-chankle shall be in thy hand."
DYSART: Chinkle-chankle? That's his mouth chain?
ALAN: Yes.
DYSART: Good . . . . . Now: think of the stable. What is the stable? His Temple? His Holy of Holies?
ALAN: Yes.
DYSART: Where you wash him? Where you tend him, and brush him with many brushes?
ALAN: Yes.
DYSART: And there he spoke to you, didn't he? He looked at you with his gentle

eyes, and spake unto you?

ALAN: Yes.

DYSART: What did he say? "Ride me?" "Mount me, and ride me forth at night"?

ALAN: Yes.

DYSART: And you obeyed?

ALAN: Yes.

Alan learned how to ride by watching others. Once every three weeks, at night, he would take a horse out.

Scene 20

Dysart asks him to describe such a night in detail. Accompanied by the Equus Noise, Alan puts special sandals on Nugget's feet and, after first ritually putting the bit, or "chinkle-chankle", into his own mouth, puts it into the horse's, strapping on the bridle; no saddle, however. He leads the horse to a field. The horse resists going in. "It's his place of Ha Ha," Alan explains. Dysart tells him to make the horse go into the field.

Scene 21

"The Equus Noise dies away." The boy removes his clothing and puts a stick he calls the "manbit" into his mouth, "so's it won't happen too quick." He touches the horse all over and offers him a lump of sugar, the lump standing for the equivalent of The Last Supper. The horse is now ready to be mounted.

> *Alan, lying before Nugget, stretches out on the square. He grasps the top of the thin metal pole embedded in the wood. He whispers his god's name ceremonially.*

ALAN: Equus! . . . Equus! . . . Equus!

> *He pulls the pole upright. The actor playing Nugget leans forward and grabs it. At the same instant all the other horses lean forward around the circle, each placing a gloved hand on the rail. Alan rises and walks right back to the upstage corner, left.*

Take me!

> *He runs and jumps high on to Nugget's back.*

The horse wants to go now, but Alan restrains him. Dysart tells him not to, to ride away alone with Equus.

> *A hum from the Chorus. Very slowly the horses standing on the circle begin to turn the square by gently pushing the wooden rail. Alan and his mount start to revolve. The effect, immediately, is of a statue being slowly turned round on a plinth. During the ride, however, the speed increases, and the light decreases until it is only a fierce spotlight on*

horse and rider, with the overspill glinting on the other masks leaning in towards them.

On they ride against Equus's enemies—the "Hosts" bearing the brand names Alan has had to sell in the electrical supply house, and the "Hosts" of those who abuse the dignity and spirit of horses for their own vanity. Now they are observed by the admiring eyes of cowboys. Alan whips Nugget into a canter to "show them." *"The speed of the turning square increases."*

ALAN: . . . . . And Equus the Mighty rose against All!
His enemies scatter, his enemies fall!
TURN!
Trample them, trample them,
Trample them, trample them,
TURN!
Trample them, trample them,
Trample them, trample them,
TURN!
TURN!!
TURN!!!
 The Equus Noise increases in volume.
(*Shouting.*) WEE! . . . WAA! . . . WONDERFUL! . . .
I'm stiff! Stiff in the wind!
My mane, stiff in the wind!
My flanks! *My* hooves!
Kick night! Break night!
Mane on my legs, on my flanks, like whips!
Wind on my legs, on my flanks—whips!
Raw!
Raw!
I'm raw! Raw!
Feel me on you! *On* you! *On* you! *On* you!
I want to be *in* you!
I want to BE you forever and ever!—
Equus, I love you!
Now!—
Bear me away!
Make us One Person!
 He flogs Equus with the invisible stick.
One Person! One Person! One Person! One Person!
 He rises up on the horse's back and calls like a trumpet.
Ha-HA! . . . HA-Ha! . . . Ha-HA!
 The trumpet turns to great cries.
HA-HA! HA-HA! HA-HA! HA-HA! HA! . . . HA! . . . HAAAAA!
 He twists like a flame. Silence. The turning square comes to a stop in the same position it occupied at the opening of the act. Slowly the boy

drops off the horse's back on to the ground. He lowers his head and kisses Nugget's hoof. Finally he flings back his head and cries up to him.

AMEN!

Nugget snorts, once. Blackout.

ACT II

Scene 22

The scene begins with the same image as ended Act I. Alan gets up from his kneeling position, *"climbing lovingly up the body of the horse until he can stand and kiss it."* Dysart addresses the audience as Alan leads the horse away and returns to his room. Dysart is haunted by the image of Equus challenging his ability and right to exorcise him: "Of course, I've stared at such images before —or been stared at *by* them. But this one is the most alarming yet. It asks questions I've avoided all my professional life. Had to avoid. *Must* avoid to function. This kind of Why has no place in a consulting room."

The nurse enters to tell him that Dora is in her son's room and a row has ensued. Dysart arrives in time to see her slap Alan's face, trying to jar him out of the silent stare he has fixed on her. Dysart orders her out of the room.

Scene 23

In his office, Dysart tells Dora she must not return, that she has intruded on Alan in his most vulnerable and distressed state. She replies that she too is distressed. Psychiatry, she knows, often blames the problems of children on their parents. But she refuses to accept the blame. She and her husband have loved Alan and tried to do their best by him. No, what's happened to Alan came out of himself, she insists. Psychiatrists may use technical terms, but from her perspective the Devil is responsible. She leaves.

Scene 24

Dysart informs Alan that his mother knows nothing of what Alan has told him. Alan angrily replies that all he said in the trance was lies. Now he expects Dysart will be trying truth drugs on him, won't he?

Scene 25

Dysart tells Hester that Alan's allusion to a truth drug is a sign that he really wants one so he can have an excuse to unburden himself. Dysart intends to give Alan a pill with no drugs in it whatever. The boy, believing he has been drugged, will not just tell all but act out all and thus, afterwards, will not be able to deny what he reveals.

But Dysart is experiencing sharp moral qualms as to whether he should go through with his plan. "Can you think of anything worse one can do to anybody than take away their worship?" Equus is the passionate center of the boy's life, he explains. If he takes that away, what will Alan have left? Hester counters that what's important is that Dysart will be taking away the boy's pain. That isn't good enough for Dysart.

HESTER: Why not?

DYSART: Because it's his.

HESTER: I don't understand.

DYSART: His pain. His own. He made it. *(Pause; earnestly.)* Look . . . to go through life and call it yours—*your life*—you first have to get your own pain. Pain that's unique to you. You can't just dip into the common bin and say "That's enough!" . . . He's done that. All right, he's sick. He's full of misery and fear. He was dangerous, and could be again, though I doubt it. But that boy has known a passion more ferocious than I have felt in any second of my life. And let me tell you something: I envy it.

HESTER: You can't.

DYSART *(vehemently):* Don't you see? That's the Accusation! That's what his stare has been saying to me all this time. *"At least I galloped! When did you?"* . . . *(Simply.)* I'm jealous, Hester. Jealous of Alan Strang.

HESTER: That's absurd.

DYSART: Is it? . . . I go on about my wife. That smug woman by the fire. Have you thought of the fellow on the other side of it? The finicky, critical husband looking through his art books on mythical Greece. What worship has *he* ever known? Real worship! Without worship you shrink, it's as brutal as that . . . I shrank my *own* life. No one can do it for you. I settled for being pallid and provincial, out of my own eternal timidity. The old story of bluster, and do bugger-all . . . I imply that we can't have children: but actually it's only me. I had myself tested behind her back. The lowest sperm count you could find. And I never told her. That's all I need—her sympathy mixed with resentment . . . I tell everyone Margaret's the puritan, I'm the pagan. Some pagan! Such wild returns I make to the womb of civilization. Three weeks a year in the Peloponnesus, every bed booked in advance, every meal paid for by vouchers, cautious jaunts in hired Fiats, spongebag crammed with Entero-Vioform! Such a fantastic surrender to the primitive. And I use that word endlessly: "primitive." "Oh, the primitive world," I say. "What instinctual truths were lost with it!" And while I sit there, baiting a poor unimaginative woman with the word, that freaky boy tries to conjure the reality! I sit looking at pages of centaurs trampling the soil of Argos—and outside my window he is trying to *become one* in a Hampshire field! . . . I watch that woman knitting, night after night—a woman I haven't *kissed* in six years—and he stands in the dark for an hour, sucking the sweat off his god's hairy chest! *(Pause.)* Then in the morning, I put away my books on the cultural shelf, close up the Kodachrome snaps of Mount Olympus, touch my reproduction statue of Dionysus for luck—and go off to hospital to treat him for insanity. Do you see?

HESTER: The boy's in pain, Martin. That's all I see. In the end.

Hester suggests that Alan's stare may be not one of accusation but of adoration —that Dysart may now be a new god to the boy, or a new father. She smiles as she leaves him with this thought.

Scene 26

Dysart returns to his office to discover a note of apology from Alan, admitting all he said in the trance was true. Elated, Dysart asks the nurse to bring Alan to the room.

Scene 27

Dysart thanks Alan for the note and suggests they have a session now, even though it is very late at night. Wouldn't it be better than sleeping and risking nightmares? He hands Alan the placebo, letting him believe it is a truth drug, and tells him it will only help him do and say what he wants to do and say. While waiting for it to "take effect," Dysart intimates to Alan that he would like to stop being a psychiatrist and live in Greece with the ghosts of the old, dead gods. Alan says that gods are immortal, but Dysart tells him he knows better. Alan wonders why Dysart keeps to psychiatry if he doesn't like doing it. "Because you're unhappy," the doctor says. "So are you," retorts the boy. He apologizes. Dysart leads him to believe that his reply is a sign the drug is working. Dysart asks him to tell and show him about Jill.

Scene 28

As he tells his story to Dysart, Alan plays the events of the crucial night in flashback. Jill obviously is interested in him and she persuades him to take her to blue movies at a local theater.

Scene 29

It is the first time he has ever seen a naked girl. It isn't all he sees. His father is also in the audience. They spot each other. Frank orders his son out of the theater.

Scene 30

Alan, Jill and Frank leave the theater and walk to the bus stop, Alan protesting it is the first time he has ever been there and Jill backing him up. Frank is more concerned about formulating a satisfactory alibi to his son for his own presence there. When the bus comes, Frank orders Alan to join him, but Alan refuses, saying he intends to see Jill home. Frank gets on the bus alone, Alan seeing fear on his father's face. This upsets Alan deeply.

Scene 31

As he and Jill walk together, Alan's mind races with the implications of the revelation of this side of his father's character. He is initially angry, but talking with Jill he begins to realize that his father's impulses are the impulses of all men. This is reinforced when their walk takes them past several pubs out of which a number of men emerge. He tells Dysart, "I suddenly thought—*they all do it! All of them! . . . They're not just Dads—they're people with pricks! . . . And Dad —he's just not Dad either. He's a man with a prick, too. You know, I'd never thought about it.*"

They continue walking, finding themselves in the country. Alan keeps thinking about Frank, realizing that perhaps his mother might not satisfy his father in bed. For the first time he sympathizes with Frank, recognizing that they share a dislike for his mother's "la-di-da" affections, that they are in fact very similar. This makes him feel relieved, freer, happier. He is also happy that Jill is with him, and he begins to want to make love to her. She is receptive and tells him she knows the perfect place.

Scene 32

Her idea of a perfect place is the stables. He wants to be with her, but he shrinks from the idea of their going into the stables. She prevails on him, however.

Scene 33

They go inside. "Into the Temple? The Holy of Holies?" says Dysart. What choice has he, Alan counters. He couldn't tell her about Equus. He insists Jill close the door so the horses won't see them. They strip and embrace.

ALAN *(to Dysart):* She put her mouth in mine. It was lovely! *Oh, it was lovely! They burst into giggles. He lays her gently on the floor in the center of the square, and bends over her eagerly. Suddenly the Equus Noise fills the place. Hooves smash on wood. Alan straightens up, rigid. He stares straight ahead of him over the prone body of the girl.*
DYSART: Yes, what happened then, Alan?
ALAN *(to Dysart: brutally):* I put it in her!
DYSART: Yes?
ALAN *(to Dysart):* I put it in her!
DYSART: You did?
ALAN *(to Dysart):* Yes!
DYSART: Was it easy?
ALAN *(to Dysart):* Yes.
DYSART: Describe it.
ALAN *(to Dysart):* I told you.
DYSART: More exactly.
ALAN *(to Dysart):* I put it in her!
DYSART: Did you?
ALAN *(to Dysart):* All the way!
DYSART: Did you, Alan?
ALAN *(to Dysart):* All the way. I shoved it. I put it in her all the way.

DYSART: Did you?

ALAN *(to Dysart):* Yes!

DYSART: Did you?

ALAN *(to Dysart):* Yes! . . . Yes!

DYSART: Give me the TRUTH! . . . Did you? . . . *Honestly?*

ALAN *(to Dysart):* Fuck off!

> *He collapses, lying upstage on his face. Jill lies on her back motionless, her head downstage, her arms extended behind her. A pause.*

DYSART *(gently):* What was it? You couldn't? Though you wanted to very much?

ALAN *(to Dysart):* I couldn't . . . see her.

DYSART: What do you mean?

ALAN *(to Dysart):* Only Him. Every time I kissed her—*He* was in the way.

DYSART: Who?

> *Alan turns on his back.*

ALAN *(to Dysart):* You *know* who! . . . When I touched her, I felt *Him.* Under me . . . His side, waiting for my hand . . . His flanks . . . I refused him. I looked. I looked right at her . . . and I couldn't do it. When I shut my eyes, I saw him at once. The streaks on his belly . . . *(With more desperation.)* I couldn't feel *her* flesh at all! I wanted the foam off his neck. His sweaty hide. Not flesh. *Hide! Horse-hide!* . . . Then I couldn't even kiss her.

Jill, not understanding the source of his trouble, tells him that he shouldn't worry, that all men occasionally have problems performing sexually. Alan becomes hysterical and, brandishing the sharp horse pick, he chases her out of the stables. She dashes out the door past Nugget.

Scene 34

> *Alan stands alone, and naked. A faint humming and drumming. The boy looks about him in growing terror.*

DYSART: What?

ALAN *(to Dysart):* He was there. Through the door. The door was shut, but he was there! . . . He'd seen everything. I could hear him. He was laughing.

DYSART: Laughing?

ALAN *(to Dysart):* Mocking! . . . *Mocking!* . . .

> *Standing downstage as he stares up towards the tunnel. A great silence weighs on the square.*

(*To the silence: terrified.*) Friend . . . Equus the Kind . . . The Merciful! . . . . . Take me back again! Please! . . . PLEASE!

> *He kneels on the downstage lip of the square, still facing the door, huddling in fear.*

I'll never do it again. I swear . . . I swear! . . .

> *Silence.*

(*In a moan.*) Please!!! . . .

DYSART: And He? What does He say?

ALAN *(to Dysart: whispering):* "Mine! . . . You're mine! . . . I am yours and you are mine!" . . . Then I see his eyes. They are rolling!

Nugget begins to advance slowly, with relentless hooves, down the central tunnel.

"I see you. I see you. Always! Everywhere! Forever!"

DYSART: Kiss anyone and I will see?

ALAN *(to Dysart):* Yes!

DYSART: Lie with anyone and I will see?

ALAN *(to Dysart):* Yes.

DYSART: And you will fail! Forever and ever you will *fail!* You will see ME —and you will FAIL!

The boy turns round, hugging himself in pain. From the sides two more horses converge with Nugget on the rails. Their hooves stamp angrily. The Equus Noise is heard more terribly.

The Lord thy God is a jealous God. He sees you. He sees you forever and ever, Alan. He sees you! . . . *He sees you!*

ALAN *(in terror):* Eyes! . . . White eyes—never closed! Eyes like flames—coming —coming! . . . God seest! God seest! . . . NO! . . .

Pause. He steadies himself. The stage begins to blacken.

(Quieter.) No more. No more, Equus.

He gets up. He goes to the bench. He takes up the invisible pick. He moves slowly upstage towards Nugget, concealing the weapon behind his naked back, in the growing darkness. He stretches out his hand and fondles Nugget's mask.

(Gently.) Equus . . . Noble Equus . . . Faithful and true . . . Godslave . . . Thou —God—seest—NOTHING!

He stabs out Nugget's eyes. The horse stamps in agony. A great screaming begins to fill the theater, growing ever louder. Alan dashes at the other two horses and blinds them too, stabbing over the rails. Their metal hooves join in the stamping. Relentlessly, as this happens, three more horses appear in cones of light: not naturalistic animals like the first three, but dreadful creatures out of nightmare. Their eyes flare— their nostrils flare—their mouths flare. They are archetypical images —judging, punishing, pitiless. They do not halt at the rail, but invade the square. As they trample at him, the boy leaps desperately at them, jumping high and naked in the dark, slashing at their heads with arms upraised.

The screams increase. The other horses follow into the square. The whole place is filled with cannoning, blinded horses—and the boy dodging among them, avoiding their slashing hooves as best he can. Finally they plunge off into darkness and away out of sight. The noise dies abruptly, and all we hear is Alan yelling in hysteria as he collapses on the ground—stabbing at his own eyes with the invisible pick.

ALAN: Find me! . . . Find me! . . . Find me! . . . KILL ME! . . . KILL ME!

Scene 35

The flashback dissolves. Alan is having convulsions. Dysart rushes to keep him from doing injury to himself. Alan clings to the doctor. Dysart comforts him with assurances that Equus is gone and will not return. He puts a blanket on the boy and Alan falls asleep. Dysart looks at him sadly.

DYSART: I'm lying to you, Alan. He won't really go that easily. Just clop away from you like a nice old nag. Oh, no! When Equus leaves—if he leaves at all— it will be with your intestines in his teeth. And I don't stock replacements . . . If you knew anything, you'd get up this minute and run from me fast as you could.

> *Hester speaks from her place.*

HESTER: The boy's in pain, Martin.

DYSART: Yes.

HESTER: And you can take it away.

DYSART: Yes.

HESTER: Then that should be enough for you. . . . In the end?

DYSART *(crying out): All right! I'll take it away!* He'll be delivered from madness. *What then?* He'll feel himself acceptable! *What then?* Do you think feelings like his can be simply re-attached like plasters? Stuck on to other objects we select? *Look at him!* . . . My desire might be to make this boy an ardent husband—a caring citizen—a worshipper of abstract and unifying God. My achievement, however, is more likely to make a ghost!

After having been cured, Dysart predicts Alan will become Normal. Ordinary. He'll buy a motor scooter, work in a factory, maybe get married and, having lost what was special about him, that spiritual part of him will be dead.

DYSART . . . . . Passion, you see, can be destroyed by a doctor. It cannot be created.

> *He addresses Alan directly, in farewell.*

You won't gallop any more, Alan. Horses will be quite safe. You'll save your pennies every week, till you can change that scooter in for a car, and put the odd fifty P on the gee-gees, quite forgetting that they were ever anything more to you than bearers of little profits and little losses. You will, however, be without pain. More or less completely without pain.

> *Pause. He speaks directly to the theater, standing by the motionless body of Alan Strang, under the blanket.*

But the huge question goes on vibrating. That voice of Equus out of the cave. "Why Me?. . . . Account for Me!" All right—Who can? . . . A child is born into a world of phenomena, all equal in their power to enslave. It sniffs—it sucks— it strokes its eyes over the whole uncountable range. Suddenly one strikes. Why? Moments snap together like magnets, forging a chain of shackles. Why? I can trace them. I can even, with time, pull them apart again. But why at the start they were ever magnetized at all—just those particular moments of experience and no others—I don't know. *And nor does anyone else.* My profession is based on a total mystery! In an ultimate sense I cannot know what I do in this place —and yet I do ultimate things. Irreversible, terminal things . . . I stand in the dark with a pick in my hand, striking at heads.

> *He moves away from Alan, back to the downstage bench, and finally sits.*

I need—more desperately than my children need me—a way of seeing in the dark. What way is this? . . . *What dark is this?* . . . I cannot call it ordained of God: I can't get that far. I will however pay it so much homage. There is now, in my mouth, this sharp chain. And it never comes out.

> *A long pause. Dysart sits staring. Blackout.*

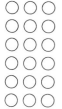

THE ISLAND

A Play in Four Scenes

BY ATHOL FUGARD, JOHN KANI AND WINSTON NTSHONA

Cast and credits appear on page 329

ATHOL FUGARD (co-author) was born June 11, 1932 in Middelburg in the semi-desert Karoo country of South Africa. His mother was an Afrikaner, his father of Irish and Hugenot descent. He studied motor mechanics at Port Elizabeth Technical College and philosophy at the University of Cape Town and spent the next three years in the Merchant Marine, mostly in the Far East. He married an actress, Sheila Meiring, and for a time they ran an experimental theater in Cape Town.

Fugard's first play was No-Good Friday *(1959), followed by* Nongogo *and then* The Blood Knot *which won its author an international reputation and reached these shores in an off-Broadway production starring James Earl Jones March 1, 1964 for 240 performances (it is about two black half-brothers, one light-skinned and one dark). His next play,* People Are Living There, *was done in Glasgow in 1968 and then in London during the 1971–72 season. His* Hello and Goodbye *appeared off Broadway with Martin Sheen and Colleen Dewhurst September 18, 1969 for 45 performances and was produced in London in the season of 1972–73. Fugard's* Boesman and Lena *was done off Broadway with James Earl Jones, Ruby Dee and Zakes Mokae June 22, 1970 for 205 performances—and was named a Best Play—a season before its subsequent London premiere. Another Fugard work,* Mille Miglia, *was aired on BBC television.*

Fugard's second Best Play, this season's The Island, *has strong mimetic as well as literary elements and is credited as a collaboration "devised" by its playwright-*

director and its actors, John Kani and Winston Ntshona. It reversed the direction of the previous Fugard Best Play by stopping in London before coming to New York, appearing under the auspices of the Royal Court Theater on a two-play schedule with the equally effective Sizwe Banzi Is Dead *by the same authors. The two plays had their American premieres this season in tandem, first at the Long Wharf Theater in New Haven, Conn., and then in alternating repertory in mini-Broadway productions at the Edison Theater.*

Fugard now lives at Schoenmakerskop near Port Elizabeth with his wife and daughter Lisa-Maria. Some of his training for what has turned out to be the triple profession of actor-director-writer was acquired at Rehearsal Room, in Johannesburg's Dorkay House (the headquarters of South Africa's Union Artists, the organization that cares for the cultural interests of non-Europeans in the Transvaal). Later, as resident director of Dorkay House, he staged the works of many modern playwrights including Steinbeck and Pinter. For the last ten years he has been associated with Serpent Players of New Brighton, Port Elizabeth, a theater workshop for black Africans experimenting in collaborative "play-making" of works dealing with the contemporary South African scene, of which both The Island *and* Sizwe Banzi *are examples. Fugard has often been a focal point of controversy in his politically controversial land and was once denied a passport by his government, in the spring of 1970, when he wanted to come to New York for rehearsals of* Boesman and Lena.

JOHN KANI and WINSTON NTSHONA (co-authors) are South African actors who collaborated in the "devising" and played all the roles of both The Island *and its companion play* Sizwe Banzi Is Dead. *They have acted together since school days, and as central figures in Serpent Players they have put on the works of a variety of authors including their own South African Wole Soyinka as well as Brecht, Strindberg and Sophocles. Kani joined Serpent in 1966, Ntshona in 1967 and both have performed in various parts of their country including the African Drama Festival in Durban.*

Rehearsals and performances of Serpent Players are customarily carried on after working hours, because "artist" is not an accepted employment category for South African blacks. There was so much demand for appearances by the Messrs. Kani and Ntshona throughout their country, however, that they finally had to leave their "regular" jobs—Kani with the Ford company and Ntshona as a factory lab assistant—to concentrate on acting, technically as "household employees" of their white colleague Athol Fugard. They soon conceived and staged Sizwe Banzi *for the special occasion of a single performance at Capetown Space Theater in October, 1972. Their one-night stand was held over for six months, after which it went on a national tour. This in turn led to an invitation from the Royal Court for a six-week London engagement together with* The Island; *and that engagement in turn lengthened to nine months in the West End and on a British tour before coming to the United States.*

Time: The present

Place: South Africa's maximum security prison for African political offenders on Robben Island in the Atlantic Ocean about seven miles from Cape Town

Scene 1

SYNOPSIS: Shaven-headed, in khaki shirts and short trousers, two prisoners —John and Winston—pantomime the grunting, *"grotesquely futile and backbreaking labor"* of digging and loading sand into wheelbarrows and then emptying those very loads onto each other's sand pile, so that *"their labor is interminable,"* obviously punitive rather than constructive. They are outdoors, but stage center is a raised area representing the inside of their prison cell, with neatly folded blankets and sleeping mats and a bucket of water with two tin mugs in one corner.

The labor continues, achingly, until a whistle gives the signal to stop. John and Winston pantomine standing side by side to be shackled together. Then, at the sound of a second whistle, *"They start to run . . . John mumbling a prayer, Winston muttering a rhythm for their three-legged race. They do not run fast enough. They get beaten . . . Winston receiving a bad blow to the eye and John spraining an ankle. In this condition they finally arrive at the cell door. Handcuffs and shackles are taken off. After being searched, they lurch into their cell. The door closes behind them. Both men sink to the floor. A moment of total exhaustion until slowly, painfully, they start to explore their respective injuries . . . Winston his eye and John his ankle. Winston is moaning softly and this eventually draws John's attention away from his ankle. He crawls to Winston and examines the injured eye. It needs attention. Winston's moaning is slowly turning into a sound of inarticulate outrage, growing in volume and violence. John urinates into one hand and tries to clean the other man's eye with it."*

Winston pushes John away, surrendering to a tantrum of fury against the guard they call Hodoshe. John warns him to be silent and not to make a fuss, and perhaps Hodoshe will take them to the quarry tomorrow, instead of to the hated sand piles.

Winston notices that John's ear is injured and attends to it. John remembers how he enjoyed taking his family to the beach the Christmas before he was arrested. Now sand has become an instrument of torture by a sadistic guard whom John would have attacked if they had been kept at the senseless labor five minutes longer.

JOHN: This morning when he said: "You two! The beach!" . . . I thought. Okay, so it's my turn to empty the sea into a hole. He likes that one. But when he pointed to the wheelbarrows, and I saw his idea . . . ! *(Shaking his head.)* I laughed at first. Then I wasn't laughing. Then I hated you. You looked so stupid, broer!

WINSTON: That's what he wanted.

JOHN: It was going to last forever, man! Because of *you.* And for *you,* because of *me.* Moer! He's cleverer than I thought.

WINSTON: If he was *God,* he would have done it.

JOHN: What?

WINSTON: Broken us. Men get tired. Hey! There's a thought. We're still alive because *Hodoshe* got tired.

JOHN: Tomorrow?

WINSTON: We'll see.

JOHN: If he takes us back there . . . If I hear that wheelbarrow . . . of yours again, coming with another bloody load of . . . eternity!

WINSTON *(with calm resignation):* We'll see.
> *Pause. John looks at Winston.*

JOHN *(with a quiet emphasis, as if the other man did not fully understand the significance of what he had said):* I *hated* you, Winston.

WINSTON *(meeting John's eyes):* I hated *you.*
> *John puts a hand on Winston's shoulder. Their brotherhood is intact. He gets slowly to his feet.*

John takes off his shirt and prepares to wash himself with their common washrag, while Winston lights the precious stump of a cigarette. John shows Winston some rusty nails he has found and retrieved for "Antigone's necklace." Winston throws the nails to the floor in disgust. It seems that they have promised to take part in the prison concert six days from now by presenting their own two-man version of *Antigone,* and John insists on using every scrap of spare time rehearsing and making the costumes.

Winston doesn't share John's enthusiasm for this project—in fact, he resists the whole idea. John throws the washrag to Winston and takes the necklace, working on it while he reviews the material for Winston's benefit.

JOHN: . . . . . Do you still remember all I told you yesterday? Bet you've bloody forgotten. How can I carry on like this? I can't move on, man. Over the whole bloody lot again! Who Antigone is . . . who Creon is . . .

WINSTON: Antigone is mother to Polynices . . .

JOHN: Haai, haai, haai . . . shit, Winston! *(Now really exasperated.)* How many times must I tell you that Antigone is the sister to the two brothers. Not the mother. That's another play.

WINSTON: Oh.

JOHN: That's all you know! "Oh."
> *He abandons the necklace and takes out a piece of chalk from a crack in the floor.*

Come here. This is the last time. S'truesgod. The last time.

WINSTON: Ag no John.

JOHN: Come! I'm putting this plot down for the last time!

John pulls Winston down beside him on the floor and diagrams the plot and characters with his chalk. King Creon represents the state. Antigone is the accused. Against Creon's edict, she has buried her traitor brother Polynices who was killed fighting against the state. In Stage One of Antigone's trial the state lays its charges against the accused. Stage Two of the trial is pleading.

JOHN: . . . . . What does Antigone plead? Guilty or not guilty?

WINSTON: Not guilty.

JOHN (trying to be tactful): Now look Winston, we're not going to argue. Between me and you, in this cell, we know she's not guilty. But in the play she pleads guilty.

WINSTON: No man John! Antigone is not guilty . . .

JOHN: In the play . . .

WINSTON (losing his temper): To hell with the play! Antigone had every right to bury her brother.

JOHN: Don't say "To hell with the play." We've got to do the bloody thing. And in the play she pleads guilty. Get that straight. Antigone pleads . . .

WINSTON (giving up in disgust): Okay do it your way.

JOHN: It's not my way! In the play . . .

WINSTON: Guilty!

JOHN: Yes, guilty.

   Writes furiously on the floor.

WINSTON: Guilty.

JOHN: Stage Three, pleading in Mitigation of Sentence. Stage Four, Sentence, State Summary, and something from you . . . Farewell Words. Now learn that.

WINSTON: Hey?

JOHN (getting up): Learn that!

WINSTON: But we've just done it!

JOHN: I've just done it. Now you learn it.

John assures Winston he'll be proud to have done the play. John shows Winston Creon's medallion that he has made, and he works on Antigone's necklace while he remembers how successfully his group once performed this play in New Brighton.

Winston claims that he has learned the plot, and when John quizzes him he gets through it almost errorlessly. Tomorrow they will start memorizing the actual words.

They prepare to sleep on their mats. John hopes they are assigned to the quarry tomorrow, because he lacks some of the material for props and costumes—rope for Winston's Antigone wig, for example. Winston wants to go to the quarry, too, so that he can try to smuggle some tobacco to a friend in solitary. John tells Winston not to be "hard-arsed" when Hodoshe comes around, to say "Ja baas" deferentially, so that maybe Hodoshe will give them both a break.

Before they go to sleep, it is John's turn to amuse them both by making up an entertaining fantasy. The night before, Winston "took them to bioscope" and invented a Glenn Ford Western. John pretends to make a telephone call to a friend at home, getting all the latest news of friends and family, passing on Winston's excited questions. Finally John asks about his own wife and children and leaves an imaginary message: "Tell her . . . this was another day. They're not very different here. We were down on the beach. The wind was blowing. The sand got in our eyes. The sea was rough. I couldn't see the mainland properly. Tell them that maybe tomorrow we'll go to the quarry. It's not so bad there. We'll be with the others. Tell her also . . . it's starting to get cold now, but the worst is still coming. *(Slow fade to blackout.)*"

Scene 2

A few days later, in the cell, John is covered with a blanket so he can't watch Winston putting on the wig and false breasts of his Antigone costume.

When Winston is ready, John comes out from under the blanket, looks at Winston and nearly collapses with laughter. This infuriates Winston, so that he *"tears off the wig and breasts, throws them down on the cell floor."* He flatly refuses to make himself an object of such mockery: "Shit man, you want me to go out there tomorrow night and make a bloody fool of myself? You think I don't know what will happen after that? Every time I run to the quarry . . . 'Nyah . . . nyah . . . Here comes Antigone! . . . Help the poor lady!' . . . Well, you can go to hell with your Antigone . . . . . I am not doing your Antigone! I would rather run the whole day for Hodoshe. At least I know where I stand with him. All he wants is to make me a boy . . . not a bloody woman."

John explains that his laughter at Winston was only to prepare him for stage fright, to get Winston ready for that inevitable opening burst of laughter: "I know those bastards out there. When you get in front of them, sure they'll laugh. . . . Nyah, nyah! . . . they'll laugh. But just remember this, brother, nobody laughs forever! There'll come a time when they'll stop laughing, and that will be the time when our Antigone hits them with her words."

Winston swears he won't play Antigone. John reminds Winston that he can't back out now, they have the best spot on the program, the finale. Winston promises not to back out, but he presses the costume into John's hands and tells him, "Take these titties and hair and play Antigone. I'm going to play Creon."

John had considered the possibility of exchanging roles, he tells Winston, but decided that Winston didn't have time to get up in the new part. John puts on the Antigone costume to give Winston a chance to laugh in his turn, but Winston won't be persuaded. Winston is skeptical about the whole project anyway. The Antigone story, he knows, is not even history but merely legend, child's play in comparison to the harsh realities of their real lives.

John calls that sort of thinking "Hodoshe's talk." He argues: "That's what he says all the time. What he wants us to say all our lives. Our convictions, our ideals . . . that's what he calls them . . . child's play. Everything we fucking do is 'child's play' . . . . . Look brother . . . I've had enough. No one is going to stop me doing Antigone."

Suddenly, they freeze at the sound of Hodoshe's voice calling John, who leaves the cell as ordered. Alone, Winston tries on his wig again, checks his reflection in the water bucket (and has to stop himself from laughing), tries a few Antigone poses, then gives the whole thing up, throwing the wig to the floor and stamping on it, crying to himself: "Shit man! If he wants a woman in the cell he must send for his wife, and I don't give a damn how he does it. I didn't walk with those men and burn my bloody passbook in front of that police station, and have a magistrate send me here for life so that he can dress me up like a woman and make a bloody fool of me."

Winston is still steaming when John returns to the cell and is so wrapped up in his own resentment that he doesn't notice a strangeness in his friend's behavior.

JOHN: Winston . . . I've got something to tell you.

WINSTON (registering John's manner for the first time): What's the matter? Hodoshe? What happened? Are we in shit? Solitary?

JOHN: My appeal was heard last Wednesday. Sentence reduced. I've got three months to go.

> Long silence. Winston is stunned.

WINSTON: Three . . .

JOHN: . . . months to go.

WINSTON: Three . . .

JOHN: Ja. That's what Prinsloo said.

WINSTON: John!

> Winston explodes with joy. The men embrace. They dance a jig in the cell. Winston finally tears himself away and starts to hammer on the cell walls so as to pass on the news to other prisoners.

Norman! Norman!! John. Three months to go. Ja . . . just been told . . .

> Winston's excitement makes John nervous. He pulls Winston away from the wall.

JOHN: Winston! Not yet, man. We'll tell them at the quarry tomorrow. Let me just live with it for a little while.

WINSTON: Okay, okay . . . . .

John was expecting trouble from Hodoshe, but the guard merely escorted him to Prinsloo's office, where John was informed that his lawyers had managed to have his sentence reduced from ten to three years. John wonders whether it mightn't be a trick to break him with false hope, since the trick with the sand and wheelbarrows didn't accomplish it. John actually signed a form stating that he had been told that he had only three more months to go, and this makes Winston certain that the reduction of sentence is real.

John remembers back almost three years ago when he and Winston first met, just after their trials. They were lined up waiting for vans to carry them off, and Winston and John chanced to be "married"—handcuffed together—before loading. Wives and families ran alongside the vans as long as they could, for last glimpses and goodbyes. The vans kept going hour after hour until many of those packed inside, including John, could no longer contain themselves and urinated in their pants. Finally they fell asleep in the vans, standing up.

JOHN: Then the docks, the boat . . . It was my first time on one. I had nothing to vomit up, but my God I tried.

WINSTON: What about me?

JOHN: Then we saw this place for the first time. It almost looked pretty, hey, with all the mist around it.

WINSTON: I was too sick to see anything, broer.

JOHN: Remember your words when we jumped off onto the jetty?

Pause. The two men look at each other.

Heavy words, Winston. You looked back at the mountains . . . "Farewell, Africa!" I've never forgotten them. That was three years ago.

WINSTON: And now, for you, it's three months to go.

Pause. The mood of innocent celebration has passed. John realizes what his good news means to the other man.

JOHN: To hell with everything. Let's go to bed.

Winston doesn't move. John finds Antigone's wig.

We'll talk about Antigone tomorrow.

John prepares for bed.

Hey Winston! I just realized. My family! Princess and the children. Do you think they've been told? Jeasus man. maybe they're also saying . . . three months! Those three months are going to feel as long as the three years. Time passes slowly when you've got something . . . to wait for . . .

Pause. Winston still hasn't moved. John changes his tone.

Look, in this cell we're going to forget those three months. The whole bloody thing is most probably a trick anyway. So let's just forget about it. We run to the quarry tomorrow. Together. So let's sleep.

Scene 3

Later that night, Winston appears to be asleep, but John is restless. He begins to count the days on his fingers. Winston sits up, watches him for a few moments, then makes John admit that he is counting the days left in prison—92. Winston counts down for him—80, 70, 60, 50, 40, then only one month left; finally, only a few days, then *tomorrow*. The idea actually hurts, and John begs Winston to stop and goes through the motions of settling himself for sleep.

Winston can't leave the thought of John's freedom. He talks on and on about how it will be, and John cannot help listening. They won't keep John here on the island for the full three months. One month before his release date he'll be taken to a mainland prison to be fed and coddled so that he'll look well at the time of his release. Finally they'll take John to the jail in Port Elizabeth, very close to home. One day they'll give him a new khaki suit and a package containing his belongings. They'll open the door, and outside his family will be waiting to take him home to New Brighton . . .

Again, the anticipation of release is too much for John, and he tries to break the spell of Winston's imagination. But Winston, no longer smiling, insists on continuing: much as his family will cater to John when he finally reaches home, he will need a form of release they cannot give him. John will slip out the back door and join his cronies, who will fix him up with the kind of woman he needs —"a really wild one!" Loudly, John denies this, but Winston insists. John sees that the thought of his freedom is driving Winston mad. John denies Winston's accusation that three months from now John will forget him.

WINSTON: . . . . . Stop bullshitting me! We've got no time left for that. There's only two months' left between us. (Pause.) You know where I ended up this morning, John? In the quarry. Next to old Harry. Do you know old Harry, John?

JOHN: Yes.

WINSTON: Yes what? Speak, man!"

JOHN: Old Harry, Cell twenty-three, seventy years, serving life!

WINSTON: That's not what I'm talking about. When you go to the quarry tomorrow, take a good look at old Harry. Look into his eyes, John. Look at his hands. They've changed him. They've turned him into stone. Watch him work with that chisel and hammer. Twenty perfect blocks of stone every day. Nobody else can do it like him. He loves stone. That's why they're nice to him. He's forgotten himself. He's forgotten everything . . . why he's here, where he comes from. That's happening to me, John. I've forgotten why I'm here.

JOHN: No.

WINSTON: Why am I here?

JOHN: You put your head on the block for others.

WINSTON: Fuck the others.

JOHN: Don't say that! Remember our ideals . . .

WINSTON: Fuck our ideals . . .

JOHN: No Winston . . . our slogans, our children's freedom.

WINSTON: Fuck slogans, fuck politics . . . fuck everything, John. Why am I here? I'm jealous of your freedom, John. I also want to count. God also gave me ten fingers, but what do I count? My life? How do I count it, John? One . . . one . . . another day comes . . . one . . . Help me, John! . . . Another day . . . one . . . one . . . Help me, brother! . . . one . . .

> John has sunk to the floor, helpless in the face of the other man's torment and pain. Winston almost seems to bend under the weight of the life stretching ahead of him on the island. For a few seconds he lives in silence with his reality, then slowly straightens up. He turns and looks at John. When he speaks again, it is the voice of a man who has come to terms with his fate, massively compassionate.

Nyana we Sizwe!

> John looks up at him.

Nyana we Sizwe . . . it's all over now . . . all over. (He moves over to John.) Forget me . . .

> John attempts a last, limp denial.

No, John! Forget me . . . because I'm going to forget you. Yes, I will forget you. Others will come in here, John, count, go, and I'll forget them. Still more will come, count like you, go like you, and I will forget them. And then one day, it will all be over.

> *A lighting change suggests the passage of time. Winston collects together their props for Antigone.*

Come. They're waiting.

JOHN: Do you know your words?

WINSTON: Yes. Come, we'll be late for the concert.

Scene 4

Winston and John convert their cell into the Antigone set by hanging blankets as a backdrop. John addresses the prison concert "audience," explaining the story: two brothers fought on opposing sides of a civil war and were killed; King Creon the victor decreed that the brother who had defended the state, Eteocles, should be buried with all honor, but the other, Polynices, was to lie in the open unburied, to be consumed by jackals; Antigone defied the decree, buried Polynices and was arrested and brought to trial. At that point begins their play, *The Trial and Punishment of Antigone.*

John disappears behind the blanket, where he and Winston change into their costumes. Then John steps out majestically in crown, pendant and draped blanket as King Creon. Addressing his people, Creon declares himself the most humble servant of his subjects, whose degree of fatness and happiness is the sole measure of the state's well being. It is the king's responsibility to promote that well being, Creon continues, and the instrument with which he performs this duty is called the law.

John, as Creon, continues to address his people: "The law defends! The law is no more or less that a shield in your faithful servant's hand to protect YOU! But even as a shield would be useless in one hand, to defend, without a sword in the other, to strike . . . so too the law has its edge. The penalty! We have come through difficult times. I am sure it is needless for me to remind you of the constant troubles on our borders . . . those despicable rats who would gnaw away at our fatness and happiness. We have been diligent in dealing with with them. But unfortunately there are still at large subversive elements . . . there are still amongst us a few rats that are not satisfied, and to them I must show this face of Creon . . . so different to the one that hails my happy people! . . . . ."

Creon calls for the accused and Winston comes from behind the backdrop dressed as Antigone in wig, necklace, false bosom and blanket wrapped around him as a skirt. Winston does not seem ludicrous in costume now, and he is letter-perfect in his lines and in his poise as he answers Creon's questions.

Antigone admits burying her brother Polynices in defiance of Creon's edict. She pleads guilty and is given a chance to speak in mitigation of her sentence. Instead of groveling, she questions Creon's right to make arbitrary laws either in the name of the state or of God.

WINSTON *(as Antigone):* When Polynices died in battle, all that remained was the empty husk of his body. He could neither harm nor help any man again. What lay on the battlefield waiting for Hodoshe to turn rotten belonged to God. You are only a man, Creon. Even as there are laws made by men, so too there are others that come from God. He watches my soul for a transgression even as your spies hide in the bush at night to see who is transgressing your laws. Guilty against God I will not be for any man on this earth. Even without your law, Creon, and the threat of death to whoever defied it, I know I must die. Because of your law and my defiance, that fate is now very near. So much the better. Your threat is nothing to me, Creon. But if I had let my mother's son, a Son of the Land, lie there as food for the carrion fly Hodoshe, my soul would never have known peace. Do you understand anything of what I am saying, Creon?

JOHN *(as Creon):* Your words reveal only that obstinacy of spirit which has brought nothing but tragedy to your people. First you break the law. Now you insult the state.

WINSTON: Just because I ask you to remember that you are only a man?

JOHN: And to add insult to injury you gloat over your deeds! No, Antigone, you will not escape with impunity. Were you my own child you would not escape full punishment.

WINSTON: Full punishment? Would you like to do more than just kill me?

JOHN: That is all I wish.

WINSTON: Then let us not waste any time. Stop talking. I buried my brother. That is an honorable thing, Creon. All these people in your state would say so too, if fear of you and another law did not force them into silence.

JOHN: You are wrong. None of my people think the way you do.

WINSTON: Yes they do, but no one dares tell you so. You will not sleep peacefully, Creon.

JOHN: You add shamelessness to your crimes, Antigone.

WINSTON: I do not feel any shame at having honored my brother.

JOHN: Was he that died with him not also your brother?

WINSTON: He was.

JOHN: And so you honor the one and insult the other.

WINSTON: I shared my love, not my hate.

JOHN: Go then and share your love among the dead. I will have no rats' law here while yet I live.

WINSTON: We are wasting time, Creon. Stop talking. Your words defeat your purpose. They are prolonging my life.

JOHN *(as Creon, again addressing the audience):* You have heard all the relevant facts. Needless now to call the state witnesses who would testify beyond reasonable doubt that the accused is guilty. Nor, for that matter, is it in the best interests of the state to disclose their identity. There was a law. The law was broken. The law stipulated its penalty. My hands are tied. Take her from where she stands, straight to the Island! There wall her up in a cell for life, with enough food to acquit ourselves of the taint of her blood.

WINSTON *(as Antigone, to the audience):* Brothers and sisters of the Land! I go now on my last journey. I must leave the light of day forever, for the Island, strange and cold, to be lost between life and death. So, to my grave, my everlasting prison, condemned alive to solitary death.

> *Winston tears off his wig and confronts the audience as Winston, not Antigone.*

Gods of our fathers! My Land! My Home! Time waits no longer. I go now to my living death, because I honored those things to which honor belongs.

> *The two men take off their costumes and then strike their "set." They then come together, and, as in the beginning, their hands come together to suggest handcuffs and their right and left legs to suggest ankle chains. They start running . . . John mumbling a prayer and Winston a rhythm for their three-legged run. The siren wails. Fade to blackout.*

ALL OVER TOWN

A Play in Two Acts

BY MURRAY SCHISGAL

Cast and credits appear on page 334

MURRAY SCHISGAL was born in East New York, Brooklyn, on Nov. 25, 1926. His father had immigrated to this country from Vilna. Schisgal left Thomas Jefferson High School at 17 to serve with the United States Navy in World War II. He was 20 when he returned to civilian life to pursue his education at night and to work at odd jobs including playing sax and clarinet in a small combo. He was graduated from Brooklyn Law School in 1953 and hung out his shingle on Delancey Street. In 1956 he left the practise of law to teach at the James Fenimore Cooper Junior High School in East Harlem, and in 1959 he received his B.A. degree from the New School for Social Research.

Schisgal's first professionally-produced work for the stage was the double bill The Typists *and* The Tiger *put on in 1960 in London and in 1963 off Broadway, where it won Vernon Rice and Outer Circle awards. His early work included* Ducks and Lovers *(London, 1961) and* Knit One, Purl Two *(Boston, 1963). His full-length* Luv *was produced in 1963 in London and in 1964 for 901 performances on Broadway, where it was named a Best Play of its season.*

Schisgal's subsequent New York credits are as follows: off Broadway, Fragments *(a program of two one-act plays entitled* The Basement *and* Fragments, *1967); Broadway,* Jimmy Shine *(1968),* A Way of Life *(1969, in previews),* The Chinese *and* Dr. Fish *(a program of two one-act plays, 1970),* An American Millionaire *(1974) and finally this season's* All Over Town *which won Schisgal his second Best Play citation.*

Schisgal is also the author of a TV play, The Love Song of Barney Kempinski, *and a screen play,* The Tiger Makes Out. *He lives in New York City with his wife and two children.*

The following synopsis of All Over Town *was prepared by Jeff Sweet.*

Time: *The present*

Place: *The Morris family's duplex apartment on Manhattan's Upper East Side*

ACT I

Scene 1: Morning

SYNOPSIS: The curtain rises on the Morrisses' living room, two stories high with staircases connecting to each end of a second-floor balcony running the width of the stage. There are many doors entering on both levels. On the first floor, going from stage right to stage left, are the following: a guest room (to be Louie's room), the front door, the bottom of one staircase, a second guest room (to be Philomena's), a pair of sliding doors into the dining room, a door to the kitchen, the bottom of the other staircase and a door to the study. On the second floor balcony are more doors, from from stage right to stage left: an arched recess leading to Millie the maid's room, a door to the linen closet, three bedroom doors, a slightly recessed door to the bathroom and a window. The living room itself is tastefully furnished by people accustomed to living well.

At rise, Dr. Morris, an eminent psychiatrist, is roaming from room to room searching for his cordovan wing-tipped shoes. While he is offstage hunting, his daughter Sybil answers the front door admitting her fiancé, Charles Kogan. Charles is a social worker who is enlisting her father's help on the Louie Lucas case. Louie Lucas is a young man who has fathered nine illegitimate children by five women (all of whom are on welfare). Lucas is supposed to appear at the apartment this morning so that Dr. Morris and Charles can meet and talk to him. The mothers only revealed Lucas's name when the Welfare Department threatened to cut off their checks.

Sybil, who also dabbles in social work, sympathizes with Charles over the resistance their clients often put up against being helped. She tells him how deeply she respects him for being a civil service employee. Unfortunately, they cannot be married on a civil service employee's salary. He suggests that perhaps he should leave social work and go into business, but she insists that he is much too dedicated to do that.

Dr. Morris appears, still looking for his shoes. Also looking are his wife BeeBee and their Swedish maid, Millie. Millie is sent offstage to continue the search as

Dr. Morris spots Charles and suggests they go into the study to prepare to meet Lucas. Charles exits into the study and a harried Dr. Morris suddenly cools himself out by placing his palms together, assuming a serene expression and going, "Ommm!" as in a yoga chant. He exits into the study.

BeeBee confides in her daughter her fear that Dr. Morris, her husband, is having a nervous breakdown. He hasn't been himself lately—making these strange sounds, giving up his private patients and offering his services to the Welfare Department. Sybil explains to her mother that her father is dissatisfied with his work and thinking of becoming a Buddhist. "Why a Buddhist?" BeeBee wonders. "We have no friends who are Buddhists!"

As Sybil tries to explain, Colonel Martin Hopkins, their house guest, enters from his bedroom on the second floor. He is dressed in khaki and swaggers militarily down the stairs, marvelling at the glories of the morning ("Reminds me of the mornings we used to have in Korea"). Hopkins enters into the discussion about Dr. Morris's state of mind, expressing surprise at the announcement of the doctor's impending conversion to Buddhism. Sybil explains that her father has begun to feel that modern psychiatry cannot meet today's overwhelming social problems, and that Buddhism may be his only spiritual alternative. She asks the colonel and her mother to be as supportive of Dr. Morris as possible, helping him believe in the value of his psychiatric work. Sybil goes up to the colonel's room to retrieve the scarf he has "forgotten."

As soon as she is offstage, Colonel Hopkins and BeeBee are revealed to the audience as lovers. BeeBee assures him her husband knows nothing of their affair. For a moment, they share regrets that each married another (the colonel's wife, Philomena—whose name he keeps forgetting—is at present in the hospital "having her back straightened out"). Still they think perhaps the adulterous element of their relationship is responsible for the special thrill they feel together. As BeeBee writes a get-well card to her lover's wife, Col. Hopkins confirms their assignation for that night in the study.

Sybil reappears with the colonel's scarf. Hopkins and BeeBee repair to the dining room for breakfast. The doorbell rings. It is Lewis, *"a young black man, wearing a garish hockey shirt and corduroy slacks."* He's delivering a package which he holds out to Sybil—but Sybil instantly assumes he is Louie Lucas, keeping his appointment with her father.

SYBIL: Come in, please. Daddy's expecting you.

LEWIS *(somewhat surprised):* Daddy's expecting me? My, my, that's very thoughtful of your daddy. *(He looks about.)* And I do like how he lives. Huhu.

SYBIL: He's in the study but before I get him I do want you to know that I sincerely sympathize with you, Mr. Lucas.

LEWIS: Mr. Who?

SYBIL: Mr. Lucas. But I'll call you Louie, if you like.

LEWIS: Yeah, you call me Louie, I'd like that.

SYBIL: I'm Sybil Morris.

> *She shakes his hand, then changes handshake to a soul-brother handclasp, pumping his hand up and down.*

Doctor Morris's daughter. I know your entire case.

LEWIS: Ah, you know my entire case. That's . . . What case are you talking about?

SYBIL: The nine illegitimate children from the five different women. *(She sits on the sofa.)*

LEWIS: The nine illegitimate children from the five different women. Oh, that case. You're talking about that case. Well, I have to tell you, Sybil, that was one of my best cases. I have had cases that were worse, much worse!

SYBIL: You must lead a fascinating life.

LEWIS: Well, I don't like to boast but the last woman who said that to me had two big black bouncing baby boys.

SYBIL *(laughing uncomfortably):* I'd better be careful, then.

She crosses her legs, pulls herself back and sits up rigidly.

Lewis is amused by her earnestness and doesn't attempt to correct her misimpression. He begins to play the part of Louie and she, flustered and fascinated by his manner and what she supposes to be his reputation, retreats up to her room, trying to manage it so that he can't look up her skirt.

Charles and Dr. Morris enter, also assuming that Lewis is Louie Lucas, introducing themselves (the doctor still in his stocking feet). Dr. Morris begins to berate Lewis for his supposed abuse of disadvantaged women. "If those women went to bed with me, they were not disadvantaged," Lewis insists, "they were advantaged."

MORRIS: We'll see about that. Fortunately for you your case is unique enough to fall under the purview of the city's new rehabilitation program.

CHARLES: Our primary aim is to help you, Mr. Lucas.

LEWIS: That's what I've been hearing all morning and I still ain't got no help.

MORRIS: In good time. But let it be understood at the start that we are not going to sit idly by and support your . . . your misdeeds with welfare checks while you hop from bed to bed like some mad little oversexed bullfrog!

Charles laughs. Lewis turns to him. Charles stops laughing abruptly.

CHARLES: There are laws that hold a man responsible for his actions, Mr. Lucas.

MORRIS: And if necessary we will use those laws.

CHARLES: We will use those laws.

LEWIS *(he starts to rise):* I got enough help for this morning.

MORRIS: Sit down and be patient.

He does so. Morris paces.

I want to suggest the following. I'd like you to spend a few weeks in this house. Under my direct observation. You'll be comfortably sheltered and fed. A clothing allowance will be given to you by the Welfare Department. We'll start a program of intensive therapy. As I explained to Mr. Kogan before you arrived, if I can get through to you, the most flagrant case of social irresponsibility I have encountered in twenty-five years, then I will have the courage to resume my practise. Otherwise . . . I'll have to act accordingly. Now, will you cooperate, Mr. Lucas?

PAMELA PAYTON-WRIGHT, CLEAVON LITTLE, CAROL TEITEL, BARNARD HUGHES
(ON SOFA), ZANE LASKY AND WILLIAM LE MASSENA IN "ALL OVER TOWN"

LEWIS: I'll cooperate all I can, Doctor, but if I'm stuck here for a few weeks I'll be suffering grievous financial deprivation. I think you gentlemen should know that I am at present enjoying a relatively high standard of living.

CHARLES: According to our files, Doctor, Mr. Lucas has not been gainfully employed since 1971.

LEWIS: Oh, is that so?

CHARLES *(holds up file papers):* I have it here.

LEWIS: Well, your files, Mr. Kogan, are grossly in error. I have been gainfully and uninterruptedly employed since Tuesday.

CHARLES: You can be prosecuted for failure to . . .

MORRIS: Charles, we could give him a per diem of twenty dollars.

CHARLES: We could give you a per diem of twenty dollars.

MORRIS: Will that suffice, Mr. Lucas?

LEWIS: Gentlemen, you have just hired yourself a first-class genuine misfit.

Dr. Morris begins to ask Lewis about the five women, trying to ascertain if their being white had anything to do with his going for them. Lewis answers with quips and jokes which do little beyond confusing Dr. Morris and Charles further.

Millie enters to tell the doctor she cannot find his shoes anywhere. Lewis pulls them out of the package he is carrying, claiming he found them sitting outside the door. Dr. Morris tells Millie to prepare a room for Lewis as he'll be staying awhile, then Charles and the doctor (who is waging a battle to get into his shoes) return to the study to confer in private.

Millie finds herself alone with the man she believes to be the notorious Louie Lucas.

MILLIE *(moving towards him):* I know all about you, Lewie Lucas, so don't make yokes vit me. Five vomen you already make pregnant.

LEWIS: And if I put my magic eye on you, Millie girl, you're going to be numbers six and seven.

MILLIE: You t'ink every voman who looks at you goes on the bed vit you?

LEWIS: Huhu. Some of them goes on the floor with me.
    Lights cigar with table lighter.

MILLIE: You got the wrong customer, mister. Dot is not my t'ing. You vant your lunch, I vill give you your lunch but dot is all you're getting from dis voman.

LEWIS: Fair enough. That is fair enough. Now let me see, for lunch I'd like to have . . . ham-hocks, collard greens, black-eyed peas and a pan of golden brown corn bread.

MILLIE: Are you yokin' vit me?

LEWIS: No, girl, I'm not yokin' with you.

MILLIE: Vot is a ham-hock?

LEWIS: Vot is a ham-hock? Vot is a yoke?

MILLIE: A yoke is a yoke. But vot is a ham-hock?

LEWIS: A ham-hock is a ham-hock.

MILLIE: I told you already I don't know vot is a ham-hock!

LEWIS *(rises; crosses to right):* Well, you go down to the supermarket, Millie

girl, and you ask the man behind the meat counter for a bag full of ham-hocks, and when you come back here I'll introduce you to the infinite joys of soul food.
MILLIE: I go but I don't have to do dis.
We hear voices from dining room.
Dis is not my vork.

BeeBee and Hopkins enter from the dining room. Millie introduces them to Louie-Lewis, then exits, muttering, into the kitchen. Hopkins and Lewis do not hit it off. BeeBee begs off going horseback riding with the colonel, promising they'll have lunch together. The colonel exits in a huff.

BeeBee, consumed with curiosity, tries to get the secret of Louie-Lewis's success with white women. He tells her he fixes them with his magic eye and whispers, "Eeny, meeny, miny, moe, catch a nigger . . ." She puts her hand over his mouth and makes him promise never to say "that word" again. He agrees on condition she get him the new wardrobe the doctor promised him.

As BeeBee is getting Lewis's sizes, Sybil enters upstairs from her bedroom and comes down to the living room, knitting. "It's going to be a jumper for one of your children," she tells him. "I'm going to start knitting things for needy children everywhere. All power to the people." Funny thing—just as BeeBee has changed her plans, Sybil has changed hers as well. She has decided to skip her good works for the day to stay with Louie. BeeBee and Lewis exchange flirtatious looks and the doctor's wife exits to buy the clothing.

Sybil seizes the moment for a serious conversation. Is he still on good terms with the mothers of his children? Lewis assures her, "We couldn't be closer. We meet once a month in back of a saloon and we all get stoned together."

Sybil wants to know if there's anything she can do to help him. Well, he has this pawn ticket . . . Say no more, she'll redeem it for him with pleasure. Charles enters to see Lewis's arm around his fiancée's shoulder. Charles suggests to Sybil that they go some place to talk in private. She suggests that they talk in the taxi on the way to the pawn shop. A little befuddled, Charles exits with her.

Dr. Morris enters wondering where everyone else has gone. They're running "all over town," Lewis replies. Dr. Morris takes the opportunity to open his heart to Lewis.

MORRIS: . . . . . It is my belief, it is my profound belief, that it is too late.
LEWIS: What's too late?
MORRIS: Everything's too late.
LEWIS: Oh.
MORRIS: You see, there's no longer the determination in our city, the faith to reverse the processes of disintegration that are taking place.
Sits down beside Lewis.
What we have to do, Louie, is evolve in our thinking a new sense of social responsibility and begin believing again that rehabilitation is possible.
LEWIS: I told you, Doctor, I'd be willing to cooperate.
MORRIS: Good. I don't want to become a Buddhist, Louie.
LEWIS: You don't want to become a Buddhist?

MORRIS: It's difficult. Very difficult. My body aches from all that exercising and my stomach hasn't felt right since I stopped eating meat. But what are the alternatives? Do you see what I mean?

LEWIS *(suspiciously):* Hu.

MORRIS: Good. Then you do understand. Don't let me down now. I'm counting on you.

LEWIS: Huhu.

MORRIS *(moving toward study; turns):* By the way, have you heard the latest?

LEWIS: What's that?

MORRIS: A mountain of sludge is moving in from the ocean onto our beaches. In a year or two our streets will be covered with sludge. We'll have to wade through the stuff in hip boots. Sludge. Incredible. It's going to be incredible.

Morris exits into the study, leaving Lewis a test to take. Almost instantly the front doorbell rings. Lewis opens it to be confronted by the real Louie Lucas, "*a young white man, with Afro hair style . . . . . in paint-splattered striped coveralls.*" Lewis pretends to Louie that he is Dr. Morris and that Louie is to stay in a guest room for a couple of weeks so that he can be analyzed. He tells him that if he doesn't cooperate, he'll be arrested for going to the movies on welfare money.

The first question Lewis has is how Louie gets his way with so many women. Louie replies, "I say, 'I love you very much and as soon as I get a little bread together, we'll get married.' " Lewis shoves Louie into the guest room downstage right, giving him the test to take and telling him not to unlock the door unless someone knocks three times. Louie wonders if he might have a glass of orange juice and Lewis barks that this is not a Riviera hotel, slamming the door shut.

Michael, the cook, and his wife Jackie enter carrying groceries and chattering away in French. They are surprised to see Lewis and quickly repair to the kitchen.

The phone rings and Lewis, pretending to be Dr. Morris, answers. It's the colonel's wife, Philomena. Lewis advises her to check out of the hospital to keep an eye on her husband who, he tells her is having an affair with his (that is to say, Dr. Morris's) wife. He hangs up and beams at the audience as lights black out.

Scene 2: Noon

Sybil, in riding togs, and BeeBee are sitting side by side on the couch knitting, BeeBee very ineptly. BeeBee wonders why Sybil's engagement to Charles has dragged on so long. Sybil says she can't see being married to Charles yet. First she wants to accomplish something of true social significance.

Millie enters from the kitchen to announce that Louie-Lewis's ham-hocks are ready and disappears upstairs, muttering to herself. BeeBee goes to the door of the guest room and knocks.

BEEBEE: . . . . . Your lunch is on the table. Would you like to have a drink first?

LEWIS *(opens door slightly: he is wearing a caftan robe):* Do you know how to make a Honkey cocktail?

BEEBEE: A Honkey . . .

LEWIS: Two ounces rum, two ounces gin, two ounces whiskey, a dash of grenadine and a crushed cherry.

Starts to close door.

And stir the contents with your finger.

BEEBEE: With my finger?

LEWIS: That's the Honkey part!

And he closes door.

BEEBEE: If you don't object . . .

She moves to bar to pour drink.

The poor boy was overwhelmed with gratitude when I gave him his new clothes.

SYBIL *(rises; crosses to her):* We do have to be careful, Mommy.

BEEBEE: Why is that?

SYBIL: Daddy hasn't analyzed Louie's case as yet. We don't know what drove him to impregnate those women.

BEEBEE: You don't think he's . . .

SYBIL: It's possible. For all we know he could be a violent rapist.

BEEBEE: Dear me. Sybil, I want you to go straight to your room. I'll deal with Louie Lucas myself.

SYBIL *(sits in swivel chair):* But, Mommy, I have more experience than you. I should deal with Louie Lucas.

BEEBEE: I wouldn't hear of it. What if he assaulted you?

SYBIL: I'd resist as best I could until my life was endangered and then I'd give in.

BEEBEE: You'd give in? No, no. If one of us has to give in, I prefer it to be me!

And she bolts down part of the drink she has mixed for Lewis.

SYBIL: Mommy, you're making me very angry. I'm the one who should have to give in.

BEEBEE *(moves to Sybil):* But, dear, at my age I have less to lose if I give in. Be practical!

SYBIL: Mommy, if you don't let me give in . . .

Lewis suddenly enters, resplendently dressed in riding togs.

LEWIS: Ahhhhhhh!

Both women scream in fright, BeeBee turning to him and Sybil jumping to her feet.

Good afternoon, ladies. Is my cocktail poured?

BeeBee gives him his drink as Sybil gives him the item she redeemed for him at the pawnshop—an expensive watch. How did he have money enough to buy it?

LEWIS: . . . . . I did not spend all my time making babies, BeeBee. I have been involved in several speculative enterprises over the years and there were occasions when I was able to buy myself a few little trinkets.

SYBIL: What kind of enterprise were you in?

LEWIS: Oh, I used to own a bicycle shop across the street from a nursing home in the Bronx. I figured a lot of the old folks would like to keep themselves physically fit by bike riding in the neighborhood.

SYBIL: Was it successful?

LEWIS: Huhu. I made one miscalculation. The street separating my bike shop from the nursing home was Pelham Parkway. They never could make it across.

He still has hopes for a business career. BeeBee tells him that Charles has been interested in going into business but that Sybil has prevented him because of her belief that Charles should stick to socially valuable work. Lewis tells her it's possible to do both.

Dr. Morris enters, takes the test Louie completed from Lewis and gives the man he believes to be his patient yet another test, stopping for a second to admire the transformation in Lewis's appearance. "It's what I've been saying for years: change the environment and you can change the person."

He returns to the study. Lewis shoves the new test under the guest room door, saying in a voice loud enough so that the confined Louie can hear him, "Louie Lucas, Doctor Morris has another test for you to take. It is a test that will challenge all your mental faculties!" Then he returns to the women, who ask him what his new business venture will be as they exit into the dining room, closing the door behind them.

Louie, wearing the clothes Lewis originally wore, enters to make a phone call to a girl friend, telling her of his situation. Then he makes another phone call— to another girl friend. He is interrupted by Millie's entrance from upstairs. She demands to know who he is. He tells her.

MILLIE (*she stops in front of him; stares at his face*): Vot did you do vit your face?

LOUIE: What's the matter with my face?

MILLIE: It's vhite.

LOUIE: I just washed it.

Points to his room.

MILLIE: And it becomes vhite?

LOUIE: Oh, that. I use an eczema-cream.

MILLIE: I never heard such a t'ing.

. . . . . *Examines his face with her hand.*

LOUIE: It works fairly well. It's funny but . . . I like you. (*He takes her hand in his.*)

MILLIE: You do?

LOUIE: There's something between us.

MILLIE (*pulls hand away*): Vot's between us?

LOUIE: I don't know. I feel comfortable with you.

MILLIE: Vot is the name of that eczema-cream?

LOUIE: Snow White. You can buy it in Woolworth's.

MILLIE: Snow Vhite vorks vonders.

LOUIE (. . . . . *moves to his room*): Look, I have to take another test for Doctor Morris. Why don't you come into my room so we can talk?

MILLIE *(follows him):* I should do the beds . . .

LOUIE *(backing into room):* Only for a minute. I don't know what it is but I like you. I really like you. Are you married?

MILLIE: I have not even had a nibble.

>*She enters room. Louie closes door, laughing nervously.*

Colonel Hopkins enters calling for BeeBee. Dr. Morris enters from the study asking the whereabouts of Louie Lucas. Hopkins can't tell him. Dr. Morris tells Hopkins that the test scores prove Louie is a genius. Hopkins replies that Lucas has been flirting with BeeBee. Dr. Morris wonders why he would do that? "Your wife happens to be an extraordinarily attractive woman," says the colonel. "She is?" Dr. Morris replies. The colonel asks him why he, his old buddy (whose life, as he reminds Morris, he saved in World War II) has changed so. Dr. Morris tells him of his spiritual depression at the state of the world. Seeking a philosophy to help him cope, he has turned to the Buddhist teachings of a Riverside Drive guru named Maharishi Bahdah.

MORRIS: . . . . . Martin, I can put myself into a profound peaceful trance in less than thirty seconds.

HOPKINS: The hell you can.

MORRIS: Watch. Watch. Time this out.

>*He sits on the floor, downstage, near Hopkins, legs tucked under him, presses air from stomach, exhaling loudly, three times, raises hands above head and brings them down to his knees with an Ommmmmmm chant, settling and freezing in a lotus-position.*

HOPKINS: Lionel? Lionel? You did it, man. I thought you were . . .

>*Checking wrist watch.*

You brought that mother in . . . in under eighteen seconds Lionel? Lionel?

>*He rises.*

That's enough now, Lionel.

>*He taps him on the shoulder. Dr. Morris falls back, still frozen in trance. Hopkins catches him, lays him gently on his back.*

Wow! You're . . . I said . . . Now look here, Lionel, I can't be playing games here with you.

>*He pushes him on left knee, Dr. Morris falls over on his right; runs around and pushes Morris on his right knee and Morris tips over on his left; angrily.*

Come on now, Lionel. Enough is enough. You cut that out. You . . .

>*Stands stiffly over him; a military shout.*

Now you shape up or ship out! You hear me? When I say fall in, I want to hear those rifle straps pop!

>*He grabs him under arms, drags him towards study, rocking him up and down.*

Come on, Lionel. Come on, man. I'm going to get you out of here. I'll put you in the pantry if you don't snap out of it!

>*He lays him down, left of coffee table.*

You're deliberately provoking me and I will not allow you or any man to deliberately . . . provoke . . .

> *He sets Dr. Morris upright, pulling his sweater up on his head in the process.*

Oh, the hell with you.

> *With his foot, he pushes Dr. Morris on his back and starts towards staircase, right.*

BeeBee enters. The colonel, upset that she has broken their date and is lunching instead with Lewis, threatens to leave her. He exits into his room.

BeeBee sees her husband on the floor. She calls Sybil and Lewis. Sybil explains her father is in a trance and will come back on his own. For now he needs privacy. She and BeeBee and Lewis haul him into the study.

As soon as they are offstage, Louie's head pops out of the guest room. He tells Millie the coast is clear and she enters wearing only bloomers and an undershirt and a blissful expression. Louie tells her that when he gets enough money together they will be married. He adds, "I'll be with you tonight." Euphorically she puts on her uniform while singing "I'm in Love with a Wonderful Guy" in Swedish. She exits into her room upstairs.

Lewis enters from the dining room to answer the phone. It is his former employer, Mr. Demetrius. Pretending to be Dr. Morris, Lewis tells him that he has indeed received his shoes. "That handsome young black man delivered them to me." Obviously, from Lewis's reactions, Demetrius's evaluation is somewhat harsher.

Lewis tells Demetrius on the phone: "Well, I suggest that instead of denigrating that young man's reputation you keep a closer eye on your wife. I hear she's a hot little dish. I daresay I wouldn't mind having a fling at her myself. I wouldn't mind at all. Heh, heh, heh. Bye-di-bye, Mr. Demetrius."

He hangs up and goes to the guest room to check on Louie's progress on the second test. Louie tells him he's doing fine and again requests some orange juice. Hearing BeeBee and Sybil on their way into the room, Lewis quickly joins Louie in the guest room, closing the door.

The doorbell rings. Millie comes rushing down the stairs—still dressing—to answer it. She stops halfway down, as Sybil has opened it first. It's Charles, whom Sybil has called away from a full agenda at the office. She says she has important news. Millie interrupts with *her* important news—she is giving two weeks notice to get married to someone who shall remain nameless. She exits to her room.

Charles wants to know why he has been called. Sybil tells him Louie-Lewis has a wonderful business opportunity in which she wants him to invest $10,000 of the $11,000 he has managed to save. With the money he's sure to earn, they'll be able to get married. Charles is not enthusiastic about the idea. Lewis enters at this moment to make his pitch.

LEWIS: . . . . . A long time ago I asked myself what business do we need in the ghetto areas of our city, what business do we need in Harlem. What business do the people need, forget about the businessman. And I said to myself, "They need a place where they can go and forget their troubles, they need a place to relax, to socialize, to meet one another on an interpersonal level and not on a competitive dog-eat-dog level."

CHARLES: May I ask now, what business you're referring to?

LEWIS *(getting cigar from cigar box):* You may ask, and I may tell you. I am referring to a tap-dancing school.

CHARLES *(looks to others dumbly, then back to Lewis):* You want to open a tap-dancing school . . . in Harlem?

LEWIS: Exactly. And not only do I want to open a tap-dancing school in Harlem, but once our capital is recouped I want to open tap-dancing schools in all the ghetto areas of our city. We have to get those disadvantaged people off the streets and get them back to tapping again.

Charles remains skeptical. A touch of hysteria has also entered his manner. Lewis suggests that Charles might change his mind if he had a talk with his (Lewis's) business manager Harold P. Hainsworth. Sybil tells Charles they plan to get her father and the colonel in as business partners, too. Charles agrees to see Hainsworth and leaves to return to his work.

Lewis and Sybil leave too, to go horseback riding. BeeBee is about to join them, but Michael and Jackie, the cook and his wife, enter and BeeBee has new dinner instructions for them. There will be an extra person to dinner. Also, they must stock up on the fixings for Honkey cocktails. She exits.

A tapping is heard from the upstairs terrace window. It is a burglar Michael has enlisted to rob the Morrises so he can take Jackie to Amagansett and open a French restaurant with her. She has reservations about the plan, but Michael overrides them with a glowing portrait of their future. He sends her back to the kitchen and lets Laurent in.

Michael tells Laurent, who is the world's most nearsighted burglar, that the safe is in the master bedroom. Laurent is to hide in the linen closet until he gives the signal by knocking three times. Laurent will do the job while Michael and Jackie are serving dinner to the Morrises and their guests.

Laurent gets into the closet and Michael returns to the kitchen as the doctor enters. Dr. Morris knocks on the guest room door. Louie reports from behind the door that he is almost finished with the test. The doctor is in a fine mood and is about to leave when the doorbell rings. He opens the door to Philomena, the colonel's Southern wife, who has rushed over in her wheelchair. She wants to know if her husband and BeeBee are having an affair. Dr. Morris tells her the idea is preposterous and that in fact her husband had suggested that BeeBee was having an affair with his patient Louie Lucas (also preposterous). Somewhat mollified, Philomena explains the wheelchair as being necessitated by her bad back, but she had bolted over when she thought her husband was straying. She asks if she might stay awhile. Dr. Morris tells her yes, then excuses himself to go to his appointment with his guru.

Louie enters, startling Philomena, who screams, startling Louie. Philomena drops her glasses in the process. Louie returns them to her and introduces himself. She asks him if he is having an affair with BeeBee. He says no.

LOUIE: . . . . . It's funny but . . . I like you.

PHILOMENA: You like me?

LOUIE: There's something between us.

PHILOMENA: What could there possibly be between us?

LOUIE: I don't know yet. It's a feeling I have. Your voice . . . Did you ever have any voice training?

PHILOMENA: Why . . . I studied voice for years.

LOUIE: Wow, isn't that wild.

PHILOMENA: I was training for an operatic career when I met my husband.

LOUIE: I'm a big opera nut. That's my one big hang-up. I go every chance I get.

PHILOMENA: Well, that is a coincidence.

He begins to sing a passage. She joins in. Both are swept away by the emotion of the moment. He wheels her into his room, closing the door behind as the curtain falls.

ACT II

Scene 1: Afternoon

A few hours later, Louie wheels out a half-dressed, contented, still singing Philomena. He tells her he loves her and that as soon as she is divorced and he gets some money together they will be married. "I'll be with you tonight," he adds and closes the door.

Her husband enters from his room carrying a suitcase. He is startled to see her.

HOPKINS: Philomena! What are you doing here . . . without your clothes on?

PHILOMENA: I . . . What do you think I am doing here? I have come to spend the weekend with my friends, Doctor and Mrs. Morris.

Puts on her eye-glasses.

HOPKINS: But your back . . .

PHILOMENA (*takes blouse from arm of chair, waves for Hopkins to turn around, and puts it on*): My back has never felt better. I have never felt better. Didn't you hear me singing? When was the last time you heard me singing?

HOPKINS: That would be . . . twenty-three years ago.

PHILOMENA: Yes, Martin. Twenty-three years ago. The first night of our honeymoon. I haven't sung a note since that memorable occasion.

HOPKINS: What made you start up again?

PHILOMENA (*moving wheelchair to upstage*): That's for me to know and you to find out.

Notices his suitcase.

You're not planning to cut your visit short, are you?

HOPKINS: Do you know where I was going, sweetheart? To the hospital. To be with you.

PHILOMENA: Were you?

HOPKINS: This very minute.

PHILOMENA: Martin, you wouldn't be overly distressed if I started divorce proceedings, would you?

HOPKINS: Philomena, sweetheart, what are you saying?

PHILOMENA: I'm saying I have fallen in love with another man.

HOPKINS: Another . . . But how could you? You've been on your back for the past six months.

PHILOMENA (she wheels herself to upstage guest room): Let us say he is rather an unusual man.

HOPKINS: He would have to be. (He laughs.) Who is he, Philomena?

PHILOMENA (opening door to her room): When the time is appropriate you'll know. Not before. If you stay, Martin, please continue to use the upstairs guest room.

> She backs wheelchair into room singing "Fish gotta swim, birds gotta fly . . ." and closes door.

HOPKINS: This is sheer idiocy. Philomena, open this door. I demand to know who he is.

> He knocks on her door three times. Louie opens door, looks out, shuts door at sight of Hopkins. Laurent opens linencloset center doors, looks out, closes doors. Hopkins turns to downstage guest room door as it slams shut and linencloset doors as they slam shut.

Through the front door come BeeBee and Sybil in high spirits. Sybil goes to her room to change, reminding her mother to tell her when Louie-Lewis returns. Hopkins tells BeeBee that Philomena is asking for a divorce. BeeBee guesses that Philomena suspects him of having an affair with her and is trying to break it up by robbing him of the adulterous aspect which has given them such pleasure. Hopkins can't concentrate on the thought of his wife with BeeBee present and so desirable. She promises to be with him that night if he invests $10,000 in Lewis's dancing school. The colonel begins to protest when Dr. Morris enters with news of more calamities from the outside world and fruits and nuts for his guru, who will be joining them for dessert that night. Dr. Morris tells Hopkins that the tests have convinced him that Louie-Lewis is a genius, and on the basis of that he has decided to invest the $10,000 in the tap-dancing school.

Lewis enters, his body a little battered from horseback riding. BeeBee goes to her room. The colonel, suitcases in hand, returns to his room. Dr. Morris tells Lewis of his decision to invest and goes into his study. Lewis calls to Dr. Morris that his business manager, Mr. Hainsworth, will be joining them for dinner at BeeBee's request. Passing through from study to kitchen, Dr. Morris asks Lewis for the other test. While Dr. Morris is offstage, Lewis gets the completed exam from Louie.

> Dr. Morris enters from kitchen, eating yoghurt.

LEWIS: . . . . . Got the test right here, Doctor.

MORRIS: Good. Put it on the table. I've been thinking about you and your difficulties, Louie.

> Puts yoghurt on table beside swivel chair.

And I can't for the life of me reconcile what I see with what I read in your files. Please make yourself comfortable and tell me what comes to you.

Morris fluffs a pillow on sofa and lies down.

LEWIS *(sits on sofa):* Well, Doctor, if I can raise the money to start a business of my own . . .

MORRIS: Let's not go into that. What I would like to hear about is what disturbs or depresses you and those five women you impregnated because you refuse to use contraception.

LEWIS *(lying on sofa next to Morris with head at other end):* Well, Doctor, it's like this. Where I was born we didn't receive any sex education. Everything we learned about sex we had to learn out on the streets. But my momma would never let me go out on the streets, so to this day I am wholly ignorant of the birds and the bees and the things between the knees.

MORRIS *(sitting up):* Louie, is it that you have no intention of telling me the truth, or is it that you don't know the truth?

LEWIS *(sitting up):* Well, to tell you the truth, Doctor, I'm a little confused by the truth as it specifically pertains to the truth.

MORRIS: Then I suggest you lie there till you're unconfused. You think and think hard. If you can't come up with some honest answers, I'll have to ask you to leave. *(Rises.)*

LEWIS: You have to give me . . .

MORRIS *(picks up yoghurt and moves to study):* Think it over. I have a letter to write to the American Indian Committee. I hear they're planning to reclaim South Dakota and part of Oklahoma. And if California slips into the San Andreas Fault . . . there goes the West. We'll be a country without a West.

Dr. Morris exits. Lewis summons Louie into the living room to get from him the appropriate answers to Dr. Morris's questions. Louie tells him that he and his girl friends don't believe in contraception. "We think to give birth to something, to create something, is an affirmation of one's humanity." He goes on to describe a history of perpetual randiness.

LOUIE: I mean, women are terrific, Doctor.

LEWIS: Uh-uh!

LOUIE: I get so aroused when I'm with them . . .

LEWIS: Uh-uh-uh!

LOUIE: I get into this cosmic thing.

LEWIS: What cosmic thing?

LOUIE: It's like I feel I'm floating up in outer space.

LEWIS: Can't you float up in outer space if you use a rubber? Or does that weigh you down too much?

LOUIE: It's what I said before. We have to affirm our humanity. We have to fight back and refuse to be a statistic. When I'm in bed with a woman I'm not working for the Commission on Population Growth. *(He laughs nervously.)*

LEWIS: So this is your way of fighting the system, is that it?

LOUIE *(crossing to him):* Yes, in effect it is. You could say I'm the last revolutionary left. But instead of using guns and bombs I use sex as my weapon.

LEWIS: Well, that's a *mighty* powerful weapon you got there, Lucas.

Having gotten what he wanted, Lewis begins to lead Louie back to his room, promising finally to feed him something. The phone rings. Lewis answers. It is one of Louie's girl friends. Upset that Louie has endangered his plan by making contact with the outside world, Lewis hangs up on the girl and orders Louie to return to his room and strip and give him his clothes so as to restrict his mobility.

With Louie stripping in his room, Lewis is now faced with the appearance of a ragingly amorous Millie who gives him a flower and reconfirms her date that night with Louie. She throws herself (literally) into Lewis's arms, and it is in this position Dr. Morris finds them as he enters from the study. They disengage and Lewis begins to repeat Louie's sexual philosophy to Dr. Morris as they head for the study. Philomena has watched them exit and asks Millie who was with the doctor. "Louie Lucas," Millie replies.

PHILOMENA *(all color leaving her face):* But . . . But . . . Millie, that couldn't be Louie Lucas. Louie Lucas is a young white boy . . . isn't he?

MILLIE: Sometimes he is vhite and sometimes he is black. But mostly he is black.

PHILOMENA *(rises):* Mostly he's . . .

MILLIE: He has a formula to remove the black from his face. They sell it in the Voolvorth's.

PHILOMENA: Oh . . . Oh . . . Ohhh, shit!
She gasps and faints into wheelchair; both leg-rests shoot up, backrest reclines, as she falls into chair.

Millie summons Dr. Morris to aid Philomena. Dr. Morris dispatches Millie to get his bag and fetch Hopkins. The doorbell rings. He opens the door and Demetrius, Lewis's former shoemaker-employer, enters in a rage. So, he says, Dr. Morris would like to make it with his wife, hunh? He lifts the befuddled doctor in his arms just as Philomena is regaining consciousness. Still bellowing, the shoemaker deposits Dr. Morris on top of the screaming Philomena. Both Dr. Morris and Philomena faint, and Demetrius exits.

Millie emerges from the master bedroom upstairs with the doctor's bag and knocks on Hopkins's door three times (which causes Laurent to peep out myopically for a second). Hopkins follows Millie downstairs as BeeBee emerges in a bathrobe from the bathroom. They are all surprised to see an unconscious Dr. Morris lying on top of an unconscious Philomena. Hopkins assumes this is another of Dr. Morris's trances. Sybil enters from her bedroom as BeeBee and the colonel wheel the double-loaded chair into Philomena's room. Millie extracts smelling salts from the doctor's bag, leaving the bag on a table. They all pile into Philomena's room and close the door with a slam.

Laurent shuffles myopically downstairs and somehow manages to cut the telephone wire. As he returns to his hiding place, Lewis enters, not seeing him. Lewis makes sure the coast is clear before signalling Louie to open the door.

Meanwhile, in trying to get back into the linen closet, Laurent has caught his neck in the door. He screams. Frightened, Lewis jumps. Just then, Louie opens the door and Lewis bounds into the guest room, slamming the door at the same time Laurent slams *his* door shut. The lights black out.

Scene 2: Evening

Sybil is mixing Honkey cocktails, preparing for the guests to come. Millie enters from Philomena's room with the news that Philomena is resting.

BeeBee enters and summons Michael and Jackie to tell them that there will be yet two more to dinner. Michael protests that there will not be enough in case someone should want seconds, but BeeBee tells him to make do. Michael and Jackie exit as BeeBee exits into Philomena's room. The doorbell rings.

Sybil goes to the front door to admit Charles. He tries to persuade her to let him keep out of investing in Lewis's school, but she is firm. A Honkey cocktail does nothing to improve his mood.

Hopkins and Dr. Morris enter from the master bedroom and come downstairs. They have been trying to sort out some of the baffling events of the day, to little avail. BeeBee emerges from Philomena's room. Dr. Morris tells Hopkins to take it easy and Hopkins asks BeeBee for a stiff drink.

Lewis enters from Louie's room dressed in a dinner jacket and carrying Louie's clothing in a bed sheet. He asks Millie to take care of the bundle for him. She responds with an enthusiasm that leaves him physically wobbly. She then exits. Lewis turns down BeeBee's offer of a Honkey cocktail in favor of a wine spritzer.

The doorbell rings and he opens it to introduce Mr. Hainsworth, "a recent graduate from the N.Y.U. School of Law and one of the most astounding minds in the financial world today." Mr. Hainsworth is flamboyantly gay. Lewis makes introductions while Hainsworth gives a running critique of the decoration of the apartment, the guests' clothes, hairstyles and perfume. With Lewis's urging, Hainsworth pulls out papers saying that they must be signed that night or they will lose the choice location Lewis has in mind for the Lewis Franklin Dancing Academy. (He explains that Lewis Franklin is Louie Lucas's legal name.)

The potential investors are a little hesitant about jumping in so quickly. Hainsworth remarks that if he'd known they weren't going to do business, he would have stayed home to be rubbed down by his masseuse. "You should see me after a rub-down from my masseuse, Colonel. Mauve. My skin turns to a bright Regency mauve. I look irresistible."

Millie interrupts this turn in the conversation by announcing dinner. Everyone repairs to the dining room, closing the doors behind.

Michael and Jackie enter, Michael about to set their plan in motion by signalling Laurent. At this moment, Louie springs from his room with only a towel around his waist, hoping to persuade the man he thinks is the doctor to return his clothes. Michael quickly hides, but Louie spots Jackie. "It's funny but I like you," he says. Michael pops up indignantly and Louie retreats to his room.

Michael knocks three times on the linen closet door and Laurent pops out. Laurent tells Jackie that the jewels will be hidden in the doctor's bag. Michael exits into the master bedroom. Laurent embraces Jackie (after some directional assistance from her) telling her he is doing this for love of her. Michael reappears and dispatches Jackie to the kitchen to continue the serving of the dinner. Michael exits with Laurent into the master bedroom to continue the caper.

Louie, very hungry, enters to grab some food which has been left in the living room. At the same time, Hainsworth enters from the dining room to fetch the papers. He stops in his tracks at the sight of the half-naked Louie. He introduces himself. Louie explains his situation.

LOUIE: Doctor Morris took all of my clothes so I can't get out. He refuses to feed me. I haven't had anything to eat or drink in two days. I'm really going through hell in this house.

HAINSWORTH: There. There. Perhaps I can help you.

LOUIE: Would you? I'm so hungry I could eat a horse.

HAINSWORTH: That may not be necessary. You wait here. I'll be out with gobs of food.

He moves to kitchen.

LOUIE: Orange juice, Hal.

HAINSWORTH: Shhh.

LOUIE: I'm dying for a glass of orange juice.

HAINSWORTH: I'll squeeze the oranges myself. Don't go 'way now.

He exits into kitchen.

Francine, one of Louie's girl friends, arrives at the door, very pregnant. Louie leads her to his room to tell her of his trials.

Hopkins and BeeBee enter from the dining room. Hopkins, who has just given Lewis his check, is still steamed at the thought of his wife having a lover. BeeBee reminds him that the two of them still have their evening together to look forward to. Hopkins forgets about Philomena for the moment and demands that BeeBee join him now in the study. She tells him to wait for her there, that she'll be with him shortly. As Hopkins disappears, Hainsworth enters from the kitchen carrying a tray of food for Louie.

BEEBEE: Oh, Mr. Hainsworth. Are you bringing Philomena her dinner?

HAINSWORTH: Philomena?

BEEBEE: I'll get Millie to do that. You don't . . .

HAINSWORTH: No, please, let me. Philomena is ravenous.

BEEBEE: How considerate. I'll go and help Louie with the others. Don't be long now.

Exits into dining room, closing doors. Hainsworth looks about.

HAINSWORTH: Louie? Louie? Are you hiding from me?

Philomena enters from upstage guest room. She is wearing a white nightgown and robe; her hair hangs loosely on her back . . . . . She is barefoot.

PHILOMENA: Hey! Are you Louie Lucas?

HAINSWORTH: Not that I know of.

PHILOMENA: Where is Louie Lucas?

HAINSWORTH: I couldn't say. Are you Philomena?

PHILOMENA: Yes, I am. Philomena Carswell Hopkins. And you're . . .

HAINSWORTH: Harold Prinkley Hainsworth. Louie Lucas's personal manager.

PHILOMENA: I take it then that Louie Lucas is definitely colored.

HAINSWORTH: Are you from the South?

PHILOMENA: My family has lived in Macon, Georgia, for over seven generations.

HAINSWORTH *(broadly):* Well, girl, dat boy's as black as de ace of spades.

PHILOMENA: No matter. If you see him, would you please tell him I must speak to him. I'll be in my room. Your little girl is weak, Daddy.

> *She looks upwards.*

Have mercy on her. She has fallen in love with a darkie.

> *Exits into her bedroom.*

Hainsworth starts looking for Louie again as Jackie runs from the kitchen upstairs into the master bedroom. Lewis comes out of the dining room to tell Hainsworth to return and finish business. Hainsworth protests that he is about to feed Louie, but Lewis takes the tray from him saying he'll take care of that and sends Hainsworth back into the dining room to tend to business. Lewis is about to give Louie the food when Michael and Jackie swoop down from the master bedroom and snatch it from him. (Jackie had run up to tell Michael that a portion was missing.) Michael apologizes and tells him there's not enough for seconds, dispatches Jackie with the food to finish serving the dinner and returns to the master bedroom.

The doorbell rings and Dr. Morris comes out from the dining room to answer it. It is his guru, Bahdah, *"a small paunchy man wearing a white cotton dhoti and white turban, black shoes and socks revealed,"* who will be leaving the next day to take up permanent residence in Tibet.

MORRIS: . . . . . This is a patient of mine, Mr. Bahdah. Mr. Louie Lucas or Franklin or . . . He has several names.

BAHDAH: That makes the two of us. First I vos Goldberg, then I vos Kincaid and finally I am Bahdah. Glad to meet you, young man. *(He shakes his hand.)*

LEWIS: Glad to meet you, Mr. Bahdah.

BAHDAH: You should come vit me to Ti*bit.*

LEWIS *(looks to guest room door):* I might just have to . . .

BAHDAH *(taking them both by the arm and bringing them forward):* You know, everybody should come vit me to Tibit. Forty years ago ven I vos in the wholesale carpet business I asked myself two qvestions: qvestion number one: vot is the meaning of human existence? Qvestion number two: is vot I'm doing in the wholesale carpet business human existence? No, vos my affirmative answer. And since that day I have searched from the highways to the byways until I recognized the ultimate truth of human existence.

MORRIS: What is that, Mr. Bahdah?

BAHDAH: Don't be a shmuck and ask stupid qvestions!

MORRIS: Wisely put. Oh, wisely put.

Morris leads Bahdah into the dining room. Millie pops out of the kitchen. Lewis asks for and gets the key to his-Louie's room (Louie has locked the door). He tells Millie he will meet her in her room in five minutes as BeeBee appears to tell him his presence is needed in the dining room. He returns to the table with BeeBee as Millie starts up the stairs to her room, undressing on the way.

The colonel comes out of the study, impatient for BeeBee, asks Millie when dinner will be finished. Millie tells him the meal will soon be over, as she exits. Philomena comes out of her room. There is an awkward pause when she and the colonel see each other. They stiffly say goodnight and return from whence they came.

Louie and Francine enter from his room. He is dressed in her clothes and she is wearing his towel. Francine goes over his plan. He is to leave. She will wait fifteen minutes, then call Dr. Morris and demand clothes. They will meet at her apartment. She returns to Louie's room. Louie is about to leave but hears the others coming. The study being closer to where he is at the moment, he dives into there. Lewis, Charles and Sybil enter. Charles is dazed from having been successfully hustled by Lewis and Sybil into signing the check. Not feeling well, he bolts for the upstairs bathroom, followed by an attentive Sybil.

LEWIS (opens Louie's room with the key): Okay, Louie Lucas. Now you're in for it. Now we're going to have a man-to-man . . .

> He exits into guest room. There is a loud scream from Francine. He rushes back onstage, closing door after him. Stands stunned.

PHILOMENA (entering from upstage guest room): Did I . . . are you Louie Lucas?

> Lewis doesn't move. Philomena moves to him and leads him back to her room.

Where have you been? I've been waiting for you all evening. If you're a colored man, you're a colored man. You should have told me from the onset. We'll manage. We'll go away somewhere. Africa. Would you like to go to Africa?

> She exits with him, closing door. Louie exits from study, slamming door shut. He angrily pulls at his dress, shouts at Hopkins through closed door, making fists at door; his tights are at his ankles.

LOUIE: You filthy beast! You dirty old man! (Pulls up tights.) Look what you did to my stockings!

> Lewis enters from upstage guest room, coat half off—we hear Philomena singing—Lewis slams door shut, shouts at Philomena through closed door.

LEWIS: You keep singing, Ma'm. And I'm . . . I'm . . .

> He turns to see Louie pulling up his tights; to Louie, moving after him.

I'm going to whip your ass!

> Lewis chases Louie around room; Louie manages to keep sofa between them.

Who's that fat naked girl in your room? When did she get here?

LOUIE: She's my best girl friend.

LEWIS: She's going to be your last girl friend.

> Louie runs into his guest room and backs slowly out, holding up his

> *hand for Lewis to stop. We hear Francine breathing heavily—La Maze method. Lewis stares through open door, wide-eyed, breathing sympathetically along with her.*

Francine is about to have the baby. Louie asks Lewis to deliver it. Lewis says he will if Louie goes home now.

LEWIS: . . . . . Come back tomorrow.
LOUIE: Tell Francine I love her very much and as soon as I get a little bread . . .
> *Lewis slams door shut on him.*
HAINSWORTH *(enters from dining-room with briefcase):* Lewis! We did it, Lewis! The three checks are in here. *(Looks about.)* Where's Louie Lucas?
LEWIS *(moving into dining-room):* He just left in some funky old dress! *(And exits.)*
HAINSWORTH: Oh, my God! I knew it!
> *He grabs umbrella and exits, shouting.*
Louie? Louie . . . ?
> *Hopkins enters from study; dazed expression on his pale face: his jacket and shirt have been torn to shreds. Jackie enters from kitchen, wearing a coat; bumps into Hopkins, turning him around; runs up left staircase. Hopkins collapses into swivel chair.*
JACKIE: Pardon, monsieur. Pardon . . .
> *Lewis enters from dining room, followed by Dr. Morris, BeeBee and Bahdah. They move to downstage guest room.*
MORRIS *(moving to study):* Where is she?
LEWIS: In my room.
MORRIS *(exits into guest room):* Does she have a personal physician?
LEWIS: He doesn't make house calls.
BEEBEE *(exits into guest room):* The poor girl . . .
BAHDAH *(napkin at chin):* I vos a nurse in the Second World War. But we had no pregnancies!
> *Exits into guest room.*
MORRIS *(coming back to doorway):* Phone for an ambulance, Louie.
LEWIS: Right away, Doctor.
> *He picks up phone; sees wire has been cut.*
The line's dead.
MORRIS *(offstage):* Never mind. Get my medicine-bag! Upstairs!
> *Lewis runs up right staircase. Michael exits from master bedroom; Jackie and Laurent are behind him. Michael is carrying the medicine-bag with jewels in it.*

Lewis grabs the bag from their hands. Dr. Morris tells him it's too late for the bag and that he should run out and find a working phone to call for an ambulance. Just as Lewis is about to leave, Millie pops out of her room dressed in a nightie, beckoning him. The next instant, Philomena has popped out from her room, calling for her lover.

"As soon as I get a little bread together we'll get married," Lewis assures them.

"We'll *all* get married!" And he dashes out the front door, still carrying the medicine-bag. Lights black out.

Scene 3: The following morning

BeeBee, Sybil and Charles—much the worse for the previous evening's wear —are answering questions put to them by Detective Peterson. Upon the birth of Francine's baby they realized that Lewis could not have been the father and thus could not be Louie Lucas. Now they're positive Lewis is responsible for the theft of the jewels. Charles, in a vaguely suicidal mood, tells Sybil he has decided he doesn't want to get married and turns for solace to a small bottle of Milk of Magnesia.

Kirby, another detective, enters with Louie. Louie is overjoyed at the news that Francine gave birth to a boy, bringing his total to seven girls and three boys. They put him in the room he's spent so much time in once more. He again asks for orange juice as they close the door. "He's not what I expected," Sybil comments.

The colonel and his wife enter from his room. They are leaving for her parents' home in Macon. She gives him permission to say goodbye. "All this reminds me of the day we packed up and left Nam," he begins. "There was a tear in my eye and a lump in my . . ." "Oh don't, Martin," Philomena interrupts. Millie is also leaving, returning to Sweden. Sybil tells her Louie Lucas is in the other room.

MILLIE: Wich vun?

BEEBEE: The white one.

MILLIE: The vhite vun is vorse than the black vun.
        Shakes BeeBee's hand and then picks up trunk, turning upstage to go.
Okay. Goodbye, Mrs. Morris. Many t'anks. I am going home vhere dere vill be no more Louie Lucases. And dot vill be . . . Doctor Morris!
        She stops in mid-speech, dropping trunk and gaping at the sight of Dr. Morris coming out of his room. He is dressed in bright orange safron dhoti, sandals; small canvas bag hangs from his shoulder, a braided Tibetan skullcap on his head.

BEEBEE *(crossing to stairs):* Lionel!

SYBIL *(crossing to stairs):* Oh, Daddy! Please don't go to Shigatse, Tibet!

MORRIS *(comes down left staircase and hands BeeBee piece of paper):* There. There. Be brave. Don't make it more difficult for me than it is. I wrote down the name of the ashram I'll be staying at. Unfortunately, we're not permitted to communicate with the outside world for five years.

BEEBEE: Won't we ever see you again?

MORRIS: In New Delhi. On (today's date), 1980.

SYBIL: Daddy . . .

MORRIS *(crossing to entrance door):* I'll make reservations for the both of you at the Shigatse Hilton. Don't fret. Don't fret.

Lewis shows up in the middle of all this with the doctor's bag and a folder. He explains how he fell into being Louie Lucas; also that, after getting the ambulance, he went home to bed, not realizing the jewels were in the bag until

20 minutes ago. The police ask how he got the bag and he tells them he got it from Jackie. Detective Peterson announces that the alarm is out for Jackie and Michael and that it is his belief that Lewis is in the clear.

The detectives leave as Lewis tells Charles that the location for the dancing academy has been secured and that they are well on their way to becoming rich. Louie enters from his room, spots Lewis and, still thinking he is Dr. Morris, thanks him for delivering the baby and kisses him on the cheek.

LEWIS (getting up, crossing to Morris): I don't know why those women chase after you, Louie Lucas. You kiss like an uptight woodpecker.

LOUIE: You can't hurt my feelings, Doctor. I'm too happy.

MORRIS: I take it you're Louie Lucas.

LOUIE: That's right. Who are you?

MORRIS: I'm Doctor Morris.

LOUIE: Doctor Morris?

LEWIS (putting an arm around Morris's shoulder): This is my father.

LOUIE: You're putting me on.

LEWIS: Dad, it'd be a pity if you gave up on this boy.

MORRIS: If there was one chance in a million . . .

LEWIS: You were wrong about me. You could be wrong about him.

MORRIS: I was wrong about you, Lewis. And I could be wrong about . . .
        Crosses to Louie; Louie laughs nervously.
My God, what a challenge. I'll do it. BeeBee, I'll cancel my reservations to Shigatse.
        Crosses to her; they embrace.

LOUIE: Does this mean I can't go home?

LEWIS: That's what it means, Louie. My daddy's taking over.

Hopkins apologizes to Lewis for his suspicions. Lewis accepts the apology and suggests they all go into the dining room for breakfast. Millie decides she'll stay long enough to "see vhat the black vun is like." Charles and Sybil decide it's time they get married. Philomena tells the colonel she's decided she wants children. It isn't too late. After all, she was born when her mother was 47. "Didn't she want you any sooner?" Hopkins asks. Louie gets Dr. Morris's permission to visit Francine after breakfast, promising to come back. He tells them his seducing days are over. "I have to start conserving my energy or I'll be wiped out by the time I'm fifty."

Everyone but Lewis and the doctor have exited into the dining room.

MORRIS: Do you think there's any hope, Lewis?

LEWIS: Oh, there's hope, Doctor, but we can't let ourselves despair with the ups and downs of city life.
        Laurent comes out from behind drapes and picks up medecine-bag with
        jewels.
Only if we have faith in each other and continue to believe in the infinite resources of the human heart, then and only then . . .

He claps his hands three times. Laurent, on the balcony, drops the bag into Lewis's waiting arms.
Do we stand a ghost of a chance.

They repair to the dining room for breakfast, closing the doors behind them as the curtain falls.

THE RITZ

A Comedy in Two Acts

BY TERRENCE McNALLY

Cast and credits appear on page 338

TERRENCE McNALLY was born in St. Petersburg, Fla., Nov. 3, 1939 and grew up in Corpus Christi, Texas. He received his B.A. in English at Columbia where in his senior year he wrote the varsity show. After graduation he was awarded the Harry Evans Travelling Fellowship in creative writing. He made his professional stage debut with The Lady of the Camellias, *an adaptation of the Dumas story produced on Broadway in 1963. His first original full-length play,* And Things That Go Bump in the Night, *was produced on Broadway in 1965 following a production at the Tyrone Guthrie Theater in Minneapolis.*

McNally's short play Tour *was produced off Broadway in 1968 as part of the* Collision Course *program. In the next season, 1968–69, his one-acters were produced all over town:* Cuba Si! *was staged off off Broadway in the ANTA Matinee series;* Noon *formed part of the Broadway program* Morning, Noon and Night; *off Broadway a program of two McNally one-acters—*Sweet Eros *and* Witness*— opened that fall; and in early winter his one-acter* Next *opened with Elaine May's* Adaptation *on a bill which was named a Best Play of its season.*

McNally's second Best Play, Where Has Tommy Flowers Gone?, *had its world premiere at the Yale Repertory Theater before opening off Broadway in 1971. His third,* Bad Habits, *was produced off off Broadway in 1973 by New York Theater Strategy, directed then and in its off-Broadway and Broadway phases last season by Robert Drivas. Another full-length McNally play,* Whiskey, *was produced off off Broadway in 1973 but hasn't yet reached the commercial theater.*

The Ritz is McNally's fourth straight Best Play out of his last four commercial theater productions. It had its pre-Broadway premiere, not in one of the smaller

*New York theaters which have launched so many new McNally works, but at the
Yale Repertory Theater last season under the working title* The Tubs.
   McNally, a bachelor, now lives in New York City.

Time: Now

Place: A men's bathhouse in New York City

ACT I

*SYNOPSIS: Before the curtain rises the lights go to black. We can hear
sobbing and the drone of prayers and the dying voice of Old Man Vespucci,
who is surrounded by his grieving family. He has only one thought before he
dies: "Get Proclo!" Proclo is his son-in-law; he orders his family "Get Proclo!!"
with his dying, revengeful breath.*

   *The lights come up, revealing the inside of the Ritz, a men's bathhouse,
behind a scrim. The impression is of many corridors with rows of doors, with
numbers of men moving in and out and along the corridors.* "One of the most
important aspects is this sense of men endlessly prowling the corridors outside
the numbered doors. The same people will pass up and down the same
corridors and stairways over and over again. After a while, you'll start to think
some of them are on a treadmill. Most of them are dressed exactly alike, i.e.
they are wearing bathrobes. A few men wear towels around their waists. Every
so often we see someone in bikini underwear or an additional accoutrement,
such as boots or a vest."

Two young attendants—Tiger and Duff—are sweeping, making beds, etc.
Every so often the voice of Abe, the manager, intrudes over a speaker system
with instructions for the attendants on the various floors, or reporting the
arrival of a client, or an announcement for the guests, like "Just a reminder
that every Monday and Thursday is Buddy Night at the Ritz. So bring s
friend. Two entrances for the price of one."

The lights dim and a curtain comes down representing the Ritz's entrance
area, with the manager Abe in his booth. Here is where *"The various patrons
will pay, check their valuables, receive a room key and then be buzzed through
the inner door adjacent to the booth."*

Abe announces a patron's room number and admits him; then answers a
question on the phone. Another patron arrives, dripping wet from the rain
outside, and is admitted. Another comes along carrying a Valet Pack and a
bag from Zabar's Delicatessen (all part of the costume he intends to wear in
tonight's Ritz talent show). He is Claude Perkins, an old customer.

ABE: I thought you'd sworn off this place.
CLAUDE: I thought I had, too.
ABE: You got homesick for us, right?

CLAUDE: I didn't have much choice. I don't speak Spanish, so the Continental is out. The Club Baths are just too far downtown, I'm boycotting the Beacon, Man's Country's had it and I've been barred from the Everard.

ABE: You've been barred from the Everard?

CLAUDE: They'll regret it.

ABE: Nobody gets barred from the Everard. How'd you manage that?

CLAUDE: There was this man there.

ABE: A fat man, right?

CLAUDE: Fat? He was the magic mountain. He drove me into one of my frenzies. I went berserk and I kicked his door in. So they threw me out and told me never to come back. I was willing to pay for it. I just wanted to talk to him.

Abe buzzes Claude in through the door, just before Gaetano Proclo hurries in. Proclo is carrying a suitcase and a box of Panettone; he's overweight and is wearing *"a wet raincoat, a cheap wig, a big bushy moustache and dark glasses."* He explains to Abe that he needs to cash a check to pay an impatiently waiting taxi, because he came on from Cleveland in such a hurry he didn't have time to get some money. Proclo identifies himself with a card reading "Proclo Sanitation Services, Gaetano Proclo, President," but Abe is reluctant to cash a check for him. Proclo takes off his disguise to show Abe he is on the level and explains further: "My brother-in-law is a maniac and he's going to kill me tonight. If you don't let me in there I'm going to be a dead person. Please, mister, you are making a grown man cry. I'm begging you. It's a matter of life and death!"

Abe relents and decides to give Proclo a $10 bill, as Chris enters. Chris *"wears jeans, a blue nylon windbreaker and a bright purple shirt. . . . . also, he is wearing a policeman's whistle and a 'popper' holder around his neck."* Proclo hurries out to pay the honking cab driver, while Chris, obviously one of the regulars at the Ritz, signs in.

CHRIS: How's that gorgeous son of yours?

ABE: You're too late. He's getting married.

CHRIS: That's terrific. Give him my love, will you?

ABE: Sure thing, Chris.

CHRIS: Does he need anyone to practise with?

ABE: He's been practising too much. That's why he's getting married.

CHRIS: Compared to me, Abe, she'd have to be an amateur.
      He returns the registration book.

ABE: Ronald Reagan! Aw, c'mon Chris!

CHRIS: You know, he used to be lovers with John Wayne.

ABE: Sure he was.

CHRIS: Right after he broke up with Xavier Cugat.

ABE: People like you think the whole world's queer.

CHRIS: It's lucky for people like you it is.

Proclo comes back for change—the taxi driver can't change a ten. He goes out again as Chris enters the bathhouse, blowing his whistle and shouting, "All right, men! Up against the wall! This is a raid!"

Michael Brick, a rugged looking young man, asks for a room in a voice that is, surprisingly, a high boyish treble. He wants the room for only three or four hours but is told he must take it for a minimum of twelve hours for a charge of $10. He takes the room and questions Abe as to whether a fat, balding, middle-aged man just came in. Abe won't talk about his clients, but he's willing to let Michael into the Ritz, once he makes sure that Michael isn't a policeman, (he's a private detective on a case). Abe warns Michael that with his high voice he'd better "stay out of the steam room. It gets pretty wild in there."

As Michael is buzzed through the door, Googie Gomez—an attractive, animated creature with Spanish accent and style to match—makes her entrance. She's using a copy of *Variety* to protect herself from the rain and is carrying wig box and wardrobe bag. She's trying to keep rain spots off her dress, while cursing Tex Antoine, the TV weather man, for giving her a wrong forecast on this, "the biggest night of my life." She's closely followed by Proclo, whom she doesn't notice at first. When she does, *"there is a marked change in her behavior and vocabulary."*

GOOGIE: Joe Papp. Hello, Mr. Papp. It's a real pleasure to meet you. I seen all your shows. Uptown, downtown, in the park. They're all fabulous. *Fabulosa!* And I just know, in my heart of hearts, that after you see my show tonight you're going to want to give me a chance at one of your wonderful theaters. Uptown, downtown, in the park. I'll even work the Mobile Theater. Thank you for coming, Mr. Papp. Excuse me, I got a little laryngitis. But the show must go on, *si?*

PROCLO: My name isn't Papp.

GOOGIE: You're not Joe Papp?

PROCLO: I'm sorry.

GOOGIE: But you are a producer?

PROCLO: No.

GOOGIE: Are you sure?

PROCLO: Yes.

GOOGIE: That's okay. I heard there was gonna be a big producer around tonight and I wasn't taking any chances. You never know. It's hard for me to speak English good like that. *(A new outburst.)* Aaaaiiieee! My God, not the hairs! *Cono!* *(Her hands are hovering in the vicinity of her head.)* Okay. Go ahead and say it. It's okay. I can take it. Tell me I look like shit.

PROCLO: Why would I want to say a thing like that to such an attractive young lady?

GOOGIE: You boys really know how to cheer a girl up when she's dumps in the down.

She gives Proclo a kiss on the cheek.

My boyfriend Hector see me do that: *ay! cuidado!* He hates you *maricones*, that Hector! He's a ball breaker with me, too, mister. You know why you're not a producer? You're too nice to be a producer. But I'm gonna show them all, mister, and tonight's the night I'm gonna do it. *(Googie is moving towards the door.)* One day you gonna see the name Googie Gomez in lights and you gonna say to

yourself "Was that her?" And you gonna answer yourself, "That was her!" But you know something, mister? I was *always* her. Just nobody knows it. *Yo soy Googie Gomez, estrellita del futuro!*
    Googie is buzzed through the door and is gone.

Proclo is astonished to see a woman admitted to the all-male bathhouse and is told by Abe that Googie sings in the Ritz's night club, known as The Pits (it is only one of the Ritz's many facilities which include "movies, TV, swimming pool, steam room, sauna, massage table, discotheque, bridge, amateur night and free blood tests every Wednesday"). Another woman approaches dressed in rough male attire—it's only the accountant, Maurine, who is admitted without ceremony.

Proclo has come here to hide, he tells Abe, who assures him no one will bother him if he locks his door and stays in his room. Abe tells Proclo he can register under any name he chooses, so Proclo signs himself in as "Carmine Vespucci, Bensonhurst, Brooklyn"—the name of the brother-in-law who's sworn to kill him. As Abe buzzes Proclo in, the admitting area disappears and we see the interior of the Ritz with its two levels of corridors.

Tiger is sweeping on the lower level. Chris comes in, exchanges greeting with him, promises to liven things up. Claude comes in, sees Proclo and befriends him, promising to show him to his room.

Duff shows Chris to his usual room, 240, on the upper level near the steam room. Chris announces his presence loudly: "There will be an orgy in Room 240 in exactly four minutes!", then goes inside his room and closes the door.

Meanwhile, Claude has led Proclo to his own room, not Proclo's, and he plies Proclo with the food he has brought. Proclo weighs 226 and has triggered Claude's strange fascination with fat people. Claude begins singing "Jelly Roll Baby" to Proclo and wrestling with him. At first completely confused and finally alarmed, Proclo calls for help. Tiger lets himself into the room with a passkey.

TIGER *(pulling Proclo off Claude):* Okay, fat man! Leave the little guy alone! What are you trying to do? Pull his head off?
    He takes Proclo's key.
Let me see your key. 196! Now get down there and don't cause any more trouble. What do you think this is? The YMCA?
    He puts Proclo's suitcase in the corridor and turns back to Claude.
I'm sorry, sir. It won't happen again.
    CLAUDE *(moaning happily):* I certainly hope not.
    TIGER: Get down there, man! *(He goes.)*
    PROCLO: He ought to be locked up!
    The crowd of patrons are all looking at Proclo.
Hello. Whew! I just had quite a little experience in there. I think that guy's got a problem. People like that really shouldn't be allowed in a place like this.
    Stony silence from the patrons.
What unusual pants. They look like cowboy chaps.
    PATRON IN CHAPS: They are cowboy chaps.

Proclo manages to grasp the fact that he is somehow off on the wrong foot, and he retreats downstairs while the group of patrons melts away.

Michael Brick, the handsome detective with the squeaky voice, comes to the phone booth to report to his client, who is waiting in the bar across the street. It turns out that Michael's client is the real Carmine Vespucci, Proclo's vengeful brother-in-law.

MICHAEL *(into the phone):* Mr. Vespucci? My name is Michael Brick. I'm with the Greybar Detective Agency. You hired my partner to get something on a Mr. Gaetano Proclo, only my partner's sick so I'm taking over the case for him. I'm calling you from the Ritz. I just got here. Now let me see if I've got his description right. A balding middle-aged fat man? That's not much to go on, but I'll do my best.
> *Googie enters and signals to him.*
One of those transvestites is standing right next to me. Now you just stay by the phone in that bar across the street and I'll get back to you.

GOOGIE: *Ay, que cosa linda!*

MICHAEL *(into the phone):* I can't talk now. I think he's surrounding me for unnatural things.
> *Michael hangs up, gives Googie a horrified look and hurries off.*

Tiger comes in, and Googie finds out he was only joking when he told her a big producer was coming to see the show tonight. Furious, she contracts instant laryngitis and threatens to leave Tiger and Duff in the lurch to do the show alone if no producer shows up.

Proclo is still looking for his room, Number 196, and Duff shows him where it is. It's very small and still very messy from the previous tenant. Proclo is complaining about the strange man upstairs, when Tiger arrives with a broom and a change of linen for 196. Tiger tells Duff about the problem with Googie. Duff goes on an errand, and Tiger gives Proclo a friendly warning to stay out of Room 205.

PROCLO: What's in 205?

TIGER: That room I had to pull you out of. You could hurt comeone doing that.

PROCLO: Now just a minute! I thought that guy was taking me to my room! You don't think I went in there because I wanted to?

TIGER *(dawning on him):* You trying to tell me he's a chubby chaser?

PROCLO: A chubby what?

TIGER: Someone who likes . . . *(He gestures, indicating great bulk.)*

PROCLO: You mean like me?

TIGER: You're right up his alley.

PROCLO: I knew someone like that once. I just never knew what to call him. "Get away from me, Claude!" is all I could come up with. A chubby chaser! That's kind of funny. Unless, of course, you happen to be the chubby they're chasing. Room 205. Thanks for the tip. I'll avoid it like the plague.

Duff comes back and suggests that Proclo (whom they think is named Vespucci because of the register) pretend to be a big showman so that Googie will do her act. Proclo agrees to help them out—he rather likes Duff and Tiger, though he can't tell them apart.

Michael the detective is knocking on doors looking for Proclo. He looks into Claude's room. Claude informs Michael he's "resting" (a euphemism for "not interested") and slams the door in Michael's face.

Michael knocks on two other doors and looks into the rooms. Each time he's so startled by what he sees that he jumps back into the corridor. Finally he happens to enter the steam room and catapults himself back out in rhythm with the swing of the door.

Proclo has finished changing and is putting his wig on when there's a knock at his door—it's Claude pretending to be room service. Proclo peers through a crack, sees who it is and fastens the door firmly. Trying to entice Proclo, Claude throws Hershey bars, Milky Ways and other candy through the transom. Proclo accuses Claude of being a chubby chaser, Claude admits it but refuses to budge from the corridor outside Proclo's door. Claude tries singing; he asks Proclo's name and manages to fit "Vespucci" into the lyric of the "Maria" song.

To get rid of Claude, Proclo promises to meet him in his room in five minutes.

CLAUDE: Five minutes then. Room 205. If you're not up there, I'm gonna come down here and break your knees. Don't push your luck with Claude Perkins.

He goes. His name seems to have struck a distant bell for Proclo.

PROCLO: Claude Perkins. It can't be the same one. Claude Perkins. That's all I need. He's dead. He has to be dead. Claude Perkins.

Proclo opens the door and looks out. No sign of Claude. Without realizing it, he shuts the door behind him and locks himself out.

Oh no! Come on, will you? Open up. Damn! *(Calling off.)* Boys! Boys! You with the keys! Yoo hoo! Yoo hoo!

Proclo is suddenly aware of a patron who is just looking at him and smiling.

Hello. Just clearing my throat. Ahoo! Ahoo! Too many cigarettes. Ahoo! Hello there. I hear the Knicks tied it up in the last quarter.

PATRON: Crisco.

PROCLO: What?

PATRON: Crisco oil party.

PROCLO: Crisco oil party?

PATRON: Room 419. Pass it on.

PROCLO: Pass what on?

PATRON: And bring Joey.

PROCLO: Who's Joey?

PATRON: You know Joey. But not Chuck. Got that?

PROCLO: Crisco oil party. Room 419. I can bring Joey but not Chuck.

PATRON: Check.

PROCLO: What's wrong with Chuck?

Patron whispers something in Proclo's ear. Proclo's eyes grow wide. He

can't wait to get out of there.
Chuck's definitely out! If you'll excuse me now . . . !

The patron leaves, and Proclo thinks things over: perhaps he's just imagining things, he hasn't seen anything specifically outrageous, and maybe he's overly conditioned by the fact that "people are just more normal in Cleveland." He hears an announcement about a telephone call for "Joe Namath" and decides to follow it up—but what he finds at the source is Chris. Chris doesn't realize that Proclo is both straight and square. He thinks Proclo is lonely and tries to find someone for him, but Proclo declines with thanks.

Chris offers to show Proclo around. Proclo confesses to Chris that he's not what Chris thinks he is.

CHRIS: Baby, you're very much in the minority around here.
PROCLO: That's what I'm afraid of.
CHRIS: Or maybe you're not and that's why I'm having such rotten luck tonight. What are you? A social worker or something?
PROCLO: You mean *everybody* here is . . . ?
CHRIS: Gay. It's not such a tough word. You might try using it some time.
PROCLO: Nobody is . . . the opposite?
CHRIS: I sure as hell hope not. I didn't pay ten bucks to walk around in a towel with a bunch of Shriners.
PROCLO: What about Tiger and Duff?
CHRIS: What about them?
PROCLO: I thought they were normal.
CHRIS: They are normal. They've also been lovers for three years.
PROCLO: I'm sorry. I didn't mean it like that.
CHRIS: Yes, you did.
PROCLO: Yes, I did.
CHRIS: I'll tell you something about straight people, and sometimes I think it's the only thing worth knowing about them. They don't like gays. They never have. They never will. Anything else they say is just talk.
PROCLO: That's not true.
CHRIS: Think about it.

Proclo apologizes, pleads his confusion in a strange place, his knowing his brother-in-law is planning to kill him. The whole Vespucci family hates Proclo and regards him as a sissy anyway—except for his wife Vivian. Proclo tells Chris about the father's dying words—"Get Proclo"—and there's a big sum of family money involved, too, that the brother-in-law would like to get his hands on.

Chris advises Proclo to hide out in his own room. No one, not the brother-in-law, not the chubby chaser nor the singer who thinks he's a producer will bother him at the Ritz unless he stands out in the hall, inviting attention. Chris vanishes into the steam room. Proclo's curiosity about what goes on in there gets the better of him, and he goes into the steam room too. After a long pause, he comes bursting out calling for Duff, who unlocks the door of Proclo's room with his master key. Duff reminds Proclo that the performance will start soon, then exits. Proclo decides not to go to Googie's show, figuring she's probably a female impersonater, anyway.

Michael comes back to the phone, calls Vespucci, reports that he can't find anyone who fits Proclo's description. He tells Vespucci he's based in Room 101. Googie comes in, and Michael runs away from her.

Googie barges in to Proclo's room to warn him that her orchestra sometimes plays off key. She tells Proclo some of her past theater experience: fired from the original cast of *The Sound of Music* the first day of rehearsals, later fired from *Camelot,* and all because of her arch-enemy, a company manager named Seymour Pippin. Googie tries to flirt with Proclo, but she only frightens him because he still thinks she may be a male in drag.

Googie hears her music beginning and departs. Proclo refuses to follow her until he sees Claude on a upper level and decides he is the same Claude Perkins Proclo knew in the Army. Proclo rushes off after Googie, the lesser of two evils.

The night club setting flies in, as Abe is introducing the performers: first Duff, then Tiger, then Googie. *"Googie bursts on and launches into her first number. She is very bad but very funny. it's the kind of number you watch in disbelief. Sincerity is what saves her. Such a lack of talent is appalling, yes, but it does come straight from the heart. Tiger and Duff are doing their best, too. They dance well enough and they look pretty good up there."*

Googie's opening number is "Ev'rything's Coming Up Roses." She works through it energetically, her shoe flying off when she kicks for emphasis.

> *When the number ends, during the applause, we see Proclo run across pursued by Claude. Googie, followed by Tiger and Duff, goes after them.*

GOOGIE: Hey, wait a minute! Where are you going? I was just gonna introduce you!

> *They are gone. Suddenly the figure of a very wet, very angry balding middle-aged fat man comes storming into Googie's spotlight.*

CARMINE: I'm Carmine Vespucci of the Bensonhurst Vespuccis. I want a room in this here whorehouse and I don't want any shit.

> *There is a mighty roll of drums as Scarpia's theme from* Tosca *is heard. A crack of cymbals. Curtain.*

ACT II

Some time later, Carmine comes along the corridor outside Michael's room. Carmine knocks on Michael's door.

CARMINE: Brick? Are you in there, Brick? It's Vespucci. Don't open. I don't want anyone to see us. If you can hear me, knock once. If you can't, knock twice. Are you there, Brick?

> *Michael knocks once.*

Good. Our signals are working. Now listen to me, have you seen that balding fat brother-in-law of mine yet?
Michael knocks twice.
What does that mean? No?
Michael knocks once.
Okay, I think I read you. Now I know he's in here somewhere. What I don't know is how you could miss him. He's a house. Listen, Brick, none of these fruits tried to pull anything with you, did they?
Michael knocks twice.
You can thank Our Blessed Lady for that. Meet me in 102 in fifteen minutes. Knock three times. Got that?
Michael knocks three times.
Not now, stupid, *then.* And you don't have to worry about him leaving this place, leaving it in one piece I should say. I got all my men outside. Ain't that great, Brick? Hunh?
Michael knocks once.
I knew you'd like that. Keep looking.

Carmine returns to his own room and begins to undress, divesting himself of several weapons he's carrying. Proclo, Googie, Duff and Tiger are running in and out on various errands, and so is Claude, who is looking high and low for his "Vespucci." Proclo reaches the safety of his room and begins hurriedly packing; he's had enough of the Ritz, he's going home to Cleveland, come what may.

As Proclo looks for the exit, Claude appears. Proclo's only escape is the steam room, and he goes in there carrying his suitcase, his box of Panettone and his clothes. Claude enters the steam room after him.

Meanwhile, Googie is running around, looking for Claude and crying revenge because he ruined her act by chasing the "producer" out of the night club. She's pounding on all the doors, and one of them is opened by the patron wearing chaps.

PATRON IN CHAPS: Howdy, pardner.
GOOGIE: Don't howdy me, you big leather sissy!
She pushes him back into the room.
You think I don't know what goes on around this place? All you men going hee-hee-hee, poo-poo-poo, hah-hah-hah! I get my boy friend Hector in here with his hombres and he kill you all!
She is heading for the steam room.
DUFF: You can't go in there!
TIGER: Googie, no!
Googie storms into the steam room, Tiger and Duff following. The door closes behind them. A moment later, Googie lets out a muffled yell.
GOOGIE: *Pendego!*
Patrons start streaming out. Googie comes right out after them. She has Claude firmly in tow.
There will be no more hee-hee-hee, poo-poo-poo, hah-hah-hah around this place tonight!

CLAUDE: You're hurting me!

She slings Claude across the hall.

GOOGIE: I'm just getting started!

Tiger and Duff attempt to subdue her.

CLAUDE: You could use a good psychiatrist, mister!

GOOGIE: What you call me?

TIGER: He didn't mean it!

GOOGIE: What you call me?

TIGER: Tell her you're sorry!

CLAUDE: I haven't seen such tacky drag since the Princeton Varsity Show!

GOOGIE: Tacky drag?

CLAUDE: Thirty years ago, sonny!

Googie has gotten herself into a good street fighting position by now. With a blood-curdling yell she leaps for Claude and chases him off, Tiger and Duff close behind. The stage is bare for a moment.

CLAUDE *(off):* Help!

From the yell, it sounds as if Googie's got him. The steam room door opens and Chris comes out.

CHRIS: I'm going straight.

Suddenly the steam room door slams open and Proclo, or what's left of him, staggers out. He is fully dressed, wearing the wig, dark glasses and moustache from his first entrance, and carrying his suitcase. He has visibly wilted. He doesn't seem to know where he is.

PROCLO: I don't believe this whole night.

CHRIS: Were you in there for all that?

Proclo just nods.

Where?

Proclo just shrugs.

You don't want to talk about it?

Proclo just shakes his head.

Proclo has decided to move to Central Park. Michael comes along the corridor and overhears Chris address Proclo as "Vespucci". Chris makes a move to attract Michael, but it is Proclo in whom Michael takes a sudden interest and leads into his room. Michael mistakenly thinks that Proclo, disguised in his wig and mustache, is his client Carmine Vespucci, whom he's spoken to on the phone and behind a closed door but never actually seen.

MICHAEL: Now this is what I thought we'd do. Get under the bed.

PROCLO *(beginning to cry):* Another one!

MICHAEL: All right, stay there. We'll pretend you're him and I'm me and the real you is under the bed.

PROCLO *(tears are really flowing):* Only this one's the worst.

MICHAEL: Now get the picture. The lights are low, he's moving down the hallway and he sees me leaning against the door. I flex for him. Pecks and biceps are supposed to be a turn-on. Don't ask me why. I catch his eye. I've got a cigarette dangling from my lips, I put one knee up, I wink, I kind of beckon with my head and finally I speak. "See something you like, buddy?" That's the tough guy approach.

Proclo is curious about Michael's high voice. He asks about it and in the course of questioning learns of his brother-in-law Vespucci's actual presence in the Ritz, Michael's identity as a hired detective, and the plan to entice the "middle-aged, balding, fat man" into Room 101 where Michael and "Vespucci" hiding under the bed can capture him. Playing his role of Vespucci, Proclo hides under Michael's bed.

Meanwhile, Chris is moving down the corridor knocking on doors and by chance arrives at the real Carmine Vespucci's. In still another case of mistaken identity, Carmine assumes that Chris is his hired detective keeping his appointment, and that Chris's campy manner is part of his detective pose. Carmine wants to set a trap for his brother-in-law: Chris is to entice Proclo into making advances. Carmine will be hiding under the bed—"And then I pop out, catching you both in the act and whammo! I got him."

Chris begins to get an inkling of what is going on when Carmine identifies himself as Vespucci and explains that Proclo married his sister: "Twenty years she thinks she's happily married, my sister, but the truth is it's twenty years she's been a martyr, that woman. My sister is a saint and she don't even know it. I'll tell you one thing: with Poppa gone now . . . *(He breaks into uncontrollable sobs.)* . . . Poppa, God bless him . . . I ain't sharing Vespucci Sanitation Services and Enterprises, Inc., with no fairy!"

Carmine intends to catch Proclo in an unnatural act this very night and kill him in a crime of passion. Chris takes matters into his own hands, turns out the lights and leaves Carmine waiting under the bed for his prey with the door of his room ajar. Chris then knocks on Michael's door, where the detective has set exactly the same sort of trap.

Chris is not too surprised to find Proclo hiding under Michael's bed: "Why not? Everybody else is. I always wondered what you straight guys did together. Now that I know, I'm glad I'm gay." He manages to communicate to Proclo—without enlightening Michael—that his brother-in-law Carmine is inside the Ritz looking for Proclo and carrying a gun.

Googie comes down the corridor and knocks on Michael's door. Chris dives under the bed for safety's sake. Michael opens the door a crack, sees that it's Googie and dives under the bed himself.

Proclo, with no room now to hide, hears Googie's voice outside the door and opens it. Googie dashes in, pushes Proclo onto the bed and lies on top of him, persuading: "You know why you don't like women? Because you never tried it, that's all. Or maybe you did and that's why. She was a bad woman. Forget her. Believe me, *chico,* it don't hurt. It's nice. It's very nice. Just lie back and Googie's gonna show you how nice."

Googie sings "Besame Mucho," and *"almost involuntarily, under the bed, Michael and Chris join in the singing."* Proclo, terrified, insists "This isn't going to work out, Mr. Googie!" Googie now understands that Proclo is mistaking her for a man in drag and easily proves the contrary. But Proclo has other demanding problems, as he tells Googie: his brother-in-law is trying to kill him, and there are others hiding under the bed.

When Michael and Chris show themselves, Googie is at first furious and then begins to understand that there's more to all of this than a sexual romp. Proclo informs her he's not a producer. Googie makes a grab for him, pulls off his wig, mistakes him for her old enemy Seymour Pippin and attacks him. Michael and Chris pull Googie away from Proclo just as Carmine knocks on the door. All but Michael dive under the bed as Carmine storms into the room where Michael, still believing that Proclo is Carmine and now assuming that Carmine is probably Proclo, does his seduction act as planned.

MICHAEL *(going into his muscle-flexing routine):* See something you like, buddy?

CARMINE: What the—?

MICHAEL: You new around here, Mac?

CARMINE: You're not Brick! Where's Brick? What have you done to him?

MICHAEL: Lie down.

CARMINE: Get your hands off me!

> *Michael shoves Carmine into the bed. Googie cries out.*

GOOGIE: Ow! *Ay, cono!*

PROCLO: Sshh!

CARMINE: What the—?

MICHAEL: Relax.

CARMINE: Somebody's under there!

MICHAEL: Just stretch out on the bed, now.

CARMINE: What are you doing in here?

MICHAEL: Just relax: I'm trying to seduce you.

CARMINE: Get your hands off me, you goddamn Greek, or I'll lay your head open.

MICHAEL *(pinning Carmine down):* Is it him, Mr. Vespucci?

PROCLO: Yes!

CARMINE: Vespucci? I'm Vespucci.

MICHAEL: Is it?

PROCLO: Yes, yes! It's him! It's him!

CARMINE: I know that voice!

> *He leans over the bed just as Googie rolls out.*

What the hell is this? One of them goddamn transvestitites, sure you are!

GOOGIE: Seymour Pippin!

> *She is attacking Carmine, swatting him with a pillow.*

CARMINE: Fight fair, you faggot!

> *Michael knocks Carmine out with a karate blow.*

MICHAEL: Hi-ya!

> *Carmine falls onto the bed. Proclo groans.*

GOOGIE: Aw, shit! Why you do that? I was gonna fix his wagon for him good!

MICHAEL: He's out cold, Mr. Vespucci.

PROCLO: Just get me out of here.

CHRIS: And we were starting to have so much fun!

GOOGIE: You know something? This man is not Seymour Pippin either. He sure got a mean face though! I wonder who he is.

Proclo tries to explain who Carmine is. Michael, still not understanding who's who, gives away the full details of the plot against Proclo, and Proclo tries to strangle him. Googie and Chris stop him and also take away Michael's camera to prevent any attempt at blackmail. Michael goes off after them, leaving Proclo alone with Carmine, who is still unconscious.

Proclo goes into Carmine's room, takes all Carmine's clothes and gives them to Tiger with orders to burn them. Then he tries to revenge himself on the unconscious Carmine by shouting in the corridor: "Fat man in 101! Come and get it."

Elated at having foiled his brother-in-law's plot, Proclo picks up his suitcase and heads out, bound for Cleveland. He's stopped when Michael, answering the phone, informs him that his wife, Vivian Proclo, waiting in the bar across the street, has decided to come into the Ritz after her husband, wearing a man's coat and hat. Once again, Proclo is desperate, but Tiger reassures him that women aren't permitted in the Ritz and his wife will never get past Abe at the door. Meanwhile, Googie comes in and out on her way to do her second show, and Michael follows her off.

Looking for any port in a storm, Proclo goes back into his room. Claude, who has been stalking him, follows Proclo into the room. Claude recognizes Proclo as someone he knew in the Army—they used to do an act together, pantomiming Andrews Sisters records with a third soldier. Proclo manages to repulse Claude, who leaves just as the public address system announces a newcomer for Room 253—obviously, Proclo's wife Vivian has passed as a man.

There is nothing left for Proclo but resorting to prayer. The patron in chaps goes into the room where Carmine is just beginning to regain consciousness. The three entertainers run on and off, still trailed by Michael. Chris comes in and out, on his way to check out the newcomer in 253.

> On the second level we see Vivian. She is wearing a man's hat and raincoat over her black pants suit. She carries a shopping bag. Chris approaches her.

CHRIS: I had a hunch it would be bad, but nothing like this. (To Vivian.) Welcome to the city morgue.

> Vivian recoils and lets out one of her giant sobs: an unearthly sound.

VIVIAN: AAaaaaaeeeeee!

CHRIS: Forget it, mister, that's not my scene!

> Opening the door to the steam room.

Avon calling!

> He goes in. Claude has approached Vivian in the corridor.

CLAUDE: Looking for 253?

> Vivian nods, stifling her sobs.

Right this way.

> *He leads her to his own room, of course, carefully concealing the number as they enter. He slams the door and starts to sing.*

"Jelly roll baby

You're my jelly roll man . . ."

> *Vivian really lets out a big sob as he starts moving toward her.*

VIVIAN: Aaaaiiiieeeee!

> *No sooner does she scream than Vivian faints dead away on Claude's bed.*

In the meantime, Carmine has regained consciousness, pulled himself together and shot off the lock of his door. He sees that someone has taken his clothes and runs off swearing threats against Proclo.

Claude is trying to revive Vivian, but he's in a hurry because this is amateur night at the Ritz, and Claude is entering the talent contest. He finds a mink coat in Vivian's shopping bag and tries it on.

Carmine points his gun at Chris, still believing that Chris is his hired detective Brick, and demands to know the whereabouts of his brother-in-law. Chris directs him to Claude's room and makes his escape.

Claude takes one look at hefty Carmine and starts his jelly-roll song. But Carmine is having none of it, and Claude is lucky to escape, taking with him his clothes and Vivian's mink. Carmine sees that the inert figure on the bed is his sister Vivian, not Proclo, and tries to revive her.

Proclo is sitting helplessly in his room waiting for Carmine to find him and kill him. Chris tries to buck him up. Claude comes by in his mink coat, and they all move off together.

Carmine revives Vivian, who is horrified by what she's seen so far, thus doubling her brother Carmine's determination to kill everybody in sight. Vivian disguised herself as a man to save her beloved, like Gilda in *Rigoletto,* but now she just wants to go home.

VIVIAN: Take me home, Carmine, please.

CARMINE: Home? But he's here. I can prove it to you.

VIVIAN: I don't want proof. I just want to go back to Cleveland.

CARMINE: With a man like that?

VIVIAN: I don't care. He's my husband.

CARMINE: I'm gonna kill the son of a bitch when I find him.

VIVIAN: No killing, Carmine. I don't want killing.

CARMINE: All he's done to you.

VIVIAN: He hasn't done anything to me.

CARMINE: That's what you think. Now I want you to get out of here and take a cab back to Brooklyn. Leave that husband of yours to me.

VIVIAN: I'm not going!

CARMINE: Then stay in here and don't let anyone in.

VIVIAN: No!

CARMINE: This is between him and me, Viv!

VIVIAN: If you hurt him, I'll never speak to you again!
CARMINE: It's Poppa's honor that's at stake!
VIVIAN: Poppa's dead!
This statement causes them both to collapse into sobs.
CARMINE: Poppa! He's stained the Vespucci honor!

Proclo has dishonored Vivian, too, Carmine insists. Vivian threatens to shoot herself; but suddenly she discovers that her mink coat is missing, a mink that Proclo gave her for their anniversary. Carmine goes off in search of Proclo and Vivian goes off in search of her missing mink.

Running by on their way to the night club, Proclo, Claude and Chris are planning to do the Andrews Sisters routine for the talent show. Carmine enters, and Proclo hides behind Claude. Chris directs Carmine to the steam room. Vivian enters in time to see the trio exiting with her mink, and she follows in pursuit. Claude enters the steam room and all the other patrons come running out, pursued by Carmine brandishing his gun.

The scene changes to the night club with the talent show in progress. A contestant draped in balloons is trying to sing "Life Is Just a Bowl of Cherries" while patrons run across the stage chased by Vivian and Carmine. The contestant finishes his number bravely. Googie, an unflustered MC, introduces the last act.

GOOGIE: Our last contestant is Mr. Claude Perkins and partners recreating their famous Army act. Hit it, boys!
> *Music is heard. It is a 1940s sounding swing orchestra. A spotlight picks up Claude in his WAC uniform, Proclo in his wife's mink coat and a long blonde wig, and Chris in an elaborate makeshift gown made from sheets. The Andrews Sisters are heard singing one of their big hits, "The Three Caballeros." Claude, Chris and Proclo begin to pantomime to the record and jitterbug.*
>
> *At first, Proclo is all nerves and Claude does a Herculean job of covering for him. But as the number progresses, we see Proclo getting better and better as the act comes back to him. After a while, he's close to enjoying himself.*

The trio continues with "The Three Caballeros" while all the patrons reappear, chased across the stage and up the aisle by Vivian and Carmine. As the number builds to a climax, Carmine fires a shot in the air which brings the act to a halt and creates pandemonium among the Ritz patrons. Waving his weapon, Carmine forces everybody to line up for his inspection. Carmine orders the group across the stage, which reveals Claude and Proclo with his face turned away.

> *Claude approaches Carmine.*
CLAUDE: You really know how to mess up an act, you know that, mister?
CARMINE: Christ, another one!
CLAUDE: I'm an entertainer. Pantomime acts are coming back, you'll see.
CARMINE: In the meantime, you're still a transvestitite. Move!

> *Only Proclo remains now. Carmine is savoring every moment of his humiliation.*

I guess that makes it you. Look at you. I could vomit. Jesus, Mary and Joseph! Is that her mink?

> *Proclo turns around. Not only is he wearing the mink and the Patty Andrews wig, he has added the dark glasses and the moustache. He nods.*

Give it back to her.

> *Proclo shakes his head.*

VIVIAN: I don't want it now. That's not Gaetano. I just want to go home.

CARMINE: Okay, Gaetano, the jig's up. Take that crap off. The wig, the glasses, the moustache, the mink. Everything. I'm giving you three. *(To the others.)* I want you all to meet my splendid brother-in-law, Gaetano Proclo.

MICHAEL: That's not Mr. Proclo! He is!

CARMINE: Who is?

MICHAEL: You are!

> *Carmine spins around. Proclo bites his wrist and grabs the gun. The others subdue Carmine. For a few moments he is buried as they swirl about him. Vivian just sobs hysterically.*

CARMINE: Get your hands off me! This time you've really done it, Gaetano!

PROCLO: Shut up, Carmine.

Proclo has the upper hand now. Tiger, Duff and Chris subdue Carmine. Proclo tries to comfort and reassure his wife, but Vivian is still in the mood to greet the situation with her piercing cries. Finally she manages to get some words out: "My husband, the man in the mink coat! I can't wait to go to Bingo with you like that next week but I won't be there if God is merciful because I'm going to have a heart attack right here."

Proclo's behavior is grounds for annulment, Carmine assures his sister, but this information doesn't seem to make Vivian any happier. Proclo protests his innocence: he's here only because this is where the cab driver chose to bring him.

Vivian begs Proclo not to mention the Ritz in his next confession—she seems ready for some sort of reconciliation. Proclo continues to protest that he hasn't done anything to confess, but the negative is hard to prove.

Maurine, the Ritz's accountant, comes in and, surprisingly, hands Carmine the week's balance sheet. Vivian grabs it away from her brother and discovers that the Ritz is a subsidiary of Vespucci Enterprises; the Vespuccis own it. Vivian now wants to know what kind of a cab brought Proclo here. It was an Aida Cab, Vivian learns, a company also owned by the Vespuccis. Vivian questions Proclo about the cab driver's appearance.

PROCLO: He stuttered and smoked pot.

VIVIAN: Cousin Tito! I should've guessed. It's going to be very hard to forgive you for this, Carmine.

CARMINE: What's to forgive! I don't want no forgiving!

VIVIAN: Now take the hit off him, Carmine.

CARMINE: Vivian!

VIVIAN: Take it off!

CARMINE: No!

VIVIAN: If you don't take it off, Carmine, I am gonna tell Frankie di Lucca about you muscling into the Bingo concession at the Feast of St. Anthony and then Frankie di Lucca is gonna put a hit out on you and you are gonna end up wearing cement shoes at the bottom of the East River and then there will be even more grief and less peace in our fucking family than there already is!

PROCLO: I am married to an extraordinary woman!

CARMINE: You wouldn't do this to me, sis!

VIVIAN: You know me, Carmine.

CARMINE: Vivian!

VIVIAN: I swear it, Carmine. *Lo giuro.*

CARMINE: *Non giura,* sis!

VIVIAN: *Lo giuro,* Carmine. *Lo giuro,* the Bingo and the cement shoes.

CARMINE: "Get Proclo." You heard Poppa.

VIVIAN: I've got Proclo, Carmine. Now take the hit off!

CARMINE: I'll lose face.

VIVIAN: Not under the East River!

CARMINE *(writhing in defeat):* Aaaaiiieee!

VIVIAN: Now take the hit off him, Carmine! Is it off?

> *Carmine nods.*

On Poppa's grave?

> *He shakes his head.*

I want it on Poppa's grave and I want it forever!

> *He shakes his head.*

I'm calling Frankie di Lucca.

CARMINE: It's off on Poppa's grave!

VIVIAN *(finally breaking down):* Poppa! All right, now I forgive you.

Vivian further demands that Carmine and Proclo forgive each other and kiss as brothers. At Vivian's insistence, Proclo finally agrees: "I forgive you, Carmine. With a little luck nobody's gonna die in your family for a long, long time and we won't have to see each other for another twenty years. Just be sure to send the checks."

They approach each other for a ritual kiss of peace, but when Proclo gets close enough Carmine lets go a punch in the stomach. In return, Proclo knees Carmine in the groin.

> *Carmine goes down. The others give a mighty cheer and congratulate Proclo.*

PROCLO *(amazed):* I did it. I did it. *(Now jubilant.)* I won. I didn't fight fair but I won! *(To Carmine.)* You can go *va fangool* yourself, Carmine. People like you really do belong in garbage. People like me just marry into it. Get him out of here, men!

CHRIS: Bring her up to the steam room, girls!

> *The others pounce on Carmine who is protesting mightily and drag him off.*

CARMINE: I'm coming back here and I'm gonna kill every last one of you fairies!
CHRIS: Sure you are, Nancy!
> *It is a gleeful, noisy massed exit.*

Vivian wants Proclo to collect his clothes and come home with her, but Proclo isn't quite ready to forgive and forget. He is tired of being hounded by the Vespuccis. He wants to be respected, he wants to be called a "sanitary engineer" instead of a garbage man. Finally Proclo decides that whatever else he wants—and he wants a lot—he wants to go back home to Cleveland with Vivian.

Claude enters with three trophies; their Andrews Sisters act has won the talent contest. As Vivian and Proclo return to his room to pack and get ready to leave, Googie comes in followed by Tiger and Duff, who are apologetic about having lied to her about a big producer in the audience. Michael follows them in and informs Googie that his uncle is a dinner theater producer. Googie decides to try for a part in his *Oklahoma.* On their way out, Michael confides the name of his producer-uncle to Tiger and Duff: Seymour Pippin.

Chris comes in to say goodbye and to tell Proclo they've dressed Carmine up and called the police to come get him. Vivian asks Proclo to do something about Carmine, to see that he is all right before they go. Proclo agrees.

PROCLO: On Poppa's grave.
VIVIAN *(a new outburst of grief):* Poppa! *(Exits.)*
PROCLO *(calling off to her):* Not your Poppa's. Mine!
> *As Proclo starts off, a policeman races on. Proclo stops to watch with a contented smile. Chris blows his whistle, and the policeman runs up to the steam room, where he finds Carmine bound and gagged and dressed in a green brocade ball gown.*
>
> *Claude sees Carmine, too, and sings his "Jelly Roll" song as he plays tug-o'-war with the policeman over Carmine. Patrons are filling the halls. Duff and Tiger start making fresh beds. And Proclo just smiles.*
CHRIS: Orgy! Orgy! Orgy in 240!
> *The lights are fading. The play is over. Curtain.*

SEASCAPE

A Play in Two Acts

BY EDWARD ALBEE

Cast and credits appear on page 338

EDWARD ALBEE was born March 12, 1928, in Washington, D.C. Two weeks after his birth he was adopted by a branch of the Keith-Albee theater family. He attended several schools including Rye Country Day, Lawrenceville, Valley Forge Military Academy and Choate, and he spent a year and a half at Trinity College. In 1958 he wrote The Zoo Story *which was produced in German in West Berlin in 1959; then by Actors Studio before its off-Broadway presentation in 1960. Other Albee plays produced off Broadway were* The Sandbox *(1960),* Fam and Yam *(1960),* The American Dream *(1961),* Bartleby *(a one-act opera in collaboration with James Hinton Jr. and William Flanagan, based on a Herman Melville story) and* The Death of Bessie Smith *(1961).*

Albee made his Broadway debut with Who's Afraid of Virginia Woolf? *(1962), a Best Play of its season and the winner of the Drama Critics Award, and in 1966 a successful movie. His* Tiny Alice *(1964) was named a Best Play, as was his* A Delicate Balance *(1966), which also won him the Pulitzer Prize in drama. His later work has included four adaptations:* The Ballad of the Sad Cafe *(1963) from the novella by Carson McCullers;* Malcolm *(1966) from the novel by James Purdy; a musical adaptation of* Breakfast at Tiffany's *which closed in tryout in 1966, and* Everything in the Garden *(1967) based on a play by Giles Cooper. His most recent original plays were the program of one-acters* Box *and* Quotations From Chairman Mao Tse-Tung *(1968),* All Over *(1971) and this season's* Seascape, *his fourth*

Best Play and second Pulitzer Prize winner and the first premiere production of an Albee play on Broadway directed by the author himself.

Albee is a member of the National Institute of Arts and Letters and the board of directors of the Montauk Writers' Colony. He is a bachelor and lives in New York City.

Time: The present

Place: A sand dune

ACT I

SYNOPSIS: Nancy and Charlie, married, middle-aged in a well-tended sort of way, are relaxing in the shelter of a sand dune on an ocean beach very like those of Long Island. *"Bright sun. They are dressed informally. There is a blanket and a picnic basket. Lunch is done; Nancy is finished putting things away."*

A jet plane roars across the sky. Nancy comments, "Such noise they make." Charlie adds, "They'll crash into the dunes one day. I don't know what good they do." It's a litany they they repeat to each other each time a plane comes over.

It's pleasant on the beach nevertheless, and Nancy suggests they could stay among the dunes for the rest of their lives.

CHARLIE: Here?

NANCY *(expansive)*: Yes!

CHARLIE: Right here on the beach. Build a . . . a tent, or a lean-to.

NANCY *(laughs gaily)*: No, silly, not this very spot! But *here*, by the shore.

CHARLIE: You wouldn't like it.

NANCY: I would! I'd love it here! I'd love it right where we are, for that matter.

CHARLIE: Not after a while you wouldn't.

NANCY: Yes, I *would*. I love the water, and I love the air, and the sand and the dunes and the beach grass, and the sunshine on all of it and the white clouds way off, and the sunsets and the noise the shells make in the waves, and, oh, I love every bit of it, Charlie.

CHARLIE: You wouldn't. Not after a while.

NANCY: Why wouldn't I? I don't even mind the flies and the little . . . sand fleas, I guess they are.

CHARLIE: It gets cold.

NANCY: When?

CHARLIE *(lies down)*: In the winter. In the fall even. In spring.

NANCY *(laughs)*: Well, I don't mean this one, literally . . . not all the time. I mean go from beach to beach . . . live by the water. Seaside nomads, that's what we'd be.

CHARLIE *(curiously hurt feelings)*: For Christ's sake, Nancy!

But Nancy persists. They could try all the beaches . . . the Gulf, South America, the South Seas. Nancy begs Charlie to pretend he'd like it, but Charlie doesn't dare; she might hold him to it. Besides, he doesn't want to run from beach to beach—he wants to relax and do nothing. He irritates Nancy by lying there and insisting "I just . . . want . . . to . . . do . . . nothing."

Nancy doesn't intend to waste what's left of her life doing nothing (she busies herself gathering picnic things, just to emphasize her point). Charlie feels that after all their years together they've earned a rest. Nancy doesn't see it that way. She hasn't raised their children and come all this way along the path of life just to sink into a kind of living purgatory of letting go, giving up mentally and physically, sleeping out their lives in the old folks' home.

NANCY: . . . . . I think the only thing to do is to *do* something.

CHARLIE *(nice):* What would you like to do?

NANCY *(far away):* Hm?

CHARLIE: Move from one sandstrip to another? Live by the sea from now on?

NANCY *(great wistfulness):* Well, we have nothing holding us, except together; chattel? Does chattel mean what I think it does? We *have* nothing we *need* have. We could do it; I would so like to.

CHARLIE *(smiles):* All right.

NANCY *(sad little laugh):* You're humoring me; it *is* something I want, though; maybe only the principle. *(Larger laugh.)* I suspect our children would have us put away if we announced it as a plan—beachcombing, leaf huts. Even if we did it in hotels they'd have a case—for our *reasons.*

CHARLIE: Mmmmmmm.

NANCY: Let's merely have it for today . . . and tomorrow . . . and . . . who knows: continue the temporary and it becomes forever.

CHARLIE *(relaxed; content):* All right.

Another jet flies over and Nancy and Charlie repeat their comments. Nancy remembers that when Charlie was a boy he wanted to live in the sea. Charlie admits that once he wished he could spend all day under water, as though he had gills. Nancy remembers that she wanted to be a pony at one time, but she soon changed her mind and decided she wanted to be a woman: "I wanted to grow up to be that, and all it had with it." She's momentarily distracted by the sight of some people way down the beach, but she soon returns to her point. She has probably realized her ambition, she has become a woman and created her pyramid of husband, children and grandchildren.

Charlie isn't really listening to Nancy. His replies are perfunctory, and suddenly he goes back to the subject of living under water: "I used to go way down; at our summer place; a protected cove. The breakers would come in with a storm, or a high wind, but not usually. I used to go way down. and try to stay. I remember before that, when I was tiny, I would go in the swimming pool, at the shallow end, let out my breath and sit on the bottom; when you let out your breath —all of it—you sink, gently, and you can sit on the bottom until your lungs need air. I would do that—I was so young—sit there, gaze about . . . . ."

Later on, at 12 or 13, Charlie "would go into the water, take two stones, as large as I could manage, swim out a bit, tread, look up one final time at the sky . . . relax . . . begin to go down. Oh, twenty feet, fifteen, soft landing without a sound, the white sand clouding up where your feet touch, and all around you ferns . . . and lichen. You can stay down there so long! You can build it up, and last . . . so long, enough for the sand to settle and the fish come back. And they do —come back, all sizes, some slowly, eyeing past; some streak, and you think for a moment they're larger than they are, sharks, maybe, but they never are, and one stops being an intruder, finally—just one more object come to the bottom, or living thing, part of the undulation and the silence. It was very good."

Nancy urges Charlie to try it right now, "Be young again!" But Charlie refuses, with the excuse that some casual observer, like the couple sunning themselves on the sand nearby, will think he's drowning. He admits he hasn't tried it in too long a time, not since he was 17. Nancy urges him again to do it, to "reconfirm," but Charlie is content with his memory. As for Nancy, she'd never let a chance for an experience escape her.

NANCY: . . . . . There isn't that much. Sex goes . . . diminishes; well, it becomes a holiday and rather special, and not like eating, or going to sleep. But that's nice too—that it becomes special—*(Laughs gaily.)* Do you know, I had a week when I thought of divorcing you?

CHARLIE *(quite surprised, vulnerable; shakes his head)*: No.

NANCY: Yes. You were having your thing, your melancholia—poor darling— and there I was, brisk and thirty, still pert, learning the moles on your back instead of your chest hairs.

CHARLIE *(relieved, if sad)*: Ah. Then.

NANCY *(nods)*: Umh-hum. Then. Rereading Proust, if I have it right. Propped up in bed, all pink and ribbons, smelling good, not all those creams and looking ten years married as I might have, and who would have blamed me, but fresh, and damned attractive, if I have to say it for myself; propped up in bed, literate, sweet-smelling, getting familiar with your back. One, two, three moles, and then a pair of them, twins, flat black ones . . .

CHARLIE *(recalling)*: *That* time.

The deeper Charlie sank into inertia, the more alive Nancy felt. She managed to stay busy, play the helpful wife and weather the difficulty—though she did suspect that there might be another woman. Charlie denies this emphatically. Nancy goes on to remember that it caused her to think for the first time about what it might be like for her to have an affair with another man, and what that man would be like. She thought about divorce for only a short time, then forgot about it. She did some pondering about the loneliness of sleeping with a husband who is thinking about another woman.

Charlie tells Nancy again that he's never been with another woman; he means it, and Nancy believes him. Charlie adds, "I think one time, when you and I were making love—when we were nearly there, I remember I pretended it was a week or so before, one surprising time we'd had, something we'd hit upon by accident or decided to do finally; I pretended it was the time before, and it was quite good that way."

Nancy listens to this in some wonderment: "You pretended I was me." Then she decides, "Well; perhaps I was," and again she tries to persuade Charlie to go into the water. The nearby couple seems to have disappeared, though for a time Nancy had an idea they were moving nearer. Then Nancy sees them, sunning halfway up the dune: they look odd to Nancy.

Nancy would like to try a dive herself but wouldn't dare without Charlie. She admits that Charlie has taken good care of her over the years and given her all that she wanted, including children and a comfortable life. Charlie is so self-satisfied about this that Nancy remarks bitterly, "Well, we'll wrap you in the flag when you're gone, and do taps," hurting Charlie's feelings. He feels that he *has* made an effort to do well for Nancy, an effort which shouldn't be dismissed with a petulant remark.

Nancy admits that her petulance is brought on like the swelling from a bee sting by remarks about their having *had* a good life. They should still be *having* a good life. Nancy insists, they have a lot left beside watching their children's lives.

CHARLIE: . . . . . What?!

NANCY: Two things!

CHARLIE: Yeah?

NANCY: Ourselves and some time. Charlie; the pyramid's building by itself; the earth's spinning in its own fashion without any push from us; we've done all we ought to—and isn't it splendid we've enjoyed so much of it.

CHARLIE *(mild irony):* We're pretty splendid people.

NANCY: Damned right we are, and now we've got each other and some time, and all *you* want to do is become a vegetable.

CHARLIE: Fair, as usual.

NANCY *(shrugs):* All right: a lump.

CHARLIE: We've earned . . .

NANCY *(nods):* . . . a little rest. My God, you say that twice a day, and sometimes in between. *(Mutters.)* We've earned a little *life,* if you ask *me.*
   Pause.
Ask me.

CHARLIE *(some rue):* No; you'd tell me.

NANCY *(bold and recriminating):* Sure! 'Course I would! When else are we going to get it?

CHARLIE *(quite serious; quite bewildered):* What's to be gained? And what would we really get? Some . . . illusion, I suppose; some smoke. There'd be the same sounds in the dark—or similar ones; we'd have to sleep and wonder if we'd waken, either way. It's six of one, except we'll do it on familiar ground, if *I* have *my* way. I'm not up to the glaciers and the crags, and I don't think you'd be . . . once you got out there.

NANCY *(grudging):* I do admit, you make it sound scary—first time away to camp, sleeping out, the hoot owls and the goblins. Oh, that's scary. Are you telling me you're all caved in. Charlie?

CHARLIE *(pause; considers the fact):* Maybe.

NANCY *(pause while she ponders this):* Then . . . what's the difference? You make it ugly enough, either way. The glaciers and the crags? At least we've never *tried that.*

CHARLIE *(trying to justify, but without much enthusiasm):* There's comfort in settling in.

> *Pause.*

NANCY: Small.

> *Pause.*

CHARLIE *(final):* Some.

> *A silence. Leslie appears, pops up, upper half of trunk, upstage, from behind the dune. Neither Charlie nor Nancy sees him. Leslie looks at the the two of them, pops back down out of sight.*

NANCY *(to bring them back to life again):* Well. I've got to do some post cards tonight; tell all the folks where we are.

The brief glimpse of Leslie has shown him to be a scaly, green-colored sea lizard of some sort, with humanoid limbs and body but reptilian features and appendages. Nancy and Charlie, not having seen Leslie, continue their small talk about post cards. While they are speaking, Leslie and his female counterpart Sarah come to the top of the dune, revealing their whole bodies which are of human size but scaled and plate-jointed and ending in large, saurian tails.

> *Charlie senses something behind him. He turns his head, sees Leslie and Sarah. His mouth falls open; he is stock still for a moment, then, slowly getting on all fours, he begins, very cautiously, to back away. Nancy sees what Charlie is doing, is momentarily puzzled. Then she looks behind her. She sees Leslie and Sarah.*

NANCY *(straightening her back abruptly):* My goodness!

CHARLIE *(on all fours; ready to flee):* Ohmygod.

NANCY *(great wonder):* Charlie!

CHARLIE *(eyes steady on Leslie and Sarah):* Oh my loving God.

NANCY *(enthusiasm):* Charlie! What *are* they?!

CHARLIE: Nancy, get back here!

NANCY: But Charlie . . .

CHARLIE *(deep in his throat; trying to whisper):* Get back here!

> *Nancy backs away until she and Charlie are together.*

(Whispering.) Get a stick!

NANCY *(interest and wonder):* Charlie, what are they?

CHARLIE *(urgent):* Get me a stick!

NANCY: A what?

CHARLIE *(louder):* A stick!

NANCY *(looking about; uncertain):* Well . . . what *sort* of stick, Charlie?

CHARLIE: A stick! A wooden stick!

NANCY *(begins to crawl):* Well, of course, a wooden stick, Charlie; what other kinds of sticks *are* there, for heaven's sake? But, what sort of stick?

CHARLIE *(never taking his eyes off Leslie and Sarah):* A big one! A big stick!
NANCY *(none too happy about it):* Well . . . I'll *look.* Driftwood, I suppose . . .

Leslie makes a movement which panics Charlie into crying, "Get me a gun!" But Nancy is more curious than frightened. She finds a ludicrously small stick, and as she hands it to Charlie she can't help commenting, "They're magnificent!"

Leslie clears his throat. The sound terrifies Charlie, who takes Nancy in his arms, brandishes his stick and prepares to sell their lives as dearly as possible. *"Leslie takes a step forward, stops, bends over and picks up a large stick, four feet long and stout; he brandishes it and clears his throat again."* The odds against Charlie have increased, it seems, and he can think of nothing to do except tell Nancy one last time that he loves her.

Leslie raises his stick in a gesture of invincible power. *"Leslie and Sarah slowly begin to move toward Charlie and Nancy. Suddenly the sound of the jet plane again, lower and louder this time. Leslie and Sarah react as animals would; frozen for an instant, tense seeking of the danger, poised, every muscle taut, and then the two of them, at the same instant and with identical movements—paws clawing at the sand, bellies hugging the earth—they race back over the dune toward the water."*

Nancy is momentarily speechless. Charlie comments that they've never been closer to "the glaciers and the crags" in their lives; but then he decides that Leslie and Sarah must have been hallucination—brought on, for example, by the liver paste they had for lunch. Yes—the liver paste spoiled in the sun and poisoned them, Charlie insists: "We ate the liver paste and we died."

Leslie and Sarah reappear over the top of the dune. Nancy, seeing them, can only laugh. Charlie tenses up again at the lizards' approach, and this time Nancy takes charge.

NANCY: Charlie, there's only one thing for it. Watch me now; watch me carefully.
CHARLIE: Nancy . . .
    Nancy smiles broadly; with her feet facing Leslie and Sarah, she slowly rolls over on her back, her legs drawn up, her hands by her face, fingers curved, like paws. She holds this position, smiling broadly.
NANCY: Do *this,* Charlie! For God's sake, do *this!*
CHARLIE *(confused):* Nancy . . .
NANCY: It's called "submission," Charlie! I've seen it in the books. I've read how the animals do it. Do it, Charlie! Roll over! Please!
    Charlie hesitates a moment, looks at Leslie and Sarah.
Do it, Charlie!
    Slowly, Charlie smiles broadly at Leslie and Sarah, assumes Nancy's position.
CHARLIE *(finally):* All right.
NANCY: Now, Charlie, smile! And mean it!
    Curtain.

ACT II

Immediately following, Leslie and Sarah are consulting about the peculiar behavior of the two human beings. The lizards decide it's probably a submission pose but might be a trick, so they approach warily. Charlie is more and more panicked.

> *Leslie stops, leans forward toward Charlie and sniffs him several times. Then he straightens up and pokes Charlie in the ribs with his foot paw. Charlie makes an involuntary sound, but holds his position and keeps smiling. Leslie looks at Nancy, sniffs her a little, pokes her too. She holds position and wags her hands a little. Leslie surveys them both, then turns and ambles back to Sarah.*

SARAH: Well?

LESLIE: Well . . . they don't look very . . . formidable—in the sense of prepossessing. Not young. They've got their teeth bared, but they don't look as though they're going to bite. Their hide is funny—feels soft.

SARAH: How do they smell?

LESLIE: Strange.

SARAH: Well, I should suppose *so.*

LESLIE *(not too sure):* I guess it's *safe.*

SARAH: Are you *sure?*

LESLIE *(laughs a little):* No, of course not. *(Scratches his head.)*

NANCY *(sotto voce):* What are they doing?

CHARLIE: It poked me; one of them poked me; I thought it was all over.

NANCY *(not to be left out):* Well, it poked *me,* too.

CHARLIE: It *sniffed* at *me.*

NANCY: Yes. Keep where you are, Charlie; don't move. It sniffed at *me,* too.

CHARLIE: Did you smell it?

NANCY: Yes; fishy. And beautiful!

CHARLIE: Terrifying!

NANCY *(agreeing):* Yes: beautiful.

Leslie and Sarah are undecided what to do next, though Leslie makes it clear that he is boss and will do the deciding, while Sarah is sweetly submissive. Leslie comes over and pokes Charlie again, and this time Charlie cries out. Leslie clears his throat and states "Pardon me," and Nancy urges Charlie to speak to the lizard. Charlie doesn't want to—if he speaks to it he'll have to accept it as real.

Nancy and Sarah make the first contact with an exchange of hellos. Charlie finally, reluctantly, says hello to Leslie, but both males are very much on their guard. Each couple suspects the other of wanting to kill and eat the other. When they find this isn't the case, they relax enough to introduce themselves, exchanging names.

Charlie assures the couple from the sea that they aren't accustomed to eating their own kind, particularly when it speaks English. Leslie doesn't eat his own kind either and is a bit offended at any suggestion that he might. Nancy explains that they usually cook their food before eating it, anyhow, but of course the lizards don't understand what she means.

Nancy decides to greet the lizards properly and explains the significance of shaking hands.

NANCY: I give you my hand and you give me your . . . what *is* that? What is that called?

LESLIE: What?

NANCY *(indicating Leslie's right arm):* That there.

LESLIE: It's called a leg, of course.

NANCY: Oh. Well, we call this an arm.

LESLIE: You have four arms, I see.

CHARLIE: No; she has two arms. *(Tiny pause.)* And two legs.

SARAH *(moves closer to examine Nancy with Leslie):* And which are the legs?

NANCY: These here. And these are the arms.

LESLIE *(a little on his guard):* Why do you differentiate?

NANCY: Why do we differentiate, Charlie?

CHARLIE *(quietly hysterical):* Because they're the ones with the hands on the ends of them.

NANCY *(to Leslie):* Yes.

SARAH *(as Leslie glances suspiciously at Charlie):* Go on, Leslie. Do what Nancy wants you to. *(To Nancy.)* What is it called?

NANCY: Shaking hands.

CHARLIE: Or legs.

LESLIE *(glowers at Charlie):* Quiet.

CHARLIE *(quickly):* Yes, sir.

LESLIE *(to Nancy):* Now; what is it you want to do?

NANCY: Well . . .

    A glance at Charlie, both reassuring and imploring.

. . . you give me your . . . that leg there, that one, and I'll give you my . . . leg, or arm, or whatever, and we'll come together by our fingers . . . these are your fingers . . .

LESLIE: Toes.

NANCY: Oh, all right; toes.

    Shakes hands with Leslie.

Leslie is puzzled by this ceremony. Sarah wants to try it and does. Leslie at last understands that the earth people aren't immediately dangerous to him, but he also sees that things might be different if either he or Charlie panics. He asks Charlie what frightens him, and Charlie gives him a short list ending somewhat offensively with "Great . . . green . . . creatures, coming up from the sea."

To Leslie and Sarah, Nancy and Charlie also look peculiar—for one thing, the lizards can't understand the purpose of the humans' outer covering. Nancy tries to explain its multiple functions of warmth, style and modesty, She goes so far as to show the lizards her "secondary sex organs," her breasts, which the lizards lack. The lizards are fascinated; Charlie disturbed and upset. Sarah remembers once seeing a school of whales, with their young attached "to devices I *think* were very much like those of yours." Sarah herself has produced hundreds of children by means of laying eggs.

CHARLIE: You . . . lay eggs.
SARAH: Certainly! right and left.
       A pause.
NANCY: Well.
LESLIE *(eyes narrowed):* You, um . . . you don't lay eggs, hunh?
CHARLIE *(incredulous):* No! Of course not!
LESLIE *(exploding):* There! You see!? What did I tell you!? They don't even lay eggs!
NANCY *(trying to save the situation):* How many . . . uh . . . eggs have you laid, Sarah?
SARAH *(thinks about it for a bit):* Seven thousand?
NANCY *(admonishing):* Oh! Sarah!
SARAH: No?
NANCY: Well, I dare say! Yes! But, really!
SARAH: I'm sorry?
NANCY: No! Never that!
CHARLIE *(to Leslie, with some awe):* Seven thousand! Really?
LESLIE *(gruff; the usual husband):* Well, *I* don't know. I mean . . .
NANCY: What do you *do* with them, Sarah? How do you take *care* of them?
SARAH: Well . . . they just . . . float away.
NANCY *(chiding):* Oh, Sarah!
SARAH: Some get eaten—by folk passing by, which is a blessing, really, or we'd be inundated—some fall to the bottom, some catch on growing things; there's a disposition.
NANCY: Still!
SARAH: Why? What do *you* do with them?
NANCY *(looks at her nails briefly):* It's different with us, Sarah. In the birthing, I mean; I don't know about . . . well, how you go about it!
SARAH *(shy):* Well . . . we couple.
LESLIE: Shhh!
NANCY: Yes; I thought. And so do we.
SARAH *(relieved):* Oh; good . . . . .

Nancy explains gestation and the bearing, usually, of one baby at a time. The lizards are amazed that humans care for their young for as long as 18 years before letting them go. Charlie tries to explain that humans *love* their children, and soon he perceives that the lizards don't know what love is, nor indeed do they understand the concept of emotion. Nancy tries to explain what emotion is by calling off the names of several: "Fear. Hatred. Apprehension. Loss. Love." Charlie angers Nancy by insisting that emotions can't be put into words. He tries another way.

CHARLIE *(to Leslie and Sarah):* Maybe *I* can do it. How did you two get together? How'd ya meet?

LESLIE: Well, I was just going along, one day, minding my own business . . .

SARAH: Oh, Leslie! *(To Charlie.)* I was reaching my maturity, and so, naturally, a lot of males were paying attention to me—milling around—you know—preening and snapping at each other and generally showing off, and I noticed one was hanging around a little distance away, not joining in with the others . . .

LESLIE: That was me.

SARAH: . . . and I didn't pay too much attention to him, because I thought he was probably sickly, or something, and besides, there were so many others, and it was time to start coupling . . .

LESLIE: *You* noticed me.

SARAH: . . . when, all of a sudden! There he was, right in the middle of them, snapping away, really fighting, driving all the others off. It was quite a rumpus.

LESLIE *(an aside to Charlie):* They didn't *amount* to much.

SARAH *(shrugs):* And so . . . all the others drifted away . . . and there he was.

LESLIE: They didn't *drift* away: I drove them away.

SARAH: Well, I suppose that's true. *(Bright.)* Show them your scar, Leslie! *(To Charlie and Nancy.)* Leslie has a marvelous scar!

LESLIE *(proud):* Oh . . . some other time.

SARAH: And there he *was* . . . and there *I* was . . . and here we *are.*

CHARLIE: Well, yes! That proves my point!

LESLIE: What?

    Pause.

CHARLIE: About *love. (Pause.)* He *loved* you.

Leslie wanted Sarah specifically, Charlie insists, because he loved her—but Leslie still fails to understand. Charlie questions Leslie about coupling with others. Leslie insists "I've coupled in my time," but he won't admit to actual events. Nancy is angry at Charlie for taking this whole tack and becomes even angrier when Charlie asks the same question of Sarah: has *she* coupled with anyone else? Leslie answers for her: no. Finally Sarah agrees: no, she hasn't.

Still Leslie fails to understand what Charlie is getting at about love and emotion. Frustrated, Charlie tells Leslie he has no grasp of conceptual matters so that Charlie "might as well be talking to a fish." This produces instant anger and aggression in Leslie; evidently the lizards don't think well of fish.

CHARLIE: What's the matter with fish all of a sudden?

LESLIE *(real middle-class, but not awful):* For one thing, there're too many of them; they're all over the place . . . racing around, darting in front of you, picking at everything . . . moving in, taking over where you live . . . and they're stupid!

SARAH *(shy):* Not all of them; porpoises aren't stupid.

LESLIE *(still wound up):* All right! Except for porpoises—they're stupid! *(Thinks about it some more.)* And they're dirty!

CHARLIE *(mouth open in amazement and delight):* You're . . . you're prejudiced! Nancy, he's . . . You're a bigot! *(Laughs)* You're a goddamn bigot!

LESLIE *(dangerous):* Yeah? What's that?

NANCY: Be careful, Charlie.

LESLIE *(not amused):* What *is* that?

CHARLIE: What? A bigot?

LESLIE: I don't know. Is that what you said?

CHARLIE *(right on with it):* A bigot is somebody who thinks he's better than somebody else because they're different.

LESLIE:*(brief pause; anger defused):* Oh; well, then; that's all right. I'm not what you said. It's *not* because they're different: it's because they're stupid and they're dirty and they're all over the place!

CHARLIE *(parody of studying and accepting):* Oh. Well, that's all right, then.

NANCY *(wincing some):* Careful, Charlie.

LESLIE *(absorbed with his own words):* Being different is . . . interesting; there's nothing implicitly inferior or superior about it. *Great* difference, of course, produces natural caution; and if the differences are too extreme . . . well, then, reality tends to fade away.

NANCY *(an aside; to Charlie):* And so much for conceptual matters.

Sarah notices the broad sky and birds for the first time; birds are a bit alarming, and Leslie goes through his instinctive protective motions, placing himself on guard. Sarah doesn't understand how the birds manage to fly; they remind her of swimming rays.

Nancy in her turn is thinking of how much fun it will be to tell others about the lizards' first experience of the upper world. Charlie can only believe that others, including their own children, will think they've lost their minds. Leslie finally abandons his guard duty, but he is still apprehensive and distrustful. Trying to ease the situation any way she can, Nancy informs Leslie that nothing matters anyway because according to Charlie they're dead, poisoned by liver paste: "I mean, we *have* to be dead, because Charlie has decided that the wonders do not occur; that what we have not known does not exist; that what we cannot fathom cannot be; that the miracles, if you will, are bedtime stories; he has taken the leap of faith, from agnostic to atheist; the world is flat; the sun and the planets revolve about it, and don't row out too far or you'll fall off."

Leslie doesn't believe they're dead. Sarah, trying to be helpful, informs Nancy that Charlie isn't dead; Nancy is suitably grateful for the information. If Charlie and Nancy are dead (as Leslie understands it), Leslie is only an illusion, and Leslie believes that he does, in reality, exist. Charlie tries to hammer Descartes's theory into Leslie but doesn't have patience enough to be a good teacher. Charlie calls death a release, a fitting end, and Nancy replies by kissing Charlie ardently, as an affirmation that they are both still alive and all right.

A jet plane roars over again, terrifying the lizards. Their fear moves Nancy to pity and Charlie to some reassurance. Charlie tries to explain what an airplane is, again unsuccessfully. He tells Leslie: "Give us a machine and there isn't anywhere we don't go. Why, we even have a machine that will . . . go down there; under water."

Leslie is most interested in the fact that Charlie has been under water. Nancy tells them about Charlie's boyhood diving, but Charlie angrily deprecates the experience, calls for Nancy to stop talking about it.

CHARLIE *(to Leslie and Sarah):* It was just a game; it was enough for a twelve-year old, maybe, but it wasn't . . . finding out, you know; it wasn't *real.* It wasn't enough for a memory.
> *Pause. Shakes his head.*

SARAH *(to Nancy; quietly): Is* he all right?

NANCY *(her eyes and mind on Charlie):* Hm?

CHARLIE *(barely controlled rage; to Leslie):* Why did you come up here in the first place?

LESLIE *(too matter-of-fact):* I don't know.

CHARLIE *(thunder):* COME! ON!

LESLIE: I don't know! *(To Sarah; too offhand.) Do* I know?

SARAH *(yes and no):* Well . . .

LESLIE *(final):* I don't know.

SARAH: We had a sense of not belonging any more.

LESLIE: Don't, Sarah.

SARAH: I should, Leslie. It was a growing thing, nothing abrupt, nor that anything was different.

LESLIE *(helpless):* Don't go on, Sarah.

SARAH: . . . in the sense of having changed; but . . . *we* had changed . . . *(Looks about her.)* . . . all of a sudden, everything . . . down there . . . was terribly . . . interesting; I suppose; but what did it have to do with *us* any more?

LESLIE: Don't, Sarah.

SARAH: And it wasn't . . . comfortable any more. I mean, after all, you make your nest, and accept a whole . . . array . . . of things . . . and . . . we didn't feel we *belonged* there any more. And . . . what were we going to do?!

CHARLIE *(after a little; shy):* And that's why you came up.
> *Leslie nods glumly.*

Down there, Leslie and Sarah discussed the pros and cons and decided to come up. This puts Charlie in mind of eons of evolution: "What do they call it . . . the primordial soup? The glop? That heartbreaking second when it all got together, the sugars and the acids and the ultraviolets, and the next thing you knew there were tangerines and string quartets." Somewhere in between, they were all swimming around together, Leslie's ancestors as well as Charlie's (Leslie doesn't accept this, but he goes along with it, humoring Charlie; Sarah is fascinated). Nancy tries to explain that individual creatures began to develop individual characteristics over long periods of time—a tail, for example.

LESLIE *(quite dry):* I've always had a tail.

NANCY *(bright):* Oh, no; there was a time, way back, you didn't. Before you needed it you didn't have one.

LESLIE *(through his teeth):* I have *always* had a *tail.*

SARAH: Leslie's very proud of his tail, Nancy . . .

CHARLIE: You like your tail, do you?

LESLIE *(grim; gathers his tail in front of him):* I have *always* had a *tail.*

SARAH: Of course you have, Leslie; it's a lovely tail.

LESLIE *(hugging his tail in front of him; anxiety on his face):* I have. I've always had one.

Charlie is equally proud that he *doesn't* have a tail, that he has mutated. He tries to explain to Leslie about the "crowning moment" of evolution when "some . . . slimy creature poked his head out of the muck, looked around and decided to spend some time up here." Again, Leslie fails to believe or understand, but Charlie keeps on: "Part of what he became didn't fancy it on land, and went back down there, and turned into porpoises and sharks, and manta rays and whales . . . and you."

The process is still going on, Charlie insists, and he urges Leslie to stay up here on the land. Nancy adds that the advantage of being an advanced evolutionary type like herself over, say, a rabbit, is that she uses tools, creates art and is aware of mortality—all of which makes her more interesting. Charlie defines one who lacks these advantages as a "brute beast." Leslie senses, somewhat justifiably, that the phrase is aimed at him, in condescension.

Actually, Charlie isn't entirely sure how he feels about Leslie. Maybe Charlie envies the emotional freedom of the brute beast. In any event, he decides: "I want you to know about *all* of it; I'm impatient for you. I want you to experience the whole thing! The full sweep!" He asks Sarah how she'd feel if Leslie went away and she knew he was never coming back. Nancy calls Charlie heartless and relentless, but Charlie persists until Sarah understands the meaning of his question and begins to sob. She has now lost her brute-beast innocence and has acquired some of the human being's awareness of mortality.

Leslie tries to comfort Sarah, as Sarah sobs, "I want to go *back!*" Furious that Charlie has made Sarah cry, *"Leslie begins to choke Charlie. . . . . his arm around Charlie's throat. It has the look of slow, massive inevitability, not fight and panic."* Charlie is done for, except that Sarah joins Nancy's pleas for Leslie to stop. He finally does so with a final angry "Don't you talk to me about brute beast." Charlie sinks to the sand, but he is all right.

LESLIE *(attempts a quiet half-joke):* It's . . . rather dangerous . . . up here.

CHARLIE *(looks him in the eye):* Everywhere.

LESLIE: Well. I think we'll go back down now.

NANCY *(hand out; a quiet, intense supplication):* No!

LESLIE: Oh, yes.

NANCY: No! You mustn't!

SARAH *(as a comfort):* Leslie says we must.
    Leslie puts paw out.

NANCY: No!
    Charlie takes it.

LESLIE: This *is* how we do it, isn't it?

SARAH *(watching; tentative):* Such a wonderful thing to want to do.

LESLIE *(tight; formal):* Thank you very much

CHARLIE *(eyes averted):* You're welcome.

NANCY: NO!

LESLIE *(sighs):* Well.

> *Leslie and Sarah start moving to the upstage dune to exit.*

NANCY *(in place):* Please?

> *Nancy moves to follow them.*

SARAH: It's all right; it's all right.

NANCY: You'll have to come back . . . sooner or later. You don't have any choice. Don't you know that? You'll have to come back up.

LESLIE *(sad smile): Do* we?

NANCY: Yes!

LESLIE: *Do* we have to?

NANCY: Yes!

LESLIE: Do we *have* to?

NANCY *(timid):* We could *help* you. Please?

LESLIE *(anger and doubt):* How!

CHARLIE *(sad, shy):* Take you by the hand? You've got to *do* it—sooner or later.

NANCY *(shy):* We *could* help you.

> *Leslie pauses; descends a step down the dune; crouches; stares at them.*

LESLIE *(straight):* All right. Begin.

> *Curtain.*

SAME TIME, NEXT YEAR

A Comedy in Two Acts

BY BERNARD SLADE

Cast and credits appear on page 344

BERNARD SLADE was born May 2, 1930 in St. Catherines, Ontario, the son of an aircraft mechanic. He left Canada at age 5 for England, where he went to school until he was 18, after which he returned to Canada as an actor. He worked in stock and TV for a decade. He also became a producer when, in 1954, he opened and maintained a theater in Canada between Vineland and Niagara Falls.

In 1957 Slade branched out into writing. His first produced work was the hour-long TV play The Long, Long Laugh, *the first of many Slade TV scripts seen in Canada, England and all three American networks. It was six more years before his debut as a playwright with* Simon Says Get Married *at the Crest Theater in Toronto, followed by* A Very Close Family *at the Manitoba Theater (also produced as a two-hour TV play).* Same Time, Next Year *is his Broadway debut and his third produced play.*

Slade's writing credits also include the feature film Stand Up and Be Counted. *He now lives in Los Angeles and is married, with two children: Laurel, 19, and Christopher, 16.*

Time: 1951–1975

Place: A guest cottage of a country inn in Northern California

ACT I

Scene 1: A day in February, 1951

SYNOPSIS: George and Doris are lying in a double bed in a large, comfortable cottage bed-sitting room of a Spanish-style inn near Mendecino, north of San Francisco. The room features a grand piano and a fireplace as well as sofa, dressing table, etc. Doors lead to the bathroom and to the cottage's entrance and patio. *"The room's aura of permanence is not an illusion. The decor has been the same for the past 25 years and will not change for the next 25."*

George tries to creep out of bed and put his clothes on one item at a time, as he finds them, without disturbing Doris. He's managed a jacket and two socks, when Doris informs him she's awake and reaches for her slip to put it on under the covers. George is uneasy about having spent the night with Doris (and only just now learns what her name is) but admits that it was "the most beautiful, wonderful crazy thing that's ever happened to me."

DORIS: It was—nice. Especially the last time.

GEORGE: I'm an animal. I don't know what got into me. What was the matter with the first two times?

DORIS: What? Oh—well, the first time was kinda fast and the second—look, I feel funny talking about this.

GEORGE: It was a very beautiful thing, Doris. There was nothing disgusting or dirty in what we did.

DORIS: Then how come you look so down in the dumps?

GEORGE: My wife is going to kill me.

DORIS: How is she going to find out?

GEORGE: She knows.

DORIS: You said she was in New Jersey.

GEORGE: It doesn't matter. She knows.

DORIS: How?

GEORGE: Was it as incredible for you as it was for me?

DORIS: Boy, do all men like to talk about it a lot afterwards?

GEORGE: Why? You think I'm some sort of pervert or something?

DORIS: No, I just wondered. See, I was a virgin when I got married. At least sort of.

GEORGE: Sort of?

DORIS: Well, I was pregnant but I don't count that.

GEORGE: Doris, that counts.

DORIS: I mean it was by the man I married.

George has discovered a disturbing fact: he loves Doris, even though he suspects she's never read *Catcher in the Rye* (and she didn't graduate from high school). And George also is happily married. His whole love life has presented these awkward problems, even though he has the methodical mind of a C.P.A. Doris is a Roman Catholic who grew up in a large Italian family, and she too is suffering pangs of guilt. She's thinking about going to confession, while George is thinking about making love to her again.

A knock on the door sends them into a panic. Doris grabs her hat and her clothes and climbs out of the window. George goes to the door and squeezes outside into the hall so that whoever is there can't see into the room. George returns with the breakfast tray—it was only the waiter—and Doris follows him back into the room through the door.

George informs Doris that he comes out here from New Jersey every year to go over the books of a friend in the wine business. He assures Doris that this is his first infidelity. Doris has already guessed that this is the first time for him, because of "the way you tried to get your pants off over your shoes and then tripped and hit your head on the coffee table. Little things like that."

While Doris tries some breakfast, George elaborately confesses a deception: he told Doris he was married with two children, whereas in reality he has three children. He thought the lie would make him seem less married. George's wife never accompanies him on his yearly trip because she doesn't like to fly. George managed to meet Doris by sending a steak over to her table in the dining room the night before "Usually I never do that sort of thing. I have a friend who says that life is saying 'yes'. The most I've ever been able to manage is 'maybe'."

DORIS: I really should be going, the nuns will be wondering what happened to me.

GEORGE: Nuns?

DORIS: Yeah. It didn't seem right to bring up when we met yesterday in the restaurant, but I was on my way to retreat.

GEORGE: Retreat?

DORIS: It's right near here. I go every year at this time when Harry takes the kids to Bakersfield.

GEORGE: What's in Bakersfield?

DORIS: His mother. It's her birthday.

GEORGE: She doesn't mind that you don't go?

DORIS: No, she hates me.

GEORGE: Why?

DORIS: I got pregnant.

GEORGE: Her son had something to do with that.

DORIS: She blocks that out of her mind. You see, he was in his first year of dental college and he had to quit and take a job selling waterless cooking. And so now every year on her birthday I go on retreat.

GEORGE: To think about God?

DORIS: Well, Him too, sure. See, I have three little kids. I got pregnant the first time when I was eighteen and so I never really had any time to think about what I think. Never mind . . . sometimes I think I'm crazy.

GEORGE: Why?

DORIS: Well, take my life. I live in a two-bedroom duplex in downtown Oakland, we have a 1948 Kaiser, a blonde three-piece dinette set, Motorola TV, and we go bowling at least once a week. I mean what else could anyone ask for? But sometimes things get me down, you know? It's dumb!

George and Doris find each other very sympathetic. Naturally, they're curious about each other's lives and spouses. But rather than going on and on about their lives at home, George proposes "I'll tell you two stories, one showing the best side of my wife and the other showing the worst. Then you do the same about your husband and then let's forget that. Okay?"

Doris agrees, so George tells her about his wife Phyllis's uncanny knack of knowing even at long distance when George is misbehaving (that's his "bad" story). On the other hand, Phyllis helped George conquer his feelings of inadequacy simply by marrying him.

Then it's Doris's turn to tell George one good thing and one bad thing about her husband Harry. The bad thing is that she once heard Harry say that the best years of his life were in the Army (even though he spent three years in a prison camp). The good thing is that he tries to be friends with the children, to the point of overdoing it.

Through a slip of the tongue, George reveals that his wife's name is really Helen, not Phyllis—George was being extra discreet in giving Doris the wrong name. Doris offers to show George pictures of her children. Sitting side by side on the sofa, they exchange snapshots and anecdotes.

GEORGE (looking at a snap in his hand): Why is this one's face all scrunched up?

DORIS: Oh, that's Paul. It was taken on a roller coaster. Isn't it natural looking? Right after that he threw up.

GEORGE: Yeah, he's really something. I guess he looks like Harry, huh?

DORIS: Both of us really. What's your little girl's name?

GEORGE: Debbie. That was taken on her second birthday. We were trying to get her to blow out the candles.

DORIS: She has her hand in the cake.

GEORGE: Yeah, neat is not her strong suit.

DORIS: You have great looking kids, George.

GEORGE: Thank you. So do you.

DORIS: Thank you.

> They hand back the photographs which each immediately replaces where they came from. They gaze at one another, move into an awkward embrace which becomes extremely passionate. They pull apart.

(Removing her hat and rising.) Okay. But this is the last time.

> Curtain.

Scene 2: A day in February, 1956

In the same room at the same time of year five years later, George has brought all the symbols of celebration—cake, champagne, even a sign proclaiming "Happy 5th". It's George and Doris's fifth annual rendezvous, which George tells Doris is "one of the best ideas you ever had." Doris doesn't feel she can take the credit for it, "It was just something we stumbled into."

They catch up on each other's lives: Doris has dyed her hair blonde and joined the Book of the Month Club, while George has moved to a converted barn in Connecticut. George's family has increased by a baby girl (he has brought pictures). George is looking forward to his "one beautiful weekend every year with no cares, no ties and no responsibilities," but just as they embrace the phone rings. It's George's daughter Debbie calling to say that she's lost a tooth and wishes her father were with her to help her find it again. Otherwise, Debbie fears, the tooth-fairy will never know.

This reminder of homely matters turns George's guilt feelings up to a high level. Trying to forget, George suggests they tell their usual "good" and "bad" stories about their spouses. Doris's "good" story about Harry is that he went bankrupt selling real estate. Harry's "good" story about Helen is that she never told anyone he fainted when he saw his son Chris gash his knee. But the stories aren't much help.

GEORGE: . . . . . Instead of leaving at my usual time would you mind if I left earlier?

DORIS: When did you have in mind?

GEORGE: Well, there's a plane in half an hour.

DORIS: You want to leave twenty-three hours early?

GEORGE: Look, I know how you feel, I really do, and I wouldn't even suggest it if you weren't a mother. I mean I wouldn't even think of it if this crisis hadn't come up.

> *He moves his suitcase to the bed and starts packing through the following.*

Oh, it's not just the tooth-fairy but she could have swallowed the tooth. It could be lodged God knows where. Now I know this leaves you up in the air but there's no reason for you to leave too. The room's all paid for—have you seen my hairbrush? Anyway, I'm probably doing you a favor. If I did stay I wouldn't be very good company.

> *Doris throws the hairbrush at him. It sails past his head and crashes into the wall. There is a pause.*

You feel somewhat rejected, right? I can understand that but I want you to know my leaving has nothing to do with you and me. Doris, I have a sick child at home. This is an emergency.

DORIS: Will you stop it. It's got nothing to do with the goddamn tooth-fairy. You're just feeling guilty and the only way you think you can deal with it is by getting as far away from me as possible.

GEORGE: Okay, I feel guilty. Is that so strange? Doris, we're cheating! Once a year we lie to our families and sneak off to a hotel in California and commit adultery. Not that I want to stop doing it! But yes, I feel guilt. I admit it.

DORIS: You admit it! You take out ads. You probably stop strangers on the street. I'm surprised you haven't had a scarlet "A" embroidered on your jockey shorts! You think that by talking about it you can excuse what you're doing. So you wander around like an open nerve saying, "I'm cheating but look how guilty I feel so I must really be a nice guy!" And to top it all, you have the incredible arrogance to think you're the only one in the world with a conscience. Well, that doesn't make you a nice guy. You know what that makes you? A horse's ass.

GEORGE: You know something? I liked you a lot better before you joined the Book of the Month Club.

If George leaves, Doris isn't sure she's willing to make a date for next year. George doesn't seem to be making the same kind of commitment as Doris. Doris actually thought about George quite a few times during the year, and this disturbed her. She decided maybe she'd better not keep the rendezvous.

DORIS: . . . . . But then I thought I at least owed you an explanation. So I came. When you walked in the door I knew I couldn't do it. That no matter what the price I am willing to pay it.

GEORGE: I feel so guilty!

DORIS: Then why don't you leave?

GEORGE: Doris, I love you. I know I'm no bargain. I suspect I'm deeply neurotic, but I do love you and I would very much love to stay.
  She turns to him and smiles. They move into each other's arms.
What are we going to do?

DORIS: Touch and hold on very tight . . . until tomorrow.
  Curtain

Scene 3: A day in February, 1961

George has his raincoat and hat on and has just arrived, in the same room five years later. He's on the phone talking to his mother. From hints that his wife Helen has thrown around, the mother has deduced that George is having trouble with impotency. He refuses to go into the matter with her except to inform her that he is going to consult an expert and will soon be O.K. He slams down the receiver and goes into the bathroom to change.

Doris comes in. She calls for George who tells her he'll be right out. Doris lights the fire and is facing away from George when he comes out of the bathroom wearing his pajamas. When she turns to greet him, he sees that she is very obviously pregnant (at least eight months, she believes). George is crestfallen, but Doris insists: "Honey, it's not that tragic. We'll just have to find some other way to communicate . . . . . I look forward to this weekend all year for a lot of reasons besides sex."

Doris suggests they break the ice by exchanging confidences about each other. She goes first: she tells George she's been having sex dreams about making love with him under water.

GEORGE: I can't swim.

DORIS: Do you mean literally?

GEORGE: Of course literally! When I tell you I can't swim I simply mean I can't swim.

DORIS: Okay, I just asked. How come?

GEORGE: I just never learned when I was a kid. Helen found out when she pushed me off a dock and I almost drowned but my kids don't even know. When we go to the beach I pretend I'm having trouble with my trick knee.

DORIS: You have a trick knee?

GEORGE: No. They don't know that either.

DORIS: You see, it worked. Now we're talking just like two people who have made love and everything.

George decides to tell Doris what's on his mind: his wife Helen seems to have lost interest in sex. He claims that her drive is decreasing while his is increasing. When Doris observes "That's odd. Usually it's the other way around," George goes on the defensive. He can't stand Helen's sense of humor. He illustrates: "We'd come home from a party and we'd had a few drinks and we went to bed and we started to make love. Well, nothing happened—for me—I couldn't— Well, you get the picture. It was no big deal. We laughed about it. Then about half an hour later, just as I was about to fall asleep, she said, 'It's funny, when I married a C.P.A. I always thought it would be his eyes that would go first.' "

Doris perceives at once that his own impotence is George's real problem. She's curious about how it happened and whether he blames his wife, but George isn't very outgiving on this subject. He'd rather talk about Doris's pregnancy. Doris tells George she feels "Catatonic, incredulous, angry, pragmatic and finally maternal" (she was confined to bed for the first three months, took a correspondence course and now has her high school diploma).

In spite of Doris's condition, George finds himself becoming aroused. Doris is flattered and pleased, but George of course feels guilty about his desires. He tries to release his sexual tension by playing the piano—he plays it surprisingly well. Doris decides that maybe they could figure out some way to make love, but when they kiss and embrace she suddenly doubles over with a labor pain.

GEORGE: My God, what have I done?

DORIS: What have *you* done?

GEORGE: I brought it on. My selfishness.

DORIS: You didn't have anything to do with it.

GEORGE: Don't treat me like a child, Doris!

DORIS: Will you stop getting so excited.

GEORGE: Excited? I thought I had troubles with my sex life before. Can you imagine what this is going to do to it?

DORIS: George, will you—

She is stopped by a pain.

I think I'd better lie down.

She lies back on the bed.

GEORGE: What kind of a man am I? What kind of man would do a thing like that?

DORIS: May I say something?

GEORGE: Look, I appreciate what you're trying to do, but nothing you can say will make me feel any better.

DORIS: I'm not trying to make you feel any better. I'm gonna have a baby.

Doris begs George to calm down and get on the phone while she goes into the bathroom. Frantically, George phones the desk, torn between getting action and keeping up the pretense that he and Doris are married. George sets it up so the desk is phoning Doris's doctor to meet her at the hospital, which is some distance away—but this plan has to be abandoned. The baby is on its way. Doris orders George to get the nearest doctor on the phone, any doctor. The nearest turns out to be on the golf course down the road, but even that is too far away. There's no time; the baby is arriving. Doris is frightened. George comforts her; he's stopped thinking about himself, regained his self-possession; in charge now and ready to do his best. He goes into the bathroom for a pile of towels, comes back at once and reassures Doris: "Honey, we're going to have a baby . . . . . I'm going to need your help. Give me your hand. Look into my eyes. You're going to be fine. There's nothing to worry about, we're together. You think I play the piano well? Wait 'til you see the way I deliver babies." *Curtain.*

ACT II

Scene 1: A day in February, 1965

Four years later, in the same room at the same time of year, George is unpacking. He has brought a bottle of Chivas Regal and pours himself a drink. *"Doris enters in jeans, turtle neck, Indian necklace, headband, long hair and sandals. She is carrying a daisy which she has picked up along the way."* George is a bit astonished at her appearance but embraces her, whereupon her first words to him are, "Hey, man! What do you say? So, you wanta fuck?"

George is somewhat put off by this opener, but they are soon catching up on what's happened to them in the past year. George has moved from Connecticut to Beverly Hills, where's he's doing very well as a business manager. Doris is going to college at Berkeley. She felt "restless and undirected" and felt that school might give her a chance to "find out who the hell I am." She considers the protest meetings and demonstrations against the war part of her education.

GEORGE: Demonstrations aren't going to stop the war.

DORIS: You have a better idea?

GEORGE: Look, I didn't come up here to discuss politics.

DORIS: Well, so far you've turned down sex and politics. You want to try religion?

GEORGE: I think I'll try a librium.

DORIS: How come you're so uptight?

GEORGE: That's another expression I hate.

DORIS: Uptight?

GEORGE: There's no such word.

DORIS: You remind me of my mother when I was nine years old I asked her what "fuck" meant and do you know what she said? "There's no such word."

GEORGE: And now you've found out there is you feel compelled to use it in every other sentence?

DORIS: George, what's bugging you?

GEORGE: Bugging me? I'll tell you what's "bugging" me? The blacks are burning down the cities, there's a Harvard professor telling my kids the only way to happiness is to become doped up zombies, and I have a teenage son with hair so long that from the back he looks exactly like Yvonne De Carlo.

DORIS: That's right, honey. Let it all hang out.

Among other things George objects to are the "indecent" way his daughter dresses and sex movies. Doris reminds him of their own "fifteen one-night stands," but George prefers to remember the night he delivered Doris's baby, a girl, who's now healthy, noisy, and spoiled.

Doris prods George to tell his "bad" story about his wife Helen. This year's tale is about a cocktail date at a client's house, where Helen urinated on the rug and lost George the account. Doris accuses George of acting and looking stuffy and George admits he's not "a faddist . . . . . like those middle-aged idiots with bell bottom trousers and Prince Valiant haircuts who go around yelling 'Ciao!' " Times and standards are changing so fast that George is confused, but he knows he doesn't like what's happening.

His confusion is suddenly appealing to Doris, and she sits on his knee; but her warmth is short-lived because she soon discovers George voted for Barry Goldwater for President. George is wracked by frustration, while trying to explain that if he had his way he'd bring the war to an end by bombing the enemy: "Wipe the sons of bitches off the face of the earth."

Doris is shocked. George was a Stevenson liberal and now, in Doris's eyes, he's little better than a Fascist.

DORIS: You're advocating mass murder!

GEORGE: Doris—drop it, okay! Just—drop it!

DORIS: You stand for everything I'm against!

GEORGE: Then maybe you're against the wrong things!

DORIS: You used to believe in the same things I do.

GEORGE: I changed.

DORIS: Why?

GEORGE: Because Michael was killed!

DORIS: Oh, my God. How?

GEORGE: He was trying to get a wounded man onto a Red Cross helicopter and a sniper killed him.

DORIS: When?

GEORGE: We heard at a July Fourth party. Helen went completely to pieces. I didn't feel a thing. I thought I was in shock and it would hit me later. It never did. The only thing I've been able to feel is blind anger. Isn't that something? He was my son, I loved him—I've been unable to shed a tear over him. Doris, I'm sorry about—everything. Lately I've been a bit on edge and—It just seems to be one—damn thing—after . . .

> *They embrace. Curtain.*

Scene 2: A day in February, 1970

> *Doris and George are sitting up in bed. She is doing a crossword puzzle. He is reading the sports section of a newspaper. After a few moments, they put down their papers and look at each other.*

DORIS: It's amazing how good it can be after twenty years, isn't it?

GEORGE: Honey, if you add up all the times we've actually made it together we're still on our honeymoon.

DORIS: Did I tell you I'm a grandmother?

GEORGE: No, but I think you picked a weird time to announce it. Anyway, you're the youngest-looking grandmother I've ever had a peak experience with.

DORIS *(gets up and crosses to dressing table):* My mother thanks you, my father thanks you, my hairdresser thanks you and my plastic surgeon thanks you.

> *She sits at dresser, peers into mirror, starts to brush hair and apply makeup.*

When Harry says "You're not the girl I married" he doesn't know how right he is.

GEORGE: Didn't Harry like your old nose?

DORIS: Harry thinks this is my old nose.

GEORGE: He never noticed?

DORIS: Pathetic, isn't it? . . . . .

That's Doris's "bad" story about Harry for this year. George's is about Helen putting sleeping pills in her ears. As George gets up and dresses, the phone rings —it's for Doris, something about a party for 60 guests. She now owns and runs a catering business, and she is so busy this weekend that she had to leave this number, but George needn't worry about Harry finding out. Harry still thinks Doris goes on retreat.

This year it's George's turn to be wearing blue jeans and spouting jargon. He's using terms like "high tension level" and "anxiety reduction." Doris guesses that George has picked them up in analysis.

GEORGE: . . . . . One day I took a look at my hundred and fifty thousand dollar house, the three cars in the garage, the swimming pool and the gardeners. I asked myself did I really want the whole status trip? So—I decided to try and find out what I did want and who I was.

> *Doris has gotten lounging pajamas from her suitcase and exited into the bathroom.*

DORIS *(offstage):* And you went from analysis to Esalen to Gestalt to Transactional to encounter groups to Nirvana.

GEORGE: Doris, just because some people are trying to widen their emotional horizons doesn't make the experience any less valid. I've learned a lot.

DORIS *(offstage):* I've noticed. For one thing, you learned to talk as if you're reasoning with someone about to jump off a high ledge.

She enters and crosses to George for help with her zipper.

GEORGE: Sometimes to compensate for my former emotionalism I tend to overcompensate and tend to lose some of my spontaneity. I'm working on that.

DORIS: I'm glad to hear it. What else have you learned?

GEORGE: I've learned that behind the walls I've built around myself I can be a very warm, caring, loving human being.

DORIS: I could have told you that twenty years ago . . . . .

Helen responded to George's analysis first in anger, then by taking up pottery. They live simply now, and George supports them by playing piano in a cocktail lounge.

The phone rings again—another business problem for Doris, who settles it with authority. She has gone beyond mere Women's Liberation to a quest for more and more power; she's a successful businesswoman now and is buying another store.

George argues that men and women are both victimized by the same circumstances; besides, he's given up the whole money-and-success routine. Doris fears their lives are becoming unsynchronized, but she feels she now has everything in her grasp that she wants—except Harry her husband, who disappeared four days ago.

George angers Doris by asking her how she feels about that, as though he were probing her psyche. Doris challenges George to carry out his policy of total honesty by telling his wife Helen about their annual affair, and George insists that Helen could probably take it now. Finally Doris admits that Harry's departure has made her feel "like I've been kicked in the stomach . . . . . Angry, hurt, betrayed and—okay, a little guilty. But boy, I resent the fact that he's making me feel guilty." She resents it because she didn't love Harry any the less when he was a business failure, and she doesn't see why he should love her the less because she's a business success.

George advises Doris that Harry probably feels his masculinity is threatened. Doris isn't sure she wants Harry back—and she toys with the thought that she and George might make a good couple. George senses that she really doesn't mean this—she still loves Harry—but she needs reassurance that she is still attractive. "You're as feminine as you've always been," George tells her, cheering her up and forcing her to admit that maybe she isn't as liberated as she'd thought.

Doris has brought their dinner from her own catering service, "the choicest, most expensive French delicatessen in San Francisco." She has it in the trunk of her car, but before she goes to get it she gives George his instructions.

DORIS: . . . . . Set the table, light the candles, and when I come back make me laugh.

GEORGE: I'll try.

DORIS: Don't worry. If you can't make me laugh just hold my hand.

    Doris exits. After a few moments, the phone rings. George hesitates for
    a moment before answering.

GEORGE: Hello. No, she's not here right now. Who's calling, please? Harry!
—Hold on a moment, please.

    He hesitates for a few moments.

Hello—Harry, we're two adult, mature human beings and I've decided to be
totally honest with you . . . No, Doris is not here right now but I'd like to talk
to you . . . I know you and Doris have been having difficulties lately and . . . We're
very close friends. I've known Doris for twenty years and through her I feel as
if I know you . . . Well, we've been meeting this same weekend for twenty years
—The Retreat? Well, we can get into that later but first I want you to know
something. She loves you, Harry—she really loves you—I just know, Harry
. . . Look, maybe if I told you a story she just told me this morning it would help
you understand. A few months ago Doris was supposed to act as a den mother
for your ten year old daughter and her Indian guide group. Well, she got hung
up at the store and was two hours late getting home. When she walked into the
house she looked into the living room and do you know what she saw? A rather
overweight, balding, middle-aged man with a feather on his head sitting cross-
legged on the floor very gravely and gently telling a circle of totally absorbed little
girls what it was like to be in a World War II Japanese prison camp. She turned
around, walked out and sat in her car and thanked God for being married to a
man like you . . . Are you still there, Harry? Well, sometimes married people get
into an emotional straitjacket and find it difficult to express how they truly feel
about each other. Total honesty is the key. Yes, I've known Doris for twenty years
and I'm not ashamed to admit that it's been one of the most intimate, satisfying
experiences of my life . . . My name? My name is Father Michael O'Herlihy.

    Curtain.

Scene 3: A day in February, 1975

Same place, five years later, Doris is looking into the mirror figuring out how
to make herself look younger, when George enters. They embrace. They're in a
reflective mood, remembering how it has been with them over the years, how they
once felt so insecure, how they have matured but are still strongly attracted to
one another.

George has gone back to figures, teaching accounting at U.C.L.A., and Doris
has sold her business. She now pursues all the usual leisure activities including
visiting her grandchildren—and she helped pull Harry through a mild heart
attack. She's been asked to run for local office on an independent ticket. Doris
tells this year's "good" story about Harry: "When they were wheeling him out
of intensive care he looked up at the doctor and said, 'Doc, give it to me straight.
After I get out of here will I be able to play the piano?' The doctor said, 'Of
course.' And Harry said, 'Funny, I couldn't when I came in.' The thing is, Harry
never makes jokes but he saw how panicky I was and he wanted to make me feel
better."

George asks about their emotional relationship and is told it has become "comfortable." Doris notices that George hasn't brought any luggage this time, and George admits he didn't bring any. This time he can't stay. George's wife Helen has known about this annual tryst for ten years—a close friend, Connie, finally told George that Helen knew. And George further informs Doris that his wife Helen has died (curiously, Doris shares George's feeling of loss). The children were a great help in getting George through a bad time. George once phoned Doris for comfort, but he deliberately hung up before the phone could be answered.

DORIS: I wish you'd spoken to me.

GEORGE: I didn't want to intrude. I didn't feel I had the right.

DORIS: My God, that's terrible. We should have been together.

GEORGE: I've been thinking about us a lot lately. Everything we've been through together. The things we've shared. The times we've helped each other. Did you know we've made love a hundred and thirteen times? I figured it out on my Bomar calculator.

He is fixing fresh cups of coffee.

It's a wonderful thing to know someone that well. You know, there is nothing about you I don't know. It's two sugar, right?

DORIS: No, one.

GEORGE: So I don't know everything about you. I don't know who your favorite movie stars are and I couldn't remember the name of your favorite perfume. I racked my brain but I couldn't remember.

DORIS: That's funny. It's My Sin.

GEORGE: But I do know that in twenty-four years I've never been out of love with you. I find that incredible. So what do you say, Doris, you want to get married?

DORIS *(lightly)*: Married? We shouldn't even be doing this.

GEORGE: I'm serious.

DORIS *(looking at him)*: Oh dear, you are.

GEORGE: What did you think I was—just another summer romance? A simple "yes" will do.

DORIS: There's no such thing.

GEORGE: What is it?

DORIS: I was just thinking of how many times I've dreamed of you asking me this. It's pulled me through a lot of bad times. I want to thank you for that.

GEORGE: What did you say to me all those times?

DORIS: I always said "yes".

GEORGE: And you're hesitating now?

Pause.

Do you realize I'm giving you the opportunity to marry a man who has known you for twenty-four years and cannot walk by you without wanting to grab your ass?

DORIS: You always were a sweet talker.

GEORGE: That's because if I told you how I really felt about you it would probably sound like a medley of cliches from popular songs. Will you marry me?

DORIS *(pause):* I can't.

GEORGE: Why not?

DORIS: I'm already married.

She is too fond of Harry to leave him; furthermore, she can't break up her family. George kicks himself for having helped patch up their trouble five years ago. Doris always suspected that George did it because he was afraid a free Doris might ask for a permanent commitment.

Doris reminds George that they'll have each other every year, "Same time, same place"—their arrangement is still on. But George needs a wife, he tells Doris: if not Doris, then perhaps Connie. But Connie's not the kind to permit her husband an annual rendezvous with another woman.

The thought of never seeing George again upsets Doris, and once again George begs her to marry him. But Doris has decided once and for all: she can't leave Harry.

George wishes he could think of something that would "make you burst into tears and come away with me," but he can't, and he has a plane to catch. He has one last question.

GEORGE: Who *were* your favorite movie stars?

DORIS: Cary Grant, Alan Ladd and Turhan Bey.

GEORGE: You've come such a long way.

DORIS: We both have.

GEORGE: I can't believe this is happening to us.

> *He exits quickly, shutting the door behind him. Doris stands for a moment trying to absorb the shock of his departure. Doris finally can contain her tears no longer. She throws herself face down on the bed. The door crashes open and George bursts into the room with his suitcase.*

Okay, I'm back Goddamit!

DORIS: What about Connie?

GEORGE: Connie's eighty-nine years old!

> *Doris laughs.*

Look, I wanted you to marry me and I figured if you thought someone else wanted me I might stand a better chance . . . I was desperate, okay? Look, for once in my life I wanted a happy ending. Listen, I don't want to talk about it any more. I'm back and I'm going to keep coming back every year until our bones are too brittle to risk contact.

> *Doris and George embrace. Curtain.*

A CHORUS LINE

A Musical in One Act

CONCEIVED BY MICHAEL BENNETT

BOOK BY JAMES KIRKWOOD AND
NICHOLAS DANTE

MUSIC BY MARVIN HAMLISCH

LYRICS BY EDWARD KLEBAN

Cast and credits appear on pages 358, 360

MICHAEL BENNETT (conception) was born in 1943 in Buffalo, N.Y., where his father was a machinist and he attended high school. He played a youngster in West Side Story *and then became a dancer with performing credits which include the choruses of* Subways Are for Sleeping, Here's Love *and* Bajour. *He was the choreographer for* Henry, Sweet Henry *(1967) and was nominated for a Tony then and ten subsequent times, winning for both his choreography and his co-direction of* Follies *(1971) and his choreography of* Seesaw *(1973), a show which also won him this season's Los Angeles Drama Critics Circle award for the year's best direction of a musical.*

Bennett's other credits include the musical staging of Promises, Promises *(1968),* Coco *(1969),* Company *(1970) and the direction of the straight play* Twigs *(1971).* A Chorus Line *was his second authorship credit (his first was* Seesaw*) and he also choreographed and directed this 1975 New York Drama Critics award-winner and Best Play. Bennett is a bachelor and lives in New York City.*

JAMES KIRKWOOD (co-author of book) was born into show business in 1930 in Los Angeles as the son of theatrical parents (Lila Lee and James Kirkwood Sr.). He was educated at various schools and served as a radarman on a transport in the Korean War. He started his career as a performer in the comedy team of Jim Kirkwood and Lee Goodman which played major cabarets. In addition to many stage roles in New York and on tour, he played in the TV serial Valiant Lady *for four years.*

In 1961 Kirkwood wrote his first novel, and his published works include There Must Be a Pony! *(which the author dramatized as a touring vehicle for Myrna Loy, and which has been sold to the movies),* Good Times/Bad Times *(also sold to the movies),* American Grotesque *(a non-fiction account of the Garrison-Shaw case in New Orleans) and the new* Some Kind of Hero. *On Broadway, Kirkwood wrote a sketch for* Dance Me a Song *(1950), a revue which he also appeared in; the short-lived* UTBU *(1966, whose title initials stand for Unhealthy To Be Unpleasant); and this season's* P.S. Your Cat Is Dead! *(see its entry in the "Plays Produced on Broadway" section of this volume) which he published as a novel after first writing it as a play.* A Chorus Line *is Kirkwood's first Best Play and first work for off Broadway. He is a bachelor and lives in Easthampton, L.I.*

NICHOLAS DANTE (co-author of book) was born Nov. 22, 1941 in New York City, the son of a Transit Authority employee. He quit Cardinal Hayes High School to go onto the stage as a dancer, changing his name from Conrado Morales to his present stage name. After many jobs in night clubs, stock companies, etc., he found himself in St. Louis in 1965 doing a succession of ten musicals (it was here that he decided he could write better shows than the ones he was appearing in and began to try). In New York, Dante danced in the choruses of Applause, Smith, Ambassador *and other stage and TV productions before achieving his first professional author's credit for* A Chorus Line. *Dante is a bachelor who lives in New York City and is a Nicheren Shoshu Buddhist.*

MARVIN HAMLISCH (music) was born in New York City in 1943 and was educated at the Juilliard School of Music and Queens College. He is best known as a motion picture composer who swept three 1974 Academy Awards, receiving the Oscars for best song and best score (The Way We Were) *and best adaptation* (The Sting). A Chorus Line *is Hamlisch's first work for the theater. He is a bachelor and commutes between Los Angeles and New York.*

EDWARD KLEBAN (lyrics) was born in New York City April 30, 1939, the son of an attorney. He was educated at Music and Art High School and Columbia, where he studied music and wrote the score for the varsity show. He joined Columbia Records, producing both classical and pop records, and later worked for six years with Goddard Lieberson producing original cast albums of Broadway shows. About ten years ago he joined the BMI Musical Theater Workshop under the direction of Lehman Engel, and he has become a lyricist as well as a composer, contributing lyrics to The Desert Song *and* Irene *as well as songs off off Broadway, on TV and for the movies (in the new* The Hindenburg). *A Chorus Line is his debut as a lyricist for an entire show in the professional theater, and he's written both the music and the lyrics for another stage musical, with production planned for next season. Kleban is a bachelor and lives in New York City.*

Our method of representing A Chorus Line *in these pages differs from that of the other Best Plays. The musical appears here in a series of photographs with selections from the text of the script and lyrics, recording the overall "look" of its visually expressive concept and characters, as well as its story structure and literary style.*

The photographs of A Chorus Line *depict scenes as produced by Joseph Papp and directed and choreographed by Michael Bennett, as of the opening May 21, 1975 at the New York Shakespeare Festival Public Theater, with scenery by Robin Wagner, costumes by Theoni V. Aldredge and lighting by Tharon Musser. Our special thanks are tendered to the producer and his press representatives, Merle Debuskey, Bob Ullman and Norman Berman, for making available these selections from Martha Swope's excellent photographs of the show.*

A CHORUS LINE

Time: The present
Place: Here, an audition

SYNOPSIS—1. A director-choreographer, Zach (Robert LuPone, *below, foreground*), is auditioning dancers for the chorus line of a Broadway show. "God I hope I get it," sing the many aspirants, expressing the desire of each and of all, "I really need this job, please God I need this job, I've got to get this job." But Zach needs only eight dancers for his line. After seeing them perform, Zach finally picks nine women (*below*) and eight men, seventeen candidates to keep trying for the eight roles.

2. The dancers present their photos and resumes (*above*), but Zach (*right*) wants to know even more about them. Zach explains: "I'm looking for a strong dancing chorus. . . . But there are some small parts that have to be played by the dancers I hire. . . . . I don't want to give you just a few lines to read. I think it would be better if I knew something about you—about your personalities. So, I'm going to ask you some questions. And I want to hear you talk. Treat it like an interview. I don't want you to think you have to perform. I just want to hear you talk and be yourselves. And everybody just relax—as much as you can."

None of the dancers wants to be the first to submit to Zach's questions, so Zach picks one of the men at random: Mike (*opposite page, top*). To get Mike talking, Zach questions him about his background. Mike was the last of twelve children in a family with an Italian background.

3. At age 4, Mike (Wayne Cilento, *above*) was taken to watch his big sister's dancing class. He kept telling himself, "I can do that," until one day his sister couldn't go to class and Mike took her place. Mike sings:

"I stuff her shoes   I can do that (*dances*)
  With extra socks   I got to class
  Run seven blocks   And had it made
  In nothin' flat   And so I stayed
  Hell, I can do that   The rest of my life. . . . . "

4. Bobby (Thomas J. Walsh, *left*) is next. He pours out stories of growing up as an oddball in a middle class family. "As I got older I kept getting stranger and stranger. I used to go down to this busy intersection near my house at rush hour and direct traffic. I just wanted to see if anybody'd notice me. That's when I started breaking into people's houses — Oh, I didn't steal anything—I'd just rearrange their furniture." Bobby's father was ashamed of his son's awkwardness at sports, and his mother failed to understand him. He dreamed of a spectacular suicide, "But then I realized—to commit suicide in Buffalo is redundant."

5. Sheila (Carole Bishop, *right*) is called downstage by Zach.

ZACH: Closer.

SHEILA (*walks further downstage*): Can I sit in your—lap?

ZACH: Do you always come on like this?

SHEILA: No, sometimes I'm aggressive . . . Actually I'm a Leo . . .

ZACH: What's that supposed to mean?

SHEILA: It means the other eleven months of the year have to watch out . . . I'm very strong.

ZACH: Maybe too strong.

SHEILA: Am I doing something you don't like? I mean, you told me to be myself.

ZACH: Just bring it down.

SHEILA: Bring what down?

ZACH: Your attitude. Tell me about your parents.

Sheila's mother wanted to be a dancer, but when Sheila's father wouldn't permit it she made Sheila a dancer instead, taking her to ballets, encouraging her. Sheila's family life was a disaster. But in contrast, as she sings, "Everything was beautiful at the ballet. . . . . I was happy . . . at the ballet."

6. Bebe (Nancy Lane, *left*) joins Sheila in the song. She sings:
"Mother always said I'd be very attractive
When I grew up . . . when I grew up
'Different,' she said,

               'with a special something
And a very, very personal flair,'
And though I was eight or nine. . . .
I hated her. . . . .
Different is nice, but it sure wasn't pretty
'Pretty' is what it's about
I never met anyone who was different
Who couldn't figure that out. . . . ."

7. Maggie (Kay Cole, *above, right*) joins Sheila and Bebe in reminiscing about parents: "I don't know what they were for or against really, except each other. I was born to save their marriage and when my father came to pick my mother up at the hospital he said, 'Well, I thought this was going to help. But I guess it's not . . .' Anyway, I did have a fantastic fantasy life. I used to dance around the living room with my arms up like this. My fantasy was that it was an Indian Chief . . ." Maggie sings:

> "It was an Indian Chief and he'd say,
> 'Maggie, do you wanna dance?'
> And I'd say, 'Daddy, I would love to . . .'
> Ev'rything was beautiful at the ballet
> Raise your arms, and someone's always there
> Yes, Ev'rything was beautiful at the ballet
> At the ballet
> At the ballet . . ."

8. Kristine (Renee Baughman, *below, right foreground*) is next, and she's very nervous. Her husband Al (Don Percassi, *below, left foreground*), who's also trying out for the chorus, helps her explain herself to Zach. Kristine always wanted to be a performer: "Only it's funny, I never wanted to be Ann Miller . . . I wanted to be—Doris Day. But, I had this little, a . . ." Al finishes the sentence for her: "Problem." Kristine's problem was, she couldn't sing.

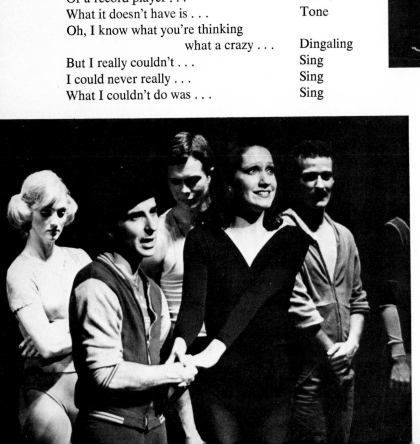

KRISTINE (*sings*):	AL (*sings*):
What I couldn't do was . . .	Sing
I have trouble with a . . .	Note
It goes all around my . . .	Throat
It's a terrifying . . .	Thing
See I really couldn't hear	
Which note was lower or was . . .	Higher
Which is why I disappear	
If someone says "Let's start a . . .	Choir"
Hey, when I begin to . . .	Squeak
It's a cross between a . . .	Shriek
And a quiver or a . . .	Moan
It's a little like a . . .	Croak
Or a record player . . .	Broke
What it doesn't have is . . .	Tone
Oh, I know what you're thinking	
what a crazy . . .	Dingaling
But I really couldn't . . .	Sing
I could never really . . .	Sing
What I couldn't do was . . .	Sing

9. Mark (Cameron Mason, *left on opposite page*) says, "I get the feeling most of you always knew what you wanted to do. Me—I didn't." One day he found a medical book in his father's library and became fascinated with it. Once Mark used the book to diagnose correctly his own appendicitis. He tried to solve the new physical problems of adolescence with the book, but he only became more confused and alarmed. Finally a priest set him straight. Mark joins the rest of the company in their group reminiscences in a song number called "Hello Twelve, Hello Thirteen, Hello Love."

10. Connie (Baayork Lee, *above, in foreground*) sings of her problem:

"Four foot ten
Four foot ten
That's the story of my life
I remember when everybody
was my size
(*Speaks*) Boy, was that great. But then everybody started moving up and—there I was, stuck at . . .
(*Sings*) Four foot ten
Four foot ten

I used to hang from the
parallel bars by the hour
Hoping I'd stretch
Just an inch more"

Connie explains: "I was into dancing then, and I was good. And I wanted so much to group up to be a prima ballerina." She decided to go out for cheerleader, but they told her, "No dice, you'd get lost on the football field. The pom-pons are bigger than you."

11. Diana (Priscilla Lopez, *left*) remembers her first day of acting class, "up on the stage with our legs around everybody" pretending to be riding a bobsled. Diana sings about it:
"Ev'ry day for a week we would try to
 Feel the motion . . . feel the motion
 Down the hill
 Ev'ry day for a week we would try to
 Hear the wind rush . . . hear the wind rush
 Feel the chill
 And I dug right down the bottom of my soul
 To see what I had inside
 Yes, I dug right down to the bottom of my soul
 And I tried . . . I tried!"
The others in the class could "feel" the bobsledding. The teacher turned to Diana and asked, "Okay, Morales. What did you feel?" Diana sings her reply:
"And I said . . . 'Nothing,
 I'm feeling nothing,'
 And he says, 'Nothing
 Could get a girl transferred.'
 They all felt something
 But I felt nothing
 Except the feeling
 That this bullshit was absurd. . . .'"
So Diana decided The Method wasn't for her and transferred to another acting class.

13. Judy (Patricia Garland, *left*) remembers her embarrassment when her mother would appear in public with rollers in her hair. Judy sings:
"But the thing that made my daddy
                               laugh so much
Was when I used to jump and dance
                    around the living room. . . .
But then when I was fifteen
The most terrible thing happened
The Ted Mack Amateur Hour
             held auditions in St. Louie
And I didn't hear about it
                 till after they were gone
And I nearly killed myself
Nearly killed myself
I tried to walk
        in front of a speeding streetcar.
And I remember noticing boys
                 for the first time . . .
(*Speaks.*) Anyway, I remember practising kisses with Leslie. She was my best girl friend. Did any of you ever practise kissing with another girl?
(*Sings.*) So that when the time came
             you'd know how to? . . . . ."

12. Don (Ron Kuhlman, *left, on opposite page*) worked a Kansas City night club at 15 and befriended the stripper, who boasted "dynamic, twin forty-fours. Well, she really took to me. I mean, we did share the same dressing room." Don sings:

"Anyway, she used to come and pick me up
And drive me to work nights
Well, the neighbors would all be hanging outside
Of their windows
And she'd drive up in this big pink Cadillac
And . . . smile."

Don would come out "in my little tuxedo and my tap shoes in hand and we'd drive off down the block with her long, flaming red hair just blowing in the wind."

ALL (*sing*): Hello twelve, hello thirteen, hello love. . . .

14. The adolescence of Greg (Michel Stuart, *left*) was a series of badly timed, inconvenient erections in school, on the bus, etc.

GREG: And then there was the time I was making out in the back seat with Sally Ketchum. We were necking and I was feeling her boobs and after about an hour or so she said . . .
(*Sings*) Oooohhh! Don't you want
to feel anything else?
. . . and I suddenly thought to myself: "No, I don't."
ZACH: Did that come as a surprise to you?
GREG: I guess, yeah. It was probably the first time I realized I was homosexual and I got so depressed because I thought being gay meant being a bum all the rest of my life. . . . .

15. Richie (Ronald Dennis, *right foreground*) sings:
"Gimme the ball
 Gimme the ball
 Gimme the ball, yeah!
 I was so enthusiastic
 The yearbook is filled
                 with my pictures
And I was lucky 'cause I got
A scholarship to college
So I went. . . . .
And I was scared."

ALL (*sing*): Shit, Richie
RICHIE (*sings*): Scared
ALL: Shit, Richie
RICHIE: Scared. . . . .
GIRLS: My braces gone
BOYS: My pimples gone
ALL: My childhood's gone
        Goodbye
        Goodbye twelve
        Goodbye thirteen
        Goodbye fourteen
        Goodbye fifteen
        Goodbye sixteen
        Goodbye seventeen
        Hello love

16. Val (Pamela Blair, *above*), tells how she left home for New York at 18, ambitious to become a Rockette: "I could do a hundred and eighty degree split and come up tapping the Morse Code." But Val didn't have the looks to match her talent, as she sings in "Dance Ten, Looks Three":

"Dance ten, looks three
And I'm still on unemployment
Dancing for my own enjoyment
That ain't it kid . . . that ain't it
Dance ten, looks three
Is like to die
Left the theater and
Called the doctor for
My appointment to buy . . .
Tits and ass
Bought myself a fancy pair
Tightened up the derriere
Did the nose with it
All that goes with it
Tits and ass
Had the bingo-bongos done

Suddenly I'm getting nash-nal tours
Tits and ass won't get you jobs
Unless they're yours
Didn't cost a fortune neither
Didn't hurt my sex life either. . . . .
Tits and ass
Where the cupboard once was bare
Now you knock and someone's there
You have got 'em, hey
Top to bottom, hey
It's a gas
Just a dash of silicone
Shake your new maracas
                              and you're fine
Tits and ass can change your life
They sure changed mine."

17. Cassie (Donna McKechnie, *above center*) and Zach were once more than friends, and Zach sends the others out for a break so he can talk to Cassie alone. He tells her, "You're too good for the chorus"—she was a featured Broadway dancer but couldn't act well enough to make it in movies and TV. Now she wants to get back to dancing any way she can: "Yes, I'm putting myself on your line. I don't want to wait on tables. . . . ." Cassie sings "Music and the Mirror":

> "God, I'm a dancer
> A dancer dances!
> Give me somebody to dance with
> Give me a place to fit in
> Help me return to the world of the living
> By showing me how to begin
> Play me the music
> Give me the chance to come through
> All I ever needed was the music and the mirror
> And the chance to dance for you. . . . ."

Zach insists: "You shouldn't have come. You don't fit in. You don't dance like anybody else—you don't know how."

18. **Paul** (Sammy Williams, *below right*) was questioned briefly before the break. Now Zach calls him back to say, "I really like the way you dance." Paul tells Zach how he began to like musicals at age 7 or 8 when his father would take him to the movies on 42nd Street. The memory troubles him too: "I'd have to move up front—'cause I couldn't see—I wear contact lenses now . . . I'd move up front and these strange men would come and sit beside me and 'play' with me. I never told anyone because—well, I guess it didn't matter."

Paul would often find himself dancing, copying the musicals: "I was always being Cyd Charisse. . . . . I always knew I was gay, but that didn't bother me. What bothered me was that I didn't know how to be a boy." He had a very difficult time at school and finally quit, "trying to find out who I was and how to be a man. You know, there are a lot of people in this world who don't know how to be men. And since then, I found out that I am one."

Paul found a job as a "pony" in a drag show. One night his parents paid a surprise visit to the theater to say goodbye before the show went on tour. "We were doing this oriental number and I looked like Anna May Wong. I had these two great big chrysanthemums on either side of my head and a huge headdress with gold balls hanging all over it. I was going on for the finale and going down the stairs and who should I see standing by the stage entrance but my parents. . . . . I freaked. I didn't know what to do. I thought to myself: 'I know, I'll just walk quickly past them like all the others.' So I took a deep breath and started down the stairs and just as I passed my mother I heard her say, 'Oh, my God.' Well . . . I died. But what could I do? I had to go on for the finale. . . . . After I'd finished dressing and taking my makeup off, I went back downstairs. And there they were standing in the middle of all these . . . and all they said to me was please write, make sure you eat and take care of yourself. And just before my parents left, my father turned to the producer and he said: 'Take care of my son . . .' That was the first time he ever called me that . . . I . . . ah. I . . . ah."

19. Zach calls the dancers back and leads them (*above and on opposite page, at top*) in a unison number with his assistant (Clive Clerk, *above, left foreground*). Zach orders: "I don't want anybody to pull my eye." The dancers have memorized a rhythmic chant: "*Change,* step, step, point, point, point, *flick, step, kick, touch,* change, walk, walk. . . . ."

Zach is hypercritical of Cassie's dancing: "Too high with the leg, Cassie. . . . . Too much plie, Cassie . . . Don't pop the hip, Cassie," finally stopping to tell her (*opposite page, at bottom*), "You're distorting the combination, Cassie. Cool it. Pull in. Dance like everyone else." But when Cassie does, it hurts Zach to see it. They were lovers once, and Zach neglected her for a chance to direct a play. He thinks she should have the same burning desire to excel at all costs. But Cassie tells Zach: "We're all special. . . . . I'd be happy to be dancing in that line. Yes, I would . . . I'll take the chorus . . . if you'll take me."

Zach orders other routines. Suddenly Paul falls on a turn. He has reinjured a damaged knee and is carried offstage in pain. Zach forces the others to consider what will happen to them when they can no longer dance. Some express private terrors, and finally Diana comments: "Listen, who knows anything? It's just something you're gonna have to wait and see." And she says it another way, singing the lyrics of a song: "Kiss today goodbye . . . and point me toward tomorrow."

20. At last, it's time for Zach to pick the eight dancers for the show: "Before I start eliminating, I just want to say I think you're all terrific. You've been wonderful about going through all this today. I wish I could hire all of you, but I can't. Will the following people please step forward: Don . . . Greg . . . Al . . . Diana, no, I'm wrong, back in line . . . Kristine . . . Bebe . . . Sheila . . . Connie . . . Maggie. Front line, thank you very much for coming and I'm sorry." The front line exits, leaving Val, Mike, Richie, Judy, Diana, Mark, Cassie and Bobby standing on the stage. Zach continues: "Rehearsals begin September Twenty-second. We will rehearse for six weeks with a two-month out-of-town tryout. Our New York opening will be sometime mid-January. . . . And I'm very glad we are going to be working together."

The play is over, but the cast appears on the stage, costumed for a traditional finale (*below*). The song is entitled "One." All sing:

> "She walks into a room and you know you must
> Shuffle along, join the parade
> She's the quintessence of making the grade
> This is what ya call trav'lling
> Oh, strut your stuff
> Can't get enough
> Of her
> Love her
> I'm a son of a gun
> She is one of a kind." (*Curtain*)

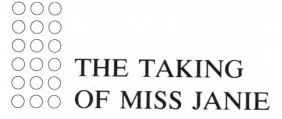

THE TAKING
OF MISS JANIE

A Play in One Act

BY ED BULLINS

Cast and credits appear on pages 364–365

*ED BULLINS was born in Philadelphia July 2, 1935 and educated at business school and various colleges. From 1952 to 1955 he served in the Navy. His first professionally produced stage work was a program of three one-act plays—*The Electronic Nigger, Clara's Ole Man *and* A Son, Come Home—*presented off Broadway in 1968 by American Place. His next was also a one-actor,* The Gentleman Caller, *on a 1969 off-Broadway program. Later in this same season, in April 1970, his full-length* The Pig Pen *appeared in an American Place production off Broadway. It dramatized a party which happened to take place on the night Malcolm X was killed (the party is a recurring symbol in Bullins's work) and his 1975 Best Play and New York Drama Critics Circle award-winner* The Taking of Miss Janie *is a sequel to it.*

Bullins has continued to write plays about the black experience in works produced off and off off Broadway: In the Wine Time, In New England Winter *(1971),* Street Sounds, The Fabulous Miss Marie, The Duplex *(1972),* The Corner, Goin' a Buffalo *and* House Party *(1973). In addition to his 1975 Best Play citation and Critics award for best American play, he has been the recipient of Obie and Vernon Rice awards and Rockefeller and Guggenheim fellowships.*

Time: The 1960s

Place: California and elsewhere

SYNOPSIS: The stage is uncluttered and represents *"an abstract depiction of cheap living spaces"* over the period of a decade and a continent in such cities as Los Angeles, San Francisco, New York, Boston, etc. Now there is a rollout bed in the foreground, on which Monty is lying half-covered with a sheet. Monty is in his middle 20s, black, *"a student type but with a street background.* Sitting on the edge of the bed is Janie, a blonde white girl also in her 20s. She is *"a California beach girl turned perennial student. An air of innocence. Moody. Reflective. Too all-American looking and well-scrubbed to be overtly sexy, but very attractive to men."*

At the moment Janie is very upset, very close to tears.

JANIE *(not looking at him at first):* It's sad . . . so sad . . . I don't even understand it . . . Once you said . . . no . . . no . . . many times you've told me . . . that anything's possible . . . But I wouldn't believe you. I *couldn't* believe you . . . You made the world, life, people . . . *everything* . . . seem so grim . . . And I knew it couldn't be that way . . . It couldn't . . . Even while I felt sad most of the time. Even while I suffered and had what you called "The Blues" . . . Even though I didn't understand why you refused to give in to sadness . . . to feeling down and beat . . . I . . . I still didn't believe, Monty. I didn't. I still didn't believe that I have so little understanding of the world . . . Oh, Monty, I have so little understanding of people and life . . . and I don't know *you,* who I thought was my friend, at all . . . And now . . . and now I don't know what to believe any more . . . or know what to do next. We've been friends for such a long time. Such a long time . . . Ten years? . . . God, it's been that long . . . I don't know what I'll do now . . . I don't know what's going to happen to me . . . For such a long time I thought of you as one of my few friends. A special friend, really. Do you understand that, Monty? . . . My special friend . . . And now you rape me . . . you rape me!

> *She begins to cry softly. Monty raises his head from the pillow, then reaches over and pulls her to him and kisses her until she quiets. She doesn't resist. She catches her breath.*

Oh, Monty . . . Monty . . . why . . . why?

MONTY *(annoyed):* Why what?

JANIE *(surprised):* What did you say? . . . What did you mean by that?

> *Silence except for a tinny sounding radio playing the Beatles off somewheres.*

Monty . . . please . . . what did you mean? I don't understand . . .

MONTY *(accusing):* You understand, Janie . . . You've always understood, Miss Janie.

Monty hasn't called her by her special name, "Miss Janie," in years. He took her simply because he wanted her—he declares—and he stalks her again. He upsets her by calling her a "whining white bitch," insists that she's always known that some day their relationship would come to this. He arouses her again, though she begs him not to.

The lights change and there are slides and sounds of a college campus; a slide of Monty and Janie as 1950s collegians.

> *The slide holds for a moment, then the light comes up on Monty and Janie as they play out the scene.*

JANIE: Hello. You're in my Creative Writing class, aren't you?

MONTY: Yeah . . . I think so.

JANIE: I loved the poetry you read today.

MONTY: Thanks.

JANIE: But it was so bitter.

MONTY: Oh.

JANIE: Do you call that Black poetry?

MONTY: Hey . . . my name's Monty.

JANIE: Mine's Janie.

MONTY: Please to meet'cha, Miss Janie.

JANIE *(surprised):* What did you say?

MONTY: What did ya think I said?

JANIE *(curious):* Why did you say that?

MONTY: Oh, just a little joke of mine, I guess.

JANIE *(confused):* You guess? . . . But I don't think I . . .

MONTY: Let's just keep it between ourselves, huh?

JANIE *(thoughtful):* If you say so . . . But I don't think I understand you very well.

Monty insists on calling Janie "Miss" but asks her to a party at his place this evening. Janie is somewhat coy about coming but finally accepts, hoping that Monty will read some poetry that is a little less despairing, a little less scary.

The lights come up in Monty's apartment, as party music is heard. Monty is in the kitchen attending to last-minute details, while his roommates, Len and Rick, are indulging in *"their daily ritual of debate."* Both are light-skinned blacks in their early 20s. Len *"wears Levis and sandals; he has a large, uncombed 'natural.' Rick wears a black suit, white shirt, white bow tie and white bucks. His head is shaven and glistens. He wears eye glasses that glisten also."*

Rick is animated in his argument, referring to the white man as the "devil" who has kept the black man in slavery for 400 years; calls Len "negro" meant as a deprecatory expression, and insists that he wants "self-determinism" and 10 per cent of the U.S. land area in addition to "freedom, justice and equality."

The doorbell rings, and Rick goes to answer it; it's Janie, wearing dark glasses. Rick believes she must have the wrong address and slams the door in her face. Monty goes to let Janie in. She's nervous, but Monty pulls her inside. Rick greets Janie coldly, Len greets her warmly. Janie disappears into the kitchen with Monty to make the avocado dip.

Rick calls Janie a "devil lady." Len reminds him he knew this was going to be a mixed gathering and challenges him to leave if he doesn't like it. Rick refuses to accept the situation, and at the same time he refuses to leave.

LEN: But you not gonna be draggin' the party, are ya, man?

RICK: Me a drag? On the contrary, my brother. There would be little or no party if it wasn't for me. Have the times of your young lives. I just simply don't have to accept the validity of this scene, that's all.

LEN: And why not, man?

RICK: Because it's phony, irrelevant and it comes straight out of some of you so-called negroes' fantasy bags.

LEN: Awww, Rick, man. Just listen to that . . . You are goin'a be a big drag tonight.

RICK: Relax, brother Len. I'm here . . . naturally. I'm in the room. You'all got your scene goin'. Swell. I just ain't gonna deal with it like I'm a part of it. I'm checkin' yawhl out . . . dig?

LEN: Aww, you jive turkey. Monty and I are just lookin' for some good times. We don't want to get into all that Black crap tonight . . .

Janie comes in, wearing an apron and passing the guacamole. Impolitely, Rick informs her he won't eat anything she's touched. Rick tries to anger Janie by insulting her because of her whiteness, but Janie keeps cool. Monty comes in. Rick persists in putting Janie in the position of an enemy, a member of what he calls the Zionist Youth Conspiracy. This makes Janie laugh—she is of German extraction, not Jewish.

Monty answers the doorbell. It's Peggy—black, in her early 20s, *"speaks in an affected manner to conceal her Southern background. Tender. Sensitive . . . . . She wears a sweater and Levis. Her hair is cut short in a boyish Afro; she wears glasses."* Peggy is somewhat taken aback by Janie's presence here, but she swallows it with a pinch of sarscasm. She has brought over some of her own poetry to read. Monty and Len go to the kitchen. Rick and Peggy greet each other warmly, ignoring Janie.

PEGGY: Haven't seen you in a month of gospel bird days, brother.

RICK: Just tryin' to be Black here in the white wilderness of North America, sister.

> Rick and Peggy embrace and give an approximation of a traditional African greeting.

It's sure good to see your Black self here, sister.

PEGGY: It's good to have my Black self here, brother. But who's this pale thing on the couch belong to?

JANIE (on couch; apprehensive): Did you two say something? are you speaking about me?

RICK: You'll have to get Monty to explain this beast to you, Sister Peg. If I had my way I'd po' gasoline on the blonde, brown-eyed devil and watch it burn.

JANIE *(stands):* Oh, I wish you all wouldn't talk like that. You have such a strange sense of humor. I guess I just have to learn to become hep.

PEGGY *(with raised eyebrows):* Hep?

> *Janie takes off the apron and goes behind Peggy and tries to tie it on her.*

JANIE: Here . . . Peggy . . . maybe you'd like to help out Monty some. I'm not very good in the kitchen.

PEGGY *(pushes Janie away):* Hey, woman . . . Why don't you be cool?

Monty and Len come back from the kitchen, as the doorbell rings again. Len opens the door to Lonnie *("White. Late 20s. Hides an uneasiness behind a super-cool pose")* and Sharon *("White. Brunette. Pretty. A California lotus-eater. Early 20s").* Peggy reacts momentarily against the arrival of two more whites. Rick is concerned about the gumbo Monty's preparing. Monty assures him there's none of Rick's despised pork in it.

Sharon and Lonnie aren't together, it turns out—Sharon is Len's guest and Lonnie is Janie's "ole man, kinda" and was invited by her. Rick continues speaking out against the evils of pork. Monty can barely hide his annoyance at Lonnie's presence. Len and Sharon are locked in private conversation. Lonnie is cool.

The doorbell rings again. It's Flossy, a black sister in her early 20s, *"a woman of the streets but not a whore,"* eager for a party. She greets Monty warmly, kissing him. Meanwhile, Lonnie is trying to establish his credentials as an insider—he's a jazz musician who plays the horn in a combo.

RICK: We are in the time of the fall of America. We are witnesses to the end.

> *Music plays and some of the couples are in a semi-dance movement. The lights change in color and depth, and the shadows deepen as the room takes on a surreal quality.*

LONNIE: I always did say spades really knew how to party.

MONTY: Hey, man. Check yourself with that spade crap.

JANIE: Oh, Monty . . . he didn't mean nothin'.

RICK *(to Lonnie):* Say devil . . . how did you ever learn how to play Black music?

LONNIE: You mean jazz, man.

LEN: That's what the brother said, man.

SHARON: Len, you're not going to start anything, are ya?

LONNIE: I just went to school . . . and learned a little and started playin', man.

RICK: He went to school to learn how to play our music. Check that out, brothers.

FLOSSY: I'm scarfish as a bear. Where's the grease, honey?

MONTY: In the kitchen, baby. It should be ready by now. Hey, everybody . . . food's on.

RICK: I never knew Germans could play jazz.

LONNIE: Maybe Germans can't, man, but I'm Jewish.

Rick tries to make something heavy out of Lonnie and Janie as a German-Jewish pair, but they refuse to be drawn into a discussion about it. The way Rick sees it, "Jews are fraternizing and lying down with their executioners and exterminators. Woe woe woe . . . the last days of civilization are at hand."

The lights deepen even more. Through the door comes Mort Silberstein, *"a post-beatnik mythic figure . . . . . wears a greasy vest, a black bowler hat, baggy grey tweed pants, red suspenders, white sneakers and a short-sleeved denim shirt . . . . . He has on dark glasses and affects an unkempt beard."*

Mort Silberstein dances a rock horah and passes out marijuana cigarettes. Blacks and whites seem to drift into separate groups. Then the characters are singled out in turn by a colored spotlight while they express what's on their minds. After each monologue there is to be a scene, or encounter, or exchange between the speaker and other characters in which the time and place is flexible, often flashing forward from the party into future times and places.

Monty is the first to "give his rap" in the spotlight. He boasts that he's merely using Janie (though she may perhaps believe she's using him). In Monty's opinion, she's a tease who's only pretending to be interested in black poetry: "Tells me she loves my mind. Haaa . . . I wouldn't have much of a mind if I believed her. She came to my party, the one where I invited her, and told her corny little boy friend where she'd be. Who does she think she is? She can't make a fool out of me. She's mine even if she doesn't know it yet. And I'm gonna take her when I'm ready. And the time's right. That's right, get her. Take her, get her, have her . . . whatever I gotta do. I dig her blonde lookin' self. And I don't care how long it takes to get her. I got all the time in the world. 'Cause the world is what you make it."

Mort steps into the spotlight with Monty and begs him to pay $10 more than the usual price for a lid. Mort needs the extra money, he says, to attend Civil Rights rallies of Martin Luther King and Malcolm X; Mort figures Monty practically owes him the extra money.

The lights go down on the two men and come up on Janie smoking her joint. She wants Monty as a friend because he's sensitive and talented. Lonnie is just a bad habit she wants to break, "So it isn't Lonnie that keeps me from letting Monty have his way with me. Nor is it because Monty's black and I'm white. Gee . . . I think colored people are neat. And I've made it with black guys before. And I guess I'll do it some more. But not with Monty. He's a friend. A lifelong friend, I hope. And I know that men and women more often than not sacrifice their friendship when they become lovers. So I'll be true to Monty. To keep our friendship alive. And perhaps our relationship will mature into the purest of loves one day. An ideal black/white love. Like sweet grapes change with age and care into a distinctive bouquet upon choice, rare wines."

Monty steps into the light with Janie, who's appealing to him for help. She has no one else to turn to or even talk to; she needs an abortion. She and Lonnie have broken up, and besides she's at U.C.L.A. now and it would be very awkward to have the baby, both for herself and for her family.

Monty agrees to help, to drive her down to Tijuana or somewhere else and then put her up at his place afterwards (he now has his own pad, without roommates).

MONTY: . . . . . You can even pretend that you're my woman.

JANIE: You're such a good friend, Monty.

MONTY *(serious):* You know I've always loved you, Janie.

JANIE *(places her fingers across his lips):* Shhssss . . . Monty . . . please . . . don't say things that we'll both regret later.

MONTY: Why does it have to be this way between us, Janie?

JANIE: I don't know. It's just that I think of you as somebody special for me. And I refuse to spoil that secret, special feeling.

MONTY: You're wrong, you know, Miss Janie.

On top of everything else, Janie is broke, and Monty agrees to advance her the money for the trip. She confesses she's beginning to like his pet name for her— "Miss Janie". Monty picks her up and carries her off.

The spotlight comes up on Peggy. Peggy remembers how one day Monty took Peggy to the courthouse and married her, with Len as best man. Peggy really loved Monty—and still does—but she knows he has never given himself completely to any woman, not even to Janie. Peggy remembers their troubled marriage, their child which they put up for adoption, all the details of their "heavy trip" which was nevertheless worth it because "loneliness is a fatal disease . . . . . And you know . . . even the pain was sweet through the bitter."

Flossy joins Peggy, trying to console her by telling her that no man is worth her suffering. What Peggy resents most is the intrusion of white people into their lives and emotions—she knows because she solaced herself by marrying a white man after she broke with Monty. Peggy is also aware that Flossy had a thing going with Monty. Flossy admits: "Well, you know that my thing is making it with my friend-girl's ole men, honey."

The light comes up on Monty and Janie. Janie has come to visit Monty's and Peggy's home in San Francisco. Flossy has come in to keep Monty company while Peggy is at work. Monty begins to make love to Flossy in spite of Janie's presence. Janie voices her disappointment at not finding the old, easy friendship of school days.

JANIE: . . . . . I didn't know you had someone besides me . . . somebody real . . . somebody black and sensual as the night who would blot out my pale image like a cloud covering a dim, far constellation.

Lights down on Janie and Monty. Flossy returns to Peggy's area.

FLOSSY: That Monty was a no-good nigger. He'd sit that ole white girl in one room and have her read his poetry and stuff while he screwed me until my tongue hung out in the next room. Chile . . . it was a scream. With those thin walls you could hear a roach pee on a soda cracker . . . and the stains on the couch. What did you have in your head when you saw that, girl?

PEGGY: Ha ha . . . I was ignorant. I thought that the cats kept gettin' up there and were messin' around.

FLOSSY: Ooeeee . . . and the way Monty would sock it to me, girl, that lil white broad musta thought we were tearin' down the house with all that humpin'. I knew she'd be gettin' hot as a ten cent pistol cause when we'd come out she'd turn all red lookin' and her eyes would be waterin'.

PEGGY: Yeah . . . and when I got home from work at midnight everybody would still be lookin' funny. Smiling secretly to yourselves. Damn, I was dumb. I thought it was because of the wine and pot.

FLOSSY: Nigger men ain't no good, Peggy. We sisters should start takin' those niggers' heads off behind the stuff they be pullin' on us.

PEGGY: Maybe so . . . maybe so . . . at least I could agree with you at one time. When I cared about men. But I'm a liberated lesbian now. See, I had to learn to cope with the world the best way I could. Sister power is where it's at!

FLOSSY: Right on!

PEGGY *(tender)*: You're still my friend, ain't you, Flossy?

> *The two women embrace and kiss passionately, then walk off into the shadows hand-in-hand.*

Lights up on Lonnie, who confides that in those times with Janie they tended to feed on each other's weaknesses instead of backing each other up. Janie was too obsessed with the idea of going to college to pay Lonnie the kind of attention he wanted. Lonnie knows he's not a big-time musician but he makes out well enough with the engagements he's able to get in and around Los Angeles: "And being around spades all the time in the music business I gets to know them, you see. They okay, if they keep their distance and know their place. Some of my best friends . . . you know? But you got to give them dudes credit. They got lots of the broads psyched out. They got a whole super stud/super spade thing goin' for them."

Janie had three abortions while she and Lonnie were together, and Lonnie felt guilty about them: "I told her that she was killing our future. She said she was afraid of the future. And she was never happy with me after that." Lonnie dropped her when she became a drag. He then took up a religion called Baha'i World Faith.

Rick joins Lonnie in the spotlight. Rick again calls Lonnie a devil, and Lonnie resents it, accusing Rick of having it in for everybody. Rick insists that Israel is soon to fall and the black man's time to rule the world has come. "Allah will sweep you white devils into the sea," Rick informs Lonnie humorlessly. Lonnie, disgusted with this kind of talk, departs, leaving Rick alone and believing that he has won some kind of small victory.

The lights change, and it's now Len's turn to step into the spotlight and declare himself. Len considers himself a great teacher who inspired both Monty and Rick to take the paths they've chosen, firing Rick up by telling him about black nationalism, starting him on a revolutionary career which is destined to rise to pinnacles in the 1960s and then subside. "Don't put down nationalism," Len advises. It's the flame that lit the fire in Rick's "ambitious heart" and it's "the stuff that fuels revolutions. Agreed? . . . One can even say that the Zionists are the nationalists of Israel, couldn't one? And that Al-Fatah and other Arab terrorist organizations are the nationalists of Occupied Palestine. Nationalism translated means national liberation, wherever that nation stands. But these are arguments that will take too long to deal with. Tonight you are looking into some of the makings of the sixties . . . which, of course, went to make the seventies.

Just think . . . at this moment in our story, the Kennedys have still to be disposed of, Malcolm X hasn't passed from the scene, Watts has to happen, Martin Luther King Jr. must go to the mountain . . . never to return. . . . ."

Len ends his diatribe with "Remember, more political and cultural phenomena came out of Southern California in the mid-century than Richard Nixon and Walt Disney."

Sharon joins Len in the spotlight. Len tells her he is an intellectual, not a revolutionary, he can try conclusions with any fanatic or radical without letting his feelings get involved. Sharon's revolt was an emotional one, she tells Len; she doesn't want him to think of her as a tramp, but in her teens she gave herself to more than 70 men before she stopped counting. Len assures her it's nothing to feel guilty about, it was just part of the times.

Len comforts Sharon and then moves away as Sharon stays in the spotlight and tells how she and Len were married at a dull church wedding with family and friends in dutiful attendance. Len and Sharon settled into a flat near City College where Len was taking five years to complete a two-year course. They gave a million parties, had lots of fun and tried to get used to each other. Sharon remembers that "It was pretty terrible for a while. We even broke up a number of times. But that's history now. We're back together and are making it. We have a pretty large son now who is spoiled bad as hell and looks just like Len. Len's got his own business now. I kid him about his Marxist days now that he's a working capitalist but he reminds me that he's really an intellectual. We're one of the lucky couples. We made it. But it took a lot of doing. And let me tell you, it's not easy being married to a Blackman . . . even if he's an intellectual or not. But we're making it."

Sharon is joined by Mort Silberstein, who calls her "the girl who lays all the spades in town then adds racial suicide to cultural injury by marrying one." Sharon feels insulted. Mort accuses her of betraying her Jewish heritage. Sharon in turn accuses Mort of living with a girl from Germany instead of a Jewish girl, the kind he could marry and start a family with. Mort wants no part of a girl who would tie him down or put him to work supporting her. As for Janie—who has enough money of her own to support Mort—she's too middle-class for his taste, and a goy as well. The German Mort is living with is at least a Marxist.

Sharon concludes: "You ex-Hasidic Jews are all nuts. Leave me alone, will ya? I have a baby who is half Black. That's the only reality I can deal with now. I don't care who killed Jesus."

Sharon and Mort disappear as the lights come up and it's Flossy's turn to comment: "Some party, heh? I come to all of Monty's parties. Some are better than this one . . . and some are worse. I don't live around here. Hardly no black people do except the ones you see here tonight. That's why it's such an integrated scene. Mostly college dudes and broads. Sure is phony, huh? But I like Monty . . . . ."

Monty and Flossy make it together once in a while, and Monty doesn't look down on Flossy because she's not an intellectual and doesn't know the big words. Monty may turn out O.K., Flossy believes, if he doesn't get too involved with white women.

Janie joins Flossy and is at once put down for being white. Janie indicates to

Flossy that she doesn't consider herself a rival for Monty's physical attentions. Flossie relents a bit and decides to teach Janie a thing or two. She takes Janie into the corner as the light comes up on Rick.

Rick criticizes his roommates' attachment to white girls. They are all in a war, Rick declares, and his friends are loving the enemy. Rick decides he wants to get out of this Babylon, this group, as soon as the party's over and he can hitch a ride downtown.

Peggy comes into the light and offers Rick a ride. He accepts, but he can't resist lecturing her about her two marriages, one to a black man (Monty) and one to a white man. He accuses her of attending wine-and-pot parties to impress white people, who've turned Peggy into a sort of a freak.

Peggy denies this: "No, Rick. Don't distort things so much. We didn't party to impress white girls. Or anybody. They were just there, that's all. And we wanted them there. The girls . . . and the boys. Our heads were into that then. It was the thing to do. We believed in America. The whole trip. And America was boring and we were young. We were just thinking that that was the best way to have a good time . . . . ."

Rick keeps at her.

RICK: But to have this Western madhouse of North America drive you into becoming a freak, sister.

PEGGY: Freak! You call me a freak? Well look what happened to you, Rick. You became something called a Cultural Nationalist. Hahh! In fact, you thought you invented it. And when the media pumped your head full of your own bull you wigged out on a Section Eight trip. What was it now? . . . Torturing young Black women? Freaking out? Oh, I know . . . or at least what I heard . . . you were under stress and had been keeping your thing together with speed cause those other comic opera political clowns . . . The Big Black Cats . . . were on your case after the big-shoot-out and assassination out at U.C.L.A. . . .

RICK: Hey! Hey! . . . you got it all wrong and backwards. You don't know what you're talkin' about, sister. In fact, you are incorrect! So why don't you just keep quiet about all that? It ain't even happened yet. So be cool.

PEGGY: But you haven't let me tell all of your future yet, brother Rick.

RICK: I already know my future. It is going to be glorious!

PEGGY: If you think so, Rick. If you think so. But do you know what?

RICK: What's that, sister?

PEGGY: We all failed. Failed ourselves in that serious time known as the sixties. And by failing ourselves we failed in the test of the times. We had so much going for us . . . so much potential . . . Do you realize it, man? We were the youth of our times . . . And we blew it. Blew it completely. Look where it all ended. Look what happened?

They are looking out front at the audience.

We just turned out lookin' like a bunch of punks and freaks and fuck-offs.

RICK: It has been said: "That if one doesn't deal with reality then reality will certainly deal with them."

PEGGY: Amen.

RICK: But I am not allowing myself to be held to blame. I am not allowing myself to be other than glorious. History will vindicate me.

PEGGY: Hey, man . . . you know, you never left yesterday. You're confused like all of us. . . . .

Rick decides he doesn't want a ride after all, and Peggy decides to stay here, too, and begin her future with Monty by making love to him. Mort Silberstein steps into the spotlight, as the lights fade on the other two. Mort judges that this is the worst party of the decade, and it's the fault of "the creator of this mess" for mixing in so many disparate elements: "Jews, niggers, politics, Germans, time philosophy, memory, theme, sociology, past, drugs, history, sex, present, women, faggots, men, dikes, phonys, assholes." Mort doesn't want to try to sort it all out; he's just "a beat poet from the fifties" who is concerned only about the fix he wants and needs $10 for.

Monty comes in to tell Mort Silberstein he's going to drop him. If Mort keeps hanging around he'll get somebody killed.

MORT *(turns away):* Awww . . . you spades.
    Monty grabs Mort by the collar.
MONTY: If you say that again I'll crush your filthy nose.
MORT: See what I mean? See what I mean? It always comes to this with you guys. Shit, man! We lost people in Mississippi too, hero. Where were you at Kent State, huh, Freedom River? I been with you for a long time and on a long, long trip . . . from Scottsboro and back . . . and now you coppin' out with mashin' my nose and talkin' that Third World Black People's crap. The Arabs ain't Black, man? You ain't got no place in Palestine! You can't even go to Algiers no more! . . . And the Egyptians sold your mammy!
    Monty punches him. Mort begins to cry.
The whole goddamn world has gone and went fuckeroo . . . and I don't care. I'm sick and need a fix and I don't give a fuck no more about nothin'. Kiss my Lower East Side ass, blackie.
MONTY *(shouting):* I don't want to be a whiteman, do you hear me, Mort Silberstein? I don't want to be a token Jew even. I'm me. You understand? It's taken a long time but I know that now.
MORT *(screaming):* All I know is that I am a Zionist junkie . . . and I don't give a shit for fertilizer . . . but what are you still gettin' your rocks off a blonde meat for and still talkin' that Black shit!
MONTY: Shut up! Shut up your goddamn mouth before I kill ya.
MORT *(quieter, serious):* You can't kill me any more than you can kill the last century. I'm in your head, nigger, like your nightmares.
MONTY *(scared):* No! Nothin's in my head except Congo drums and Freeway sounds and the A train bearing down on 125th Street.
    They wrestle about the stage. The other party members move about as if sleepwalking.

Monty and Mort Silberstein shout socio-political catchwords at each other like curses. Monty hits and hits again at Mort until Mort is unconscious. The others at the party come to life, as though after a dream brought on by a bad drug trip.

Lonnie and Peggy and then Len and Sharon leave the party as couples.

Flossy kisses Monty goodbye and Rick decides to go along with her. Monty comments, "This is the beginning of the sixties . . . but it seems like forever. And I'm so goddamn tired already. We got a long way to go, ain't we?" Rick agrees, and he and Flossy oblige Monty by dragging out the inert form of Mort Silberstein as they leave.

Janie comes out of the kitchen wearing dark glasses and tells Monty again that it's hard to believe that after all these years of friendship he would suddenly turn and rape her. Monty feels that he never really had the chance before, even though everybody has always thought Janie was an easy mark for Monty. The contrary has been the case. They've been good, true friends, and something in that friendship is lost in the rape.

Monty begins to unbutton Janie's clothes.

MONTY: . . . . . If our signs were compatible I'd probably have tried to marry you.

JANIE: Oh, no, you've always been too color conscious.

MONTY: Yeah . . . you're right.

JANIE: Remember the friend we had who hanged herself?

MONTY: Sure. How can I forget? We were a couple of her closest friends, or so we thought.

JANIE: She just went up on Mount Tamaipais and tied a rope to a tree branch and swung off.

MONTY: Are you going to scream and fight me, Miss Janie?

JANIE: I know you too well, don't I, Monty? I'd feel so icky doing something like that.

    The lights dim. He fully undressed her.

MONTY: I never wanted anyone as much as I have wanted you.

JANIE: Don't tell me what you tell all the others.

MONTY: You . . . I'm going to enjoy this very, very much.

JANIE: She just put the noose over her head and felt her spirit dance away.

    Monty pushes her back on the couch as he tears the last of her clothes away and the lights go down to blackness. Curtain.

THE NATIONAL HEALTH

A Play in Two Acts

BY PETER NICHOLS

Cast and credits appear on page 322

PETER NICHOLS was born in Bristol, England, in 1927 and made early ac-
quaintance with the stage assisting his mother, a contralto, in concert performances.
His father was a salesman. Nichols was educated at Bristol Grammar School and
performed his military service in the Far East. He studied at the Bristol Old Vic
School and worked for five years as an actor in repertory in various English cities.
He later trained as a teacher. While teaching at a London primary school in 1959,
Nichols wrote his first play, Walk on the Grass, *which shared a prize in a BBC*
competition and was produced on TV. Thirteen of his TV plays have reached
production, including The Hooded Terror, *which was later done in a stage version*
by the Bristol Old Vic. On the large screen, Nichols is the author of Catch Us if
You Can *and co-author of* Georgy Girl.

Nichols's first West End and Broadway play, A Day in the Death of Joe Egg,
was first produced by the Glasgow Citizens' Theater and was subsequently brought
to London where it won an award as the best new play of 1967. It was produced
on Broadway February 1, 1968 for 154 performances and was named a Best Play
of its season. Soon afterward it was made into a motion picture. Nichols's second
play was The National Health, *first presented by the National Theater and winning*
him the Evening Standard award for the best London play of 1969; and now, in
its American production on Broadway via the Long Wharf Theater in New Haven,
his second Best Play citation. Nichols's third play was Forget-Me-Not Lane,
produced in London in the 1971 season and in America at the Long Wharf Theater
and the Mark Taper Forum in Los Angeles, with Arvin Brown directing both

productions. A new Nichols playscript, The Freeway, *was produced in London this season, as was his* Harding's Luck, *a stage adaptation of a novel. Nichols is married with four children and lives in London.*

Time: The present

Place: The men's ward of a British hospital

ACT I

Scene 1

SYNOPSIS: The ward is dimly lit, but dawn is breaking and the light grows as Cleo Norton, a West Indian Staff Nurse, checks various patients, one seriously ill and being drip-fed, one crying out in his sleep, one groaning, another snoring. Ash, the patient in Bed 21, gets up and starts rummaging in his locker. Tyler— another patient with both legs amputated—comes on in a wheelchair. They greet each other and the Staff Nurse. This wakens another patient, Foster, Bed 22.

FOSTER: Morning.
ASH: Good morning to you, friend.
FOSTER: He likes to make a row.
ASH: Who's that?
FOSTER: Whosit—just been through—
ASH: Tyler.
FOSTER: What a voice.
ASH: Wonderful spirit, though, considering—
FOSTER: Oh, yes.
> *Ash stands checking his gear. Foster glances round, sees that Bed 23 is empty.*
Where's Mr. Lucas then?
ASH: Of course, you didn't hear. You get a wonderful sleep.
FOSTER: I do, yes.
ASH: Very enviable. He went in the night.
FOSTER: Transferred. In that condition? Never.
ASH *(quietly):* Passed on. First I knew was the screens going round, then the resuscitation unit and the heart-machine . . . quite a pantomime but . . . n.b.g. . . . I regret to say.
FOSTER: I'm blowed.
ASH: The orderly cleaned him and wheeled him off . . .
FOSTER: I suppose it was a blessing.
ASH: A happy release, yes. I must find myself a basin before the headlong rush of the Gadarene swine.

Ash goes off, and Staff Nurse Norton comes on with a trolley of wash bowls. Another patient, Ken, is heard coughing offstage. Ken wanders through the ward smoking a cigarette. Rees, an old man in Bed 24, wakes up. He is a medical doctor as well as a patient, and he offers a comment on Ken.

REES: He smokes too much, that boy.
FOSTER: Morning, Doctor.
REES: Killed this fellow too, the cough.
FOSTER: Mister Lucas?
REES: Smoked too much.
FOSTER: With a chest like his, yes.
REES: Sixty-five, you know, that's all he was. I'm eighty-two, but I could have knocked spots off him.
FOSTER: I hope I'll be as fit as you at eighty-two.
REES: No, he's dead. He died last night.
FOSTER (louder): I say if I'm as fit as you at eighty, I shan't complain.
REES: Eighty-*two*.
FOSTER: Ah!
> *Rees leans back. Mackie wakes in Bed 26. He groans and Foster looks at him.*

Cheer up, sir, you're still alive.
MACKIE: So I see. More's the pity.
FOSTER: But Lucas has gone. That should please you.
MACKIE: A step in the right direction.
> *Rees and Foster laugh. Rees leans back again. Foster lies back.*

Scene 2

As the light grows, the patients occupy themselves with reading, listening to the radio by means of earphones, etc. Sweet, "*a plump English nurse wearing glasses,*" comes in and screens off Bed 23. A new patient, Loach, wanders in, is given pajamas and is directed to Bed 23 to change into them.

Ash is weaving a basket to occupy his time. Nurse Lake, a West Indian like the Staff Nurse, comes in wheeling a laundry cart to strip Ken's bed—Ken, 19, has been cured of multiple fractures and is being discharged.

FOSTER: Doing a spot of work on your basket?
ASH: I hope I never see another basket, to be quite frank.
> *An old woman in a flowered dress and white hat comes on and goes to Mackie's bed.*

OLD WOMAN: Good morning, I have a message for you. It's that God gave his only begotten Son that whosoever believeth in Him should not perish but have everlasting life.
MACKIE: He's welcome to it.
OLD WOMAN: Isn't it wonderful news? The best ever. There is no death.

MACKIE: I'm dying.
OLD WOMAN: Dying only to live.

The old woman goes from bed to bed, delivering her message and dropping a card off to each patient. Rees believes her message is about a taxi sent by his wife to take him home. Foster humors her, up to a point.

Loach comes out from behind his screens, changed into pajamas and carrying his clothes. The old woman wanders off. Rees, still hallucinating a taxi waiting to take him home, believes Loach is bringing him his clothes and tries to take them from him. Sweet comes in and subdues Rees, reminding the old man that he's a patient now, not a doctor.

The screens are removed from Loach's bed. Sweet takes Loach's clothes when she exits, also taking a full ash tray from the top of the ward's stove in passing.

Ash, still working on his basket, briefs the new patient as to the others in the ward. Rees, it seems, is the victim of a stroke, sometimes thinking clearly and sometimes in the grip of his taxi delusion.

ASH: In the corner, Mister Flagg: bladder trouble and complications. He was in theater yesterday. I find, if they keep you in the end beds, you can prepare to meet your maker.
LOACH: That end?
ASH: Where they can reach you easily.
LOACH: I'm only third from the end.
ASH: We all start *off* near the end. Under observation. But we slowly work our way along to the furthest window by the balcony.
LOACH: Long as we know.
ASH: That bed just happened to fall vacant this morning.
      Sweet crosses from right to left, returning emptied ash tray to stove on the way.
Next to you on the other side Desmond Foster, coronary. Young for that, only forty. Then me, Mervyn Ash, tummy ulcer.
      Offers his hand. Loach shakes it.
Been here a fortnight so far. On a blotting paper diet. Tapioca, semolina, boiled fish, chicken. The merest glimpse of semolina makes me heave. Always has. Don't ask me why.
      Lake crosses left to right. Loach is paying no attention. He looks frightened. Ash observes him closely. Loach pulls himself together.
LOACH: Who's the old boy by the door?
ASH: Mister Mackie. They've pulled him through once or twice but he's lost the will.

Tyler, the double amputee, comes through the ward in his wheelchair. Lake comes in, orders Loach to go take a bath; Loach resents her peremptory manner because of her color: "No blackie pushes me around."

The young patient about to be discharged after recovering from a motor bike accident, Ken, comes into the ward to say goodbye. His girl has come to meet him with his bike. Sweet expects that Ken will be back soon—he's already been in twice with injuries from bike accidents. Ken scatters brash, disrespectful remarks around and takes his leave. Loach goes off to his bath. The religious old woman comes in and out, and the others turn their attention to their private diversions.

Scene 3

An orderly, Barnet, comes into the ward pushing an empty wheelchair and joshing the patients. He tries to get Rees up and walking a few steps, but Rees soon urinates in his trousers and starts to struggle in fright. Accidentally, Rees hits Ash with his flailing arm and knocks Ash down. With Sweet's help, Barnet gets Rees back into bed. Mackie reproaches them all for keeping Rees alive.

Scene 4

In a bluish light, screens are placed downstage center, as though forming the background for a small stage. Barnet adopts the part of narrator for the scene which follows, an episode of a hospital-drama soap opera the patients are watching on TV, presented as a play-within-the-play, a double pastiche of hospital reality and TV cliches.

In the TV drama, Staff Nurse Cleo Norton has felt the touch of young Dr. Neil Boyd's fingers. She is strongly attracted to him, and vice versa. Sweet and Lake come in with cloaks covering their nurses' uniforms, taking up the dialogue on cue from the narrator.

SWEET: . . . . . I feel so honored you finally managed to come to tea. You're certainly hard to get, Beth Lake—

LAKE: Being a nurse and a married woman isn't any rest cure, believe me, Joyce Sweet.

SWEET: Just give me the chance.

LAKE: Don't be in a hurry, Joyce. You're young yet.

NARRATOR: "Beth flashed her large, gleaming, widely-spaced teeth."

SWEET *(sits on bed):* Guess I'm just the marrying kind, Beth. Listen, Beth.

LAKE: What is it, Joyce?

SWEET: Your husband drives a bus full of white passengers and you look after a ward full of white patients—Don't you ever get hopping mad, Beth?

LAKE: Mad? No, Joyce. Why?

SWEET: But you think of the way some white people treat colored people, I wonder you're not tempted to turn off their saline solutions or something . . .

LAKE: Oh no, those people shouldn't be hated. They should be pitied. And understood.

SWEET: And when you think that the Health Service would pack up tomorrow if you all went back where you came from. I'm surprised you bother to stay, Beth, honestly!

Staff Nurse Cleo Norton comes in, now wearing her sexy uniform.

NARRATOR: "Cleo Norton breezed back into the room, her pert figure now trimly encased in the crisp uniform. She grinned a sunny welcome."
STAFF: Hullo, Joyce, hullo, Beth.

The three are gossiping, when Lake reveals that she saw Neil Boyd holding hands with Sister McPhee. This sends Staff Nurse Norton off in tears of jealousy. Lake kicks herself for having told, but then she remembers that the older Dr. Boyd is "bitterly opposed to mixed marriages" and young Dr. Neil Boyd is "unusually respectful" of his father. The two "stare at each other wordlessly" as the soap opera scene comes to an end, with the nurses resuming their ordinary appearances and orderlies striking the screens of the "set".

Scene 5

Ash is sitting in the armchair by the stove. All the patients' temperatures are being taken, and Lake and Sweet are attending to other necessary details of care.

Loach comes in looking for a cigarette; Ash supplies one, while telling Loach how depressed and bored he became on the outside with his drearily mechanical occupation as a clerk. Ash wanted to be a teacher but could get nowhere in this profession because of "A matter of preferment. Nepotism. Muggins here didn't give the secret handshake, never got tiddly in the right golf club. I didn't have the bishop's ear. You scratch my back, I'll scratch yours. I wasn't smarmey enough by half."

Ash shows Loach a picture of his son, now in a good school in Kent where he'll learn the right accent to break into the inner circle of influence. Ash warns Loach that it can get very tedious here in the hospital. Loach is sure that "They can't keep you in here. If you don't want to stay."

ASH: They'll fix you up, don't worry.
Sweet goes to Bed 26.
LOACH: Once they find out who I am. Once they can tell me that, I'll be out of here like a . . . what d'you call it . . . ?
ASH: Who you are?
LOACH: Once the police get on to that.
ASH: Who you *are?*
LOACH: Not that I want the police sticking their noses into my business. I didn't *ask* them, know what I mean?
Sweet eases Mackie.
MACKIE: Oh, hell! This is hell.
LOACH: But soon as they put me straight on that, I'm off. They try to get me to take the cure, they got another think coming.

Lake silences Loach by giving him a thermometer to put into his mouth. Ash's and Loach's temperatures are recorded by Lake and Ash gets into his bed as the scene ends.

Scene 6

The orderlies set up an armchair-and-fireplace area for another episode in the TV hospital drama. The older Dr. Boyd, sitting by the fire and cleaning his pipe, admonishes his son, young Dr. Neil Boyd, that black and white may mix in heaven, but not in North London. Sister McPhee, not Staff Nurse Norton, is the one for Neil (his father insists), but the younger Boyd announces that he means to marry Staff Nurse Norton, and he's told Sister McPhee as much. The elder Dr. Boyd, in a thick Scottish accent, reminds his son that it was his mother's dying wish that he marry Mary McPhee (his childhood sweetheart), "And now ye say ye're taking a wee colored girl to wife and . . . Mary is to be left on the shelf. At thirty. Have you thought of that, son? While you're so busy with your noble sentiments? Have you given a thought to puir wee bonnie Mary at the age of thirty? Have ye?"

Blackout, as the orderlies strike the armchair-fireplace setting.

Scene 7

At another dawn the patients are sleeping, some of them crying out in their sleep. As they wake, Rees is still hallucinating a taxi come to take him home. Mackie tells Rees there's no taxi, challenges him to "Die with dignity, for Christ's sake." Foster advises Rees to obey the nurses and do whatever he is told.

Flagg gets out of bed and takes a tentative step. Rees does the same, but falls. Foster and Ash go their assistance, getting both men back into bed, calming them down.

ASH: Snuggle down, now, leave it to the doctors.
REES: I *am* a doctor.
ASH: I know, yes.
REES: See the way I fell down? I didn't think . . . went to walk and . . . in my youth I ran like a rabbit . . . I was Area High Jump Champion. *(Cries.)*
ASH: There, there . . .
    Staff enters, crossing quickly with a tray and a hypodermic.
STAFF: All right?
ASH: Thank you, Staff . . .
REES: I beg your pardon. We're a highly emotional people. Ask anyone.
MACKIE: Sentimental and sloppy if you ask me.
ASH: We *didn't* ask you, Mister Mackie.
REES: Much obliged to you.
ASH: Sleep well.

Rees asks for a urine bottle, and Staff Nurse Norton attends to it. Loach, feeling dry and chilly, wants something to drink—preferably a drop of brandy. The Staff Nurse is offering Loach a sleeping draught and has just settled Rees down when she sees that Rees has just died. She turns off Rees's bedside light and exits. Barnet comes on in a travelling spotlight, as though on cue, wheeling a trolley covered with a white cloth.

BARNET *(whips off cloth, shows articles as he names):* Wash bowl, sponges, nail brush and file. Safety razor, scissors, tweezers. Cotton-wool, carbolic soap, shroud.

Covers it again.

Covered with a sheet, 'case one of the other patients catching a butcher's thinks it's all for him. So anyway I get the call. Ward such-and-such, bed so-and-so. Screens already up, of course.

Nurses have been putting screens round Rees's bed. now they strike Bed 24 and locker 24 from behind screens . . . . .

First you strip the patient down, then you wash him spotless with carbolic. Cut the nails—they can scag the shroud. Shave the face and trim the head. Comb what's left. Well, relatives don't want to find themselves mourning a scruff. Now the cotton-wool. Can anyone tell me what I do with that?

Reacts to woman in audience.

You're right, madam, absolutely right. Been making that answer all your life and for the first time it's accurate, not just vulgar. Yes. We have to close the apertures, the points that might evacuate bodily fluids. Miss one out, they'll raise Cain in the mortuary . . . . .

Barnet elaborates further details. An Oriental nurse comes in, and he pats her as she passes. Another vehicle—*"like a stretcher but with a looped hood"*—comes rolling on, and Barnet goes to meet it.

BARNET: . . . . . I must say this in all seriousness. Everything within reason is done to spare you the sight of an actual cadaver. This hooped cover, the screens. A screened passageway is put up all the way to the door, as with royalty going to the toilet.

Nurse enters, crosses, waiting for trolley.

You've heard about that, haven't you? If the monarch is unusually tall, attentive observers can spot the coronet bobbing up and down all the way to the velvet convenience.

Pushes hooped trolley upstage, Nurse catches it and takes it behind screens.

No, I don't wish to give the wrong impression. I'm sure I speak for my colleagues throughout the business when I say that we show every conceivable respect the deceased is due. We may hate the sight of them when they're living but once they've passed on, they get the full going-over. And I don't know about you, but I find that thought consoling. Whatever kind of shit is thrown at us during our long and dusty travail, we can at least feel confident that, after our final innings, as we make our way to that last great pavilion in the sky—no, come on—we shall be a credit to Britain's barbers, the National Health and—last but by no means least—our mothers. Thank you very much indeed.

Exit to music. Nurses remove screens. Rees's bed and locker have gone. Blackout.

Scene 8

Everyone in the ward is in bed but Ash. Sweet brings in the mail: a get-well card for Flagg, a letter to Ash from his son at school explaining why he can't visit his father just now. Ash asks to be moved up into the bed vacated by Ken, the motorcyclist who went home. Nurse Lake tells him to ask Sister.

Old Dr. Boyd comes in, making the rounds accompanied by Sister McPhee, an Indian student and a woman doctor named Bird. Dr. Boyd comments on Flagg's prostate problems, quizzing the other medical personnel as he goes along. He diagnoses Loach's trouble as "brewer's measles" (alcoholism); they've obtained Loach's name, told it to him and at least he now knows who he is. Dr. Boyd decides Loach needs as oesophagoscopy and schedules him for the operating theater the next day.

Dr. Boyd passes over Foster because Foster isn't one of "his". Now it is Ash's turn.

BOYD *(scans Ash's X-rays):* How are you in yourself?

ASH: Not so dusty, sir, but then I never feel what-you-call on top of the world. My doctor wrote down all my symptoms, then he said "By George, you're a mess on paper."

BOYD: Worry about yourself?

ASH: I get depressed. I abhor my work.

BOYD: Find a hobby. Brass rubbings, basket making. Take some interest.

> *Boyd presses on Ash's stomach. Ash cries out.*

Tell you what, your tummy's not much better. I want you in theater tomorrow, do a bit of crochetwork.

ASH: *Physically* I'm not too bad, sir.

BOYD: Take away a bit of your stomach. You'll learn to do without it.

ASH: I thought I was on the mend.

BOYD: Much the best.

> *Moves down. They follow.*

Mister's duodenal's failed to respond to a medical regimen. So what shall we do? Come on, come on, scream and hide our faces?

BIRD: Polya gastrectomy?

BOYD: At last. Of course he's a case, you can see that. Talk a gramophone to scrap by the look of him. Next, Sister?

> *Takes papers, glances at them, makes for the right.*

(As he goes.) Ah, morning, Mister. Bum any better?

> *Exit right with Bird, nurses, Sister and student. As Bird exits she drops her papers—Lake and Sweet pick them up and follow her off right.*

LOACH: You won't see me down no theater. Soon as they bring me in my clothes, I'll be off. They can't keep me here against my will.

ASH: I thought I was on the mend.

FOSTER: He'll fix you up. You trust him.

ASH *(crosses to armchair and sits):* Oh, he's a first-rate man, Mister Boyd. I'm taken aback, that's all—

LOACH: Is he a gen bloke, me old mate?
FOSTER: Harley Street.
LOACH: Go on—
FOSTER: We get the best here, don't you worry. All for the price of a stamp.
ASH: No moving towards the balcony now.

They discuss the pros and cons of smoking, while Ash can only think, "Three weeks of semolina down the drain." He gets into bed to conserve his strength. The nurses set screens around Beds 21 and 23 so that Ash and Loach can change into operating-room garb. Meanwhile, the other patients settle down to watch another "episode" in the continuing TV drama of young Dr. Neil Boyd and his romance with Staff Nurse Norton.

Scene 9

Neil and Staff Nurse Norton enter the Boyd home, represented again by the armchair and fireplace. Neil mixes Staff a drink. They've been to a concert and this is the first time Neil has brought her to his home (his father is in Edinburgh for a lecture).

With Barnet interpolating narration as in the previous "episode" of this play-within-a-play, Neil admits that his father doesn't approve of interracial romances, and "I can't risk doing anything that would upset him. He's too valuable to society." Staff is a bit jealous of Mary McPhee, but Neil, kissing her, assures her Mary is only a family friend.

Neil tries to make love to Staff, who refuses him her body because "I'll never do anything dirty before marriage."

Old Dr. Boyd enters unexpectedly, just as Neil experiences some kind of violent seizure of pain in his back, which he tries to conceal. The episode ends with the three staring at each other, as the lights go to black and the screens and living room props are taken off.

Scene 10

Barnet comes in with a trolley to shave Ash for surgery, commenting in a long monologue on some of the exotic emotional quirks of those in the healing profession. The nurses have moved Ash's bed and locker down toward the end of the row, not up toward the window, and now they move him to a trolley to be wheeled off.

Michael, an orderly, is coughing and smoking. Flagg is assisted to the armchair, carrying his drainage bottle. Sweet borrows a cigarette from Foster for Flagg, but when Loach asks for one it is refused him; he's booked for the operating room. Loach is fearful, but Foster reassures him he's only going to be examined. Loach signed some sort of permission form, and he's afraid of what may be in the unreadable fine print.

Loach is finally shifted to a trolley and wheeled out. Flagg is still smoking while Foster and Mackie watch and chat. Foster reminisces about Sunday picnics and visits to Hampton Court.

FOSTER: . . . . . I find a particular interest in the servants' quarters. I say to the wife, you'd have been here, love, a skivvy for life, and I'd have been one of an army of gardeners scything the lawn from dawn to dusk. But these lords are only holding on by our permission and when they've served their purpose, they'll be out. Not that I've anything against them personally but we're not living in the Dark Ages with Queen Victoria sitting in state. This is the twentieth century, d'you agree?

> *Eats orange.*

MACKIE: The armies of democracy on the move.

FOSTER: Pardon?

MACKIE: Columns of minibuses . . . moving up the motorways . . . from Hampton Court to Woburn Abbey . . . Woburn Abbey to Windermere . . .

FOSTER: Why should they have it all to theirselves?

MACKIE: . . . a world of lay-bys, drive-ins, pull-ups . . .

FOSTER: Better than when my Dad was a boy, never got his nose outside the street he—

MACKIE: You a socialist?

Foster is a socialist, yes, but not a communist—he doesn't want to do away with religion, for example, though he never goes to church except to look at the stained glass. Mackie agrees that socialism has brought them clean sheets to die in, but he wishes they wouldn't work so hard to keep him alive. He is in too much pain: he has terminal stomach cancer.

Barnet and Michael—still coughing a lot—bring Ash back to his new bed, unconscious and with drip and drain equipment. Mackie suspects that Ash has been brought back only to die. Sister notices Mackie's depression and offers him the services of a chaplain, which he refuses, remarking that "Jesus Christ lived in a largely unpopulated world" and might evaluate human life somewhat differently today.

MACKIE: If somebody doesn't let us die—or prevent others being born—there are going to be seventy million British by the turn of the century—

SISTER: I shall get you a sedative.

> *She goes off. Lake re-enters and tidies Bed 23.*

MACKIE: And thirty million cars . . . this scept'rd isle with its rivers poisoned . . . beaches fouled with oil . . . the sea choked with excrement . . . the polluted air alive with supersonic bangs . . . that what you want? The socialist Nirvana?

FOSTER: You're a whining Winnie, I know that.

MACKIE: But—abortion—euthanasia—birth control won't be enough. *(Flagg groans.)* . . . some government will have to have the guts to stop people coming in . . . filling the country—Enforced emigration too.

> *Points at Flagg. Lake looks and sees some blood in the urine.*

FOSTER: Nurse. The bottle.

MACKIE: Fill the empty spaces in Australia, Canada.

LAKE: Sister.

MACKIE: Manpower must be directed where it's needed . . .

SISTER *(re-enters, crosses to Flagg):* Better let him have a rest.

She and Lake help Flagg back to bed.

MACKIE: Break the power of the unions and make people do what they're told . . . close down the luxury trades, put a stop to gambling and vice . . . send the croupiers to work in penal colonies . . . get the striptease girls back to the farms . . .

> *Barnet and Michael bring Loach up the front steps, with Sweet attending. Take him to Bed 23. Nurse re-enters, waits and clears trolley when Loach is lifted from it by Michael and Barnet.*

Because, you see, it's not only a question of the natural resources of the land . . . there's a spiritual cancer too.

BARNET: Dear oh dear! She sowing discontent again?

MACKIE: A nation doesn't grow great on material greed without a sense of duty . . . Churchill knew this, he got the best from us, inspired us with purpose . . . National Service turned boys into men . . . the world's finest youth club . . .

> *Slowly lights go down on the rest of the ward and only Mackie remains lit. In the darkness, Loach and Flagg are settled and Barnet, Sister Sweet, Nurse, Michael and Lake go off with trolley.*

. . . but now the Chatterley Set are destroying our moral fiber with liberalism . . . fornication . . . pederasty, drug-taking condoned by the church . . . remember the fall of the Roman Empire, as Mr. Carson of Woolwich Holdings was saying to me . . .

> *Lake comes on with a hypodermic. She cleans his arm. He doesn't notice her.*

Mixed marriages advocated on television . . . which God never intended . . . proved scientifically that some races are genetically inferior . . . no good sullying sound stock with an alien strain . . . jazz dancing and . . .

> *Lake injects a sedative.*

. . . factory farming . . . but first—let the old go . . . give us the gas chambers and we will finish the job . . .

> *Lake has gone off. A hand bell tinkles. Sister comes on ringing it, and all available nurses and orderlies bring on vases of flowers as the light grows to a warm summer evening.*

SISTER: Ready for visitors?

> *Sister looks at the effect. It satisfies her. She nods at the audience and goes off. It looks like a flower show. And the visitors come. Most of them go through the ward and out. Two women sit at Flagg and Foster's beds. Mackie sleeps. Lake comes on with a trolley of tea. Curtain.*

ACT II

Scene 1

The patients are sitting up in bed or, like Ash, sitting in one of the armchairs, reading. The nearby cries of a premature baby remind them all that the National Health watches over them from the cradle to the grave.

Loach has had two teeth out and now knows his wife's name as well as his own, though he takes little pleasure in remembering how she has always tried to make him stop drinking. Ash argues that he should stop, but Loach won't consider it. He used to drink for pleasure; now he drinks for medicine.

Flagg hobbles in, no longer wearing his drains but attended by Lake. Flagg has a note from his brother about a letter he's just received, mailed in 1943 but delayed for decades by the Post Office—which now wants Flagg's brother to reimburse it for the subsequent rise in the price of postage.

Loach reminisces about his service as a batman with the engineers in India and Africa. His educated countrymen looked down on him even out there, although "the British ought to stand together against the wogs. Perhaps if we had, we might still have the Empire, right? But it's like I say, these doctors just the same. They turn round and tell you to jack in smoking, half the time they're smoking more than what you or I do."

Flagg wants to know what's on TV today, learns its "Coronation Street" and not wrestling. Ash, exasperated, throws his half-finished basket downstairs. He exclaims against the unfairness of losing his job because of a mental breakdown his job caused. "I suppose what got me through was the thought of my boy, my adopted boy," Ash tells Loach. "My wife couldn't have children. We're separated now, it never went too swimmingly. I was awarded custody."

But the boy is going his own way now, Ash admits, leaving his father pretty much alone. Ash is now comforted only by his study of religion and his belief in reincarnation.

Foster joins the group, hobbling with a walking stick, with Lake assisting. Ash calls to someone to throw his basket back, and it is returned to him. Ash's stomach has recovered enough from the operation so that he's able to eat a boiled egg, and his bad case of eczema seems to be under control.

They chat, and Lake comes back, offering the urine bottle. Mackie refuses it and starts his complaining.

MACKIE: I drift off and nearly sleep and one of these happy days I shan't come back.

ASH: Now, now . . .

MACKIE: But someone's always calling me back for a cup of tea or . . . a bottle . . . an overdose of the right drug is what I want.

LOACH: Whining Winnie's off.

FOSTER: We want a lecture, we'll ask for one.

ASH: Try to count your blessings.

MACKIE: You count them. I'm too busy coping with the pain . . . they wouldn't kill a pig like this . . .

ASH: Human life and a pig's life—

MACKIE: I've no regard for life itself, only the quality of life . . . should be clinics where you could get your death as you get a library book—

FOSTER (sings): "Tell us the same old story."

MACKIE: The Eskimos let their old die in peace.

FOSTER: The Eskimos haven't got a health service.

Mackie continues his observations—"Too many rats in a cage will tear each other to pieces"—but the others successfully drown him out by singing the Gaumont British theme song in unison. All at once, Mackie begins to cry out in genuine pain, and Sister, Lake and Nurse come in to attend to him and take him to his bed.

Foster believes in making the best of things, no matter what; he isn't letting his bad heart get him down, he still means to enjoy outings with his wife and five children as best he can. It's different for Mackie, Ash observes; Mackie has the disease with the awful name: *cancer.*

FOSTER: But you look at Mr. Tyler. *(To Loach.)* Diabetic in the wheel chair. Nine times in here in the last two years and every time an amputation. First his toes, then his feet, then his legs—
LOACH: All right, me old mate.
ASH: Wonderful spirit!
FOSTER: There you are. Life and soul. And always busy with something useful.
ASH *(nodding):* Last few days he's been learning Mah Jong.
LOACH: Got to keep smiling.
ASH: But highly intelligent people can be more sensitive.
FOSTER: They've got no right to be.

Barnet and Lake come in to straighten up the ward and ready the patients for Matron's rounds.

Scene 2

Mackie is groaning. The ward is brightly lit as Sweet comes in, followed by Matron with Sister in attendance. Matron *"is regal, smiling, but wastes no time."*

MATRON *(to Mackie):* Good morning. How are you today?
    Mackie groans.
Keep smiling. Soon be out of here. *(To Ash.)* Good morning, how are you today?
ASH: Morning, Matron, not so dusty, thank you—
MATRON: That's the style—
ASH: When you consider half my tummy's been—
MATRON: Keep it up.
ASH: —taken away.
    Mackie groans. Everyone looks at him, except Matron.
MATRON *(to Flagg):* Good morning. How are you getting along?
FLAGG: Eh?
MATRON: Are they treating you well?
FLAGG: Not too bad.
MATRON: That's right.
FLAGG: Though I'd like to go to a toilet—you know—
MATRON: Sister—
FLAGG: —toilet with a decent chain.

MATRON: Get this patient a bedpan.
SISTER: Nurse Lake—
LAKE: Sister?
SISTER: Get Mr. Flagg a bedpan.
LAKE: Nurse Sweet—
MATRON: Good morning, how are you?
LAKE: Get Mr. Flagg a bedpan.
LOACH: Well, miss, I get these cramps—
MATRON *(looking at her watch):* Good.
LOACH: In my leg.
SWEET: Mister Barnet—
MATRON: Soon be out of here.
LOACH: I don't want the cure.
BARNET *(coming on):* Hallo?
SWEET: Bedpan for Mr. Flagg.
BARNET: Right.
> *Sweet exits.*
Morning, Matron.
MATRON: Good morning, how are you getting on?
FOSTER *(without removing earphones):* Lovely, Matron, everything's lovely—
> *Barnet has gone off.*
MATRON: That's what we like to hear, isn't it, Sister? Get well soon. We need the beds.
> *Goes off with Sister and Lake.*

Flagg protests that he doesn't need the bedpan, he meant only that he'd like to use a real toilet for a change, some time. But the attendants insist: if Matron says he needs a bedpan, he needs it. They go behind the screens to make him use it.

Dr. Bird comes in, checks Mackie, finds him very ill, orders screens for him and then a transfer to the terminal ward. Dr. Bird departs, dropping papers, with Sweet behind her picking them up. Sweet and Barnet wheel Mackie out on his bed.

Matron comes back on her way down the other side of the ward and orders the chairs arranged more neatly. Her orders are passed along like a chain reaction, as before. Sweet takes Mackie's locker out, as Matron describes how they are planning to redecorate the ward soon with all the most modern colors and equipment.

MATRON *(notices Mackie's bedspace):* Another one gone there, Sister?
SISTER: It looks like it.
MATRON: Good, good. Keep them moving.
> *Goes off left with nurses and Barnet. Flagg farts.*
LOACH: Dear, oh Lord!
ASH *(amused):* Musical evening.
FOSTER: Her Majesty gone?

LOACH: She's gone, yes.

ASH: Desmond, I've just this minute noticed something.

FOSTER: What?

ASH: I'm in the end bed.

> *They look. They see that this is true. They find nothing to say. Barnet comes dowstage. Spotlight finds him.*

BARNET: Running spot man? You wouldn't know a running spot if you had them all over you. At the end, Mr. Mackie's heart stopped three times and three times they brought him back. They were fetching the artificial respirator when it stopped again and some daring soul decided to call it a day. I'm sure I speak for all those who knew him in life when I say that he will be remembered as an evil-tempered, physically repulsive old man. But—now the pump's been allowed to pack up, the flesh has receded, that puffiness has gone, an altogether younger face has appeared. You can see how—once—someone might even have fancied him.

> *Looks at audience, then exits.*

Scene 3

The area downstage is brilliantly lit, and Dr. Boyd and Sister McPhee enter dressed for the operating room. This is yet another episode in the TV hospital drama of young Dr. Neil Boyd and dark-skinned Staff Nurse Cleo Norton.

As Dr. Boyd and Sister McPhee scrub up for the operation, it is revealed that Staff Nurse Norton is giving a kidney to save Dr. Neil's life—"Because her life wouldna be worth living without him," Sister remarks sententiously, and adds "I know how she feels." Dr. Boyd blames himself for not diagnosing his son's condition sooner because they had quarreled and weren't speaking: "I thought the odor of sanctity was in my nostrils and all the time it was the stench of racial prejudice."

Sister McPhee informs old Dr. Boyd that Neil doesn't love her, nor does she love Neil. Hinting broadly that age is no barrier to love, Sister McPhee makes Dr. Boyd understand it is *him* she loves (but for 30 years she has "never dared to hope").

Dr. Boyd realizes what a fool he has been, but Sister bolsters his ego by reminding him that he and he alone can save his son's life with a kidney operation. Sister helps Dr. Boyd get ready for the operating room with equipment that jumps out of a machine at the touch of a button, ready-sterilized. The scene ends with Dr. Boyd and Sister McPhee happy in the certain knowledge of their mutual devotion, music swelling, orderlies striking the soap-opera props and set.

Scene 4

A black orderly brings a game trolley into the ward and exits. Flagg and Ash get out of their beds, as Sweet comes on to encourage the others to move about as much as they can. Loach is getting tired of all the tests and the blood samples. Ash sets chairs at the trolley and sits down with Flagg, resuming a game of

Monopoly where it had been left off. Loach joins them.

Flagg likes to grow things; he used to plant trees for the Parks Department. Loach once worked for the Parks Department too, as a caterer.

Barnet comes in and tries to create some excitement by reminding Loach that he was once in prison, trying to get him to discuss prison life. But Loach doesn't oblige. The game is going against him and finally he gives up, much to Ash's concern. Ash is trying to encourage Loach to pull himself together generally: "Now come on. You promised me. What did you promise? That you'd summon up your courage and face the cure. Then, once you're better—and it won't take long, you're half way there already—then you'll come and lodge at my place and I shall help you to keep the pledge."

A West Indian chaplain dressed in Anglican vestments comes in looking for Mackie and is told he's too late. The chaplain joins the patients and sits, talking about his service in the hospital. Like the doctors and nurses he is overworked; too many details to attend to, too much muddled bureaucracy. The Old Woman comes into the ward with her Gospel message but departs at the sight of the chaplain. The chaplain likes to talk about England's chances in the cricket matches and at Wimbledon, but Flagg intrudes with the subject of capital punishment and its chances of being restored. People came to his street with some sort of petition about it.

FLAGG: I said: hanging's too good for them. They ought to be slowly tortured to death . . . any ruffian that has a go at a little girl or police constable . . . ought to be taken limb from limb, I said . . .

CHAPLAIN: I don't know that I could altogether agree with that. *(Smiles at Flagg.)* Not altogether.

ASH: Nor I. I don't believe in cruelty.

CHAPLAIN: Quite.

ASH: They should be strung up. It's quick and merciful.

CHAPLAIN: So many different sides to every question. Well—*(Rises.)*—I must love you and leave you. At least a dozen bods in this ward marked C. of E. Most of them turn out to be Greek Orthodox, I daresay. *(Looks at card.)* Mister, Mackie, yes. Mister Ash—wasn't it?

ASH: Yes, Chaplain.

CHAPLAIN: And you're Mister—

LOACH: Loach.

FLAGG: Flagg.

CHAPLAIN *(ticking names):* Wonderful. Now. Mister Foster—

ASH: Having forty winks.

CHAPLAIN: Better have a word.

ASH: Let me bring you a chair. You're not allowed to sit on the bed.

Chaplain and Ash go to Foster's bed, Ash bringing an upright chair.

CHAPLAIN: Oh, yes, we don't want to break the rules. These nurses put the fear of *God* into me.

Laughs and sits as Ash returns to Monopoly trolley.

Come along, squire, wakey, wakey. Mister Foster . . .
> *Shakes Foster to wake him. Foster falls sideways, his head lolling over, the phones still on.*

The Chaplain rises and supports Foster's body, calling for the nurses. Sweet comes in and takes charge of the situation, ordering the games put away and the patients back to their beds.

Scene 5

Barnet places the screens around Foster and the nurses go to work on him, trying to revive him. Barnet advises the other patients to watch TV.

The lights change, and two operating tables are wheeled on, together with an abundance of equipment. It is another "scene" in the continuing drama of the Boyds and Sister McPhee. This is the operating room scene with Dr. Boyd performing a kidney transplant from Staff Nurse Norton to his son Neil, surrounded by a team, with Sister McPhee assisting. This time, however, there is no dialogue; and the reality of Foster's emergency distracts from the fiction, as equipment to treat cardiac arrest is brought on and Sweet, the Indian student, Lake and Dr. Bird attempt to save him. The wrench to operate the oxygen cylinder is missing from the resuscitation equipment—"Typical balls up," Barnet comments—and Lake goes to get it.

While they continue to work on Foster behind the screens and the patients try to concentrate on the TV drama, Barnet takes a microphone and provides a narration for the "kidney transplant" in the soap opera: "In the terrible loneliness of the operating theater, so many times she had stood beside him, this grizzled man with the strangely tender eyes, whose love she had never dared to crave." Barnet continues in this vein, as Dr. Boyd and Sister McPhee proceed with the fictional operation.

Back in reality, one of the screens falls away revealing Foster lying on the floor beside his bed and the medical staff working on him. Barnet comments: "All going as well as can be expected but not so nice for the other patients. Which is where the telly is a great step forward. Keep their minds off what's going on next door."

The team working on Foster finally slows down, then places his body back on the bed and begins to disperse, taking the equipment. The Old Woman comes in to deliver once again her message of everlasting life; Sweet and Michael have gone for the hooded trolley, which soon carries Foster off.

Meanwhile, in the TV show, *"Boyd raises his head to the anesthetist, who gives thumbs-up. The scrum parts to allow Boyd to emerge. Music triumphant. He goes to instruments trolley and removes gloves. McPhee takes and throws them on to tray. He removes his mask. The attendants are wheeling away the patients. As the instruments trolley is wheeled off, Sister takes Boyd's pipe from pocket and puts it into his mouth. Together they circle and he partners her in a pirouette. They dance off as the music ends."*

The Chaplain crosses Foster's name off his list and exits. Barnet is called downstairs for an accident case in Bed 7. Loach is called out for another blood test. An accident patient is wheeled through the ward: it's Ken, the cyclist, back after another crash. Now it is Ken's turn to receive the attentions of the resuscitation team.

Scene 6

Barnet comes in with an oxygen cylinder. It seems that Ken swerved to avoid a dog and caused a collision of buses that killed or injured 60 people—the accident ward is crammed full. Nurse Sweet comes in and informs Barnet that they've managed to pull Ken through again. They won't need the oxygen.

BARNET: He must have nine lives.
>*Doctors return from Ken's bedspace with their machines. Sweet smiles and goes toward right.*

Go on, run!

SWEET *(turns):* I beg your pardon?

BARNET: You're all of a flutter. Say you're not.

SWEET: Why should I be?

BARNET: After some of those noises used to come from the screens—

SWEET *(delighted):* I beg your pardon—?

BARNET: —when you were giving him a bed-bath.

SWEET: I didn't hear that remark.
>*Goes to help other nurses off right.*

BARNET: Now say there's nothing bent about the healing arts.
>*Turns to push his oxygen cylinder off.*

Scene 7

Ash wakes at dawn, gets out of bed, puts on his robe and starts to work on his basket.

>*Ken crawls in on all fours. His head is still bandaged and he wears gown and slippers. He hides from Ash then raises both fists and points his index fingers. He imitates gunfire.*

ASH: Now, Kenny, old son, what are you up to, eh?
>*Ken is now an idiot. His efforts at speech are incoherent but the others are used to his condition and talk over the noise.*

Come and sit by Uncle Mervyn . . . see what he's doing with his funny old basket. I bet you've never seen a basket that shape. No more have I.
>*Ken laughs at it. He puts it on his head.*

You could use it for that, I suppose, yes.
>*Laughs and takes it back. Ken goes to stove and begins shovelling coke into the grate.*

That's right. You like doing that, don't you? Not too much, though, it's warm today.

Ash obviously enjoys this new relationship with Ken—it makes him feel somewhat like a teacher again. Flagg comes in dressed in street clothes and carrying a case, waiting for an ambulance to take him home. He is now cured and feels perfectly able to walk. Sweet comes in, bringing Ken a construction toy.

Barnet comes in and makes disparaging remarks about Ash's basket and Ken's probable future. Loach comes in, also dressed for the outside world, in time to hear Ash resenting the fact that he's forced to waste his time doing things he hates, like making baskets, when he would be able to make a real contribution as a teacher.

Barnet smuggles a small bottle of spirits to Loach, who pays Barnet for this and some horse-race bets, then takes a swig. Loach is going home in the same ambulance as Flagg, who lives in Islington and remembers fondly how it used to be before they tore down the Agricultural Hall, when they still held exhibitions of country produce. Loach now feels a wince of pain in his leg but ignores it, boasting to the others that he used to be a sahib out in Asia, with 50 bearers.

Tyler is carried through the ward, his condition worse now but still showing his "wonderful spirit" by flinging a word of encouragement to Ken. Flagg and Loach finally leave with handshakes and conventional invitations to "drop in some time" on the outside.

> *Ash looks at the ward. Only his bed remains. He goes to Ken and sits on the floor.*

ASH: D'you know, son, we speak the most beautiful language in the world? That's our heritage. The tongue that Shakespeare spake. Yet most of the people you meet can utter nothing better than a stream of filth. I'm not sorry to see him go. I mean, I did my best, but he clung like a limpet. Mind you, I think one should be able to mix without actually lowering standards. Like the time I took my slum boys camping.

> *Ken laughs, Ash ruffles his hair.*

Yes, I did. What's more, I tried an experiment. Paired them off with college boys. Nicely spoken lads, you know. And the ragamuffins visibly *rose*, they actually raised themselves. But—this is the crux of the matter, son—the college lads were totally unscathed. And that's the secret of the governing class. The secret of the Royal Family. Clever boy, there's a clever boy. *(Ken laughs.)* And when I was a teacher I was privileged to know many of the Royal Family personally. No side at all. Regal bearing, yes, but not the snobbery of the newly rich. Simple dignity. Which is what is missing from so much of life today. Grace. Style. We're all the same, we need something fine to which to aspire. We want to rise, not sink in the bog. My hat, the old queen! She'd come inspecting. We'd spit-and-polish everywhere. Gym, library, canteen, even the toilets. Know what she'd ask to see? The brush cupboards.

> *Ken finishes making toy. Ash laughs at the recollection. Ken laughs at his laughter.*

There isn't nearly enough of that sort of spirit about these days.

Scene 8

> *Music. Lights and a pantomime transformation. A carpeted staircase comes down and two bridal pairs appear—Dr. Boyd and Sister McPhee, Neil and Staff Nurse Norton, the grooms in kilts, the brides in white. Full company appears throwing confetti and streamers and waving Union Jacks. The chaplain comes on as a bishop, mitred and golden. An acolyte bears his train. Matron calls for cheers from whole company. Bridal party shakes hands with chaplain. Acolyte turns to audience. It is Barnet.*

BARNET: It's a funny old world we live in and you're lucky to get out of it alive.
> *Bridal couples exit.*

BARNET:

A double wedding ends our pantomime,
Two hearts transplanted in the nick of time,
Our nursing staff, yes madam, you're so right,
Under the doctor both will spend the night.

The ship of state sails on a bit becalmed,
Though matron on the bridge is not alarmed,
Until the sails swell out above the boom,
She trusts her coolies in the engine room.

As for the rest there's not a lot to say,
They're born, they live and then get wheeled away,
The lucky ones,
Don't ask me what it means,
See you again one day behind the screens.

> *Music and dance stop suddenly. Patients, hospital staff and Barnet go behind screens. Curtain.*

THE WAGER

A Play in Three Acts

BY MARK MEDOFF

Cast and credits appear on page 365

MARK MEDOFF *was born in 1940 in Mt. Carmel, Ill., the son of a physician (his father) and a psychologist (his mother). He grew up in Florida and spent his undergraduate years at the University of Miami, moving on to Stanford, Calif., for his M.A. in English. His first play,* The Kramer, *was produced in 1973 under an Office for Advanced Drama Research grant at American Conservatory Theater in San Francisco and subsequently in the New Theater for Now series at the Mark Taper Forum in Los Angeles. His next,* The Wager, *was done at Stanford Repertory Theater and the Berghof Playwright's Workshop. His third play,* When You Comin' Back, Red Ryder? *was produced off off Broadway at the Circle Repertory Theater last season before moving up to a commercial off-Broadway production and its author's professional debut, opening December 6, 1973 for a run of 302 performances in which it was named a Best Play of its season and won an Obie Award for distinguished playwriting and the Outer Critics Circle John Gassner award as the outstanding new playwriting of the year.*

Medoff brought The Wager *into New York production off off Broadway at the Manhattan Theater club in January, 1974. Again his work took the long step to commercial production, opening off Broadway October 21, 1974 for a run of 104 performances and again was named a Best Play of its year.*

Medoff has received a Guggenheim Fellowship in playwriting, and he is an associate professor of English at New Mexico State University which gave him its Westhafer Award in spring 1974, its highest faculty recognition. He is also an actor who has played the leading role in his own Red Ryder *both in Chicago (where he won an award) and New York. Other Medoff works,* The Odyssey of Jeremy Jack *and* Four Short Plays *are in publication by the Dramatists Play Service. He lives in Las Cruces, New Mexico with his wife Stephanie and his daughter Debra.*

Time: *The present*

Place: *A university in northern California, the apartment of two graduate students*

ACT I

Scene 1: Thursday evening

SYNOPSIS: The usual sofa, coffee table, desk and chair are part of the living room furnishings of the apartment shared by Leeds and Ward, graduate student roommates. The room to the bedroom area is up right, to the hall up center and to the breakfast bar and kitchen up left. There is an "athletic area" up right with basketball hoop, dart board and "toy box" full of equipment; down left is a messy desk area with papers, bulletin board, etc.

Leeds enters from the bedroom. He is *"a man who seems purposely careless in his dress and, more importantly, a man who enters a room and by his gaze and bearing makes the inhabitants of the room uneasy."* He is wearing a T-shirt over which is strapped a shoulder holster and revolver as he approaches the desk. He carries a pipe, not to smoke but as *"a focus of energy, perhaps even a means of controlling a dangerous explosiveness raging beneath his very cool exterior."* Leeds takes hold of the audience with his eyes and addresses them directly, *"not so much to help the audience understand where the play will begin, but to let the audience know who he is and who they are in relation to him."*

LEEDS: When Honor Stevens's husband started down toward the pool, Ward suggested to Honor that he had better go, hoping to insinuate to her that either more existed between them than did, or that he was fully aware of what she was fully aware of: that there existed between them more than her husband suspected. And by leaping up when young Professor Stevens came onto the patio and diving hastily into the pool, Ward hoped to suggest to Stevens that he didn't want Stevens to suspect that anything existed between him and his wife because that's exactly what he hoped to suggest. Ward swam forty quick laps, careful to occasionally glance up at very unathletic Stevens, who seemed oblivious to Ward, convincing Ward that Stevens wanted him to think he didn't suspect anything so he could trap Ward who wouldn't have any idea he was suspected. But Ward suspected everything, and when Honor didn't glance at him once, he was sure that he was right—or if he wasn't, that Honor was convinced he was.

Blackout. In the darkness the sound of a bouncing basketball is heard. When the lights come up, Ward is dribbling the ball. *"He is wearing a bathing suit which displays his body and sexual apparatus to best advantage; he is bullish . . . . . he is a man who works from hedged bets."*

Ward sinks a basket and then approaches Leeds with a proposition: he will bet Leeds $400 that he can seduce Honor Stevens within five days. Ward has his eye on Honor—besides, he has made it with every other woman in the building, and now it's Honor's turn.

Leeds is worried that if Honor's husband finds out Leeds will lose his daily 7:30 A.M. ride to class. He calls his roommate "a mechanical penis taking a master's degree in Physical Education," and Ward in his turn taunts Leeds.

WARD *(in Leeds's ear):* She can't stand you, Leeds. Think about that. Think about the way she's always tearing you to shreds. Think about what I'll do to her for you.

LEEDS: Why would I want to bet against you then?

WARD: Because I need the incentive, goddamn it! I'm tired of balling all these chicks without any incentive!

Leeds ignores him. Ward backs off, turns suddenly.

How 'bout a buck I get her by midnight?

LEEDS: Why not be done with it, Ward, and simply admit you want any justification you can come up with for wreaking havoc, creating misery and indulging your psychopathic sexual appetite?

WARD: Justification! Of what? *For* what? Justify nothing to no one, Leeds. Just do!

Taking command of the conversation, Leeds insists on betting Ward $500 that there's no point to Ward's seducing Honor Stevens. Ward doesn't accept the bet, but Leeds arbitrarily gives Ward only five seconds to make his point.

WARD: The point to it, Leeds—the point to it is that I *want to do it.*

LEEDS: How do you know you want to do it? You have two seconds left.

WARD: I feel it.

LEEDS: Wrong, and your time's up—sorry. We don't feel reasons, Ward.

WARD: No?

LEEDS: We think reasons.

WARD: Gee.

LEEDS: And in coming to conclusions—even "I want"—there has to be some mental justification process. If you cannot justify, simply mentally, how you know you want, you cannot know, to begin with, *that* you want and therefore cannot want.

Holding out a flat palm to Ward.

You owe me five hundred dollars. Pay up.

Ward slaps the basketball into Leeds's palm and moves away.

WARD: That's very interesting, Leeds.

LEEDS: I'm glad.

Leeds takes a pump valve from the desk.

WARD: You are certainly an interesting person.

Leeds inserts the valve into the ball and presses down on it. The air escapes. Ward does a long take, first on empty space, then on Leeds. (Finally.) That's my basketball, Leeds.

Leeds stares at him. The air escapes.

LEEDS *(finally removing the valve):* That *was* your basketball. It is now your deflated piece of rubber.

Leeds dumps the basketball on the floor. It is dead.

WARD: Well, you're takin it down to the gas station, goddamn it, and gettin it blown back up.

LEEDS: Fine. And now that we've exchanged these little pleasantries, Ward, let's get down to it. I will bet you double or nothing on the five hundred you owe me that—

WARD: The five hundred I owe you . . .

LEEDS: Yes, Ward, the five hundred you owe me. And you either bet, pay up, or I'm going to murder you.

Leeds stands and casually crosses his arms, one hand going unseen beneath his shirt to the shoulder holster.

So, what'll it be? Will you bet, will you pay up, or will you be murdered?

WARD *(jocularly defiant):* Murdered.

Leeds draws the revolver from beneath his shirt, checks the cylinder to be sure the bullet is in the right chamber, and aims at Ward's face. Ward snorts and turns and strolls toward his toy box. Leeds alters his aim and fires at one of Ward's pictures, hitting it squarely between the eyes. Ward dives frantically behind the couch.

Frightened and deflated like his basketball, Ward offers to pay Leeds—but Leeds still holds out for a double-or-nothing wager. He reassures Ward that there was only one bullet in the gun, he need not fear being shot: "If I had wanted to kill you, Ward, you'd be dead; just as, if I ever *do* want to kill you, you *will* be dead."

They finally agree on the bet: double or nothing on the $500 that Ward can seduce Honor Stevens—but if her husband tries and/or succeeds in an attempt on Ward's life within 48 hours after the seduction, Ward loses, even though the seduction may have been accomplished.

Ward doesn't think the bet is fair, but Leeds tells him "I don't believe in fair." Ward is playing with a football, when there is a knock on the door. Ward knows that it is Honor Stevens, coming to get help for a calculus exam. Ward tries to persuade Leeds to get out and give him a chance with Honor, but Leeds insists on staying and working on correcting his pile of Freshman themes, to make it tough for Ward.

Ward opens the door for Honor Stevens. *"Though she is not now, it appears she has been crying. She is a very attractive young woman in a simple, sophisticated way and has about her a hardness that is past being a 'fun' facade. She is not intimidated by Leeds . . . . . their exchanges are head-on duels between nearly equal cynics, with only occasional respites on her part."*

Ward escapes to the bedroom before Honor enters. She greets Leeds, then informs him that she'd like him out of here. When Leeds protests that he's deeply involved in the themes, Honor declares: "You're not deeply involved in a god-damn thing. Now get the hell out of here."

Before Leeds can reply, there's another knock at the door. It is Honor's husband, Ron Stevens, *"conservatively dressed, a young scientist, without wit, but a very intelligent, well educated man who is so nearly guileless that he is almost hopelessly vulnerable to the likes of Leeds, Ward and Honor."*

Ron wants to see Honor outside, but Leeds immediately engages his attention by calling Ron "Stevens" and demanding that he be addressed as "Leeds" rather than the less formal "John." This makes Ron feel unwanted and increases his awkwardness in conversation with the other two.

Ward enters from the bedroom in tennis clothes, including sweat bands. He greets Honor, then notices Ron.

WARD: Ron! What a nice surprise.

HONOR: Surprise?

LEEDS: Yes, Ward, what kind of surprise?

WARD: Well . . . that Ron is with you.

LEEDS: Ah! Yes, that *is* surprising. Stevens, why are you with me?

RON: I'm not. I'm with Honor.

LEEDS: Then no wonder Ward is surprised.

WARD: Who said he's with you?

LEEDS: You did. You said, "Well, that Ron is with you" after I—

WARD: I meant that Ron is with Honor.

LEEDS: Then why didn't you say so?

WARD: I did say so, Leeds.

LEEDS: Oh, no you didn't. And we're not falling for the ole I did say so Leeds trick, either. Why shouldn't they be together?

WARD: Because I have to help Honor study for her calculus exam.

LEEDS: What the hell's that got to do with Stevens?

WARD: Nothing.

LEEDS *(fixing on Ron):* Then why are you here, Stevens?

RON: I . . . just stopped in to say that I'm going out for ice cream for everybody.

HONOR *(coldly; the implication being that she'll hasten his exit):* I'll get the bowls.

The three men track her with their eyes as she exits to the kitchen.

Leeds proceeds with his intention of confusing and exasperating Ward. Honor comes back with the bowls and tries to arrange matters so that she can study for the exam. Leeds hassles Ron about who is going to pay for the ice cream, and about whether Ron is capable of fetching it. Finally Leeds decides to accompany

Ron on the errand, if only to leave the other two alone.

Ward immediately embarks on his seduction, but he is interrupted almost at once by Leeds coming back for a question about the ice cream. When Leeds is gone, Ward hovers over Honor, nudging her with little attentions and cliches, but Honor remains unmoved. Ward tries harder.

WARD: Honor, let me be honest with you. I think I'm . . . falling in love with you.

HONOR: Falling in love . . . Have you ever wondered, Ward, why we *fall* in love? Why always that sense of entrapment and doom? . . . Why don't we ever *rise* to love?

WARD *(pause):* I think, then, that I'm . . . rising in love with you.

HONOR: That's . . . that's beautiful, Ward.

WARD: Well, it may not be beautiful, but I mean it from my heart.

HONOR: That's another image I adore.

WARD *(pressing on):* What do you feel for me, Honor?

HONOR: Contempt.

Ward refuses to believe that she's serious, but he switches abruptly to the frontal attack: he wants to make love with her, because it would be fun. Honor informs him that her husband Ron would like her to make love with *him,* too, but she's refused him for the past five years because she doesn't love him. She tells Ward she married Ron "because I was eighteen and because he was there; because I wanted to go away from where I was and he was going somewhere."

She has now decided that she doesn't want to follow where Ron is headed—to some quiet backwater of a campus where he can serve humanity with the study of science. Honor has decided she wants to live her own life, and for a starter she will not finish her Masters in Elementary Education because she doesn't want to be a school teacher after all.

WARD *(seductively):* Why don't ya divorce him?

HONOR *(returning from a mental distance to the sheer reality of Ward):* Because two weeks ago when I suggested a divorce . . . *(Putting the onus on Ward.)* . . . he threatened various forms of radical behavior.

WARD: You didn't believe him, did you?

HONOR: Actually, Ward, I didn't give it a whole lot of thought either way.

WARD: My point exactly . . . Come to bed with me.
   Ward addresses the bedroom.

HONOR: All right, Ward.

WARD: You will? What if they catch us?

HONOR: I guess that's a chance we'll have to take.
   She exits to the bedroom.

WARD *(at the bedroom door):* Honor . . . come to bed. Come share my bed, come . . . share my life.
   Ward stares after her a moment, then swings into action. He grabs up one of his dumbbells and does several quick presses with each arm. He

grabs a breath mint and pops it into his mouth as he exits after her. Blackout.

Scene 2: Seventeen minutes later

The lights come up, as Ward re-enters the living room from the bedroom, adjusting his sweat bands.

WARD: O.K., let's move 'em out.
> *He goes to his toy box and takes a very thick notebook out. He sits on the couch and turns well past the middle of the notebook. He begins to check off and write the particulars called for.*

Honor Stevens . . . Caucasian . . . married . . . Volkswagon . . . *(Calling toward the bedroom.)* Hey, how old are you?

HONOR *(soberly):* Twenty-three. Why?

WARD *(to himself, absently):* Why what? *(Writes her age.)* . . . student . . . total expenditure? *(Thinks a moment, then with a certain pride.)* None. *(He stares toward the bedroom, evaluating her.)* About a C-minus . . . *(Double-checks his appraisal.)* Yeah—a C-minus.

Honor enters—she knows Ward is rating her, but Ward won't disclose her "grade". Leeds and Ron return with the ice cream, Ron insisting on making a grand entrance. They had trouble both with the car and finding a place to buy the ice cream. They could get only French vanilla; they bought it from a youth in a restaurant. Ron claims vanilla is Honor's favorite flavor; Honor denies this. Ward and Honor insist that Ron and Leeds should act out the scene of buying the ice cream. They refuse to let Leeds play himself—Ron will play Leeds, and Leeds will play the youngster. They act out the scene with Ron portraying an arrogant, demanding Leeds and Leeds making the most of his secondary role as the half-defiant, half-sniveling youth. He wouldn't sell them anything but cones, so they bought the three-gallon container by paying for 87 cones, which was Ron's lightning calculation of its contents.

Leeds dishes out the ice cream—by now become a bit soupy—while Ron reminisces, sentimentally, about Honor's favorite ice cream. The day they bought the old car they wanted to celebrate by driving out to a place called Roy's, Ron remembers, "just for the heck of it—to have a root beer float. But you were afraid that a six-year-old car with fifty thousand miles on it wouldn't make it out to Roy's, so why didn't we just go across the street from the car lot to this drug store and have an ice cream cone. And I said, probably all they've got is chocolate, strawberry and vanilla. And you said, that's all right because vanilla was really your favorite anyway. You remember that."

Honor doesn't remember, but since Ron seems desperate to make the point she declines to argue.

> *Leeds takes his ice cream and goes to his desk. Ward gets a bowl for himself and one for Honor, then sits with her on the couch. Ron gets*

himself a bowl and moves toward the couch, assuming that he'll sit beside Honor. Ward, however, has spread himself in such a way that the couch is full. Ron takes one of the stools from the breakfast bar and sits on the other side of Honor from Ward. Leeds and Ward take a slurping mouthful of the soupy stuff. Honor eats . . . and finally Ron eats, having tried to remain as stoic and cool in the face of the slurping as possible. As Ron's spoon touches his lips, Leeds and Ward simultaneously do a big:

LEEDS and WARD: *Yummy!*

RON: It's all right?

    Simultaneously:

LEEDS: *Yech!*　　　　　　　　　　　　WARD: *Blah!*

RON: Don't you like it really?

    Simultaneously:

LEEDS: *Terrific!*　　　　　　　　　　WARD: *Great!*

RON: Is it?

    Simultaneously:

LEEDS: *Blah!*　　　　　　　　　　　　WARD: *Yech!*

HONOR *(amused in her unamused way):* Oh all right, stop it. It's fine, Ron.

WARD: Sure it's *fine,* Ron. Isn't it, Leeds?

LEEDS: Fine? Well, I don't—Fine . . . That's the word you're pushing? *(Rolls it around.)* Fine . . . Fine . . .

WARD: That's it on the nose, wouldn't you say?

LEEDS: No.

WARD: What?

LEEDS: Adequate. It's adequate—

WARD: Adequate!

LEEDS: . . . soup.

WARD: Ah! Adequate soup. You've pinpointed it!

LEEDS: Yes, it's adequate soup—

WARD: But—

LEEDS: —but lousy ice cream

WARD *(just a beat behind Leeds):* —lousy ice cream. You're right, Leeds. I hate to admit it, but you really hit it that time.

Honor half-heartedly reassures Ron that the others are only joking, but Leeds immediately leaps in with fulsome praise for Ward as a basketball hero who was offered three scholarships and a convertible in exchange for his prowess. Ron notes calmly that he has received 12 scholarship offers, with the observation "Half the morons in the world can get an athletic scholarship." But almost at once Ron is feeling sorry for himself: "They didn't have a special section of the cafeteria where I could eat . . . steak—for *free.* They didn't even have a special section where I could eat steak if I paid for it. You know why? . . . . . Because they didn't serve steak in our lousy section of the lousy cafeteria. And even if they did, I couldn't have afforded it on my lousy academic scholarship."

Ward challenges Ron to an imaginary one-on-one scoring duel of basketball.

Leeds taunts Ron: "Go ahead, it'll be fun. Afterward you can quiz him in microbiology." Leeds takes the referee's whistle. All the imaginary plays and referee's decisions go against Ron, who enters into the spirit of the thing hoping they'll play fair with him but finding, of course, that they're just trying to make a fool of him in front of Honor. Honor is shaking with laughter. Ron, furious, takes up his jacket and exits.

Now the most vulnerable person present, Ward, becomes the target.

LEEDS: Nice going, big guy. Just like the year you made All American. Tell Honor about the year you made All American.
> *Ward glances at Leeds to see if Leeds will permit him to heave a little bullshit.*
WARD: Yeah, well I made a few of—
LEEDS: Liar.
WARD: Oh yeah?
LEEDS: Ward just didn't have it. The first time one of those big boys whacked him in the nose on a rebound, old Ward boy, he just packed it up. So long bouncy-ball.
WARD: Get off it, will ya! *(To Honor.)* He doesn't know. I just decided since I was goin into coaching I'd better concentrate on—
LEEDS: —On bullshit.
WARD: I oughta know, *Leeds.*
LEEDS: And I'm sure you do, *Ward.* You didn't want to get marked up. You saw you didn't have it, so rather than chance jeopardizing your major industry, you—
WARD: *So what?*
LEEDS: So that was laudably realistic of you.
WARD: Yeah, but so what?
HONOR: Ron was Phi Beta Kappa.
WARD: What the hell's that got to do with anything?
HONOR: Oh. I don't know; just that he achieved the highest honor in his field and you evidently failed miserably at more than one—
WARD: I got "Best Looking" in the yearbook.
HONOR: Ron got "Most Intelligent" in his.
LEEDS: And you of course got "Most Likely to Succeed" in yours.
HONOR: Yes. That's right.
LEEDS: At what?
HONOR: There were no specifications.
LEEDS: How're ya doin?
HONOR: I'm sorting out my options.
LEEDS: Ah, so that's what you're doing.

Ward boasts about some of his other achievements. Honor rebukes them both for teasing Ron, but her heart is not in it. Finally it is Leeds, not Ward, whom she challenges: ". . . . . In a perverse way I've come to find it amusing that you are so frightened of me . . . . . What would you say, I wonder, if one day, by prior agreement—we'd have to work through agents of course—we would walk stripped and unarmed into an empty room somewhere?"

Leeds shakes his head. Honor says goodnight to Ward and exits.

LEEDS: How's the wager stand?

WARD: I screwed her.

LEEDS: Big deal.

WARD: Look, I've had a little more experience with women than you have.

LEEDS: So have most ninth graders.

WARD: Yeah? And to what do you attribute your lack of experience?

LEEDS: Lack of success . . . What the hell's this got to do with anything? How was she in bed?

WARD: What the hell's that got to do with anything?

LEEDS: I'm thinking of writing your biography. How was she?

WARD: I gave her a C-minus.

LEEDS: What's wrong with her.

WARD: She just *lays* there.

LEEDS: Hmph.

WARD: But I guess they can't all be A's and B's.

LEEDS: No, I guess not.

Handing Ward a banana.

From all us guys, Ward, who have to take a steady diet of C-minuses, I want to present this token of our gratitude to you for knocking off a C-minus now and then and saving us that little extra wear and tear on our bodies.

WARD *(putting the banana back on the coffee table):* You think you're very goddamn clever, don't you Leeds?

LEEDS: Yes I do, Ward, but *you* think I think I'm cleverer than you think I am, when in fact you think I'm cleverer than I am. And that's one of the reasons why I'm king and you clean the stables.

But Ward makes Leeds feel sexually inferior, there's no getting around that. They will time the 48 hours in which Ron may try to kill Ward from 9 P.M., an hour ago when the first part of the bet was won, so that Ward has only 47 more hours to go. Ward offers to double the bet that he'll seduce Honor again within that time, and Leeds accepts. *"Ward snaps the banana in half in Leeds's face. Blackout."*

ACT II

Late the following afternoon, Friday, Leeds comes into the empty living room with a pile of themes and drops them on his desk. Ward looks in cautiously from the bedroom, surprised to find Leeds home at this hour. Leeds claims he wasn't feeling well so Ron Stevens drove him home.

When Leeds insists on going into the bedroom, Ward tips his roommate off that Honor is in there. Leeds calls out, and Honor appears in the bedroom doorway.

Leeds informs Honor that Ron is home, then goes and gets a pillow and lies down on the couch.

Honor insists on questioning Leeds about how Leeds feels about her. Leeds's answer is: "I don't hate you. I don't care enough about you to hate you. I don't even care enough about you to care about you."

Honor wonders whether Leeds means to tell Ron about her relations with Ward, and Leeds's reply is enigmatic. Finally her questions anger Leeds: "Look, you little trollop, I don't care what you do *with* Ward or *to* Stevens. In fact, I don't care so much that in order for me *to* care, I'd have to pay off a minus caring debt so large that it would take me longer than I care to spend just to reach the point where I didn't care so I could start thinking up reasons why I might care. My only interest in this whole thing is whether or not Ward gets murdered."

There's a knock on the door—it's Ron, who is surprised to see Honor. Honor says she came home early to go over an exam with Ward.

RON: Why didn't you let me know you were here when Leeds got here? Didn't he tell you that I was here too?

WARD *(staring at Leeds):* Yeah, but he said you were coming right over.

RON: I didn't say I was coming over.

LEEDS *(stares at Honor a moment; then at Ron):* But I assumed you would because you're of a type who will come to see how a neighbor's feeling.

RON: How do you feel?

LEEDS: Within the limits of relative absolutes, terrible. Of course, if one cared to attack relative absolutes—

RON: If you don't mind—not now.

LEEDS: Perhaps some other time.

RON: Come home, Honor.

HONOR: Why, Ron?

RON: Why not?

HONOR: Because I'm supposed to be in school.

RON: But you're not, so you can come home.

HONOR: But this is scheduled as time when I'm not at home; therefore, I shouldn't have to be there.

WARD: What happened, Ron, was we got sidetracked into a very interesting discussion . . . *In fact,* why don't we ask Ron what he thinks?

LEEDS: Fine. What do you think, Stevens?

RON: About what?

LEEDS: Don't ask me. Ask Ward.

RON *(advancing on Ward and staring him dead in the eye):* About what?

WARD: About . . . whether it's colder in the winter or . . . on the farm.

RON *(continuing to stare dead at Ward, the scientific part of his mind simultaneously at work on an answer):* I'd say it's colder in the winter.

LEEDS: Some day when you've got a year or two, I'd be more than a little bit interested in how you arrived at that conclusion.

RON: I can tell you in one sentence: It's colder in the winter because the amount

of space winter occupies is greater than the space occupied by all the farms on earth. *(To Honor.)* I'm going home, Honor.
> *Pause.*

HONOR: I'm going to stay here awhile.

Ron leaves, and Ward gets Leeds to go into the bedroom, leaving him alone with Honor. Ward asks Honor if she'd like to drive out to the beach with him, but Honor refuses to answer. Irritated, Ward goes into the kitchen for a snack. When Leeds comes back into the room, Honor stares at him, then grabs her purse and exits. Ward is puzzled when he comes back and finds Honor gone. Leeds taunts him, gives him no help.

Leeds goes back into the bedroom, and there's a knock on the door. Ward hopes it's Honor but is somewhat flustered to find that it's Ron. Ron informs Ward he's neither stupid nor blind. Ward can figure out for himself what Ron means by that.

Leeds comes back, and to avoid conversation with Ron he pretends to be searching for an imaginary dog. Ron insists on talking to Leeds alone, and so Leeds, resigned, sends Ward out to get pizza.

Ron asks Leeds point-blank whether Honor has been seeing Ward and sleeping with him. Leeds tells him frankly that Ward says yes, she has. Ron absorbs the blow, while *"Leeds fights as the scene goes on to maintain his distance, to keep his detachment from this man who nevertheless touches him in ways he doesn't want to be touched."*

Leeds makes Ron understand that Ward doesn't love Honor, but that there's no chance of their relationship being innocent of physical consummation. Leeds admits to Ron that he finds Ron boring, because Ron is normal, while Leeds is admittedly insane. But the point of this discussion, Leeds emphasizes, isn't what he thinks of Ron, but what Ron is going to *do,* now that he has found out about Ward and Honor.

Ron and Leeds contemplate the consequences of 1) Ron committing suicide, 2) Ron killing Honor and 3) Ron killing both Honor and himself, but none of these alternatives seems entirely satisfactory. Finally Leeds suggests, "How about . . . killing Ward," but Ron objects, "If I killed him I'd defeat my purpose by losing my own life." Leeds argues that it might provide a kind of exorcism, but Ron is not interested.

Abruptly Ron changes roles and becomes the inquisitor, asking Leeds about his emotional relationships with his parents, particularly his mother.

RON: . . . . . I'm just trying to determine what kind of relationship you had with her. I mean, I assume she was—I mean, you know, did you—

LEEDS: —have coitus with her?

RON: *No!* Were you close to each other?

LEEDS: No. I was close to my father. I used to side with him against her.

RON: Why?

LEEDS: Because he scared me and she didn't. I loved her but I admired him.

RON: That's a very interesting distinction—between loving and admiring. Why did you love her and only admire him?

LEEDS: Not "only," Stevens, not "only." When I say I admired him, I mean I really admired the man.

RON: Okay—why?

LEEDS: Because he could resist feeling for other people.

RON: And so to protect *yourself* from a hostile world, you emulate your father. Do you think that's healthy?

LEEDS: Don't try to switch roles with me, Stevens! A guy like you trying to be forthright hasn't got a chance.

RON: Because I'm weak?

LEEDS: Weak in the sense of great strength, Stevens. But essentially because you're boring.

RON: And I suppose killing Ward would make me honest and interesting . . . and strong in the sense of great *weak*ness . . . Is that right, Leeds?

LEEDS: I don't know, Stevens . . . . .

Ron reminds Leeds that the purpose of any action he might take would be to prevent Honor from sleeping with Ward again. Leeds warns Ron against taking any sensible action, because that would place him among the majority, the 52 out of 60 who are the "crucified" meek.

RON: . . . . . Let's carry it to its positive extension: What happens to those other eight people? Those other eight people—

LEEDS: —Those other eight people, Stevens, disguise themselves as eggplants and make little kids throw up at the dinner table.

RON: Are you insane, so therefore sensible?

LEEDS: I am meticulously insensible to the point of being compulsively, fastidiously sensible; therefore insane.

RON: I'm beginning to see.

LEEDS: I almost hope you're not.

RON: Why not?

LEEDS: Because I'm afraid I want you to so much. *(Catching himself too late; in too deep; trying to jump out.)* Listen, Stevens, you wouldn't be interested in a little plan I've got to scare the shit out of Ward, would you?

Ron doesn't know, he knows only that he doesn't want to lose Honor. Leeds assures Ron he's already lost her, to Ron's great distress.

Ward comes in with a large pizza. Contrarily, Leeds has now decided he doesn't want any. Ward, trying to stay on Ron's good side, offers him the pizza, but Ron doesn't want it either. As Ron departs and Leeds goes to the kitchen to get some yoghurt, Ward is literally and foolishly left holding the pizza. Ward demands that Leeds take it back for a refund, but Leeds casually throws some money at Ward to pay for it. Ward drops Leeds's change into Leeds's yoghurt, to get his attention. Ward is going downtown on his bicycle.

WARD: . . . . . I'm goin to buy a body shirt I saw. A see-through job. Very tough on guys with good bodies.

LEEDS: I think I'll stay here in case Stevens comes back looking for you.

WARD: Whudduya mean? What'd you tell him?

LEEDS: I told him to hide in the toilet and the next time you sit down to carve up your brain with a straight razor.

WARD: You know something, Leeds: I think this Stevens thing is getting to you. Guilt over Constipation multiplied by fear of Losing the Wager equals an Uptight Madman.

LEEDS: The only thing that's getting to me is the fear that Stevens isn't going to murder you.

WARD: That's very nice—thanks. And don't bother telling me you don't believe in nice.

LEEDS: What kind of presumption is that? Who said I don't believe in nice?

WARD: Do you?

LEEDS: Certainly not.

Ward hangs around badgering Leeds about the strange ways they have of communicating—or not communicating—with each other. Finally Ward departs, having been commanded by Leeds to pick him out a tie, no stripes, and if Leeds likes it he'll pay for it.

Soon there's a knock on the door—it's Honor. *"The seriousness of whatever thoughts she was thinking while she was sitting out there on the stairs is reflected in her stance, her face."* Leeds makes it plain that he's not happy to see her. Honor knows that Leeds has told Ron about her affair with Ward. She and Ward have decided on a trip to Tijuana for an instant divorce, but Honor is worried. Ron owns a gun, and she wonders what he might do. Leeds informs Honor: "I don't know either. But I hope he at least makes an attempt on Ward's life, and at best I hope he kills Ward . . . and, for that matter, you too."

Honor takes this suggestion in stride. She confides to Leeds that, with Ward, she had an orgasm for the first time in her life, but Leeds, knowing that Ward gave her only a C-minus, doesn't believe her and tells her so. Honor admits that Leeds is right, and Leeds tries to dismiss her, but she stands her ground.

HONOR: May I ask you a personal question? At this point, it seems only fair.

LEEDS: I don't believe in fair.

HONOR (starting for the door): No, obviously not.

LEEDS: One question.

HONOR (pause): Are you queer?

For a moment, Leeds is immobile, then slowly he turns to her.

LEEDS: No, I don't think so. I hope not, anyway. I don't want to be . . . The ultimate irony in my relationship with Ward is that I don't want any of my organs in any of his, or vice versa.

HONOR: Have you ever loved a woman?

LEEDS: A woman—no. I've endured several for short periods of time, but loved one—no, I don't think so. Rather fond of a girl from Greece coupla years ago. Got run over by a truck.

HONOR: That's too bad.

LEEDS: Especially for her. Loved a little girl once. We were twelve and we went steady for two weeks.

Honor understands the relationship only too well—innocent affection, giving her his identity bracelet, shaking hands with her every day outside the home room, and then, after two weeks, losing her to another boy. Leeds took it like a man: "I shook hands with her when she gave me the word that last day, and I made a perfect military turn, marched to my gym class, started a fight with the fourth toughest kid in school and got the crap beat out of me."

Leeds hints that maybe Honor's marriage to Ron is a little like that. Honor replies with a question.

HONOR: Don't you *want*, John?
LEEDS: No.
HONOR: Don't lie to me. This is so nice now.
LEEDS *(retreating into words; playing with the syntax):* This is so nice now. Now this is so nice.
HONOR: What's happened since that little girl?
LEEDS: I've developed what seems to be an overly simplistic distaste for particular types of human relationships.
HONOR: I didn't mean to imply that many other things have not contributed to your paralysis.
LEEDS: Is nice so now this.
HONOR: What do you want, John?
LEEDS: Now?
HONOR: That's right.
LEEDS: To be hermetically sealed in sheet metal.
HONOR: What do you want, John? Now.
LEEDS: Not you, Honor.
HONOR: You're lying.
LEEDS: No. I'm not.

Honor isn't quite sure what she's trying to do; Leeds is sure she's going about it the wrong way. He accuses her of trying to drive him out of his mind, but she claims she's merely trying to preserve her own sanity, and she now knows she's been trying to get closer to Leeds for several months.

Leeds's reaction is to shy away, and Honor wonders what Leeds has to lose.

HONOR: Are you afraid you'll be less successful with me than Ron or Ward?
LEEDS *(with a defensive, angry laugh):* Now why the hell did you ask that? Couldn't you ask first if it's some quaintly moral concern for your moronic husband or because I don't want sloppy seconds or sevenths or twenty-thirds or whatever the hell it would be?
HONOR: I *asked* what seemed the most relevant question!
LEEDS: Well, it wasn't!
HONOR *(laughing):* You're not being very convincing.

LEEDS: Don't laugh at me!

HONOR: But you're funny.

LEEDS: The most relevant question is: Are you worth the aggravation that trying to *keep* you would cause me once I'd *gotten* you?

HONOR: And you don't think I am?

LEEDS *(moving away from her to his desk area; absently picking up a handful of themes)*: No. Christ no!

HONOR *(advancing on him)*: I see you, little boy.

> *She touches the side of his face, presses her hand gently there.*

LEEDS: Please don't touch me.

HONOR *(leaving her hand on his face)*: If you didn't want me to to touch you, you wouldn't say please.

LEEDS: Don't touch me!

> *She kisses him, and for several seconds he almost responds; but then he pushes her away with his free hand and smacks her across the face with the pack of themes. Shaken, he sits in his desk chair. Pause.*

HONOR: If you think you've just made some kind of grand gesture, you're out of your mind.

> *She moves for the door.*

LEEDS: *Honor.*

HONOR: *Yes.*

LEEDS: I have a wager with Ward that says he can plow you within forty-eight hours of eight o'clock last night—which he did with forty-seven hours to spare—and that Stevens will either make an attempt on his life or murder him.

After a beat or two of silence, Honor remarks "That's very amusing" and continues on her way out, passing Ward who is on the way in, carrying his packages. Ward wants to know what Honor was doing here. Leeds feeds Ward's ego by telling him Honor wants to divorce Stevens and move in here with Ward. Leeds also lets Ward know that Ron is very upset.

Ward is worried about what to do with Honor and about Ron, and he starts pounding a baseball into a glove to help him think, while Leeds fools with one of the darts. Ward tries to laugh off his troubles, but Leeds won't let him. When there is a knock at the door Ward tries to escape to the bedroom but isn't quick enough to hide himself before Ron enters. But it is Leeds whom Ron fixes with a cold, angry stare. Sensing that he's in the clear for the time being, Ward goes out, with the excuse of getting some beer for everybody.

Honor has told Ron that Leeds has something to say to Ron. Leeds tries to focus Ron's anger on Ward by mentioning the plans for a divorce, but Ron will not be distracted. He understands this whole affair is really Leeds's fault, and Ron is determined to kill Leeds, not Ward. Honor has told Ron all about the wager.

LEEDS: . . . . . How does that make this whole thing my fault? I mean, sure—I'm imaginative but am I *that* imaginative?

RON: No, you're not that imaginative, John.

LEEDS: Leeds.

RON: You're just that dangerous and *stupid.*

LEEDS: You don't say.

RON: No, I do say. You think I'm kidding about killing you, don't you? You think this whole thing is pretty funny. Well, you can't just go around doing these things to people.

> *He heads for the door.*

LEEDS: What things?

RON *(stopping): Crummy* things!

> *He starts for the door again.*

LEEDS: Where are you going?

RON *(at the door):* You'll find out.

> *Ron exits. Leeds holds a moment, absently fingering the dart in his hand. He looks after Ron, looks away, then snaps off the light just inside the wall of the breakfast bar, blacking out the stage.*

ACT III

Scene 1: Seconds later

Ron re-enters the dimly-lit room carrying a submachine gun, peering around for Leeds.

Leeds, behind the breakfast bar, throws his dart into the dart board. When Ron turns at the sound, Leeds presses his revolver into Ron's back. Ron is forced to put down his weapon, leaning it against a bar stool. He claims, somewhat ashamedly, that he keeps it for hunting ducks.

Leeds casually informs Ron that his revolver isn't loaded. Ron makes a move for the submachine gun and Leeds for the box of ammunition in his desk, but Ron is quicker and now it is Leeds's turn to put down his weapon.

Leeds can scarcely believe that Ron means to kill him. Ron means it, all right —but when he points the gun at Leeds he can't bring himself to pull the trigger. Ron puts the gun on the coffee table and slumps into a chair.

Leeds suggests to the now disconsolate Ron that perhaps he would be able to kill Ward instead. But no—in his present mood, Ron has decided "I'm going to do the truly noble thing . . . I'm going to bow out like a man." Leeds's comment is: "That is so marvelous a thing to do because it's so purposelessly, magnificently, munificently, magnanimously *ig*noble." Leeds is relieved because for a minute there Ron almost made him feel something—but now he has recovered his cool.

Ward comes back—he hasn't brought beer after all. Ron takes up the submachine gun, and Ward ducks out into the hall. But Ron is angrier at Leeds than at Ward, and he finally goes out, passing nervous Ward in the hall but offering him no harm.

Ward comes back in and starts getting some things together. He's has enough of this situation, he'll accompany Honor as far as the airport on her way to Tijuana and then slip away to Santa Barbara for the weekend "sacked out with one of my old B-pluses." Ward wants no part of any submachine gun and doesn't feel that he owes Honor anything.

Honor comes in. Dutifully, Ward asks her for a kiss, but she ignores him. She informs them that Ron has gone to let off steam by shooting up their old car with his gun. Leeds comments, "I am going to fall on my knees right here, Honor, and I am going to pray that when Stevens starts spraying bullets at that very symbol of your years together that he doesn't spray any, by mistake, at Ward's two-hundred-dollar, three-month-old Italian ten-speed bicycle."

The suggestion so upsets Ward that he grabs his putter and runs off to defend his property, and Leeds follows to observe what happens.

Left alone, Honor goes to the pizza box on the breakfast bar, takes out a section and bites off a large piece which crams her mouth full. Ron comes in, entering silently and startling her. His gun misfired and he couldn't shoot the car, so he's decided to wash it instead—he can't have her driving to the airport in a dirty car.

Ron is glad the gun didn't fire, because he might have ricocheted himself to death—much Honor would have cared, Ron observes. Maybe as much as three on a scale of ten. Honor assures him she'd have cared seven, setting up a sense of closeness that Ron tries to exploit. He can't understand why and where they failed in their marriage.

RON: . . . . . We had so much fun.
HONOR: Did we, Ron?
RON: God, yes—don't you remember?
HONOR: No, I don't.
RON: Sure you do.
       He begins to sing the first bars of a four- or five-year-old love song.
HONOR *(cutting him off):* I don't remember!
RON: Honor . . .
HONOR *(in effect, "Please don't get to me now"):* No!
RON *(pause):* How did I fail you?
HONOR *(with a small, pained laugh):* Perfectly.
RON: How, Honor?
HONOR: Oh, God, Ron, don't start *asking* me things like that.
RON: Honor, please . . .
HONOR: I failed you.
RON: Talk to me, Honor.
HONOR: Honor Honor . . .
RON: I need to know.
HONOR: My *God!* Our colossal, basic, ground-level ineptitude!
RON: What do you mean? I don't—
HONOR: *Yours!*
RON: What do you—
HONOR: Yours.
       Silence.
RON: My ineptitude. Not yours.
HONOR: Of course mine; ours.
RON: All right . . . I'm sorry.
HONOR: I know you are. I know you are. I am too.

Ron begs for honesty between them. He offers to try harder, but she repulses him, calling him boring.

RON: Don't you understand?—I love you.

HONOR: So what? What kind of big goddamn deal is that, I love you? Everybody says that like it's some big goddamn deal. *So what! I hate you!*

RON: *I'll help you be whatever you want to be.*

HONOR: *I don't want to be married to you any more, Ronald.*
      Silence. They stare at each other.
Go home, Ronny.
      Ron starts for the door, stops.

RON: Are you sleeping here tonight?

HONOR: What's the difference?

RON: The difference is that tonight you're still married to me. And I know that's just quaint as hell, but if you can see your way clear not to humiliate me any further in front of that jackass you're going off with tomorrow, I would appreciate it.

HONOR: It doesn't matter where I sleep, Ronald.

RON: Yes—it does. It matters to me.

HONOR: Everything matters to you, Ronald. Everything has always mattered to you, hasn't it?

RON: Yes.

HONOR: That's very nice, Ronald. But it's no goddamn good.

They are interrupted by the return of the two roommates, Ward trying to carry off the situation, Leeds seeing at once that something has passed between Honor and Ron. Ward decides he's going to help Ron wash the car, and they go out together. "*Silence. Honor holds with her face to the wall, her back to Leeds. Leeds continues to stare at her. Finally, evidently having gotten herself reasonably enough together to leave the apartment, she starts to cross for the door. As she comes abreast of Leeds, though, she suddenly lets out a cry and crashes one fist down against his shoulder. He does not move. She crashes the other fist down against his other shoulder. He still does not move. In a flurry, she swings first one arm at him again and then the other. Almost metronomically, he catches in his hands first one fist and then the other. He turns her wrists back and she goes to her knees and he goes with her. He holds her viselike until she stops struggling and then he releases her hands.*

"*She presses herself to him, her hands not around him but together and pressed by their two chests. And now he holds her loosely for some seconds before he must break from her. He moves away, in his movement a sense of desperate flight.*"

Ron and Ward come back, quarreling. Ward confronts Ron with the information that he and Honor are going to sleep here tonight. Ron informs Honor she's sleeping at home. They leave it up to Honor, who decides: "I'm sleeping at home." But Leeds taunts her, and she decides to punish Ron and Leeds at one and the same time—she'll sleep at home, taking Ward with her. She exits. Ward, showing no sympathy whatever for Ron (and with only 47 minutes left of the wager time) gets his toothbrush and follows her.

Leeds orders Ron to turn off the lights, which Ron does. Leeds wants to go to sleep, but Ron wants to talk about the ironic humor of his situation. He and Honor didn't love each other when they got married. He knows this, because his mother told him so at the time.

RON: . . . . . But funnier than that, Leeds—maybe forty *times* funnier than that is that I grew to *really* love her and she didn't grow to really love me. God, that's funny. Now tonight she says it's no big deal that I love her, because she hates me, and I want to point out to her that she's always hated me and that I've just found out that I've known it for five and a half years. Chuckle anywhere along here that you feel like it, Leeds. Here's the point, though, Leeds—and needless to say—this is the very funniest part of all: Now she won't even *tolerate* me any more! *(Pause.)* She's screwed up, boy, I'm telling you. *(Pause.)* God, somebody's gotta take care of her or she's gonna be in a helluva lot of trouble. *(Pause.)* And that's the part that I don't think's so funny.
    A long pause.
What have you got to say, Leeds?
    He sits at the desk.
LEEDS: Stevens, please don't sit in my chair.
    Blackout.

Scene 2: Saturday morning

When the lights come up it is morning. Ron is still sitting at Leeds's desk, wide awake, while Leeds is asleep on the couch. Ward comes in from the hall in his bathrobe, carrying clothes and toothbrush. Ward goes on in to the bedroom, leaving Ron to digest the highly indigestible surmise that Ward is naked under the robe and therefore must have slept that way all night with Honor in their apartment.

Ron goes into the bathroom as Ward comes out and tells Leeds he has won the bet, made love to Honor again successfully, three minutes before the end of the time limit: "Double or nothing on double or nothing on the five hundred I didn't owe you, Leeds, equals nothing. Victory!"

Ward exits as Honor comes in. Ron joins them and asks immediately if she slept naked. She tells him no, but Ron doesn't believe her.

Ward comes in to say he wants to get going to the airport, but Honor wants to tell Ron something first: Ward isn't going with her to Tijuana, he's going to Santa Barbara. Honor refused to sleep with Ward last night (so that Ward lied about winning the bet) and she has no intention of living with him after her divorce.

Leeds demands his winnings: $2,000. Ward denies there was ever anything at stake, and this infuriates Ron. His marriage was at stake, he reminds them, and he slaps first Ward and then Honor.

LEEDS: Who's gonna pay? That's the question? Who's gonna pay for the ice cream, who's gonna pay for the pizza, who's gonna pay for your marriage?

Somebody's gotta pay, right, Stevens?

RON: Oh, but not you, Leeds. Not you. No, Because—

LEEDS: Because that's all that's been at stake here, right? Just *your* marriage. Right?

HONOR: What else was at stake, John?

WARD: I gotta catch a plane.

RON: Yeah—what was at stake for *you,* Leeds?

LEEDS: We're not talking about me.

HONOR: *I'm* talking about you. You can't be the perennial neuter Director of Personnel.

LEEDS: Somebody's gotta do it.

HONOR: *Not in my life! (To Ron.)* Don't imagine, Ronald, that I don't choose to do what I do. One of these days I hope I'll be able to tell you why.

RON: Yeah, well don't expect me to be around to listen.

HONOR: I hope you're not.

RON: I won't be.

Ron has decided he will go to Israel and fight against the Arabs. He has finally decided one thing for sure: he doesn't want to be like Leeds, or Ward—or Honor. This is his ultimate rejection of them, and he goes.

Ward insists that he must get to the airport. Honor makes it clear that she isn't going with him, gives him the keys to the car and sends him on his way alone. Then she turns to Leeds.

HONOR: If that hunk of sheet metal insists on standing there, I'm going to have to go through it.

LEEDS: No.

HONOR: No more words, John.

LEEDS: I've told you I don't want you, I've told you not to touch me, and I'm telling you to get out.

HONOR: Words.

LEEDS: Get out!

HONOR: Words. No more words, John.

LEEDS: Please get out.

HONOR: No more words. *(Pause.) Silence!*
       Silence.

LEEDS: I've told so many lies in my life that I no longer know when I'm telling the truth any more. *(Pause.)* I'm afraid.
       Pause.

HONOR: Wanna make a bet, John?
       A long pause.

LEEDS: Sure.
       Curtain.

A GRAPHIC GLANCE

Hirschfeld is represented exclusively by the Margo Feiden Galleries, New York, New York

3+1

RAUL JULIA IN THE REVIVAL OF "WHERE'S CHARLEY?"

JOHN STANDING AND MAGGIE SMITH IN THE REVIVAL OF NOEL COWARD'S
"PRIVATE LIVES"

SANDY DENNIS, GERALDINE PAGE AND CAROLE SHELLEY IN "ABSURD PERSON SINGULAR"

SAM WATERSTON AND LIV ULLMANN IN THE REVIVAL OF IBSEN'S "A DOLL'S HOUSE"

ROBERT PRESTON, BERNADETTE PETERS, ROBERT FITCH AND LISA KIRK IN "MACK AND MABEL"

JACK GWILLIM AND INGRID BERGMAN IN THE REVIVAL OF W. SOMERSET MAUGHAM'S "THE CONSTANT WIFE"

OPPOSITE: JAMES EARL JONES IN THE REVIVAL OF JOHN STEINBECK'S "OF MICE AND MEN"

CHITA RIVERA, JERRY ORBACH AND GWEN VERDON IN THE MUSICAL "CHICAGO"

ANGELA LANSBURY IN THE REVIVAL OF "GYPSY"

BEN GAZZARA IN THE REVIVAL OF EUGENE O'NEILL'S "HUGHIE"

THE CAST OF "THIEVES": MARLO THOMAS AND RICHARD MULLIGAN (FORE-GROUND) SURROUNDED BY DAVID SPIELBERG, WILLIAM HICKEY, ANN WEDGE-WORTH (ON BALCONY), CHARLES MAYER, IRWIN COREY (IN GLASSES), ALICE DRUMMOND, HEYWOOD NELSON AND PIERRE EPSTEIN (ON BALCONY)

PAUL SHYRE AS H. L. MENCKEN IN "BLASTS AND BRAVOS: AN EVENING WITH H. L. MENCKEN"

OPPOSITE: ELIZABETH ASHLEY IN THE REVIVAL OF TENNESSEE WILLIAMS' "CAT ON A HOT TIN ROOF"

S. J. PERELMAN, WHOSE "THE BEAUTY PART" WAS REVIVED OFF BROADWAY

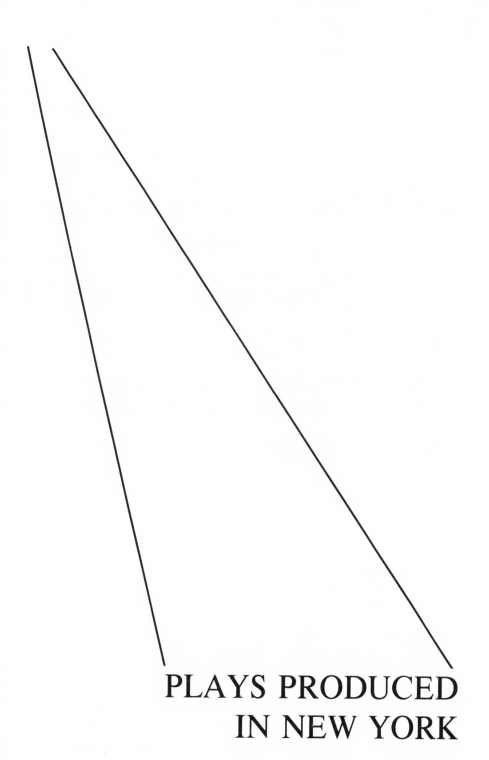

PLAYS PRODUCED
IN NEW YORK

PLAYS PRODUCED ON BROADWAY

Figures in parentheses following a play's title indicate number of performances. The figures are acquired directly from the production office in each case and do not include previews or extra non-profit performances.

Plays marked with an asterisk (*) were still running on June 2, 1975. Their number of performances is figured from opening night through May 31, 1975.

In a listing of a show's numbers—dances, sketches, musical scenes, etc.—the titles of songs are identified by their appearance in quotation marks (").

HOLDOVERS FROM PREVIOUS SEASONS

Plays which were running on June 3, 1974 are listed below. More detailed information about them appears in previous *Best Plays* volumes of appropriate years. Important cast changes since opening night are recorded in the "Cast Replacements" section of this volume.

*Grease (1,375). Musical with book, music and lyrics by Jim Jacobs and Warren Casey. Opened February 14, 1972.

Don't Bother Me, I Can't Cope (1,065). Musical revue by Micki Grant. Opened April 19, 1972. (Closed October 17, 1974)

*Pippin (1,113). Musical with book by Roger O. Hirson; music and lyrics by Stephen Schwartz. Opened October 23, 1972.

A Little Night Music (600). Musical suggested by Ingmar Bergman's film *Smiles of a Summer Night;* book by Hugh Wheeler; music and lyrics by Stephen Sondheim. Opened February 25, 1973. (Closed August 3, 1974)

Irene (604). Revival of the musical with book by Hugh Wheeler and Joseph Stein; from an adaptation by Harry Rigby; based on the original play by James Montgomery; music by Harry Tierney; lyrics by Joseph McCarthy; additional lyrics and music by Charles Gaynor and Otis Clements. Opened March 13, 1973. (Closed September 7, 1974)

*Raisin (658). Musical based on Lorraine Hansberry's *A Raisin in the Sun;* book by Robert Nemiroff and Charlotte Zaltzberg; music by Judd Woldin; lyrics by Robert Brittan. Opened October 18, 1973.

Good Evening (438). Two-man revue with music; written and performed by Peter Cook and Dudley Moore. Opened November 14, 1973. (Closed November 30, 1974)

*Candide (519). Musical revival with new book by Hugh Wheeler adapted from Voltaire; music by Leonard Bernstein; lyrics by Richard Wilbur; additional lyrics by Stephen Sondheim and John Latouche. Opened December 11, 1973 off Broadway at the Chelsea Theater Center where it played 48 performances through January 20, 1974; transferred to Broadway March 10; 1974 matinee.

A Moon for the Misbegotten (314). Revival of the play by Eugene O'Neill. Opened December 29, 1973. (Recessed July 13, 1974) Reopened September 3, 1974. (Closed November 17, 1974)

Lorelei (321). Musical based on the musical *Gentlemen Prefer Blondes* (book by Anita Loos and Joseph Fields, music by Jule Styne, lyrics by Leo Robin, based on Miss Loos's collection of stories); new book by Kenny Solms and Gail Parent; new music by Jule Styne; new lyrics by Betty Comden and Adolph Green. Opened January 27, 1974. (Closed November 3, 1974)

Bad Habits (273). By Terrence McNally. Opened February 4, 1974 off Broadway where it played 96 performances through April 28, 1974; transferred to Broadway May 5, 1974 for 177 additional performances. (Closed October 5, 1974)

Noel Coward in Two Keys (140). Program of two plays by Noel Coward: *Come Into the Garden Maud* and *A Song at Twilight*. Opened February 28, 1974. (Closed June 29, 1974)

New York Shakespeare Festival Lincoln Center. 1973–74 schedule of five programs ended with **Short Eyes** (156). By Miguel Piñero. Opened February 28, 1974 off Broadway where it played 54 performances; transferred to Broadway May 23, 1974 for 102 additional performances. (Closed August 4, 1974)

Over Here! (348). Musical with book by Will Holt; music and lyrics by Richard M. Sherman and Robert B. Sherman. Opened March 6, 1974. (Closed January 4, 1975)

My Fat Friend (288). By Charles Laurence. Opened March 31, 1974. (Closed December 7, 1974)

Thieves (312). By Herb Gardner. Opened April 7, 1974. (Closed January 5, 1975)

Words and Music (128). Revue by Sammy Cahn; lyrics by Sammy Cahn; music by various composers. Opened April 16, 1974. (Closed August 3, 1974)

My Sister, My Sister (119). By Ray Aranha. Opened April 30, 1974. (Closed August 11, 1974)

Circle in the Square. 1973–74 schedule of four programs ended with **Scapino** (121). Adapted from Molière's *Les Fourberies de Scapin* in The National Theater of Great Britain Young Vic production. Opened May 18, 1974. (Closed August 1, 1974)

*The Magic Show (422). Musical with book by Bob Randall; music and lyrics by Stephen Schwartz; magic by Doug Henning. Opened May 28, 1974.

PLAYS PRODUCED JUNE 1, 1974–MAY 31, 1975

Gypsy (120). Revival of the musical with book by Arthur Laurents; music by Jule Styne; lyrics by Stephen Sondheim; suggested by the memoirs of Gypsy Rose Lee. Produced by Barry M. Brown, Edgar Lansbury, Fritz Holt and Joseph Beruh at the Winter Garden. Opened September 23, 1974. (Closed January 4, 1975)

Uncle Jocko; Kringelein; Cigar . . . . .John C. Becher George; Mr. Goldstone . . . . . . Don Potter	Clarence (and His Classic Clarinet) . . . . Craig Brown Balloon Girl . . . . Donna Elio

Baby Louise	Lisa Peluso	Little Rock	Jay Smith
Baby June	Bonnie Langford	San Diego	Dennis Karr
Rose	Angela Lansbury	Boston; Bourgeron-Couchon	Serhij Bohdan
Chowsie	Peewee	Gigolo	Edith Ann
Pop; Phil	Ed Riley	Waitress	Patricia Richardson
Weber	Charles Rule	Miss Cratchitt; Mazeppa	Gloria Rossi
Herbie	Rex Robbins	Agnes	Denny Dillon
Louise	Zan Charisse	Pastey	Richard J. Sabellico
June	Maureen Moore	Tessie Tura	Mary Louise Wilson
Tulsa	John Sheridan	Electra	Sally Cooke
Yonkers	Steven Gelfer	Maid	Bonnie Walker
L.A.	David Lawson		

Newsboys: Craig Brown, Anthony Marciona, Sean Rule, Mark Santoro. Hollywood Blondes: Pat Cody, Jinny Kordek, Jan Neuberger, Marilyn Olson, Patricia Richardson.

Standby: Miss Lansbury—Mary Louise Wilson. Understudies: Messrs. Robbins, Becher—Ed Riley; Miss Charisse—Patricia Richardson; Misses Wilson, Cooke, Rossi—Bonnie Walker; Miss Moore— Jan Neuberger; Misses Peluso, Langford—Donna Elio; Mr. Sheridan—Steven Gelfer; Messrs. Riley, Rule—Don Potter; Mr. Potter—Charles Rule.

Directed by Arthur Laurents; original New York production directed and choreographed by Jerome Robbins; choreography reproduced by Robert Tucker; musical director, Milton Rosenstock; scenery and lighting, Robert Randolph; costumes, Raoul Pène du Bois; Miss Lansbury's costumes, Robert Mackintosh; orchestrations, Sid Ramin, Robert Ginzler; dance music arrangements, John Kander; production stage manager, Kathleen A. Sullivan; stage manager, Moose Peting; press, The Merlin Group, Ltd., Sandra Manley.

Time: The early 1920s to the early 1930s. Place: Various cities throughout the U.S.A. The play was presented in two parts.

Gypsy was originally produced on Broadway 5/21/59 for 702 performances.

The list of musical numbers in *Gypsy* appears on page 338 of *The Best Plays of 1958–59.*

Cat on a Hot Tin Roof (160). Revival of the play by Tennessee Williams. Produced by the American National Theater and Academy in The American Shakespeare Theater Production, Michael Kahn artistic director, at the ANTA Theater. Opened September 24, 1974. (Closed February 8, 1975)

Margaret	Elizabeth Ashley	Sookey	Sarallen
Brick	Keir Dullea	Dixie	Kathy Rich
Mae	Joan Pape	Big Daddy	Fred Gwynne
Gooper	Charles Siebert	Reverend Tooker	Wyman Pendleton
Big Mama	Kate Reid	Doctor Baugh	William Larsen

Children: Jeb Brown, Sukey Brown, Amy Borress.

Standbys: Misses Ashley, Pape—Caroline McWilliams; Mr. Dullea—Michael Zaslow. Understudies: Miss Reid—Carol Gustafson; Mr. Gwynne—William Larsen; Messrs. Pendleton, Larsen— Robert Horen; Miss Rich—Amy Borress.

Directed by Michael Kahn; scenery, John Conklin; costumes, Jane Greenwood; lighting, Marc B. Weiss; production stage manager, Edward P. Dimond; stage manager, Robert Horen; press, Seymour Krawitz, Patricia McLean Krawitz, Fred Hoot.

Time: 1954. Place: A delta plantation. The play was presented in two parts.

Cat on a Hot Tin Roof was first produced on Broadway 3/24/55 for 694 performances. This production, which was previously produced last summer at Stratford, Conn., is its first professional New York revival of record.

Michael Zaslow replaced Keir Dullea 2/3/75.

Scapino (176). Return engagement of the revival adapted by Frank Dunlop and Jim Dale from Molière's *Les Fourberies de Scapin.* Produced by Eugene V. Wolsk and Emanuel Azenberg in The Young Vic production at the Ambassador Theater. Opened September 27, 1974. (Closed March 2, 1975)

Scapino	Jim Dale	Waiters	George Connolly, Norman Abrams
Headwaiter	Barry Michlin	Waitress	Holly Villaire

Carlo	John Horn	Geronte	J. Frank Lucas
Ottavio	Christopher Hastings	Leandro	Phil Killian
Sylvestro	Gavin Reed	Zerbinetta	Hattie Winston
Giacinta	Connie Forslund	Nurse	Bertha Sklar
Argante	Ian Trigger		

Standby: Messrs. Trigger, Lucas—Arnold Soboloff. Understudies: Mr. Dale—John Horn; Messrs. Reed, Horn, Miss Sklar—George Connolly; Messrs. Hastings, Killian—Tom Fitzsimmons; Misses Forslund, Winston, Villaire—Kathryn Grady.

Directed by Frank Dunlop; scenery and costumes, Carl Toms; lighting, Tharon Musser; music, Jim Dale; production stage manager, Lawrence Spiegel; stage managers, Lani Sundsten, Norman Abrams; press, Merle Debuskey, Susan L. Schulman.

Place: Naples. The play was presented in two parts.

This Young Vic production of *Scapino* was produced in New York twice during the 1973-74 season: off Broadway in repertory 3/12/74 for 10 performances and on Broadway by Circle in the Square 5/18/74-8/1/74 for 121 performances.

Arnold Soboloff replaced John Horn 2/25/75.

Medea and Jason (1). Free adaptation by Eugenie Leontovich of the Robinson Jeffers verson of Euripides's *Medea*. Produced by Catherine Ellis at the Little Theater. Opened and closed at the evening performance October 2, 1974.

Nurse	Lilla Skala	4th Woman	Diane Burak
Herikles	Philip McKeon	5th Woman	Ellen Farran
Helios	James Spies	Medea	Maria Oho
Tutor	Al Hill	Creon	Chet Doherty
1st Woman	Glen Lincoln	Jason	Richmond F. Johnson
2d Woman	Millette Alexander	Messenger	David MacEnulty
3d Woman	Roz Vallero		

Soldiers: David MacEnulty, E. Lynn Nickerson, Faustino Rothman, Henry Tunney.

Directed by Eugenie Leontovich; choreography, Nora Peterson; scenery, Alan Beck; costumes, sound and music, Thom Edlun; lighting, Lee Goldman; production coordinator, Tatiana Survillo; production stage manager, Susan Chase; press, Lee Solters, Milly Schoenbaum.

The play was presented in two parts.

The Robinson Jeffers version of *Medea* from which this new work was freely adapted was produced on Broadway 10/20/47 for 214 performances with Judith Anderson in the title role. It was revived 5/2/49 for 16 performances at the City Center and 11/28/65 for 77 performances off Broadway.

Mack & Mabel (65). Musical with book by Michael Stewart; music and lyrics by Jerry Herman; based on an idea by Leonard Spigelgass. Produced by David Merrick at the Majestic Theater. Opened October 6, 1974. (Closed November 30, 1974)

Eddie	Stanley Simmonds	Mabel Normand	Bernadette Peters
Mack Sennett	Robert Preston	Mr. Kleinman	Tom Batten
Lottie Ames	Lisa Kirk	Mr. Fox	Bert Michaels
Ella	Nancy Evers	Iris	Marie Santell
Freddie	Roger Bigelow	William Desmond Taylor	James Mitchell
Charlie Muldoon	Christopher Murney	Phyllis Foster	Cheryl Armstrong
Wally	Robert Fitch	Serge	Frank Root
Frank Wyman	Jerry Dodge		

Grips: John Almberg, Roger Bigelow, George Blackwell, Frank Bouley, Gerald Brentte, Lonnie Burr, Chet D'Elia, Igors Gavon, Jonathan Miele, Don Percassi, Frank Root.

Mack Sennett Bathing Beauties: Cheryl Armstrong, Claudia Asbury, Sandahl Bergman, Chrystal Chambers, Nancy Dafgek, Prudence Darby, Elaine Handel, Paula Lynn, Patricia Michaels, Carol Perea, L.J. Rose, Rita Rudner, Marianne Selbert, Jo Speros, Pat Trott, Geordie Withee.

Understudies: Mr. Preston—Igors Gavon; Miss Peters—Marie Santell; Miss Kirk—Patricia Michaels; Mr. Mitchell—Roger Bigelow; Mr. Dodge—Frank Root; Mr. Murdey—Lonnie Burr; Mr. Batten—Frank Bouley; Mr. Michaels—Jonathan Miele; Miss Evers—L.J. Rose; Mr. Fitch—Don Percassi; Mr. Simmonds—George Blackwell; Swing Dancers—Helen Butleroff, Richard Maxon.

Directed and choreographed by Gower Champion; musical direction and vocal arrangements, Don Pippin; scenery, Robin Wagner; costumes, Patricia Zipprodt; lighting, Tharon Musser; orchestrations, Philip J. Lang; incidental and dance music, John Morris; associate choreographer, Buddy Schwab; production supervisor, Lucia Victor; associate producer, Jack Schlissel; production stage manager, Marnel Sumner; stage manager, Tony Manzi; press, Solters, Sabinson & Roskin, Inc., Bud Westman, Joshua Ellis.

The story of producer Mack Sennett and his star, Mabel Normand, treated as a frustrated love affair, in parallel with the growth of silent film comedy.

ACT I

Scene 1: The Sennett Studios, 1938
"Movies Were Movies" . . . . Mack
Scene 2: The Brooklyn studio, 1911
"Look What Happened to Mabel" . . . . Mabel, Wally, Charlie, Frank, Grips
Scene 3: Mack's office, Brooklyn
"Big Time" . . . . Lottie, the Family
Scene 4: En route to California
"I Won't Send Roses" . . . . Mack
"I Won't Send Roses" (Reprise) . . . . Mabel
Scene 5: Los Angeles, 1912
"I Wanna Make the World Laugh" . . . . Mack, Company
Scene 6: On the set
"I Wanna Make the World Laugh" (Reprise) . . . . Mack, Company
Scene 7: The Orchid Room of the Hollywood Hotel, 1919
"Wherever He Ain't" . . . . Mabel, Waiters
Scene 8: On the set
"Hundreds of Girls" . . . . Mack, Bathing Beauties

ACT II

Scene 9: Mack's new office, 1923
Scene 10: The studio early next morning
"When Mabel Comes in the Room" . . . . Company
"My Heart Leaps Up" . . . . Mack
Scene 11: A pier, New York
"Time Heals Everything" . . . . Mabel
Scene 12: "Vitagraph Varieties of 1929" and the terrace of William Desmond Taylor's home
"Tap Your Troubles Away" . . . . .Lottie, Girls
Scene 13: Mack's office—then Mabel's home
"I Promise You a Happy Ending" . . . . Mack
Scene 14: The Sennett Studio, 1938

Flowers (24). Program of pantomime devised by Lindsay Kemp. Produced by Herman and Diana Shumlin and Merrold Suhl in association with Larry Parnes at the Biltmore Theater. Opened October 7, 1974. (Closed October 26, 1974)

The Boy . . . . David Meyer	Woman in Red . . . . .Jack Birkett
The Groom . . . . Neil Caplan	Waiter . . . . Tony Maples
The Mother . . . . Arlene Phillips	Tap Dancer . . . . Robert Anthony
Woman in Silver . . . . Lindsay Kemp	The Angel . . . . David Haughton

Directed and designed by Lindsay Kemp; lighting, Lindsay Kemp, John Spradbery; original sound, Andrew Wilson; scenery supervision, Leo B. Meyer; lighting supervision, James Gleason; assistant to the producers, Julie Chanova; assistants to the director, Lindsay Levy, Celestino Coronado; production stage manager, John Spradbery; press, Gifford/Wallace, Inc.

Place: A prison—a cemetery—a cafe in Montmartre—a garret—and a theater. The play was presented in two acts.

Episodes of sex deviation and transvestism performed in mime and said to be suggested by Jean Genet's *Notre Dame des Fleurs*. A foreign play previously produced in London.

*Absurd Person Singular (271). By Alan Ayckbourn. Produced by The Theater Guild and the John F. Kennedy Center for the Performing Arts in association with Michael Codron at The Music Box. Opened October 8, 1974.

Jane	Carole Shelley	Marion	Geraldine Page
Sidney	Larry Blyden	Eva	Sandy Dennis
Ronald	Richard Kiley	Geoffrey	Tony Roberts

Standbys: Misses Shelley, Page, Dennis—Marilyn Clark; Messrs. Blyden, Kiley, Roberts—Wayne Carson.

Directed by Eric Thompson; scenery, Edward Burbridge; costumes, Levino Verna; lighting, Thomas Skelton; produced by Philip Langner and Armina Marshall; production stage manager, Frederic de Wilde; stage manager, Wayne Carson; press, Joseph Wolhandler, Terry Fay.

Place: A town in England. Part I: Christmas Past. Part II: Christmas Present. Part III: Christmas to come.

Comedy about three couples representative of the British upper, middle and lower (but upward-mobile) classes who get together every Christmas Eve for a party that is never wholly successful. A foreign play previously produced in London.

Fritz Weaver replaced Richard Kiley 3/10/75. Curt Dawson replaced Tony Roberts 5/12/75. Paul Shyre replaced Larry Blyden 5/19/75.

Circle in the Square. Schedule of four programs. **The National Health** (53). By Peter Nichols; in the Long Wharf Theater Production. Opened October 10, 1974. (Closed November 24, 1974) **Where's Charley?** (76). Musical revival based on Brandon Thomas's play *Charley's Aunt*; book by George Abbott; music and lyrics by Frank Loesser. Opened December 20, 1974. (Closed February 23, 1975) **All God's Chillun Got Wings** (53). Revival of the play by Eugene O'Neill. Opened March 20, 1975. (Closed May 4, 1975). And *Death of a Salesman*, revival of the play by Arthur Miller, scheduled to open 6/19/75. Produced by Circle in the Square, Theodore Mann artistic director, Paul Libin managing director, at the Circle in the Square Joseph E. Levine Theater.

THE NATIONAL HEALTH

Staff Nurse Norton	Rita Moreno	Nurse Lake	Olivia Cole
Ash	Richard Venture	Woman	Mary Fogarty
Rees	William Swetland	Barnet	Leonard Frey
Foster	George Taylor	Dr. Boyd	Richard McKenzie
Flagg	Louis Beachner	Neil	Sean G. Griffin
Mackie	Emery Battis	Sister McPhee	Veronica Castang
Tyler	Stephen Mendillo	West Indian Student	Tazewell Thompson
Ken	Paul Rudd	Dr. Bird	Shirley Bryan
Nurse Sweet	Suzanne Lederer	Matron	Joyce Ebert
Loach	John Braden	Chaplain	David H. Leary

Nurses and Orderlies: Carlos Carrasco, David Derosa, Alice Nagel, Christinea Whitmore.

Directed by Arvin Brown; scenery, Virginia Dancy Webb; costumes, Whitney Blausen; lighting, Ronald Wallace; original music, Terrence Sherman; dialect coach, Elizabeth Smith; production stage manager, Anne Keefe; stage manager, Randall Brooks; press, Merle Debuskey, Leo Stern.

Time: The present. Place: The men's ward of a British hospital. The play was presented in two parts.

Satirical treatment of hospital life and man's common fate in a series of episodes. A foreign play previously produced in London and in New Haven, Conn.

Patricia Manceri replaced Rita Moreno 11/74.

A Best Play; see page 257.

WHERE'S CHARLEY?

Brassett . . . . Louis Beachner	Sir Francis Chesney . . . . Peter Walker
Jack Chesney . . . . .Jerry Lanning	Mr. Spettigue . . . . Tom Aldredge
Charley Wykeham . . . . Raul Julia	Donna Lucia D'Alvadorez . . . . . Taina Elg
Kitty Verdun . . . . .Carol Jo Lugenbeal	Reggie . . . . Dennis Cooley
Amy Spettigue . . . . Marcia McClean	

Students, Young Ladies: Pamela Burrell, Jacqueline Clark, Dennis Cooley, Karen Jablons, Jack Neubeck, Craig Sandquist, Leland Schwantes, Miriam Welch.

The Sextet: Ann Barak violin, David Everhart cello, Hugh Loughran viola, Donald Palma bass, Vladimir Weisman violin, Tom Pierson harpsichord and piano.

Understudies: Mr. Julia—Dennis Cooley; Miss McClean—Miriam Welch; Mr. Lanning—Jack Neubeck; Miss Lugenbeal—Karen Jablons; Miss Elg—Pam Burrell; Mr. Aldredge—Leland Schwantes; Mr. Walker—Craig Sandquist; chorus—David-James Carroll, Martha Deering.

Directed by Theodore Mann; choreography, Margo Sappington; musical direction and new arrangements, Tom Pierson; scenery, Marjorie Kellogg; lighting, Thomas Skelton; costumes, Arthur Boccia; production stage manager, Randall Brooks; stage manager, James Bernardi.

Time: Summer, 1892.

Where's Charley? was first produced on Broadway 10/11/48 for 792 performances and in a return engagement 1/29/51 for 48 additional performances. It was revived 5/26/66 for 8 performances by the City Center Light Opera Company.

The synopsis of scenes and list of musical numbers in *Where's Charley?* appears on page 389 of *The Best Plays of 1948–49.*

ALL GOD'S CHILLUN GOT WINGS

Mickey (Child) . . . . .Jimmy Baio	Mickey . . . . .Tom Sminkey
Joe (Child) . . . . Robert Lee Grant	Jim Harris . . . . Robert Christian
Jim (Child) . . . . Carl Thomas	Ella Downey . . . . Trish Van Devere
Shorty (Child) . . . . Tommy Gilchrist	Wino . . . . Chuck Patterson
Ella (Child) . . . . .Susan Jayne	Mrs. Harris . . . . Minnie Gentry
Shorty . . . . Ken Jennings	Hattie Harris . . . . Vickie Thomas
Joe . . . . .Tim Pelt	Harmonica Player . . . . .Craig Wasson

Children: Ginny Binder, Beatrice Dunmore, Helen Jennings, Kathy Rich, Derrel Edwards. Street People: Alice Nagel, Ted Snowdon, Arthur French, Verona Barnes, Robert Earl Jones, Gracie Carroll. Singers: Chuck Patterson, Craig Wasson.

Standby: Miss Van Devere—Judith Barcroft, Understudies: Messrs. Pelt, Christian—Chuck Patterson; Messrs. Jennings, Sminkey—Craig Wasson; Messrs. Grant, Thomas—Derrel Edwards; Miss Jayne—Ginny Binder; Misses Thomas, Gentry—Verona Barnes.

Directed by George C. Scott; scenery, Ming Cho Lee; costumes, Patricia Zipprodt; lighting, Thomas Skelton; production stage manager, Randall Brooks; stage manager, James Bernardi.

Act I, Scene 1: A corner in Lower New York, years ago, the end of an afternoon in spring. Scene 2: The same, nine years later, the end of an evening in spring. Scene 3: The same, five years later, a night in spring. Scene 4: The street before a church in the same ward, a morning some weeks later. Act II, Scene 1: A flat in the same ward, a morning two years later. Scene 2: The same, at twilight some months later. Scene 3: The same, a night some months later.

O'Neill's drama of the interracial marriage of childhood sweethearts, with tragic consequences, was first produced off Broadway at the Provincetown Playhouse, May 15, 1924. This is its first professional New York revival of record.

Hosanna (24). By Michel Tremblay; translated by John Van Burek and Bill Glassco. Produced by Norman Kean in association with John C. Goodwin and Tarragon Theater, Toronto, at the Bijou Theater. Opened October 14, 1974. (Closed November 3, 1974)

Hosanna . . . . Richard Monette	Cuirette . . . . Richard Donat

Directed by Bill Glassco; design, John Ferguson; lighting, Vladimir Svetlovsky; New York design supervisors—Ken Billington lighting, Stuart Wurtzel scenery, Molly Harris Campbell costumes; production stage manager, Penelope Ritco; press, Les Schecter Associates, Henry Luhrman.

Time: The present. Place: A Montreal apartment. Act I: In the early hours of the morning. Act II: Immediately thereafter.

A transvestite and his leather-jacketed lover reveal their innermost longings and fears, said to be symbolic of French Canadian politics. A foreign play previously presented in French in Montreal and in English in Toronto.

Brief Lives (53). Return engagement of the one-man performance by Roy Dotrice as John Aubrey. By Patrick Garland; adapted from the works of John Aubrey. Produced by Paul Elliott, Ellen Brandt and David Lonn at the Booth Theater. Opened October 16, 1974. (Closed December 1, 1974 matinee)

Directed by Patrick Garland; scenery, Julia Trevelyan Oman, supervised by Neil Peter Jampolis; press, Jean Dalrymple.

Time: 1697, the year of Aubrey's death. Place: Mistress Byerley's lodgings in Dirty Lane, Bloomsbury. The play was presented in two parts.

Brief Lives, with Roy Dotrice, was previously produced on Broadway 12/18/67 for 16 performances and was later produced in London and Australia.

Dreyfus in Rehearsal (12). By Jean-Claude Grumberg; adapted by Garson Kanin. Produced by David Merrick at the Ethel Barrymore Theater. Opened October 17, 1974. (Closed October 26, 1974)

Morris	Allan Arbus	Zalman	Harry Davis
Michael	Peter Kastner	Myriam	Tovah Feldshuh
Mendl	Avery Schreiber	Dr. Wasselbaum	Anthony Holland
Arnold	Sam Levene	Yanek	Michael Pendrey
Zina	Ruth Gordon	Bronislaw	Rex Williams

Standby: Miss Gordon—May Muth. Understudies: Messrs. Kastner, Arbus, Pendrey, Holland—Jerry Sroka; Miss Feldshuh—Ellen Sherman; Messrs. Levene, Davis, Williams, Schreiber—Loney Lewis.

Directed by Garson Kanin; scenery, Boris Aronson; costumes, Florence Klotz; lighting, Jennifer Tipton; translator consultant, Daphne Swabey; associate producer, Jack Schlissel; production stage manager, Murray Gitlin; stage manager, May Muth; press, Solters, Sabinson & Roskin, Inc., Bud Westman.

Time: 1931. Place: Vilna, Poland. Act I, Scene 1: An evening in March. Scene 2: Two weeks later. Scene 3: One week later. Scene 4: The following evening. Act II, Scene 1: An afternoon in April. Scene 2: A week later, evening. Scene 3: An evening in May.

A Jewish dramatist and actors rehearse a play about the Dreyfus case while another tide of anti-Semitism rises outside the doors of their theater. A foreign play previously produced in Paris.

*Equus (253). By Peter Shaffer. Produced by Kermit Bloomgarden and Doris Cole Abrahams in association with Frank Milton at the Plymouth Theater. Opened October 24, 1974.

Martin Dysart	Anthony Hopkins	Dora Strang	Frances Sternhagen
Alan Strang	Peter Firth	Horseman; Nugget	Everett McGill
Nurse	Mary Doyle	Harry Dalton	Walter Mathews
Hester Salomon	Marian Seldes	Jill Mason	Roberta Maxwell
Frank Strang	Michael Higgins		

Horses: Gus Kaikkoen, Philip Kraus, Gabriel Oshen, David Ramsey, John Tyrrell.

Standby: Mr. Hopkins—Alan Mixon. Understudies: Mr. Firth—Thomas Hulce; Mr. Higgins—Walter Mathews; Misses Sternhagen, Seldes—Mary Doyle; Misses Maxwell, Doyle—Dale Hodges; Messrs. Mathews, McGill—Philip Kraus; Horses—Michael Wieben.

Directed by John Dexter; scenery and costumes, John Napier; lighting, Andy Phillips; sound, Marc Wilkinson; mime, Claude Chagrin; American supervision—Howard Bay scenery & lighting, Patricia Adshead costumes; production stage manager, Robert L. Borod; stage manager, Nicholas Russiyan;

press, John Springer Associates, Inc., Louis Sica.

Time: The present. Place: Rokeby Psychiatric Hospital in Southern England. The play was presented in two parts.

A young man's obsessive fascination for horses intrudes upon his sex life, with tragic consequences which are explored by a doctor attempting to help him. A foreign play previously produced in London.

A Best Play; see page 133

New York Shakespeare Festival Lincoln Center. Schedule of four programs. **Mert & Phil** (41). By Anne Burr. Opened October 30, 1974. (Closed December 8, 1974) **Black Picture Show** (41). By Bill Gunn; music and lyrics by Sam Waymon. Opened January 6, 1975. (Closed February 9, 1975) **A Doll's House** (56). Revival of the play by Henrik Ibsen; new version by Christopher Hampton. Opened March 5, 1975. (Closed April 20, 1975) **Little Black Sheep** (33). By Anthony Scully. Opened May 7, 1975. (Closed June 1, 1975) Produced by the New York Shakespeare Festival Lincoln Center, Joseph Papp producer, at the Vivian Beaumont Theater.

ALL PLAYS—Associate producer, Bernard Gersten; press, Merle Debuskey, Faith Geer.

MERT & PHIL

Mert	Estelle Parsons	George	Norman Ornellas
Phil	Michael Lombard	Lavoris	Beverlee McKinsey
Mother	Marilyn Roberts	Beauty Lady	Marie Wallace
Lucille	Rhoda Gemignani		

Standbys: Misses Parsons, Gemignani—Marcia Haufrecht; Messrs. Lombard, Ornellas—George Dzundza. Understudies: Miss Roberts—Lucy Lee Flippen; Misses McKinsey, Wallace—Elaine Kerr.

Directed by Joseph Papp; scenery, Santo Loquasto; costumes, Theoni V. Aldredge; lighting, Martin Aronstein; production stage manager, D. W. Koehler; stage manager, Michael Chambers.

Time: Now. Place: Here. The play was presented in two parts.

Emotional impact of a mastectomy on a middle-aged woman and her marriage of 20 years' duration.

BLACK PICTURE SHOW

Vocalist	Sam Waymon	Rita	Carol Cole
J.D.	Albert Hall	Philippe	Paul-David Richards
Alexander	Dick Anthony Williams	Jane	Linda Miller
Norman	Graham Brown		

Hospital Attendants: William Leet, Marvin Beck.

Musicians: Sam Waymon keyboards, John Betsch drums, John Blake violin, Frank Clayton bass, George Davis Jr. guitar, Nadi Qamar percussion.

Understudies: Messrs. Richards, Leet, Beck—Doug Rowe; Miss Cole—Ethel Ayler; Miss Miller —Hilary Beane; Mr. Hall—Tucker Smallwood; Messrs. Hall, Williams—Bill Cobbs.

Directed by Bill Gunn; music conducted by Sam Waymon; scenery, Peter Harvey; costumes, Judy Dearing; lighting, Roger Morgan; production stage manager, Dyanne Hochman; stage manager, Osborn E. Scott Jr.

Time: Now. Place: A hospital psychiatric unit, Bronx, N.Y. The play was presented without intermission.

How and why it all went wrong for a black poet and playwright looking back over his life from the vantage point of its last day.

MUSICAL NUMBERS: "I'm So Glad" (Overture). "Mose Art" (2d Movement), "Bird of Paradise," "Variation on 'Chopin in E Minor'," "Memory," "Black Picture Show" (lyrics by Bill Gunn), "Mose Art (1st Movement), "Bitch in Heat," "Digits," "Science Fiction," "I Feel So Good" (lyrics by Bill Gunn), "Vintage '51," "Afghanistan," "Terminate."

A DOLL'S HOUSE

Torvald Helmer	Sam Waterston	Helene	Judith Light
Nora	Liv Ullmann	Errand Boy	Michael Chambers
Mrs. Kristine Linde	Barbara Colby	The Helmers' Children:	
Dr. Rank	Michael Granger	Bob	Gibby Gibson
Nils Krogstad	Barton Heyman	Emmy	Paula Gibson
Anne-Marie	Helen Stenborg	Ivar	Wayne Harding

Standbys: Miss Ullmann—Virginia Vestoff; Mr. Waterston—Drew Snyder. Understudies: Messrs. Granger, Heyman—James Gallery; Miss Colby—Zina Jasper; Misses Stenborg, Light—Sloane Shelton.

Directed by Tormod Skagestad; scenery, Santo Loquasto; costumes, Theoni V. Aldredge; lighting, Martin Aronstein; Tarantella choreographed by Donald Saddler; press assistant, Sally Campbell.

Place: The Helmers' Flat. Act I: Christmas Eve. Act II: Christmas Day. Act III: The day after Christmas.

This Christopher Hampton version of the Ibsen play was previously produced on Broadway 1/13/71 for 89 performances.

LITTLE BLACK SHEEP

Priests of the Society of Jesus:		Michael George	John Christopher Jones
Father Finley	Joseph Warren	Willie Schmidt	Stefan Schnabel
Jack Hassler	Ken Howard	Sister Mary Charles	Diane Kagan
Johnnie Rock	Edward Grover	Henry Morlino	Pierre Epstein
Vinnie Caputo	Gastone Rossilli		

Understudies: Messrs. Jones, Rossilli—Douglas Jones; Messrs. Howard, Grover—Will Lyman; Messrs. Warren, Schnabel, Epstein—Tom Toner.

Directed by Edward Payson Call; scenery, David Mitchell; costumes, Theoni V. Aldredge; lighting, Martin Aronstein; production stage manager, Jason Steven Cohen; stage manager, John Beven.

Time: June 1968. Place: The Jesuit House of Study, New Haven, Conn. The play was presented in two parts.

Times and emotions are out of joint within the cloister as they are outside it, where the assassination of Robert Kennedy has just taken place.

Tubstrip (22). By A.J. Kronengold. Produced by K.G. Productions, Ltd., in association with Mark Segal at the Mayfair Theater. Opened October 31, 1974. (Closed November 17, 1974)

Brian	Calvin Culver	Kevin	Michael Kearns
Darryl	Jade McCall	Richie	Edward Rambeau
Andy	Walter Holiday	Dusty	John Bruce Deaven
Wally	Jake Everett	Bob	Dick Joslyn
Tony	Gerald Grant		

Directed by Jerry Douglas; scenery, Leo B. Meyer; costumes, Jim Faber; lighting, Edward I. Byers; production stage manager, Robert Lo Bianco; associate producer, Fred Walker; press, Max Eisen.

Comedy set in a steambath and dealing with homosexuals. Previously produced in tryouts off Broadway and on national tour.

Mourning Pictures (1). By Honor Moore; music by Susan Ain. Produced by Samuel H. Schwartz in the Lenox Arts Center/Music-Theater Performing Group production at the Lyceum Theater. Opened and closed at the evening performance November 10, 1974.

Margaret	Kathryn Walker	David	Daniel Landon
Maggie	Leora Dana	Drs. Rumbach, Cassidy,	
Philip	Donald Symington	Berryman, Potter	Philip Carlson
Abigail	Leslie Ackerman	Singer	Dorothea Joyce

Musicians: Amy Rubin electric and acoustic piano, John Carbonne acoustic and fender base, Sue Ann Kahn soprano and alto flute, Joe Passaro percussion.

Directed by Kay Carney; scenery, John Jacobsen; costumes, Whitney Blausen; lighting, Spencer Mosse; producers for Lenox Arts Center/Music Theater Performing Group, Lyn Austin, Mary Silverman; production stage manager, Frank Marino; stage manager, Duane Mazey; press, The Merlin Group, Ltd., Harriett Trachtenberg, Elizabeth Rodman.

Place: Connecticut, New York and Washington, D.C. Part I: March-May. Part II: June-September. A play with music about a 27-year-old poet observing the slow death of her mother caused by cancer.

MUSICAL NUMBERS—Part I: "What Will She Leave Me?", "It's Such a Beautiful Day," "What Are You Saying About Me Now?", "Sweet Clear Sun." Part II: "The Garden, "Wait Until the Sun," "I Want to Go Home," "Paul Arrives," "There Is a Birthday."

The New Phoenix Repertory Company. Schedule of three revivals.**Love for Love** (24). By William Congreve. Opened November 11, 1974. (Closed November 30, 1974) **The Rules of the Game** (12). By Luigi Pirandello; translated by William Murray. Opened December 12, 1974. (Closed December 21, 1974). **The Member of the Wedding** (12). By Carson McCullers. Opened January 2, 1975. (Closed January 11, 1975) Produced by the Phoenix Theater, T. Edward Hambleton and Michael Montel managing directors, Stephen Porter and Harold Prince artistic directors, at the Helen Hayes Theater.

PERFORMER	"LOVE FOR LOVE"	"THE RULES OF THE GAME"	"THE MEMBER OF THE WEDDING"
Glenn Close	Angelica	Neighbor	Janice
Patricia Conwell	Jenny		
David Dukes	Scandal	Guido Venanzi	
George Ede	Sir Sampson	Filippo	Mr. Addams
Marge Eliot	Servant		Berenice Sadie Brown
Joel Fabiani	Valentine	Barelli	
Clarence Felder	Streetsweeper	Neighbor	
Peter Friedman	Ben	Marquis Migliorili	
Munson Hicks	Jeremy	Meme	
Nicholas Hormann	Trapland	Coco	Jarvis
Marybeth Hurt	Miss Prue		Frankie Addams
Charles Kimbrough	Tattle	Dr. Spiga	
Jeanette Landis	Nurse	Clara	Doris
Marcella Lowery			Sis Laura
Eamon MacKenzie			John Henry West
John McMartin	Foresight	Leone Gala	
Charlotte Moore	Mrs. Frail		Mrs. West
Fred Morsell	Buckram	Neighbor	T.T. Williams
Ernest Thomas	Snap		Honey Camden Brown
Ellen Tovatt	Mrs. Foresight	Neighbor	
Joan Van Ark		Silia Gala	
Tim Wilson			Barney MacKean

The Elizabeth Enterprise in *Love for Love*: Lucy Cross, David Hart, Mary Springfels.

Understudies—*Love for Love*: Messrs. Ede, Morsell—Clarence Felder; Messrs. Fabiani, Friedman —Nicholas Hormann; Messrs. Dukes, Hormann—Fred Morsell; Messrs. Kimbrough, McMartin— Munson Hicks; Mr. Hicks—Ernest Thomas; Misses Close, Hurt—Patricia Conwell; Misses Tovatt, Moore—Jeanette Landis; Miss Landis—Marge Eliot. *The Rules of the Game*: Mr. McMartin— Munson Hicks; Miss Van Ark—Glenn Close; Mr. Dukes—Peter Friedman; Messrs. Kimbrough, Ede —Clarence Felder; Mr. Fabiani—Nicholas Hormann; Miss Landis—Marybeth Hurt. *The Member of the Wedding*: Miss Eliot Marcella Lowery; Miss Hurt—Glenn Close; Master MacKenzie—Master John E. Dunn; Mr. Ede—Clarence Felder; Messrs. Morsell, Thomas—Charles Turner; Miss Moore —Jeanette Landis.

ALL PLAYS—Scenery, Douglas Higgins; lighting, Ken Billington; production stage manager, Robert Beard; stage managers, Jonathan Penzner, Elisabeth W. Seley; press, Mary Bryant, Bill Evans.

LOVE FOR LOVE—Directed by Harold Prince; costumes, Franne Lee; incidental music, Paul

Gemignani; songs, Hugh Wheeler, Paul Gemignani; assistant director, Ruth Mitchell.

Place: Valentine Legend's lodgings and the Foresight country home in Kensington. The play was presented in three parts.

Love for Love was produced on Broadway 3/31/25 and the following season 9/14/25. Its last New York revival was the Theater Guild's, with John Gielgud, 5/26/47 for 48 performances.

THE RULES OF THE GAME—Directed by Stephen Porter; costumes, Nancy Potts.

Time: 1918. Act I: Silia Gala's apartment, evening. Act II, scene 1: Leone Gala's house, next morning, Scene 2: Early the following morning.

The Rules of the Game, about a husband avenging a supposed insult to his wife in a duel, is the play the actors are rehearsing in Pirandello's *Six Characters in Search of an Author*. Its only previous professional New York production of record took place off Broadway during the 1960–61 season.

THE MEMBER OF THE WEDDING—Directed by Michael Montel; costumes, Donald Brooks; incidental music, Charles Strouse.

Time: August 1945. Place: A small Southern town. Act I: A late afternoon in August. Act II: Afternoon of the next day. Act III, Scene 1: The wedding day—afternoon of the day following Act II. Scene 2: 4 A.M. the next morning. Scene 3: Late afternoon, the following November.

The Member of the Wedding was first produced on Broadway 1/5/50 for 501 performances. This is its first professional revival.

NOTE: In addition to its regular programs, The New Phoenix Repertory Company presented a series of 5 special "Side Shows" at Playhouse II for engagements limited to 6 performances each, as follows: *Knuckle* by David Hare, 1/23/75–1/26/75; *Dandelion Wine* by Ray Bradbury, adapted by Peter John Bailey, 2/6/75–2/9/75; *Meeting Place* by Robert Lord, 4/24/75–4/27/75; *Macrune's Guevara* by John Spurling, 5/8/75–5/11/75; *Flux* by Susan Miller, 5/22/75–5/27/75.

*Sherlock Holmes (219). Revival of the play by Arthur Conan Doyle and William Gillette. Produced by arrangement with the governors of the Royal Shakespeare Theater, Stratford-Upon-Avon, England, in the Royal Shakespeare Company production at the Broadhurst Theater. Opened November 12, 1974.

Madge Larrabee	Barbara Leigh-Hunt	Billy	Sean Clarke
John Forman	Harry Towb	Doctor Watson	Tim Pigott-Smith
James Larrabee	Nicholas Selby	Jim Craigin	Morgan Sheppard
Terese	Pamela Miles	Thomas Leary	Keith Taylor
Sidney Prince	Trevor Peacock	"Lightfoot" McTague	Joe Marcell
Alice Faulkner	Mel Martin	Parsons	Arthur Blake
Sherlock Holmes	John Wood	Sir Edward Leighton	John Keston
Professor Moriarty	Philip Locke	Count von Stalburg	John Bott
John	Michael Mellinger	Newsboy	Robert Cook
Alfred Bassick	Martin Milman	Violinist	Christopher Tarlé

Londoners and Others: Wendy Bailey, Joseph Charles, Alan Coates, Robert Cook, Joe Marcell, Michael Walker.

Directed by Frank Dunlop; scenery and costumes, Carl Toms; lighting, Neil Peter Jampolis; music arrangements, Michael Lankester; presented in the United States through the cooperative efforts of James Nederlander, Inc., The Shubert Organization, Kennedy Center Productions, Inc., Adela Holzer, Eddie Kulukundis and Victor Lurie; production stage manager, George Ronde; press, Michael Alpert Public Relations, Marilynn LeVine, Ellen Levene.

Time: 1891. Place: London. Act I, Scene 1: Drawing-room at the Larrabees, evening. Scene 2: Professor Moriarty's underground office, morning. Scene 3: Sherlock Holmes's apartment in Baker Street, evening. Act II, Scene 1: The Stepney gas chamber, midnight. Scene 2: Doctor Watson's consulting room in Kensington, the following evening.

This Doyle-Gillette Sherlock Holmes was last produced on Broadway 11/25/29 for 45 performances with Gillette in the title role, at which time it was described by Burns Mantle as follows: "This 'hitherto unpublished episode in the career of the great detective, showing his connection with the strange case of Miss Faulkner,' relates the adventures attending the roundup of Professor Moriarty and his gang of crooks, including James and Madge Larrabee, who were holding Miss Faulkner in the expectation of collecting blackmail." A foreign production previously presented in London.

Clive Revill replaced Philip Locke, Dennis Cooney replaced Tim Piggott-Smith, Christina

Pickles replaced Barbara Leigh-Hunt, Lynne Lipton replaced Mel Martin, Tony Tanner replaced Trevor Peacock, Richard Lupino replaced Harry Towb, Ron Randell replaced Nicholas Selby 2/4/75. Patrick Horgan replaced John Wood 4/22/75. John Neville replaced Patrick Horgan 5/13/75.

Sizwe Banzi Is Dead (159). Opened November 13, 1974. And **The Island** (52). Opened November 24, 1974. Repertory of two plays devised by Athol Fugard, John Kani and Winston Ntshona. Produced by Hillard Elkins/Lester Osterman Productions/Bernard Delfont/Michael White, by arrangement with The English Stage Company Limited, in The Royal Court Theater Production at the Edison Theater. (Repertory closed May 18, 1975)

PERFORMER	"SIZWE BANZI IS DEAD"	"THE ISLAND"
John Kani	Styles; Buntu	John
Winston Ntshona	Sizwe Banzi	Winston

Directed by Athol Fugard; scenery, Stuart Wurtzel; costumes, Bill Walker; lighting, Ronald Wallace; design consultant, Douglas Heap; Lester Osterman Productions—Lester Osterman, Richard Horner; production stage manager, Nina Seely; stage manager, Bryan Young; press, Solters/Sabinson/Roskin, Bud Westman, Ted Goldsmith.

Both plays presented without intermission; foreign plays previously produced in South Africa, London, and the Long Wharf Theater, New Haven, Conn.

Sizwe Banzi Is Dead is about the inner conflict of a South African Bantu who could profit greatly by switching passbooks (identity cards) with a dead man but hates to lose his own identity in doing so.

The Island is an anecdote of miserable prison life in a maximum-security lockup for political offenders, where two cellmates prepare a version of *Antigone* for the annual prison show.

A Best Play; see page 157

Sgt. Pepper's Lonely Hearts Club Band on the Road (66). Musical conceived and adapted by Robin Wagner and Tom O'Horgan; music and lyrics by John Lennon and Paul McCartney. Produced by Robert Stigwood in association with Brian Avnet and Scarab Productions, Inc. at the Beacon Theater. Opened November 17, 1974. (Closed January 5, 1975)

Maxwell's Silver Hammermen:
Jack . . . . Allan Nicholls
Sledge . . . . William Parry
Claw . . . . B.G. Gibson
Billy Shears . . . . Ted Neeley
Lucy . . . . Alaina Reed
Flattop . . . . Walter Rivera
Sun Queen; Lovely Rita; Polythene Pam;
    Sgt. Pepper . . . . . . David Patrick Kelly
Strawberry Fields . . . . Kay Cole

Hammeroids: Blake Anderson, Edward Q. Bhartonn, Arlana Blue, Ron Capozzoli, Michael Meadows, Stoney Reece, Jason Roberts.

Sgt. Pepper's Lonely Hearts Club Band: Billy Schwartz electric and acoustic guitar, banjo, probo; Richie Resnicoff electric, acoustic and electric 12-string guitar, mandolin; Bobby Cranshaw, electric bass; Peter Phillips piano, clavinet, fender-rhodes, organ; Allen Herman drums; Hank Jaramillo percussion; Phil Davis moog synthesizer, arp string synthesizer, E-flat cyclotron; Lloyd Michels lead trumpet, piccolo trumpet, flugel horn, soprano recorder; Victor Paz jazz trumpet, flugel horn, claves; Wayne Andre lead trombone, euphonium, bass trombone, alto recorder; Alan Raph bass trombone, tuba, trombone; Peter Gordon french horn, wagner tuba, maracas, tenor recorder; Paul Fleisher saxophones, clarinet, flute, unicycle; Ruben Rivera cello, tamborine, maestro.

Understudies: Mr. Neeley—David Patrick Kelly; Misses Cole, Reed—Stoney Reece; Mr. Kelly—Michael Meadows.

Directed by Tom O'Horgan; music arranged and conducted by Gordon Lowry Harrell; scenery, Robin Wagner; costumes, Randy Barcelo; lighting, Jules Fisher; sound, Abe Jacob; executive producer, Peter Brown; associate producers, Gatchell and Neufeld; presented at the Beacon Theater by Steven Singer, Steve Metz and Howard Dando; production supervisor, Richard Scanga; press, Rogers & Cowan, Leee Black Childers.

Rock musical spectacle based on the Beatles' record album *Sgt. Pepper's Lonely Hearts Club Band,* with 17 McCartney-Lennon songs added to the record's original 12.

ACT I

Opening	Orchestra
"Sgt. Pepper's Lonely Hearts Club Band"	Hammermen
"With a Little Help From My Friends"	Billy, Hammermen
"Nowhere Man"	Hammermen
"With a Little Help From My Friends" (Reprise)	Billy, Hammermen
"Lucy in the Sky With Diamonds"	Lucy, Billy, Hammermen
"I Want You"	Billy, Lucy, Hammermen
"Come Together"	Lucy, Flattop, Friends
"Nowhere Man II"	Hammermen
"Sun Queen"	Company
"Lovely Rita"	Rita, Billy, Hammermen, Lucy
"Polythene Pam"	Rita, Billy, Hammermen, Lucy
"She Came in Through the Bathroom Window"	Hammermen (featuring Jack)
"You Never Give Me Your Money"	Billy, Rita, Hammermen, Lucy
"Lovely Rita" (Reprise)	Billy, Rita, Hammermen, Lucy
"Her Majesty"	Billy
"A Day in the Life"	Billy
"She's Leaving Home"	Hammermen (featuring Claw)
"Strawberry Fields Forever"	Strawberry, Billy
"Getting Better"	Billy, Strawberry, Hammermen

ACT II

Opening	Orchestra
"Because"	Billy, Strawberry
"When I'm Sixty-four"	Billy, Strawberry
"Because" (Reprise)	Billy, Strawberry
"Good Morning, Good Morning"	Hammermen
"Being for the Benefit of Mr. Kite"	Hammermen, Lucy
"Oh Darling"	Strawberry
"Fixing a Hole"	Billy
"Oh Darling" (Reprise)	Strawberry
"Being for the Benefit of Mr. Kite II"	Hammermen
"Mean Mr. Mustard"	Lucy
"Maxwell's Silver Hammer"	Hammermen
"Being for the Benefit of Mr. Kite III"	Hammermen
"Carry That Weight"	Hammermen
"Golden Slumbers"	Billy
"Carry That Weight" (Reprise)	Hammermen
"The Long and Winding Road"	Billy
"Get Back"	Sgt. Pepper, Billy, Lucy, Hammermen
"Sgt. Pepper's Lonely Hearts Club Band" (Reprise)	Company
The End	Company

Fame (1). By Anthony J. Ingrassia. Produced by James J.C. Andrews and Tony Zanetta for Mainman at the John Golden Theater. Opened and closed at the evening performance, November 18, 1974.

Cast: Studio Official, Louis B. Mayer, Tadlock, TV News Reporter—Rudy Hornish; Diane Cook —Ellen Barber; Makeup Man, Young Gable, Richard Ronson, Young Priest—Robert Miano; Eunice, Eva, Luba—Bibi Besch; Madge, Louella O. Parsons, Helen Harvey—Nancy Reardon; Bill, Ned, Milton, Sonny—Lawrie Driscoll; Ed Aimes, Private Dick, Danny Grant, Walter, Sam, Newspaper Reporter—Jeremy Stevens; Established Movie Actress in TV, Meg, An Established Actress, Telephone Operator, Woman With Fur at Party, Mrs. Hodges—Christine Lavren.

Directed by Anthony J. Ingrassia; scenery, Douglas W. Schmidt; costumes, Jeffrey B. Moss; lighting, Martin Aronstein; sound, Chuck London; associate producer, Shirley Rappoport; production stage manager, R. Derek Swire; stage manager, Peter von Mayrhauser; press, Les Schecter Associates.

Time: See the U.S.A. in Your Chevrolet. Place: America. The play was presented in two parts. The life story of a performer, based on the life and career of Marilyn Monroe.

Saturday Sunday Monday (12). By Eduardo de Filippo; English adaptation by Keith Waterhouse and Willis Hall. Produced by Barry M. Brown, Fritz Holt and S. Spencer Davids by arrangement with The National Theater of Great Britain at the Martin Beck Theater. Opened November 21, 1974. (Closed November 30, 1974)

Antonio	Walter Abel	Giulianella	Francesca Bartoccini
Rosa	Sada Thompson	Virginia	Minnie Gordon Gaster
Peppino	Eli Wallach	Federico	Gary Sandy
Aunt Meme	Jan Miner	Luigi Ianniello	Ron Holgate
Raffaele	Michael Vale	Elena	Nina Dova
Attilio	Amos Abrams	Catiello	Michael Enserro
Maria	Susan Merson	Michele	Terry Hinz
Roberto	William McCauley	Dr. Cefercola	Sam Gray
Rocco	Jeff Giannone		

Understudies: Misses Thompson, Miner—Nina Dova; Messrs. Abel, Enserro, Wallach—Sam Gray; messrs. Gray, Hinz, Holgate, Vale—John Grigas; Messrs. Abrams, Giannone, McCauley, Sandy—Richard DeFabees; Misses Dova, Gaster, Merson—Saax Bradbury; Miss Bartoccini—Susan Merson.

Directed and designed by Franco Zeffirelli; lighting, Roger Morgan; original National Theater costume designs, Raimonda Gaetani; production stage manager, William Dodds; stage manager, John Grigas; press, The Merlin Group, Ltd., Cheryl Sue Dolby.

Time: The present. Place: The Priore family's apartment in Naples. Act I: Saturday. Act II: Sunday. Act III: Monday.

A well-to-do Neopolitan family's life and problems presented as comedy. A foreign (Italian) play previously produced in London.

As You Like It (8). Revival of the play by William Shakespeare. Produced by Hurok in association with Herman and Diana Shumlin by arrangement with the National Theater of Great Britain in the Clifford Williams Production at the Mark Hellinger Theater. Opened December 3, 1974. (Closed December 8, 1974 matinee)

Duke Senior	Michael Beint	Touchstone	Nigel Hawthorne
Frederick	Gilbert Wynne	Sir Oliver Martext	Christopher Robb
Amiens; Hymen	Ian Hanson	Corin	John Gay
Jaques	John Nettleton	Silvius	Geoffrey Burridge
Le Beau	Dennis Edwards	William	John Dallimore
Charles	John Flint	1st Forest Lord	David Mace
Oliver	David Howey	Rosalind	Gregory Floy
Jaques de Boys	Adam Kurakin	Celia	David Schofield
Orlando	Paul Hastings	Phebe	Christopher Neame
Adam	Blake Butler	Audrey	Gordon Kaye
Dennis	Rod Willmott		

Lords and Pages: John Dallimore, Raymund Dring, Andrew Johns, Adam Kurakin, David Mace, Jeff Murray, Christopher Robb, Rod Willmott.

Musicians: Geoff Driscoll woodwind, leader; Hywell Thomas organ, Mike Barker bass guitar, Bill Castle drums.

Directed by Clifford Williams; design, Ralph Kotai; lighting, Robert Ornbo; music, Marc Wilkinson; fight director, William Hobbs; production stage manager, Robert Findlay; stage manager, Michael Joyce; press, Gifford/Wallace, Inc.

The play was presented in two parts.

This all-male performance of Shakespeare's comedy was previously produced in London and on tour in the United States. The play itself was last produced here last season by New York Shakespeare Festival in Central Park, 6/21/73 for 28 performances.

London Assurance (46). Revival of the play by Dion Boucicault; adapted by Ronald Eyre. Produced by James M. Nederlander, Eddie Kulukundis, Roger L. Stevens by arrangement with Eddie Kulukundis in The Royal Shakespeare Company production at the Palace Theater. Opened December 5, 1974. (Closed January 12, 1975)

Cool	Anthony Pedley	Pert	Sue Nicholls
Martin	Tom Owen	James	Andy Mulligan
Charles Courtly	Roger Rees	Grace Harkaway	Polly Adams
Dazzle	Bernard Lloyd	Mark Meddle	John Cater
Sir Harcourt Courtly	Donald Sinden	Lady Gay Spanker	Elizabeth Spriggs
Maximilian Harkaway	Glyn Owen	Adolphus Spanker	Sydney Bromley
Solomon Isaacs	Leon Sinden	Jenks	Douglas Anderson

Standbys: Miss Adams—Marion Lines; Mr. Pedley—Stephen Gordon. Understudies: Mr. Cater—Douglas Anderson; Messrs. Leon Sinden, Anderson, Tom Owen, Mulligan—Stephen Gordon; Mr. Lloyd—Andy Mulligan; Miss Spriggs—Sue Nicholls; Mr. Rees—Tom Owen; Donald Sinden—Anthony Pedley; Messrs. Glyn Owen, Bromley—Leon Sinden.

Directed by Euan Smith; scenery, Alan Tagg; costumes, David Walker, Michael Stennett; lighting, Robert Ornbo; assistant director, Howard Panter; music arrangements, Guy Woolfenden; scenery and costume supervision, Mason Arvold; production manager, John Wallbank; stage manager, Michael Cass Jones; press, Michael Alpert Public Relations, Ellen Levene, Marilynn LeVine, Anne Weinberg, Warren Knowlton.

Time: Mid-19th century. Act I, Scene 1: An anteroom in Sir Harcourt Courtly's house in Belgrave Square, London, a morning in early summer. Scene 2: The lawn before Oak Hall, Gloucestershire, noon the next day. Scene 3: A drawing room at Oak Hall, late afternoon two days later. Act II, Scene 1: The drawing room, after dinner. Scene 2: The lawn before Oak Hall, later that night. Scene 3: The drawing room, later.

Comedy about an aging widower in pursuit of the fair sex, written in 1841 and first produced in New York in that year. Its last professional New York production was as a comedy with music 2/18/37 for 5 performances. The present production was produced in London by The Royal Shakespeare Company during the 1970–71 season and on tour this season in Canada and the U.S.

Who's Who in Hell (8). By Peter Ustinov. Produced by Alexander H. Cohen and Bernard Delfont at the Lunt-Fontanne Theater. Opened December 9, 1974. (Closed December 14, 1974)

Elbert C. Harland	George S. Irving	Arnold J. Pilger	Josef Sommer
Arlo Forrest Buffy	Beau Bridges	The Frenchman	Jim Oyster
Ilse	Olympia Dukakis	Galina Chubkina	Christina Pickles
Samuel E. McWhirter	Bob Lawrence	General Mike O'Henry	G. Wood
Sir Augustus Ludbourne	Joseph Maher	Bundy Harris	Erin Connor
Boris Vassilievitch Krivelov	Peter Ustinov		

Standbys: Messrs. Ustinov, Sommer, Wood—Jim Oyster; Messrs. Irving, Maher—Miller Lide; Mr. Lawrence—Dino Shorte; Misses Pickles, Dukakis—Jane Groves; Miss Connor—Barbara Cohen.

Directed by Ellis Rabb; scenery, Douglas W. Schmidt; costumes, Nancy Potts; lighting, John Gleason; production associate, Hildy Parks; associate producer, Roy Somlyo; production supervisor, Jerry Adler; stage manager, Barbara Cohen; press, Richard Hummler.

The play was presented in three parts.

Topical comedy set in an anteroom of hell, or maybe heaven, immediately after a young assassin has murdered the President of the United States and the Chairman of the U.S.S.R. on a visit to Disneyland.

In Praise of Love (199). By Terence Rattigan. Produced by Arthur Cantor at the Morosco Theater. Opened December 10, 1974. (Closed May 31, 1975)

Lydia Cruttwell	Julie Harris	Mark Walters	Martin Gabel
Sebastian Cruttwell	Rex Harrison	Joey Cruttwell	Peter Burnell

Standbys: Messrs. Harrison, Gabel—Paul Sparer; Miss Harris—Joan Bassie. Understudy: Mr. Burnell—Bill Biskup.

Directed by Fred Coe; scenery and lighting, Jo Mielziner; costumes, Theoni V. Aldredge; production stage manager, Mortimer Halpern; stage manager, Bill Biskup; press, Arthur Cantor Associates, George Willard.

Time: During the past year. Place: The Cruttwell flat in the Islington section of London. Act I: Six o'clock on a spring evening. Act II: Seven o'clock the following evening.

A self-centered husband doesn't realize his wife is suffering from a terminal illness—or does he? A foreign play previously produced in London.

God's Favorite (119). By Neil Simon. Produced by Emanuel Azenberg and Eugene V. Wolsk at the Eugene O'Neill Theater. Opened December 11, 1974. (Closed March 23, 1975)

Joe Benjamin	Vincent Gardenia	David Benjamin	Terry Kiser
Ben Benjamin	Lawrence John Moss	Mady	Rosetta LeNoire
Sara Benjamin	Laura Esterman	Morris	Nick LaTour
Rose Benjamin	Maria Karnilova	Sidney Lipton	Charles Nelson Reilly

Standbys: Messrs. Reilly, Moss—Ken Olfson; Miss Karnilova—Jo Flores Chase. Understudies: Mr. Gardenia—Richard Kuss; Mr. Kiser—Philip Cusack; Miss LeNoire—Mary Rio Lewis; Miss Esterman—Ellen Ruskin; Mr. LaTour—Phil Lindsay.

Directed by Michael Bennett; scenery, William Ritman; costumes, Joseph G. Aulisi; lighting, Tharon Musser; production stage manager, Tom Porter; stage manager, Philip Cusack; press, Solters/Sabinson/Roskin, Milly Schoenbaum, Bud Westman.

Place: The Benjamin mansion on the North Shore of Long Island. Act I, Scene 1: Midnight. Scene 2: Two weeks later. Act II: The Holocaust after.

Comedy, the Biblical Job story cast in a contemporary setting.

Of Mice and Men (61). Revival of the play by John Steinbeck. Produced by Elliot Martin in association with Mortimer Levitt at the Brooks Atkinson Theater. Opened December 18, 1974. (Closed February 9, 1975)

George	Kevin Conway	Curley's Wife	Pamela Blair
Lennie	James Earl Jones	Slim	David Gale
Candy	Stefan Gierasch	Carlson	Pat Corley
The Boss	David Clarke	Whit	James Staley
Curley	Mark Gordon	Crooks	Joe Seneca

Standby: Miss Blair—Linda Martin. Understudies: Messrs. Jones, Seneca—Frankie Faison; Mr. Conway—Pat Corley; Mr. Gierasch—David Clarke; Mr. Gordon—James Staley; Messrs. Corley, Staley, Gale, Clarke—Lanny Flaherty.

Directed by Edwin Sherin; scenery, costumes and lighting, William and Jean Eckart; production stage manager, Harry Young; press, Seymour Krawitz, Patricia McLean Krawitz.

Time: The 1930s. Place: Southern California. Act I, Scene 1: Bank of the Salinas River. Scene 2: Bunkhouse. Scene 3: Bunkhouse. Act II, Scene 1: Crook's room. Scene 2: Hayloft. Scene 3: Bank of the Salinas River.

Steinbeck's drama was first produced on Broadway 11/23/37 for 207 performances, when it won the Critics Award and was named a Best Play of its season. This is its first professional New York revival other than a musical version produced off Broadway in the season of 1957–58.

Good News (16). Musical revival with book by Laurence Schwab, B.G. De Sylva and Frank Mandel; words and music by (B.G.) De Sylva, (Lew) Brown and (Ray) Henderson; adapted by Abe Burrows. Produced by Harry Rigby and Terry Allen Kramer at the St. James Theater. Opened December 23, 1974. (Closed January 4, 1975)

Bill Johnson	Gene Nelson	Beef Saunders	Joseph Burke
Tom Marlowe	Scott Stevensen	Bobby Randall	Wayne Bryan

Pooch Kearney	Stubby Kaye	Slats	Jimmy Brennan
Flo	Rebecca Urich	Sylvester	Tommy Breslin
Millie	Paula Cinko	Prof. Kenyon	Alice Faye
Pat	Jana Robbins	Connie Lane	Marti Rolph
Babe O'Day	Barbara Lail	Muffin	Margaret
Windy	Terry Eno	Colton Player	Ernie Pysher

Acrobats: Lisa Guignard, Mary Ann Lipson, Ernie Pysher, Jeff Spielman. Happy Days Quartet: Tim Cassidy, Randall Robbins, Scott Stevensen, David Thome. Baton Twirlers: Tim Cassidy, Lynda Goodfriend, Lisa Guignard. Tap Dancers: Terry Eno, Jimmy Brennan.

Coeds: Paula Cinko, Robin Gerson, Lynda Goodfriend, Lisa Guignard, Anne Kaye, Mary Ann Lipson, Sally O'Donnell, Rebecca Urich, Marcia Lynn Watkins. The Boys: Michael Austin, Jimmy Brennan, Tim Cassidy, Ernie Pysher, Randall Robbins, Jeff Spielman, David Thome. Alternates: Kathel Carson, David Fredericks.

Understudies: Miss Faye—Jana Robbins; Mr. Nelson—Randall Robbins; Messrs. Kaye, Breslin— Jimmy Brennan; Miss Rolph—Anne Kaye; Mr. Stevensen—Terry Eno; Miss Robbins—Paula Cinko; Miss Lail—Rebecca Urich; Mr. Bryan—Tommy Breslin; Mr. Burke—Ernie Pysher; Miss Cinko— Marcia Lynn Watkins; Miss Urich—Sally O'Donnell; Mr. Eno—David Thome; Mr. Brennan—Tim Cassidy.

Directed by Abe Burrows; musical numbers staged by Donald Saddler; musical direction, Liza Redfield; scenery, Donald Oenslager; costumes, Donald Brooks; lighting, Tharon Musser; orchestrations, Philip J. Lang; sound, Tony Alloy; musical supervision & vocal arrangements, Hugh Martin, Timothy Gray; dance & incidental music composed and arranged by Luther Henderson; assistant choreographer, Arthur Faria; associate producers, Robert Anglund, Stan Hurwitz and Frank Montalvo; production stage manager, Phil Friedman; stage manager, Craig Jacobs; press, Henry Luhrman Associates.

Time: The mid-1930s. Place: On and around the campus of Tait College.

Good News was first produced on Broadway 9/6/27 for 551 performances. This, its first New York revival, has been re-set a decade later and presented with its original score augmented by additional De Sylva, Brown & Henderson songs.

ACT I

*Asterisk indicates song added to the original score

Overture	Orchestra, Company
"He's a Ladies' Man"	Pat, Millie, Flo, Students
"The Best Things in Life Are Free"	Prof. Kenyon, Students
"Just Imagine"	Connie, Pat, Millie, Flo
"Happy Days"	Tom, Pat, Millie, Flo, Sylvester, Boys
*"Button Up Your Overcoat"	Bobby, Babe
"Lucky in Love"	Connie, Tom, Students
*"You're the Cream in My Coffee"	Prof. Kenyon, Johnson
"Varsity Drag"	Babe, Students
*"Together"	Prof. Kenyon
"Tait Song"	Johnson, Pooch, Students
"Lucky in Love" (Reprise)	Company

ACT II

"Today's the Day"	Girls
"Girl of the Pi Beta Phi"	Pat, Girls
"Good News"	Prof. Kenyon, Connie, Students
*"Keep Your Sunny Side Up"	Pooch, Boys
"The Best Things in Life Are Free" (Reprise)	Connie, Tom
*"Life Is Just a Bowl of Cherries"	
"I Want to Be Bad"	Prof. Kenyon
"The Professor and the Students"	Prof. Kenyon, Pooch, Company
Finale	Company

All Over Town (176). By Murray Schisgal. Produced by Adela Holzer at the Booth Theater. Opened December 29, 1974.

Millie . . . . .Pamela Payton-Wright	Jackie Boyssan . . . . Patti Perkins
Sybil Morris . . . . Jill Eikenberry	Laurent . . . . Gerrit de Beer
Dr. Lionel Morris . . . . . . Barnard Hughes	Philomena Hopkins . . . . . . Polly Holliday
Beebee Morris . . . . Carol Teitel	Demetrius; Detective Kirby . Richard Karron
Charles Cogan . . . . Jim Jansen	Mr. Harold P. Hainsworth . . . Every Hayes
Col. Martin Hopkins . . William LeMassena	Francine . . . . Hershey Miller
Lewis . . . . .Cleavon Little	Maharishi Bahdah . . . . . . .Michael Gorrin
Louie . . . . Zane Lasky	Detective Peterson . . . . Barney Martin
Michael Boyssan . . . . Joseph Leon	

Understudies: Messrs. Hughes, Gorrin, Martin—Joseph Leon; Misses Holliday, Teitel—Ruth Baker; Messrs. Little, Hayes—Joseph Keyes; Misses Eikenberry, Payton-Wright, Perkins, Miller—Carol Nadell; Mr. Leon—Barney Martin; Messrs. Jansen, Lasky, Karron, de Beer—Chip Zien.

Directed by Dustin Hoffman; scenery, Oliver Smith; costumes, Albert Wolsky; lighting, John Gleason; production stage manager, Frank Marino; stage managers, Barbara-Mae Phillips, Ron Abbott; press, Michael Alpert Public Relations, Ellen Levene, Marilynn LeVine.

Time: The present. Place: The Morris family's duplex apartment on Manhattan's Upper East Side. Act I, Scene 1: Morning. Scene 2: Noon. Act II, Scene 1: Afternoon. Scene 2: Evening. Scene 3: The following morning.

Mistaken identity holds sway over a farce about a sexually gifted misfit and the sociologists trying to rehabilitate him.

George S. Irving replaced Barnard Hughes 3/11/75. Ron O'Neal replaced Cleavon Little 5/26/75. A Best Play; see page 169

The Hashish Club (11). By Lance Larsen. Produced by John Voight and Susan Bloom, an Elmer and Jalmia Production, Terrence Shank and Robert Waters associate producers, at the Bijou Theater. Opened January 3, 1975. (Closed January 11, 1975)

Tom Eren . . . . Lance Larsen	Doc Trane . . . . .Dennis Redfield
Jack Cutter . . . . Jack Rowe	Maston Kantaylis . . . . . . .Michael Stefani
Dean Potter . . . . .Gar Campbell	

Standbys: Messrs. Larsen, Stefani—Michael Hawkins; Messrs. Rowe, Campbell, Redfield—Dan Plucinski.

Directed by Jerome Guardino; production and special effects designed by Russell Pyle; supervising designers: Stuart Wurtzel scenery, Ken Billington lighting, Sara Brook costumes; production stage manager, Robert Vandergriff; press, Betty Lee Hunt Associates, Stanley F. Kaminsky.

A planned drug trip goes awry and produces violence. Previously produced by The Company Theater in Los Angeles.

*The Wiz (169). Musical based on L. Frank Baum's The Wonderful Wizard of Oz; book by William F. Brown; music and lyrics by Charlie Smalls. Produced by Ken Harper at the Majestic Theater. Opened January 5, 1975.

Aunt Em . . . . Tasha Thomas	Tinman . . . . Tiger Haynes
Toto . . . . Nancy	Lion . . . . Ted Ross
Dorothy . . . . Stephanie Mills	Gatekeeper . . . . Danny Beard
Uncle Henry; Lord High	The Wiz . . . . Andre De Shields
Underling . . . . .Ralph Wilcox	Evillene . . . . .Mabel King
Tornado . . . . .Evelyn Thomas	Soldier Messenger . . . . Carl Weaver
Addaperle . . . . Clarice Taylor	Winged Monkey . . . . Andy Torres
Scarecrow . . . . Hinton Battle	Glinda . . . . Dee Dee Bridgewater

Munchkins: Phylicia Ayers-Allen, Pi Douglass, Joni Palmer, Andy Torres, Carl Weaver. Yellow Brick Road: Ronald Dunham, Eugene Little, John Parks, Kenneth Scott. Crows: Wendy Edmead, Frances Morgan, Ralph Wilcox. Kalidahs: Phillip Bond, Pi Douglass, Rodney Green, Evelyn Thomas, Andy Torres. Poppies: Lettie Battle, Leslie Butler, Eleanor McCoy, Frances Morgan, Joni Palmer. Field Mice: Phylicia Ayers-Allen, Pi Douglass, Carl Weaver, Ralph Wilcox. Emerald City Citizens: Lettie Battle, Leslie Butler, Wendy Edmead, Eleanor McCoy, Frances Morgan, Joni Palmer, Evelyn Thomas, Philip Bond, Ronald Dunham, Rodney Green, Eugene Little, John Parks, Kenneth Scott, Andy Torres.

Pit Singers: Frank Floyd, Sam Harkness, Jozella Reed, Tasha Thomas.

Standbys: Miss Mills—Arnetia Walker; Miss Taylor—Butterfly McQueen. Understudies: Mr. Haynes—Ralph Wilcox; Mr. Battle—Pi Douglas; Miss Taylor—Jozella Reed; Miss King—Tasha Thomas; Miss Thomas—Dee Dee Bridgewater; Miss Bridgewater—Phylicia Ayers-Allen; Swing Dancer/Singers—Cynthia Ashby. Otis Sallid.

Directed by Geoffrey Holder; choreography and musical numbers staged by George Faison; musical direction & and vocal arrangements. Charles H. Coleman; scenery, Tom H. John; costumes, Geoffrey Holder; lighting, Tharon Musser; orchestrations, Harold Wheeler; dance arrangements, Timothy Graphenreed; production stage manager, Charles Blackwell; stage managers, Henry Velez, Jerry Laws; press, The Merlin Group, Ltd., Sandra Manley.

Soft-rock musical version of the Oz story, with an all-black cast.

ACT I

Prologue: Kansas
"The Feeling We Once Had" . . . . Aunt Em
Tornado Ballet . . . . Company
Scene 1: Munchkin Land
"He's the Wizard" . . . . .Addaperle, Munchkins
Scene 2: Oz countryside
"Soon as I Get Home" . . . . .Dorothy
"I Was Born on the Day Before Yesterday" . . . . Scarecrow, Crows
"Ease on Down the Road" . . . . .Dorothy, Scarecrow, Yellow Brick Road
Scene 3: Woods
"Slide Some Oil to Me" . . . . Tinman, Dorothy, Scarecrow
Scene 4: Jungle
"Mean Ole Lion" . . . . Lion
Scene 5: Kalidah Country
Kalidah Battle . . . . Friends, Kalidahs, Yellow Brick Road
Scene 6: Poppy field
"Be a Lion" . . . . Dorothy, Lion
Lion's Dream . . . . Lion, Poppies
Scene 7: Emerald City
Emerald City Ballet ("Pssst") . . . . Friends, Company
   Music by Timothy Graphenreed and George Faison
Scene 8: Throne room
"So You Wanted to Meet the Wizard" . . . . .The Wiz
"To Be Able to Feel" . . . . Tinman

ACT II

Scene 1: West Witch Castle
"No Bad News" . . . . Evillene
Scene 2: Forest
Funky Monkeys . . . . Monkeys
Scene 3: Courtyard
"Everybody Rejoice" . . . . Friends, Winkies
   Music and lyrics by Luther Vandross
Scene 4: Emerald City gate
Scene 5: Throne room
"Who Do You Think You Are?" . . . . Friends
"Believe in Yourself" . . . . .The Wiz
Scene 6: Fairgrounds
"Y'all Got It!" . . . . .The Wiz
Scene 7: The outskirts
Scene 8: Quadling Country
"A Rested Body Is a Rested Mind" . . . . .Glinda
"Believe in Yourself" (Reprise) . . . . .Glinda
"Home" . . . . .Dorothy

Shenandoah (167). Musical based on the original screen play by James Lee Barrett; book by James Lee Barrett, Peter Udell and Philip Rose; music by Gary Geld; lyrics by Peter

Udell. Produced by Philip Rose, Gloria and Louis K. Sher at the Alvin Theater. Opened January 7, 1975.

Charlie Anderson . . . . John Cullum	Reverend Byrd; Tinkham . . . Charles Welch
Jacob . . . . Ted Agress	Sam . . . . Gordon Halliday
James . . . . .Joel Higgins	Sgt. Johnson . . . . Edward Penn
Nathan . . . . Jordan Suffin	Lieutenant . . . . .Marshall Thomas
John . . . . .David Russell	Carol . . . . Casper Roos
Jenny . . . . Penelope Milford	Corporal . . . . Gary Harger
Henry . . . . .Robert Rosen	Marauder . . . . Gene Masoner
Robert (The Boy) . . . . Joseph Shapiro	Engineer . . . . Ed Preble
Anne . . . . Donna Theodore	Confederate Sniper . . . . .Craig Lucas
Gabriel . . . . .Chip Ford	

The Ensemble: Tedd Carrere, Stephen Dubov, Gary Harger, Brian James, Robert Johanson, Sherry Lambert, Craig Lucas, Gene Masoner, Paul Myrvold, Dan Ormond, Casper Roos, J. Kevin Scannellin Scannell, Jack Starkey, E. Allen Stevens, Marshall Thomas, Matt Gavin (Swing).

Understudies: Mr. Cullum—Edward Penn; Mr. Agress—Gene Masoner; Mr. Higgins—Marshall Thomas, Paul Myrvold; Mr. Suffin—Craig Lucas, Matt Gavin; Mr. Russell—Matt Gavin, Robert Johanson; Miss Milford—Betsy Beard; Mr. Rosen—Robert Johanson, Craig Lucas; Mr. Shapiro—Jeffrey Rea; Miss Theodore—Kay Coleman; Mr. Ford—Brent Carter; Mr. Welch—Ed Preble; Mr. Halliday—Robert Rosen; Mr. Penn—Casper Roos; Mr. Thomas—Tedd Carrere; Mr. Roos—J. Kevin Scannell; Mr. Harger—Robert Johanson; Messrs. Masoner, Preble—E. Allan Stevens.

Directed by Philip Rose; choreography, Robert Tucker; musical direction, Lynn Crigler; scenery, C. Murawski; costumes, Pearl Somner, Winn Morton; lighting, Thomas Skelton; orchestrations, Don Walker; dance arrangements, Russell Warner; production stage manager, Steve Sweigbaum; stage manager, Arturo E. Porazzi; press. Merle Debuskey, Leo Stern.

Time: During the Civil War. Place: The Shenandoah Valley, Virginia. Act I: Spring. Act II: Autumn.

A prosperous, independent farmer and his sons refuse to take sides in the Civil War until events force them to do so. Previously produced as the motion picture *Shenandoah,* starring James Stewart, and in this musical stage version at the Goodspeed Opera House, East Haddam, Conn.

ACT I

Prologue: "Raise the Flag of Dixie" . . . . .Confederate and Union Soldiers
"I've Heard It All Before" . . . . .Charlie Anderson
"Pass the Cross to Me" . . . . The Congregation
"Why Am I Me?" . . . . Boy, Gabriel
"Next to Lovin' (I Like Fightin')" . . . . Jacob, James, Nathan, John, Henry
"Over the Hill" . . . . Jenny Anderson
"The Pickers Are Comin" . . . . .Charlie Anderson
"Next to Lovin' " (Reprise) . . . . Jacob, James, Nathan, John Henry, Jenny
"Meditation" . . . . .Charlie Anderson
"We Make a Beautiful Pair" . . . . Anne, Jenny
"Violets and Silverbells" . . . . Jenny, Sam, the Family
"It's a Boy" . . . . .Charlie Anderson

ACT II

"Freedom" . . . . .Anne, Gabriel
"Violets and Silverbells" (Reprise) . . . . James, Anne
"Papa's Gonna Make It Alright" . . . . .Charlie Anderson
"The Only Home I Know" . . . . Corporal, Soldiers
"Papa's Gonna Make It Alright (Reprise) . . . . Jenny
"Meditation" (Reprise) . . . . .Charlie Anderson
"Pass the Cross to Me" (Reprise) . . . . The Congregation

*The Ritz (150). By Terrence McNally. Produced by Adela Holzer at the Longacre Theater. Opened January 20, 1975.

Abe	George Dzundza	Carmine Vespucci	Jerry Stiller
Claude Perkins	Paul B. Price	Vivian Proclo	Ruth Jaroslow
Gaetano Proclo	Jack Weston	Pianist	Ron Abel
Chris	F. Murray Abraham	Policeman	Bruce Bauer
Googie Gomez	Rita Moreno	Crisco	Richard Boccelli
Maurine	Hortensia Colorado	Sheldon Farenthold	Tony de Santis
Michael Brick	Stephen Collins	Patron in Chaps	John Remme
Tiger	John Everson	Patron From Sheridan Sq.	Steve Scott
Duff	Christopher J. Brown		

Standbys: Miss Jaroslow—Vera Lockwood; Messrs. Weston, Stiller—George Dzundza. Understudies: Miss Moreno—Hortensia Colorado; Mr. Collins—Bruce Bauer; Messrs. Everson, Brown—Steve Scott; Messrs. Abraham, Price—John Remme; Mr. Dzundza—Richard Boccelli.

Directed by Robert Drivas; scenery & costumes, Lawrence King and Michael H. Yeargan; lighting, Martin Aronstein; production stage manager, Larry Forde; stage manager, Steve Beckler; press, Michael Alpert Public Relations, Marilynn LeVine, Ellen Levene.

The play was presented in two parts.

Comedy about a fugitive from gangster family vengeance, a straight hiding out in a gay Turkish bath. Previously produced by the Yale Repertory Theater, New Haven, Conn.

Robert Drivas replaced F. Murray Abraham 5/12/75. F. Murray Abraham replaced Robert Drivas 5/26/75. George Dzundza replaced Jack Weston 3/3/75. Jack Weston replaced George Dzundza 3/17/75.

A Best Play; see page 194

*Dance With Me (144). By Greg Antonacci. Produced by Ted Ravinett and Steve Rubenstein at the Mayfair Theater. Opened January 23, 1975.

Tommie Sincere	Annie Abbott	Wendell Crunchall	Scott Robert Redman
Honey Boy	Greg Antonacci	Goldie Pot	Deborah Rush
Jimmy Dick II	John Bottoms	Smitner Tuskey	Stuart Silver
Thumbs Bumpin	Peter Frumkin	Don Tomm	Skip Zipf
Judy Jeanine	Patricia Gaul	Bulldog Allen	Joel Zwick

Understudy: Girls—Wendy Ellen.

Directed and choreographed by Joel Zwick; scenery and lighting, Scott Johnson; costumes, Susan Hum Buck; sound, Theater Technology; music consultant, Peter Frumkin; production stage manager, Robert H. Keil Jr.; press, Max Eisen, M.J. Boyer, Judy Jacksina.

Time: The present. Place: A subway station. The play was presented in two parts.

Comedy with music, a loser tries to recapture the innocent past in memory, performed by the La Mama Plexus Company. Previously produced as *Dance Wi' Me* by the La Mama Experimental Theater Club and the New York Shakespeare Festival Public Theater.

Seascape (65). By Edward Albee. Produced by Richard Barr, Charles Woodward and Clinton Wilder at the Sam S. Shubert Theater. Opened January 26, 1975. (Closed March 22, 1975)

Nancy	Deborah Kerr	Leslie	Frank Langella
Charlie	Barry Nelson	Sarah	Maureen Anderman

Standbys: Misses Kerr, Anderman—Augusta Dabney; Mr. Nelson—William Prince; Mr. Langella—Allen Williams.

Directed by Edward Albee; scenery and lighting, James Tilton; costumes, Fred Voelpel; production stage manager, Mark Wright; stage manager, Charles Kindl; press, Betty Lee Hunt Associates, Maria C. Pucci, Stanley F. Kaminsky.

The play was presented in two parts.

Middle-aged couple preparing to enjoy "the golden years" encounters two lizard-like, humanoid creatures beginning to evolve from the sea.

A Best Play; see page 213

Man on the Moon (5). Musical with book, music and lyrics by John Phillips. Produced by Andy Warhol in association with Richard Turley at the Little Theater. Opened January 29, 1975. (Closed February 1, 1975)

Dr. Bomb	Harlan S. Foss	Celestial Choir:	
Ernie Hardy	Eric Lang	Mercury; Miss America	Brenda Bergman
Leroy (Little Red Box)	Mark Lawhead	Mars	John Patrick Sundine
President; King Can	Dennis Doherty	Neptune	Jennifer Elder
Angel	Genevieve Waite	Pluto	E. Lynn Nickerson
Venus	Monique Van Vooren	Saturn	Jeanette Chastonay

Standbys: Messrs. Doherty, Foss—John Patrick Sundine; Miss Van Vooren—Brenda Bergman; Miss Waite—Jennifer Elder; Misses Bergman, Elder—Jeanette Chastonay.

Musicians: Ben Aronov organ, harp; Harvey Estrin woodwinds; Bob Milliken trumpet; Jay Leonhart bass; Jeff Layton guitars; Hank Jaramillo drums; Warren Hard percussion.

Directed by Paul Morrissey; musical direction, Karen Gustafson; scenery, John J. Moore; costumes, Marsia Trinder; lighting, Jules Fisher; musical arrangements, Michael Gibson, Jim Tyler; sound, Gary Harris; costume design supervision, Michael Yeargan; production stage manager, Michael Maurer; press, Michael Sean O'Shea, Robert M. Zarem.

Of bombs and the space age, written by a former member of the singing group known as The Mamas and the Papas. The play was presented without intermission.

MUSICAL NUMBERS

Scene 1: Earth
Prologue . . . . Dr. Bomb
"Boys From the South" . . . . Ernie
"Midnight Deadline Blastoff" . . . . Ernie
"Mission Control" . . . . Dr. Bomb, Ernie, Leroy, President, Miss America
"Speed of Light" . . . . Ernie, Leroy
Scene 2: Canis Minor
"Though I'm a Little Angel" . . . . Angel
"Girls" . . . . King Can, Venus, Angel
"Canis Minor Bolero Waltz" . . . . King Can, Venus, Angel
"Starbust" . . . . Angel
"Penthouse of Your Mind" . . . . King Can
"Champagne and Kisses" . . . . Venus
"Star Stepping Stranger/Convent" . . . . Ernie, Angel
"My Name Is Can" . . . . King Can
"American Man on the Moon" . . . . Angel
Scene 3: The moon
"Welcome to the Moon" . . . . Company
"Sunny, Sunny Moon" . . . . Venus, Dr. Bomb
"Love Is Coming Back" . . . . Angel Ernie
"Truth Cannot Be Treason" . . . . Leroy
"Place in Space" . . . . Ernie, Angel
Scene 4: Earth
"Family of Man" . . . . Dr. Bomb
"Yesterday I Left the Earth" . . . . Company
"Stepping to the Stars" . . . . Company

Private Lives (92). Revival of the play by Noel Coward. Produced by Arthur Cantor by arrangement with H.M. Tennent, Ltd. at the Forty-sixth Street Theater. Opened February 6, 1975. (Closed April 26, 1975)

Sybil Chase	Niki Flacks	Amanda Prynne	Maggie Smith
Elyot Chase	John Standing	Louise	Marie Tommon
Victor Prynne	Remak Ramsay		

Standbys: Miss Smith—Laura Stuart; Messrs. Standing, Ramsay—Colin Hamilton. Understudies:

Miss Flacks—Marie Tommon; Miss Tommon—Nancy Aiello.

Directed by John Gielgud; scenery, Anthony Powell; costumes, Germinal Rangel, Beatrice Dawson; lighting, H.R. Poindexter; production manager, Mitchell Erickson; stage manager, Robert Crawley; press, Carl Samrock, C. George Willard.

Time: The late 1920s. Act I: The terrace of a hotel in France, a summer evening. Act II: Amanda's flat in Paris, a few days later, evening. Act III: The same, next morning.

Noel Coward's comedy was first produced on Broadway 1/27/31 for 256 performances. It has subsequently been revived on Broadway 10/4/48 for 248 performances and 12/4/69 for 204 performances, and off Broadway 5/19/68 for 9 performances. This production opened in London 9/21/72 and came to New York from a 17-week tour of the U.S. and Canada.

Hughie, by Eugene O'Neill, and **Duet**, by David Scott Milton (31). Program of two one-act revivals. Produced by Jay Julien in association with Sidney Eden at the John Golden Theater. Opened February 11, 1975. (Closed March 8, 1975)

HUGHIE

Night Clerk . . . . Peter Maloney   "Erie" Smith . . . . Ben Gazzara

Time: Between 4 and 5 A.M. of a day in the summer of 1928. Place: The lobby of a small hotel off Times Square.

DUET

Leonard Pelican . . . . Ben Gazzara

Time: The present. Place: The lobby of the 43d Street Hotel off Times Square.

Directed by Martin Fried; scenery, Kert Lundell; costumes, Ruth Morley; lighting, Marc B. Weiss; associate producer, Norman A. Levy; production stage manager, Franklin Keysar; press, Merle Debuskey, Leo Stern.

O'Neill's *Hughie* was first produced on Broadway 12/22/64 for 51 performances. This, its first professional New York revival, was previously produced in Chicago and elsewhere. *Duet* was previously produced by American Place Theater 3/9/70 for 35 performances as a two-character play entitled *Duet for Solo Voice*.

The Night That Made America Famous (47). Musical revue with music and lyrics by Harry Chapin. Produced by Edgar Lansbury and Joseph Beruh in association with The Shubert Organization at the Ethel Barrymore Theater. Opened February 26, 1975. (Closed April 6, 1975)

Alexandra Borrie	Delores Hall
Harry Chapin	Sid Marshall
Stephen Chapin	Gilbert Price
Tom Chapin	Ernie Pysher
Mercedes Ellington	Bill Starr
Kelly Garrett	Lynne Thigpen

Understudies: Harry Chapin—Tom Chapin; Miss Garrett—Alexandra Borrie; Miss Hall—Lynne Thigpen; Mr. Price—Sid Marshall; Mr. Starr—Ernie Pysher; Misses Borrie, Thigpen—Mercedes Ellington.

Orchestra: Stephen Chapin conductor, keyboards; Tom Chapin guitars, banjo, harmonica; Jim Chapin percussion; Howie Fields drums; Doug Walker lead guitar; John Wallace assistant conductor, bass; Mike Masters cello; Buzz Brauner woodwinds; Harry Cykeman violin.

Directed by Gene Frankel; choreography, Doug Rogers; musical direction, Stephen Chapin; multimedia under the direction of Joshua White; scenery, Kert Lundell; costumes, Randy Barcelo; lighting, Imero Fiorentino; lighting supervision, Fred Allison; multimedia consultants, Imero Fiorentino Associates; multimedia executed by Jim Sant'Andrea; dance arrangements, John Morris; audio, Michael Solomon; associate producer, Nan Pearlman; production stage manager, Herb Vogler; press, Gifford/Wallace, Inc.

Program of dramatized songs written and sung by recording star Harry Chapin, many of them making social comment and most of them in the rock or country style. The play was presented in two parts, with songs of the 1960s in Act I and of the 1970s in Act II.

ACT I—Prologue—Company; "Six String Orchestra"—Harry Chapin, Company; "Give Me a Road"—Company; "Sunday Morning Sunshine"—Chapin, Company; "It's My Day"—Kelly Garrett; "Give Me a Cause"—Company; "Welfare Rag"—Delores Hall, Bill Starr, Gilbert Price, Company; "Better Place To Be"—Chapin, Company; "Give Me a Wall"—Company; "Peace Teachers" —Miss Garrett; "Pigeon Run"—Price; "Changing the Guard"—Price; "When I Look Up"—Miss Hall; "Sniper"—Chapin, Company.

ACT II—"Great Divide"—Chapin; "Taxi"—Chapin, Miss Garrett; "Cockeyed John"—Company; "Mr. Tanner"—Chapin, Price; "Maxie"—Miss Garrett; Fugue: "Love Can't"—Starr, "When Maudey Wants a Man"—Miss Hall, "I'm a Wonderfully Wicked Woman"—Miss Garrett; "Battleground Bummer"—Price; "Stoopid"—Starr; "Cat's in the Cradle"—Chapin, Company; "Cockeyed John" (Reprise), "Give Me My Dream"—Company; "Too Much World"— Starr, Price, Chapin, Misses Garrett, Hall, Company; "As I Grow Older"—Miss Garrett; "Beginning of the End"—Company; Epilogue: "The Night That Made America Famous"—Harry, Company.

Clarence Darrow (18). Return engagement of the one-man performance by Henry Fonda in a play by David W. Rintels; based on *Clarence Darrow for the Defense* by Irving Stone. Produced by Mike Merrick and Don Gregory at the Minskoff Theater. Opened March 3, 1975. (Closed March 22, 1975)

Directed by John Houseman; scenery and lighting, H.R. Poindexter; production stage manager, George Eckert; stage manager, Bernie Baker; press, Seymour Krawitz, Patricia McLean Krawitz.

The play was presented in two parts. It was previously presented on Broadway 3/26/74 for 22 performances in a run which was ended prematurely by the star's illness.

Goodtime Charley (104). Musical with book by Sidney Michaels; music by Larry Grossman; lyrics by Hal Hackady. Produced by Max Brown and Byron Goldman in association with Robert Victor and Stone Widney at the Palace Theater. Opened March 3, 1975. (Closed May 31, 1975)

Henry V; 2d Soldier . . . . Brad Tyrrell	Charley . . . . Joel Grey
Charles VI; 2d English Captain;	Archbishop . . . . Jay Garner
Herald; 3d Soldier . . . . . . Hal Norman	Gen. de la Tremouille . . . . . Louis Zorich
Isabella of Bavaria . . . . Grace Keagy	Agnes Sorel . . . . Susan Browning
Queen Kate . . . . Rhoda Butler	Joan of Arc . . . . Ann Reinking
Phillip of Burgundy; 1st English	Minguet . . . . Richard B. Shull
Captain; Chef; Guard . . . . Charles Rule	3d English Captain;
Yolande . . . . Peggy Cooper	1st Soldier . . . . Kenneth Bridges
Marie . . . . Nancy Killmer	Louis . . . . Dan Joel
Pope . . . . Ed Becker	Estelle . . . . Kathe Dezina

Servants: George Ramos, Ross Miles, Pat Swayze, Cam Lorendo. Jesters: Andy Hostettler, Gordon Weiss. Citizen Trio; Soldier Trio; Peasant Trio; Hostile Trio: Kenneth Bridges, Brad Tyrrell, Ed Becker.

Singers: Rhoda Butler, Peggy Cooper, Kathe Dezina, Nancy Killmer, Jane Ann Sargia, Ed Becker, Kenneth Bridges, Hal Norman, Charles Rule, Brad Tyrrell.

Dancers: Andy Hostettler, Cam Lorendo, Dan Joel, Glen McClaskey, Ross Miles, Tod Miller, Sal Pernice, George Ramos, Pat Swayze, Gordon Weiss, Jerry Yoder.

Standby: Mr. Grey—Austin Pendleton. Understudies: Miss Reinking—Susan Browning; Miss Browning—Rhoda Butler; Mr. Shull—Kenneth Bridges; Mr. Garner—Hal Norman; Mr. Zorich— Charles Rule; Miss Keagy—Peggy Cooper; Miss Cooper—Nancy Kilmer; Misses Butler, Killmer, Dezina—Jane Ann Sargia; Messrs. Tyrrell, Norman, Rule, Becker—Kenneth Bridges.

Directed by Peter H. Hunt; dances and musical numbers staged by Onna White; musical direction and incidental music, Arthur B. Rubinstein; scenery, Rouben Ter-Arutunian; costumes, Willa Kim; lighting, Feder; orchestrations, Jonathan Tunick; dance music, Daniel Troop; associate to Miss White, Martin Allen; production manager, Peter Stern; stage managers, Bruce W. Stark, Lee Murray; press, Max Eisen, Barbara Glenn, Judy Jacksina.

Musical version of the historical drama of Joan of Arc and the Dauphin, Charles, whom she placed on the throne of France.

ACT I

Scene 1: Prologue, Charley's nightmare, March 6, 1429
"History" . . . Henry V, Charles VI, Isabella, Kate, Phillip, Yolande, Marie, Pope, Ensemble
Scene 2: Charley's bedroom at Chinon, that morning
"Goodtime Charley" . . . . Charley, Ensemble
Scene 3: Great hall, immediately after
"Visions & Voices" . . . . Joan
Scene 4: Charley's study, that evening
"Bits and Pieces" . . . . Charley, Joan
"To Make the Boy a Man" . . . . Joan
Scene 5: Before a tapestry, immediately after
"Why Can't We All Be Nice?" . . . . Charley, Agnes
Scene 6: Council chamber, three weeks later, April
"Born Lover" . . . . Charley
Scene 7: A nearby grove at twilight
"I Am Going to Love" . . . . Joan
Scene 8: Castles of the Loire, subsequent weeks
"Castles of the Loire" . . . . Joan, Soldiers
     (music by Arthur B. Rubinstein)
Scene 9: Reims Cathedral, late May, 1429
"Coronation" . . . . Charley, Joan, Ensemble

ACT II

Scene 1: A formal garden, late summer
"You Still Have a Long Way to Go" . . . . Joan, Charley
Scene 2: Chinon courtyard, the following spring
"Merci, Bon Dieu" . . . . .Minguet, Agnes
Scene 3: A bank of the Vienne River, immediately after sunset
Scene 4: Confession booth, a week later
"Confessional" . . . . General, Archbishop
Scene 5: Cell in Rouen, May 30, 1431
"One Little Year" . . . . Joan
Scene 6: Cell and war tent, that same day, simultaneously
Scene 7: Great hall, three weeks later
Scene 8: Epilogue, 32 years later, February 28, 1461
"I Leave the World" . . . . .Charley

The Lieutenant (9). Musical with book, music and lyrics by Gene Curty, Nitra Scharfman and Chuck Strand. Produced by Joseph S. Kutrzeba and Spofford J. Beadle at the Lyceum Theater. Opened March 9, 1975. (Closed March 16, 1975)

Lieutenant . . . . Eddie Mekka
Judge; OCS Sergeant . . . . . . Gene Curty
Recruiting Sergeant; Senator . . . Joel Powers
1st General . . . . .Chet D'Elia
2d General . . . . Eugene Moose
3d General . . . . .Danny Taylor
Chaplain; 1st Congressman . . Don McGrath
Captain . . . . Walt Hunter

G.I.; 2d Reporter . . . . .Tom Tofel
Clergyman; 1st Reporter . . . . .Jim Litten
2d Congressman; Prosecutor . Burt Rodriguez
3d Reporter . . . . Jo Speros
Defense Attorney . . . . Gordon Grody
New Recruit . . . . Alan K. Siegel
Dance Captain . . . . .Jim-Patrick McMahon

"C" Company: Jim Litten (Sergeant), Steven Boockvor, Clark James, Jim-Patrick McMahon, Joseph Pugliese, Burt Rodriguez, Tom Tofel.
Musicians: John Angelori rhythm guitar, Alan Bowin organ, Mark Cianfrani lead guitar, Joe DiCarlo drums, James Marino bass guitar, Chuck Strand piano.
Standby: Mr. Grody—Dan Kruger. Understudies: Swing Dancer—Marius Hanford; Mr. Curty—

Steven Boockvor; Mr. Rodriguez—Gene Curty; Mr. Grody—Walt Hunter; Mr. Taylor—Clark James; Miss Speros—Beth Kennedy; Mr. Tofel—Dan Kruger; Mr. Litten—Jim-Patrick McMahon; Mr. Mekka —Joseph Pugliese; Mr. Hunter—Burt Rodriguez; Messrs. Powers, McGrath—Danny Taylor; Mr. Siegel—Tom Tofel.

Directed by William Martin; choreography, Dennis Dennehy; musical direction, Chuck Strand; scenery & costumes, Frank J. Boros; lighting, Ian Calderon; arrangements, Chuck Strand, Gus Montero; sound, Bill Merrill; production stage manager, Bruce Hoover; stage manager, Phillip Moser; press, Alan Eichler, Marilyn Percy.

The time and place alternate between Vietnam and the United States over a three-year period. The play was presented without intermission.

Self-described as "a rock opera," based on the My Lai incident. Previously produced at the Queens, N.Y., Playhouse.

MUSICAL NUMBERS

"The Indictment" . . . . .Lieutenant, Judge
"Join the Army" . . . . Lieutenant, Recruiting Sergeant, Recruits
"Look for the Men With Potential" . . . . .Generals
"Kill" . . . . .OCS Sergeant
"I Don't Want to Go Over to Vietnam" . . . . .Lieutenant, "C" Company
"Eulogy" . . . . Chaplain
"At 0700 Tomorrow" . . . . Captain, "C" Company
"Massacre" . . . . Captain, Lieutenant, "C" Company, Vietnamese
"Something's Gone Wrong" . . . . Captain, Lieutenant
"Twenty-Eight" . . . . .Generals, Captain, Lieutenant
"Let's Believe in the Captain" . . . . .Generals
"Final Report" . . . . 1st General
"I Will Make Things Happen" . . . . G.I.
Two Years Later
"He Wants to Put the Army in Jail" . . . . Senator, 1st & 2d Congressmen, Clergyman
"There's No Other Solution" . . . . .Generals
"I'm Going Home" . . . . .Lieutenant, "C" Company
"We've Chosen You, Lieutenant" . . . . .Generals
"The Star of This War" . . . . Reporters, Lieutenant
"On Trial for My Life" . . . . .Lieutenant
"The Conscience of a Nation" . . . . .Prosecutor
"Damned No Matter How He Turned" . . . . .Defense Attorney
"On Trial for My Life" (Reprise) . . . . .Lieutenant
"The Verdict" . . . . Judge, Jurors
Finale . . . . New Recruit, Recruiting Sergeant, Company

The Rocky Horror Show (32). Musical with book, music and lyrics by Richard O'Brien. Produced by Lou Adler in the Michael White production at the Belasco Theater. Opened March 10, 1975. (Closed April 6, 1975)

Popcorn Girl (Trixie) . . . . .Jamie Donnelly	Columbia . . . . Boni Enten
Janet . . . . .Abigale Haness	Magenta . . . . .Jamie Donnelly
Brad . . . . .Bill Miller	Frank . . . . Tim Curry
Narrator . . . . .William Newman	Rocky . . . . Kim Milford
Riff-Raff . . . . Ritz O'Brien	Eddie; Dr. Scott . . . . .Meat Loaf

Understudies: Meat Loaf—David P. Kelly; Misses Haness, Donnelly—Pamela Palluzzi; Messrs. Miller, Milford—Robert Rhys.

Directed by Jim Sharman; musical direction, D'Vaughn Pershing; scenery, Brian Thomson, supervised by Peter Harvey; costumes, Sue Blane, supervised by Pearl Somner; lighting, Chipmonck; sound, Abe Jacob; assistant director, Nina Faso; associate producer, John Beug; arrangements, Richard Hartly; production stage manager, David H. Banks; stage manager, August Amarino; press, Michael Alpert Public Relations, Ellen Levene, Marilynn LeVine, Anne Weinberg, Warren Knowlton.

Lampoon of the movies, presented cabaret-style without intermission. A foreign play previously produced in London and Los Angeles.

MUSICAL NUMBERS

"Science Fiction" . . . . Trixie
"Wedding Song" . . . . Brad, Janet
"Over at the Frankenstein Place" . . . . Brad, Janet
"Sweet Transvestite" . . . . Frank
"Time Warp" . . . . Magenta, Columbia, Riff-Raff, Narrator
"The Sword of Damocles" . . . . Rocky
"Charles Atlas Song" . . . . Frank
"What Ever Happened to Saturday Night" . . . . Eddie
"Charles Atlas Song" (Reprise) . . . . Frank
"Eddie's Teddy" . . . . Dr. Scott, Columbia, Company
"Once in Awhile" . . . . Brad
"Planet Shmanet Janet" . . . . Frank
"It Was Great When It All Began" . . . . Company
"Super Heroes" . . . . Company
"Science Fiction" (Reprise) . . . . Trixie
"Sweet Transvestite" (Reprise) . . . . Company
"Time Warp" (Reprise) . . . . Company

The Misanthrope (94). Revival of the play by Molière; adapted by Tony Harrison. Produced by David Merrick and The John F. Kennedy Center in The National Theater From Great Britain production. Opened March 12, 1975. (Closed May 31, 1975)

Alceste	Alec McCowen	Acaste	Nicholas Clay
Philinte	Robert Eddison	Clitandre	Albert Roffrano
Oronte	Gawn Grainger	Basque	Daniel Thorndike
Célimène	Diana Rigg	Official of the Academie	Stephen Williams
Eliante	Louie Ramsay	Dubois	Peter Needham
Arsinoé	Gillian Barge		

Understudies: Mr. McCowen—Alfred Karl; Miss Rigg—Carole Menferdini; Messrs. Addison, Thorndike—John Straub; Messrs. Grainger, Williams, Needham—Tom McLaughlin; Mr. Clay—Josef Warik; Mr. Roffrano—Patrick Watkins; Misses Barge, Ramsay—Claudia Wilkens.

Directed by John Dexter; design, Tanya Moiseiwitsch; lighting, Andy Phillips; musical arrangements, Marc Wilkinson; production stage manager, Alan Hall; stage manager, Claudia Wilkens; press, Solters/Roskin, Inc., Bud Westman.

Time: 1966. Place: Célimène's house in Paris. The play was presented in two parts.

The Misanthrope modernized to the Gaullist France of the mid-1960s. *The Misanthrope* was last revived on Broadway in the Richard Wilbur version by APA 10/9/68 for 86 performances.

*Same Time, Next Year (92). By Bernard Slade. Produced by Morton Gottlieb, Dasha Epstein, Edward L. Schuman and Palladium Productions at the Brooks Atkinson Theater. Opened March 13, 1975.

Doris	Ellen Burstyn	George	Charles Grodin

Standbys: Miss Burstyn—Rochelle Oliver; Mr. Grodin—Joe Ponazecki.

Directed by Gene Saks; scenery, William Ritman; costumes, Jane Greenwood; lighting, Tharon Musser; associate producers, Ben Rosenberg, Warren Crane; stage manager, Kate Pollock; press, Solters/Roskin, Inc., Milly Schoenbaum.

Place: A guest cottage of a country inn in Northern California. Act I, Scene 1: A day in February, 1951. Scene 2: A day in February, 1956. Scene 3: A day in February, 1961. Act II, Scene 1: A day in February, 1965. Scene 2: A day in February, 1970. Scene 3: A day in February, 1975.

A happily married (to other people) couple decides to repeat an adulterous rendezvous at the same time and place every year, in six amorous comedy scenes mirroring the changing facts and conditions of their lives over 25 years.

A Best Play; see page 228

Don't Call Back (1). By Russell O'Neil. Produced by Charles Bowden, Slade Brown and Jim Milford at the Helen Hayes Theater. Opened and closed at the evening performance, March 18, 1975.

Jason Croydon	Richard Niles	Crowbar	Mark Kologi
Miriam Croydon	Arlene Francis	Trucker	Robert Hegez
Gregory Schaeffer	Stanley Grover	Claire	Catherine Byers
Clarence	Dorian Harewood		

Directed by Len Cariou; scenery, Oliver Smith; costumes, Whitney Blausen; lighting, John Gleason; electronic sound, Ken Guilmartin; associate producer, Morgan Holman; production stage manager, Donald Christy; stage manager, Frank Di Elsi; press, Seymour Krawitz, Patricia McLean Krawitz, Barbara Carroll.

Time: The present. Place: A Park Avenue duplex apartment in New York City. Act I, Scene 1: A spring night, 10:30 P.M. Scene 2: The following morning, 7:30 A.M. Act II, Scene 1. Immediately following. Scene 2: Three hours later. Scene 3: That same evening, 7 P.M.

Thriller, an actress is terrorized in her own home by her son and his friends.

Doctor Jazz (5). Musical with book, music and lyrics by Buster Davis; additional music and lyrics by King Oliver, Howard Melrose, Jack Coogan, J.L. Morgan, Eubie Blake, E. Ray Goetz, Harry von Tilzer, A.J. Piron, Swanstone, McCarren and Morgan. Produced by Cyma Rubin at the Winter Garden Theater. Opened March 19, 1975. (Closed March 22, 1975)

Steve Anderson	Bobby Van	Georgia Sheridan	Lillian Hayman
Jonathan Jackson Jr.	Jack Landron	Edna Mae Sheridan	Lola Falana
Henry; Rudy; Harry	Paul Eichel	Lead Dancer	Hector Jaime Mercado
Harriet Lee	Peggy Pope	Pete	Eron Tabor

Georgia's Girls: Bonita Jackson, Michele Simmons, Annie Joe Edwards. Harriet's Girls: Gail Benedict, Sarah Coleman, Maggy Gorrill, Kitty Jones, Diana Mirras, Sally Neal, Yolanda R. Raven, Catherine Rice. The Group: Bruce Heath, Bonita Jackson, Sally Neal, Yolanda R. Raven, Michele Simmons. Showgirls: Sarah Coleman, Kitty Jones. Spasm Band: Quitman D. Fludd III, Bruce Heath, Hector Jaime Mercado, Jeff Veazey.

Dancers: Gail Benedict, Quitman D. Fludd III, Maggy Gorrill, Bob Heath, Bruce Heath, David Hodo, Bonita Jackson, Michael Lichtefeld, Diana Mirras, Sally Neal, Yolana R. Raven, Catherine Rice, Michele Simmons, Dan Strayhorn, Jeff Veazey.

Singers: James Braet, Annie Joe Edwards, Paul Eichel, Marian Haraldson, Evelyn McCauley, Eron Tabor.

Onstage Musicians: George Davis Jr., Dennis Drury, John Gill, Vince Giordano, Haywood Henry, Danny Moore, Sam Pilafian, Candy Ross, Bob Stewart, Allan Vache, Warren Vache Jr., Earl Williams, Francis Williams.

Understudies: Mr. Van—Eron Tabor; Miss Falana—Sally Neal; Miss Hayman—Annie Joe Edwards; Miss Pope—Evelyn McCauley; Mr. Landron—Quitman D. Fludd III; Swing Dancers—Marshall Blake, JoAnn Ogawa.

Directed and choreographed by Donald McKayle; entire production supervised by John Berry; musical direction & vocal arrangements, Buster Davis; scenery and costumes, Raoul Pène du Bois; lighting, Feder; sound, Abe Jacob; associate orchestrators, Dick Hyman, Sy Oliver; dance music arrangements & incidental music, Luther Henderson; associate musical director, Joyce Brown; scenic coordinator, Mason Arvold; costume coordinator, David Toser; production stage manager, Michael Turque; stage manager, Marnel Sumner; press, David Powers.

The birth and development of jazz in New Orleans, Chicago and other places, told in the story of a young man with a trumpet.

ACT I

Scene 1: A brothel quarter in New Orleans, 1917
"Doctor Jazz" . . . . Steve, Musicians, Spasm Band
    (words and music by King Oliver and Howard Melrose)
"We've Got Connections" . . . . Steve, Georgia, Harriet

Scene 2: The street
Scene 3: Georgia's salon
"Georgia Shows 'em How" . . . . Georgia, Georgia's Girls
Scene 4: Harriet's boudoir
Scene 5: The street
"Cleopatra Had a Jazz Band" . . . . Steve, Ballyhoo Band
    (words by Jack Coogan, music by J.L. Morgan)
"Juba Dance" . . . . Edna Mae, Spasm Band
Scene 6: Georgia's garden
Scene 7: The Palace of Pleasure
"Charleston Rag" . . . . Jonathan's Band, Harriet's Girls
    (by Eubie Blake)
"I've Got Elgin Watch Movements in My Hips" . . . . Edna Mae
"Blues My Naughty Sweetie Gave to Me" . . . . Ballyhoo Band
    (by Swanstone, McCarren and Morgan)
Scene 8: Shanghai Theater
"Good-Time Flat Blues" . . . . Georgia
    (by A.J. Piron)
Scene 9: Harriet's office
Scene 10: Shanghai Theater stage
"Evolution Papa" . . . . Edna Mae, Lead Dancer, Troupe
Scene 11: Backstage
"Rehearsal Tap" . . . . Group
"Blues My Naughty Sweetie Gave to Me" (Reprise) . . . . Steve
"I Love It" . . . . Edna Mae
    (words and music by E. Ray Goetz and Harry von Tilzer)
Scene 12: Harriet's office
"Anywhere the Wind Blows" . . . . Steve

ACT II

Scene 1: The dressing room—the Lenox Club
Scene 2: The Lenox Club
"Those 'Sheik-of-Araby' Blues" . . . . Singers, Dancers
"Look Out for Lil" . . . . Edna Mae, Dancers
Scene 3: The dressing room
Scene 4: In front of a New York theater
"Swanee Strut" . . . . Steve
Scene 5: Dressing room—a New York Theater
Scene 6: On stage
"All I Want Is My Black Baby Back" . . . . Edna Mae
Scene 7: Dressing room
"Everybody Leaves You" . . . . Steve
Scene 8: On stage
"Free and Easy" . . . . Edna Mae, Company
"I Love It" (Reprise) . . . . Steve, Edna Mae

A Letter for Queen Victoria (16). By Robert Wilson; music by Alan Lloyd in collaboration with Michael Galasso. Produced by The Byrd Hoffman Foundation at the ANTA Theater. Opened March 22, 1975. (Closed April 6, 1975)

George Ashley	Christopher Knowles
Stefan Brecht	Cynthia Lubar
Julia Busto	James Neu
Kathryn Cation	Scotty Snyder
Andrew De Groat	Sheryl Sutton
Alma Hamilton	Robert Wilson

Musicians: Michael Galasso 1st violin, Susan Krongold 2d violin, Kevin Byrnes violin, Laura Epstein cello, Kathryn Cation flute.
Directed by Robert Wilson; choreography, Andrew De Groat; scenery & costume supervision,

Peter Harvey; lighting supervision, Beverly Emmons, assisted by Carol Mullins; musical direction, Michael Galasso; verbal tape constructions, Christopher Knowles; introductory letter, Stefan Brecht; Sundance Kid speech, Christopher Knowles; Act III dialogue, Cynthia Lubar; 1st speech of China-man, James Neu; slide, Francis Brooks; stage manager, Terrence Chambers; press, The Merlin Group Ltd., Sandra Manley.

The play was presented in two parts with intermission between Acts III and IV. Self-described as an opera; an avant garde, stream-of-consciousness form of theater, without continuity in its succession of dramatic, musical and choreographic effects,

INTRODUCTION: Queen Victoria—Alma Hamilton; others—Kathryn Cation, Stefan Brecht, Christopher Knowles, Robert Wilson. ACT I: Pilots—Brecht, James Neu; Billy—Miss Cation; Warden—Scotty Snyder; Chris—Christopher Knowles; others—Sheryl Sutton, Cynthia Lubar, George Ashley, Brecht. ACT II: Civil War Soldier—Miss Sutton; Warden—Snyder; Chris—Knowles; others—Ashley, Brecht, Misses Lubar, Cation. ACT III: Brecht, Snyder, Ashley, Knowles, Neu, Andrew De Groat, Julia Busto, Misses Sutton, Cation, Lubar. ENTR'ACTES: Wilson, Knowles. ACT IV: Billy—Miss Cation; Chris—Knowles; George—Ashley; Pilots—Neu, Brecht; others—Neu, Snyder, Brecht, Misses Sutton, Lubar.

Marcel Marceau (24). One-man program of pantomime by Marcel Marceau. Produced by Ronald Wilford at City Center 55th Street Theater. Opened March 25, 1975. (Closed April 13, 1975)

Presentation of cards, Pierre Verry; stage manager, Antoine Casanova; press, Herbert H. Breslin, Inc., Marvin R. Jenkins, Merle Hubbard.

Marcel Marceau's last New York appearance was 4/18/73 at the City Center for 23 performances.

In this engagement each program consisted of selections from the following Marceau repertory, presented in two parts.

Style Pantomimes: Walking, Walking Against the Wind, Walking in Water, the 1,500 Meter, The Optical Illusion, The Staircase, The Tight Rope Walker, The Circus, The Public Garden, The Bill Poster, The Kite, The Man and His Boat, The Magician, The Circus Performer, The Sculptor, The Painter, The Cage, The Bureaucrats, The Hands, Luna Park, Rememberances, The Side Show, The Pickpocket's Nightmare, The Carnival, The Angel, Contrasts, The Maskmaker, The Seven Deadly Sins; Youth, Maturity, Old Age and Death; The Japanese Pantomimes (The Sculptor and the Samurai), The Tango Dancer, The Small Cafe, The Dice Players, The Four Seasons, The Dream, The Creation of the World, The Trial, A Sunday Walk, Abel and Cain, The Dress-Memories of a Past Love, The Post Office, The Duel in Darkness, Shadow and Light, Revolt of the Robot, At the Clothier's, The Tug of War, The Bicycle Race.

Bip Pantomimes: Bip in the Subway, Bip and the Bumble Bee, Bip Travels by Train, Bip Travels by Sea, Bip as a Skater, Bip Hunts Butterflies, Bip Plays David and Goliath, Bip at a Ballroom, Bip Commits Suicide, Bip as a Soldier, Bip at a Society Party, Bip as a Street Musician, Bip as a China Salesman, Bip as a Fireman, Bip as a Baby Sitter, Bip as a Jeweller's Apprentice, Bip as a Professor of Botany, Bip as a Tailor in Love, Bip Dreams He Is Don Juan, Bip at an Audition, Bip as a Matador, Bip and the Dynamite, Bip as a Tragedian, Bip as a Lion Tamer, Bip the Illusionist, Bip Looks for a Job, Bip in the Modern and Future Life; Bip, King of Sports; Bip at the Athletic Club; Bip Pays Tribute to the Silent Film Actors; Bip, the Bank Employee, Dreams of a Better World; Bip Has a Sore Finger, Bip Has a Date, Bip as a Concert Artist.

We Interrupt This Program... (7). By Norman Krasna. Produced by Alexander H. Cohen at the Ambassador Theater. Opened April 1, 1975. (Closed April 5, 1975)

Amanda Williams	Holland Taylor	Jason Taylor	Marshall Borden
Sam Williams	Brandon Maggart	Father Murray	George Hall
Benny	Tony Major	Lt. Burke	Frederick Coffin
Dave	Dino Shorte	Sonny Seaver	Albert Hall
Kenny	Charles Turner	Louise Fletcher	Theta Tucker
Howie	Howard Rollins Jr.	Patrolman Walker	Don Creech
Jim	J.W. Smith	Mister Johnson	John D. Seymour
Luke	Taurean Blacque	Mrs. Johnson	Abby Lewis
Al Seaver	Dick Anthony Williams	Laura Woodley	Susan Kendall Newman
Stage Manager	Stanley Brock	Albert Woodley	James Ray Weeks
Man in Brown Suit	Taylor Reed	Detective Louis Harris	Lloyd Hollar
Gunga Din	Miller Lide		

Understudies: Mr. Williams—Howard Rollins Jr.; Albert Hall—Dino Shorte; Messrs. Coffin, Reed —Stanley Brock; Mr. Blacque—Tony Major; Mr. Hollar—Charles Turner; Messrs. Major, Shorte— Jimmy Smith; Messrs. Brock, Borden, George Hall, Seymour—Jim Cavanaugh; Misses Taylor, Lewis —Esther Benson; Miss Tucker—Stephannie Hampton Howard; Messrs. Creech, Weeks—Miller Lide; Miss Newman—Barbara Cohen.

Directed by Jerry Adler; scenery, Robert Randolph; costumes, Pearl Somner; lighting, Marc B. Weiss; sound, Jack Shearing; production associate, Hildy Parks; associate producer, Roy A. Somlyo; presented in association with ABC Entertainment; production stage manager, Murray Gitlin; stage manager, Robert O'Rourke; press, David Powers, Martha Mason.

Time: Tonight. Place: The stage of the Ambassador Theater in New York City. The play was presented without intermission.

Mystery thriller, a simulated take-over of the theater just after the "performance" begins, as a gang of criminals holds the audience hostage for the release of a friend in prison.

P.S. Your Cat Is Dead! (16). By James Kirkwood. Produced by Richard Barr, Charles Woodward and Terry Spiegel at the John Golden Theater. Opened April 7, 1975. (Closed April 20, 1975)

Vito	Tony Musante	Carmine	Antony Ponzini
Kate	Jennifer Warren	Janie	Mary Hamill
Jimmy	Keir Dullea	Wendell	Bill Moor
Fred	Peter White		

Standbys: Mr. Dullea—Peter White; Mr. Musante—Antony Ponzini. Understudies: Misses Warren, Hamill—Sharon De Bord; Messrs. White, Moor, Ponzini—Duncan Hoxworth.

Directed by Vivian Matalon; scenery and lighting, William Ritman; costumes, Frank J. Boros; associate producer, Neal Du Brock; produced in cooperation with the Buffalo Studio Arena Theater; production stage manager, Mark Wright; press, Betty Lee Hunt associates, Maria C. Pucci, Stanley Kaminsky.

Time: New Year's Eve. Place: Jimmy Zoole's loft apartment in New York City. Act I, Scene 1: Late evening. Scene 2: Thirty minutes later. Act II: Later the same night.

The burglary of his apartment isn't quite the last straw for an actor having a bad day; the last straw is the captured burglar's persistent effort to seduce him into trying a homosexual experience. Previously produced at the Buffalo, N.Y. Studio Arena Theater.

The Constant Wife (32). Revival of the play by W. Somerset Maugham. Produced by Arthur Cantor by arrangement with H.M. Tennent, Ltd. Opened April 14, 1975. (Closed May 10, 1975)

Mrs. Culver	Brenda Forbes	Marie-Louise Durham	Carolyn Lagerfelt
Bentley	Richard Marr	John Middleton FRCS	Jack Gwillim
Martha Culver	Delphi Lawrence	Bernard Kersal	Paul Harding
Barbara Fawcett	Marti Stevens	Mortimer Durham	Donald Silber
Constance Middleton	Ingrid Bergman		

Standbys: Miss Bergman—Jillian Lindig. Misses Forbes, Lawrence—Constance Dix. Understudies: Mr. Gwillim—Joe Hill; Miss Stevens—Jillian Lindig; Miss Lagerfelt—Sigourney Weaver; Messrs. Harding, Silber—Richard Marr.

Directed by John Gielgud; scenery, Alan Tagg; costumes, Beatrice Dawson; lighting, H.R. Poindexter; production manager, Mitchell Erickson; production stage manager, David Taylor; stage manager, Joe Hill; press, Gertrude Bromberg, C. George Willard.

Time: The late 1920s. Place: The drawing room of John Middleton's house in Harley Street, London. Act I: A summer afternoon. Act II: A few weeks later, late afternoon. Act III: Afternoon, one year later.

Maugham's comedy of marital fidelity/infidelity was first produced in New York during the 1926–27 season and last produced during the 1951–52 season. This production was previously presented in London and on tour in the U.S.A.

*Bette Midler's Clams on the Half Shell Revue (88). Revue devised as a showcase for Bette Midler. Produced by Aaron Russo in association with Ron Delsener at the Minskoff Theater. Opened April 17, 1975

| Bette Midler | Michael Powell Ensemble |
| Lionel Hampton | The Harlettes |

Directed and choreographed by Joe Layton; musical direction, Don York; scenery & costumes, Tony Walton; lighting, Beverly Emmons; sound, Stan Miller; associate choreographer, André De Shields; orchestrations, Jimmie Haskell; production coordinator, Fritz Holt; stage manager, George Boyd; press, Howard Atlee, Candy Lee.

Broadway, rock, ballad, gospel and other musical numbers in a cabaret-style revue tailored to fit a Bette Midler concert. The show was presented in two parts.

*Rodgers & Hart (22). Musical revue with music by Richard Rodgers; lyrics by Lorenz Hart; concept by Richard Lewine and John Fearnley. Produced by Lester Osterman Productions (Lester Osterman, Richard Horner) in association with Worldvision Enterprises, Inc. at the Helen Hayes Theater. Opened May 13, 1975.

Barbara Andres	Mary Sue Finnerty
Jimmy Brennan	Laurence Guittard
Wayne Bryan	Stephen Lehew
David-James Carroll	Jim Litten
Jamie Donnelly	Virginia Sandifur
Tovah Feldshuh	Rebecca York

Standbys: Kevin Daly, Pamela Peadon, David Thomé.

Directed by Burt Shevelove; choreography, Donald Saddler; musical direction & vocal arrangements, Buster Davis; scenery, David Jenkins; costumes, Stanley Simmons; lighting, Ken Billington; principal orchestrator & dance music arranger, Luther Henderson; additional orchestrations, Jim Tyler, Bill Brohn, Robert Russell Bennett; assistant choreographer, Arthur Faria; production stage manager, Mortimer Halpern; stage manager, Bryan Young; press, Seymour Krawitz, Patricia McLean Krawitz, Barbara Carroll.

Collection of 98 Rodgers & Hart numbers from shows, movies, etc. of the 1920s, 1930s and 1940s, produced as a revue with romantic numbers grouped in the first part and satirical ones in the second.

MUSICAL NUMBERS—The following Rodgers & Hart songs, listed in alphabetical order, were performed in part or in toto: "At the Roxy Music Hall," "Babes in Arms," "Bewitched, Bothered and Bewildered," "Blue Moon," "Blue Room," "Bye and Bye," "Can't You Do a Friend a Favor?", "Careless Rhapsody," " 'Cause We Got Cake," "Come With Me," "Dancing on the Ceiling," "Dear Old Syracuse," "Did You Ever Get Stung?," "Do I Hear You Saying?", "Down by the River," "Easy to Remember," "Ev'rybody Loves You," "Ev'rything I've Got."

Also "Falling in Love With Love," "The Flower Garden of My Heart," "From Another World," "The Gateway of the Temple of Minerva," "The Girl Friend," "Give It Back to the Indians," "Glad to Be Unhappy," "Great Big Town," "Happy Hunting Horn," "Have You Met Miss Jones?," "He and She," "He Was Too Good to Me," "The Heart Is Quicker than the Eye," "Here in My Arms," "How About It?", "How Was I to Know?", "I Could Write a Book," "I Didn't Know What Time It Was," "I Married an Angel," "I Wish I Were in Love Again," "I'll Tell the Man in the Street," "Imagine," "Isn't It Romantic?", "It Never Entered My Mind," "It's Got To Be Love," "I've Got Five Dollars."

Also "Johnny One Note," "Jupiter Forbid," "The Lady Is a Tramp," "Love Me Tonight," "Love Never Went to College," "A Lovely Day for a Murder," "Lover," "Manhattan," "Me for You," "Mimi," "Mountain Greenery," "My Funny Valentine," "My Heart Stood Still," "My Prince," "My Romance," "No Place But Home," "Nobody's Heart," "Nothing But You," "Oh, Diogenes," "On a Desert Island With Thee," "On Your Toes," "Quiet Night," "Sentimental Me," "She Could Shake the Maracas," "A Ship Without a Sail," "The Shortest Day of the Year," "Sing for Your Supper," "Slaughter on Tenth Avenue," "Soon," "Spring Is Here."

Also "Take Him," "Ten Cents a Dance," "There's a Small Hotel," "This Can't Be Love," "This Funny World," "This Is My Night to Howl," "Thou Swell," "The Three B's," "To Keep My Love Alive," "A Tree in the Park," "Two-a-Day for Keith," "Wait Till You See Her," "Way Out West," "What's the Use of Talking?", "Where or When," "Where's That Rainbow?", "Why Can't I?", "With a Song in My Heart," "You Always Love the Same Girl," "You Are Too Beautiful," "You Mustn't Kick It Around," "You Took Advantage of Me," "You're Nearer," "Zip."

PLAYS WHICH CLOSED
PRIOR TO BROADWAY OPENING

Plays which were organized in New York for Broadway presentation, but which closed during their tryout performances, are listed below.

I Got a Song. Musical with book by E.Y. Harburg and Fred Saidy; music by Harold Arlen, Vernon Duke, Sammy Fain, Burton Lane, Jay Gorney, Earl Robinson; lyrics by E.Y. Harburg. Produced by Joel Schenker and Claire Nichtern in a pre-Broadway production at the Studio Arena Theater, Neal Du Brock executive producer, Buffalo, N.Y. Opened September 26, 1974. (Closed October 20, 1974)

D. Jamin-Bartlett	Bonnie Franklin
Alan Brasington	Miguel Godreau
Norma Donaldson	Gilbert Price

Musicians: Marty Henne conductor, keyboard; Lee Carroll, guitar; Lynn Harbold drums; Frank Primerano bass; Tony Carere flute, clarinet; Tony Ragusa, percussion.

Directed by Harold Stone; choreography, Geoffrey Holder; musical direction and vocal arrangements, Marty Henne; design, R.J. Graziano; costumes, Theoni V. Aldredge; lighting, Thomas Skelton; orchestrations, Tony Ragusa; associate producer, Paul Repetowski; production stage managers, Donald Walters, Steven Zweigbaum; press, Max Eisen, Elsa Hoppenfeld.

Self-described in a subtitle as "a view of life and times through the lyrics of E.Y. Harburg," who is the lyricist of all the musical numbers listed below, except as noted (composers' names appear in parentheses).

ACT I—"Look to the Rainbow" (Burton Lane), "I Got a Song" (Harold Arlen), "Great Day Coming Manana" (Lane), "Brother, Can You Spare a Dime?" (Jay Gorney), "April in Paris" (Vernon Duke), "Let's Take a Walk Around the Block" (Arlen; co-lyricist, Ira Gershwin), "Necessity" (Lane), "The Money Cat" (Arlen), "When the Idle Poor Become the Idle Rich" (Lane), "Happiness Is a Thing Called Joe" (Arlen), "Silent Spring" (Arlen), "The Eagle and Me" (Arlen), "The Monkey in the Mango Tree" (Arlen), "Jump, Children, Jump" (Sammy Fain), "Noah" (Arlen), "We're Off to See the Wizard" (Arlen).

ACT II—"We're Off to See the Wizard" (Reprise), "Napoleon" (Arlen), "Ain't It de Truth" (Arlen), "Leave de Atom Alone" (Arlen), "We're in the Same Boat, Brother" (Earl Robinson), Love Medley—"If This Isn't Love" (Lane), "The World Is Your Balloon" (Fain), "Old Devil Moon" and "Right as the Rain" (Arlen), "Over the Rainbow" (Arlen), Eagle Dance (musical medley), "That Great Come-and-Get-It-Day" (Lane), "It's Only a Paper Moon" (Arlen; co-lyricist, Billy Rose).

Miss Moffat. Musical based on Emlyn Williams's play *The Corn Is Green*; book by Emlyn Williams and Joshua Logan; music by Albert Hague; lyrics by Emlyn Williams. Produced by Eugene V. Wolsk, Joshua Logan and Slade Brown in a pre-Broadway tour at the Shubert Theater, Philadelphia. Opened October 7, 1974. (Closed October 18, 1974)

Champ	Rudolf Lowe	Mr. Jones	Lee Goodman
Ty	Jaison Walker	Mrs. Sprode	Anne Francine
Absie	Nat Jones	Miss Ronberry	Dody Goodman
Zeke	Gian Carlo Esposito	Senator	David Sabin
Morgan Evans	Dorian Harewood	Bessie Watty	Marion Ramsey
Jim	Kevin Dearinger	Miss Moffat	Bette Davis
Jerry	Randy Martin	Ol Mr. Pete	Avon Long
Larry	Michael Calkins	Marse Jeff	Gil Robbins

Others: Wendell Brown, Vicky Geyer, Yolande Graves, Helen Jennings, Betty Lynd, Pamela Palluzzi, Lacy Darryll Phillips, Sandra Phillips, Janet Powell, Christine Tordenti.

Directed by Joshua Logan; musical staging, Donald Saddler; musical direction, Jay Blackton;

scenery and lighting, Jo Mielziner; costumes, Robert Mackintosh; orchestrations, Robert M. Freedman; associate producer, Jim Milford; press, Merle Debuskey.

The Williams play on which the musical is based was originally produced on Broadway 11/26/40 for 477 performances and was named a Best Play and received the Drama Critics Circle award. It was revived 5/3/43 for 56 performances and 1/11/50 for 16 performances. Miss Davis, who starred in this musical production (set in the Southern United States at the turn of the century) played the same role in the 1946 motion picture version.

MUSICAL NUMBERS—"A Wonderful Game," "A Wonderful Game" (Reprise), "Pray for the Snow," "Here in the South," "Tomorrow," "Tomorrow" (Reprise), "There's More to a Man Than His Head," "Time's A-Flyin'," "Here in the South" (Reprise), "You Don't Need a Nailfile in a Cornfield," "There's More to a Man Than His Head" (Reprise), "The Words Unspoken," "Peekaboo, Jehovah," "The Words Unspoken" (Reprise), "Go, Go, Morgan," "I Can Talk Now," "If I Weren't Me," "What Could Be Fairer Than That?," "The Debt I Owe," "I Shall Experience It Again."

PLAYS PRODUCED
OFF BROADWAY

Some distinctions between off-Broadway and Broadway productions at one end of the scale and off-off-Broadway productions at the other end were blurred in the New York theater of the 1970s. For the purposes of this *Best Plays* listing, the term "off Broadway" signifies a show which opened for general audiences in a mid-Manhattan theater seating 299 or fewer during the time period covered by this volume and 1) employed an Equity cast, 2) planned a regular schedule of 7 or 8 performances a week and 3) offered itself to public comment by critics at designated opening performances.

Occasional exceptions of inclusion (never of exclusion) are made to take in visiting troupes, borderline cases and a few non-qualifying productions which readers might expect to find in this list because they appear under an off-Broadway heading in other major sources of record.

Figures in parentheses following a play's title indicate number of performances. These figures are acquired directly from the production office in each case and do not include previews or extra non-profit performances.

Plays marked with an asterisk (*) were still running on June 1, 1975. Their number of performances is figured from opening night through May 31, 1975.

In a listing of a show's numbers—dances, sketches, musical scenes, etc.—the titles of songs are identified by their appearance in quotation marks (").

Most entries of off-Broadway productions which ran fewer than 20 performances are somewhat abbreviated.

HOLDOVERS FROM PREVIOUS SEASONS

Plays which were running on June 1, 1974 are listed below. More detailed information about them appears in previous *Best Plays* volumes of appropriate years. Important cast changes since opening night are recorded in a section of this volume.

*The Fantasticks (6,281; longest continuous run of record in the American theater). Musical suggested by the play *Les Romantiques* by Edmond Rostand; book and lyrics by Tom Jones; music by Harvey Schmidt. Opened May 3, 1960.

*Godspell (1,684). Musical based on the Gospel according to St. Matthew; conceived by John-Michael Tebelak; music and lyrics by Stephen Schwartz. Opened May 17, 1971.

El Grande de Coca-Cola (1,114). Musical revue in the Spanish language written by the cast; based on an idea by Ron House and Diz White. Opened February 13, 1973. (Closed April 13, 1975)

*The Hot l Baltimore (943). By Lanford Wilson. Opened March 22, 1973.

Moonchildren (394). Revival of the play by Michael Weller. Opened November 4, 1973. (Closed October 20, 1974)

When You Comin' Back, Red Ryder? (302). By Mark Medoff. Opened December 6, 1973. (Closed August 25, 1974)

*****Let My People Come** (700). Musical revue with music and lyrics by Earl Wilson Jr. Opened January 8, 1974.

Roundabout Theater Company. 1973–74 schedule of five programs ended with **The Circle** (96). Revival of the play by W. Somerset Maugham. Opened March 26, 1974. (Closed June 16, 1974)

The Sea Horse (128). By Edward J. Moore. Opened April 15, 1974. (Closed August 4, 1974)

The Ridiculous Theatrical Company. 1973–74 schedule of two programs ended with **Camille** (113). Revival of the play by Alexandre Dumas; adapted by Charles Ludlam. Opened May 13, 1974. (Closed October 27, 1974)

Jacques Brel Is Alive and Well and Living in Paris (125). Revival of the revue based on Jacques Brel's lyrics and commentary; production conception, English lyrics and additional material by Eric Blau and Mort Shuman; music by Jacques Brel. Opened May 17, 1974. (Closed September 1, 1974)

The American Place Theater. 1973–74 schedule of four programs ended with **The Year of the Dragon** (29). By Frank Chin. Opened May 22, 1974. (Closed June 15, 1974)

PLAYS PRODUCED, JUNE 1, 1974–MAY 31, 1975

Negro Ensemble Company. 1973–74 schedule of three programs ended with **In the Deepest Part of Sleep** (32). By Charles Fuller. Produced by the Negro Ensemble Company, Douglas Turner Ward artistic director, Robert Hooks executive director, Frederick Garrett administrative director, at the St. Marks Playhouse. Opened June 4, 1974. (Closed June 30, 1974)

Maybelle	Mary Alice	Lyla	Michele Shay
Reuben	Todd Davis	Ashe	Charles Weldon

Directed by Israel Hicks; scenery and costumes, Mary Mease Warren; lighting, Susan Chapman; production assistant, Sandra Ross; production stage manager, Harrison Avery; press, Howard Atlee, Clarence Allsopp, Meg Gordean.

Time: Phildelphia, April 1956, Wednesday. Place: Philadelphia. The play was presented in two parts.

An emotionally disturbed mother upsets her family, in particular her adolescent son.

Some People, Some Other People and What They Finally Do (16). Revue by Jordan Crittenden; incidental music by Stephen Lawrence. Produced by Ruth Kalkstein and Sidney Annis, John Allen associate producer, at Stage 73. Opened June 5, 1974. (Closed June 16, 1974)

Directed by Charles Aidman; scenery, John Lee Beatty; costumes, Reef Pell; lighting, Joel Grunheim; production stage manager, Duane Mazey; press, Gerald Siegal, Ronni Chasen. With Lois Battle, Rod Browning, Jordan Crittenden, Carol Morley.

Revue of comedy episodes "with very little music."

The World of Lenny Bruce (137). One-man show conceived and performed by Frank Speiser; based on the life and works of Lenny Bruce. Produced by Norman Twain in association with Michael Liebert by special arrangement with Marvin Worth at the Players Theater. Opened June 11, 1974. (Closed October 6, 1974)

Directed by Frank Speiser; press, Jeffrey Richards.
The play was presented in two parts entitled *The Words of Lenny Bruce* and *The Trial of Lenny Bruce.*
In the first part author-performer Speiser appears as the night club comedian in one of his routines; in the second he reenacts Bruce's handling of his own defense in his obscenity trial.
Ted Schwartz replaced Frank Speiser for the final two weeks of the run, 9/24/74–10/6/74.

New York Shakespeare Festival. Summer schedule of outdoor programs of two revivals of plays by William Shakespeare. **Pericles, Prince of Tyre** (24). Opened June 20, 1974; see note. (Closed July 21, 1974) **The Merry Wives of Windsor** (24). Opened July 25, 1974; see note. (Closed August 25, 1974) Produced by New York Shakespeare Festival, Joseph Papp producer, at the Delacorte Theater in Central Park.

BOTH PLAYS—Associate producer, Bernard Gersten; scenery, Santo Loquasto; lighting, Martin Aronstein; press, Merle Debuskey, Norman L. Berman; produced in cooperation with the City of New York, Hon. Abraham D. Beame mayor, Hon. Edwin L. Weisl administrator of parks, Hon. Irving Goldman commissioner of cultural affairs.

PERICLES, PRINCE OF TYRE

Gower (Chorus) . . . . . . Barnard Hughes	Marina . . . . Marybeth Hurt
Kingdom of Antioch:	1st Fisherman . . . . Richard Ramos
Antiochus . . . . Lex Monson	2d Fisherman . . . . Lex Monson
His Daughter . . . . Carol Cole	3d Fisherman . . . . Ted Swetz
Thaliard . . . . Lenny Baker	Knight of Tharsus . . . . . Armand Assante
Messenger . . . . Steven Burleigh	Knight of Macedon . . . . Gastone Rossilli
Kingdom of Tyre:	Knight of Antioch . . . . Juan Palma
Pericles . . . . Randall Duk Kim	Knight of Mytilene . . . . Steven Burleigh
Helicanus . . . . Graham Brown	Knight of Ephesus . . . . Lenny Baker
Escanes . . . . Ted Swetz	City of Ephesus:
City-State of Tharsus:	Diana . . . . Carol Cole
Cleon . . . . Richard Ramos	Cerimon . . . . Tom Toner
Dionyza . . . . Dimitra Arliss	Philemon . . . . Michael Hammond
Leonine . . . . Armand Assante	Companion to Thaisa . . . . Helen Stenborg
1st Pirate . . . . Roland Sanchez	City-State of Mytilene:
2d Pirate . . . . Kenneth Marshall	Lysimachus . . . . Gastone Rossilli
3d Pirate . . . . Bob Harders	Pander . . . . Graham Brown
Kingdom of Pentapolis:	Bawd . . . . Sasha von Scherler
Simonides . . . . Tom Toner	Boult . . . . Lenny Baker
Thaisa . . . . Charlotte Moore	Companion to Marina . . . . . . Rise Collins
Lychorida . . . . Helen Stenborg	

Lords and Ladies: Steven Burleigh, Patricia Carney Conwell, Rise Collins, Jane Dentinger, Richard Hamburger, Michael Hammond, Bob Harders, Kenneth Marshall, Juan Palma, Roland Sanchez, Angela Sargeant, Ted Swetz, Pilar Zalamea.
Musicians: Fred Hand lute, 12-string guitar; George Mgrdichian, oud; John Bergano dumbeg.
Directed by Edward Berkeley; costumes, John Conklin; music, William Penn; dances, Dennis Nahat; production stage manager, D.W. Koehler; stage manager, Jason Steven Cohen.
The play was presented in two parts. The only New York production of record of *Pericles* in this century was off off Broadway in CSC repertory in the 1970–71 season.

THE MERRY WIVES OF WINDSOR

Robert Shallow	Tom Toner	Mistress Quickly	Marilyn Sokol
Abraham Slender	Lenny Baker	John Rugby	Danny DeVito
Sir Hugh Evans	George Pentecost	Doctor Caius	David Hurst
George Page	George Hearn	Fenton	Frederick Coffin
Sir John Falstaff	Barnard Hughes	Mistress Page	Marcia Rodd
Bardolph	Ernest Austin	Mistress Ford	Cynthia Harris
Pistol	Jaime Sanchez	Frank Ford	Joseph Bova
Nym	Dennis Tate	Robin	Matthew Douglas Anton
Peter Simple	Michael Tucker	John & Robert	Richard Hambuger,
Ann Page	Deborah Offner		Michael Hammond
Host	Kenneth McMillan	William Page	Stephen Austin

Villagers: Michael Austin, Linda Howes, Reginald Vel Johnson, Sam McMurray, David Wier, Alan Woolf.

Directed by David Margulies; costumes, Carrie F. Robbins; music, Robert Dennis; dances, Donald Saddler; production stage manager, John Beven; stage manager, Osborne Scott.

The play was presented in two parts. The last professional production of record of *The Merry Wives of Windsor* in New York was on Broadway 4/14/38 for 4 performances.

NOTE: In this volume, certain programs of off-Broadway companies like the New York Shakespeare Festival in Central Park are exceptions to our rule of counting the number of performances from the date of the press coverage. When 'he official opening takes place late in the run of a play's public performances (after previews), we count the first performance of record, not the press date, as opening night. Press date for *Pericles* was 6/30/74, for *The Merry Wives of Windsor* 7/30/74.

Why Hanna's Skirt Won't Stay Down (137). By Tom Eyen (see note). Produced by Michael Harvey in the Theater of the Eye Repertory Company 1974 production at the Top of the Village Gate. Opened July 1, 1974. (Closed October 27, 1974)

Hanna	Helen Hanft	Barker	William Duff-Griffin/
Arizona	Steven Davis		Neil Flanagan/Jerome Eyen
Sophie	Mary Carter		

Directed by Neil Flanagan and Tom Eyen; scenery, T.E. Mason; costumes, Patricia Adshead; lighting, Gary Weathersbee; production stage manager, Gary Keeper; press, Alan Eichler.

Two linked comedies about two sisters, one a 42d Street movie ticket-taker and the other a suburban Avon lady.

NOTE: This material originated as an Eyen trilogy entitled *The Three Sisters From Springfield, Illinois.* The third part of the trilogy was added to the program under the title *What Is Making Gilda So Gray?* 10/1/74 for 12 performances with Carleton Carpenter and Alix Elias in the two roles of the one-actor, about the conflict been the fantasy and real lives of a man and wife, staged as a radio play with sound effects.

Roundabout Theater Company. Schedule of six programs. **The Burnt Flowerbed** (48). By Ugo Betti; translated by Henry Reed. Opened July 2, 1974; see note. (Closed August 11, 1974) **All My Sons** (60). Revival of the play by Arthur Miller. Opened September 27, 1974; see note. (Closed November 17, 1974) **The Rivals** (79). Revival of the play by Richard Brinsley Sheridan. Opened December 3, 1974; see note. (Closed February 9, 1975) **Rosmersholm** (32). Revival of the play by Henrik Ibsen. Opened December 3, 1974; see note. (Closed December 29, 1974) **James Joyce's Dubliners** (80). By J.W. Riordan; music and lyrics by Philip Campanella; based on *My Brother's Keeper* by Stanislaus Joyce. Opened February 25, 1975; see note. (Closed May 4, 1975) ***What Every Woman Knows** (5). Revival of the play by James M. Barrie. Opened May 28, 1975; see note. Produced by Roundabout Theater Company, Gene Feist producing director, Michael Fried executive producer.

THE BURNT FLOWERBED

Giovanni	. . . . Paul Sparer	Raniero	. . . . David Byrd
Tomaso	. . . . Brian Davies	Rosa	. . . . Lauren Frost
Luisa	. . . . Jane White	Nicola	. . . . Salem Ludwig

Directed by Paul Aaron; scenery, Holmes Easley; costumes, Mimi Maxmen; lighting, Timothy Harris; musical supervision, Philip Campanella; sound, Gary Harris; production stage manager, Ron Antone; press, David Guc.

Time: The recent past. Place: A country house near a European frontier. Act I: Early evening. Act II: That night. Act III: Just before dawn.

New York professional premiere of Ugo Betti's 1952 suspense drama about an aging political leader beset by his own onetime followers. A foreign play previously produced in Italy and elsewhere.

ALL MY SONS

Joe Keller	. . . . Hugh Marlowe	Chris Keller	. . . . Drew Snyder
Dr. Jim Bayliss	. . . . . Kenneth Kimmins	Bert	. . . . Matthew Barry
Frank Lubey	. . . . Rik Pierce	Kate Keller	. . . . Beatrice Straight
Sue Bayliss	. . . . Janet Sarno	Ann Deever	. . . . Catherine Byers
Lydia Lubey	. . . . Jane Dentinger	George Deever	. . . . Tom Keena

Directed by Gene Feist; scenery, Holmes Easley; costumes, Mimi Maxmen; lighting, Richard Winkler; sound, Gary Harris; original score, Philip Campanella; production stage manager, Ron Antone; press, Gerald Siegel/Ronni Chasen.

Time: Late August, 1947. Place: The back yard of the Keller home in the outskirts of an American town. Act I: Evening. Act II: The same evening as twilight falls. Act III: Two o'clock the following morning. The play was presented in two parts with the intermission following Act II.

All My Sons was first produced on Broadway 1/29/47 for 328 performances. It was revived off Broadway in the 1949–50 season.

THE RIVALS

Thomas; David	. . . . Arthur Anderson	Sir Anthony Absolute	. . Christopher Hewett
Fag	. . . . Michael Tucker	Capt. Jack Absolute	. . . . . Richard Monette
Lucy	. . . . Elizabeth Owens	Faulkland	. . . . Dennis Lipscomb
Lydia Languish	. . Kathleen O'Meara Noone	Bob Acres	. . . . George Pentecost
Julia	. . . . Susan Watson	Sir Lucius O'Trigger	. . . . . . John Newton
Mrs. Malaprop	. . . . Jane Connell		

Directed by Michael Bawtree; scenery, Holmes Easley; costumes, Susan Benson; lighting, Clarke Dunham; original score, Philip Campanella; sound, Gary Harris; production stage manager, Ron Antone.

Time: An early summer's day in the late 18th century. Place: Bath. The play was presented in two parts.

The last major New York revival of *The Rivals* was the Walter Hampden-Mary Boland production 1/14/42 for 54 performances. It was revived off Broadway during the 1952–53 season and was adapted into the musical *All in Love* 11/10/61 for 141 performances.

ROSMERSHOLM

Rebekka West	. . . . Jane White	Johannes Rosmer	. . . . Bill Moor
Miss Helseth	. . . . Virginia Payne	Ulrik Brendel	. . . . Stefan Schnabel
Professor Kroll	. . . . Stephen Scott	Peter Mortensgaard	. . . . . Steven Gilborn

Directed by Raphael Kelly; scenery, Stuart Wurtzel; costumes, Patrizia von Brandenstein; lighting, Timmy Harris; production stage manager, J.R. Grant.

Time: The late 1800s. Place: Rosmersholm, an old estate in Norway. The play was presented in two parts.

The most recent professional New York revival of *Rosmersholm* was off Broadway 4/11/62 for 119 performances.

JAMES JOYCE'S DUBLINERS

John Joyce	Stan Watt	Stannislaus Joyce	Ty McConnell
Mary Joyce	Ruby Holbrook	William Murray	Walter Klavun
James Joyce	Martin Cassidy	Josephine Murray	Justine Johnson

Young Jimmy Joyce, Butcher Boy, Mike O'Brien—Michael Hagerty; Kate Murray, Mrs. Parker, Young Woman—Erika Petersen; Holohan, Alleyne, Gallagher, Capuchine Priest, Dempsey, Henchy —Don Perkins; Fitzpatrick, Father Conmee, Sheehy, Old Jack, Dowd—Frank Hamilton; D'Arcy, Bartender, Brother Kenny, Matt Calahan, Dodd—Kent Rizley.

Directed by Gene Feist; scenery, Holmes Easley; costumes, Christina Giannini; lighting, Ian Calderon; sound, Gary Harris; production stage manager, Ron Antone.

Time: A ten-year period at the turn of the century. Place: Dublin. The play was presented in two parts.

Episodes from James Joyce's life based on his brother's book and other writings, with the inclusion of ballads and other songs.

WHAT EVERY WOMAN KNOWS

James Wylie	Jeff Rubin	John Shand	Michael Goodwin
Alick Wylie	Jack Bittner	Comtesse de la Briere	Grayson Hall
David Wylie	Ron Frazier	Lady Sybil Tenterden	Susan Tabor
Maggie Wylie	Fran Brill	Mr. Venables	Ronald Drake

Directed by Gene Feist; scenery, Holmes Easley; costumes, Charles Gelatt; lighting, Ian Calderon; original score, Philip Campanella; sound, Gary Harris; production stage manager, Robert A. Lowe; press, Gerald Siegel, Valerie Warner.

ACT I: The house of the Wylies, who are the proprietors of a granite quarry in northern Scotland, evening, late summer. Act II: A barber shop in Glasgow, serving as John Shand's committee rooms, election night, autumn, six years later. Act III, Scene 1: Mr. Shand's house in London, late spring, two years later. Scene 2: The same, a few days later. Act IV: The country estate of the Comtesse de la Briere, early afternoon three weeks later, early summer. The play was presented in two parts with the intermission between Acts II and III.

The last major New York revival of *What Every Woman Knows* starred Helen Hayes at New York City Center 12/22/54 for 15 performances.

In addition to its regular schedule, Roundabout Theater Company presented *A Musical Merchant of Venice* (12), book by William Shakespeare, music by Jim Smith, lyrics by Tony Tanner, directed by Tony Tanner, scenery Sandro La Ferla, costumes Dwayne Moritz, lighting Lewis Mead, with Gary Beach, Randy Hornish, Cara Duff-McCormick, Mary Ann Robbins, Danny Sewell, Albert Verdesca, Sel Vitella, John Thomas Waite, Phyllis Ward, Mark Winkworth, in a showcase production at Stage Two at the end of the season, 6/1/75–6/13/75.

This season Roundabout Theater Company expanded from one to two theaters known as Stage One (the new theater) and Stage Two. *All My Sons, The Rivals, James Joyce's Dubliners* and *What Every Woman Knows* played Stage One; *The Burnt Flowerbed* and *Rosmersholm* played Stage Two.

NOTE: In this volume, certain programs of off-Broadway companies like Roundabout Theater Company are exceptions to our rule of counting the number of performances from the date of the press coverage. When the official opening takes place late in the run of a play's public performances (after previews), we count the first performance of record, not the press date, as opening night. Press date for *The Burnt Flowerbed* was 7/24/74, for *All My Sons* 10/28/74, for *Rosmersholm* 12/15/74, for *The Rivals* 1/13/75, for *James Joyce's Dubliners* 3/24/75, for *What Every Woman Knows* 6/3/75.

Naomi Court (73). By Michael Sawyer. Produced by Leonard Schlosberg in association with Jean Dalrymple at Manhattan Theater Club Stage 73. Opened September 10, 1974. (Closed December 26, 1974; transferred to off off Broadway)

Lenny	Terry Alexander	Mr. Berry	Michael M. Ryan
David	Jordan Charney	Harper	Brad Davis
Miss Dugan	Sally Gracie		

Directed by Ira Cirker; scenery and lighting, Andrew Greenhut; stage manager, K.C. Schulberg; press, Saul Richman.

Prologue: Outside Naomi Court, 3 A.M. today. Act I, Scene 1: Miss Dugan's apartment, 12:30 P.M. yesterday. Scene 2: Miss Dugan's apartment, four hours later. Act II, Scene 1: David's apartment, early evening. Scene 2: David's apartment, later that evening. Epilogue: Outside Naomi Court, 3 A.M. today.

Two separate episodes—one of wrenching loneliness and one of sex perversion and menace—are connected by their setting, Naomi Court, an apartment building scheduled to be torn down and nearly vacated. Previously produced 8/21/74 off off Broadway in this same production.

The Advertisement (12). By Natalia Ginzburg; translated by Henry Reed. Produced by Nicholas John Stathis in the Classic Theater Production at the Provincetown Playhouse. Opened October 3, 1974. (Closed October 20, 1974)

Directed by David Black; scenery, Donald L. Brooks; consultant, Maurice Edwards; stage manager, Karen Sundbergh; press, Alan Eichler. With Julia Curry, Maria Ruberto, Harvey Solin, Ali Jones.

In modern Rome, an abandoned wife advertises for a young woman companion, who finally falls in love with the ex-husband. A foreign play previously produced in Italy and in London by the National Theater.

New York Shakespeare Festival Public Theater. Schedule of six programs and six guest residency programs. Public Theater productions: **Where Do We Go From Here?** (36). By John Ford Noonan. Opened October 5, 1974; see note. (Closed November 3, 1974) **The Last Days of British Honduras** (43). By Ronald Tavel. Opened October 22, 1974; see note. (Closed November 24, 1974) **In the Boom Boom Room** (31). Revised version of the play by David Rabe. Opened November 20, 1974; see note. (Closed December 15, 1974) **Kid Champion** (48). By Thomas Babe. Opened January 28, 1975; see note. (Closed March 9, 1975). **Fishing** (46). By Michael Weller. Opened February 1, 1975; see note. (Closed March 9, 1975) *****A Chorus Line** (54). Musical conceived by Michael Bennett; book by James Kirkwood and Nicholas Dante; music by Marvin Hamlisch; lyrics by Edward Kleban. Opened April 15, 1975; see note.

Guest residency programs: **The Measures Taken** (102). Revival of the play by Bertolt Brecht in the Shaliko Company production; English version by Eric Bentley; music by Hanns Eisler. Opened October 4, 1974; see note. Recessed January 19, 1975 after 89 performances and reopened April 13, 1975 in repertory with **Ghosts** (37). Revival of the play by Henrik Ibsen in the Shaliko Company production; translated by Rolfe Fjelde. Opened March 6, 1975; see note. (Repertory closed May 18, 1975). **The Sea Gull** (42), revival of the play by Anton Chekhov, opened January 8, 1975, and **Our Late Night** (38) by Wallace Shawn, opened January 9, 1975. Repertory of two programs in The Manhattan Project productions. (Repertory closed April 5, 1975) **Alice in Wonderland** (20). Return engagement of The Manhattan Project production of the Lewis Carroll book. Opened April 15, 1975. (Closed April 26, 1975) **Endgame** (12) Return engagement of The Manhattan Project production of the play by Samuel Beckett. Opened April 29, 1975. (Closed May 10, 1975) Public Theater programs and guest residencies produced by New York Shakespeare Festival Public Theater, Joseph Papp producer, at the Public Theater.

ALL PLAYS—Associate producer, Bernard Gersten; press, Merle Debuskey, Bob Ullman, Norman L. Berman.

WHERE DO WE GO FROM HERE?

Remo Weinberger	Gabriel Dell	Robert M. Cleery	Charles Parks
Johann Sebanstian Fabiani	Jake Dangel	Winnifred Winowski	Jane Sanford
Whimsey	Danny De Vito	Heather Weinberger	Anna Shaler
Coriolanus T. O'Shea	Kenneth McMillan		

Directed by David Margulies; scenery and costumes, Robert Yodice; lighting, Roger Morgan; music, Kirk Nurock; production stage manager, Richard S. Viola.

Time: The dead of winter, mid-December, early evening. Place: The living room of a four-room apartment two stories above the streets of a downtown section of Boston, Mass. The play was presented in two parts.

Comic and melodramatic incidents concerning a transvestite and his friends.

THE LAST DAYS OF BRITISH HONDURAS

Capt. Henry	Hannibal Penney	Angel Ruz Covarrubias	Daniel Hedaya
Danyon Paron Jr.	Stephen Collins	Walter	Frankie Faison
Al Balam	Marc Vahanian	Joseph Austin	Norman Matlock
The Prisoner	Don Blakely	Dennis Simons	F.M. Kimball
The Amerind	Ray Barry	Suzanne	Sheila Gibbs
Lornette Wilson	Lisa Richards	Charlie	Leroy Lessane

Directed by David Schweizer; scenery, Paul Zalon; costumes, Timothy Miller; lighting, Ian Calderon; production stage manager. Jack Caputo.

Time: Sept. 9 and 10, 1970. Place: British Honduras. C.A.; Stann Creek Town; The Hummingbird Forest; Lubaatun, steps of the pyramid. The play was presented in two parts.

Science fiction exploration and surmise of the reasons for the disappearance of Mayan civilization in the 12th century.

IN THE BOOM BOOM ROOM

Chrissy	Ellen Greene	Vikki	Missie Zollo
Harold	Tom Quinn	Ralphie	David Cromwell
Susan	Gwendolyn Brown	Al	Christopher Lloyd
Guy	Philip Polito	Helen	Helen Hanft
Eric	Fred Grandy	Irene	Aleta
Sally	Lynn Oliver	The Man	Peter Victor
Melissa	Patricia Gaul		

Bar Patrons: Madison Arnold, Ken Kliban, Gloria Lord.

Directed by Robert Hedley; scenery, David Mitchell; costumes, Milo Morrow; lighting, Martin Aronstein; choreography, Baayork Lee; production stage manager, Ken Glickfeld.

Time: The mid-1960s. Place: Philadelphia. The play was presented in two parts.

Revised version of last season's Drama Critics Award runner-up *Boom Boom Room*, about the life and times of a go-go dancer.

KID CHAMPION

Tom	Christopher Allport	Devoted Hack	Jerry Zaks
Lord Jim	Matthew Cowles	Porter	Flloyd Ennis
Manager	David Margulies	Alice	Anna Levine
Kid Champion	Christopher Walken	Simon L. Renfrew	Kenneth McMillan
Zinko	Don Scardino	Celebrity; Woman	Patricia Stewart
Cop	Anthony Mannino	Photographer; Cop	T. Richard Mason
Stage Manager	Gene Fanning	Groupie	Shelly Batt
Fan; Mailboy	Tom Happer	Jill McDill	Kathryn Walker
Marylou	Mary Elaine Monti	Mom	Sasha von Scherler

Narcs: Flloyd Ennis, Gene Fanning, Tom Happer. Roadies, Groupies, etc.: Kevin Geer, Bertina Johnson, Anthony Mannino, Anne O'Sullivan, William Russ, Ilsebet Tebesli. Cops: Anthony Mannino, T. Richard Mason.

Directed by John Pasquin; scenery, Douglas W. Schmidt; costumes, Theoni V. Aldredge; lighting, William Mintzer; music, Jim Steinman; lyrics, Thomas Babe, Jim Steinman; musical direction and arrangements, Steven Margoshes; production stage manager, Richard S. Viola.

Time: Late 1969 to spring 1970. Act I, Scene 1: Backstage, an auditorium in Cleveland. Scene 2: Hotel room in Akron, the next day. Scene 3: Men's room, an auditorium in Akron, the following day.

Scene 4: Limousine in the streets, Pittsburgh, two days later. Scene 5: Green room of the Civic Arena, Pittsburgh, the following day. Scene 6: The concert stage, Civic Arena, immediately following. Act II, Scene 7: Villa near Acapulco, six months later. Scene 8: Townhouse in Manhattan, one month later. Scene 9: Head table, ACLU banquet, one month later. Scene 10: Apartment, the East Village, one month later. Scene 11: Penthouse in Manhattan, an hour later. Scene 12: Kitchen in a house, Abilene, Kan., three weeks later.

The downfall of a star in the popular rock music world.

FISHING

Robbie	Guy Boyd	Mary-Ellen	Kathryn Grody
Bill	Tom Lee Jones	Dane	John Heard
Shelly	Lindsay Crouse	Reilly	Edward Seamon
Rory	Raymond J. Barry		

Directed by Peter Gill; scenery and costumes, Pat Woodbridge; lighting, Ian Calderon; stage manager, John Beven.

Time: 1974. Place: The Pacific Northwest. Act I, Scene 1: Bill and Shelly's cabin. Scene 2: In front of the cabin. Act II, Scene 1: The look-out over the Pacific Ocean. Scene 2: Bill and Shelly's cabin.

Purposeless young people, somewhat older now than this same author's student *Moonchildren*, looking for a function and meaning in their lives.

A CHORUS LINE

Roy	Scott Allen	Don	Ron Kuhlman
Kristine	Renee Baughman	Bebe	Nancy Lane
Sheila	Carole Bishop	Connie	Baayork Lee
Val	Pamela Blair	Diana	Priscilla Lopez
Mike	Wayne Cilento	Zach	Robert LuPone
Butch	Chuck Cissel	Mark	Cameron Mason
Larry	Clive Clerk	Cassie	Donna McKechnie
Maggie	Kay Cole	Al	Don Percassi
Richie	Ronald Dennis	Frank	Michael Serrecchia
Tricia	Donna Drake	Greg	Michel Stuart
Tom	Brandt Edwards	Bobby	Thomas J. Walsh
Judy	Patricia Garland	Paul	Sammy Williams
Lois	Carolyn Kirsch	Vicki	Crissy Wilzak

Directed and choreographed by Michael Bennett; co-choreographer, Bob Avian; musical direction & vocal arrangements, Don Pippin; scenery, Robin Wagner; costumes, Theoni V. Aldredge; lighting, Tharon Musser; orchestrations, Bill Byers, Hershy Kay, Jonathan Tunick; music coordinator, Robert Thomas; production stage manager, Jeff Hamlin.

Time: Now. Place: Here; an audition. The play was presented without intermission.

A Broadway director is selecting a chorus for his show; he narrows the applicants down to 17 dancers, of whom he must pick eight.

A Best Play; see page 242

MUSICAL NUMBERS

"I Hope I Get It"	Company
"Joanne"	Mike
"And . . ."	Bobby, Richie, Val, Judy
"At the Ballet"	Sheila, Bebe, Maggie
"Sing!"	Kristine, Al
"Hello Twelve, Hello Thirteen, Hello Love"	Company
"Nothing"	Diana
"Dance: Ten, Looks: Three"	Val
"The Music and the Mirror"	Cassie
"One"	Company
"The Tap Combination"	Company

"What I Did for Love" . . . . Diana, Company
"One" (Reprise) . . . . Company

THE MEASURES TAKEN

Control Commission . . . . . . Tom Crawley,   Jane Mandel, Jerry Mayer
        Susan Topping, Mary Zakrzewski   Pianist . . . . Warren Swenson
Agitators . . Jim Carrington, Chris McCann,

Directed by Leonardo Shapiro.
Revival by N.Y.U.-based troupe of Brecht's 1930 play about four Soviet agitators reporting on a mission to Mukden. This is its first professional New York production of record.

GHOSTS

Regina Engstrand . . . . Jane Mandel   Mrs. Helen Alving . . . . . . Mary Zakrzewski
Jacob Engstrand . . . . Jerry Mayer   Osvald Alving . . . . Chris McCann
Pastor Manders . . . . Tom Crawley

Directed by Leonardo Shapiro; design, Jerry Rojo; costumes, Theodora Skiptares; production coordinator, Jim Carrington.
The last off-Broadway revival of *Ghosts* was the Roundabout's 3/13/73 for 89 performances.

THE SEA GULL

Irina . . . . Saskia Noordhoek Hegt   Paulina . . . . Avra Petrides
Kostya . . . . Larry Pine   Masha . . . . Karen Ludwig
Petrusha . . . . John Ferraro   Trigorin . . . . Gerry Bamman
Nina Zaretchnaya . . . . . Angela Pietropinto   Dorn . . . . Tom Costello
Shamraev . . . . John Holms   Medvedenko . . . . David Laden

Directed by Andre Gregory; produced by Lyn Austin; scenery, Ming Cho Lee; costumes, Nanzi Adzima; translation consultant, Laurence Senelick; lighting, Victor En Yu Tan; production stage manager, Jeff Hamlin.
Place: Sorin's country estate. The play was presented in two parts.
Chekhov's play was last revived in New York last season by the Roundabout Theater Company, 12/18/73 for 105 performances.

OUR LATE NIGHT

With Gerry Bamman, Tom Costello, John Ferraro, Saskia Noordhoek Hegt, Karen Ludwig, Angela Pietropinto, Larry Pine.
Directed by Andre Gregory; produced by Lyn Austin; scenery, Douglas W. Schmidt; costumes, Ara Gallant; lighting, Victor En Yu Tan; production manager, Jeff Hamlin.
Place: An apartment high above a city. The play was presented without intermission.
Anecdotes and episodes of disgust, lewdness and perversion in a party scene.

ALICE IN WONDERLAND

With Gerry Bamman, Tom Costello, Saskia Noordhoek Hegt, Angela Pietropinto, Larry Pine.
Directed by Andre Gregory; produced by Lyn Austin; scenery & costumes, Eugene and Franne Lee.
This *Alice in Wonderland* was first produced 10/8/70 for 119 performances and has appeared in return engagements off and off off Broadway every season since.

ENDGAME

With Gerry Bamman, Tom Costello, Saskia Noordhoek Hegt, Larry Pine.
Directed by Andre Gregory; produced by Lyn Austin.
This *Endgame* was produced off off Broadway 2/2/73 and 4/11/74.

1974–75 workshop or work-in-progress productions at the Other Stage included *Heat* (10) by William Hauptmann, directed by Barnet Kellman, scenery William Stabile, lighting Cheryl Thacker, with Doug Ball, Guy Boyd, Joseph Carberry, Stephen Clark, Marjorie Erdreich, opened 12/1/74; *Apple Pie* (10) musical by Myrna Lamb, music by Nicholas Meyers, directed by Rae Allen, dances by Baayork Lee, scenery David Mitchell, costumes Milo Morrow, lighting Roger Morgan, with Ellen Barber, Robert Guillaume, Mike Kellin, Lucille Patton, Gloria Valenza, opened 1/19/75; *Time Trial* (10) by Jack Gilhooley, directed by Peter Maloney, with Graham Beckel, Robert Burgos, Jayne Haynes, Jeffrey Pomerantz, Ellen Sandler, Diane Sitwell, Tracey Walter, opened 3/23/75.

Among guest residencies at the New York Shakespeare Public Theater was a spring season of children's theater by the Meri Mini Players, a troupe of child actors under the direction of Meridee Stein. They alternated performances of *Alice Through the Looking Glass* and *Looice*, the latter a new musical with book and lyrics by Benjamin Goldstein, music by Philip Namanworth, edited by Meridee Stein.

In Joseph Papp's Public Theater there are many separate auditoriums. *The Measures Taken* played the Little Theater. *Where Do We Go From Here, Fishing* and *A Chorus Line* played the Estelle R. Newman Theater. *The Last Days of British Honduras* played the Other Stage. *In the Boom Boom Room* and *Kid Champion* played the Florence S. Anspacher Theater. *The Sea Gull, Our Late Night, Alice in Wonderland* and *Endgame* played Martinson Hall.

NOTE: In this volume, certain programs of off-Broadway companies like New York Shakespeare Public Theater are exceptions to our rule of counting the number of performances from the date of the press coverage. When the official opening takes place late in the run of a play's public performances (after previews), we count the first performance of record, not the press date, as opening night. Press date for *The Measures Taken* was 10/15/74, for *Where Do We Go From Here!* 10/27/74, for *The Last Days of British Honduras* 11/5/74, for *In the Boom Boom Room* 12/4/74, for *Kid Champion* 2/19/75, for *Fishing* 2/12/75, for *Ghosts* 4/2/75, for *A Chorus Line* 5/21/75.

The Chelsea Theater Center of Brooklyn. Schedule of four programs. **Hothouse** (32). By Megan Terry. Opened October 15, 1974; see note. (Closed November 10, 1974) **Yentl the Yeshiva Boy** (48). Based on a short story by Isaac Bashevis Singer; adapted by Leah Napolin and Isaac Bashevis Singer. Opened December 17, 1974; see note. (Closed January 26, 1975) **Santa Anita '42** (32). By Allan Knee. Opened February 27, 1975 matinee. (Closed March 16, 1975) **Polly** (32). Revival of the musical by John Gay; freely adapted by Robert Kalfin; music newly realized by Mel Marvin. Opened April 29, 1975; see note. (Closed May 25, 1975) Produced by The Chelsea Theater Center of Brooklyn, Robert Kalfin artistic director, Michael David executive director, Burl Hash productions director, at the Brooklyn Academy of Music.

HOTHOUSE

Jody Duncan	Kathleen Tolan	Andy Anderson	R.A. Dow
David Gordan	Michael Cornelison	Doll Jensen	Carol Morley
Ma Sweetlove	Dorothy Chace	Lorna	Barbara Tarbuck
Banty	Dermot McNamara	Scoogie	Kelly Fitzpatrick
Roz Duncan	Helen Gallagher	Jack Duncan	Brad Sullivan

Directed by Rae Allen; scenery, Lawrence King; costumes, Vernon Yates; lighting, William Mintzer; production stage manager, Clint Jakeman; press, Leslie Gifford.

Time: Late spring, about 1953. Place: The fishing village of Edmonds, near the city of Seattle, in the state of Washington. Act I: Late afternoon to late at night. Act II: The next morning. Act III: Between 12 and 1 A.M. that night.

Action and interaction of three generations of alcoholic women.

YENTL THE YESHIVA BOY

Yentl—Tovah Feldshuh; Reb Todrus, Fulcha, Musician, Cantor, Shepsel the Messenger—Bernie Passeltiner; Rivka, Necheleh, Chambermaid—Mary Ellen Ashley; Lemmel, Yussel, Musician, Wedding Jester, The Mohel—Leland Moss; Reb Nata, Musician, Groinem Zelig—Reuben Schafer; Nehemiah, Rabbi Sheftl—Albert M. Ottenheimer; Mordecai, Feitl—Hy Anzell; Zisheh, Shmuel, Dr, Chanina—Stephen de Pietri; Nachum, Chaim, Musician—Charles McKeane; Gershon, Luzer, Laibish, Musician, Moishe the Coachman—Elliot Burtoff; Lazar, Feivl, Musician, Dr. Solomon—Ron

Lagomarsino; Treitl, Reb Alter—Herman O. Arbeit; Avigdor—John V. Shea; Pelte, Raizeleh—Susan Andre; Berel, Finkl—Kathleen Heaney; Avram, Dovid—Brian Kannard; Shimmel, Zelda-Leah—Madeline Shaw; Hadass—Neva Small; Frumka—Natalie Priest; Pesheh—Blanche Dee; Yachna—Rita Karin; Zlateh—Elaine Grollman.

Directed by Robert Kalfin; music composed by Mel Marvin; scenery, Karl Eigsti; costumes, Carrie F. Robbins; lighting, William Mintzer; engagement and wedding, courtesy of Patricia Birch; production stage manager, Ginny Freedman.

Time: 1873. Place: The villages of Yanev, Zamosc and Bechev in Poland. The play was presented in two parts.

Dramatization of Singer story of a young Jewish girl who disguises herself as a boy in order to pursue learning.

SANTA ANITA '42

3d Immigration Official; FBI Agent; Announcer . . . . Frank Anderson	Tamako . . . . Lani Gerrie Miyazaki
Teacher . . . . Henry Kaimu Bal	Mother; Serenader; Mrs. Yamato . . . . Mary Mon Toy
2d Immigration Official; Dressmaker; Committeewoman . . . . Beth Dixon	Paul . . . . Stephen D. Newman
1st Immigration Official; Barker;	Michael . . . . Sab Shimono
Announcer; FBI Agent . . . William Knight	Satoru . . . . Conrad Yama
Father; Serenader . . . . . Tom Matsusaka	Chi Chi . . . . Peter Yoshida

Directed by Steven Robman; scenery, Jeremy Unger; costumes, Carol Oditz; lighting, David Sackeroff; produced by special arrangement with Claire Nichtern; production stage manager, Abbe Raven.

Americans of Japanese ancestry interned in a California race track in World War II.

POLLY

Poet; Morano (alias Macheath) . . . . . . Stephen D. Newman	Polly Peachum . . . . Betsy Beard
1st Player; Old Woman Cook; LaGuerre . . . . Roy Brocksmith	Damaris; Indian Wife . . . Mary Ellen Ashley
2d Player; Culverin . . . . . Alexander Orfaly	Mrs. Ducat . . . . Fran Stevens
3d Player; Flimzy; Old Woman Maid;	Reginald . . . . Ruff Ruff
Indian Wife . . . Prudence Wright Holmes	1st Footman; Vanderbluff . . . . Igors Gavon
Sra. Crochetta; Jenny Diver . Patricia Elliott	2d Footman; Dagger; Indian . . . Brent Mintz
4th Player; Capstern; Indian . . . John Long	Messenger Indian . . . . . . Robert Manzari
Diana Trapes . . . . Lucille Patton	Hacker . . . . George F. Maguire
Mr. Ducat . . . . Edward Zang	Cutlace; Indian . . . . Brian James
	Cawwawkee . . . . Richard Ryder
	Pohetohee . . . . William J. Coppola

Musicians: Clay Fullum harpsichord, harmonium; Bob Haley trumpet, piccolo trumpet; Allan Kaplan trombone; Artie Kruger flute, oboe; Roger Morgan cello; Denise Semenovich, violin.

Directed by Robert Kalfin; musical direction, Clay Fullum; scenery, Robert U. Taylor; costumes, Carrie F. Robbins; lighting, William Mintzer; musical staging, Elizabeth Keen; orchestration, Mel Marvin, Ken Guilmartin; fight director, R.D. Colter; dialect coach, Gordon A. Jacoby; production stage manager, Lewis Rosen.

Place: The West Indies. Act I, Scene 1: A pier. Scene 2: Mr. Ducat's House. Act II, Scene 1: The view of an Indian country. Scene 2: The pirates' aerie. Scene 3: A hidden place. Act III, Scene 1: The Indian camp. Scene 2: In a wood. Scene 3: A mountain pass (the field of battle). Scene 4: The Indian camp from another view.

Polly is John Gay's sequel to *The Beggar's Opera*. Written in 1729, it has Macheath saved from hanging and deported to the West Indies, followed by Polly Peachum; he takes up piracy, she bawdry. Its only previous revival of record was 10/10/25 at the Cherry Lane Theater.

NOTE: In this volume, certain programs of off-Broadway companies like The Chelsea Theater Center are exceptions to our rule of counting the number of performances from the date of the press coverage. When the official opening takes place late in the run of a play's public performances (after previews), we count the first performance of record, not the press date, as opening night. Press date for *Hothouse* was 10/23/74 matinee, for *Yentl the Yeshiva Boy* 12/20/74 matinee, for *Santa Anita '42* 2/18/75, for *Polly* 5/8/75 matinee.

New York Shakespeare Festival Lincoln Center. Schedule of three programs. **Richard III** (90). Revival of the play by William Shakespeare. Opened October 20, 1974. (Closed December 22, 1974) **A Midsummer Night's Dream** (62). Revival of the play by William Shakespeare. Opened January 19, 1975. (Closed March 16, 1975) ***The Taking of Miss Janie** (32). By Ed Bullins. Opened May 4, 1975. Produced by New York Shakespeare Festival Lincoln Center, Joseph Papp producer, at the Mitzi E. Newhouse Theater.

ALL PLAYS—Associate producer, Bernard Gersten; press, Merle Debuskey, Faith Geer, Sally Campbell.

RICHARD III

Richard III . . . . .Michael Moriarty	1st Murderer; Ratcliffe . . . . . Barry Snider
Clarence; Tyrrel . . . . .George Hearn	2d Murderer; Cardinal
Brakenbury; Bishop of Ely . . John Wardwell	Bourchier . . . . David Tabor
Hastings . . . . Tom Toner	Catesby . . . . .Stephen D. Newman
Lady Anne . . . . Marsha Mason	Richard, Duke of York . . . . Stephen Austin
Edward IV; Lord Mayor . . . .Patrick Hines	Edward V . . . . .David Jay
Elizabeth . . . . Barbara Colby	Messenger; Page . . . . Gregg Almquist
Rivers . . . . Howland Chamberlin	Priest; Surrey . . . . .Joseph Corral
Dorset . . . . .Robert Lesser	Norfolk . . . . .David Downing
Grey . . . . .Martin Shakar	Richmond . . . . Marco St. John
Buckingham . . . . .Paul Winfield	Oxford . . . . .Kurt Garfield
Stanley (Earl of Derby) . . . . Maury Cooper	Blunt . . . . K.C. Wilson
Margaret . . . . Betty Henritze	Herbert . . . . Powers Boothe
Mistress Shore . . . . .Robyn Goodman	Brandon . . . . Steve Karp

Lords, Guards, Citizens: Gregg Almquist, Powers Boothe, Joseph Corral, Gene Galusha, Kurt Garfield, Ellen Novack, K.C. Wilson.

Directed by Mel Shapiro; design, John Conklin; lighting, Roger Morgan; unit setting, Santo Loquasto; production stage manager, Jason Steven Cohen; stage manager, D.W. Koehler.

The play was presented in two parts. *Richard III* was last revived in New York by New York Shakespeare Festival in Central Park 6/25/70 for 20 performances.

Jane Marla Robbins replaced Marsha Mason 11/19/74. Robyn Goodman replaced Jane Marla Robbins 11/26/74. Ellen Novack replaced Robyn Goodman 11/26/74. Stephen D. Newman replaced Paul Winfield 11/26/74. Steve Karp replaced Stephen D. Newman 11/26/74. Gene Galusha replaced Steve Karp 11/26/74.

A MIDSUMMER NIGHT'S DREAM

Hippolyta . . . . .Marlene Warfield	Francis Flute . . . . Edward Herrmann
Theseus . . . . Dan Hamilton	Nick Bottom . . . . .Richard Ramos
Philostrate . . . . William Robertson	Peter Quince . . . . Tom Toner
Egeus . . . . Jack Davidson	Cobweb . . . . Stephen Austin
Hermia . . . . .Toni Wein	Puck . . . . Larry Marshall
Lysander . . . . Michael Sacks	Titania . . . . Kathleen Widdoes
Demetrius . . . . .Richard Gere	Oberon . . . . .George Hearn
Helena . . . . Lucy Lee Flippen	Peaseblossom . . . . Timmy Michaels
Snug . . . . Jack R. Marks	Moth . . . . Arthur De Lorenzo
Robin Straveling . . . . David Harscheid	Mustardseed . . . . Gwendolyn Smith
Tom Snout . . . . Roberts Blossom	

Attendants on Theseus and Hippolyta: Frank Ammirati, Michael Cornelison, Tom Everett, Carolyn McCurry, Ellen Novack.

Directed by Edward Berkeley; musical staging, Donald Saddler; music composed by William Penn; design, Santo Loquasto; lighting, Jennifer Tipton; production stage manager, Jason Steven Cohen.

The play was presented in two parts.

A Midsummer Night's Dream was last produced on the New York professional stage 1/20/71 for 62 performances in the Royal Shakespeare Company production.

THE TAKING OF MISS JANIE

Monty	Adeyemi Lythcott	Sharon	Lin Shaye
Janie	Hilary Jean Beane	Lonnie	Sam McMurray
Rick	Kirk Kirksey	Flossy	Dianne Oyama Dixon
Len	Darryl Croxton	Mort Silberstein	Robert B. Silver
Peggy	Robbie McCauley		

Directed by Gilbert Moses; co-produced by Henry Street Settlement's New Federal Theater, Woodie King Jr. producer; scenery, Kert Lundell; costumes, Judy Dearing; lighting, Richard Nelson; production stage manager, Osborne Scott.

Time: The 1960s. Place: California and elsewhere. The play was presented without intermission. The rape of a white girl by a black friend at a party is a symbol of race relations and conditions. A Best Play; see page 245

The Wager (104). By Mark Medoff. Produced by Richard Lee Marks, Henry Jaffe and William Craver at the Eastside Playhouse. Opened October 21, 1974. (Closed January 19, 1975)

Leeds	Kristoffer Tabori	Honor	Linda Cook
Ward	Kenneth Gilman	Ron	John Heard

Directed by Anthony Perkins; scenery, David Mitchell; lighting, Neil Peter Jampolis; costume coordinator, Mary Beth Regan; production stage manager, Peter Lawrence; press, Marilynn LeVine.

Time: The present. Place: A university in northern California, the apartment of two graduate students. Act I, Scene 1: Thursday evening. Scene 2: Seventeen minutes later. Act II: Late Friday afternoon. Act III, Scene I: Seconds later. Scene 2: Saturday morning.

Cool, acidulous philosophy student goads his roommate into seducing a married woman by means of a bet, which gives rise to a series of bitterly ironic consequences.

Carolyn Hurlburt replaced Linda Cook 11/74.

A Best Play; see page 278

The American Place Theater. Schedule of three programs. **The Beauty Part** (36). Revival of the play by S.J. Perelman. Opened October 23, 1974; see note. (Closed November 23, 1974) **Killer's Head** and **Action** (34). Program of plays by Sam Shepard. Opened April 4, 1975 (see note). (Closed May 3, 1975) ***Rubbers** and **Yanks 3 Detroit 0 Top of the Seventh** (17). Program of one-act plays by Jonathan Reynolds. Opened May 16, 1975; see note. Produced by The American Place Theater, Wynn Handman director, at The American Place Theater.

BOTH PLAYS—Associate director, Julia Miles; literary advisors, Joel Schechter, Cassandra Medley; press, David Roggensack.

THE BEAUTY PART

ACT I

Scene 1: Library of Mr. & Mrs. Milo Weatherwax

Mike Mulroy	Ron Faber	Milo Weatherwax	Joseph Bova
Octavia Weatherwax	Bobo Lewis	Lance Weatherwax	Peter Kingsley

Scene 2: April Monkhood's apartment, two days later

Fussfeld	Mitchell Jason	Lance	Peter Kingsley
April Monkhood	Susan Sullivan		

Scene 3: Office of Hyacinth Beddoes Laffoon, a week later

Bunce	Armand Assante	Vishnu	Jerrold Ziman
Van Lennep	Mitchell Jason	Hyacinth Beddoes Laffoon	Joseph Bova
Hagedorn	Ron Faber	Lance	Peter Kingsley

Scene 4: Goddard Quagmeyer's studio, several days later

Goddard Quagmeyer	Jerrold Ziman	Lance	Peter Kingsley

Mrs. Gloria Krumgold   . . . Cynthia Harris
Mr. Seymour Krumgold   . . Mitchell Jason
Scene 5: April Monkhood's apartment, half an hour later
Maurice Blount   . . . . Ron Faber
Boris Pickwick   . . . . .Jerrold Ziman
Kitty Entrail   . . . . Bobo Lewis

Harry Hubris . . . . .Joseph Bova
Rob Roy Fruitwell   . . . . Armand Assante

Vernon Equinox   . . . . . Armand Assante
And April, Mr. Krumgold, Mrs. Krumgold,
Lance, Rob Roy, Hubris.

ACT II

Scene 1: Rising Sun Employment Agency, Santa Barbara, two weeks later.
Mrs. Younghusband   . . . . Cynthia Harris
Hubris   . . . . .Joseph Bova

Lance as Wing Loo   . . . . . Peter Kingsley

Scene 2: Kitchen of the Fingerhead residence, five days later
Wing Loo   . . . . Peter Kingsley
Grace Fingerhead   . . . . . Cynthia Harris
Curtis Fingerhead   . . . . Ron Faber

Fish Market Boy . . . . . . Armand Assante
Emmett Stagg   . . . . Mitchell Jason
Hubris as Wing Loo's Father . .Joseph Bova

Scene 3: Conservatory, the Pasadena estate of Nelson Smedley, three days later
Wormser   . . . . .Jerrold Ziman
Lance   . . . . Peter Kingsley

April   . . . . Susan Sullivan
Nelson Smedley   . . . . .Joseph Bova

Scene 4: Whirlaway Scenic Studio, Los Angeles, two days later
Rowena Inchcape   . . . . Bobo Lewis
Lance   . . . . Peter Kingsley
Virgil Rukeyser   . . . . . . Mitchell Jason
Wagnerian   . . . . Armand Assante

Quagmeyer   . . . . .Jerrold Ziman
Bimbo . . . . Cynthia Harris
Hennepin . . . . Ron Faber
April   . . . . Susan Sullivan

Scene 5: A television studio, Los Angeles, three days later
Camera Man   . . . . .Jerrold Ziman
Hanratty   . . . . Mitchell Jason
Bailiff   . . . . Ron Faber
Judge Rinderbrust   . . . . . . .Joseph Bova

Roxana DeVilbiss   . . . . . . Cynthia Harris
Joe Gourielli . . . . Armand Assante
April   . . . . Susan Sullivan
Lance   . . . . Peter Kingsley

Scene 6: A wedding chapel, New York, a month later
Press PhotographersJerrold Ziman, Ron Faber
Lance   . . . . Peter Kingsley
April   . . . . Susan Sullivan
Octavia Weatherwax   . . . . Bobo Lewis

Mrs. Lafcadio Mifflin   . . . . Cynthia Harris
Milo Wealtherwax   . . . . . . .Joseph Bova
Roxana DeVilbiss   . . . . . . Cynthia Harris

Directed by James Hammerstein; scenery, Fred Voelpel; costumes, Pearl Somner; lighting, Roger Morgan; production stage manager, Gigi Cascio; stage manager, Mary E. Baird.

Perelman comic odyssey, about a rich man seeking something better in life than money, was originally produced on Broadway 12/26/62 for 85 performances.

KILLER'S HEAD

Mazon   . . . . Richard Gere

ACTION

Shooter . . . . .R.A. Dow
Lupe   . . . . Marcia Jean Kurtz

Liza . . . . Dorothy Lyman
Jeep . . . . Richard Lynch

Directed by Nancy Meckler; scenery, Henry Millman; costumes, Susan Denison; lighting, Edward M. Greenberg; production stage manager, Gigi Cascio; stage manager, Mary E. Baird.

Killer's Head is an 8-minute monologue of the thoughts of a man strapped into the electric chair waiting to be executed. Action presents four strange celebrants on a bleak Christmas Eve under symbolic stresses as they attempt to pass the time; it was previously produced in London by the Royal Court Theater.

RUBBERS

Republicans:
Mr. Clegg   . . . . Charles Siebert

Mr. Mutrix . . . . Lou Criscuolo
Mr. Damiano   . . . . .Robert Lesser

Mr. Tomato; Mr. Fermrlnr . Michael Prince	Mr. Pard . . . . .MacIntyre Dixon
Mr. P. Vlitsiak . . . . Mitchell Jason	Mr. Townsend . . . . .Albert Hall
Mr. Bapp . . . . .William Bogert	Mr. Austin . . . . John Horn
Democrats:	Miss Sinkk . . . . Lane Binkley
Mrs. Brimmins . . . . . . Laura Esterman	Pages . . . . Warren Sweeney, Jaime Tirelli

Place: The Assembly Chamber of the state legislature.

YANKS 3 DETROIT 0 TOP OF THE SEVENTH

Emil "Duke" Bronkowski . Tony Lo Bianco	Lincoln Lewis III . . . . Albert Hall
Lawrence "Beanie" Maligma . Lou Criscuolo	Guido Morosini . . . . .Robert Lesser
Old Salt . . . . Mitchell Jason	Brick Brock . . . . .William Bogert
Lucky Johnson . . . . John Horn	Baseball Players . . . . . . .Warren Sweeney,
Donna Luna Donna . . . . Lane Binkley	Jaime Tirelli

Directed by Alan Arkin; scenery, Henry Millman; costumes, Susan Denison; lighting, Roger Morgan; production stage manager, Franklin Keysar; stage manager, Mary E. Baird.

Rubbers caricatures the state legislative process as an eager-beaver lady from Brooklyn introduces and pushes her offensive bill commanding the display of contraceptives in drug stores. *Yanks 3 Detroit 0 Top of the Seventh* presents exactly that situation to an aging pitcher with a perfect game so far, which he doesn't have the confidence to complete.

Straws in the Wind: A Theatrical Look Ahead, a collection of new sketches and songs by American dramatists, was produced by American Place 2/21/75–3/22/75 for 34 subscription performances but closed before being offered for review. It contained sketches by Donald Barthelme, Marshall Brickman, Brock Bower and Peter Stone; songs by Betty Comden and Adolph Green, Cy Coleman, Ira Gasman, Galt MacDermot, Billy Nichols and Stephen Schwartz. Directed by Phyllis Newman; musical direction, Lanny Meyers; scenery, Peter Harvey; costumes, Ruth Morley; lighting, Roger Morgan; assistant to the director, Otis S. Sallid; with Tovah Feldshuh, Carol Jean Lewis, Brandon Maggart, Josh Mostel, George Pentecost.

In addition to its regular schedule, American Place presented a series entitled *Our American Humorists* in their theater's Sub Plot Cafe, as follows: *Jean Shepherd and the America of George Ade* 11/1/74 for 4 performances; *At Sea With Benchley, Kalmar & Ruby* 12/6/74 for 16 performances; *Jean Shepherd Plays Jean Shepherd* 1/30/75 for 5 performances; *We're in the Money* (humor and songs of the Depression) 3/27/74 for 5 performances.

NOTE: In this volume, certain programs of off-Broadway companies like The American Place Theater are exceptions to our rule of counting the number of performances from the date of the press coverage. When the official opening takes place late in the run of a play's public performances (after previews), we count the first performance of record, not the press date, as opening night. Press date for *The Beauty Part* was 11/4/74, for *Killer's Head* and *Action* 4/15/75, for *Rubbers* and *Yanks 3 Detroit 0 Top of the Seventh* 5/29/75.

The Chelsea Theater Center of Brooklyn. Schedule of four "Westside World Series" Manhattan programs. **La Carpa de los Rasquachis** (The Tent of the Underdogs) (32). By El Teatro Campesino in the El Teatro Campesino de Azatlán production. Opened October 24, 1974. (Closed November 18, 1974). **The Wild Stunt Show** (129). Return engagement of the revue by the Madhouse Company of London. Opened October 25, 1974. (Closed January 20, 1975) **San Francisco Mime Troupe** repertory of two programs: **The Mother** (21), adapted from the Maxim Gorky novel by Bertolt Brecht, translated by Lee Baxandall, music by Hanns Eisler and the San Francisco Mime Troupe, opened November 20, 1974; and **The Great Air Robbery** (14), by the San Francisco Mime Troupe, songs by Phil Marsh, opened November 24, 1974. (Repertory closed December 23, 1974). Produced by The Chelsea Theater of Brooklyn, Robert Kalfin artistic director, at the Westside Theater (two stages including the basement cabaret called The Brooklyn Navy Yard).

LA CARPA DE LOS RASQUACHIS

Felix Alvarez	Jose Delgado
Lily Alverez	Ernesto Hernandez
Allen David Cruz	Charles Martinez

Edgar Sanchez   Andres Valenzuela Gutierrez
Socorro Cruz   Daniel Villalva
Sal Bravo   Diana Rodriguez

Directed by El Teatro Campesino; music by El Teatro Campesino; press, Leslie Gifford.
Chicano farmworkers' collective theater dramatizes their victimization by the landlords in a combination of the English and Spanish languages, often employing the *corrido,* or ballad, style.

THE WILD STUNT SHOW

The Madhouse Company: Oscar Oswald
Hamlet MacWallbanger   Prof. Tommy Shand
Marcel Steiner   Nina Petrovna

A revue evolved in April 1971 by former performers in The Ken Campbell Show (an entertainment which toured London's pubs and streets), of which only one charter member, Marcel Steiner, appears in this company. A foreign play previously produced in London at the Royal Court and in New York by The Chelsea Theater Center of Brooklyn 4/9/74 for 21 performances.

THE MOTHER and THE GREAT AIR ROBBERY

Both plays performed, directed, designed and produced by the San Francisco Mime Troupe.
The Mother was presented in 14 scenes. Its drama of a mother who is radicalized by the bosses' ill treatment of her son was last produced in Civic Repertory 11/19/35 for 36 performances.
The Great Air Robbery was presented in three acts. A science fiction fantasy about enemies from space depleting the terrestrial air supply.

Bullshot Crummond (8). By Ron House, John Neville-Andrews, Alan Shearman, Diz White and Derek Cunningham; from an idea by Ron House and Diz White. Produced by Gil Adler and Jack Temchin in The Low Moan Spectacular production at Theater Four. Opened October 29, 1974. (Closed November 3, 1974)

Scenery and costumes, Mary Moore; associate producers, Allen Stanton, Howard Bellin; production manager, Jonathan Gardner; press, David Powers, William Schelble. With Alan Shearman, John Neville-Andrews, Ron House, Louisa Hart, Diz White.
Satire on the Bulldog Drummond type of thriller. A foreign play previously produced in London.

I'll Die If I Can't Live Forever (81). Musical with original book concept by Karen Johnson; music and lyrics by Joyce Stoner; additional book material by William Brooke; additional music by William Boswell. Produced by Patrick Stoner at The Improvisation. Opened October 31, 1974. (Closed February 2, 1975)

Gabrielle Schwartz . . . . . . .Gail Johnston   Jonathan Winslow . . . . .Tom Hastings
Heather O'Malley . . . . . Maureen Maloney   Ted Thornton . . . . Michael David Laibson
Jenette Morrison . . . . Nancy Reddon   Pianist . . . . Mark T. Long
Dan Craig . . . . .Don Bradford

Musical staging, Joyce Stoner; musical direction and arrangements, William Boswell; design, Irving Milton Duke; stage manager, Dale Lally; press, Al Davis.
Self-described in the subtitle as "a stage struck revue," satirizing the hopes and fears of aspirants auditioning for a show.

ACT I

"The Opening Number" . . . . Company
"The Improvisation" . . . . Company
Flashback:
  "Joys of Manhattan Life" . . . . Jonathan, Gabby, Ted
  "Where Would We Be Without Perverts?" . . . . Company

"My Life's a Musical Comedy" . . . . Gabby, Jonathan
"We're Strangers Who Sleep Side by Side" .Jenette, Ted
"The Roommate Beguine" . . . . Heather, Dan
"A Is For" . . . . Gabby
"Take Me!" . . . . Company
"There's Always Someone Who'll Tell You 'No' " . . . . Jonathan
"Twenty-four Hours From This Moment" . . . . Company

ACT II

The revue within the revue continues:
"The Improvisation" . . . . Company
"Ode to Electricity" . . . . Company
"I'm in Love" . . . . Heather
"I'm So Bored" . . . . Company
"My Place or Yours?" . . . . .Jenette, Ted
"Who Do We Thank!" . . . . Company
"Let's Have a Rodgers and Hammerstein Affair" . . . . . . .Jenette, Heather, Jonathan, Ted
"Less Is More and More" . . . . .Gabby, Dan
"I Hate Football" . . . . .Jenette
"They Left Me" . . . . Heather
"It's Great To Be Gay" . . . . Company
"I'll Die If I Can't Live Forever" . . . . Company
"The Finale" . . . . Company
"The Great White Way" . . . . Company

How to Get Rid of It (9). Musical with book and lyrics by Eric Blau; music by Mort Shuman; based on *Amedée* by Eugene Ionesco. Produced by 3W Productions, Inc., Stan Swerdlow executive producer, at the Astor Place Theater. Opened November 17, 1974. (Closed November 24, 1974)

Directed by Eric Blau; scenery and costumes, Don Jensen; lighting, Ian Calderon; music arranged and conducted by Wolfgang Knittel; production stage manager, G. Allison Elmer; press, Saul Richman. With Matt Conley, Carol L. Hendrick, Lorrie Davis, David Vogel, Joseph Neal, Janet McCall, Vilma Vaccaro, James Doerr, Mike Dantuono, Edward Rodriguez, Joe Masiell, Muriel Costa-Greenspan.

A hidden corpse growing larger and larger symbolizes a married couple's deteriorating relationship.

The Prodigal Sister (40). musical with book by J.E. Franklin; music by Micki Grant; lyrics by J.E. Franklin and Micki Grant. Produced by Woodie King Jr. at the Theater de Lys. Opened November 25, 1974. (Closed December 29, 1974)

Jackie	.Paula Desmond	Lucille	.Saundra McClain
Mother	.Frances Salisbury	Slick; Pallbearer	. Kirk Kirksey
Mrs. Johnson	.Esther Brown	Rev. Wynn; Employment Man	. Frank Carey
Sissie	. Ethel Beatty	Hot Pants Harriet	. Joyce Griffen
Jack	. Leonard Jackson	Dr. Patten; Caesar; Jackie's	
Essie; Baltimore Bessie	. . . .Louise Stubbs	Boyfriend	. Victor Willis

Prostitutes, Employment Girls, Dowahs, Country Girls, City Girls, Policemen, Country Boys, City Men: Ethel Beatty, Saundra McClain, Joyce Griffen, Judy Dearing, Yolande Graves, Larry Lowe, Rael Lamb.

Directed by Shauneille Perry; choreography, Rod Rodgers; musical direction, Neal Tate; production design, C. Richard Mills; costumes, Judy Dearing; associate producer, Ed Pitt; presented by special arrangement with Lucille Lortel Productions, Inc.; production stage manager, Dan Early; stage manager, Regge Life; press, Samuel Lurie.

The play was presented without intermission in a series of scenes called Beats. Beat 1: A country road. Beat 2: Jackie's house. Beat 3: Big city. Beat 4: Employment office. Beat 5: City street. Beat 6: Bessie's casket factory and house of ill repute. Beat 7: Jackie's house. Beat 8: Jackie's house.

Adventures and tribulations in the big city, previously produced off off Broadway by the New Federal Theater.

MUSICAL NUMBERS

"Slip Away" . . . . Jackie, Dowahs
"Talk, Talk, Talk" . . . . Mother, Mrs. Johnson, Dowahs
"Ain't Marryin' Nobody" . . . . Jackie, Dowah's
"If You Know What's Good for You" . . . . Jackie
"First Born" . . . . Mother, Sissie
"Woman Child" . . . . Mother, Jackie's Spirit
"Big City Dance" . . . . Company
"If You Know What's Good for You" (Reprise) . . . . Jackie
Employment Office Dance . . . . Company
"Sister Love" . . . . Slick
Hot Pants Dance . . . . Hot Pants, Company
"Remember Caesar" . . . . Caesar
"Superwoman" . . . . Lucille
Flirtation Dance . . . . Jackie, Caesar, Hot Pants
"Look at Me" . . . . Sissy
"I Been Up in Hell" . . . . Jackie, Company
"Thank You Lord" . . . . Family, Reverend, Company
"Remember" . . . . Jackie
"Celebration" . . . . Company
"The Prodigal Has Returned" . . . . Company
"Celebration" (Reprise) . . . . Company

Bil Baird's Marionettes. Schedule of two marionette programs. **Peter and the Wolf** (77). Revival with book by A.J. Russell; music by Serge Prokofiev; lyrics by Ogden Nash; conceived by Bil Baird. And **Holiday on Strings**, by Alan Stern, created by Bil Baird. Opened December 6, 1974. (Closed February 9, 1975) **Alice in Wonderland** (51). Musical with book by A.J. Russell; music by Joe Raposo; lyrics by Sheldon Harnick; based on the story by Lewis Carroll. And **Bill Baird's Variety**. Opened March 1, 1975. (Closed April 13, 1975) Produced by The American Puppet Arts Council, Arthur Cantor executive producer, at the Bil Baird Theater.

PUPPETEER	"PETER AND THE WOLF"	"ALICE IN WONDERLAND"
Peter Baird	Owl; Weasel; Duck; Hunter; Crow	White Rabbit; Tweedledee; Frog Footman; 1st Creature; Lobster; Violet
Rebecca Bondor	Mouse; Bird	Alice; Turtle; Cheshire Cat; Dormouse; 2d Creature; Whiting
Tim Dobbins	Grandpa; Crow; Beaver	
Olga Felgemacher	Peter; Rabbit; Cat; Hunter; Bee	Alice Queen; Tiger Lily; Turtle; 3d Creature; Caterpillar
Steven Hansen	Humphrey; Frogs	Duchess; Walrus; Knave of Hearts; Humpty Dumpty; March Hare; Five of Spades; Mock Turtle
William Tost	Wolf; Hunter; Squirrel	Fish Footman; Tweedledum; Mad Hatter; King; Lobster; Violet
Steven Widerman		Three of Spades; Executioner; Cook; Carpenter; Violet

PERFORMER		
Mary Case		Alice
Merry Flershem		Person in the Forest

Singing voices in *Peter and the Wolf:* George S. Irving—Wolf; William Tost—Humphrey.
Singing Voices in *Alice in Wonderland:* George S. Irving—Duchess; Sheldon Harnick—White

Rabbit, March Hare, Tweedledee; Rose Mary Jun, Ivy Austin, Margery Gray—Violet trio; William Tost—Mad Hatter, Tweedledum, Whiting; Margery Gray—Dormouse; Bil Baird—Mock Turtle, Walrus, Caterpillar.

BOTH PROGRAMS—Designed and produced by Bil Baird; directed by Paul Leaf; scenery, Howard Mandel; associate producer, Susanna Lloyd Baird; artistic associate, Frank Sullivan; Carl Harms, production manager; press, Arthur Cantor, C. George Willard.

PETER AND THE WOLF—Lighting, Carl Harms; music adapted & arranged by Paul Weston; incidental music, Paul Weston; musical director & special arrangements, Alvy West; assistant to Messrs. Weston & Nash, Sheldon Harnick.

The Prokofiev music adapted and visualized with marionettes and one live actress.

HOLIDAY ON STRINGS—A story of Christmas and the winter holidays.

ALICE IN WONDERLAND—Lighting, Peggy Clark.

A new musical *Alice* with the Tenniel drawings visualized in marionettes, and with Alice appearing both as a puppet and a live actress.

BIL BAIRD'S VARIETY—Perennial exhibition of "puppet virtuosity embodying many styles and types."

The Ridiculous Theatrical Company. Schedule of two programs. **Stage Blood** (45). By Charles Ludlam. Opened December 8, 1974. (Closed February 9, 1975) ***Bluebeard** (32). By Charles Ludlam. Opened April 18, 1975. Produced by The Ridiculous Theater Company at the Evergreen Theater.

BOTH PLAYS—Directed by Charles Ludlam; scenery, Bobjack Callejo; lighting, Richard Currie; production stage manager, Richard Gibbs; press, Alan Eichler, Marilyn Percy.

STAGE BLOOD

Carleton Stone; Gilbert Fey	. . Jack Mallory	Jenkins	John D. Brockmeyer
Carleton Stone Jr.	Charles Ludlam	Edmund Dundreary	Bill Vehr
Helga Vain	Lola Pashalinski	Elfie Fey	Black-Eyed Susan

Costumes and graphics, Arthur Brady.

Act I: A theater in Mudville, U.S.A., opening day. Act II: Various places around the theater, the following day, Act III: Later that night.

Farce in the Ridiculous Theater style about a troupe of players attempting to put on *Hamlet*.

BLUEBEARD

Mrs. Maggott	Jack Mallory	Rodney Parker	Bill Vehr
Sheemish	John D. Brockmeyer	Miss Cubbidge	Lola Pashalinski
Lamia	Mario Montez	Hecate	Richard Currie
Baron Khanazar		Hecate's Train .	Arthur Brady, Richard Gibbs
von Bluebeard	Charles Ludlam	Serpent	Larry
Sybil	Black-Eyed Susan		

Costumes, Mary Brecht, Arthur Brady, Bobjack Callejo, Mario Montez.

A mad scientist performing experimental sexual surgery on beautiful young women, with the customary absurdist styling of this troupe.

Pretzels (120). Revue by Jane Curtin, Fred Grandy and Judy Kahan; music and lyrics by John Forster. Produced by Burry Fredrik and Walter Boxer in the Phoenix Theater production at Theater Four. Opened December 16, 1974. (Closed March 30, 1975)

Jane Curtin

John Forster

Timothy Jerome

Judy Kahan

Directed by Patricia Carmichael; scenery, Stuart Wurtzel; costumes, Clifford Capone; lighting, Ken Billington; dance sequence, Francis Patrelle; projections, Eugene Lowery; production stage manager, Susie Corton; press, Mary Bryant, Carl Samrock, Bill Evans.

Songs and sketches of contemporary urban problems.

Jane Ranallo and Sandy Faison replaced Jane Curtin and Judy Kahan 3/18/75.

PART I: "Pretzels"—Company; Unemployment—Jane Curtin, Timothy Jerome, Judy Kahan; "Take Me Back"—Jerome; Cosmetology—Misses Curtin, Kahan; "Sing and Dance"—Miss Kahan, Jerome; Wild Strawberries—Miss Curtin, Jerome; "Jane's Song"—Miss Curtin; The Waitress—Miss Curtin, Jerome; "The Cockroach Song"—John Forster, Jerome, Miss Curtin.

PART II: Richie and Theresa—Miss Curtin, Jerome; Monologue—Miss Curtin; "Classical Music" —Forster; Tim Vander Beek—Jerome, Misses Curtin, Kahan; Leohmann's—Misses Curtin, Kahan; "The Reunion"—Company.

Broadway Dandies (8). Cabaret revue staged and produced by Robert Johnnene at the International Cabaret Theater. Opened December 17, 1974. (Closed December 22, 1974)

Choreography, Henry Le Tang; musical direction, Don Whisted; scenery, Wilfred Surita; costumes, Cheena Lee; press, Saul Richman. With Marilyn Anderson, Sharon Bruce, Robert Fitch, Diane Nicole, Hal James Pederson, Michael Radigan, Janet Saunders, Don Swanson, Susan Swanson, Teddy Williams.

Self-described as "a musical romp through New York."

Hotel for Criminals (15). Conceived and written by Richard Foreman; music by Stanley Silverman. Produced by Lyn Austin, Mary Silverman and Charles Hollerith in the Music-Theater Performing Group production at the Exchange Theater (Westbeth). Opened December 30, 1974. (Closed January 12, 1975)

Judex . . . . Ken Bell		Vampire Gang:	
Fantomas . . . . Paul Ukena		M. Gaston . . . . Luther Enstad	
Helene . . . . Lyn Gerb		Alain Duchamp . . . . Robert Schlee	
Irma Vep . . . . .Lisa Kirchner		Julot l'Enjoleur . . . . Ray Murcell	
Max . . . . Gene West		Dr. Lacloche . . . . Paul Ukena Jr.	

Parisians: Victor Abravaya, Katherine Alport, Glenn Barrett, Roxy Dawn, Steven Guimond.

Musicians: Michael Sussman clarinet, Sue Palma flute, Louis Oddo percussion, Sandy Strenger violin, Rolla Durham trumpet, Steve Johns tuba, Ed Flower guitar, Glenn Kenereich trombone.

Directed by Richard Foreman; musical direction, Roland Gagnon; scenery and lighting, Richard Foreman; costumes, Whitney Blausen; orchestrations, Stanley Silverman; production associate, Kenneth Jansen; press, Kenneth Jansen.

Time: 1902. Place: Paris.

Vampire fantasies in a turn-of-the-century atmosphere, with musical ornamentation.

Salome (30). Adapted by Lindsay Kemp from the play by Oscar Wilde. Produced by New York Theater Ensemble in association with Alan Eichler and Ron Link at 62 E. Fourth Street Theater. Opened January 8, 1975. (Closed February 16, 1975)

Acrobat; Salome's Page . . . Robert Anthony		Salome . . . . Lindsay Kemp	
Bride; Young Syrian . . . . . . Tony Maples		Blind Angel; Jokaanan . . . David Haughton	
Fool; Narraboth . . . . .Neil Caplan		Mad King; Herod . . . . David Meyer	
Man With a Whip; Naaman . .Robin Martin			

Directed, designed and illuminated by Lindsay Kemp; music composed and performed by William Hellermann; scenery, Chris Sedimaur; lighting, David Andrews; stage manager, Jeremy Switzer; press, Howard Atlee, Owen Levy.

All-male version of the Wilde play, embellished with tableaux and pantomime.

*Diamond Studs (158). Musical based on the life of Jesse James; book by Jim Wann; music and lyrics by Bland Simpson and Jim Wann. Produced as a special project by The Chelsea Theater Center of Brooklyn, Robert Kalfin artistic director, Michael David executive director, Burl Hash productions director, at the Westside Theater Opened January 14, 1975.

The Southern States Fidelity Choir:
  Jesse James (guitar) . . . . Jim Wann
  Gov. Thomas Crittendon
    (piano) . . . . Bland Simpson
  Bob Ford (12-string guitar) . . . John Foley
  Allen Pinkerton (percussion) . Mike Sheehan
  Maj. Edwards (bass) . . . . . . Jan Davidson
The Red Clay Ramblers:
  Zerelda Samuels; Cole
    Younger (banjo) . . . Tommy Thompson

Jim Younger (mandolin) . . . . Jim Watson
Bob Younger (fiddle) . . . . Bill Hicks
Dr. Samuels (piano) . . . . . . Mike Craver
And Friends:
William Clark Quantrill . . . . Scott Bradley
Zee James . . . . Joyce Cohen
Frank James . . . . Rick Simpson
Belle Starr . . . . Madelyn Smoak
Tourist . . . . Frances Tamburro

Directed by John L. Haber; musical numbers staged by Patricia Birch; music consultant, Mel Marvin; design adviser, Larry King; stage manager, Brenda Mezz; press, Leslie Gifford, Betty Lee Hunt.

A self-described "saloon musical" based on the career of Jesse James and other Western characters, with adaptations of traditional songs mixed in with the newly-composed numbers.

ACT I—(Songs marked with an asterisk (*) are based on traditional American folk music) "Jesse James Robbed This Train," "These Southern States That I Love," *"The Year of Jubilo", "The Unreconstructed Rebel" (by Jan Davidson), "Mama Fantastic," "Saloon Piano," "I Don't Need a Man to Know I'm Good," "Northfield Minnesota," *"King Cole," *"New Prisoner's Song," *"K.C. Line," "Cakewalk Into Kansas City."

ACT II—*"When I Was a Cowboy," "Pancho Villa," "Put It Where the Moon Don't Shine," "Sleepy Time Down South," "Jesse James Robbed This Train" (Reprise), *"Bright Morning Star," "When I Get the Call," "Cakewalk Into Kansas City" (Reprise).

Blasts and Bravos: An Evening with H.L. Mencken (46). One-man performance by Paul Shyre; adapted by Paul Shyre. Produced by Edgar Lansbury, Joseph Beruh and Torquay Company at the Cherry Lane Theater. Opened January 16, 1975. (Closed February 23, 1975)

Design, Eldon Elder; incidental music, Robert Rines; production stage manager, Clint Jakeman; press, Gifford/Wallace, Inc.

Time: 1930. Place: The study of H.L. Mencken's home in Baltimore, Md. The play was presented in two parts.

Shyre as H.L. Mencken in a personal portrait adapted from the works of the noted journalist.

Lovers (118). Musical with book and lyrics by Peter del Valle; music by Steve Sterner. Produced by Phillip Graham-Geraci and Michael Brown at the Players Theater. Opened January 27, 1975. (Closed May 11, 1975)

Freddie . . . . Martin Rivera
Eddie . . . . Michael Cascone
Harry . . . . John Ingle

Dave . . . . Robert Sevra
Spencer . . . . Reathel Bean
George . . . . Gary Sneed

Directed by Peter del Valle; lighting, Paul Sullivan; costumes, Rêve Richards; graphics, Keith Rabedeau; sound, Eugene Hide; production stage manager, Rick Claflin; press, Henry Luhrman Associates, Les Schecter.

An affirmation of homosexuality and homosexual love. Previously produced off off Broadway by Tosos.

ACT I

"Lovers" . . . . Company
"Look at Him" . . . . Freddie, Eddie
"Make It" . . . . Harry, Dave
"I Don't Want to Watch TV/Twenty Years" . . . . Company
"Somebody, Somebody Hold Me" . . . . Dave
"Belt & Leather" . . . . Harry, Dave

"There Is Always You" . . . . George
"Hymn" . . . . Company
"Somehow I'm Taller" . . . . Freddie, Eddie, Company

ACT II

"Role-Playing" . . . . Spencer, George, Freddie, Eddie
"Argument" . . . . George, Spencer
"Where Do I Go From Here?" . . . . .Freddie, George, Harry, Dave
"The Trucks" . . . . Spencer, Harry, Company
"Don't Betray His Love" . . . . George, Company
"You Came to Me as a Young Man" . . . . Spencer
"Lovers" (Reprise) . . . . Company
"Somehow I'm Taller" (Reprise) . . . . Company

Royal Shakespeare Company. Repertory of four programs. **Summerfolk** (13). Revival of the play by Maxim Gorky; English version by Jeremy Brooks and Kitty Hunter Blair. Opened February 5, 1975. **Love's Labour's Lost** (13). Revival of the play by William Shakespeare. Opened February 13, 1975. **King Lear** (16). Shortened version of the play by William Shakespeare. Opened February 25, 1975. **He That Plays the King** (8). Recital compiled from the works of William Shakespeare by Ian Richardson. Opened March 29 matinee. (Repertory closed April 6, 1975). Produced by The Brooklyn Academy of Music by arrangement with the governors of the Royal Shakespeare Theater, Stratford-Upon-Avon, England, in the Royal Shakespeare Company production, at The Brooklyn Academy of Music.

PERFORMER	"SUMMERFOLK"	"LOVE'S LABOUR'S LOST"	"KING LEAR"	"HE THAT PLAYS THE KING"
Sheila Allen			Goneril	
Robert Ashby	Ryumin	Longaville		
Annette Badland	Sasha			
Roger Bizley	Gentleman in a Top Hat		Kent	
Doyne Byrd	1st Beggar			
Gavin Campbell	Kropilkin	Forester		
Janet Chappell	Lady in Yellow	Katharine		
Tony Church	Suslov	Don Adriano	Lear	Chorus III; Henry IV; Henry VI; Macbeth; Gravedigger; Lear
Mark Cooper	Cadet			
Lynette Davies	Yulia	Maria	Regan	
Jeffrey Dench		Sir Nathaniel	Gloucester	
Michael Ensign	Zimin	Dumaine		
Susan Fleetwood	Kaleria	French Princess		Chorus II; Princess Katharine; Lady Anne; Lady Macbeth; Cordelia; Constance

Maroussia Frank	Woman With Bandaged Cheek			
Patrick Godfrey	Dudakov	Boyet		
Wilfred Grove	Man in Check Suit	French Lord		
Mike Gwilym	Vlass	Costard	Edgar	Prince Hal; Henry V; Hamlet
Denis Holmes		Dull		
Louise Jameson	Sonya	Jaquenetta	Cordelia	
Charles Keating			Edmund	
Estelle Kohler	Varvara	Rosaline		
John Labanowski	2d Beggar	Marcade		
Martin Lev		Moth		
Ian Richardson	Shalimov	Berowne		Chorus I: Richard II; Richard III; Doctor; Claudius; Gloucester; Osric
Norman Rodway	Bassov	Holofernes		
Sebastian Shaw	Dvoetochie			
David Suchet	Zamislov	Ferdinand	Fool	
Norman Tyrrell	Pustobaika			
Margaret Tyzack	Maria			
Anthony Vanden Ende			Servant	
Albert Welling	Semyonov			
Janet Whiteside	Olga			
Emma Williams	Young Lady in Pink			

Navarre Lords, Forester, Villagers in *Love's Labour's Lost:* Annette Badland, Doyne Byrd, Gavin Campbell, John Labanowski.

Musicians—*Summerfolk:* Donald Hollington accordion, Michael Lewin guitar, Laurie Wise mandolin, balalaika. *Love's Labour's Lost:* Gordon Bennett trumpet, William Grant oboe, Roger Hellyer bassoon, Peter Morris horn, Robert Pritchard trumpet, Ian Reynolds flute, John Riley percussion, David Statham horn, Robin Weatherall percussion. *King Lear* and *He That Plays the King*—Robin Weatherall.

ALL PLAYS—Artistic director, Trevor Nunn; direction, Peggy Ashcroft, Peter Brook, Trevor Nunn; musical directors, Michael Tubbs, Gordon Kember; press, Charles Ziff.

SUMMERFOLK—Directed by David Jones; design, Timothy O'Brien, Tazeena Firth; music composed and arranged by Carl Davis; lighting, Stewart Leviton; assistant director, Howard Davies; stage managers, Maggie Whitlum, Giles Barnabe.

Act I: The Bassovs' summer villa, evening. Act II, Scene 1: Outside the Bassovs' villa, early evening the next day. Scene 2: A picnic in the woods, a few days later. Act III: Outside the Bassovs' villa, a few weeks later.

Gorky's play about the up-and-coming Russian bourgeoisie on a holiday at the turn of the century was written in 1904 but has never had a professional New York production of record.

LOVE'S LABOUR'S LOST—Directed by David Jones; design, Timothy O'Brien, Tazeena Firth; music by William Southgate; lighting, Stewart Leviton; stage managers, Maggie Whitlum, Giles Barnabe.

The play was presented in two parts. The most recent professional New York production of this play was 6/9/65 by New York Shakespeare Festival in Central Park.

KING LEAR—Directed by Buzz Goodbody; design, Anna Steiner; music, Michael Tubbs; lighting, Brian Harris; stage managers, Maggie Whitlum, Giles Barnabe.

The play, abbreviated to 140 minutes running time, was presented in two parts.

This version of *King Lear* was produced in Stratford-Upon-Avon's "The Other Place" (Buzz Goodbody artistic director) for audiences of school children. The full play was last produced in New York last season, with James Earl Jones in the New York Shakespeare Festival production in Central Park.

HE THAT PLAYS THE KING—Music composed by Guy Woolfenden; stage manager, Hal Rogers.

Part I—The Histories: "The Crown Imperial" from *Henry V,* "The Hollow Crown" from *Richard II,* "Uneasy Lies the Head That Wears a Crown" from *Henry IV,* "The Crown of Victory—Crown Matrimonial" from *Henry V,* "The Shepherd King" from *Henry VI,* "King Macchiavel" from *Richard III,* "The Empire Unpossessed" from *Richard III.*

Part II—The Tragedies: "The Throne of Blood" from *Macbeth,* "The Prince of Players" from *Hamlet,* "The Conscience of the King" from *Hamlet,* "Most Sovereign Reason" from *Hamlet,* "The Royal Fool" from *King Lear,* "Let Kings Assemble" from *King John.*

Of the various auditoria under the Brooklyn Academy of Music Roof, the Opera House housed *Summerfolk* and *Love's Labour's Lost,* the Leperq Space *King Lear* and the Music Hall *He That Plays the King.*

The Ramayana (6). New interpretation in English by Gopal Sharman of the Indian epic by Valmiki for a one-woman show with Jalabala Vaidya. Produced by Robert Hendrickson at the Barbizon-Plaza Theater. Opened February 6, 1975. (Closed February 15, 1975)

Created and directed by Gopal Sharman; lighting and sound, Anasuya Vaidya; New York production directed by Helen Breed; scenery, John C. Macgregor; sound, John W. Ackley III; New York presentation by arrangement with The Akshara Theater, New Delhi, India, and Hartwick College, Oneonta, N.Y.; press, Betty Lee Hunt Associates.

The play was presented in two parts.

The Ramayana was written in Sanskrit 5,000 years ago and is an epic of man's ascension to divinity. Its present adaptation for a one-woman performance by Miss Vaidya is a foreign play previously produced in New Delhi and elsewhere including tours of American campuses.

Four Friends (1). By Larry Kramer. Produced by Michael Harvey at the Theater de Lys. Opened and closed at the evening performance, February 17, 1975.

Directed by Alfred Gingold; scenery and lighting, Duane F. Mazey; costumes, Tom Fallon; production manager, Duane F. Mazey; press, Alan Eichler. With Robert Stattel, Ronald Hale, John Colenback, Jeremiah Sullivan, Jill Andre, Brad Davis, Jane Hallaren, Sharon Laughlin.

Four former Yale roommates and their loves 15 years out of college.

*The National Lampoon Show (128). Cabaret revue with words and lyrics by the cast, overlooked by Sean Kelly; music by Paul Jacobs. Produced by Ivan Reitman at the New Palladium. Opened March 2, 1975.

John Belushi	Gilda Radner
Brian Doyle-Murray	Harold Ramis
Bill Murray	

Directed by Martin Charnin; music performed by Paul Jacobs; production supervised by Dale Anglund; lighting, Lowell Sherman; sound, Abe Jacob; press, Gifford/Wallace, Inc.

A topical revue in the broad satirical style of *National Lampoon's Lemmings,* devised under the same auspices.

The Negro Ensemble Company. Schedule of two programs and four limited engagements.

The First Breeze of Summer (80). By Leslie Lee. Opened March 2, 1975. (Closed April 27, 1975; to be transferred to Broadway 6/10/75) **A Season-Within-a-Season**. Four one-week limited engagements of new plays: **Liberty Call** (8) by Burial Clay, opened April 29,

1975 (closed May 4, 1975); **Sugar Mouth Sam Don't Dance No More** and **Orrin** (8) by Don Evans, opened May 6, 1975 (closed May 11, 1975); **The Moonlight Arms** and **The Dark Tower** (8) by Rudy Wallace, opened May 13, 1975 (closed May 18, 1975); **Welcome to Black River** (8) by Samm Williams, opened May 20, 1975 (closed May 25, 1975) *****Waiting for Mongo** (16). By Silas Jones. Opened May 18, 1975. Produced by The Negro Ensemble Company, Douglas Turner Ward artistic director, Robert Hooks executive director, Frederick Garrett administrative director, at St. Marks Playhouse.

THE FIRST BREEZE OF SUMMER

Gremmar	Frances Foster	Sam Greene	Carl Crudup
Nate Edwards	Charles Brown	Briton Woodward	Anthony McKay
Lou Edwards	Reyno	Rev. Mosely	Lou Myers
Aunt Edna	Barbara Montgomery	Hope	Petronia
Milton Edwards	Moses Gunn	Joe Drake	Peter DeMaio
Hattie	Ethel Ayler	Gloria Townes	Bebe Drake Hooks
Lucretia	Janet League	Harper Edwards	Douglas Turner Ward

Directed by Douglas Turner Ward; produced in association with Woodie King Jr.; scenery, Edward Burbridge; costumes, Mary Mease Warren; Lighting, Sandra L. Ross; production stage manager, Horacena J. Taylor; press, Howard Atlee, Clarence Allsopp, Meg Gordean, Owen Levy.

Time: The present. Place: A small city in the Northeast. Act I: Thursday afternoon through Friday night in June. Act II: The following Saturday afternoon through Sunday night.

A black family is moving into the middle class and beyond, while its matriarch remembers her difficult past, taking pleasure in the memory of the three men who fathered her children, as she helps to ease her grandson's emotional tensions in the present.

A SEASON-WITHIN-A-SEASON

Liberty Call

John Wilheart	Samm Williams	Opium Man; Bartender	George Campbell
H.O.B. Rothschild II	Michael Jameson	1st Girl	Naola Adair
Mama Sun	Thelma Carter	2d Girl	Elaine Jackson
Lt. Priest	Ramon Rafiur	1st Marine	Sam Finch
		2d Marine	Suavae Mitchell

Directed by Anderson Johnson; wardrobe supervision, Shirley Garrett Smith; coordinator, Steve Carter; lighting, Sandra Ross.

Black and white trying to share an experience but ending in hostility.

Sugar-Mouth Sam Don't Dance No More

Verda Mae Hollis	Lea Scott	Sammy	Carl Gordon

Orrin

Wilma	Lea Scott	Kenny	Eric Coleman
Orrin	Taurean Blacque	Alex	Carl Gordon

Directed by Helaine Head.

In *Sugar-Mouth Sam,* a former lover returns and tries again, but leaves once more. In *Orrin,* a middle-class prodigal son returns as a street-wise dope pusher.

The Moonlight Arms

		The Dark Tower	
Rena	Charliese Drakeford	Joe	Arthur French
Roy	Charles Brown	Philip	Charles Brown

Directed by Osborne Scott.

The Moonlight Arms is the bickering of a mismatched husband and wife. *The Dark Tower* places in conflict a clean-cut young poet and a shabby old artist.

Welcome to Black River

		D.J.	Taurean Blacque
Mama Liza	Juanita Bethea	David Jack	Clayton Corbin
Lou Mae	Marcella Lowery	Mordicah	Peter DeMaio
Anna Lee	Lea Scott	Amos	Carl Gordon

Directed by Dean Irby.

Sharecropping, poverty and racism in North Carolina in 1958.

WAITING FOR MONGO

Virgil . . . . Reyno
Preach; Mongo . . . . Bill Cobbs
Viana . . . . Bebe Drake Hooks
Sadie Mae . . . . Barbara Montgomery
Bill . . . . Roland Sanchez
Teach . . . . Ethel Ayler
Doodybug . . . . Adolph Caesar
Doc . . . . Graham Brown
Argus . . . . Samm Williams

Klansmen: Samm Williams, George Campbell, Sam Finch.
Directed by Douglas Turner Ward; scenery and costumes, Mary Mease Warren; lighting, Sandra L. Ross; production stage manager, Horacena J. Taylor.
A self-styled "nightmare comedy" about reality and fantasy mixed up in the situation of a black rapist hiding from his would-be captors and awaiting rescue.

Wings (9). Musical based on Aristophanes's *The Birds;* book, music and lyrics by Robert McLaughlin and Peter Ryan. Produced by Stephen Wells at the Eastside Playhouse. Opened March 16, 1975. (Closed March 23, 1975)

Pisthetairos . . . . Jerry Sroka
Euelpides . . . . David Kolatch
Butler Bird; Insurance
    Salesman; Hercules . . . . . . David Pursley
Epops . . . . Jay E. Raphael
Procne . . . . Mary Sue Finnerty
Cardinal; Barbarian God . . . . Peter Jurasik
Male Tanager . . . James Howard Laurence
Female Tanager;
    Birdwatcher . . . . Maureen Sadusk
Large-Breasted Bushtit;
    Poet . . . . Barbara Rubenstein
Dickcissel . . . . Nicholas Stannard
Eagle; Construction Boss;
    Prometheus . . . . Dan Held
Macaw . . . . Brenda Gardner
Parrot; Iris . . . . Robin Wesley
Flamingo; Soothsayer . . . . . Sally Mitchell
Penguin; Land Developer;
    Zeus . . . . Stuart Pankin

Directed by Robert McLaughlin; musical numbers staged by Nora Christiansen; musical direction, Larry Hochman; scenery and lighting, Karl Eigsti; costumes, Shadow; associate producers, R.E. Lee Jr., Charles Walton; orchestrations and vocal arrangements, Bill Brohn; production stage manager, Peter Lawrence; press, Mary Bryant, Bill Evans.
Place: A mountain top.
The Aristophanes comedy about two Athenians in search of miracles among the gods and birds —never professionally produced in New York in modern times—set to music.

ACT I

"Call of the Birds" . . . . Procne, Epops, Birds
"O Sacrilege" . . . . Birds
"The Human Species" . . . . Macaw, Parrot, Eagle, Birds
"Time to Find Something to Do" . . . . Pisthetairos, Birds
"First I Propose" . . . . Pisthetairos
"First I Propose" (Reprise) . . . . Epops, Birds
"Comfort for the Taking" . . . . Birds
"You'll Regret It!" . . . . Pests
"How Great It Is To Be a Bird" . . . . Epops, Birds

ACT II

"Rah Tah Tah Tio Beep Doo Doo" . . . . Birds
"The Wall Song" . . . . Male Tanager, Epops, Birds
"Take to the Air" . . . . Birds
"Iris the Fleet" . . . . Iris
"Iris the Fleet" (Reprise) . . . . Iris, Pisthetairos, Birds
"The Great Immortals" . . . . Macaw, Butler Bird, Cardinal, Birds
"Wings" . . . . Company
"We're Gonna Make It" . . . . Pisthetairos, Prometheus, Euelpides
Finale . . . . Company

*Be Kind to People Week (79). Musical with book, music and lyrics by Jack Bussins and Ellsworth Olin. Produced by J. Arthur Elliot in the Quinton Raines production at the Belmont Theater. Opened March 23, 1975.

Hope Healy	Naura Hayden	Grenoldo	Grenoldo Frazier
Norman	Kenneth Cory	Bobby	Bobby Lee
Alan	Alan Kass	Dana	Dana Lorge
Dan	Daniel Brown	Randy	Randy Martin
Nell	Nell N. Carter	Maureen	Maureen Moore
Judy	Judy Congress		

Directed by Quinton Raines; musical direction, Jeremy Stone; choreography, Bobby Lee; scenery, Bruce Monroe; lighting, Centaur Productions, Anguss Moss; vocal arrangements, John Franceschina; musical arrangements, Jack Gale; production stage manager, John Brigleb; press, Herb Striesfield.

Well-meaning heroine tries to unite all pressure groups such as women's libbers, peace marchers, hardhats, etc.

ACT I: Newspaper Office—Grenoldo Frazier, Randy Martin, Judy Congress, Kenneth Cory, Naura Hayden; Political Club—Daniel Brown, Bobby Lee; "What Ever Happened to the Good Old Days"—Brown, Lee, Martin, Frazier; New York Streets—Cory, Miss Hayden; "I Will Give Him Love"—Cory, Miss Hayden; City Hall-Brown, Cory, Misses Congress, Hayden; "Mad About You Manhattan"—Brown, Miss Congress; Taxi—Martin, Lee, Cory, Maureen Moore, Miss Hayden; Outside Burlesque House—Cory, Miss Hayden; Bijou Burlesque—Nell N. Carter, Alan Kass, Dana Lorge, Cory, Miss Hayden; "I Have a Friend at the Chase Manhattan Bank"—Miss Lorge; Outside Burlesque House—Miss Hayden, Cory; Bed Sty—Frazier, Cory, Misses Carter, Hayden; "All I Got Is You"—Cory, Miss Hayden; Talk Show Studio—Kass, Brown, Lee, Cory, Miss Hayden: Outside Studio—Cory, Miss Hayden: "I'm in Like With You"—Cory; Unemployment Office—Cory, Kass, Brown, Frazier, Lee, Martin, Misses Hayden, Congress, Lorge, Moore; New York Street—Cory, Miss Hayden; "When We See a Pretty Girl We Whistle"—Cory, Brown, Frazier, Lee, Martin, Misses Hayden, Carter, Congress, Lorge, Moore: "Ecology"; Hope's Apartment—Cory, Miss Hayden; "I Will Give Him Love" (Reprise)—Miss Hayden.

ACT II: New York Street—Martin, Lee, Kass, Brown, Frazier, Misses Hayden, Congress, Moore, Lorge; Jail—Lee, Frazier, Cory, Miss Hayden; "All I Got Is You"—Lee, Frazier; "I Need You"—Cory; Taxi—Lee, Martin, Miss Moore; "I'm in Like With You" (Reprise) and "To Love Is to Live" (Duet)—Martin, Miss Moore: Psychiatrist's Office—Kass, Misses Lorge, Hayden; "Freud is a Fraud"—Kass; Park—Cory, Miss Hayden: "Black Is Beautiful"—Cory, Brown, Frazier, Lee, Martin, Misses Hayden, Carter, Congress, Lorge, Moore; On the Town—Cory, Kass, Brown, Misses Hayden, Carter, Lorge; Night Club—Cory, Brown, Martin, Misses Hayden, Congress, Moore, Lorge; "A Smile Is Up" (special arrangement by Grenoldo Frazier)—Frazier; "To Love Is to Live" (Reprise)—Miss Carter: "You're Divine"—Miss Hayden; New York Street—Cory, Miss Hayden; Finale ("Be Kind to People Week," "I'm in Like With You" (Reprise), "A Smile Is Up" (Reprise), "Be Kind to People Week" (Reprise)—Company.

In Gay Company (13). Musical revue with music and lyrics by Fred Silver. Produced by MCB Company at Upstairs at Jimmy's. Opened April 4, 1975. (Closed April 13, 1975)

Directed by Sue Lawless; musical direction, John Franceschina; additional dialogue, Les Barkdull; design, Michael J. Hotopp, Paul de Pass; stage manager, Les Barkdull; press, Gifford/Wallace, Inc. With Candice Earley, Rick Gardner, Cola Pinto, Gordon Ramsey, Robert Tananis.

Self-described as "a try-sexual musical revue." Previously presented off off Broadway this season at The Little Hippodrome.

The National Theater of the Deaf. Program of two plays. **The Dybbuk,** revival of the play by S. Ansky, based on the translation by Joseph Landis; and **Priscilla, Princess of Power,** based on a script by James Stevenson, adapted by the company under the supervision of Ed Waterstreet Jr. (8). Produced by The Brooklyn Academy of Music in the O'Neill Center's National Theater of the Deaf production, David Hays producing director, at the Leperq Space. Opened April 7, 1975. (Closed April 13, 1975)

PERFORMER	"THE DYBBUK"	"PRISCILLA, PRINCESS OF POWER"
Robert Blumenfeld	Khonnon Voice	
Linda Bove	Gittel	Priscilla
Bernard Bragg	Reb Sender	Dr. Schlock
Elaine Bromka	Young Woman; Voice	Narrator
Joseph A. Castronovo	Meyer	
Julianna Field	Nurse	Mrs. Colson
Patrick Graybill	Rabbi Azrielke	Jelly Bean Boss
Timothy Near	Leye Voice	Dental Assistant
Freda Norman	Leye	
Rico Peterson	Rabbi Voice	
Joe Sarpy	Messenger	
Timothy Scanlon	Khonnon	Chuck
Andrew Vasnick	Old Man	
Gunilla Wagstrom	Elderly Woman	
Ed Waterstreet Jr.	Hennakh	

Balloons and Gangsters in *Priscilla, Princess of Power*: Robert Blumenfeld, Joseph A. Castronovo, Freda Norman, Rico Peterson, Joe Sarpy, Andrew Vasnick, Gunilla Wagstrom, Ed Waterstreet Jr.

The Dybbuk directed by John Broome; *Priscilla, Princess of Power* directed by Ed Waterstreet Jr.; scenery, David Hays; costumes, Fred Voelpel; lighting, Guy Bergquist; production stage manager, Guy Bergquist; stage manager, Jerry Kelch; press, Arts Counterparts, Inc., William Schelble.

Plays adapted for performance by and for the deaf, with the principals using sign language for dialogue while guest actors speak the words aloud. *The Dybbuk* was last presented professionally in New York in Yiddish by the Jewish State Theater of Bucharest 9/19/72 for 8 performances. *Priscilla, Princess of Power* is a comedy about America's sugary diet, written and performed in comic-book style.

Philemon (48). Musical with book and lyrics by Tom Jones; music by Harvey Schmidt. Produced by Portfolio Productions at Portfolio Studio. Opened April 8, 1975. (Closed May 18, 1975)

Andos . . . . Michael Glenn-Smith	Wife . . . . Leila Martin
Marsyas . . . . Virginia Gregory	Commander . . . . Howard Ross
Servillus . . . . Drew Katzman	Kiki . . . . Kathrin King Segal
Cockian . . . . Dick Latessa	

Musicians: Ken Collins keyboard, guitar; Bill Grossman percussion, french horn; Penna Rose keyboard, recorder.

Staged by Lester Collins; musical direction, Ken Collins; costumes, Charles Blackburn; stage manager, Janet Watson; press, David Powers.

Story of a clown masquerading as a Christian zealot and caught by his role so that he suffers martyrdom, based on an occurrence in Antioch in 287 A.D. The play was presented in two parts.

ACT I

"Within This Empty Space" . . . . Company
"The Streets of Antioch" . . . . Cockian, Commander
"Gimme a Good Digestion" . . . . Cockian, Kiki
"Don't Kiki Me" . . . . Kiki, Cockian
"I'd Do Almost Anything to Get Out of Here and Go Home" . . . . . . Cockian, Commander
"He's Coming" . . . . Prisoners
"Antioch Prison" . . . . Prisoners
"Name: Cockian" . . . . Cockian, Company

ACT II

"I Love Order" . . . . Commander, Company
"My Secret Dream" . . . . Andos, Cockian, Prisoners
"I Love His Face" . . . . Marsyas, Cockian
"Sometimes" . . . . Cockian, Prisoners

"The Protest" . . . . Company
"The Nightmare" . . . . Cockian, Company
"Love Suffers Everything" . . . . Wife
"The Confrontation" . . . . Cockian, Commander, Company
"Love Suffers Everything" (Reprise) . . . . Company
"Within This Empty Space" (Reprise) . . . . Company

The Magic of Jolson! (5). Musical with book by Pearl Sieben; additional music by Richard DeMone: additional lyrics by Pearl Sieben. Produced by Sieben Productions at the Provincetown Playhouse. Opened April 9, 1975. (Closed April 13, 1975)

Production devised and directed by Isaac Dostis; musical direction, Richard DeMone; scenery & projections, Chuck Hoefler; lighting, Ralph Madero; press, Saul Richman. With Norman Brooks, Linda Gerard, John Medici.
A musical tribute to Al Jolson including an impersonation of him in some of his famous song numbers.

Augusta (9). By Larry Ketron. Produced by Gerald Seiff and Geoffrey Winters at Theater de Lys. Opened April 20, 1975. (Closed April 27, 1975)

Directed by David Black; scenery, Barry F. Williams; costumes, Jennifer von Mayrhauser; lighting, Daniel Flannery; production stage manager, Peter von Mayrhauser; press, Betty Lee Hunt. With Jill Andre, Anthony Call, Kenneth Harvey, Faith Catlin, Jeffrey DeMunn, Elizabeth Franz.
A teacher's fondness for an ex-boxer; sex and melodrama in a Georgia setting.

A Matter of Time (1). Musical with book by Hap Schlein and Russell Leib; music and lyrics by Philip F. Margo. Produced by Jeff Britton at the Playhouse Theater. Opened and closed at the evening performance, April 27, 1975.

Directed and choreographed by Tod Jackson; musical direction & vocal & dance arrangements, Arnold Gross; scenery, David Guthrie; lighting, Martin Aronstein; sound, Jack Shearing; orchestrations, Elliot Gilman; production stage manager, Janet Beroza; press, Max Eisen, M.J. Boyer. With David-James Carroll, Jane Robertson, Glory Van Scott, Joe Masiell, Carol Estey, Miriam Welch, Joyce Nolen, Leland Schwantes, Dennis Michaelson, Douglas Bentz, Charise Harris, Donald M. Griffith, Elliott Lawrence, Suellen Arlen, Rosamond Lynn, Linda Willows.
The New Year refuses to come in on the evening of Dec. 31.

Parto (21). By Maria Isabel Barreno and Gilda Grillo; adapted from *The Three Marias: New Portuguese Letters* by Maria Isabel Barreno, Maria Teresa Horta and Maria Velho da Costa. Produced by Lois D. Sasson and Olive P. Watson at Washington Square Church. Opened April 28, 1975. (Closed May 18, 1975)

Mother Abbess	Natalie Gray	Eunuchs	Loremil Machado, Jelom Vieira
Maria	Carole Leverett	Mariana	Sherry Mathis
Coleta	Coleta	Joana	Donna Faye Isaacson
Ana	Ruth Truran	Monica	Carol Cole
Dona Brites	Muriel Miguel		

Musicians: Marie Truran organ, Edwina Tyler percussion.
Directed by Gilda Grillo; scenery and costumes, Hortense Guillemard; lighting, Marilyn Rennagel; production stage manager, Elizabeth Holloway; stage manager, P. Delurier; press, Shirley Herz.
Scene 1: The final vows of Mariana. Scene 2: Joana's visit to Mariana in the convent. Scene 3: Marriage. Scene 4: Mariana, Joana and the Cavalier. Scene 5: Mariana's lament and Joana. Scene 6: Marians's abortion in the Witch's cave. Scene 7: The awakening of Monica. Scene 8: Mariana and Dona Brites in Mariana's cell, and the nuns. Scene 9: Monica's monologue to her husband. Scene 10: Metamorphosis—The Visit, The Tasks, The Rape, The Flight. Scene 11: Joana and Monica, Mariana and Dona Brites. Scene 12: Joana, Monica and the Commune of Women.
Feminist outcry against the condition of women, in a drama of a nun seduced and abandoned by a cavalier, based on material from a contemporary book.

*Women Behind Bars (36). By Tom Eyen. Produced by Alan Eichler, Ron Link and Craig Baumgarden at the Astor Place Theater. Opened May 1, 1975.

Pat Ast	Helen Hanft
Sharon Ann Barr	Madeleine Le Roux
May Boylan	Hope Stansbury
Ann Collier	Mary-Jennifer Mitchell
Maria DeLanda	Walker Stuart
Leslie Edgar	

Directed by Ron Link; scenery, Herbert Nagle; lighting, Lawrence Eichler; stage manager, Jack Kalman; press, Alan Eichler.

Comedy takeoff of women's-prison movies. Previously produced this season off off Broadway by Theater of the Eye Repertory Company.

The $ Value of Man (8). Musical written by Christopher Knowles and Robert Wilson; music by Michael Galasso. Produced by The Brooklyn Academy of Music in The Byrd Hoffman Foundation production at the Leperq Space. Opened May 9, 1975. (Closed May 18, 1975)

Directed by Christopher Knowles and Robert Wilson; choreography, Andrew De Groat; scenery, Gregory Payne, Terrence Chambers, Charles Dennis; costumes, Richard Roth; lighting, Carol Mullins; sound, Jan Kroeze; production coordinator, James Finguerra; press, Charles Ziff. With a cast of 60.

Another round of Wilson's highly imaginative comments on the world around us.

The Glorious Age (9). Musical with book by Cy Young and Mark Gordon; music and lyrics by Cy Young. Produced by Jane Manning and Carol McGroder in association with Wendell Minnick at Theater Four. Opened May 11, 1975. (Closed May 18, 1975)

Directed by John-Michael Tebelak; musical direction, Robert W. Preston; scenery, Stuart Wurtzel; costumes, Jennifer von Mayrhauser; lighting, Barry Arnold; arrangements & orchestrations, Stephen Reinhardt; special movement, Dick Stephens; production stage manager, Suzanne Egan; press, Gifford/Wallace Inc., Tom Trenkle. With Stuart Pankin, George Riddle, Clyde Laurents, Susan Willis, Barry Pearl, Paul Kreppel, Laurie Faso, Robin Wesley, D'Jamin Bartlett, Carol Swarbrick, W.M. Hunt, Don Scardino.

Musical fantasy of the Crusades and medaeval times.

OFF OFF BROADWAY
AND ADDITIONAL PRODUCTIONS

Here is a comprehensive sampling of off off Broadway and other experimental or peripheral 1974–75 productions in New York. There is no definitive "off-off-Broadway" area or qualification. To try to define or regiment it would be untrue to its fluid, exploratory purpose. The listing of more than 550 programs below is as inclusive as reliable sources will allow, however, and takes in almost all Manhattan-based, new-play-producing, English-language organizations listed by the Theater Development Fund and the Off-Off-Broadway Alliance—plus many others.

Producing groups are identified in **bold face type**, in alphabetical order, with artistic policies and the name of the managing director given whenever these are a matter of record. Examples of outstanding 1974–75 programs—and in many cases a group's whole 1974–75 schedule—are listed with play titles in capital letters. Often these are works in progress with changing scripts, casts and directors, usually without an engagement of record (but an opening or early performance date is included when available).

Actor's Place at St. Luke's Emphasis on audience involvement. Frank Mosier, director.

INDIAN written and directed by Frank Mosier. March, 1975.

The Actors Studio. Development of talent in productions of new and old works. Arthur Penn and Lee Strasberg, artistic directors.

OLD TIMES by Harold Pinter. October 16, 1974. Directed by the cast; with Will Hare, Sandra Seacat, Hildie Brooks.
CHRISTMAS SHOW. December, 1974. Directed by Anna Strasberg.
THE LADIES AT THE ALAMO. May 29, 1975. Written and directed by Paul Zindel.

Afro-American Studio. Express the black experience in terms of theater. Ernie McClintock, artistic director (and director of all productions).

TABERNACLE by Paul Carter Harrison. June, 1974.
A HAND IS ON THE GATE by Roscoe Lee Browne. November, 1974.
ACIFE AND PENDABIS by Daniel Owens. November 21, 1974.
EL HAJJ MALIK by N.R. Davidson. May 9, 1975.
EVOLUTION OF A SISTER '75 (one-woman show). May 17, 1975. With Francine Major.

Afro-American Total Theater. Developing and producing the work of black artists. Hazel Bryant, artistic director.

CHILDREN'S MUSE COUNTEE CULLEN GREAT STORYTELLER SERIES. January, 1975. With Geraldine Fitzgerald.
MA LOU'S DAUGHTERS by Gertrude Greenridge. March, 1975. Directed by Mical Whit-' aker.

Amas Repertory Theater. Creative arts as a powerful instrument of peaceful change, towards healthier individuals. Rosetta LeNoire, founder and artistic director.

HOUND DOG PARTY (annual variety show by workshop members). June 9, 1974.
TWO DAUGHTERS by Hy Ray Bush Jr. Directed by Charles Briggs.
ALL OVER NOTHING by Fred Light. Directed by Charles Kakitsakis. October, 1974.
BAYOU LEGEND by Owen Dodson. January, 1975. Directed by Shauneille Perry.
BUBBLING BROWN SUGAR by Lofton Mitchell and Rosetta LeNoire. February, 1975. Directed by Bob Cooper.
GOD'S TROMBONES by James Weldon Johnson. April, 1975. Directed by John Barracuda.

American Center for Stanislavski Theater Art (ACSTA) Development of the Stanislavski method in the American Theater. Sonia Moore, director.

THE CHERRY ORCHARD by Anton Chekhov, translated by Irene and Sonia Moore. February, 1975. Directed by Sonia Moore.
THE BIRTHDAY PARTY by Harold Pinter. May 23, 1975. Directed by Len Silver.

American Ensemble Company. Interested in literary value of plays; concerned with entertaining, as well as stimulating thoughts of audiences. Robert Petito, artistic director.

BREAK A LEG (musical revue) written and directed by Robert Petito. April, 1975

American Theater Company. New works done, but accent on the American theater's heritage.Richard Kuss, artistic director.

IT PAYS TO ADVERTISE by Megrue and Hackett. October 10, 1974. Directed by Ellis Santone.
AARON BURR by Charles A. Haslett. November 21, 1974. Directed by Richard Harden.

NO GREATER LOVE (program of one-act plays): GLADYS AND VICTOR by Stephen Levi, directed by Ellis Santone; and THIS PIECE OF LAND by Lou Rivers, directed by Georgia Fleenor. December, 1974.
THE UNDISCOVERED COUNTRY by Stephen Levi. December, 1974. Directed by Ellis Santone.
GETTYSBURG by Percy MacKaye. December, 1974. Directed by John Hagan.
PONTEACH by Major Robert Rogers. January 23, 1975. Directed by Richard Kuss.
SOMETHING THAT MATTERS by Don Flynn. March, 1975. Directed by John Hagan.
THE PRIVATE SECRETARY by William Gillette. April 17, 1975. Directed by Richard Kuss.

Brooklyn Academy of Music. In addition to its commercial-theater schedule, this organization occasionally finds room for experimental productions of the avant garde. Harvey Lichtenstein, executive director.

BLACK THEATER ALLIANCE FESTIVAL schedule included: YESTERDAY, TODAY, TOMORROW presented by The Weusi Kuumba Troupe. December 27, 1974. AID TO DEPENDENT CHILDREN by Umar Bin Hussan. January 10, 1975. Directed by Helaine Head; presented by New Federal Theater. THE LONG BLACK BLOCK presented by New Heritage Repertory. January 24, 1975.

Byrd Hoffman School of Byrds. Ongoing workshops in theater experiment, often culminating in commercial-theater productions. Robert Wilson, director. (See *A Letter for Queen Victoria* entry in the "Plays Produced on Broadway" and *The $ Value of Man* entry in the "Plays Produced off Broadway" sections of this volume.)

Central Arts Ministry of Central Presbyterian Church. An open community of artists. Bill Silver, director of Arts Ministries.

FROGS by Carl Morse. January, 1975. Directed by James Barbosa; performed by The Medicine Show.
AFTER DINNER OPERA COMPANY by Richard Schotter. January, 1975. Directed by Barbara Vann; performed by The Medicine Show.
TOVARICH by Jacques Deval. February, 1975. Directed by Bob Livingston.
UP IN THE AIR, BOYS by Robert Dahdah and Mary Boylan. March, 1975. Directed by Robert Dahdah.
ONE CENT PLAIN (musical) by Marvin Gordon, music by Ted Simons. May 9, 1975. Directed by Randal Hoey.

Circle Repertory Theater Company. Purpose is to make the action of the play become the experience of the audience. Marshall W. Mason, artistic director.

ONE PERSON by Robert Patrick, directed by Marshall W. Mason; XXX'S by Bill Hoffman, directed by Doug Dwyer; WHEN EVERYTHING BECOMES THE CITY'S MUSIC by Lance S. Belville, directed by Ron Troutman. June 11, 1974.
NOT ENOUGH ROPE by Elaine May, directed by Judd Hirsch; BUSY DYIN' by Sheila Quitten Hoffstetter, directed by Peter Schneider. June 18, 1974.
BATTLE OF ANGELS by Tennessee Williams. October 27, 1974. Directed by Marshall W. Mason.
INNOCENT THOUGHTS, HARMLESS INTENTIONS by John Heuer. December 4, 1974. Directed by Maggie Bos.
FIRE IN THE MIND HOUSE (musical) book and lyrics by Arnold Borget, music by Lance Mulcahy. December, 1974. Directed by Marshall Oglesby.
SAINT FREUD by David Roszkowski. January, 1975. Directed by Richard Steel.
THE MOUND BUILDERS by Lanford Wilson. February 1, 1975. Directed by Marshall W. Mason.
DOWN BY THE RIVER WHERE THE WATERLILIES ARE DISFIGURED EVERY DAY by Julie Bovasso. March 23, 1975. Directed by Marshall Oglesby.
SCANDALOUS MEMORIES by Harvey Perr, directed by Jered Barclay; AFTERNOON TEA by Harvey Perr, directed by John Sullivan. April 16, 1975.
HARRY OUTSIDE by Corinne Jacker. May 11, 1975. Directed by Marshall W. Mason; with Lois Smith, Kevin McCarthy, Tanya Berezin, Jonathan Hogan, Alfred Hinckley, Shelly Batt, Denise Lute.

The Classic Theater. Theater as intense, heightened reality. Herb Barnett, artistic director.

DANTON'S DEATH by Georg Buechner. December, 1974. Directed by Maurice Edwards.
A VIEW FROM THE BRIDGE by Arthur Miller. February, 1975. Directed by Herb Barnett.
THE PHYSICISTS by Friedrich Duerrenmatt. March, 1975. Directed by Maurice Edwards; with Ed Crowley, Mae Marmy, Gerald McGonagil, Robert Milton, Anna Minot, Wendy Nute.
THE PROMISE by Aleksei Arbuzov, translated by Ariadne Nicolaeff.

Colonnades Theater Lab. Resident repertory company with an in-training program for actors. Emphasis on new playwrights. Michael Lessac, artistic director.

A CONVENTION OF TUBA PLAYERS CONVENES IN FAT CITY and WHO HAS SEEN THE COLOR OF THE WIND by Louis Phillips. June 20, 1974. Directed by Michael Lessac.
SECOND WIND by David Morgan. April 20, 1975. Directed by Michael Lessac; with Louis Giambalvo, Charlie Stavola, Jacqueline Cassel.
A MONTH IN THE COUNTRY by Ivan Turgenyev. May 23, 1975. Directed by Michael Lessac; with Louis Giambalvo, Charlie Stavola, Jacqueline Cassel, Tom V. Tammi, Bill E. Noone, Kathleen O'Meara Noone.

The Comedy Stage Company. Actors, directors and audience interested in the revival of modern and traditional comedies. Tim Ward, director.

THE MISER by Molière. December, 1974. Directed by Tim Ward.
THE BIRTHDAY PARTY by Harold Pinter. February, 1975. Directed by Tim Ward; with Michael Sears.
THE REAL INSPECTOR HOUND by Tom Stoppard and THE MARRIAGE PROPOSAL by Anton Chekhov. May, 1975. Directed by Tim Ward.

Common Ground. Developing theater programs by a collaborative process known as "progression". Norman Taffel, artistic director.

THE ANALYSIS conceived and performed by the group. December, 1974.
EIGHT PEOPLE by Michael Kirby. February, 1975. Directed by Norman Taffel.
COMBINE written and directed by Norman Taffel. May, 1975.

Corner Loft Theater (The Friday Theater Foundation). Concentration on presentation and performance of new plays by American playwrights and of little-known and rarely-performed plays of world writers. Michael Shurtleff, artistic director.

SPIRIT YOUR WIFE AWAY TO THE WOODS by Michael Shurtleff, directed by Bryan Hull; with Jackie King, Robert McIlwaine, James Pettibone, Sonja Sepsee, Lenore Sherman; TELL ME YOU DON'T LOVE ME, CHARLIE MOON! by Michael Shurtleff, directed by Dakota DeSmet, with William Perley, Toby Nelson, Sharon Ernster, Jeffrey Marsh; IN THE COUNTRY'S NIGHT by Michael Shurtleff, directed by Hope Arthur, with Johana Durham, Donald Silva. October, 1974.
OASIS by Michael Shurtleff. November 22, 1975. Directed by Patricia Carmichael.
THE RUFFIAN ON THE STAIR by Joe Orton, directed by Marc Gass, with Stanton Coffin, Peter Boyden, Gail Kellstrom; THE COLLECTION by Harold Pinter, directed by Steve Jobes, with John Fedinatz, Rick Jeffers, Anita Sorel, Richard Stack. December, 19, 1975.
NOW by Michael Shurtleff. January, 1975. Directed by Dina Boogaard.
WHO ARE YOU by Michael Shurtleff. February, 1975. Directed by Gail Kellstrom.
THE FREAKOUT by Michael Shurtleff, directed by Dennis Goldfarb; MRS. DALLY HAS A LOVER by William Hanley, directed by Diane Gold; RED CROSS by Sam Shepard, directed by Curtiss W. Sayblack.
LIFE AMONG THE YOUNG PEOPLE (program of one-act plays). May 16, 1975. Directed by Bob Bass, Curtiss W. Sayblack, Dina Boogaard, Steve Jobes; with Lenore Sherman, Roger Grey, Jacqueline King, Stanton Coffin, Beege Barkett.
WHERE THERE'S HOPE (program of one-act plays). May, 1975. Directed by Bob Bass, Diane Gold, Steve Jobes, F.R. McCall; with Jackie King, Hal Rosen, Judy Briane, Toby Nelson, Rich Rosdal, Bryce Holman.

Counterpoint Theater Company. Purpose is to maintain high standards of excellence in the service of plays of distinction, through theatrical productions of enduring value. Howard Green, artistic director.

SPOON RIVER ANTHOLOGY by Edgar Lee Masters, adapted by Charles Aidman. September, 1974.
FINGERNAILS BLUE AS FLOWERS by Ronald Ribman, directed by Gonzalo Madurga; BURIAL OF ESPOSITO by Ronald Ribman, directed by Howard Green. December, 1974.
UNCLE VANYA by Anton Chekhov. February, 1975. Directed by Gonzalo Madurga.
NO EXIT by Jean-Paul Sartre. April, 1975. Directed by Howard Green.

The Courtyard Playhouse Foundation. Eclectic policy of searching for "a good play", new ones preferred but not exclusively. Houses Little People's Theater Company for quality in children's theater. Kenneth R. Eulo, artistic director.

THE WHITE APE. September, 1974.
FINAL EXAMS by Ken Eulo. December, 1974.
TAKE THE FIRST SUBWAY TO SIBERIA by David Toll. March, 1975.
HOT FUDGE by Martin Low. May, 1975.

CSC Repertory Theater. A permanent company performing classics reinterpreted for modern audiences in rotating rep, at the Abbey Theater, a 255-seat thrust-stage house. Christopher Martin, artistic director (and director of all productions)

EDWARD II by Christopher Marlowe.
HEDDA GABLER by Henrik Ibsen, English version by Christopher Martin.
THE TEMPEST by William Shakespeare.
THE SERVANT by Robin Maugham.
THE MAIDS by Jean Genet, translated by Bernard Frechtman.
THE DWARFS by Harold Pinter.
THE LADY'S NOT FOR BURNING by Christopher Fry.
ANTIGONE by Jean Anouilh.
WOYZECK by Georg Buechner, English version by Christopher Martin.

The Cubiculo and Cubiculo III. Experiments in the use of theater, dance, music, etc. housed in four studios and two stages. Phillip Meister, artistic director.

SMITH, HERE! and ROSENSWEIG, FC by Ed Greenberg. June, 1974. Directed by Donald Austitz; with Stanley Brock, Susan Baum, Robert Dale Martin, Norman Sample, Lee Terri.
THE KISSOFF and BLUEBERRY MOUNTAIN by John Herzfeld. June, 1974. Directed by Sara Harte; with Connie Forslund, William Andrews, Ryan Listman, David Pendleton, Lynn Laury.
THE RISE AND FALL OF BURLESQUE HUMOR FROM ARISTOPHANES TO LAUGH-IN written and directed by Dick Poston; with Marilyn Wassell, Joe Elic, Dick Poston.
FALLING APART (one-act) by Monte Merrick. November, 1974.
THE DARK MOON AND THE FULL and SUNDAY MORNING BRIGHT AND EARLY by Joe Hart. November, 1974.
THE SEAGULL, directed by Phillip Meister. December 5, 1974.
THE FIRST, THE MIDDLE AND THE LAST by Israel Horovitz. December, 1974.
HEARTBREAK HOUSE by George Bernard Shaw. January 9, 1975. Directed by Robert Elston; with Elizabeth Perry, Catherine Byers, Kent Broadhurst, Robert Gaus, Allan Rich.
HOLMES AND MORIARTY and THE WILD MAN OF BORNEO by Allen Sternfield. January, 1975. Directed by Bret Lyon.
RAFFERTY, ONE BY ONE by Rolf Fjelde. February, 1975. Directed by John Davis.
BLOOD WEDDING by Federico Garcia Lorca. March 6, 1975. Directed by Phillip Meister.
JUDAS by Robert Patrick. March, 1975. Directed by Eric Concklin.
STICK OF INCENSE and MADAM ZODIAC by Michael McGrinder. March 11, 1975.
ROLLS OF GOLD written and directed by Joseph Bush.
HOORAY, WORLD WAR III IS COMING, OR THINGS ARE GETTING BETTER (musical) by Van Hoyce. April 17, 1975. Directed by Donald Honey; with Tim Cahill, Dana Coen, Sharon Hess, Gail Johnston, Jean Palmerton, Charles Leipart.
THE PETITION by Don Flynn and BIG RED & LITTLE BLUE by Gary Martin. May 1, 1975.

SWORD/PLAY by Leon Rooke. May 14, 1975. Directed by Neil Flanagan.
AIN'T THAT A SHAME by Joseph Renard. May 20, 1975. Directed by Neil Flanagan.

The Demi Gods. A company with special training in dance and music as well as theater. Joseph A. Walker, director.

YIN YANG written and directed by Joseph A. Walker music by Dorothy A. Dinroe. October, 1974.
ANTIGONE AFRICANUS written and directed by Joseph A. Walker. March, 1975.

Direct Theater. A professional company of actors and other stage artists exploring new techniques. Allen R. Belknap, artistic director.

DIRECTORS' FESTIVAL, September 8–29, 1974; PLAYWRIGHTS' FESTIVAL, October, 1974; ACTORS' FESTIVAL, November, 1974.
THE DEVILS by John Whiting. January 10, 1975. Directed by Allen R. Belknap; with Fred Martell.
RIGHT YOU ARE BY Luigi Pirandello. February, 1975. Directed by Jerry Roth; with Ralph Pape, Lisa Goodman, George McGuire, Tom Baer, Bob DelPazzo, Fred Martell.
IN THE CITY OF ANGELS by Stan Thomas. March, 1975. Directed by Charles Conwell; with Patricia Conwell, Paul Collins, Christopher Hughes, Bill Roberts, Patricia Hodges, Graham Harper.
GILGAMESH, adapted by Ross Alexander. April 24, 1975. Directed by Allen R. Belknap.

Drama Ensemble Company. Devoted to experimental plays, as outgrowths of ongoing workshops; open to new writers and directors. Roberto Monticello, artistic director.

WHO'S THERE and MORTALITY GAME, PART I written and directed by Roberto Monticello. Autumn, 1974.
THE PASSIONATE ONE by Roberto Monticello written and directed by Roberto Monticello. March, 1975.
THE ACTING TEACHER written and directed by Bob Madiero. April, 1975. With Roberto Monticello.
ENTRANCE by Elizabeth Converse. May, 1975. Directed by Roberto Monticello; with Elizabeth Converse.
ALLEGORY OF BEATRICE CENCI written and directed by Roberto Monticello. June 12, 1975; also performed in cooperation with New York City Department of Cultural Affairs June 15, 1975, Washington Square Park.

Dramatis Personae. A showcase for new, specifically oriented material. Steven Baker, director.

THE SOUND OF A DIFFERENT DRUM by A.R. Bell. September, 1974. Directed by Steven Baker.

Drifting Traffic. The production of new plays, classical plays, family theater, with a strong focus on movement. Sande Shurin, artistic director.

THE SATYR PLAY by Sophocles. December, 1974. Directed by Sande Shurin.
SWEET SUITE by Leonard Melfi, music and lyrics by Pendleton Brown and Hayden Wayne. May 31, 1975. Directed by Sande Shurin; with Leonard Melfi, Gwendolyn Brown, Charles Mayer Karp, Malcolm Groom, Jeff Hillock.

Ensemble Studio Theater. Nucleus of 16 playwrights-in-residence dedicated to supporting individual theater artists and developing new works for the stage. Curt Dempster, artistic director.

PARADES SHALL FOLLOW written and directed by Donald Marcus and Gary Nebiol. December 5, 1974.
JUST BREAKFAST by John Clarkson. Directed by Mari Gorman.
THE DOG RAN AWAY by Brother Jonathan, OSF. February, 1975. Directed by Curt Dempster; with Joseph Ponazecki, Josef Sommer, John Wardwell.

AMNESIA by Michael Shaffer. March, 1975. Directed by Charles Parks; with Bill Cwikowski, Lyle Kessler, Bevya Rosten, Richard Sherman, Melodie Somers.
THE TRANSFIGURATION OF BENNO BLIMPIE by Albert Innaurato. April 3, 1975. Directed by Robert Saidenburg.
DREAM OF A BLACKLISTED ACTOR by Conrad Bromberg. May 1, 1975. Directed by Harold Stone.

Equity Library Theater. Actors' Equity produces a series of revivals each season as showcases for the work of its actor-members. George Wojtasik, managing director.

ARMS AND THE MAN by George Bernard Shaw. October 17, 1974. Directed by Russell Treyz.
THE BOY FRIEND (musical) by Sandy Wilson. November 7, 1974. Directed by Nancy Rubin.
THE DESPERATE HOURS by Joseph Hayes. December 5, 1974. Directed by Robert Brink.
NEW GIRL IN TOWN (musical) by Bob Merrill and George Abbott. January 9, 1975. Directed by Richard Michaels.
BUS STOP by William Inge. February 6, 1975. Directed by Richard Mogavero.
DO I HEAR A WALTZ? (musical) book by Arthur Laurents, music by Richard Rodgers, lyrics by Stephen Sondheim. March 6, 1975. Directed by Delores Ferraro; with Rosalind Harris, Gail Oscar, Donald Craig.
THE ZYKOVS by Maxim Gorky. April 10, 1975. Directed by Isaac Schlambelan; with Louis Turenne, Gaetano Bongiovanni.
THE THREE MUSKETEERS (operetta) by Rudolph Friml. May 8, 1975. Directed by Charles Abbott.

ETC Theater. Produces plays by American playwrights. Improvisational techniques utilized in all shows. Rae Allen, J.J. Barry, Frank Bongiorno, artistic directors; Sheldon Patinkin, artistic consultant.

BREAK A LEG by Ira Levin. Directed by Sheldon Patinkin.
SWEETHEART written and directed by J.J. Barry.
ONCE IN A LIFETIME by George S. Kaufman and Moss Hart. Directed by Frank Bongiorno.
WAITING FOR LEFTY by Clifford Odets. April, 1975. Directed by Sheldon Patinkin.
THE BIG KNIFE by Clifford Odets. Directed by Rae Allen.

Gene Frankel Theater Workshop. Development of new works for the theater, housed this season at The Lambs. Gene Frankel, artistic director.

AMERICAN WAR WOMEN by Roma Greth. June 1, 1974. Directed by Karen Helder and Pat Mullen.
ARTHUR by Jim Peck. Directed by Lames Leigh.
THE OLD ONES by Arnold Wesker. December 7, 1974. Directed by Ben Shaktman; with Lou Gilbert, Eda Reiss Merin, Norman Rose, Tresa Hughes.
NOTES ON A LOVE AFFAIR by Frank Marcus. Directed by Michael Dimond.
THE MYSTERY OF PERICLUSE by John Cromwell. May, 1975.
FIGHT SONG (musical) by Ben Barber, Robert Lamb, John Duffy.

Greenwich Mews Theater. Encourage and promote understanding among all people, through the arts. William Glenesk, artistic director.

CRUSHES (musical) book by Jeff Hochhauser, music, lyrics by Rosemary Gimpel. July, 1974. Directed by Joseph Kavanaugh: with Michael Oakes, Bonni Baryard, Nita Novy, Joseph Ostopak, Sharon Talbot, Cynthia Jackson.
LOVE'S LABOUR'S LOST by William Shakespeare. August, 1974. Directed by Gus Kaikkonen; with Don Adriano, Erik Rhodes.
MACBETH by William Shakespeare. September, 1974. Directed by Ron Troutman; with Powers Boothe, Susanne Peters, Robert Ousley.
THE COLLECTOR by David Parker, adapted from John Fowles's novel. October, 1974.
ON THE EDGE OF SURPRISE by Dorothy Kobak. November 11, 1974. Directed by Evelyn Neinkan.
A MIDSUMMER NIGHT'S DREAM by William Shakespeare, directed by Rafael Blanco.
THE MISER by Molière, directed by Alan A. Gabor.

DARK LADY OF THE SONNETS, HOW HE LIED TO HER HUSBAND, ANNAJAN-
SKA, THE BOLSHEVIK EMPRESS by George Bernard Shaw. February, 1975. Directed by
Alan A. Gabor.

Hamm and Clov Stage Company. International repertory of new and contemporary plays,
tours abroad. David Villaire, director.

THE WIDOW'S HOUSE by David Ferguson. June 13, 1974. Directed by David Villaire; with
Ernest Abuba, Tisa Chang, Arabella Hong Young, Marion Jim, Alvin Lum, Tom Matsusaka,
Lani Gerrie Miyazaki, Peter Yoshida.
THE FALL AND REDEMPTION OF MAN by John Bowen. June, 1974.
PROGRAM OF DRAMATIZED REVOLUTIONARY SPEECHES. July 4, 1974.
STRINDBERG by Colin Wilson. November, 1974. Directed by David Villaire: with Alvah
Stanley.
TREES IN THE WIND by John McGrath. November, 1974. Directed by John Beary.
THE TRUE HISTORY OF SQUIRE JONATHON AND HIS UNFORTUNATE TREASURE
by John Arden. December, 1974. Directed by David Villaire.

Hudson Guild Theater. American classics interspersed with original and experimental
plays. P.J. Barry, artistic director.

DAYS OF WINE AND ROSES by J.P. Miller. November, 1974. Directed by P.J. Barry.
LONG DAY'S JOURNEY INTO NIGHT by Eugene O'Neill. December, 1974. Directed by
Geraldine Teagarden.
YOU'RE A GOOD MAN CHARLIE BROWN by Clark Gesner. January, 1975. Directed by
Geraldine Teagarden.
RELIEF: by George Patterson, with music by Franklin Roosevelt Underwood. February, 1975.
Directed by P.J. Barry.
HERITAGE written and directed by P.J. Barry. April, 1975.

Iglesias Theater Club. Illumination of the human pattern's relationship to the spiritual
pattern until the unity of both is defined. Alex Iglesias, director.

THE IMPORTANCE OF BEING EARNEST by Oscar Wilde. Directed by Alex Iglesias; with
Owen Lackell, Alex Iglesias, John Rengstorff, Diane Barry, Nina Kethevan.
THE PLAY'S THE THING by Ferenc Molnar. July 26, 1974. Directed by Alex Iglesias; with
R. Mack Miller, John Mitchell, Pauline Walsh, Ken Pearlman.
DON JUAN IN HELL by George Bernard Shaw. September, 1974.
THE COCKTAIL PARTY by T.S. Eliot. October, 1974.
CHORAL ASSEMBLY, HOT HOUSE, and MR. KEMPT written and directed by Richard
Taylor. December, 1974.
ABSTRACT MAGENTA by Candide Cummings. February, 1975. Directed by Andrew Louca.
DANCE OF DEATH by August Strindberg. February, 1975. Directed by Andrew Louca.
THREE COMEDIES by Rebecca Maiden, Louise Wolf, Dorothy Parker. March, 1975. Directed
by Shelly Warwick.
JOHNNY NO-TRUMP by Mary Mercier. Directed by Paul C. Iablings.
A SOP TO CERBERUS OF 500 BEAUTIFUL GIRLS by Rebecca Maiden and MRS. GOLD-
STEIN'S DAUGHTER by Louise Woolf. February, 1975. Directed by Shelly Warwick.

Interart Theater. Opportunities for women to participate in theatrical activity. Margot
Lewitin, Amy Saltz, coordinators.

WHAT'S ON TONIGHT (mixed media event) conceived and directed by Wendy Clarke. June
1, 1974
THE CINDERELLA PROJECT by The Womanrite Theater Ensemble. November, 1974.
BLOOM TREE MUSIC (improvisational evening) by Kay JeriAnn.
THE COMMON GARDEN VARIETY by Jane Chambers. November, 1974. Directed by Nancy
Rhodes.
MINSTREL SHOW conceived and directed by Amy Saltz. February, 1975.
RITE OF PASSAGE written and directed by Laura Sims. March, 1975.
THE FIRST OF APRIL by Nina Voronel. Directed by Margot Lewitin.

The Irish Rebel Theater (An Claidheamh Soluis). Dedicated to establishing an awareness among people of all ethnic backgrounds of the artistic expression of the Irish people. Larry Spiegel, artistic director.

> HOME IS THE HERO by Walter Macken. December, 1974. Directed by Larry Spiegel.
> WOOD OF THE WHISPERING by M.J. Molloy. April, 1975. Directed by Larry Spiegel.

Jean Cocteau Repertory. Located in the historic Bouwerie Lane Theater, the Jean Cocteau Repertory presents vintage and modern classics on a rotating repertory schedule. Eve Adamson, artistic director (and director of productions).

> SUDDENLY LAST SUMMER by Tennessee Williams.
> CAIN (dramatization of works by Lord Byron).
> ASTONISHMENTS pieces by Samuel Beckett, T.S. Eliot, Jeff Sheridan.
> GHOSTS by Henrik Ibsen.
> WAITING FOR GODOT by Samuel Beckett.
> NO EXIT by Jean-Paul Sartre.
> A MIDSUMMER NIGHT'S DREAM by William Shakespeare. With Lesley Appleby, Michael Fesenmeier, Kathleen Forbes, Daniel Johnson, James Payne, Craig Smith.
> THE DOCTOR IN SPITE OF HIMSELF by Molière. October, 1974.
> ROMEO AND JULIET by William Shakespeare. December 14, 1974.
> THE FIREBUGS by Max Frisch. March, 1975.
> IN THE BAR OF A TOKYO HOTEL by Tennessee Williams.
> AN EVENING WITH EDNA ST. VINCENT MILLAY. adapted and directed by Jere Jacob. May, 1975.

Jones Beach Marine Theater. Each summer, a musical classic is presented in this huge outdoor theater on Long Island. Guy Lombardo, producer.

> FIDDLER ON THE ROOF (musical) book by Joseph Stein, music by Jerry Bock, lyrics by Sheldon Harnick. June 26, 1974. Directed by John Fearnley; with Geoffrey Webb, Norman Atkins, Geraldine Brooks, Honey Sanders, Tony Slez, Ted Thurston.

Joseph Jefferson Theater Company. An eclectic policy of production, housed in the annex of The Little Church Around the Corner. Activites in 1974–75 included discussions of plays moderated by Norman Nadel, Harold Clurman and Marion Fredi Towbin. Cathy Roskam, founder.

> RIP VAN WINKLE (Boucicault version). July, 1974. Directed by Neil Flanagan; performed in cooperation with Sleepy Hollow Restorations at Tarrytown, N.Y.
> I REMEMBER MAMA by John van Druten. November 7, 1974. Directed by William Koch; with Eugenia Rawls.
> ADAM AND EVE by Seymour Reiter, music by Lor Crane. Directed by Valerie Bettis.
> AWAKE AND SING by Clifford Odets. January 23, 1975. Directed by Ernest Martin; with Frances Cheney, Jerry Jarrett, Daniel Hedaya, Linda Selmann, William Daprato, Michael Hardstark.
> WILDEFLOWERS adapted from stories by Oscar Wilde. February, 1975. Conceived and directed by William Koch.
> THE AUTUMN GARDEN by Lillian Hellman. April 17, 1975. Directed by Nancy Rubin; with Michael Ryan, Ron Tomme, Mary Mims, David Matthews, Stephanie Satie.
> PENETRATION FLATTS by Dennis Hackin. May 14, 1975. Directed by Christopher Cox.

The Judson Poets' Theater. The theater arm of Judson Memorial Church and its pastor, Al Carmines, who creates a series of new, unconventional musicals which are sometimes transferred to the commercial theater. Al Carmines, director.

> LISTEN TO ME by Gertrude Stein, music by Al Carmines. October 18, 1974. Directed by Lawrence Kornfeld.
> CHRISTMAS '74 conceived and directed by Al Carmines.
> SACRED AND PROFANE LOVE written and directed by Al Carmines. February, 1975. With Essie Borden, Lou Bullock, Terence Burk, Alice Carey, Eric Ellenburg, Lee Guilliatt, Philip

Owens, Elly Schadt, David Tice, Beverly Wideman.
THE JOURNEY OF SNOW WHITE (revival) written and directed by Al Carmines. May 29, 1975.

La Mama Experimental Theater Club (ETC). A busy workshop and showcase for experimental theater of all kinds. Ellen Stewart, director.

PIERRE OR THE AMBIGUITIES, adapted from Herman Melville's work by Walter Brown. Directed by Walter Brown; with Jon Argonne, Eugenia Bostwick, John Bowers, Bump Heeter, Ann Hennessey.
THE BIG BROADCAST ON EAST 53RD STREET by Dick Brukenfeld. June, 1974. Directed by Charles Marian.
JULIA CAESAR by Allan Causey. Directed by Gerald Bovenschein and Allan Causey.
FRAGMENTS OF A TRILOGY (MEDEA, ELECTRA, THE TROJAN WOMEN), from Greek plays, conceived and directed by Andrei Serban, music by Elizabeth Swados. June, 1974. With Stuart Baker, Patrick Burke, Natalie Gray, Richard Jackiel, Heather McDermott, Priscilla Smith, Elizabeth Swados.
THE 20TH CENTURY LIMITED by Charles Stanley. June, 1974.
SANDIGAN KALINANGANI, coordinated by Leo Ruiz. (Philippine Festival of the Arts). June, 1974.
LIPSINK, THE UNVANISHED WORKS by Sam Francisco.
THE CITY written and directed by Yutaka Higashi. August, 1974.
DANCE WITH ME by Greg Antonacci. September, 1974. Directed by Joel Zwick.
BIG MOTHER by Charles Dizenzo. September, 1974. Directed by John Vaccaro.
A MIDSUMMER NIGHT'S DREAM and MEASURE FOR MEASURE by William Shakespeare. October 20, 1974. Directed by Tisa Chang; performed by resident Chinese troupe.
ARK by Nancy Fales. October 30, 1974. Directed by Ralph Lee.
THE SHADOW OF EVIL (OR DRACULA, THE UNDEAD) written and directed by Ken Hill. October 31, 1974.
THE NOTHING KID and STANDARD SAFETY written and directed by Julie Bovasso. December, 1974.
RAGS TO RICHES TO RAGS by Paul Foster. December, 1974. Directed by Cal Yeomans.
THE GOOD WOMAN OF SETZUAN by Bertolt Brecht. February, 1975. Directed by Andrei Serban; performed as work-in-progress.
THE SWEETHEART by J.J. Barry. February, 1975. Directed by J.J. Barry and Frank Bongiorno.
ONE MAN'S RELIGION and THE PINOTTI PAPERS written and directed by H.M. Koutoukas. February, 1975.
THE MYSTIC WRITINGS OF PAUL REVERE (dance play) by Carolyn Lord. March, 1975.
THE SECRET PLACE by Garrett Morris. March 7, 1975. Directed by Bill Duke.
MADAM SENATOR by Mario Fratti, music by Ed Scott. March 20, 1975. Directed by Roger Hendricks Simon.
THE WORKSHOP by Victor Eschbach, directed by Daffi; THE PICTURE OF INNOCENCE by Victor Eschbach, directed by Lawrence Catlett.
OBA KOSO written and directed by Duro Lapido; with the Duro Ladipo National Theater.
RESONANCE conceived and directed by Jacques Chuat. March, 1975. With Marianne Marcellin.
HOTEL PARADISO by Georges Feydeau and Maurice Desvallieres. April, 1975. Directed by Tisa Chang.
THE REVENGER'S TRAGEDY by Cyril Tourneur. Directed by John Gillick.
LAZARUS by The Master of Fleury and Eric Salzman. Directed by Eric Salzman.
SPRING RITES conceived by Tom O'Horgan. April 23, 1975.
EMERGENCE directed and choreographed by Aileen Passloff and BA LET THERE BE LIGHT COW conceived and directed by Lawrence Sacharow, text by Judith Walcutt. May 29, 1975. Presented by Bard College.

Lion Theater Company. Actors' company with an eclectic repertory. Gene Nye, Garland Wright, artistic directors.

THE TEMPEST by William Shakespeare. July 10, 1974. Directed by Garland Wright; with James Rey, John Guerrasio, William Metzo, Leland Moss, Mary Wright, Keith McDermot, Gene Nye, Robert Blumenfeld, Terry Hinz.
PULLMAN CAR HIAWATHA by Thornton Wilder. July, 1974.

GAMMER GURTON'S NEEDLE. August 7, 1974. Directed by Gene Nye; with John Guerrasio, Garland Wright, Leigh Burch.
KITTY HAWK by Len Jenkin. August, 1974. Directed by Garland Wright; with Steve Karp, Gene Nye, Charles Berendt, David Bates, Joniruth White, Frank Geraci, Leland Moss, Jack Heifner.

Lolly's Theater Club. Low-admission professional productions on a schedule of new scripts, specialities, revivals, visiting troupes, etc. Laura Bivens, director.

MURDER AT THE VICARAGE adapted from the Agatha Christie book by Jay More Charles and Barbara Troy. June 21, 1974. Directed by June Plager; with Fran Harris, David Wilborn, Robb McIntire, Pamela Baldwin, Ben Phillips.
LABURNUM GROVE by J.B. Priestley. July 28, 1974. Directed by Anthony DeVito.
READING, OR THE MIDNIGHT HORROR SHOW by Joseph Dougherty. October 1974.
LOVE FROM A STRANGER by Agatha Christie. October 15, 1974. Directed by June Plager.
OLD TIMES by Harold Pinter. Directed by Chris Adler; with Michael Ruud, Nancy Campbell, Jennifer Crandall.
MURRAY'S (revue). March 21, 1975. Directed by David Rieger.
RED PEPPERS by Noel Coward, directed by Anthony DeVito, with Thomas MacGreevy, Ann Ault, Ted Ulmer, Roger Bowman, Fran Harris; A SHORT VISIT ONLY by Noel Coward, directed by Johnny King, with Ann Ault, Robert Brittany, Carol Crittendon, Keith Ryan, Monique Leboeuf, Linda Creamer. April, 1975.

The Manhattan Project. Development of theater by means of group improvising. Andre Gregory, director; Lyn Austin, producer. (See its schedule of programs in the New York Shakespeare Festival Public Theater entry in the "Plays Produced off Broadway" section of this volume.)

Manhattan Theater Club. A producing organization with three stages for productions, readings, workshop activities and cabaret. Lynne Meadow, artistic director.

NAOMI COURT by Michael Sawyer. June, 1974. Directed by Ira Cirker; with Jeffrey Giannone, Joey Faye, Sally Gracie, Nicholas Coster, Brad Davis, Earl Hammond.
BREAD AND ROSES by Maria Gioffre. Directed by Carol Kastendlecit.
THIS PROPERTY IS CONDEMNED and PORTRAIT OF A MADONNA by Tennessee Williams. Directed by Delores Ferraro.
THE MORNING AFTER OPTIMISM by Thomas Murphy. Directed by Bob Mandel; with Kevin O'Connor, Jill Eikenberry, Allan Carlsen, Sharon Spelman.
A TOUCH OF THE POET by Eugene O'Neill. Directed by David Davies; with James Noble, Flora Elkins, Ruth Klinger.
SOME PEOPLE, SOME OTHER PEOPLE AND WHAT THEY FINALLY DO by Jordan Crittendon. Directed by Charles Aidman; with Lois Battle, Rod Browning, Jordan Crittendon, Carol Morley.
NIGHT MUST FALL by Emlyn Williams. June 27, 1974. Directed by Stephen Levi.
THE CARETAKER by Harold Pinter. July 18, 1974. With Will Hare, Peter Burnell, Edward Herrmann.
ONE SUNDAY AFTERNOON by James Hagan. August, 1974. Directed by Barbara Loden; with Steve Railsback, Clinton Allmon, J.J. Quinn.
BLUES FOR MISTER CHARLIE by James Baldwin. August, 1974. Directed by Nick Latour.
PEOPLE'S LIVES (series of short scenes from works by Gorky, Arthur Miller, William Saroyan). August, 1974. Performed by Renee Baughman, Linda Canby, Jack Gerner, Judy Grebelsky, Paul Greene, Mari Gorman.
THE SUBJECT WAS ROSES by Frank D. Gilroy. September, 1974. Directed by Barry Moss.
THE PRIME OF MISS JEAN BRODIE by Jay Allen. October, 1974.
AN EVENING OF COLE PORTER (musical revue) by Norman Berman. October, 1974.
LOOK BACK IN ANGER by Paul Osborne. October, 1974. Directed by Paul Schneider.
BITS AND PIECES by Corinne Jacker. November 13, 1974. Directed by Lynne Meadow.
BLESSING by Joseph Landon. November 20, 1974. Directed by Thomas Bullard.
PHILADELPHIA STORY, THE by Philip Barry. November, 1974. Directed by Ronald Roston.
END OF SUMMER by S.N. Behrman. November 24, 1974. Directed by Ronald Roston.
THE RUNNER STUMBLES by Milan Stitt. December 13, 1974. Directed by Austin Pendle-

ton; with Alan Mixon, Nancy Donohue, Katina Mathewson, Marilyn Pfeiffer, Sloane Shelton, Robb Webb.

LOOK HOMEWARD, ANGEL by Ketti Frings. January, 1975. Directed by Jeff Bricmont.

THE SEAGULL (new English version) by Jean-Claude van Itallie. January 29, 1975. Directed by Joseph Chaikin.

BUS STOP by William Inge. January 23, 1975. Directed by Jeff Bricmont.

VALENTINE'S DAY (musical) by Ron Cowen, Seth Glassman, Saul Naishtat. February, 1975.

THE BEST IS YET TO BE by Margie Appleman. February, 1975. Directed by Delores Ferraro.

THE PORNOGRAPHER'S DAUGHTER by Jonathon Levy. February 27, 1975. Directed by John Pleshette.

BLOODSHOT WINE (songs) by Jim Steinman. March, 1975. Directed by Barry Keating.

THE SEA by Edward Bond. March 16, 1975. Directed by Robert Mandel; with Grayson Hall, John Heffernan, Arnold Soboloff, Paul Collins, Susan Sharkey.

DEATH STORY by David Edgar. March 23, 1975. Directed by Carole Rothman.

STAIRCASE by Charles Dyer. April 3, 1975. Directed by Tom Bullard.

BATTERING RAM by David E. Freeman. April 24, 1975. Directed by Stephen Pascal.

THE PAST IS A PEST by Richard Wesley and BREAKOUT by Oyamo. April 27, 1975. Directed by Harold Scott; with Bill Cobbs, Brent Jennings, Terry Alexander, Robert Stocking, Joe LoGrippo.

EAST LYNNE adapted, conceived and directed by David Chambers. May 8, 1975. With Christopher Guest, Caroline Kova, Donovan Sylvest, Mary Wright, Julie Garfield.

Matinee Theater Series. Devoted to theater experimentation, it attempts to explore new avenues of approach in acting, production and dramatic form. Lucille Lortel, artistic director.

FIRE AND ICE (program of poems by Robert Frost) arranged and directed by John Genke and Albert Takazauckas. November, 11, 1974. Performed by Theater of the Open Eye.

DRUMS AT YALE by Walter A. Fairservis Jr. December 2, 1974. Directed by Isaiah Sheffer; with Linda Martin, Lon Clark, Matthew Tobin, Gary Cookson, Joseph Jamrog, Walter A. Fairservis Jr.

THE LONG VALLEY by John Steinbeck, adapted and directed by Robert Glenn. January 6, 1974. With Aurelia DeFelice, Will Hare, J. Frank Lucas, Brandon Maggart, Alan Marlowe.

The New Dramatists. An organization devoted to playwrights; member writers may use the facilities for anything from private cold readings of their material to workshop stagings. Jeff Peters, Program Director.

NIGHTLIGHT by Barry Berg. June 4, 1974. Directed by Craig Anderson.

THE BEACH CHILDREN by John von Hartz. June 25, 1974.

THE RAG DOLL by Allen Davis III. July 16, 1974.

THE SHAFT OF LOVE by Charles Dizenzo. September 19, 1974.

LOVE ONE ANOTHER by Rose Leiman Goldemberg. October 1, 1974.

NEVER A SNUG HARBOR by David Clarke. October 13, 1974.

A SAFE PLACE by C.K. Mack. October 29, 1974.

GIVE MY REGARDS TO BROADWAY by Dennis Turner. November 20, 1974.

BREADWINNER by Marian Winters. December 17, 1974.

THE PINK PALACE by Aldo Giunta. December 19, 1974.

LEAVE OF ABSENCE by Stephen H. Foreman. January 9, 1975.

CAKES WITH THE WINE by Edward Cohen. January 19, 1975.

CARNIVAL DREAMS by Conn Fleming. January 20, 1975.

BETWEEN NOW AND THEN by Leslie Lee. February 6, 1975. Directed by Dana Roberts.

THE INN AT LYDDA by John Wolfson. February 18, 1975. Directed by Phillip Taylor.

ESTHER by C.K. Mack. March 5, 1975.

AMOUREUSE adaptation by Stuart and Anne Vaughan. March 26, 1975.

THE SALTY DOG SAGA by David Epstein. April 1, 1975. Directed by David Fox.

OAKVILLE U.S.A. by Freida Lipp. April 9, 1975.

HOCUS POCUS by Joseph Scott Kierland. April 16, 1975.

HAPPY HALLOWEEN by Kit Jones. April 24, 1975.

New Federal Theater. The Henry Street Settlement's training and showcase unit for new playwrights, mostly black and Puerto Rican. Woodie King Jr., director.

THE PRODIGAL SISTER (musical) book and lyrics by J.E. Franklin, music by Micki Grant. July 10, 1974. Directed by Shauneille Perry; with Paula Desmond, Victor Willis, Larry Lowe, Saundra McClain, Joyce Griffen, Frances Salisbury.

AS LONG AS YOU'RE HAPPY, BARBARA by Gary Lasdun. October, 1974. Directed by Otto Pirchner.

TEA by Irwin H. Lerner. January 16, 1975. Directed by Dennaro Montanino.

AID TO DEPENDENT CHILDREN by Umar Bin Hussan. January, 1975. Directed by Helaine Head.

THE SYSTEM OF GREEN LANTERN SOLOS by Barry Kaleem. February, 1975. Directed by Samm Williams.

THE TAKING OF MISS JANIE by Ed Bullins. March 13, 1975. Directed by Gilbert Moses.

DRINKWATER (musical) book and lyrics by Ifa Iyaun, music by Johnny Taylor. April 18, 1975. Directed by Denise Hamilton: with Diane Bivens, J.C. Lucas, Tora Bey, Saundra McClain, Willard Reese, Arnold Johnson.

SNAKESHIP by Joe Overstreet. April, 1975. Directed by Anderson Johnson; with Steve Cannon, Corinne Jennings.

SIDNEE, POET HEROICAL written and directed by Imamu Amiri Baraka. May 15, 1975.

The New Phoenix Repertory Company. Schedule of five experimental "Side Shows" in addition to the company's regular Broadway repertory (see The New Phoenix Repertory Company entry in the "Plays Produced on Broadway" section of this volume).

New York Shakespeare Festival Public Theater. Schedule of experimental workshop or work-in-progress productions and guest residencies, in addition to its regular productions. Joseph Papp, producer. (For its 1974–75 workshop programs, see the New York Shakespeare Festival Public Theater entry in the "Plays Produced off Broadway" section of this volume.)

New York Theater Ensemble. Organization of participating artists to encourage new theater artists and playwrights. Lucille Talayco, artistic director.

HORSE, ACID AND HAY by Louis DiGangi. June, 1974. Directed by Roy Steinberg.

SOMETIMES by Jean Granirer. June, 1974. Directed by Linda Altman.

WE ARE ALL EPICUREANS written and directed by Stan Zawatsky.

A MILD CASE OF DEATH by David Korr. Directed by Tony DeVito.

DON JUAN IN HELL by George Bernard Shaw. June 5, 1974. Directed by Ronn Muller.

PURELY COINCIDENTAL by Peter Lightstone. June, 1974. Directed by B.J. Bohack and Michael Harris.

BROTHERS AND SISTERS by James Ackerson, music by Darryl Curry. July 31, 1974. Directed by Rod Nash.

UNICORNS ARE BLUE by William Narcy. August, 1974. Directed by Dick Briggs.

THE HOLY CROSS by Carl Ticktin, I WANT TO BE WITH YOU by Michael Shurtleff, THE MAN WHO ATE PEOPLE RAW by Irving Rikon. August, 1974. Directed by J. Peter Bergman.

DISCOVERING BODIES by Richard Ohanesian, directed by Emelise Aleandri; BITCH IN AMBER by John Glines, directed by Don Anderson. August, 1974.

GLAMOR, GLORY AND GOLD by Jackie Curtis. September, 1974. Directed by Ron Link.

AGAMEMNON. September, 1974. Directed by Richard Ohanesian.

FESTIVAL OF NEW PLAYS. Schedule included SANDY by F.V. Hunt, 7300 HAMBURG-ERS LATER by George Hammer, GILBERT by David Meranze. All directed by Anne Ray-chell: WILL THE REAL YOGANANDA PLEASE STAND UP written and directed by George Birimisa; RETURN OF NOCTURNAL STROLLS by Michael Shurtleff; COCKTAIL FRANKFURTERS by Robert Reinhold; SCHLURP by Stanley Nelson, directed by Robert Logan Morrow; WELCOME TO THE MONKEY HOUSE by Kurt Vonnegut, dramatized by Michael Serzel, directed by Ron Marquette.

WOMEN BEHIND BARS by Tom Eyen. October 17, 1974. Directed by Ron Link.

HERO by Ruth Stern. December, 1974. Directed by John Sillings.

RAZZMATAZZ. December, 1974. Presented by Angels of Lights.

THE WHORE by Laurence Holder. Directed by Kirk Kirksey.

THE B-BEAVER ANIMATIONS and COME AND GO by Samuel Beckett. Directed by Lee Breuer; performed by Mabou Mines.

EROS IN EXILE by Luigia Miller. February, 1975. Directed by David Black.
COMPANY OF WAYWARD SAINTS by George Herman. February 21, 1975. Directed by Stephen Lieb.
OLD TIMES by Harold Pinter. January 31, 1975. Directed by Harve Dean.
AUNTIE J'S BOX by Margaret Harrington Tamulonis. March 14, 1975.
THE ANTS AND THE BUTTERFLIES by David McLaren.
TOGETHERNESS by Gwendolyn Gunn. Directed by Ann Meltzer.
HUNGER: (program of three one-act plays) by Warren Girarraputo, Kit Jones, Thomas Caufield. April 9, 1975. Directed by Fred Kaplan.
NIGHT WOUND by Eric Kocher. April 11, 1975. Directed by Leo Boylan.
BROTHERS AND SISTERS (musical) book, lyrics by James Ackerson. April 26, 1975. Directed by Rod Nash.
CRYSTAL PIECES and THE LIFE by Cary Pepper, directed by Keith Aldrich; SIX BILLION TRILLION by Stan Kaplan, directed by Jerry Engelbach; THE SCISSORS by Irving Glusack. April 30, 1975.
HE WHO GETS SLAPPED by Leonid Andreyev. Directed by Mark Jesserun-Lobo.
FLATBUSH TOSCA by Harvey Fierstein. May 22, 1975. Directed by Harvey Tavel.
SEX TIMES TEN adapted from *La Ronde* by Arthur Schnitzler. May 28, 1975. Directed by Bruce Abrams; with NYTE Acting Company.

New York Theater Strategy. Organization of playwrights for the production of their works. Maria Irene Fornes, president.

LANGUAGE written and directed by David Starkweather. July 10, 1974. With Paul Lieber, Jon Polito, Karen Prager, Perrin Ferris, Donna Gable, George Milno, Shelley Rogers.
HOTHOUSE by Megan Terry. August 8, 1974.
AURORA (musical) by Maria Irene Fornes. September 2, 1974. With Ken Fitch, Bob Harders, Caroline Kava, Lee Kessman, James Leon, Ed Setrakian, Lola-Belle Smith, Gayel Swymer, Camille Tibaldeo.
HE WANTS SHIH! by Rochelle Owens. March, 1975. Directed by Lawrence Kornfeld.
KING HUMPY by Kenneth Bernard. April 24, 1975. Directed by Barbara Rosoff.
GILLES DE RAIS written and directed by William M. Hoffman. May 28, 1975.

The Nighthouse. Eclectic policy of outreaching theater. David Gaard, producer.

HOT HOT HOT written and directed by William Schlottman. June, 1974.
THE IMPORTANCE OF BEING EARNEST musical version of the Oscar Wilde play written and performed by Hot Peaches.
POE: FROM HIS LIFE AND MIND by Stanley Nelson. September, 1974. Directed by Chris Cooke; with Court Van Rooten, Joanne Morris, Charles Griffin, Naomi Riseman, Patricia Kelly, Walter Wright.
THE NIGHT THOREAU SPENT IN JAIL by Jerome Lawrence and Robert E. Lee. October, 1974. Directed by Robert Davison.
NERO by Richard Vetere. November, 1974. Directed by Anthony Napoli; with Anthony Rao, Richard Abbott, Sal Allocco, Nanci Nicholson, Stephanie Saldana, D. Alexander Huderski.
MALINI by Rabindranath Tagore. January 2, 1975. Directed by Pamela DeSio.
HOLOCAUST (musical) book and lyrics by Anthony Cipolla, music by Vincent Guidice. February, 1975. Directed by Anthony Cipolla.
THE PRIVATE LIFE OF THE MASTER RACE by Bertolt Brecht. March, 1975. Directed by Rafael Blanco.
STREET CALLS. March 28, 1975. Performed by Hot Peaches.
DIALOGUE WITH A NEGRO by Mario Fratti. April, 1975. Directed by D.C. Connell.
CALIGULA by Albert Camus. May, 1975. Directed by Donald Keyes.
DIVINE ANIMALS conceived by Seamus Murphy. May, 1975.
THE SCENE (program of one-act plays). June, 1975. Directed by Chris Cooke.

Octagon. Focus revivals of rarely-performed musicals, together with some original works. Donald Oliver, artistic director; Joseph Lillis, producer.

A FUNNY THING HAPPENED ON THE WAY TO THE FORUM (musical) book by Burt Shevelove and Larry Gelbart, music and lyrics by Stephen Sondheim. June 21, 1974. Directed by Joseph Lillis; with James Gallagher, Karen Magid, David Kerkov, Michael Brown, Michelle Rosenberg, Natalia Chuma.

THE APPLE TREE (musical) book by Jerry Bock, Sheldon Harnick, Jerome Coopersmith, music by Jerry Bock, lyrics by Sheldon Harnick. July 5, 1974. Directed by Michael Brown; with Frank Juliano, Arlene Miller, Mary Boyer, Tony Reilly, Rochelle Spron, Stephen Dunne.
ANYONE CAN WHISTLE (musical) book by Arthur Laurents, music and lyrics by Stephen Sondheim. July 21, 1974. Directed by Joseph Lillis; with Karen Magid, Barbara Hartman, Leslie Minski, James Gallagher, Philip Jostrom, Robert Polenz.
POT LUCK (musical revue) conceived by Joseph Lillis. July 24, 1974. With Barbara Hartman, Karen Magid, Natalia Chuma, Cliff Watters, Leslie Minski, Bill Hedge, Jolly King.
110 IN THE SHADE (musical) book by N. Richard Nash, music by Harvey Schmidt, lyrics by Tom Jones. August 14, 1974. Directed by Leslie Magerman; with Barbara Hartman, Daniel Gerrity, James Gallagher, Bill Hedge, Cliff Watters, Jon Winder, Diane Duncan.
DRAT! THE CAT! (musical) book and lyrics by Ira Levin, music by Milton Schafer. October 14, 1974. Directed by Joseph Lillis; with Stanley Carr, Philip Jostrom, Ed Prostak, Joanne Kaplan, Robin Jacober, Audrey Levine.
PARK (musical) book and lyrics by Paul Cherry, music by Lance Mulcahy. November 8, 1974. Directed by Anthony Baksa; with Michael Bahr, Irene Frances Kling, Reed Birney, Gloria Lambert, Larry Staroff, Diane Jerger.
YOU'RE A GOOD MAN CHARLIE BROWN (musical) book, music and lyrics by Clark Gesner. November 16, 1974. Directed by Peter Simpson; with Parks Hill, Judy Reed, Gordon Cantiello, Tom Flagg, Devon Summey, Beryl Mau.
ZORBA (revised version of the musical) book by Joseph Stein, music by John Kander, lyrics by Fred Ebb. November 20, 1974. Directed by Robert Nigro; with Jim Pappas.
KABARETT written and composed by Herbert Nelson. December 13, 1974.
THE SURVIVAL OF ST. JOAN (musical) book and lyrics by James Lineberger, music by Hank and Gary Ruffin. December 19, 1974. Directed by Ray Miller; with Vicki Bennett, Clancy Cherry, Greg Macosko, Michael More, Michael Penna, David Rambo, Naomi Robin.
THE RAY MILLER MIME SHOW devised and directed by Ray Miller. January 10, 1975. With Ray Miller, David Rambo.
KNICKERBOCKER HOLIDAY (musical) book and lyrics by Maxwell Anderson, music by Kurt Weill. January 19, 1975. Directed by Dallas Alinder; with Alexander Orfaly, John Almberg, Christine Andreas, Richard Niles, Douglas Fisher.
HOLLYWOOD HATTIE AND HER CELLULOID DREAM (musical) conceived, directed and choreographed by Jack Dyville. February 6, 1975. With Wanda Drew, Michael Petro, Joseph Tripolino, Noreen Bartolomeo, Gregg Weiler.
TURKEY SALAD (musical revue featuring songs and scenes from flop Broadway musicals) conceived and directed by John Weeks. February 19, 1975. With Rick Atwell, Joan Bell, Ronn Hansen, Ross Petty, Thea Ramsey, Marsha Warner.
THE KANDER AND EBB COLORING BOOK (musical revue) conceived and directed by Joseph Lillis. March 25, 1975. With Christopher Carroll, Carolann Mary, Timothy Staton, Barbara Hartman.
TURKEY SALAD RETOSSED (second edition of *Turkey Salad*). March 25, 1975.
THE HAPPY TIME (musical) book by N. Richard Nash, music by John Kander, lyrics by Fred Ebb. March 29, 1975. Directed by J. Perry McDonald; with Ross Petty, David Rambo, Richard Beck-Meyer.

Ontological-Hysteric Theater. Avant garde theater productions written, directed and designed by the group's founder, Richard Foreman.

PANDERING TO THE MASSES by Richard Foreman. January 9, 1975.

The Open Space in Soho. A project of The Open Space Theater Experiment, Inc., they hope to serve the growing community of artists and the public who frequent the many galleries in the area. Lynn Michaels, Harry Baum, directors.

THE REFUSAL by Ransom Jeffrey. November 8, 1974. Directed by Lynn Michaels; with John Merensky, Frank Biancamano, Floyd Curtis.
THE STEAK PALACE by Bruce Serlen. May 2, 1975. Directed by Lynn Michaels; with John Benson, William Russ, Scott Griffis, Molly Adams, Diana Funk, Barbara Ganbaum.

The People's Performing Company. New, socially significant musicals. Peter Copani, Vince Gugliotti, Denise Bonenfant, directors.

AMERICA AND ITS PEOPLE (musical) by Peter Copani, David McHugh. August, 1974. Directed by Bobby Pesola; with Martin Breeson, Julia Carmen, Angel Martin, Gary Nuendel, Gail Senes, Gwen Sumter.
THE BLIND JUNKIE (musical) by Peter Copani. Directed by Frank Carucci.
STREET JESUS (musical) written and directed by Peter Copani. November, 1974.

The Performance Group. Experiments with new, collaborative and non-verbal creative techniques. Richard Schechner, director.

MOTHER COURAGE AND HER CHILDREN by Bertolt Brecht. December, 1974. Directed by Richard Schechner.

Players' Workshop. Mixture of new and classical productions drawing on Lower East Side audiences. Clay Stevenson, director.

WHOSE GOT HIS OWN by Ron Milner. September, 1974. Directed by Clay Stevenson.
TRAPS by James Whiteen. November, 1974. Directed by Clay Stevenson.

Playwrights Horizons. Purpose is to give playwrights the opportunity to see their work produced by professionals in an atmosphere devoid of commercial pressure. Robert Moss, artistic director.

FROM HERE INSIDE MY HEAD by David Rogers. Directed by Bob O'Rourke.
COWBOY PICTURES by Larry Ketron. Directed by Robert Moss.
LITTLE BIT by Harley Hackett. Directed by Charles Briggs.
CARCASS CHROME by Dennis E. Hackin. January 30, 1975.
FIRST WEEK IN BOGOTA by Robert Cessna. February 15, 1975.
THE CATCH by Philip Valcour. February 21, 1975.
MISSION by Len Jenkin. March 1, 1975. Directed by Leland Moss.
AUGUSTA by Larry Ketron. March 7, 1975. Directed by David Black.
AN EVENING WITH MA BELL (program of one-act plays) by Tony Giordano. March 15, 1975. Directed by Joseph Cali.
THE EDSEL WAS A MISTAKE by Paul Hodes. March 21, 1975. Directed by Robert Lowe.
RHINEGOLD (musical) written and directed by Barry Keating and Jim Steinman. March 29, 1975.
DEMONS: THE POSSESSION OF MERCY SHORT by Robert Karmon. April 4, 1975. Directed by David Darlow; with Linda Calson, Fred Major, Bill Cortez, Blair Cutting, Elizabeth Jones, Robert McFarland.
THE CORONER'S PLOT by David Schumaker. April 12, 1975. Directed by Alfred Gingold.
CASSEROLE by Jack Heifner. April 18, 1975.
NEWYORKNEWYORK, an omnibus of ten plays celebrating life in New York, by Anne Burr, Dennis Andersen, Ed Cohen, Allan Knee, Larry Kramer, Philip Magdalany, Marsha Sheiness, Steven Shea, Martin Sherman. April 25, 1975.
GOING OVER by Robert Gordon. May 2, 1975.
BRAIN DAMAGE by Steven Shea. May 10, 1975. Directed by Paul Cooper.
THE HOUSE WHERE I WAS BORN by Dennis Andersen. May 16, 1975. Directed by Susan Einhorn.
BEETHOVEN/KARL by David Rush. May 24, 1975. Directed by Alfred Gingold.
UNTITLED by Marsha Sheiness. June 7, 1975.
THE COMPLAINT DEPT. CLOSES AT FIVE by Ed Cohen. June 21, 1975.

Portfolio. Non-profit company set up to provide a place to experiment with original musical material. Tom Jones, Harvey Schmidt, artistic directors.

PORTFOLIO REVUE by Tom Jones and Harvey Schmidt. December 6, 1974. With David Cryer, Jeanne Lucas, Kathrin King Segal, Tom Jones, Harvey Schmidt.
PHILEMON (musical) by Tom Jones and Harvey Schmidt. January 3, 1975. Directed by Lester Collins.
CELEBRATION (musical) by Tom Jones and Harvey Schmidt. January 31, 1975. Directed by Vernon Lusby; with Gene Foote, Michael Glenn-Smith, Virginia Gregory, Ted Thurston, Bruce Cryer.

THE BONE ROOM (musical) by Tom Jones and Harvey Schmidt. February 28, 1975. Directed by John Schak; with John Cunningham, Ray Stewart, Susan Watson.

Quaigh Theater. Primarily a playwrights' theater, devoted to the new playwright, the established contemporary playwright and the modern (post-1920) playwright. William H. Lieberson, artistic director.

THE SEDUCERS (musical) by Mario Fratti, music by Ed Scott. July, 1974. Directed by Will Lieberson; with Nick Angotti, Diana Davila, Chris Gampel, Annette Hunt, Thom Koutsoukos, Danton LaPenna, Garret Nichols, Ira Rappaport, Harris Shore.
15 MINUTES OF EVIDENCE by Richard Foreman. Directed by Kate Davy. FOUR CORNERS by Helen Duberstein. Directed by Bill Lentsch. THE INCREDIBLE JULIA by Jean Reavey. Directed by John Clarkson and Nada Kokotovic. ONE PIECE SMASH by Arthur Sainer. Directed by Geraldine Lust. May 1, 1975.
LORD TOM GOLDSMITH by Victor Lipton, directed by Thom Molyneaux. PAY ATTENTION TO THE RAVEL by Donald Kvares and BIRDS by William Kushner, directed by Curtiss W. Sayblack. May 29, 1975.

Queens Playhouse. Revivals and new plays at Queens's major theater. Joseph Kutrzeba, founder.

THE AMOROUS FLEA (musical) by Jerry Devine and Bruce Montgomery, based on Molière's *The School for Wives.* June 27, 1974. Directed by Clint Atkinson; with John High, Patti Allison, Warren Pincus.
ROOM SERVICE by John Murray and Allen Boretz. July 25, 1974. Directed by Lee Watson; with Shelley Berman.
COME BACK, LITTLE SHEBA by William Inge. August 22, 1974. Directed by Marshall W. Mason; with Jan Sterling, Gil Rogers, Trish Hawkins, Roger Hill, Jon Richards.
THEATER OF TOMORROW (Series of professional showcase productions): THE JEWISH PROSTITUTE by Irving Glusack. July 29, 1974. SARA AND THE SAX by Lewis John Carlino. MRS. MINTER by Donald Kvares and TOO MUCH ANTIPASTO by John Favicchio. August 26, 1974.
THE LIEUTENANT (musical) by Nitra Scharfman, Chuck Strand, Gene Curty. September 18, 1974. Directed by William Martin; with Eddie Mekka, Mike Champagne, Leonard Feiner, Jim Litten, Joel Powers.

Section Ten. New material developed through improvisation. Andrea Balis, artistic director.

A GREAT HOSS PISTOL by Omar Shapli. September, 1974. Directed by Andrea Balis.
INSIDE LULU by Ron Cowen. April 6, 1975. Directed by Andrea Balis; with Abigail Costello, Kathryn Harrold, Sara Christiansen, Charles Pegues.

The Shaliko Company. Environmental theater group based on the primacy of the audience-actor relationship. Leonardo Shapiro, director. (See its programs in the New York Shakespeare Public Theater entry in the "Plays Produced off Broadway" section of this volume.)

South Street Theater. Developing an outdoor environmental theater on Pier 17 at the South Street Seaport Museum. Michael Fischetti, artistic director.

MOBY DICK, adapted by Michael Fischetti. June 14, 1974. Directed by Jean Sullivan; with Maurice Mee, Nicole Clark, Francesca Poston, Robert A. Kelly, Lawrence R. Johnson, Henry Stanley.
STILL LIFE by Ferenc Molnar and LANDSCAPE by Harold Pinter. December, 1974. Directed by Michael Fischetti.
MAN AND WOMAN, AN ENTERTAINMENT staged by Jack Eddleman. January, 1975. With Michael Fischetti, Jean Sullivan.

Stage Directors and Choreographers Workshop. Experimental showcase operated by the directors' and choreographers' organization. Madolin Cervantes, director.

POSTSCRIPT by Merritt Abrash.
HERO by Ruth Stern.
BLACK JESUS by Kenneth Eulo.
MASHA by Tim Kelly, adapted from a short story by Anton Chekhov.

T. Schreiber Studio. Establishing a close bond with the audience with all productions, with the widest range possible. Terry Schreiber, director.

A MIDSUMMER NIGHT'S DREAM by William Shakespeare. June 6, 1974. Directed by Terry Schreiber.
MISS JULIE by August Strindberg and SUDDENLY last summer by Tennessee Williams. September, 1974. Directed by Terry Schreiber.
PLAYBOY OF THE WESTERN WORLD by John Millington Synge. November, 1974. Directed by Bob Hall.
PINOCCHIO (musical) by Richard Bone. November, 1974. Directed by Isaac Dostis.
JOE EGG by Peter Nichols. January, 1975. Directed by Terry Schreiber; with Kelly Fitzpatrick, Jennifer Reed, Tom Leo, Pat Lavelle.
WHAT THE BUTLER SAW by Joe Orton. March 1, 1975. Directed by Bob Hall.
HAMLET by William Shakespeare. May, 1975. Directed by Terry Schreiber.
ENTERTAINING MR. SLOANE by Joe Orton. June, 1975. Directed by Robert Hall.

Theater at Noon. Dedication to the idea that there is a place for the arts in the midst of work. Sari Weisman, managing director, Michael Feingold, artistic consultant.

TWO ON A BRIDGE: TWO BLIND BEGGARS and TWO FISHERMEN by Jacques Offenbach, translated and directed by Michael Feingold. October 28, 1974. With John Long, R. Mack Miller, Jim Cunningham.
LUDLOW FAIR by Lanford Wilson. November 11, 1974. Directed by Steven Robman; with Beth Dixon, Trisha Long.
LUNCHTIME RAG (musical program). December 2, 1974.
GET OUT OF MY HOUSE (songs of the 1920s, 1930s and 1940s). December 16, 1974. Directed by Theo Barnes; with Dorian Barth, Misty Barth, Bruce Hopkins, Julie Kurnitz, Bill Reynolds, Ira Siff.
MASTER CLASS by Jonathon Levy. January 13, 1975. With Martha Schlamme.
PIONEER by Megan Terry. January 27, 1975. Directed by Harvey Tavel; with Jayne Haynes, Harvey Fierstein.
THE ITALIAN LESSON by Ruth Draper. With Diana Belshaw.
BROWN BAG BALLADS (program of songs). March 3, 1975. With Peggy Atkinson, John Williams.
WEARY OF IT ALL (musical revue). March 17, 1975. With Dennis Deal, Trisha Long, Robert Polenz.
THE GOLD STANDARD by Kenneth Koch. April 7, 1975. Directed by Robert Gainer; with Thomas Barbour, Richard Hamburger.
A SPRING AFTERNOON OF SONG. May 5, 1975. With Shelle Ackerman.

Theater at St. Clements. New plays, play readings, workshops, Music Theater Lab, full musical productions, on a highly professional level. Larry Goossen, executive producer.

NUTS by Tom Topor. June, 1974. Directed by John Margulies; with Henry Calvert, Alexander Courtney, Lynn Oliver, Lee Sanders.
WATERGATE BIZARRE (33-hour marathon reading of Watergate tapes).
THE FALL AND REDEMPTION OF MAN by John Bowen. Directed by Tom Tarpey; with Robert Blumenfeld, Kenneth Campbell, Maury Chaykin, Vivien Ferrara, Peter Kingsley, Alvah Stanley, Holly Villaire.
THREE POEMS FOR THE THEATER and TENEMENTS written and directed by Andy Trumpetter. September, 1974.
WAITING FOR GODOT by Samuel Beckett. October 1, 1974. Directed by Terry Kiser; with Jane Hallaren, Carol Kane, Larry Block, Ron Seka, Phillip James.

FIGURES IN THE SAND (program of two one-act plays) by Nathan Teitel. October 9, 1975. Directed by Nick Havinga; with Kevin O'Connor, Carol Teitel.

THE ROBBER BRIDEGROOM, adaptation of Eudora Welty, by Alfred Uhry, music by Bob Waldman. November, 1974. Directed by Gerald Freedman.

KING OF THE UNITED STATES by Jean-Claude van Itallie, music by Richard Peaslee. November 19, 1974. Directed by Allan Albert.

ENTER A FREE MAN by Tom Stoppard. December 17, 1974. Directed by Brian Murray.

DOUBLE BILL by Honor Moore and Susan Ain. February, 1975.

JOE'S OPERA by Tom Mandel. March, 1975. Directed by Robert Allan Ackerman.

FROGS presented by The Medecine Show. March 13, 1975. Directed by James Barbosa.

SET FOR LIFE by Howard Richardson. March 17, 1975. (Staged reading.)

WORKERS by Tom Griffin. April 6, 1975. Directed by Bolen High.

WAKING UP TO BEAUTIFUL THINGS (musical portfolio of songs) by Jeffrey Roy. April 23, 1975. Directed by Allen Sobek.

THE RED BLUE-GRASS WESTERN FLYER SHOW (musical) book and lyrics by Conn Fleming, music by Clint Ballard Jr. May 2, 1975. Directed by Robert Brewer.

FIRE AND ICE by Robert Frost; PRIMORDIAL VOICES; THE WOMEN OF TRACHIS by Sophocles, translated by Ezra Pound. Presented by Jean Erdman's Theater of the Open Eye. May 13, 1975.

DUCK VARIATIONS by David Mamet. May 27, 1975. Directed by Albert Takazauckas.

Theater at The Lambs. See "Gene Frankel Theater Workshop."

Theater for the New City. Specializing in experimental productions. Crystal Field, artistic director.

CHILE '73 by Mario Fratti. June, 1974. Directed by Crystal Field; with George Bartenieff.

BLAKE'S DESIGN by Kenneth Brown. Directed by Ronald Roston; with Louis Plante, Anna Brennen.

THE GREAT BEAST AND THE CONDITION OF THE WORKER. Performed by Puppet Theater of War, Dragons & Children.

BLONDE ROOTS written and directed by Seth Allen. July, 1974. With Patricia Gaul, Randy Brecker, Florie Freshman.

AMNESIA by Michael Shaffer. Directed by Lad Brown; with Jaques Hausman.

HOOSICK FALLS by Jane DeLynn. August, 1974. Directed by Mary Thompson; with Anne Ashcroft, Anthony Baksa.

THREE STREET PLAYS: IN THE FACTORY, MINDING THE STORE, UNDERCOVER COP by Robert Nichols. August, 1974. Directed by Crystal Field.

LA BELLILOTE by Emilio Cubeiro. September, 1974. Directed by Chris Kapp.

NOT AFRAID OF FALLING written and directed by Avram Patt. October, 1974.

HIGH TIME by Alan Rossett. October, 1974. Directed by William E. Hunt.

RA-D-IO (WISDOM) OR SOPHIA: PART I by Richard Foreman. December, 1974. Directed by Crystal Field.

THE FAREWELL PARTY by Drew Kalter. Directed by Dennis Pearlstein.

THEY WANT PIZZA and WINTER IN ST. CLOUD by Donald Kvares. February, 1975. Directed by Ted Mornel.

ERIC BENTLEY IN CONCERT. February, 1975.

MONDAY NIGHT VARIETIES. February, 1975. Directed by Eve Packer.

CHARLEY CHESTNUT RIDES THE IRT by Arthur Sainer. Directed by Crystal Field.

THE B-BEAVER ANIMATION. Presented by Mabou Mines.

COME AND GO, PLAY and THE LOST ONE by Samuel Beckett. March, 1975. Performed by Mabou Mines.

THE GREAT FROG MONSTER written and directed by Barry Blitstein. April, 1975. With Joseph Zwerling, Ian Mamber.

MEMPHIS IS GONE (musical) by Dick Hobson. April 19, 1975.

FAT FELL DOWN by Dan Ellentuck. April 26, 1975. Directed by Susan Gregg; with Robert Castoire, Cathy Brewer-Moore, David Patch, Maury Chaykin, Eileen Fitzpatrick.

Theater Genesis. Writers' theater; production of new American plays. Walter Hadler, artistic director.

MALECON by David Garvin. June, 1974. Directed by Phillip Price; with John Branon, Norma Chatoff, Jerry Chesnut, Jaime Sanchez, William Sanderson, Brenda Smiley, Frank Thompson.
THE CHILEAN GAME written and directed by Omar Shapli. June 26, 1974. With Polly Brooks, Bill Kleinsmith, Dennis Krausnik, Linda Prout, Lynn Weinstein.
TYPHOID MARY OR AN ENEMA OF THE PEOPLE by Steven Shea. September 18, 1974. Directed by Edward Cohen.
THE FIRST AMENDMENT (revue) conceived and performed by Los Topos. October, 1974.
THE PIONEER and PRO GAME by Megan Terry. November, 1974. Directed by Harvey Tavel.
THE SILVER BEE by Walter Hadler. December, 1974. Directed by Daffi.
HIGH JOLLY by David Garvin. February, 1975. Directed by Tony Barsha; with Elizabeth Ballard, Michael Brody, Mallory Jones, Lee Kessman, Michael Winnsett.
AGAINST THE SUN by Robert Glaudini. March, 1975. Directed by Philip Minor; with Cindy Ames, John Branon, Adam Keefe, Bernie Passeltiner, Morris Lafon.
DERELICTION-4 by Blanche Oliak and EVE by Marcia Haufrecht. April, 1975. Directed by Don Blakely.
SUBREAL written and directed by Daffi. May, 1975.
LONELY LIVES HOSTROLL by Hector Rodriguez. Directed by Tito Goya and Rick August.
SONATA written and directed by Bill Duke.
RICHARD BROWN AND THE DRAGON written and directed by Michael Winnsett.

Theater of the Riverside Church. Maintains high professional standards. Arthur Bartow, administrative director.

EXPLETIVE DELETED by Eric Bentley (edited from Watergate transcripts). June 3, 1974.
LEAVING HOME by David French. November, 1974. Directed by Arthur Bartow; with Marilyn Chris, Lenka Peterson.
MISTER RUNAWAY by Lillian Atlan, translated by Marc Prensky. January, 1975. Directed by Arthur Bartow.
SHARK by T.J. Camp III. March, 1975. Directed by Dean Irby; with James Bond III, Albert Grand Eggleston III, Arnold Johnson, Venida Evans, Bruce Strickland.
PLATONOV by Anton Chekhov. April, 1975. Directed by Mark Ross.

Theater 77. New plays preferred. Purpose is to provide opportunities for playwrights and actors to entertain in needful institutions, to find appropriate commercial vehicles for the productions. Rod Clavery, Dolores McCullough, artistic directors.

DWINDLEBERRIES by Harvey Zuckerman. June, 1974. Directed by Bob Sohne.
THE SUBSTITUTE by David L. Young. Directed by Craig Barish.
THE BILLIARD PLAYERS by Clayelle Dalferes. Directed by Craig Barish.
HELLO OUT THERE by William Saroyan. Directed by Michael Hartig.
ENCOUNTER and SOMEONE'S CRYING by Jasper Oddo. Directed by B.J. Bohack.
THE MASTER PSYCHOANALYST by Stanley Nelson. Directed by Michael Donnelly.
MUSHROOMS by Donald Kvares. Directed by Ted Mornel.
THE WALRUS SAID by Cary Pepper. Directed by Rod Clavery.
MEMORIAL by Harvey Zuckerman. Directed by Dolores McCullough.

Thirteenth Street Repertory Company. The city's only musical company focusing on new work; also children's programs. Edith O'Hara, artistic director.

OUT CRY (new version) by Tennessee Williams. June, 1974. Directed by Laura Zucker.
LOVE SONGS by Bill Weeden, David Finkle. August, 1974. Directed by Henry Banister; with Josh Burton, Pamela Dunn, Donn Roger, Kim Carlson, Gordon Grody, Harriet Stahl. In repertory with 100 MILES FROM NOWHERE by Bill Solly, choreography by Brian MacDonald and SOLLY'S FOLLIES OF 1975 by Bill Solly. Directed by Peter Gorin.
ALLUME J'ETOUFFE (comedic revues) written and directed by Jean Belville.
ALL TALKING, ALL SINGING, ALL DANCING (revue) by Fred Smith, Jim Haskins. December, 1974. Directed by Kirby Lewellen.
BOY MEETS BOY (musical) book by Donald Ward, music and lyrics by Bill Solly. January, 1975. Directed by Ron Troutman.
A LEAN AND HUNGRY PRIEST (musical) book and lyrics by Warren Kliewer, music by Don Newmark. March, 1975. Directed by Jim Payne.

THE LAST CABARET SHOW (revue) conceived and directed by Mordecai Newman. May, 1975.

Time and Space, Ltd. Experiments in writing and production. Linda Mussman, artistic director.

THE BIRTHDAY PARTY by Harold Pinter. September 14, 1974. Directed by Linda Mussman; with John Mintun, Sandra Nye Moran, Ron Harrington, Catherine Henry Lamm, Robert Brandi, Dennis Malvasi.
GHOSTS by Henrik Ibsen. Directed by Linda Mussman.
THE EXCEPTION AND THE RULE and ELEPHANT CALF by Bertolt Brecht (translated by Eric Bentley). January, 1975. Directed by Linda Mussman.
ENDGAME by Samuel Beckett. March, 1975. Directed by Linda Mussman.
EVERYTHING IS THE SAME AND EVERYTHING IS DIFFERENT, works by Virginia Woolf, Gertrude Stein, Samuel Beckett. April, 1975. Directed by Linda Mussman.

Triad Playwrights Company. Non-profit playwrights' theater that develops and produces new plays in existing performance spaces. Richard Tirotla, managing director.

THE GIRL WHO LOVED THE BEATLES by D.B. Gilles. July 9, 1974 and December 16, 1974. Directed by Alan Mixon; with Jane Campbell, Eugene Blythe.

Triangle Theater Company. Non-commercial, non-profit theater workshop. Darryl Hickman, artistic director; Pamela Lincoln, producer.

CHIP OFF OLYMPUS by Jules Tasca. Directed by Darryl Hickman.
FUNERAL PARTY by Ron McLarty. May, 1975. Directed by Darryl Hickman.

Urban Arts Corp. Dedicated to the development of theater arts and crafts skills in the black community. Vinnette Carroll, artistic director.

THE UPS AND DOWNS OF THEOPHILUS MAITLAND (musical) by Vinnette Carroll, music by Micki Grant. November 13, 1974. Directed by Vinnette Carroll.
AN EVENING OF BLACK FOLKTALES by Micki Grant. November, 1974. Directed by Vinnette Carroll.
LOVE POWER, theater event conceived by Vinnette Carroll and Micki Grant. December, 1974.
CROESUS AND THE WITCH written and directed by Vinnette Carroll, music and lyrics by Micki Grant. April, 1975.

U.R.G.E.N.T. New works (world premieres) and revivals of plays of social and political relevance. Ronald Muchnick and Nathan George, directors.

OVERNIGHT by William Inge. July 11, 1974. Directed by Nathan George; with William Mooney, Carol Potter, Arthur Roberts.
BIG FISH, LITTLE FISH by Hugh Wheeler. September 11, 1974. Directed by Richard Altman; with Mark Fleishman, Richard Seff, Ruth Livingston.
A SONG FOR NOW (revue of political and social songs from Broadway shows). October 22, 1974. Directed by Edward Roll.
IN HONORED MEMORY OF TED AND SPARKY written and directed by Jay Broad. December, 1974. (Revised version of The Killdeer).
EDGAR ALLEN POE: A CONDITION OF SHADOW (one-man show) by Jerry Rockwood. February, 1975.
e.e. AS IS (evening of e.e. cummings) adapted by William Mooney. March, 1975. Directed by Henry Kaplan; with William Mooney.
MIDNIGHT SPECIAL by Clifford Mason. April 30, 1975. Directed by Clifford Goodwin.

Voices, Inc. Productions organized for touring colleges and universities. Josephine Jackson, artistic director.

HARLEM HEYDAY by Josephine Jackson, directed by Roger Furman, and JOURNEY INTO BLACKNESS by Josephine Jackson, directed by Rod Rogers. September, 1974.

West Side Community Repertory Theater. Contemporary approaches to classical plays. Andres Castro, director (and director of all productions).

A DOLL'S HOUSE by Henrik Ibsen. September, 1974.
THE MARRIAGE OF FIGARO by Beaumarchais . February, 1975.
MRS. WARREN'S PROFESSION by George Bernard Shaw. March, 1975.
MARY STUART by Schiller. July, 1975.

Westbeth Playwrights' Feminist Collective. Develop artists and audiences for feminist theater. Delores Walker, artistic administrative director, Nancy Rhodes, producing director.

MEDEA reinterpreted by Gloria Albee. November, 1974. Directed by Pat Carmichael.
BLUE WOMEN by Susan Bruno; TOUCHPOINT by The Unity Players; Bread and Roses Company (workshop readings).
JUMPIN' SALTY (vignettes) by Gwendolyn Gunn, Delores Walker, Gayle Austin, Linda Kline, Sally Ordway, Chryse Maile, lyrics by Eve Merriam. May, 1975. Directed by Lynn Guerra.

Workshop of the Players Art (WPA Theater). 200-member company presenting works of quality, both traditional and experimental. Harry Orzello, artistic director; Daniel P. Dietrich, co-producer.

TRIAL BY JURY by Gilbert and Sullivan. June 1, 1974. Directed by Cliff Flanders.
LES DEUX AVEUGLES (THE TWO BLIND MEN) by Jacques Offenbach. June, 1974. Directed by James Nicola.
THIRD AMERICAN NEW PLAYS FESTIVAL schedule included: AND THE HONOR BE MINE by Sam David Bittman, directed by Dakota DeSmet; CURTAIN CALL by Roma Greth, directed by Pat Mullen; DEAR JOHN by Steven Somkin, directed by Zoya Khachadourian; THE DREAMER written and directed by Gabriel Oshen; FINAL RITE written and directed by Dennis Hackin; IS THERE A DOCTOR IN THE HOUSE? written and directed by Joseph Renard; L'ETAT by Jeannine O'Reilly; MEN by Stephen Holt, directed by Leonard Peters; MY NEXT GUEST IS by Thomas Molyneaux, directed by Eric Concklin; OFFENDING THE AUDIENCE by Peter Handke, directed by Ruis Woertendyke; OLD FAITHFUL by Christopher Mathewson, directed by Hugh Gittens; IN THE PUBLIC INTEREST (reading of Watergate transcripts) staged by Craig Barish; THE SAME OLD SPOT by Walter Corwin; TERROR by Hugh Gittens.
CRAIG'S WIFE by George Kelly. October, 1974. Directed by Leonard Peters; with Cara Duff-MacCormick.
ARCH written and directed by Joseph Renard.
GERONIMO by John Stuehr. November, 1974. Directed by Jamie Brown.
THEATER KALAMBUR (Polish Theater Company's only N.Y. appearance).
THE AMERICANS (evening of well-known American one-act plays): THE MOON OF THE CARIBBEES by Eugene O'Neill, directed by Ruis Woertendyke; DOROTHY PARKER—A MONTAGE, directed by John Henry Davis; TROUBLE IN TAHITI by Leonard Bernstein; I CAN'T IMAGINE TOMORROW by Tennessee Williams, directed by Craig Barish.
UNCLE TOM'S CABIN. February, 1975. Directed by Hugh Gittens; with Robert Stocking, Francine Middleton.
DUCKLING by Jeannine O'Reilly. February, 1975. With Dan Durning, Karen Hendel, Amy Lerner, Joe Pichette.
PICNIC by William Inge. April 4, 1975. Directed by Michael Dennis Moore; with Amanda Davies, Dale Robinette, Ann Whiteside, James Hillbrandt.
THE GHOST CONVENTION by Susan Dworkin. May 14, 1975. Directed by Leonard Peters.

The York Players. Each season, three or four productions of classics are mounted with professional casts; concerned with bringing classics to neighborhood residents. Janet Hayes Walker, artistic director.

GIDEON by Paddy Chayefsky. November, 1974. Directed by Janet Hayes Walker.
SCHOOL FOR WIVES by Molière. February, 1975. Directed by Janet Hayes Walker; with Douglas Barden, Alan Blue, Anne Dockery, Merle Louise, John Newton, Dickson Shaw, Jim Sprague, Michael Sullivan, Ted Theoharous.
NIGHT MUST FALL by Emlyn Williams. April, 1975. Directed by Janet Hayes Walker.

CAST REPLACEMENTS AND TOURING COMPANIES

Compiled by Stanley Green

The following is a list of the more important cast replacements in productions which opened in previous years, but were still playing in New York during a substantial part of the 1974–75 season; or were still on a first-class tour in 1974–75; or opened in New York in 1974–75 and went on tour during the season (casts of first-class touring companies of previous seasons which were no longer playing in 1974–75 appear in previous *Best Plays* volumes of appropriate years).

The name of each major role is listed in *italics* beneath the title of the play in the first column. In the second column directly opposite appears the name of the actor who created the role in the original New York production (whose opening date appears in *italics* at the top of the column). Indented immediately beneath the original actor's name are the names of subsequent New York replacements, together with the date of replacement when available.

The third column gives information about first-class touring companies, including London companies (produced under the auspices of their original Broadway managements). When there is more than one roadshow company, #1, #2, etc., appear before the name of the performer who created the role in each company (and the city and date of each company's first performance appears in *italics* at the top of the column). Their subsequent replacements are also listed beneath their names, with dates when available.

A note on bus-truck touring companies appears at the end of this section.

BAD HABITS

N.Y. Off-Bway 2/4/74
N.Y. Bway 5/5/74

Dolly Scupp; Becky Hedges Doris Roberts
 Doris Belock
 Doris Roberts 6/74
 Sasha Von Scherler 9/4/74

Jason Pepper; Hugh Gumbs Paul Benedict
 Paul B. Price
 John Heffernan 6/74

CANDIDE (revival)

Brooklyn 12/11/73
New York 3/10/74

Dr. Pangloss Lewis J. Stadlen
 Charles Kimbrough 1/20/75

Candide Mark Baker

Cunegonde Maureen Brennan

Old Lady	June Gable
Paquette	Deborah St. Darr
Maximilian	Sam Freed

CAT ON A HOT TIN ROOF (revival)

	New York 9/26/74	*Washington 2/12/75*
Margaret	Elizabeth Ashley	Elizabeth Ashley
Brick	Keir Dullea Michael Zaslow 2/3/75	Michael Zaslow
Big Daddy	Fred Gwynne	Fred Gwynne
Big Mama	Kate Reid	Kate Reid

THE FANTASTICKS

New York 5/3/60

El Gallo	Jerry Orbach
	Gene Rupert
	Bert Convy
	John Cunningham
	Don Stewart 1/63
	David Cryer
	Keith Charles 10/63
	John Boni 1/13/65
	Jack Mette 9/14/65
	George Ogee
	Keith Charles
	Tom Urich 8/30/66
	John Boni 10/5/66
	Jack Crowder 6/13/67
	Nils Hedrick 9/19/67
	Keith Charles 10/9/67
	Robert Goss 11/7/67
	Joe Bellomo 3/11/68
	Michael Tartel 7/8/69
	Donald Billett 6/70
	Joe Bellomo 2/15/72
	David Rexroad 6/73
	David Snell 12/73
	Hal Robinson 4/2/74
	Chapman Roberts 7/30/74
	David Brummel 2/18/75

Luisa	Rita Gardner
	Carla Huston
	Liza Stuart 12/61
	Eileen Fulton
	Alice Cannon 9/62
	Royce Lenelle
	B.J.Ward12/1/74
	Leta Anderson 7/13/65
	Carole Demas 11/22/66
	Leta Anderson 8/7/67
	Carole Demas 9/4/67

Anne Kaye 5/28/68
Carolyn Magnini 7/29/69
Virginia Gregory 7/27/70
Leta Anderson
Marty Morris 3/7/72
Sharon Werner 8/1/72
Leilani Johnson 7/73
Sharon Werner 12/73
Sarah Rice 6/24/74

Matt
Kenneth Nelson
Gino Conforti
Jack Blackton 10/63
Paul Giovanni
Ty McConnell
Richard Rothbard
Gary Krawford
Bob Spencer 9/5/64
Erik Howell 6/28/66
Gary Krawford 12/12/67
Steve Skiles 2/6/68
Craig Carnelia 1/69
Erik Howell 7/18/69
Samuel D. Ratcliffe 8/5/69
Michael Glenn-Smith 5/26/70
Jimmy Dodge 9/20/70
Geoffrey Taylor 8/31/71
Erik Howell 3/14/72
Michael Glenn-Smith 6/13/72
Phil Killian 7/4/72
Richard Lincoln 9/72
Bruce Cryer 7/24/73
Phil Killian 9/11/73
Michael Glenn-Smith 6/17/74
Ralph Bruneau 10/29/74

Note: As of May 31, 1975, 23 actors had played the role of El Gallo, 16 actresses had played Luisa and 19 actors had played Matt.

GODSPELL

	New York 5/17/71	*Pittsburgh 10/27/72*
Jesus	Stephen Nathan	Mark Shera
	Andy Rohrer 6/6/72	Robert Brandon
	Don Hamilton	Tom Rolfing
	Ryan Hilliard	
	Don Scardino 1/73	
	Jeremy Sage 2/74	
	Don Scardino	
	Tom Rolfing 8/74	
Judas	David Haskell	Mark Ganzel
	Bart Braverman 5/72	Tom Rolfing
	Lloyd Bremseth	Michael Hoit
	Don Scardino	
	Michael Hoit 4/75	

Note: This list of cast changes does not include numerous companies of *Godspell* organized to play single engagements in single cities. During the 1974–75 New York season casting of the major roles changed so often that the record was discontinued.

GREASE

	New York 2/14/72	*New Haven 1/22/73*

Danny Zuko	Barry Bostwick
	  Jeff Conaway 6/73
	  John Lansing 11/74
		Jeff Conaway
		  Barry Bostwick 6/73

Sandy Dumbrowski	Carole Demas
	  Ilene Graff 3/73
		Pamela Adams
		  Candice Earley

Betty Rizzo	Adrienne Barbeau
	  Elaine Petrokoff 3/73
	  Randee Heller 5/74
		Judy Kaye

THE HOT L BALTIMORE

	New York 3/22/73

Jackie	Mari Gorman
	  Jennifer Harmon 10/24/73
	  Lisa Jacobson

Bill	Judd Hirsch
	  David Groh
	  Joseph Stern
	  William Wise 7/30/74

Mr. Katz	Antony Tenuta Larry Spinelli 11/74

Girl	Trish Hawkins
	  Faith Catlin
	  Heather MacRae 10/1/74
	  Penny Peyser 5/27/75

Suzy	Stephanie Gordon Jane Lowry 1/14/75

IRENE (revival)

	New York 3/13/73	*Chicago 9/11/74*

Irene O'Dare	Debbie Reynolds
	  Jane Powell 2/6/74
	  Patricia Peadon 6/74
	  Jane Powell 6/74
	  Debbie Reynolds 9/2/74
		Debbie Reynolds
		  Jane Powell 12/28/74

Mrs. O'Dare	Patsy Kelly
	  Mary McCarty 8/2/73
	  Patsy Kelly 8/20/73
		Patsy Kelly

Madam Lucy	George S. Irving
	  Hans Conried 6/27/74
		Hans Conried
		  Lee Wallace 1/27/75

Donald Marshall	Monte Markham
	  Ron Husmann 6/4/73
		Ron Husmann
		  David Holliday

Emmeline Marshall	Ruth Warrick	Ruth Warrick Constance Carpenter 1/15/75
Jane Burke	Janie Sell Dottie Frank	Bette Glenn

Helen McFudd	Carmen Alvarez Patti Karr	Carole Bishop Kathryn Sandy
Ozzie Babson	Ted Pugh	Jess Richards

A LITTLE NIGHT MUSIC

	New York 2/25/73	*#1 Philadelphia 2/26/74* *#2 London 4/15/75*
Desiree Armfeldt	Glynis Johns	#1 Jean Simmons #2 Jean Simmons
Fredrik Egerman	Len Cariou William Daniels 2/25/74	#1 George Lee Andrews #2 Joss Ackland
Madame Armfeldt	Hermione Gingold	#1 Margaret Hamilton #2 Hermione Gingold
Count Carl-Magnus	Laurence Guittard	#1 Ed Evanko #2 David Kernan
Countess Charlotte	Patricia Elliott	#1 Andra Akers #2 Maria Aitken
Anne Egerman	Victoria Mallory	#1 Virginia Pulos #2 Veronica Page
Henrik Egerman	Mark Lambert	#1 Stephen Lehew #2 Terry Mitchell
Petra	D. Jamin-Bartlett	#1 Mary Ann Chinn #2 Diane Langton

THE MAGIC SHOW

	New York 5/28/74	*Boston 12/17/74*
Doug*	Doug Henning	Peter DePaula
Cal	Dale Soules	Pippa Pearthree
Charmin	Anita Morris	Hester Lewellen
Feldman	David Ogden Stiers Kenneth Kimmins 1/75	Paul Keith

*For tour, name of character was changed to Peter.

A MOON FOR THE MISBEGOTTEN

	New York 12/29/73	*Los Angeles 11/25/74*
Josie Hogan	Colleen Dewhurst	Colleen Dewhurst
James Tyrone Jr.	Jason Robards	Jason Robards
Phil Hogan	Ed Flanders Tom Clancy 5/20/74	Tom Clancy

MOONCHILDREN (revival)

	New York 11/4/73	*Boston 4/25/74*
Norman	Michael Sacks Lawrie Driscoll 7/74	Anthony McKay
Cathy	Carol Willard Ellen Barber 7/74	Jobeth Williams Elaine Kilden
Dick	Robert Phelps David Haskell 7/74	David Haskell Rod Gibbons 7/74
Bob Rettie	Richard Cox Don Scardino 7/74 Douglas Anderson 8/5/74	Don Scardino Tom Leopold 7/74

MY FAT FRIEND

	New York 3/31/74	*#1 Detroit 12/10/74* *#2 Philadelphia 5/19/75*
Vicky	Lynn Redgrave	#1 Lynn Redgrave #2 Tammy Grimes
Henry	George Rose	#1 George Rose #2 George Rose
James	John Lithgow	#1 John Lithgow #2 Gary Tomlin

NOEL COWARD IN TWO KEYS

	New York 2/28/74	*Ft. Lauderdale 1/13/75*
Maud Caragnani; *Carlotta Gray*	Anne Baxter	Anne Baxter
Verner Conklin; *Hugo Latymer*	Hume Cronyn	Hume Cronyn
Anna-Mary Conklin; *Hilde Latymer*	Jessica Tandy	Jessica Tandy

OF MICE AND MEN (revival)

	New York 12/18/74	*Washington 3/12/75*
George	Kevin Conway	Kevin Conway
Lennie	James Earl Jones	James Earl Jones

PIPPIN

	New York 10/23/72
Pippin	John Rubinstein Michael Rupert 11/74
Charles	Eric Berry
Catherine	Jill Clayburgh Betty Buckley 6/11/73

| *Fastrada* | Leland Palmer
Priscilla Lopez 1/6/74
Patti Karr 8/5/74 |

| *Berthe* | Irene Ryan
Lucie Lancaster 4/73
Dorothy Stickney 6/11/73
Lucie Lancaster 7/74 |

| *Leading Player* | Ben Vereen
Northern J. Calloway 2/18/74
Ben Vereen 5/7/74
Samuel E. Wright 12/74 |

PRETZELS

	New York 12/16/74	*Detroit 5/5/75*
Jane	Jane Curtin	Jane Curtin
John/Christopher	John Forster	Christopher Bankey
Tim	Timothy Jerome	Timothy Jerome
Judy/Sandy	Judy Kahan	Sandy Faison

RAISIN

	New York 10/18/73
Lena Younger	Virginia Capers
Walter Lee Younger	Joe Morton
Ruth Younger	Ernestine Jackson
Travis Younger	Ralph Carter Paul Carrington 9/3/74 Darren Green 11/74
Bobo Jones	Ted Ross Irving D. Barnes 10/1/74

SEASCAPE

	New York 1/26/75	*Los Angeles 4/2/75*
Nancy	Deborah Kerr	Deborah Kerr
Charlie	Barry Nelson	Barry Nelson William Prince 4/7/75 Barry Nelson 4/14/75
Leslie	Frank Langella	Frank Langella
Sarah	Maureen Anderman	Maureen Anderman

SUGAR

	New York 4/9/72	*Los Angeles 9/3/74*
Jerry	Robert Morse	Robert Morse

Joe	Tony Roberts	Larry Kert
Osgood Fielding Jr.	Cyril Ritchard	Gale Gordon

THIEVES

	New York 4/7/74	
Sally Cramer	Marlo Thomas	
Martin Cramer	Richard Mulligan	
Charlie	Dick Van Patten Pierre Epstein 5/27/74	
Nancy	Ann Wedgeworth Louise Lasser 10/74 Ann Wedgeworth 11/74	

WHAT THE WINE-SELLERS BUY

	New York 2/14/74	*Chicago 3/11/75*
Rico	Dick A. Williams	Gilbert Lewis
Steve Carlton	Glynn Turman	Herb Rice
Mae Harris	Loretta Greene	Loretta Greene

WHEN YOU COMIN' BACK, RED RYDER?

	New York 12/6/73
Stephen	Bradford Dourif John Lisbon Wood 3/74 Christopher Curry
Teddy	Kevin Conway Mark Medoff 7/9/74

WORDS AND MUSIC

New York 4/16/74

Sammy Cahn

Kelly Garrett
  Kay Cole

Shirley Lemmon

Jon Peck

BUS-TRUCK TOURS

These are touring productions designed for maximum mobility and ease of handling in one-night and split-week stands (with occasional engagements of a week or more). Among shows on tour in the season of 1974–75 were the following bus-truck troupes:

Bil Baird's Marionette Theater (N.Y. State Arts Council tour), six cities, 4/20/75–5/10/75
Don Juan in Hell with Ricardo Montalban, Myrna Loy, Edward Mulhare, 92 cities, 9/19/74–2/22/75

Fiddler on the Roof with Bob Carroll, 68 cities, 1/21/75–4/21/75
Give 'Em Hell, Harry with James Whitmore, 11 cities (some first-class bookings), 3/19/75–6/15/75
I Am a Woman with Viveca Lindfors, 58 cities, 10/1/74–12/15/74
The Member of the Wedding, 6 cities, 4/9/75–5/3/75
Move Over, Mrs. Markham with Julia Meade, 46 cities, 9/18/74–12/12/74
Oh, Coward with Patricia Morison, 43 cities, 1/6/75–3/22/75
Pippin, 91 cities, 9/20/74–4/6/75
The River Niger, 44 cities, 1/14/75–3/23/75
Seesaw with John Raitt, 68 cities, 9/20/74–2/15/75
The Sunshine Boys, with Robert Alda/Eddie Bracken, Arny Freeman, 92 cities, 10/11/74–4/13/75

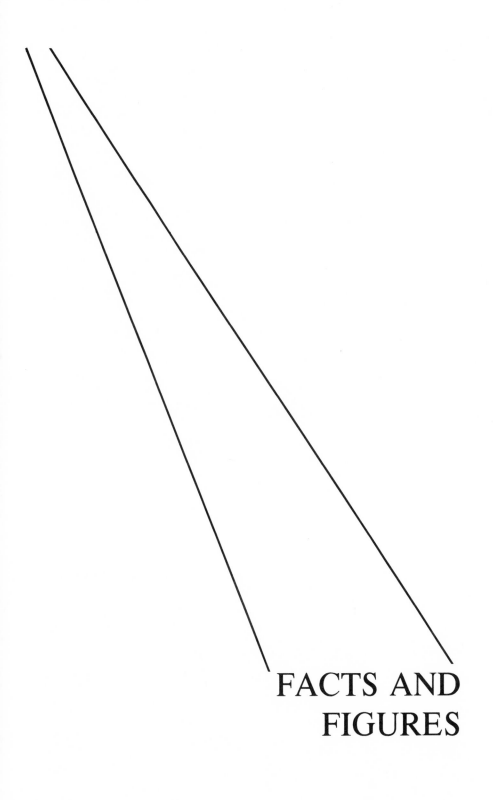

FACTS AND FIGURES

LONG RUNS ON BROADWAY

The following shows have run 500 or more continuous performances in a single production, usually the first, not including previews or extra non-profit performances, allowing for vacation layoffs and special one-booking engagements, but not including return engagements after a show has gone on tour. Where there are title similarities, the production is identified as follows: (p) straight play version, (m) musical version, (r) revival.

THROUGH MAY 31, 1975

(PLAYS MARKED WITH ASTERISK WERE STILL PLAYING JUNE 1, 1975)

Plays	Number Performances	Plays	Number Performances
Fiddler on the Roof	3,242	Cabaret	1,165
Life With Father	3,224	Mister Roberts	1,157
Tobacco Road	3,182	Annie Get Your Gun	1,147
Hello, Dolly!	2,844	The Seven Year Itch	1,141
My Fair Lady	2,717	Butterflies Are Free	1,128
Man of La Mancha	2,328	*Pippin	1,113
Abie's Irish Rose	2,327	Pins and Needles	1,108
Oklahoma!	2,212	Plaza Suite	1,097
South Pacific	1,925	Kiss Me, Kate	1,070
Harvey	1,775	Don't Bother Me, I Can't Cope	1,065
Hair	1,750	The Pajama Game	1,063
Born Yesterday	1,642	The Teahouse of the August Moon	1,027
Mary, Mary	1,572	Damn Yankees	1,019
The Voice of the Turtle	1,557	Never Too Late	1,007
Barefoot in the Park	1,530	Any Wednesday	982
Mame (m)	1,508	A Funny Thing Happened on the Way to the Forum	964
Arsenic and Old Lace	1,444	The Odd Couple	964
The Sound of Music	1,443	Anna Lucasta	957
How To Succeed in Business Without Really Trying	1,417	Kiss and Tell	956
Hellzapoppin	1,404	Bells Are Ringing	924
*Grease	1,375	The Moon Is Blue	924
The Music Man	1,375	Luv	901
Funny Girl	1,348	Applause	896
Oh! Calcutta!	1,314	Can-Can	892
Angel Street	1,295	Carousel	890
Lightnin'	1,291	Hats Off to Ice	889
Promises, Promises	1,281	Fanny	888
The King and I	1,246	Follow the Girls	882
Cactus Flower	1,234	Camelot	873
Sleuth	1,222	The Bat	867
1776	1,217	My Sister Eileen	864
Guys and Dolls	1,200		

415

Plays	Number Performances	Plays	Number Performances
No, No, Nanette (r)	861	Peg o' My Heart	692
Song of Norway	860	The Children's Hour	691
A Streetcar Named Desire	855	Purlie	688
Comedy in Music	849	Dead End	687
That Championship Season	844	The Lion and the Mouse	686
You Can't Take It With You	837	White Cargo	686
La Plume de Ma Tante	835	Dear Ruth	683
Three Men on a Horse	835	East Is West	680
The Subject Was Roses	832	Come Blow Your Horn	677
Inherit the Wind	806	The Most Happy Fella	676
No Time for Sergeants	796	The Doughgirls	671
Fiorello!	795	The Impossible Years	670
Where's Charley?	792	Irene	670
The Ladder	789	Boy Meets Girl	669
Forty Carats	780	Beyond the Fringe	667
The Prisoner of Second		Who's Afraid of Virginia	
Avenue	780	Woolf?	664
Oliver	774	*Raisin	658
State of the Union	765	Blithe Spirit	657
The First Year	760	A Trip to Chinatown	657
You Know I Can't Hear You		The Women	657
When the Water's Running	755	Bloomer Girl	654
Two for the Seesaw	750	The Fifth Season	654
Death of a Salesman	742	Rain	648
Sons o' Fun	742	Witness for the Prosecution	645
Gentlemen Prefer Blondes	740	Call Me Madam	644
The Man Who		Janie	642
Came to Dinner	739	The Green Pastures	640
Call Me Mister	734	Auntie Mame (p)	639
West Side Story	732	A Man for All Seasons	637
High Button Shoes	727	The Fourposter	632
Finian's Rainbow	725	Two Gentlemen	
Claudia	722	of Verona (m)	627
The Gold Diggers	720	The Tenth Man	623
Jesus Christ Superstar	720	Is Zat So?	618
Carnival	719	Anniversary Waltz	615
The Diary of Anne Frank	717	The Happy Time (p)	614
I Remember Mama	714	Separate Rooms	613
Tea and Sympathy	712	Affairs of State	610
Junior Miss	710	Star and Garter	609
Last of the Red Hot Lovers	706	The Student Prince	608
Company	705	Sweet Charity	608
Seventh Heaven	704	Bye Bye Birdie	607
Gypsy (m)	702	Irene (r)	604
The Miracle Worker	700	Broadway	603
Cat on a Hot Tin Roof	694	Adonis	603
Li'l Abner	693	Street Scene (p)	601

Plays	Number Performances	Plays	Number Performances
Kiki	600	Milk and Honey	543
Flower Drum Song	600	Within the Law	541
A Little Night Music	600	The Music Master	540
Don't Drink the Water	598	Pal Joey (r)	540
Wish You Were Here	598	What Makes Sammy Run?	540
A Society Circus	596	The Sunshine Boys	538
Blossom Time	592	What a Life	538
The Me Nobody Knows	586	The Unsinkable Molly Brown	532
The Two Mrs. Carrolls	585	The Red Mill (r)	531
Kismet	583	A Raisin in the Sun	530
Detective Story	581	The Solid Gold Cadillac	526
Brigadoon	581	Irma La Douce	524
No Strings	580	The Boomerang	522
Brother Rat	577	Follies	521
Show Boat	572	Rosalinda	521
The Show-Off	571	The Best Man	520
Sally	570	Chauve-Souris	520
Golden Boy (m)	568	*Candide (r)	519
One Touch of Venus	567	Blackbirds of 1928	518
Happy Birthday	564	Sunny	517
Look Homeward, Angel	564	Victoria Regina	517
The Glass Menagerie	561	Half a Sixpence	511
I Do! I Do!	560	The Vagabond King	511
Wonderful Town	559	The New Moon	509
Rose Marie	557	The World of Suzie Wong	508
Strictly Dishonorable	557	The Rothschilds	507
A Majority of One	556	Sugar	505
The Great White Hope	556	Shuffle Along	504
Toys in the Attic	556	Up in Central Park	504
Sunrise at Campobello	556	Carmen Jones	503
Jamaica	555	The Member of the Wedding	501
Stop the World—I Want to Get Off	555	Panama Hattie	501
Florodora	553	Personal Appearance	501
Ziegfeld Follies (1943)	553	Bird in Hand	500
Dial "M" for Murder	552	Room Service	500
Good News	551	Sailor, Beware!	500
Let's Face It	547	Tomorrow the World	500

LONG RUNS OFF BROADWAY

Plays	Number Performances	Plays	Number Performances
*The Fantasticks	6,281	Jacques Brel	1,847
The Threepenny Opera	2,611	*Godspell	1,684

Plays	Number Performances	Plays	Number Performances
You're a Good Man		Scuba Duba	692
Charlie Brown	1,597	The Knack	685
The Blacks	1,408	The Balcony	672
Little Mary Sunshine	1,143	America Hurrah	634
El Grande de Coca-Cola	1,114	Hogan's Goat	607
One Flew Over the		The Trojan Women (r)	600
Cuckoo's Nest (r)	1,025	Krapp's Last Tape &	
The Boys in the Band	1,000	The Zoo Story	582
*The Hot l Baltimore	943	The Dumbwaiter &	
Your Own Thing	933	The Collection	578
Curley McDimple	931	Dames at Sea	575
Leave It to Jane (r)	928	The Crucible (r)	571
The Mad Show	871	The Iceman Cometh (r)	565
The Effect of Gamma Rays on		The Hostage (r)	545
Man-in-the-Moon Marigolds	819	Six Characters in Search of an	
A View From the Bridge (r)	780	Author (r)	529
The Boy Friend (r)	763	The Dirtiest Show in	
The Pocket Watch	725	Town	509
The Connection	722	Happy Ending & Day of	
Adaptation & Next	707	Absence	504
Oh! Calcutta!	704	The Boys From Syracuse (r)	500
*Let My People Come	700		

DRAMA CRITICS CIRCLE VOTING, 1974–75

The New York Drama Critics Circle voted the British play *Equus* the best play of the season on a second ballot weighted to produce a consensus measured by points (with 3 points given to each critic's first choice, 2 for second and 1 for third), after no play received the necessary majority of first choices on the first ballot. *Equus* won with 34 points, with other points distributed as follows: *The Island* (16), *The National Health* (12), *The Taking of Miss Janie* (10), *Sizwe Banzi is Dead* (10), *Seascape* (10), *Same Time, Next Year* (4), *Summerfolk*, a Maxim Gorky play declared eligible by vote of the Circle members because this was its first New York production (4), *Saturday Sunday Monday* (3), *Absurd Person Singular* (2) *Kid Champion* (2), *Yentl the Yeshiva Boy* (2), *Black Picture Show* (1), *The First Breeze of Summer* (1), *London Assurance* (1), *Mert & Phil* (1), *The Ritz* (1).

Twenty of the 23 Circle members participated in the voting, four (Harold Clurman, Brendan Gill, Walter Kerr and Richard Watts Jr.) by proxy, which in some cases listed first choices only and therefore couldn't be included in the point-system second-ballot voting. The Circle members' 20 first choices for the best play of the season were distributed as follows: *Equus* (8)—John Beaufort, Walter Kerr, Norman Nadel, George Oppenheimer, William Raidy, Allan Wallach, Richard Watts Jr., Edwin Wilson; *The Island* (5)—Clive Barnes, Harold Clurman, Brendan Gill, Jack Kroll, Edith Oliver; *The National Health* (2)—Ted Kalem, Julius Novick; *The Taking of Janie* (2)—William H. Glover, Douglas Watt; *Saturday Sunday Monday* (1)—Henry Hewes; *Sizwe Banzi Is Dead* (1)—Martin Gottfried; *Summerfolk* (1)—John Simon.

Having named a foreign play best of bests, the Critics Circle proceeded to vote on a best American play, the first ballot producing no majority of first choices in a division as follows: *Seascape* (5)—Barnes, Gill, Hewes, Oppenheimer, Watts; *The Taking of Miss Janie* (5)—Beaufort, Clurman, Glover, Watt, Wilson; *A Chorus Line* (2)—Nadel, Novick; *Mert & Phil* (2)—Kalem, Kroll; *Black Picture Show* (1)—Gottfried; *Kid Champion* (1)—Oliver; *Yentl the Yeshiva Boy* (1)—Simon; with Kerr, Raidy and Wallach abstaining. The tie between the two front-runners on this ballot was broken by one point on the second ballot in favor of *The Taking of Miss Janie*, which thereby won the Critics citation as best American play of the season with 16 points, with other points distributed as follows: *Seascape* (15), *Same Time, Next Year* (14), *A Chorus Line* (7), *The First Breeze of Summer* (7), *Mert & Phil* (5), *Black Picture Show* (3), *Kid Champion* (3), *Yentl the Yeshiva Boy* (3), *The Sirens* (2), *Hothouse* (1), *Fishing* (1), *The Ritz* (1).

The Critics voted *A Chorus Line* the best musical of the season by a large majority of first choices on the first ballot, distributed as follows: *A Chorus Line* (16)—Barnes, Beaufort, Clurman, Gottfried, Hewes, Kalem, Kroll, Nadel, Novick, Oliver, Raidy, Simon, Wallach, Watt, Watts, Wilson; *Shenandoah* (2)—Kerr, Oppenheimer; *The Wiz* (2)—Gill, Glover.

The three Critics Circle members who did not participate in the voting either by person or by proxy are Emory Lewis (the Bergen *Record*), Hobe Morrison *(Variety)* and Marilyn Stasio *(Cue)*. Here's the way the 20 votes were distributed on the point-weighted second ballots for best play and best American play:

SECOND BALLOT FOR BEST PLAY

Critic	*1st Choice (3 pts.)*	*2d Choice (2 pts.)*	*3d Choice (1 pt.)*
Clive Barnes *Times*	The Island	Seascape	Equus
John Beaufort *Monitor*	Equus	The Taking of Miss Janie	The First Breeze of Summer
Harold Clurman *The Nation*	The Island	Sizwe Banzi Is Dead	Miss Janie
Brendan Gill *New Yorker*	The Island	Sizwe Banzi Is Dead	Equus
William H. Glover AP	Equus	Miss Janie	Summerfolk
Martin Gottfried *Post*	Sizwe Banzi Is Dead	Equus	Black Picture Show
Henry Hewes *Saturday Review*	Saturday Sunday Monday	Seascape	Equus
Ted Kalem *Time*	The National Health	Equus	Mert & Phil
Walter Kerr *Times*	No ballot		
Jack Kroll *Newsweek*	The Island	Sizwe Banzi Is Dead	The National Health

Norman Nadel Scripps-Howard	Equus	The National Health	The Island
Julius Novick *Village Voice*	The National Health	Absurd Person Singular	Equus
Edith Oliver *New Yorker*	The Island	Kid Champion	The Ritz
George Oppenheimer *Newsday*	Equus	Seascape	Same Time, Next Year
William Raidy Newhouse	Equus	Seascape	Same Time, Next Year
John Simon *New York*	Summerfolk	Yentl the Yeshiva Boy	London Assurance
Allan Wallach *Newsday*	Equus	The National Health	Same Time, Next Year
Douglas Watt *Daily News*	Miss Janie	Equus	Sizwe Banzi Is Dead
Richard Watts Jr. *Post*	Equus	Seascape	Same Time, Next Year
Edwin Wilson *Wall St. Journal*	Equus	Miss Janie	The National Health

SECOND BALLOT FOR BEST AMERICAN PLAY

Critic	*1st Choice (3 pts.)*	*2d Choice (2 pts.)*	*3d Choice (1 pt.)*
Clive Barnes	Seascape	Same Time, Next Year	The First Breeze of Summer
John Beaufort	The Taking of Miss Janie	Seascape	First Breeze
Harold Clurman	No ballot		
Brendan Gill	No ballot		
William H. Glover	Miss Janie	First Breeze	Seascape
Martin Gottfried	Black Picture Show	Same Time, Next Year	Hothouse
Henry Hewes	Seascape	The Sirens	Fishing
Ted Kalem	Mert & Phil	Miss Janie	Same Time, Next Year
Walter Kerr	Abstain		
Jack Kroll	A Chorus Line	Mert & Phil	Same Time, Next Year
Norman Nadel	A Chorus Line	Seascape	Same Time, Next Year
Julius Novick	Abstain		
Edith Oliver	Kid Champion	Miss Janie	The Ritz
George Oppenheimer	Seascape	Same Time, Next Year	First Breeze
William Raidy	Abstain		
John Simon	Yentl the Yeshiva Boy	Same Time, Next Year	A Chorus Line
Allan Wallach	Abstain		
Douglas Watt	Miss Janie	First Breeze	Same Time, Next Year
Richard Watts Jr.	No ballot		
Edwin Wilson	Miss Janie	Same Time, Next Year	Seascape

CHOICES OF SOME OTHER CRITICS

Critic	*Best Play*	*Best Musical*
Judith Crist	Same Time, Next Year	The Wiz
Alvin Klein WNYC	Equus	A Chorus Line
Stewart Klein WNEW-TV	Equus	A Chorus Line
Emory Lewis Bergen *Record*	Equus Miss Janie (best Amer. play)	A Chorus Line

Jeffrey Lyons	Same Time, Next Year	A Chorus Line
CBS Radio & WPIX-TV		
Hobe Morrison	Same Time, Next Year	A Chorus Line
Variety	Kid Champion (best Amer. play)	
Leonard Probst	Abstain	A Chorus Line
WNBC		
Virgil Scudder	Equus	The Wiz
Marilyn Stasio	Equus	A Chorus Line
Cue		

NEW YORK DRAMA CRITICS CIRCLE AWARDS

Listed below are the New York Drama Critics Circle Awards from 1935–36 through 1974–75 classified as follows: (1) Best American Play, (2) Best Foreign Play, (3) Best Musical, (4) Best, regardless of category (this category was established by new voting rules in 1962–63 and did not exist prior to that year).

1935–36—(1) Winterset
1936–37—(1) High Tor
1937–38—(1) Of Mice and Men, (2) Shadow and Substance
1938–39—(1) No award, (2) The White Steed
1939–40—(1) The Time of Your Life
1940–41—(1) Watch on the Rhine, (2) The Corn Is Green
1941–42—(1) No award, (2) Blithe Spirit
1942–43—(1) The Patriots
1943–44—(2) Jacobowsky and the Colonel
1944–45—(1) The Glass Menagerie
1945–46—(3) Carousel
1946–47—(1) All My Sons, (2) No Exit, (3) Brigadoon
1947–48—(1) A Streetcar Named Desire, (2) The Winslow Boy
1948–49—(1) Death of a Salesman, (2) The Madwoman of Chaillot, (3) South Pacific
1949–50—(1) The Member of the Wedding (2) The Cocktail Party, (3) The Consul
1950–51—(1) Darkness at Noon, (2) The Lady's Not for Burning, (3) Guys and Dolls
1951–52—(1) I Am a Camera, (2) Venus Observed, (3) Pal Joey (Special citation to Don Juan in Hell)
1952–53—(1) Picnic, (2) The Love of Four Colonels, (3) Wonderful Town
1953–54—(1) Teahouse of the August Moon, (2) Ondine, (3) The Golden Apple
1954–55—(1) Cat on a Hot Tin Roof, (2) Witness for the Prosecution, (3) The Saint of Bleecker Street
1955–56—(1) The Diary of Ann Frank, (2) Tiger at the Gates, (3) My Fair Lady
1956–57—(1) Long Day's Journey Into Night, (2) The Waltz of the Toreadors, (3) The Most Happy Fella
1957–58—(1) Look Homeward, Angel, (2) Look Back in Anger, (3) The Music Man
1958–59—(1) A Raisin in the Sun, (2) The Visit,

(3) La Plume de Ma Tante
1959–60—(1) Toys in the Attic, (2) Five Finger Exercise, (3) Fiorello!
1960–61—(1) All the Way Home, (2) A Taste of Honey, (3) Carnival
1961–62—(1) The Night of the Iguana, (2) A Man for All Seasons, (3) How to Succeed in Business Without Really Trying
1962–63—(4) Who's Afraid of Virginia Woolf? (Special citation to Beyond the Fringe)
1963–64—(4) Luther, (3) Hello, Dolly! (Special citation to The Trojan Women)
1964–65—(4) The Subject Was Roses, (3) Fiddler on the Roof
1965–66—(4) The Persecution and Assassination of Marat as Performed by the Inmates of the Asylum of Charenton Under the Direction of the Marquis de Sade, (3) Man of La Mancha
1966–67—(4) The Homecoming, (3) Cabaret
1967–68—(4) Rosencrantz and Guildenstern Are Dead, (3) Your Own Thing
1968–69—(4) The Great White Hope, (3) 1776
1969–70—(4) Borstal Boy, (1) The Effect of Gamma Rays on Man-in-the-Moon Marigolds, (3) Company
1970–71—(4) Home, (1) The House of Blue Leaves, (3) Follies
1971–72—(4) That Championship Season, (2) The Screens, (3) Two Gentlemen of Verona (Special citations to Sticks and Bones and Old Times)
1972–73—(4) The Changing Room, (1) The Hot 1 Baltimore, (3) A Little Night Music
1973–74—(4) The Contractor, (1) Short Eyes, (3) Candide
1974–75—(4) Equus, (1) The Taking of Miss Janie, (3) A Chorus Line

PULITZER PRIZE WINNERS, 1916–17 TO 1974–75

1916–17—No award

1917–18—Why Marry?, by Jesse Lynch Williams

1918–19—No award

1919–20—Beyond the Horizon, by Eugene O'Neill

1920–21—Miss Lulu Bett, by Zona Gale

1921–22—Anna Christie, by Eugene O'Neill

1922–23—Icebound, by Owen Davis

1923–24—Hell-Bent fer Heaven, by Hatcher Hughes

1924–25—They Knew What They Wanted, by Sidney Howard

1925–26—Craig's Wife, by George Kelly

1926–27—In Abraham's Bosom, by Paul Green

1927–28—Strange Interlude, by Eugene O'Neill

1928–29—Street Scene, by Elmer Rice

1929–30—The Green Pastures, by Marc Connelly

1930–31—Alison's House, by Susan Glaspell

1931–32—Of Thee I Sing, by George S. Kaufman, Morrie Ryskind, Ira and George Gershwin

1932–33—Both Your Houses, by Maxwell Anderson

1933–34—Men in White, by Sidney Kingsley

1934–35—The Old Maid, by Zoë Akins

1935–36—Idiot's Delight, by Robert E. Sherwood

1936–37—You Can't Take It With You, by Moss Hart and George S. Kaufman

1937–38—Our Town, by Thornton Wilder

1938–39—Abe Lincoln in Illinois, by Robert E. Sherwood

1939–40—The Time of Your Life, by William Saroyan

1940–41—There Shall Be No Night, by Robert E. Sherwood

1941–42—No award

1942–43—The Skin of Our Teeth, by Thornton Wilder

1943–44—No award

1944–45—Harvey, by Mary Chase

1945–46—State of the Union, by Howard Lindsay and Russel Crouse

1946–47—No award.

1947–48—A Streetcar Named Desire, by Tennessee Williams

1948–49—Death of a Salesman, by Arthur Miller

1949–50—South Pacific, by Richard Rodgers, Oscar Hammerstein II and Joshua Logan

1950–51—No award

1951–52—The Shrike, by Joseph Kramm

1952–53—Picnic, by William Inge

1953–54—The Teahouse of the August Moon, by John Patrick

1954–55—Cat on a Hot Tin Roof, by Tennessee Williams

1955–56—The Diary of Anne Frank, by Frances Goodrich and Albert Hackett

1956–57—Long Day's Journey Into Night, by Eugene O'Neill

1957–58—Look Homeward, Angel, by Ketti Frings

1958–59—J. B., by Archibald MacLeish

1959–60—Fiorello!, by Jerome Weidman, George Abbott, Sheldon Harnick and Jerry Bock

1960–61—All the Way Home, by Tad Mosel

1961–62—How to Succeed in Business Without Really Trying, by Abe Burrows, Willie Gilbert, Jack Weinstock and Frank Loesser

1962–63—No award

1963–64—No award

1964–65—The Subject Was Roses, by Frank D. Gilroy

1965–66—No award

1966–67—A Delicate Balance, by Edward Albee

1967–68—No award

1968–69—The Great White Hope, by Howard Sackler

1969–70—No Place to Be Somebody, by Charles Gordone

1970–71—The Effect of Gamma Rays on Man-in-the-Moon Marigolds, by Paul Zindel

1971–72—No award

1972–73—That Championship Season, by Jason Miller

1973–74—No award

1974–75—Seascape by Edward Albee

ADDITIONAL PRIZES AND AWARDS, 1974–75

The following is a list of major prizes and awards for theatrical achievement. In all cases the names of winners—persons, productions or organizations—appear in **bold face type**.

VILLAGE VOICE OFF-BROADWAY (OBIE) AWARDS for off-Broadway excellence, selected by a committee of judges whose members were Clive Barnes, Mel Gussow, Jack Kroll,

Michael Feingold and Julius Novick. Best play, *The First Breeze of Summer* by Leslie Lee. Distinguished playwriting, **Ed Bullins** for *The Taking of Miss Janie*, **Lanford Wilson** for *The Mound Builders*, **Wallace Shawn** for *Our Late Night*, **Sam Shepard** for *Action* and **Corinne Jacker** for **Harry Outside**. Distinguished performances, **Reyno** and **Moses Gunn** in *The First Breeze of Summer*, **Dick Latessa** in *Philemon*, **Kevin McCarthy** in *Harry Outside*, **Stephen D. Newman** in *Polly*, **Christopher Walken** in *Kid Champion*, **Ian Trigger** in *The True History of Squire Jonathan*, **Cara Duff-MacCormick** in *Craig's Wife*, **Priscilla Smith** in *Trilogy*, **Tanya Berezin** in *The Mound Builders*, **Tovah Feldshuh** in *Yentl the Yeshiva Boy*. Distinguished direction, **Lawrence Kornfeld** for *Listen to Me*, **Marshall W. Mason** for *Battle of Angels and The Mound Builders*, **Gilbert Moses** for *The Taking of Miss Janie*. Distinguished set design, **Robert U. Taylor** for *Polly*, **John Lee Beatty** for *Down by the River etc.*, *Battle of Angels* and *The Mound Builders*. Special citations, **Andrei Serban** for *Trilogy*, the **Royal Shakespeare Company** for *Summerfolk*, **Charles Ludlam** for *Professor Bedlam's Punch and Judy Show*, **The Henry Street Settlement**, **Charles Pierce**, **Mabou Mines**. Special 20-year Obies, **Judith Malina** and **Julian Beck**, **Theodore Mann** and **Circle in the Square**, **Joseph Papp**, **Ellen Stewart**, *The Fantasticks*.

ELIZABETH HULL-KATE WARRINER 1974 AWARD to the playwright(s) whose work produced within each year dealt with controversial subjects involving the fields of political, religious or social mores of the time, selected by the Dramatists Guild Council. **Terrence McNally** for *Bad Habits* and **Miguel Piñero** for *Short Eyes*.

MARGO JONES AWARD for the most significant contribution to the theater through a continuing policy of producing new plays. **Paul Weidner** and the **Hartford Stage Company**.

JOSEPH MAHARAM FOUNDATION AWARDS for distinguished New York theatrical design by American designers. Scenery design, **Robin Wagner** for *A Chorus Line*, **Robert Wilson** for *A Letter for Queen Victoria*. Costume design, **Carrie F. Robbins** for *Polly*.

DRAMA DESK AWARDS for outstanding contribution to the 1974–75 theater season. American play, *Same Time, Next Year* by Bernard Slade. Foreign play, *Equus* by Peter Shaffer. Musical, *The Wiz* by William F. Brown. Music and lyrics, **Charlie Smalls** for *The Wiz*. Director (play), **John Dexter** for *Equus*. Director (musical), **Arthur Laurents** for *Gypsy*. Actress (play), **Ellen Burstyn** in *Same Time, Next Year*. Special mention, actress (play), **Tovah Feldshuh** in *Yentl the Yeshiva Boy*. Actor (play), **Anthony**

Hopkins in *Equus*. Special mention, actor (play), **Donald Sinden** in *London Assurance*. Actor (musical), **John Cullum** in *Shenandoah*. Actress (musical), **Angela Lansbury** in *Gypsy*. Supporting actor (play), **Frank Langella** in *Seascape*. Supporting actress (play), **Frances Sternhagen** in *Equus*. Supporting actress (musical), **Donna Theodore** in *Shenandoah*. Supporting actor (musical), **Ted Ross** in *The Wiz*. Scenery design, **Carl Toms** for *Sherlock Holmes*. Lighting design, **Neil Peter Jampolis** for *Sherlock Holmes*. Costume design, **Geoffrey Holder** for *The Wiz*. Choreographer, **George Faison** for *The Wiz*. Theatrical experience, *London Assurance*, James Nederlander producer.

OUTER CRITICS' CIRCLE AWARDS for distinctive achievement in New York theater, voted by critics of out-of-town and foreign periodicals. Outstanding production, *Equus*. Outstanding ensemble playing, **Ellen Burstyn** and **Charles Grodin** in *Same Time, Next Year*. Distinguished performances, **Anthony Hopkins** in *Equus*, **John Cullum** in *Shenandoah*, **Maggie Smith** in *Private Lives*, **Geraldine Page** in *Absurd Person Singular*. Notable performances by young players, **Peter Firth** in *Equus*, **Tovah Feldshuh** in *Rodgers & Hart*, *Yentl the Yeshiva Boy* and *Dreyfus in Rehearsal*, **Chip Ford** in *Shenandoah*. Outstanding contributions to the musical theater, **The Portfolio Studio** of Tom Jones and Harvey Schmidt. Support of many outstanding productions brought to New York this season, **The Long Wharf Theater** of New Haven, Conn. and the **Arts Council of Great Britain**. The John Gassner Medallion for playwriting, **Leslie Lee** for *The First Breeze of Summer*.

CLARENCE DERWENT AWARDS for the most promising female and male actors on the metropolitan scene. **Marybeth Hurt** in *Love for Love* and **Reyno** in *The First Breeze of Summer*.

LOS ANGELES DRAMA CRITICS CIRCLE AWARDS for distinguished 1974–75 theatrical productions and performances in Los Angeles. Playwriting, **Christopher Hampton** for *Savages*, **Gardner McKay** for *Sea Marks*. Music and lyrics, **Stephen Sondheim** for *A Little Night Music*. Performances, **Andra Akers** in *A Little Night Music*, **James Gammon** in *The Dark at the Top of the Stairs*, **Colleen Dewhurst** in *A Moon for the Misbegotten*, **Betty Garrett** in *Betty Garrett and Other Songs*, **John Savage** in *One Flew Over the Cuckoo's Nest*. Directing, **Gordon Davidson** for *Savages*, **Michael Bennett** for *Seesaw*. Design, **John Gleason** (lighting) for *Savages*, **Florence Klotz** (costumes) for *A Little Night Music*, **Robert W. Zentis** (scenery) for *The New Bijou Soft Shoe*, **H.R. Poindexter** (lighting) *The Time of the Cuckoo*, **Timothy Scott** and **Patrick McFadden** for *Picnic*. Margaret Harford Award "for maintaining consistently high standards of creation and execution in design," **Robert W. Zentis**. Special awards, **Martin Magner**, the theater arts department of Los Angeles City College, **Edwin Lester**, Met Theater.

STRAW HAT AWARDS for production bests of the 1974 summer season, sponsored by Council of Stock Theaters. Achievement Award, **Rosalind Russell**. Best actor, **Patrick McNee**. Best actress, **Eileen Herlie**. Best actress (musical), **Helen Gallagher**. Best director, **John Mahon**. Best supporting actress, **Dortha Duckworth**. Best supporting actor, **Bruce Connolly**. Most promising newcomers, **Danny Aiello**, **Carol Swarbrick**.

PAUL ROBESON CITATION for outstanding creative contributions both in the performing arts and in society at large, sponsored by Actors Equity Association. **Ruby Dee** and **Ossie Davis**.

JOSEPH JEFFERSON AWARDS for distinguished shows and performances in Chicago.

Play, *The Freedom of the City* by Brian Friel. Musical, *Dance on a Country Grave*. New play, *Sexual Perversity in Chicago* by David Mamet. Performances, **Robert LuPone** in *The Tooth of Crime*, **Ben Gazzara** in *Hughie*, **Mark Medoff** and **Louise Hoven** in *When You Comin' Back, Red Ryder?*, **Bob Thompson** in *Da*, **Elaine Shore** in *The Sea Horse*, **Rebecca Clement** in *The Sound of Music*, **Eugene G. Anthony** in *George M*, the ensemble in *The Wonderful Ice Cream Suit*. Directing, **William Woodman** (play) for *The Freedom of the City*, **Patrick Henry** (musical) for *Dance on a Country Grave*. Design, **James Maronek** (scenery) for *Guys and Dolls*, **Alicia Finkel** (costumes) for *A Doll's House*. Choreography, **Ronna Kaye** for *The Sound of Music*. Citations for achievement in community theater, **Burt Ferrini** for *Steambath*, **Frank Carioti** for *The Inquiry*, the **ensemble** in *The Inquiry*.

JENNIE HEIDEN AWARD for professional work in children's theater, sponsored by the American Theater Association and the Children's Theater Association. **Bil Baird Theater**.

THE TONY AWARDS

The Antoinette Perry (Tony) Awards are voted by members of the League of New York Theaters, the governing bodies of the Dramatists Guild, Actors, Equity, the American Theater Wing, the Society of Stage Directors and Choreographers, the United Scenic Artists Union, and members of the first and second night press, from a list of up to five nominees in each category. Nominations are made by a committee serving at the invitation of the League of New York Theaters, which is in charge of the Tony Awards procedure, with the committee's personnel changing every year. The 1974–75 nominating committee was composed of Harold Clurman, Brendan Gill, William H. Glover, Leonard Harris, Henry Hewes, Joan Rubin, Isabelle Stevenson and Douglas Watt. Their list of nominees follows, with winners listed in **bold face type**.

BEST PLAY. *Equus* by Peter Shaffer, produced by Kermit Bloomgarden and Doris Cole Abrahams; *Same Time, Next Year* by Bernard Slade, produced by Morton Gottlieb; *Short Eyes* by Miguel Piñero, produced by Joseph Papp; *Sizwe Banzi Is Dead* and *The Island* by Athol Fugard, John Kani and Winston Ntshona, produced by Hillard Elkins, Lester Osterman Productions, Bernard Delfont and Michael White; *Seascape* by Edward Albee, produced by Richard Barr, Charles Woodward and Clinton Wilder; *The National Health* by Peter Nichols, produced by Circle in the Square (Theodore Mann artistic director, Paul Libin managing director).

BEST MUSICAL. *Mack & Mabel* produced by

David Merrick; *Shenandoah* produced by Philip Rose and Gloria and Louis K. Sher; *The Lieutenant* produced by Joseph S. Kutrzeba and Spofford J. Beadle; *The Wiz* produced by Ken Harper.

BEST BOOK OF A MUSICAL. *Mack & Mabel* by Michael Stewart; *Shenandoah* by **James Lee Barrett**, **Peter Udell** and **Philip Rose**; *The Lieutenant* by Gene Curty, Nitra Scharfman and Chuck Strand; *The Wiz* by William F. Brown.

BEST SCORE: *A Letter for Queen Victoria*, music and lyrics by Alan Lloyd; *Shenandoah*, music by Gary Geld, lyrics by Peter Udell; *The Lieutenant*, music and lyrics by Gene Curty, Nitra

Scharfman and Chuck Strand; *The Wiz*, music and lyrics by **Charlie Smalls**.

BEST ACTOR—PLAY. Jim Dale in *Scapino*, Peter Firth in *Equus*. Henry Fonda in *Clarence Darrow*, Ben Gazzara in *Hughie* and *Duet*, **John Kani** and **Winston Ntshona** in *Sizwe Banzi Is Dead* and *The Island*, John Wood in *Sherlock Holmes*.

BEST ACTRESS—PLAY. Elizabeth Ashley in *Cat on a Hot Tin Roof*, **Ellen Burstyn** in *Same Time, Next Year*, Diana Rigg in *The Misanthrope*, Maggie Smith in *Private Lives*, Liv Ullmann in *A Doll's House*.

BEST ACTOR—MUSICAL. **John Cullum** in *Shenandoah*, Joel Grey in *Goodtime Charley*, Raul Julia in *Where's Charley?*, Eddie Mekka in *The Lieutenant*, Robert Preston *in Mack & Mabel*.

BEST ACTRESS—MUSICAL. Lola Falana in *Doctor Jazz*, **Angela Lansbury** in *Gypsy*, Bernadette Peters in *Mack & Mabel*, Ann Reinking in *Goodtime Charley*.

BEST SUPPORTING ACTOR—PLAY. Larry Blyden in *Absurd Person Singular*, Leonard Frey in *The National Health*, **Frank Langella** in *Seascape*, Philip Locke in *Sherlock Holmes*, George Rose in *My Fat Friend*, Dick A. Williams in *Black Picture Show*.

BEST SUPPORTING ACTRESS—PLAY. Linda Miller in *Black Picture Show*, **Rita Moreno** in *The Ritz*, Geraldine Page and Carole Shelley in *Absurd Person Singular*, Elizabeth Spriggs in *London Assurance*, Frances Sternhagen in *Equus*.

BEST SUPPORTING ACTOR—MUSICAL. Tom Aldredge in *Where's Charley?*, John Bottoms in *Dance With Me*, Doug Henning in *The Magic Show*, Gilbert Price in *The Night That Made America Famous*, **Ted Ross** in *The Wiz*, Richard B. Shull in *Goodtime Charley*.

BEST SUPPORTING ACTRESS—MUSI-CAL. **Dee Dee Bridgewater** in *The Wiz*, Susan Browning in *Goodtime Charley*, Zan Charisse in *Gypsy*, Taina Elg in *Where's Charley?* Kelly Garrett in *The Night That Made America Famous*, Donna Theodore in *Shenandoah*.

BEST DIRECTOR—PLAY. Arvin Brown for *The National Health*, **John Dexter** for *Equus*, Frank Dunlop for *Scapino*, Ronald Eyre for *London Assurance*, Athol Fugard for *Sizwe Banzi Is Dead* and *The Island*, Gene Saks for *Same Time, Next Year*.

BEST DIRECTOR—MUSICAL. Gower Champion for *Mack & Mabel*, Grover Dale for *The Magic Show*, **Geoffrey Holder** for *The Wiz*, Arthur Laurents for *Gypsy*.

BEST SCENIC DESIGNER. Scott Johnson for *Dance With Me*, Tanya Moiseiwitsch for *The Misanthrope*, William Ritman for *God's Favorite*, Rouben Ter-Arutunian for *Goodtime Charley*, **Carl Toms** for *Sherlock Holmes*, Robin Wagner for *Mack & Mabel*.

BEST COSTUME DESIGNER. Arthur Boccia for *Where's Charley?*, Raoul Pène du Bois for *Doctor Jazz*, **Geoffrey Holder** for *The Wiz*, Willa Kim for *Goodtime Charley*, Tanya Moiseiwitsch for *The Misanthrope*, Patricia Zipprodt for *Mack & Mabel*.

BEST LIGHTING DESIGNER. Chipmonck for *The Rocky Horror Show*, Feder for *Goodtime Charley*, **Neil Peter Jampolis** for *Sherlock Holmes*, Andy Phillips for *Equus*, Thomas Skelton for *All God's Chillun Got Wings*, James Tilton for *Seascape*.

BEST CHOREOGRAPHER. Gower Champion for *Mack & Mabel*, **George Faison** for *The Wiz*, Donald McKayle for *Doctor Jazz*, Margo Sappington for *Where's Charley?*, Robert Tucker for *Shenandoah*, Joel Zwick for *Dance With Me*.

SPECIAL AWARDS (voted by the Tony Administration Committee). **Neil Simon** "for his over-all contribution to the theater." **Al Hirschfeld** "for 50 years of theatrical cartoons."

1974–1975 PUBLICATION
OF RECENTLY-PRODUCED PLAYS

Bacchae of Euripides. Wole Soyinka. Methuen.
Bingo. Edward Bond. Methuen (paperback).
Breeze from the Gulf, A. Farrar, Straus & Giroux (paperback).
Chez Nous. Peter Nichols. Faber & Faber (paperback).
Clarence Darrow: A One-Man Play. David W. Rintels. Doubleday.

Director of the Opera, The. Jean Anouilh. Methuen.
Don Juan. Molière; adaptation by Christopher Hampton. Faber & Faber. (paperback).
Equus. Peter Shaffer. Avon (paperback).
Foursome, The. E. A. Whitehead. Faber & Faber (paperback).
Freedom of the City, The. Brian Friel, Faber & Faber (paperback).
Good Doctor, The. Neil Simon. Random House.
Goodbye People, The. Herb Gardner. Farrar, Straus & Giroux (paperback).
Habeas Corpus. Alan Bennett. Faber & Faber (paperback).
Immortals, The. Louis Phillips. Colonnades Theater Lab (paperback).
Knuckle. David Hare. Faber & Faber.
Last of the Marx Brothers' Writers, The. Louis Phillips. Colonnades Theater Lab (paperback).
Leaving Home. David French. New Press (paperback).
Moon Dreamers, The. Julie Bovasso. Samuel French (paperback).
National Health, The. Peter Nichols. Grove Press (paperback)
People Are Living There. Athol Fugard. Oxford.
Richard's Cork Leg. Brendan Behan. Grove Press (paperback).
Saturday Sunday Monday. Eduardo De Filippo. Heinemann (paperback).
Savages. Christopher Hampton. Faber & Faber (paperback).
Sea Horse, The. Edward J. Moore. James T. White.
Seascape. Edward Albee. Atheneum.
Sense of Detachment, A. John Osborne. Faber & Faber (paperback).
Short Eyes. Miguel Piñero. Hill & Wang (paperback).
Sweet Talk. Michael Abbensetts. Methuen (paperback).
When You Comin' Back, Red Ryder? Mark Medoff. James T. White.
Zalmen, or The Madness of God. Elie Wiesel. Random House.

A SELECTED LIST OF OTHER PLAYS PUBLISHED IN 1974–75

Apple and the Square, The. Jack Gelber. Viking.
Best Short Plays 1974, The. Stanley Richards, editor. Chilton.
Buchanan Dying. John Updike. Alfred A. Knopf.
Collected Plays of Bertolt Brecht. Volume 7. Random House.
Collected Plays of Wole Soyinka. Volume 2. Oxford.
Garden of Delights. Fernando Arrabal. Grove Press (also paperback).
Killing Game. Eugene Ionesco. Grove Press (also paperback).
Kuntu Drama: Plays of the African Continuum. Paul Carter Harrison, editor. Grove (paperback).
Mary Stuart. Friedrich Schiller; adapted and translated by Stephen Spender. Faber & Faber (paperback).
Meteor, The. Friedrich Duerrenmatt. Grove (paperback).
Moon for the Misbegotten, A. Eugene O'Neill. Vintage (paperback).
Picture of Dorian Gray: A Moral Entertainment. Oscar Wilde; adapted by John Osborne. Faber & Faber (paperback).
Place Calling Itself Rome, A. Adaptation of William Shakespeare's *Coriolanus* by John Osborne. Faber & Faber (paperback).
Three Port Elizabeth Plays: The Blood Knot; Hello and Goodbye; Boesman and Lena. Athol Fugard. Viking.
Tooth of Crime, The and *Geography of a Horse Dreamer.* Sam Shepard. Grove Press (paperback).

MUSICAL AND DRAMATIC RECORDINGS OF NEW YORK SHOWS

Title and publishing company are listed below. Each record is an original New York cast album unless otherwise indicated. An asterisk (*) indicates recording is also available on cassettes. Two asterisks (**) indicate it is available on eight-track cartridges.

Behind the Fridge. (Original London Cast). Atlantic.
Billy. (Original London Cast). CBS.

Cabaret. (Original London Cast). Embassy.
Chicago. Arista.
Chorus Line, A. Columbia
Cole. (Original London Cast). RCA (2 albums).
Dr. Selavy's Magic Theater. United Artists.
Godspell. Bell (*) (**).
Good Evening. Island (*).
Goodtime Charley. RCA
Pickwick. (Original London Cast). Philips.
Lenny. Blue (2 albums).
Magic Show, The. Bell.
Mack and Mabel. ABC (*).
Shenandoah. RCA.
Wiz, The. Atlantic. (*).

THE BEST PLAYS, 1894–1974

Listed in alphabetical order below are all those works selected as Best Plays in previous volumes in the *Best Plays* series. Opposite each title is given the volume in which the play appears, its opening date and its total number of performances. Those plays marked with an asterisk (*) were still playing on June 1, 1975 and their number of performances was figured through May 31, 1975. Adaptors and translators are indicated by (ad) and (tr), and the symbols (b), (m) and (l) stand for the author of the book, music and lyrics in the case of musicals.

NOTE: A season-by-season listing, rather than an alphabetical one, of the 500 Best Plays in the first 50 volumes, starting with the yearbook for the season of 1919–1920, appears in *The Best Plays of 1968–69.*

PLAY	VOLUME	OPENED	PERFS.
ABE LINCOLN IN ILLINOIS—Robert E. Sherwood	38–39	Oct. 15, 1938	472
ABRAHAM LINCOLN—John Drinkwater	19–20	Dec. 15, 1919	193
ACCENT ON YOUTH—Samson Raphaelson	34–35	Dec. 25, 1934	229
ADAM AND EVA—Guy Bolton, George Middleton	19–20	Sept. 13, 1919	312
ADAPTATION—Elaine May; and NEXT—Terrence McNally	68–69	Feb. 10, 1969	707
AFFAIRS OF STATE—Louis Verneuil	50–51	Sept. 25, 1950	610
AFTER THE FALL—Arthur Miller	63–64	Jan. 23, 1964	208
AFTER THE RAIN—John Bowen	67–68	Oct. 9, 1967	64
AH, WILDERNESS!—Eugene O'Neill	33–34	Oct. 2, 1933	289
AIN'T SUPPOSED TO DIE A NATURAL DEATH—(b,m,l) Melvin Van Peebles	71–72	Oct. 7, 1971	325
ALIEN CORN—Sidney Howard	32–33	Feb. 20, 1933	98
ALISON'S HOUSE—Susan Glaspell	30–31	Dec. 1, 1930	41
ALL MY SONS—Arthur Miller	46–47	Jan. 29, 1947	328
ALL THE WAY HOME—Tad Mosel, based on James Agee's novel *A Death in the Family*	60–61	Nov. 30, 1960	333
ALLEGRO—(b,l) Oscar Hammerstein II, (m) Richard Rodgers	47–48	Oct. 10, 1947	315
AMBUSH—Arthur Richman	21–22	Oct. 10, 1921	98
AMERICA HURRAH—Jean-Claude van Itallie	66–67	Nov. 6, 1966	634
AMERICAN WAY, THE—George S. Kaufman, Moss Hart	38–39	Jan. 21, 1939	164
AMPHITRYON 38—Jean Giraudoux, (ad) S. N. Behrman	37–38	Nov. 1, 1937	153
ANDERSONVILLE TRIAL, THE—Saul Levitt	59–60	Dec. 29, 1959	179
ANDORRA—Max Frisch, (ad) George Tabori	62–63	Feb. 9, 1963	9
ANGEL STREET—Patrick Hamilton	41–42	Dec. 5, 1941	1,295

NECROLOGY

MAY 1974–MAY 1975

PERFORMERS

Ace, Jane Sherwood (74)—November 11, 1974
Acosta, Rodolfo (54)—November 7, 1974
Adams, Virginia (62)—March 24, 1975
Adler, Eleanor (34)—Summer 1974
Alcock, Merle (85)—March 1, 1975
Arquette, Cliff (68)—September 23, 1974
Bando, Mitsugoro (68)—January 16, 1975
Augspurg, Gus (51)—August 14, 1974
Atrash, Farid (59)—December 26, 1974
Armstrong, Sam (75)—November 1, 1974
Aragon, Teodoro (Thedy) (89)—December 30, 1974
Alsen, Elsa (94)—January 31, 1975
Alpert, Larry (56)—March 9, 1975
Alexander, Muriel (91)—Spring 1975
Baclanova, Olga (74)—September 6, 1974
Baker, Josephine (68)—April 12, 1975
Bellini, Laura (73)—January 1, 1975
Benny, Jack (80)—December 26, 1974
Bentonelli, Joseph (74)—April 6, 1975
Bergmann, Eugene J. (77)—March 15, 1975
Best, Edna (74)—September 18, 1974
Blackwell, Carlyle Jr. (61)—September 29, 1974
Blue, Ben (73)—March 7, 1975
Bradley, Truman (69)—July 28, 1974
Bradshaw, Justin (59)—October 16, 1974
Brand, Mike (27)—May 1975
Branzell, Karin (83)—December 15, 1974
Brennan, Walter (80)—September 21, 1974
Britton, Pamela (51)—June 17, 1974
Brook, Clive (87)—November 17, 1974
Brown, Johnny Mack (70)—November 14, 1974
Bruce, Betty (54)—July 18, 1974
Bruylants, Francine (75)—December 19, 1974
Burnett, Charles A. (Tiny) (86)—August 31, 1974
Burr, Bessie Fisher (82)—September 17, 1974
Cain, Perry (49)—May 1975
Calkin, Arthur (80s)—September 11, 1974
Castile, Lynn (77)—April 8, 1975
Cavanaugh, Fannie (83)—January 13, 1975
Clarke, John (69)—July 30, 1974
Cobb, Edmund (82)—August 15, 1974
Cole, Mary Keith (61)—March 16, 1975
Conte, Richard (59)—April 15, 1975
Cooper, Clarence (53)—December 6, 1974
Coppen, Hazel (50)—April 8, 1975
Cornell, Katharine (81)—June 9, 1974

Coughlin, Bill T. (81)—August 23, 1974
Courtney, Inez (67)—April 5, 1975
Courtney, Perqueta (80)—November 26, 1974
Cox, Robert (79)—September 8, 1974
Cutts, Patricia (48)—September 6, 1974
Dal Monte, Toti (81)—January 26, 1975
Dale, Harold S. (84)—October 7, 1974
Daley, Cass (59)—March 22, 1975
Daly, William (Smiley) Jr. (67)—July 24, 1974
Dante, Lionel (67)—July 30, 1974
Dare, Phyllis (84)—April 27, 1975
Dare, Zena (88)—March 11, 1975
Darvas, Lili (72)—July 22, 1974
Daufel, Andre (56)—April 22, 1975
Davis, Freeman (Brother Bones) (71)—June 14, 1974
Davis, Rufe (66)—December 13, 1974
Dawson, Elide Webb (79)—May 1, 1975
Dean, Ivor (57)—August 10, 1974
Dearing, Edgar—August 17, 1974
De Ferris, Lola (81)—July 28, 1974
Del Val, Jean (83)—March 13, 1975
DeMott, John A. (63)—March 19, 1975
De Sica, Vittorio (73)—November 13, 1974
De Vera, Cris (49)—June 25, 1974
Dierkes, John (69)—January 8, 1975
Dixon, Paul (53)—December 28, 1974
Dodge, Jerry (37)—October 31, 1974
Dodge, Roger Pryor (76)—June 2, 1974
Dodson, Lamott (Dod)—February 7, 1975
Doherty, Chester (71)—February 13, 1975
Donato, Josephine Lucchese (78)—September 10, 1974
Dorn, Philip (75)—May 9, 1975
Dunninger (82)—March 9, 1975
Elliot, Cass (33)—July 29, 1974
Emerson, Edward (65)—April 11, 1975
Fay, Brendan (54)—February 7, 1975
Feder, Sabina—March 10, 1975
Fine, Larry (73)—January 24, 1975
Finnerty, Warren (49)—December 22, 1974
Fischer, Max (65)—October 11, 1974
Fisher, Alfred (68)—May 5, 1975
Fisher, Ruth H. (60s)—August 12, 1974
Fitzharris, Edward (Fitz) (84)—October 12, 1974
Fix, Ress Jenkins (81)—January 5, 1975
Flanders, Michael (53)—April 15, 1975
Flynn, Joe (49)—July 18, 1974
Fonseca, Joseph (49)—December 12, 1974

Fontaine, Lillian (88)—February 16, 1975
Fontaine, Tony—June 30, 1974
Forbes, Mary (91)—July 23, 1974
French, Eleanor (59)—February 2, 1975
Fresnay, Pierre (77)—January 9, 1975
Frohman, Bert (74)—June 23, 1974
Gambling, John B. (77)—November 21, 1974
Garon, Norm (41)—April 13, 1975
Gauguin, Lorraine (50)—December 22, 1974
Giachetti, Fosco (70)—December 22, 1974
Giehse, Therese (76)—March 3, 1975
Glenn, Raymond (Bob Custer) (76)—December 27, 1974
Glouchevitch, Barbara (46)—July 22, 1974
Goldowsky, Dagmar (78)—February 13, 1975
Goldberg, Rubin (92)—September 7, 1974
Gordon, Bert (76)—November 30, 1974
Green, Martyn (75)—February 8, 1975
Greene, Jeanne (69)—April 14, 1975
Greenfield, Felix (57)—June 13, 1974
Gregson, John (55)—January 8, 1975
Guenther, Ruth (64)—June 25, 1974
Hadley, Reed (63)—December 11, 1974
Hale, Randolph (65)—August 9, 1974
Hamilton, Sydney (78)—May 31, 1974
Harolde, Ralf (75)—November 1, 1974
Harout, Yeghishe—June 7, 1974
Harper, George T. (72)—November 29, 1974
Harris, Bennie Michel (Little Benny) (54)—February 11, 1975
Harris, Morris O. (59)—October 16, 1974
Hart, Jack (Indian Jack) (102)—September 23, 1974
Hartnell, William (67)—April 23, 1975
Hashim, Edmund (42)—July 2, 1974
Hayden, Bob (49)—June 10, 1974
Hayes, Laurence C. (71)—November 17, 1974
Hayward, Susan (55)—March 14, 1975
Higgins, Albert (32)—January 6, 1975
Hilliard, Peter (Julian Scott) (37)—September 14, 1974
Hirose, George (75)—August 9, 1974
Hogg, Curly (57)—September 4, 1974
Houghton, Genevieve (78)—November 14, 1974
Howard, Moe (78)—May 4, 1975
Howe, Helen (70)—February 1, 1975
Hugo, Mauritz (65)—June 16, 1974
Hull, Warren (71)—September 14, 1974
Hurn, Douglas (49)—October 22, 1974
Hutchison, Muriel (60)—March 24, 1975
James, Jessie (38)—December 14, 1974
Janis, Chelle (71)—October 4, 1974
Jenkins, Allen (74)—July 20, 1974
Johns, Eric (67)—March 11, 1975
Johnson, Bess (73)—January 3, 1975
Johnson, Gladys (40s)—November 16, 1974
Johnson, S. Kenneth 2d (62)—November 1, 1974
Jones, Hazel (79)—November 12, 1974
Jones, Marjorie Dunn (86)—October 18, 1974
Jordan, Louis (66)—February 4, 1975
Justin, Morgan (47)—July 7, 1974
Kalthoum, Um (77)—February 3, 1975
Kelly, Maurice (59)—August 28, 1974

Kennedy, Bob (41)—November 5, 1974
King, Vicki Kernan (49)—January 3, 1975
Kingsley, Rex (73)—December 25, 1974
Kinsella, Walter (74)—May 11, 1975
Kinsolving, Lee (36)—December 4, 1974
Kirk, Joseph (71)—April 16, 1975
Klein, Sadie (91)—June 5, 1974
Knowles, David (27)—August 13, 1974
Koetter, Paul (76)—September 17, 1974
Kristev, George (32)—September 10, 1974
Kruger, Otto (89)—September 6, 1974
Lake, Ethel Mae (73)—March 7, 1975
Lane, Rosemary (61)—November 25, 1974
Lane, Sherry (55)—October 29, 1974
Largay, Raymond J. (88)—September 28, 1974
Larrimore, Francine (77)—March 7, 1975
Lauren, Jane (56)—December 28, 1974
Leahy, Christine Dobbins (82)—August 26, 1974
Leal, Milagros (73)—March 1, 1975
Lee, Raymond (64)—June 26, 1974
Lenihan, Burton (96)—July 1, 1974
Lewis, Darrelene (18)—May 14, 1975
Lewis, Michael (44)—March 6, 1975
Lightner, Rosella (66)—November 15, 1974
Lindsay, Kevin (51)—May 1975
Lindstrom, Erik, (68)—September 27, 1974
Lloyd, Eddie (83)—September 22, 1974
Lohr, Marie (84)—January 21, 1975
Lomax, John A. Jr. (67)—December 12, 1974
Long, Richard (47)—December 21, 1974
Lorenz, Max (72)—January 11, 1975
Lucchese, Josephine (78)—September 10, 1974
Lueders, Guenther (70)—March 1, 1975
Lyman, Rose Blaine—December 15, 1974
Macdonald, Eve March—September 19, 1974
Mackris, Orestes (75)—January 30, 1975
MacTaggart, James (46)—May 29, 1974
Mabley, Moms (Jackie) (75)—May 23, 1975
Madison, Noel (77)—January 8, 1975
Main, Marjorie (85)—April 10, 1975
Malvey, Harold (70)—March 2, 1975
March, Fredric (77)—April 14, 1975
Mark, Michael (88)—February 3, 1975
Marlowe, Alan (40)—January 5, 1975
Marshall, Charles E. (Red) (76)—April 15, 1975
Massey, Ilona (62)—August 20, 1974
Matinez, Joseph J. (82)—January 5, 1975
Matteson, Ruth (65)—February 5, 1975
McChlery, Grace (77)—May 1975
McElhone, Eloise (53)—July 1, 1974
McFarland, Nan (58)—December 31, 1974
McLean, Lex (67)—Spring 1975
Meminger, Edward Lynn (70)—April 18, 1975
Meyer, Torben (90)—May 22, 1975
Middleton, Olive (83)—October 26, 1974
Milton, Ernest (84)—July 24, 1974
Mitchell, Les (70)—January 12, 1975
Mojica, Jose (78)—September 20, 1974
Moore, Ioma Mae (Dennie Graves) (73)—August 22, 1974
Morgan, Claudia (62)—September 17, 1974
Morgan, Ray—December 29, 1974

Morrison, Effie (57)—Autumn 1974
Morrison, James W. (86)—November 15, 1974
Mosconi, Charlie (84)—March 1, 1975
Moyer, Irene—March 9, 1975
Munoz, Morayma (30)—April 7, 1975
Munsell, Jeanette (84)—September 9, 1974
Murray, Katherine (80)—August 12, 1974
Nadajan—September 20, 1974
Newsome, Carman (62)—July 18, 1974
Niesen, Gertrude (62)—March 27, 1975
Norma, Bebe (49)—December 21, 1975
Novelo, Ruben Z. (43)—June 15, 1974
O'Connor, Richard (59)—February 15, 1975
O'Donovan, Frank (74)—June 28, 1974
O'Gorman, Joe (85)—August 26, 1974
Olmsted, Gertrude (70)—January 18, 1975
Onodera, Sho (59)—October 26, 1974
Orlova, Lyubov—January 26, 1975
O'Shea, Julia (83)—October 26, 1974
Ouster, Murray (67)—Summer 1974
Pandolfi, Frank (73)—February 5, 1975
Parks, Larry (60)—April 13, 1975
Patten, Dorothy (70)—April 11, 1975
Peck, Jack (72)—October 22, 1974
Pecon, John J. (60)—March 1, 1975
Perry, Vic (54)—August 14, 1974
Peters, William (51)—January 31, 1975
Peterson, Daniel McCloud (57)—October 1, 1974
Peterson, Marjorie (68)—August 19, 1974
Phillips, Charles (25)—October 12, 1974
Pierce, Edward (80)—November 21, 1974
Pigott, Howard H. (76)—November 28, 1974
Pinkett, Willis (55)—March 13, 1975
Poliakoff, Nikolai (Coco the Clown) (78)—September 25, 1974
Pontoppidan, Clara (80s)—January 22, 1975
Porter, Alexander W. (94)—Winter 1975
Potter, Gillie (87)—Spring 1975
Pusser, Buford (36)—August 21, 1974
Quinlivan, Charles (50)—November 12, 1974
Rajamanickam, R.S. (68)—Winter 1974
Ranalli, Ralph (53)—December 23, 1974
Rao, S.V. Ranga (56)—July 19, 1974
Rathbun, Janet—March 8, 1975
Ready, Eddie—October 4, 1974
Regas, Pedro (82)—August 10, 1974
Repp, Stafford (56)—November 5, 1974
Rich, Lucius C. (Bozo Kelly) (61)—January 6, 1975
Richards, Paul (50)—December 10, 1974
Ricks, James (49)—July 2, 1974
Robbins, Jane Kiser (53)—June 24, 1974
Roberts, Roy (69)—May 28, 1975
Roecker, Edward O. (65)—May 13, 1975
Rogers, Bob—September 12, 1974
Romaine, Edith (87)—July 6, 1974
Ross, Robert (65)—July 18, 1974
Ross, Shirley (62)—March 9, 1975
Rounseville, Robert (60)—August 6, 1974
Royton, Velma (81)—July 25, 1974
St. John, Beatrice (60's)—November 4, 1974
Sanders, Felicia (53)—February 7, 1975

Sanderson, Julia (87)—January 27, 1975
Savoy, Harry (76)—November 1, 1974
Sawamura, Kunitaro (69)—November 26, 1974
Sayre, Jeffrey (73)—September 26, 1974
Schachter, Leon (74)—November 9, 1974
Schiotz, Aksel (68)—April 19, 1975
Sebring, Paul E. (84)—October 7, 1974
Sessions, Almira (85)—August 3, 1973
Shepley, Ida—Spring 1975
Shiffrin, Helen (55)—March 9, 1975
Shindell, Dario (67)—July 9, 1974
Short, Joe (Little Joe from Kokomo) (91)—December 20, 1974
Shuard, Amy (50)—April 18, 1975
Simon, Michael (80)—May 30, 1975
Slater, John (58)—January 9, 1975
Slosser, Pauline Hall (83)—October 6, 1974
Smith, Gerald (81)—May 28, 1974
Soussanin, Nicholas (86)—April 27, 1975
Stapelton, Ray (52)—November 19, 1974
Stern, Jean (84)—May 24, 1974
Stone, Dorothy (69)—September 24, 1974
Stovall, Babe (66)—September 21, 1974
Strauss, Robert (61)—February 20, 1975
Streiford, Hobart A. (63)—September 22, 1974
Striker, Richard (42)—August 1974
Sullivan, Elliot (66)—June 2, 1974
Susann, Jacqueline (53)—September 21, 1974
Sutton, Frank (51)—June 28, 1974
Tabbert, William (53)—October 19, 1974
Talbert, Rose Hershfield (91)—April 4, 1975
Talent, Bill (81)—September 23, 1974
Terry, Hazel (56)—October 12, 1974
Thimig, Helene (85)—November 7, 1974
Thomas, Edna (88)—July 22, 1974
Tierney, William A.—December 21, 1974
Triegle, Norman (47)—February 16, 1975
Truzzi, Massimiliano (71)—October 31, 1974
Tucker, Richard (60)—January 8, 1975
Tunnell, George N. (62)—May 20, 1975
Ure, Mary (42)—April 3, 1975
Usher, Graham (36)—February 3, 1975
Vague, Vera—September 14, 1974
Vasquez, Myrna (40)—February 17, 1975
Venable, Reginald (48)—June 28, 1974
Verhoeven, Paul (74)—March 22, 1975
Vincent, Larry (50)—March 8, 1975
Wadsworth, Henry (72)—December 5, 1974
Wahl, Walter Dare (78)—June 23, 1974
Wakefield, Henrietta (96)—October 23, 1974
Walker, T-Bone (64)—March 16, 1975
Warde, Anthony (66)—January 8, 1975
Warrick, Elizabeth (60)—July 14, 1974
Wattis, Richard (62)—February 1, 1975
Weil, Harry (84)—July 30, 1974
Weil, Joe (57)—December 29, 1974
Welbes, George (40)—October 17, 1974
Wery, Carl (77)—March 14, 1975
White, Joan (43)—January 30, 1975
Whitman, Chance Halliday (39)—December 20, 1974
Wickwire, Nancy (48)—July 10, 1974
Wills, Bob (70)—May 13, 1975

Wilson, Albert C. (98)—December 24, 1974
Windgassen, Wolfgang (60)—September 8, 1974
Wyle, Larry (53)—April 9, 1975
Yeats, Murray F. (65)—January 27, 1975
Young, James (51)—July 5, 1974
Yurka, Blanche (86)—June 6, 1974
Zacchini, Ernest (83)—February 20, 1975
Zides, Max (70)—February 6, 1975
Zohn, Chester E. (Chet) (71)—February 10, 1975

PLAYWRIGHTS

Achard, Marcel (75)—September 4, 1974
Adler, Jacob (B. Kovner) (101)—December 31, 1974
Code, Grant Hyde (78)—June 28, 1974
Doherty, Brian (68)—October 30, 1974
Evaguelides, Demetris (65)—February 28, 1975
Gould, John (37)—August 21, 1974
Greenwood, Walter (71)—September 13, 1974
Johnson, Greer (54)—October 30, 1974
Kaestner, Erich (75)—July 29, 1974
Kallesser, Michael (89)—March 19, 1975
Kelly, George (87)—June 18, 1974
Lagerkvist, Par (83)—July 10, 1974
Laning, Robert E. (56)—August 3, 1974
Lengyel, Melchior (95)—October 25, 1974
Linklater, Eric (75)—November 7, 1974
Luca de Texa, Juan (77)—January 11, 1975
Lyons, Harry—Winter 1975
Manhoff, Wilton (Bill) (54)—June 19, 1974
O'Brien, Kate (76)—August 13, 1974
Smith, Mrs. Ernest J. (77)—February 24, 1975
Taylor, Ethel S. (80)—March 26, 1975
Wilder, Robert (73)—August 22, 1974
Wodehouse, P.G. (93)—February 14, 1975
Young, Stanley (69)—March 22, 1975

COMPOSERS AND LYRICISTS

Anderson, Leroy (66)—May 18, 1975
Bezanson, Philip (59)—March 11, 1975
Blacher, Boris (72)—Winter 1975
Bliss, Sir Arthur (83)—March 27, 1975
Bucky, Frida Sarsen—October 2, 1974
Charlap, Mark (Moose) (45)—July 8, 1974
Crider, Ethel Osborne—April 13, 1975
Cross, Douglas (54)—January 7, 1975
Dallapiccola, Luigi (71)—February 19, 1975
De Francesco, Louis (87)—October 5, 1974
Dowell, Horace (Saxie) (70)—July 22, 1974
Evett, Robert (52)—February 4, 1975
Fairchild, Edgar (76)—February 20, 1975
Friend, Cliff (80)—June 27, 1974
Gillespie, Haven (87)—March 15, 1975
Gohman, Don (47)—Summer 1974
Greenfield, Ada G. Morley (85)—January 8, 1975
Haines, Edmund (59)—July 5, 1974
Homer, Benjamin (57)—February 12, 1975
Howard, Paul Mason (84)—January 21, 1975
Hunter, Ivory Joe (63)—November 8, 1974

Jolivet, Andre (69)—December 18, 1974
Kallman, Chester (53)—January 18, 1975
Martin, Dolphe (81)—October 2, 1974
Martin, Frank (84)—November 21, 1974
Milhaud, Darius (81)—June 22, 1974
Moritz, Edward (83)—September 30, 1974
Orient, Milt H. (56)—February 25, 1975
Parker, Ross (59)—August 2, 1974
Perl, Lothar (64)—April 28, 1975
Partch, Harry (73)—September 3, 1974
Rasbach, Oscar (86)—March 25, 1975
Samuel, Leopold (92)—March 14, 1975
Schinhan, Jan Philip (87)—March 26, 1975
Secunda, Sholom (79)—June 13, 1974
Sherwin, Manning (72)—July 26, 1974
Stewart, Ernie (61)—October 20, 1974
Stringham, Edwin (83)—July 1, 1974
Wagner, Joseph (74)—October 12, 1974
Wellesz, Egon (89)—November 9, 1974
Winfree, Richard (76)—February 24, 1975

PRODUCERS, DIRECTORS, CHOREOGRAPHERS

Arnold, Lilian (69)—June 2, 1974
Arnold, Wade—January 20, 1975
Baerwitz, Sam (82)—June 29, 1974
Barnhard, Lawrence C. (Slim) (71)—January 1, 1975
Beach, Hugh D. (61)—January 12, 1975
Benech, Rudolf F. (59)—May 3, 1975
Bennett, Compton (74)—August 13, 1974
Benthall, Michael (55)—September 6, 1974
Berry, Sidney N. (66)—February 18, 1975
Borzage, Lew (71)—December 6, 1974
Bryan, Julien H. (75)—October 20, 1974
Cahill, Paul (42)—December 28, 1974
Carlson, Keith (34)—February 12, 1975
Catrani, Catrano (61)—October 19, 1974
Charrel, Erik (80)—July 15, 1974
Chase, Cleveland B. (71)—January 17, 1975
Constable, James M. (68)—November 11, 1974
Damaskinos, Theofanis A. (75)—August 27, 1974
Davidson, Cecil (Cee) (69)—June 17, 1974
Davis, Peter (80)—August 16, 1974
De Turenne, Jean A. (77)—June 27, 1974
Doubleday, Richard (52)—January 16, 1975
Egli, Joseph E. (74)—August 2, 1974
Einfeld, S. Charles (73)—December 27, 1974
Ewing, Sherman (73)—May 15, 1975
Fanck, Arnold (85)—September 27, 1974
Ferro, Beth H. (49)—September 27, 1974
Fielden, Lionel (78)—June 1, 1974
Florance, Cassius (Babe) (65)—January 11, 1975
Ford, George D. (94)—July 24, 1974
Foster, Lewis R. (75)—June 10, 1974
Fried, Walter (69)—May 28, 1975
Galindo, Cesar Santos (65)—January 6, 1975
Georgi, Yvonne (77)—January 25, 1975
Germi, Pietro (60)—December 5, 1974
Gomez, Jerry (73)—October 17, 1974
Goodbody, Buzz (28)—April 12, 1975

Graham, William (Mecca) (74)—September 20, 1974
Griffin, Arbid (60)—September 27, 1974
Harrington, Herschel R. (75)—January 27, 1975
Hayes, James (60)—May 16, 1975
Heineman, William J. (74)—August 8, 1974
Hicks, Jack (60)—August 14, 1974
Holland, C. Maurice—November 14, 1974
Hoveler, Audrey (48)—August 19, 1974
Jacobs, Helen (53)—November 17, 1974
Jacquin, Maurice (74)—February 1974
Kalich, Jacob (83)—March 16, 1975
Kaul, Avtar (34)—July 21, 1974
Keim, Buster C. (68)—July 23, 1974
Lachman, Harry (88)—March 19, 1975
Leftwich, Alexander (66)—July 17, 1974
Levey, Jules (78)—January 2, 1975
Litvak, Anatole (72)—December 15, 1974
Lombard, Pat (61)—December 4, 1974
Lourau, Georges (76)—October 1974
Lowther, George F. (62)—April 28, 1975
Lukashok, E. David (34)—July 17, 1974
Maddock, C.B. (93)—June 17, 1974
Malipiero, Luigi (74)—February 24, 1975
Mariassey, Felix (55)—January 27, 1975
Marks, Sherman—April 4, 1975
Marshall, George (84)—February 17, 1975
McFarlane, Lillian C. (73)—February 13, 1975
Mocek, Henryk—October 21, 1973
Morelli, Antonio (69)—June 17, 1974
Ouroussow, Eugenie (66)—January 7, 1975
Palmerton, Guy (61)—March 24, 1975
Panthulu, B.R. (64)—October 8, 1974
Pardee, Chester F. (58)—October 4, 1974
Parker, Albert (87)—August 10, 1974
Pati, Pramod (42)—January 20, 1975
Peckham, John (45)—July 31, 1974
Pierson, Arthur (73)—January 1, 1975
Pumarejo, Gaspar (61)—March 25, 1975
Reichman, Thomas (30)—December 1, 1974
Reilly, William W. (53)—February 23, 1975
Reinhold, Conny (42)—October 1, 1974
Robinson, Hubbell (68)—September 4, 1974
Rodin, Gil (64)—June 17, 1974
Sandler, Jesse (57)—February 22, 1975
Sands, Larry (42)—September 9, 1974
Schneider, Stanley (45)—January 22, 1975
Severn, Gerry—June 26, 1974
Sheehan, Bailie (74)—April 1, 1975
Shukshin, Vasily (45)—October 2, 1974
Simons, Eva H. (77)—September 22, 1974
Smith, Wingate (79)—July 22, 1974
Sternfeld, Tommy (65)—October 18, 1974
Stevens, George (70)—March 8, 1975
Stevens, Rowena (68)—January 24, 1975
Ulmer, Roch—January 11, 1975
Vaught, George (46)—May 12, 1975
Victor, C. Leonard (94)—October 13, 1974
Voeller, Will H. (75)—April 3, 1975
Waller, Lee (59)—December 6, 1974
Walsh, Bill (61)—January 27, 1975
Watkins, Perry R. (67)—August 14, 1974
Wecker, Gero (51)—June 23, 1974

Wehling, Will (47)—February 4, 1975
Weingarten, Lawrence (77)—February 5, 1975
Williams, Marjorie (92)—April 1, 1975
Winik, Leslie (72)—April 26, 1975
Yamamoto, Kajiro (72)—September 28, 1974

CONDUCTORS

Andre, Franz (82)—January 19, 1975
De Parana, Luiz Alberto (46)—September 15, 1974
Diels, Hendrik (73)—Winter 1975
Francis, Nick (70)—March 1, 1975
Johnson, Thor (61)—January 16, 1975
Kelly, George F. (80)—February 26, 1975
Krips, Josef (72)—October 12, 1974
Lipkin, Arthur B. (67)—June 18, 1974
Miles, Jack (55)—June 15, 1974
Morel, Jean (72)—April 14, 1975
Spear, Sammy (65)—March 11, 1975
Vokalek, Emil (48)—April 25, 1975

DESIGNERS

Benois, Nadia (79)—December 8, 1974
Comer, Samuel M. (81)—December 28, 1974
Courtney, Elizabeth (69)—September 4, 1974
Draz, Francis K. (79)—September 20, 1974
Furse, Margaret (Maggie) (63)—July 8, 1974
Hurst, Lew (57)—January 8, 1975
Rousseau, Gladys (76)—May 21, 1975
Sullivan, James W. (65)—October 10, 1974

CRITICS

Affelder, Paul B. (59)—January 15, 1975
Budd, Nelson H. (74)—August 25, 1974
Cardus, Sir Neville (85)—February 28, 1975
Coleman, Robert Jr. (74)—November 27, 1974
Connolly, Cyril (71)—November 26, 1974
Cushing, Mary W. (80's)—October 4, 1974
Dooley, Willian G. (70)—February 15, 1975
Foster, Joseph (69)—August 27, 1974
Frankenberg, Lloyd F. (67)—March 12, 1975
Gaver, Jack (68)—December 16, 1974
Harrison, Jay S. (47)—September 12, 1974
Howes, Frank (82)—September 28, 1974
Klein, Dr. Deanne A. (40)—April 8, 1975
Kohl, John Y. (79)—August 12, 1974
Kratz, Karl L. (74)—June 20, 1974
Marquerie, Alfredo (67)—July 31, 1974
Miller, Arthur H. (81)—March 30, 1975
McCarten, John (63)—September 25, 1974
Panassie, Hugues (62)—December 8, 1974
Pieter, Ruth Yingling (80)—July 4, 1974
Raborn, George (50)—June 24, 1974
Russell, Fred H. (73)—July 20, 1974
Sheehy, T.J.M. (Tom) (56)—Winter 1974
Stehman, Jacques (62)—May 20, 1975
Sullivan, Ed (73)—October 13, 1974
Sylvester, Robert (68)—February 9, 1975
Taylor, Harvey (63)—January 17, 1975
Tyler, Parker (70)—July 24, 1974

Walton, Edith (71)—March 1, 1975
Westrup, Jack A. (70)—April 21, 1975
Whyte, Bettina F. (87)—September 24, 1974

MUSICIANS

Ammons, Eugue (Jug) (49)—August 6, 1974
Ash, Marvin (59)—August 21, 1974
Ayala, Amado (Amos) (70)—January 3, 1974
Berken, Harry (84)—October 18, 1974
Bhagavathar, Chambal Vydyanatha (78)—Winter 1975
Blade, Jimmy (67)—August 20, 1974
Boehm, Minnie W. (89)—December 8, 1974
Brown, Eddy (78)—June 14, 1974
Brunis, Georg (74)—November 19, 1974
Carney, Harry (64)—October 8, 1974
Chambers, Florence (84)—February 19, 1975
Chase, Bill—August 9, 1974
Chase, George D. (25)—June 30, 1974
Chasins, Ethel (75)—March 25, 1975
Clark, Walt—August 9, 1974
Cole, Reuben Jay (60)—February 4, 1975
DeFeis, Damon—June 30, 1974
Donovan, Martha Fisher (62)—October 6, 1974
Dunstedter, Eddie (76)—July 30, 1974
Emma, John—August 9, 1974
Flax, Hazel S. (58)—March 21, 1975
Flynn, Irving W. (66)—December 29, 1974
Furbish, Ralph E. (60)—October 8, 1974
Grandjany, Marcel (83)—February 24, 1975
Griffith, Corinne (58)—Summer 1974
Goldmark, John (69)—March 8, 1975
Goldstein, Chuck—August 18, 1974
Guillot, Yvonne (81)—April 15, 1975
Hall, Carlyle W. (68)—March 15, 1975
Harvanek, Bohuslav (70)—October 23, 1974
Huston, John (59)—April 6, 1975
Katchen, Lucille S. (71)—January 28, 1975
Krieger-Isaac, Alice (79)—October 3, 1974
La Monte, Johnny (58)—September 29, 1974
Lind, Gitta (49)—November 11, 1974
Lilienthal, Norman L. (61)—August 24, 1974
Laufkoetter, Henry (85)—September 6, 1974
Mackenzie, Alastair (58)—Winter 1974
Macpherson, Sandy (78)—Spring 1975
McIntosh, Robbie (24)—September 24, 1974
Meredith, Isabelle (71)—September 30, 1974
Moldavan, Nicholas (84)—September 21, 1974
Mooney, Joe (65)—May 12, 1975
Morrison, George Sr. (83)—November 5, 1974
Musulin, Branka (56)—January 1, 1975
Oistrakh, David (65)—October 24, 1974
Oncken, Eva von Knorring (94)—July 5, 1974
Peterson, William (46)—March 20, 1975
Pierce, Billie (67)—October 1, 1974
Puletz, Rudolph F. (66)—December 23, 1974
Rey, Don (66)—September 20, 1974
Rich, Don (32)—July 17, 1974
Robinson, Eric (65)—July 24, 1974
Roisman, Joseph (74)—October 9, 1974
Rosanoff, Lielf (96)—November 12, 1974
Rubens, Mark (74)—May 24, 1974

Sanders, Robert L. (68)—December 26, 1974
Schroeder, Gene (60)—February 16, 1975
Schnabel, Helen (63)—September 29, 1974
Schur, Maxim (67)—October 22, 1974
Smith, Cyril (65)—August 2, 1974
Shilkret, Dr. Harry H. (77)—April 2, 1975
Smith, Howard G. (63)—April 11, 1975
Smith, Roger M. (59)—February 25, 1975
Soudant, Belle Julie (88)—February 9, 1975
Stolarevsky, Mihail (70's)—December 7, 1974
Tertis, Lionel (98)—February 25, 1975
Thomas, Rene (47)—Winter 1975
Van Katwijk, Paul (89)—December 11, 1974
Wilder, Dorothea Wardell (86)—July 19, 1974
Yohn, Wallace—August 9, 1974

OTHERS

Aglgaze, Julia Cohn (73)—April 10, 1975
Lawyer for Actors Equity
Altschuler, Richard W. (67)—December 9, 1974
Film executive
Archibald, Lord (76)—February 27, 1975
Executive, Rank Productions
Armstrong, John A. (60)—July 28, 1974
Theater operator
Ash, Ingram (55)—December 28, 1974
Executive, Blaine Thompson agency
Asturias, Miguel Angel (74)—June 9, 1974
Novelist, diplomat, poet
Baker, George (59)—May 7, 1975
Walt Disney artist
Bauer, Leda V. (77)—January 7, 1975
Film story editor
Baumgarten, Edmund J. (60)—January 9, 1975
Film executive
Beardslee, Irene (87)—November 1, 1974
Goldwyn's film editor
Bernardi, Boris (70)—July 29, 1974
Theater manager
Bischoff, Samuel (84)—May 21, 1975
Hollywood producer
Blake, Robert—March 26, 1975
Company manager, English Nat'l Opera
Bothman, Fay—January 16, 1975
Talent agent
Branch, William E. (80)—February 19, 1975
Founder, Branch Clinic
Brennan, Edward H. (49)—August 17, 1974
Creator of Watts Writers Workshop
Brooks, Hugh (67)—November 6, 1974
Denver, Colo. impresario
Browne, Burton (69)—January 20, 1975
Founder, Gaslight Clubs, Inc.
Bryan, Marian Knighton (74)—December 9, 1974
Dance instructor, Sarah Lawrence
Budberg, Moura (82)—November 1, 1974
Translator
Bundy, Robert M.—August 5, 1974
Booking agent

Burns, Robert Emmett (62)—August 22, 1974
Booking agent
Caldwell, Paul N. (50)—September 28, 1974
Circus buff, collector of memorabilia
Carr, A. Selby (70)—June 14, 1974
Booking agent
Ciampi, Antonio (65)—March 11, 1975
Pres. Italian Soc. of Authors, Editors
Cochrane, Nan (77)—September 9, 1974
Story editor
Cohan, Henry (75)—February 15, 1975
Theater manager, booking agent
Cohen, Abe (76)—May 29, 1974
Executive, Shubert Theaters
Cole, Hazel B. (79)—June 20, 1974
Business manager
Coren, Leo (73)—October 19, 1974
Talent booker
Crandell, R.F. (72)—August 30, 1974
Journalist
Crosby, Larry (80)—February 12, 1975
Brother of Bing Crosby
Davis, Peter (78)—Fall 1974
General manager, Theater Guild
Depinet, Ned E. (84)—December 29, 1974
President, RKO-Radio Pictures
Doob, Oscar A. (83)—May 22, 1974
Film advertising pioneer
Dye, Barbara (52)—March 15, 1975
Cofounder, Women of Movie Industry
Ewer, Mabel S. (93)—June 30, 1974
Founder, Phila. Women's Symphony Orch.
Farrar, John Chipman (78)—November 20,
1974
Editor, founder of Farrar & Rinehart
Feist, Rabbi Milton (67)—April 23, 1975
President of two music companies
Fields, Jeanette (Mom Jen) (84)—November 28,
1974
Pioneer in resort operation
Fine, Marshall H. (48)—July 29, 1974
Founder, Nat. Assn. of Theater Owners
Fine, Max (74)—September 21, 1974
Creator of theatrical displays
Fisher, Carl (65)—December 21, 1974
General manager for Broadway shows
Frankel, Lou (63)—November 19, 1974
Journalist
Franklin, Sid S. (65)—February 1, 1975
Vocal coach, musical arranger
Frisch, Abraham H. (75)—February 23,
1975
General counsel, United Artists Circuit
Furtseva, Yekaterina (63)—October 26, 1974
Minister of Culture, Soviet Union
Geiss, Alexander (77)—July 13, 1974
Disney animator
Gent, George (49)—July 5, 1974
Journalist
Georger, Alfred M. (85)—August 20, 1974
Treasurer of, Met. Opera Assn.
Gerber, Morton (60)—January 13, 1975
President of Washington theaters

Glazer, Barney (66)—January 12, 1975
Columnist
Goldie, Sydney E. (73)—October 1, 1974
Journalist
Goldman, Mrs. Edwin F. (89)—February 13,
1975
Widow of bandmaster
Goodwin, Denis (44)—February 26, 1975
Writer, humorist
Green, Alan (68)—March 10, 1975
Writer
Griffis, Stanton (87)—August 29, 1974
Film executive, Broadway backer
Harrington, Howard D. (66)—July 25, 1974
General Manager, Detroit Symphony
Hershfield, Harry (89)—December 15, 1974
Cartoonist, humorist
Hibbs, Ben (73)—March 29, 1975
Magazine editor
Hill, Howard (76)—February 4, 1975
Professional archer
Hollingshead, Richard M. Jr. (75)—May 13,
1975
Established first U.S. drive-in
Hruby, Frank J. (90)—October 5, 1974
Founder of Hruby Conservatory
Hubbard, Thomas G. (55)—June 4, 1974
Writer
Hughes, Herman S., S.J. (59)—September 30,
1974
Founder Univ. Series, Cleveland
Hurok, Emma B. (80)—July 18, 1974
Widow of S. Hurok
Judson, Arthur (93)—January 28, 1975
Founder, Columbia Artists Mgmt.
Kalcheim, Harry (73)—November 12, 1974
Talent agent, booker
Keller, Nina (43)—August 16, 1974
Co-originator of mini-theater
Kelly, Lawrence (46)—September 16, 1974
Opera impresario
Kerr, Russell (76)—February 3, 1975
Writer, editor
King, Edith (91)—April 7, 1975
Children's School of Theater
Kingston, Al (72)—April 9, 1975
Talent agent
Kleper, Sidney H. (58)—September 27, 1974
Theatrical manager
Krieger, Lester (71)—January 6, 1975
Film and theater executive
Kriendler, I. Robert (60)—August 15, 1974
President of "21" Club
Kyatt, Philip (82)—May 10, 1975
Creator of Broadway's neon lights
Latta, C.J. (80)—October 6, 1974
Associates British Picture Corp.
Leahy, John W. (79)—March 28, 1975
Promotor of Danbury Fair
Leedy, Harry (67)—January 1, 1975
Artists' manager
Levine, Charles B. (75)—June 27, 1974
Creator of Broadway displays

Lewis, Ann (76)—January 5, 1975
West Coast *Showman's Trade Review*
Long, Lois (73)—July 29, 1974
Journalist
Longe, Jeffery (51)—October 30, 1974
Stage manager
Lopez, Joseph Messeri (72)—January 13, 1975
Maitre D at Copacabana, Stork Club
Lutz, Max (70)—January 13, 1975
Song plugger
MacDonald, J. Carlisle (80)—November 1974
Journalist, publicist
MacGregor, Robert M. (63)—November 22, 1974
Editor *Theatre Arts Books*
Madison, C.J. (67)—February 5, 1975
Elephant trainer
Markert, Gladys (71)—March 9, 1975
Publicist
Mason, Ruth Fitch (84)—December 20, 1974
Author, literary agent
McPherrin, John W. (77)—October 3, 1974
Broadway investor
McTernan, Agnes M. (56)—November 11, 1974
Editor-in-chief of *Program*
Melancon, Louis (73)—August 17, 1974
Photographer for Metropolitan Opera
Mesta, Perle (85)—March 16, 1975
Hostess, ambassadress
Mills, Jack (88)—July 19, 1974
Founder, owner of Mills Bros. Circus
Moore, Cullen—January 20, 1975
Columist, script writer
Morgan, Kay Summersby (66)—January 20, 1975
Set and costume designer
Morrison, Talmadge H. (82)—December 13, 1974
Photographer
Moskowitz, Charles C. (82)—January 18, 1975
Film executive
Newhafer, Richard (52)—October 12, 1974
Author
Oberding, Antoine (81)—October 8, 1974
Costumer
Orlin, Gean (60)—January 11, 1975
Editor, *Gotham Life Guide*
Pepper, Herman (77)—March 6, 1975
"World's greatest theatergoer"
Perkins, Albert H. (70)—February 10, 1975
Writer
Piazza, Dario (70)—September 1, 1974
Costumer
Pike, Robert (56)—November 23, 1974
Theatrical manager, press agent
Polonsky, Joe (81)—September 6, 1974
Publicist
Pritchard, Irving J. (93)—January 27, 1975
Photographer
Rapp, Charles (71)—October 8, 1974
Talent agent

Rathbone, Ouida Bergere (88)—November 29, 1974
Writer, widow of Basil Rathbone
Reese, J. Mark (31)—September 19, 1974
Talent agent
Rising, Richard (48)—September 16, 1974
Executive with M-G-M Records
Robinson, Walter W. (Wally) (46)—August 31, 1974
Writer, publicist
Rose, Charlie (88)—November 16, 1974
Boxer, "Broadway Charlie"
Rose, Rufus C. (70)—May 29, 1975
Creator, Howdy Doody marionette
Rosen, Albert H. (82)—December 15, 1974
Theatrical manager
Rosenburgh, Carleton F. (69)—September 24, 1974
Theater construction
Ross, T.J. (81)—May 27, 1975
Public relations pioneer
Savage, Charles E. (65)—September 22, 1974
Script Writer
Saville, Lewis J. (89)—January 29, 1975
British music publisher, promoter
Scheinfeld, Lou (72)—August 14, 1974
Theatrical attorney
Schymacher, Eli (87)—February 9, 1975
Theatrical mover
Sheean, Vincent (75)—March 15, 1975
Journalist, author
Shipstad, Roy (64)—January 20, 1975
Co-founder of *Ice Follies*
Shpalikov, Bennadi (37)—Winter 1975
Russian film director, scriptwriter
Silverman, Jack (86)—June 15, 1974
International Theater Restaurant
Slocum, Bill (62)—November 26, 1974
Hearst columnist
Smalls, Ed (92)—October 13, 1974
Harlem showman, Small's Paradise
Snyder, Harold—September 15, 1974
Theater manager
Spaak, Charles (71)—March 4, 1975
Screenwriter
Sprigge, Elizabeth (74)—December 9, 1974
Novelist, head of Watergate Theater
Steigman, Benjamin (85)—July 20, 1974
N. Y. High School of Music and Art
Stix, Thomas L. (78)—July 13, 1974
Agent
Sweigard, Lulu E.—August 1, 1974
Dance Division, Julliard School
Tabori, Paul (66)—November 9, 1974
Novelist, script writer
Tamagno, Caesar (63)—April 13, 1975
Monticello club, Framingham, Mass.
Thayer, Francis C. (57)—May 23, 1975
Producer of documentary films
Thompson, Helen M. (66)—June 25, 1974
Manager of NY Philharmonic
Toohey, John Latham (58)—February 9, 1975
Writer, press representative

Vanderbilt, Cornelius Jr. (76)—July 7, 1974
  Author, journalist
Van Beuren, Archbold (68)—December 8, 1974

  Founder of *Cue*
Van Sappe, Clarence (62)—April 25, 1974
  Member of John Golden Associates
Volkova, Vera (71)—May 5, 1975
  Ballet teacher for Margot Fonteyn
Vosoff, Hellen Howes (79)—February 6, 1975
  Founder, South Shore Playhouse Assn.
Wallace, Sam (68)—May 19, 1975
  Promoter for RCA Records
Wallach, Joseph (62)—October 1, 1974
  Theatrical stage manager
Walsh, Michael (70)—Summer 1974

British theatrical stage manager
Warren, Edward Alyn (54)—September 17, 1974

  Theatrical manager
Webb, James R. (64)—September 27, 1974
  Screen writer
White, Danny (67)—November 16, 1974
  Talent agent
Wiese, Henry William (70)—December 10, 1974

  Theatrical agent
Wilcox, Art (50)—September 29, 1974
  Publicist
Wutke, Louis M.—August 19, 1974
  Theater equipment specialist

INDEX

Play titles are in **bold face** and *bold face italic* page numbers refer to pages where cast and credit listings may be found.

451